THE
URBAN
SOUTH

THE URBAN SOUTH

A Bibliography

**Compiled by
CATHERINE L. BROWN**

Bibliographies and Indexes in American History, Number 12

GREENWOOD PRESS
NEW YORK • WESTPORT, CONNECTICUT • LONDON

Library of Congress Cataloging-in-Publication Data

Brown, Catherine L., 1948-
    The urban South : a bibliography / compiled by Catherine L. Brown.
        p. cm.—(Bibliographies and indexes in American history,
    ISSN 0742-6828 ; no. 12)
    Includes indexes.
    ISBN 0-313-26154-7 (lib. bdg. : alk. paper)
    1. Cities and towns—Southern States—Bibliography. 2. Human
settlements—Southern States—Bibliography. I. Title. II. Series.
Z7164.U7B69   1989
[HT123.5.S6]
016.3077 '6 '0975—dc20   89-2151

British Library Cataloguing in Publication Data is available.

Library of Congress Catalog Card Number: 89-2151
ISBN: 0-313-26154-7
ISSN: 0742-6828

First published in 1989

Greenwood Press, Inc.
88 Post Road West, Westport, Connecticut 06881

Printed in the United States of America

The paper used in this book complies with the
Permanent Paper Standard issued by the National
Information Standards Organization (Z39.48-1984).

10 9 8 7 6 5 4 3 2 1

To my parents

Thomas F. and Lucyanne Brown

Contents

Preface

This bibliography began originally as a literature search for a
research paper in urban geography under Dr. Thomas Bell, Department of
Geography at the University of Tennessee. Needless to say, it grew out
of hand. I soon discovered, as I viewed my growing stack of citation-
filled shoeboxes, that I was accumulating a resource that might be useful
for the many people interested in the various facets of southern urban
studies. I then commenced the bibliographic pursuit in earnest.

Thus, the purpose of this Urban South: A Bibliography is to
provide scholars and students with a reference document of comprehensive
dimensions to trace the literature on southern cities. My criteria for
"southern" corresponds precisely to that of the United States Bureau of
the Census, i.e., the District of Columbia and the following states:
Alabama, Arkansas, Delaware, Florida, Georgia, Kentucky, Louisiana,
Maryland, Mississippi, North Carolina, Oklahoma, South Carolina,
Tennessee, Texas, Virginia, and West Virginia. While following a
straightforward definition of "southern," my inclination to interpret
"urban" was not only less precise but also more catholic. I have felt
free to include American Indian settlements, ethnic communities, even
ghost towns, as well as other gatherings of people and buildings, whether
temporary or permanent. This is not, therefore, a strictly "citified"
urban bibliography.

Despite its breadth, this bibliography is not complete. Like you
and me, it simply begins and ends. I have attempted to bring together
material from many disciplines—as well as areas not claimed by
disciplines—in the sciences, social sciences, the arts and humanities.
I have concentrated on professional journals, books, theses and

dissertations. The vast majority of the citations in this collection are from materials readily available from any good reference library.

Finally, I would like to thank Ann Clark, who turned eleven shoeboxes of scribbly index cards into the manuscript you are about to examine. In addition, as I put this manuscript to "bed," I thank James O. Wheeler for his assistance in helping me with the final editorial details of this task. His experience in dealing with the "etiquette" of publishers has been a most welcome conclusion to this "bediquette." The only parts of this endeavor that are exclusively my responsibility are the errors.

Catherine L. Brown
Oceanside, California

THE
URBAN
SOUTH

Dissertations and Theses

Archaeology

A-1 Beidleman, Dona K., CERAMIC REMAINS AS INDICATORS OF SOCIO-ECONOMIC STATUS IN COLONIAL ST. AUGUSTINE, (M.A.: University of Florida), 1977.

A-2 Brian, Jeffrey P., WINTERVILLE: A CASE STUDY OF PREHISTORIC CULTURE CONTACT IN THE LOWER MISSISSIPPI VALLEY, (Ph.D.: Yale University), 1969

A-3 Cotter, John Lambert, ARCHAEOLOGICAL EXCAVATION AT JAMESTOWN, VIRGINIA, (Ph.D.: University of Pennsylvania), 1959.

A-4 Forman, Henry Chandee, JAMESTOWN AND ST. MARY'S: BURIED CITIES OF ROMANCE, (Ph.D.: University of Pennsylvania), 1940.

A-5 Gustafson, H. Leonard, Jr., SOME ASPECTS OF HUMAN OCCUPANCE IN COLLIERVILLE, TENNESSEE, (M.A.: Memphis State University), 1967.

A-6 Mason, Carol Ann Irwin, THE ARCHAEOLOGY OF THE OCMULGEE OLD FIELDS, MACON, GEORGIA, (Ph.D.: University of Michigan), 1963.

A-7 McMurray, Carl D., THE ARCHEOLOGY OF A MESTIZO HOUSE, (M.A.: University of Florida), 1975.

A-8 Reitz, Elizabeth Jenn, SPANISH AND BRITISH SUBSISTENCE STRATEGIES AT ST. AUGUSTINE, FLORIDA, AND FREDERICA, GEORGIA, BETWEEN 1565 AND 1783, (Ph.D.: University of Florida), 1979.

Architecture and Historic Preservation

A-9 Brown, Barbara Wilson, VICTORIAN HOUSES OF DUNN, NORTH CAROLINA, 1900-1920, (M.S.: Eastern Carolina University), 1983.

A-10 Caldwell, Joan Garcia, ITALINATE DOMESTIC ARCHITECTURE IN NEW ORLEANS, 1850-1880, (Ph.D.: Tulane University), 1975.

A-11 Campbell, Betty Jean, THE BUILDINGS OF SALEM, NORTH CAROLINA, (Ph.D.: Florida State University), 1975.

A-12 Cook, Sylvia Lorraine Rusche, THE ROCK HOUSES OF FREDERICKSBURG, TEXAS, 1846-1910, (M. Arch: University of New Mexico), 1975.

A-13 Costomiris, Joyce, ECONOMICS OF PRESERVATION: MIAMI BEACH AND PALM
      BEACH, (M.A.: Florida Atlantic University), 1983.

A-14 Cunningham, Mary C., THE DEVELOPMENT AND APPRECIATION OF HISTORIC
      ARCHITECTURE OF NATCHEZ, MISSISSIPPI, (M.A.: George Peabody Col-
      lege for Teachers), 1937.

A-15 Giuliano, Frank and Gary Michalic, CALLANWOLDE: RESTORATION, RENO-
      VATION AND ADAPTION FOR CONTEMPORARY USE, (Senior Thesis: Univer-
      sity of Georgia), 1973.

A-16 Davis, K.L., A CHRONICLE OF THE SAVOY THEATRE, LOUISVILLE, KEN-
      TUCKY,
      (M.A.: University of Louisiana), 1980.

A-17 Ethridge, Hartrison Mosley, THE BLACK ARCHITECTS OF WASHINGTON,
      D.C., 1900-PRESENT, (D.A.: Catholic University of America), 1979.

A-18 Flanagan, Hubert Livingston, THE COTTON STATES AND INTERNATIONAL
      EXPOSITION, (M.A.: University of Georgia), 1951.

A-19 Grubb, Larry Keith, ARCHITECTURAL TRENDS AND FOUNDATION PRACTICES
      IN THE DOWNTOWN LOUISVILLE AREA, (M.S.: University of Louisiana),
      1973.

A-20 Haynes, Janice C., ARCHITECTURAL PRESERVATION IN ATHENS, GEORGIA:
      A RESOLUTION OF PROGRESS AND PRESERVATION, (M.A.: University of
      Georgia), 1971.

A-21 Herzog, Lynda Vestal, THE EARLY ARCHITECTURE OF NEW BERN, NORTH
      CAROLINA, 1750-1850, (Ph.D.: University of California), 1977.

A-22 Jones, Elizabeth Fitzpatrick, HENRY WHITESTONE: NINETEENTH-CENTURY
      LOUISVILLE ARCHITECT, (M.A.: University of Louisiana), 1974.

A-23 Kapentanakos, Stephanie Anna, THE ARCHITECTURE OF NEEL REED; A
      STUDY OF THE RESIDENTIAL ARCHITECTURE OF NEEL REED IN ATLANTA,
      (M.A.: University of Georgia), 1971.

A-24 Lowry, Sandra, UNIFORMITY AND INDIVIDUALITY EXPRESSED IN THE SUB-
      URBAN RESIDENTIAL LANDSCAPES OF NORTHERN NEW CASTLE COUNTY, DELA-
      WARE, (M.A.: University of Delaware), 1981.

A-25 Mansell, Elizabeth Lloyd Meihack, THE AMERICAN TOBACCO COMPANY
      BRICK STORAGE WAREHOUSES IN DURHAM, NORTH CAROLINA, 1897-1906,
      (M.A.: University of North Carolina), 1980.

A-26 Peters, Linda Ellen, A STUDY OF THE ARCHITECTURE OF AUGUSTA,
      GEORGIA, 1735-1860, (Ph.D.: University of Georgia), 1983.

A-27 Stone, Garry Wheeler, SOCIETY, HOUSING, AND ARCHITECTURE IN EARLY
      MARYLAND: JOHN LEWGER'S ST. JOHN'S, (Ph.D.: University of Penn-
      sylvania), 1982.

Artisans and Crafts

A-28 Carel-White, Mary Allison, THE ROLE OF THE BLACK ARTISAN IN THE
      BUILDING TRADES AND DECORATIVE ARTS IN SOUTH CAROLINA'S CHARLESTON
      DISTRICT, 1760-1800, (Ph.D.: University of Tennessee), 1982.

A-29 Cook, Jane Leigh, A GEORGIAN HERITAGE: CHARLESTOWN ARTISANS AND
      CHIPPENDALE FURNITURE IN THE REVOLUTIONARY PERIOD, 1729-1785,
      (M.A.: Wake Forest University), 1985.

A-30   Green, Venus, A PRELIMINARY INVESTIGATION OF BLACK CONSTRUCTION
        ARTISANS IN SAVANNAH FROM 1820-1860, (M.A.: Columbia University),
        1982.

A-31   Pinchbeck, Raymond Bennett, THE VIRGINIA NEGRO ARTISAN AND TRADES-
        MAN, (Ph.D.: University of Virginia), 1925.

A-32   Stavisky, Leonard Price, THE NEGRO ARTISAN IN THE SOUTH ATLANTIC
        STATES, 1800-1860: A STUDY OF STATUS AND OPPORTUNITY WITH SPECIAL
        REFERENCE TO CHARLESTON, (Ph.D.: Columbia University), 1958.

Art

A-33   Crannell, Carlyn Gaye, IN PURSUIT OF CULTURE: A HISTORY OF ART
        ACTIVITY IN ATLANTA, 1847-1926, (Ph.D.: Emory University), 1981.

A-34   Latham, Tooba Kazemi, MASON MAURY AND THE INFLUENCE OF THE CHICAGO
        SCHOOL IN LOUISVILLE, (M.A.: University of Louisiana), 1975.

A-35   Salam, Cara Lu, FRENCH PORTRAITISTS: NEW ORLEANS, 1830-1860,
        (M.A.: Louisiana State University), 1967.

A-36   Stoelting, Winifred Louise, HALE WOODRUFF, ARTIST AND TEACHER:
        THROUGH THE ATLANTA YEARS, (Ph.D.: Emory University), 1978.

A-37   Thompson, N. Ruth F., A BIOGRAPHICAL CHECKLIST OF NINETEENTH CEN-
        TURY NEW ORLEANS ARTISTS, (M.A.: Louisiana State University),
        1966.

A-38   Williams, Hobie L., THE IMPACT OF THE ATLANTA UNIVERSITY EXHIBITION
        OF BLACK ARTISTS (1942-1969) ON BLACK AND NONBLACK PEOPLE, (Ed.D.:
        University of Pittsburgh), 1973.

Arts and Culture

A-39   Koch, Mary Levin, A HISTORY OF THE ARTS IN AUGUSTA, MACON, AND
        COLUMBUS, GEORGIA, 1800-1860, (M.A.: University of Georgia), 1983.

A-40   Pace, Don Mac, THE ARTS IN JACKSON, MISSISSIPPI: A HISTORY OF
        THEATRE, PAINTING, SCULPTURE, AND MUSIC IN THE MISSISSIPPI CAPITAL
        SINCE 1900, (Ph.D.: University of Mississippi), 1976.

Business and Economics

A-41   Alsobrook, David E., ALABAMA'S PORT CITY: MOBILE DURING THE PRO-
        GRESSIVE ERA, 1896-1917, (Ph.D.: Auburn University), 1983.

A-42   Alvic, Donald R., RETAIL SHOPPING OPPORTUNITY CHOICE IN A SMALL
        TOWN: AN EXAMINATION OF LENOIR CITY, TENNESSEE CONSUMERS, (Ph.D.:
        University of Tennessee), 1982.

A-43   Anderson, Alan D., URBANIZATION AND AMERICAN ECONOMIC DEVELOPMENT,
        1900-1930: PATTERNS OF DEMAND IN BALTIMORE AND THE NATION, (Ph.D.:
        Johns Hopkins University), 1973.

A-44   Argersinger, Jo Ann Eady, BALTIMORE: THE DEPRESSION YEARS, (Ph.D.:
        George Washington University), 1980.

A-45   Ashkenazi, Elliott, CREOLES OF JERUSALEM: JEWISH BUSINESSMEN IN
        LOUISIANA, 1840-1875, (Ph.D.: George Washington University), 1983.

A-46   Austin, T.C., TOBACCO MARKETING WAREHOUSES AND THEIR LOCATION IN
        THE URBAN LANDSCAPE OF THE EASTERN TOBACCO BELT OF NORTH CAROLINA,
        (M.S.: East Carolina University), 1977.

A-47   Baker, William, THE ECONOMICS OF A SMALL SOUTHERN TOWN, (Ph.D.:
        University of Alabama), 1963.

A-48   Baker, Thomas T. Jr., PARTNERS IN PROGRESS: THE GALVESTON WHARF
        COMPANY AND THE CITY OF GALVESTON, 1900-1930, (Ph.D.: Texas A & M
        University), 1979.

A-49   Belissary, Constantine, THE RISE OF THE INDUSTRIAL SPIRIT IN
        TENNESSEE, 1865-1885, (Ph.D.: University of Michigan), 1949.

A-50   Boland, Brother Herman, THE FREE MARKET OF NEW ORLEANS, (M.A.:
        Louisiana State University), 1965.

A-51   Bolding, Gary Arnold, EFFORTS TO DEVELOP NEW ORLEANS AS A WORLD
        TRADE CENTER , 1910-1948, (M.A.: Louisiana State University),
        1965.

A-52   Bouman, Clark H., INDUSTRIAL DEVELOPMENT AND SOCIAL CHANGE IN A
        SOUTHERN PLANTATION TOWN, (Ph.D.: New School for Social Research),
        1959.

A-53   Boyd, David E., THE IMPACT OF THE OFFICE WORKER ON DOWNTOWN GAINES-
        VILLE, FLORIDA, (M.A.: University of Florida), 1966.

A-54   Boykin, James Hudson, INDUSTRIAL LOCATION INFLUENCES WITHIN THE
        BALTIMORE REGION, (Ph.D.: American University), 1971.

A-55   Brouder, Saul E., ROBERT E. LUCEY: A TEXAS PARADOX, (Ph.D.:
        Columbia University), 1979.

A-56   Bruchev, Eleanor Stephens, THE BUSINESS ELITE IN BALTIMORE, 1880-
        1914, (Ph.D.: Johns Hopkins University), 1967.

A-57   Bulow, John K., AN ANALYSIS OF THE COMPETITIVE ADVANTAGES OF NORTH
        CAROLINA PORTS (M.A.: Eastern Carolina University), 1979.

A-58   Bushong, Allen D., THE PALM BEACH URBAN AREA: A GEOGRAPHIC STUDY
        OF A FLORIDA TOURIST CENTER, (M.A.: University of Florida), 1954.

A-59   Buxbaum, Richard W., THE SPATIAL STRUCTURE OF THE TOURIST ECONOMY:
        GATLINBURG, TENNESSEE, (Ph.D.: Ohio State University), 1967.

A-60   Byrd, Donald V., CHANGING FOREIGN TRADE ORIENTATIONS OF TWO
        MISSISSIPPI PORTS, (M.A.: University of Southern Mississippi),
        1967.

A-61   Campbell, Edna Fay, THE PORT OF NEW ORLEANS, (Ph.D.: Clark Uni-
        versity), 1931.

A-62   Campen, James T., NATIONAL BANKING IN KNOXVILLE, TENNESSEE, 1864-
        1913, (Ph.D.: University of Tennessee), 1981.

A-63   Carnes, Lon M., THE GEORGIA DEEPWATER PORTS AND THEIR ROLE IN THE
        ECONOMY OF THE STATE, (Ph.D.: Georgia State University), 1972.

A-64   Carpenter, Clifton C., BARRETT'S MIDWAY INC., AS A SMALL TOWN BLUE-
        GRASS CLOTHING INDUSTRY, (M.A.: University of Kentucky), 1958.

A-65   Chang, Tun-Mei Yu, AN ANALYSIS OF FAMILY INCOME AND ITS CITY-SIZE
        DIFFERENTIALS IN URBAN AREAS OF THE SOUTH, 1960-61, (Ph.D.: West
        Virginia University), 1975.

A-66   Chapman, James Emory, FACTORS IN INDUSTRIAL LOCATION IN METROPOLI-
        TAN ATLANTA, 1946-1955, (Ph.D.: University of Alabama), 1957.

A-67   Christian, Garna L., SWORD AND PLOWSHARE: THE SYMBIOTIC DEVELOP-
        MENT OF FORT BLISS AND EL PASO, TEXAS, 1849-1918, (Ph.D.: Texas
        Tech University), 1977.

A-68   Clowse, Converse Dilwarta, THE CHARLESTON EXPORT TRADE, 1717-1737,
        (Ph.D.: Northwestern University), 1963.

A-69   Colcanis, Peter, ECONOMY AND SOCIETY IN THE EARLY MODERN SOUTH:
        CHARLESTON AND THE EVOLUTION OF THE SOUTH CAROLINA LOW COUNTRY,
        (Ph.D.: Columbia University), 1984.

A-70   Cohn, Raymond L., A LOCATIONAL ANALYSIS OF MANUFACTURING IN THE
        ANTEBELLUM SOUTH AND MIDWEST, (Ph.D.: University of Oregon), 1977.

A-71   Cramer, Miles Richard, SCHOOL DESEGREGATION AND NEW INDUSTRY: THE
        SOUTHERN COMMUNITY LEADER'S VIEWPOINT, (Ph.D.: Harvard Univer-
        sity), 1962.

A-72   Crump, Cecille Evans, PROBLEMS ENCOUNTERED BY NEGRO MANAGERS IN THE
        OPERATION OF BUSINESS ESTABLISHMENTS IN NASHVILLE, TENNESSEE,
        (Ed.D.: Indiana University), 1959.

A-73   Currie, James Tyson, VICKSBURG, 1863-1870: THE PROMISE AND THE
        REALITY OF RECONSTRUCTION ON THE MISSISSIPPI, (Ph.D.: University
        of Virginia), 1975.

A-74   D'Andrea, Nicholas E., SELECTED MORPHOLOGICAL CHANGES IN INTRA-CITY
        RETAIL MOVEMENT BETWEEN DOWNTOWN MOBILE AND A MAJOR RETAIL CENTER:
        DOWNTOWN WEST, 1957-1968, (Ph.D.: University of Southern Missis-
        sippi), 1970.

A-75   Daniels, Anne Rebecca, BAYTOWN DURING THE DEPRESSION, 1919-1933,
        (M.A.: Lamar University), 1981.

A-76   Darnton, Donald Charles, THE PROBABLE IMPACT OF THE ST. LAWRENCE
        SEAWAY ON THE PORT OF BALTIMORE, MARYLAND, (Ph.D.: University of
        Michigan), 1961.

A-77   Davis, James Nathaniel Jr., EFFECTS OF INDUSTRIALIZATION UPON THE
        ECONOMY OF SEARCY, ARKANSAS: A CASE STUDY, (Ph.D.: University of
        Arkansas), 1963.

A-78   Dille, Ellwood Oakley, KNOXVILLE, TENNESSEE AS A WHOLESALE TRADE
        CENTER, (Ph.D.: Ohio State University), 1943.

A-79   Dillon, Patrick M., LOCATIONAL ASPECTS OF COMMERCIAL BANKING AT THE
        INTRAURBAN SCALE: THE CASE OF ATLANTA, (Ph.D.: University of
        Georgia), 1983.

A-80   Dodson, Mary L., SOUTHERN CITIES AND THE NATIONAL URBAN POLICY:
        ASSESSING GROWTH, DISTRESS, AND FINANCIAL ASSISTANCE IN THE URBAN
        SOUTH, (M.A.: University of North Carolina), 1980.

A-81   Dobson, Jerome E., THE CHANGING CONTROL OF ECONOMIC ACTIVITY IN THE
        GATLINBURG, TENNESSEE AREA, 1938-1973, (Ph.D.: University of Ten-
        nessee), 1975.

A-82   Doherty, Peter A., CONSUMER ATTITUDES AND PREFERENCES: A SPATIAL
        ANALYSIS OF SHOPPING BEHAVIOR IN THE ATHENS, GA. URBAN AREA,
        (Ph.D.: University of Georgia), 1974.

A-83   Dorman, Coy, MANUFACTURING IN THE WEST CENTRAL KNOXVILLE AREA,
        (M.A.: University of Tennessee), 1959.

A-84   Douglas, Edna May, AN ANALYSIS OF THE RETAIL TRADING AREA OF CHAR-
        LOTTE, NORTH CAROLINA, (Ph.D.: University of North Carolina),
        1945.

A-85 Ebert, Charles H. V., HIGH POINT'S EVOLUTION AS A FURNITURE TOWN, (M.A.: University of North Carolina), 1954.

A-86 Eisterhold, John S., LUMBER AND TRADE IN THE SEABOARD CITIES OF THE OLD SOUTH: 1607-1860, (Ph.D.: University of Mississippi), 1970.

A-87 Enedy, Joseph, THE DEPARTMENT STORE IN METROPOLITAN BALTIMORE, 1945-PRESENT: A GEOGRAPHICAL ANALYSIS, (Ph.D.: Kent State University), 1973.

A-88 Favil, James F., THE STRUCTURAL GROWTH OF THE PORT OF BALTIMORE, 1729-1814, (M.A.: University of Maryland), 1973.

A-89 Ferris, Abbott L., NORTH CAROLINA TRADE CENTERS, 1910-1940: A STUDY IN ECOLOGY, (Ph.D.: University of North Carolina), 1950.

A-90 Flemming, Douglas Lee, ATLANTA, THE DEPRESSION AND THE NEW DEAL, (Ph.D.: Emory University), 1984.

A-91 Freels, Edward Jr., INDUSTRIAL DEVELOPMENT OF THE KNOXVILLE WATER-FRONT, (M.A.: University of Tennessee), 1959.

A-92 Freeze, Richard, MASTER MILL MAN: JOHN MILTON ODELL AND INDUSTRIAL DEVELOPMENT IN CONCORD, NORTH CAROLINA, 1877-1907, (M.A.: University of North Carolina), 1980.

A-93 Fugate, Robert T. Jr., THE BANCOKENTUCKY COMPANY AND THE DEPRESSION IN LOUISVILLE--1919 TO 1932, (M.A.: University of Louisiana), 1972.

A-94 Fukawa, Kazuhisa, AN ANALYSIS OF THE RELATIONSHIP OF COMPARATIVE ADVERTISING AND CULTURE IN JAPANESE NATIVES IN THE DALLAS, TEXAS AREA, (M.A.: North Texas State University), 1979.

A-95 Fundaburk, Emma Lila, BUSINESS CORPORATIONS IN ALABAMA IN THE NINE-TEENTH CENTURY, (Ph.D.: Ohio State University), 1963.

A-96 Garofalo, Charles, BUSINESS IDEAS IN ATLANTA, 1916-1935, (Ph.D.: Emory University), 1972.

A-97 Gilbert, Geoffrey N., BALTIMORE FLOUR TRADE TO THE CARIBBEAN, 1750-1815, (Ph.D.: Johns Hopkins University), 1935.

A-98 Gilbert, James Leslie, THREE SANDS: OKLAHOMA OIL FIELD AND COM-MUNITY OF THE 1920s, (M.A.: University of Oklahoma), 1967.

A-99 Graffy, Catherine M., REHABILITATION OF AN OLD NEIGHBORHOOD RETAIL DISTRICT: A CASE STUDY OF NORTH CHARLOTTE, (M.A.: University of North Carolina), 1976.

A-100 Greb, Gregory A., CHARLESTON, SOUTH CAROLINA, MERCHANTS, 1815-1860: URBAN LEADERSHIP IN THE ANTEBELLUM SOUTH, (Ph.D.: University of California), 1978.

A-101 Green, George David, BANKING AND FINANCE IN ANTE-BELLUM LOUISIANA (1804-1861): THEIR INFLUENCE ON THE COURSE OF ECONOMIC DEVELOP-MENT, (Ph.D.: Stanford University), 1968.

A-102 Guss, Donald, THE RETAIL MERCHANTS ASSOCIATION OF LOUISVILLE, KENTUCKY: THE STUDY OF THE FUNCTION OF RMA IN THE COMMUNITY AND ITS RELATIONSHIP TO THE COMMUNITY, (M.A.: University of Louisville), 1974.

A-103 Hack, Carol Joanne, TALLAHASSEE, FLORIDA: ANALYSIS AND DELIMI-TATION OF A SMALL CITY CENTRAL BUSINESS DISTRICT, (M.A.: Florida State University), 1963.

A-104 Haskins, Ralph H., THE COTTON FACTOR, 1800-1860, A STUDY IN SOUTHERN ECONOMIC AND SOCIAL HISTORY, (Ph.D.: University of California), 1956.

A-105 Heil, Robert Eugene, THE GROWTH AND DEVELOPMENT OF FOREIGN BANKING IN THREE COMMERIAL BANKS IN MOBILE, ALABAMA, (Ph.D.: University of Alabama), 1958.

A-106 Hodge, Jo Dent, THE LUMBER INDUSTRY IN LAUREL, MISSISSIPPI, 1900-1910, (M.A.: University of Mississippi), 1966.

A-107 Hojabri-Houtry, Ahmad, ANALYSIS OF ECONOMIC AND SOCIAL FACTORS LEADING TO THE 1980 MIAMI RIOT: CONTRADICTION WITHIN ECONOMIC PROSPERITY, (D.A.: University of Miami), 1984.

A-108 Holbert, Jerry Edward, RURAL/URBAN CONFLICT OVER WATER CONTROL IN THE LOWER RIO GRANDE VALLEY OF TEXAS, (Ph.D.: Texas A & M University), 1984.

A-109 Hooks, Michael Q., THE STRUGGLE FOR DOMINANCE: URBAN RIVALRY IN NORTH TEXAS, 1870-1910, (Ph.D.: Texas Tech University), 1979.

A-110 House, Ray Smalley, AN ANALYSIS OF THE DECENTRALIZATION OF WHOLE-SALING IN THE MEMPHIS, TENNESSEE, WHOLESALE TRADE AREA FROM 1948 TO 1963, (Ph.D.: University of Mississippi), 1966.

A-111 Hughes, Sarah S., ELIZABETH CITY COUNTY, VIRGINIA, 1782-1810: THE ECONOMIC AND SOCIAL STRUCTURE OF A TIDEWATER COUNTY IN THE EARLY NATIONAL YEARS, (Ph.D.: College of William and Mary), 1975.

A-112 Jaycox, C. Melton, A PROPOSAL FOR THE MEASUREMENT OF MONTHLY RETAIL TRADE ACTIVITY IN THE WASHINGTON METROPOLITAN AREA, (M.A.: American University), 1960.

A-113 Jeffers, James Randall, BANK ASSET PORTFOLIOS AND ECONOMIC ACTIVITY, NEW ORLEANS, ATLANTA, AND HOUSTON, (Ph.D.: Tulane University), 1966.

A-114 Jewell, Jack L., THE GEOGRAPHIC ROLE OF THE HIGH-RISE OFFICE BUILDING IN THE STRUCTURE OF THE OFFICE FUNCTION IN ATLANTA, GEORGIA, (M.A.: University of Georgia), 1965.

A-115 Johnson, George Henry, RICHMOND NEGRO BUSINESSES DURING THE 1920's, (M.A.: Virginia State University), 1969.

A-116 Johnson, Keach D., THE ESTABLISHMENT OF THE BALTIMORE COMPANY: A CASE STUDY OF THE AMERICAN IRON INDUSTRY IN THE EIGHTEENTH CENTURY, (Ph.D.: University of Iowa), 1949.

A-117 Jumper, Sidney R., A GEOGRAPHIC ANALYSIS OF THE COLUMBIA, SOUTH CAROLINA, WHOLESALE MARKET, (M.A.: University of South Carolina), 1953.

A-118 Justen, Michael E., THE ECONOMIC DEVELOPMENT OF SOUTH FLORIDA, (M.A.: Florida State University), 1972.

A-119 Kelly, Larry John, SUPPLYING THE NECESSITIES OF LIFE IN OCCUPIED NEW ORLEANS--1862-65, (M.A.: Louisiana State University), 1965.

A-120 Kelly, Ruth Evlyn, 'TWIXT FAILURE AND SUCCESS: THE PORT OF GALVESTON IN THE NINETEENTH-CENTURY, (M.A.: University of Houston), 1975.

A-121 King, James Crawford, "CONTEXT WITH BEING": NINETEENTH-CENTURY SOUTHERN ATTITUDES TOWARD ECONOMIC DEVELOPMENT, (Ph.D.: University of Alabama), 1985.

A-122 Kirby, Russell S., URBAN GROWTH AND ECONOMIC CHANGE IN THE NINE-
TEENTH CENTURY SOUTH, THE HINTERLAND OF MEMPHIS, TENNESSEE, 1830-
1900, (Ph.D.: University of Wisconsin), 1981.

A-123 Kolbo, Allan D., RESPONSE OF COMMERCIAL AGRICULTURE TO URBAN IMPACT
IN RURAL-URBAN FRINGE OF BALTIMORE CITY, (Ph.D.: University of
Maryland), 1972.

A-124 Laurent, Eugene Anderson, ECONOMIC-ECOLOGIC ANALYSIS IN THE
CHARLESTON METROPOLITAN REGION: AN INPUT-OUTPUT STUDY, (Ph.D.:
Clemson University), 1970.

A-125 Lay, Elery Arnold, AN INDUSTRIAL AND COMMERCIAL HISTORY OF THE TRI-
CITIES IN TENNESSEE, (Ed.D.: George Peabody College for Teachers),
1960.

A-126 Lebsock, Suzanne D., WOMEN AND ECONOMICS IN VIRGINIA: PETERSBURG,
1784-1820, (Ph.D.: University of Virginia), 1977.

A-127 Leslie, Vernon McClean, THE GREAT DEPRESSION IN MIAMI BEACH, (M.A.:
Florida Atlantic University), 1980.

A-128 Lewis, Terry E., FRENCHTOWN: A GEOGRAPHIC SURVEY OF AN ALL-NEGRO
BUSINESS DISTRICT IN TALLAHASSEE, FLORIDA, (M.A.: Florida State
University), 1966.

A-129 Lonon, William Don, A DELIMITATION OF COLUMBIA, SOUTH CAROLINA'S
CENTRAL BUSINESS DISTRICT, (M.A.: University of South Carolina),
1969.

A-130 Logan, Byron Eugene, AN HISTORICAL GEOGRAPHIC STUDY OF NORTH CARO-
LINA PORTS, (Ph.D.: University of North Carolina), 1956.

A-131 Mainville, Linda A., BULLY TIMES IN THOMASVILLE, (Ph.D.: Florida
State University), 1983.

A-132 Marti, Bruce Edward, THE SEAPORT OF MIAMI: SITE DEVELOPMENT, THE
CONTAINER REVOLUTION, AND WATERBORN COMMERCE, (M.A.: Florida
Atlantic University), 1975.

A-133 Massengill, Stephen Edwin, WASHINGTON DUKE AND SONS, BUILDERS OF A
TOBACCO-MANUFACTURING DYNASTY IN DURHAM, NORTH CAROLINA, 1865-
1890, (M.A.: North Carolina State University), 1976.

A-134 Mayer, Arthur J., SAN ANTONIO, FRONTIER ENTREPOT, (Ph.D.: University of Texas), 1976.

A-135 Meyer, Gary, THE CALVERT CITY KENTUCKY INDUSTRIAL COMPLEX--A STUDY
IN SPATIAL INTERACTION, (M.A.: Southern Illinois Unviersity),
1965.

A-136 Miller, Frederick Byers, RICHMOND, VIRGINIA AS A WHOLESALE TRADE
CENTER: AN ANALYSIS OF ITS DEVELOPMENT AND PRESENT POSITION,
(Ph.D.: Ohio State University), 1952.

A-137 Min, Pyong Gap, MINORITY BUSINESS ENTERPRISE: A CASE STUDY OF
KOREAN SMALL BUSINESSES IN ATLANTA, (Ph.D.: Georgia State University), 1983.

A-138 Mitchell, Harry A., NEW ORLEANS AS A WHOLESALE TRADING CENTER,
(Ph.D.: University of Michigan). 1943-44.

A-139 Mowll, Jack Usher, THE ECONOMIC DEVELOPMENT OF 18TH CENTURY BALTI-
MORE, (Ph.D.: Johns Hopkins University), 1956.

A-140 McKnight, Tom L., MANUFACTURING IN DALLAS--A STUDY OF EFFECTS,
(Ph.D.: University of Wisconsin), 1955.

A-141 McNeil, Charles R., THE RED SNAPPER INDUSTRY IN PENSACOLA 1845-
1965: AN HISTORICAL PERSPECTIVE, (M.A.: University of West
Florida), 1977.

A-142 Norman, Herbert P. Jr., GOLDSBORO, NORTH CAROLINA: AN ANALYSIS OF
THE MAJOR OLD AND NEW BUSINESS DISTRICTS, (M.A.: Eastern Carolina
University). 1979.

A-143 Norsworthy, David Ray, MOBILITY EFFECTS OF INDUSTRIAL GROWTH:
TRUCTURAL CHANGE AND WORK EXPERIENCE IN A SOUTHERN PIEDMONT COM-
MUNITY, (Ph.D.: University of North Carolina), 1961.

A-144 Norsworthy, Stanley Frank, HOT SPRINGS, ARKANSAS: A GEOGRAPHIC
ANALYSIS OF THE SPA'S RESORT SERVICE AREA, (Ph.D.: University of
California), 1970.

A-145 Pacetti, Derald, SHRIMPING AT FERNANDINA, FLORIDA BEFORE 1920:
INDUSTRY DEVELOPMENT, FISHERIES REGULATION, WARTIME MATURATION,
(M.A.: Florida State University), 1979.

A-146 Papenfuse, Edward C., MERCHANTILE OPPORTUNITY AND URBAN DEVELOPMENT
IN A PLANTING SOCIETY: A CASE STUDY OF ANNAPOLIS, MARYLAND, 1763-
1805, (Ph.D.: Johns Hopkins University), 1973.

A-147 Parsons, Frieda Jean, AN INVESTIGATION OF ATLANTA AGENCIES TO
DETERMINE IF THE CITY IS POTENTIALLY A LARGE ADVERTISING CENTER,
(M.A.: University of Georgia), 1968.

A-148 Pate, J'Nell L., LIVESTOCK LEGACY: A HISTORY OF THE FORT WORTH
STOCKYARDS COMPANY, 1893-1982, (Ph.D.: North Texas State Univer-
ity), 1982.

A-149 Payne, Wayne H., THE COMMERCIAL DEVELOPMENT OF ANTE-BELLUM
ELIZABETH CITY, (M.A.: Old Dominion), 1971.

A-150 Persky, Joseph Jacob, INDUSTRIALIZATION AND URBAN GROWTH IN THE
SOUTHERN UNITED STATES, (Ph.D.: Harvard University), 1971.

A-151 Purcell, Joseph Caroll, EFFECT OF INCOME, FLUID MILK PRICES, AND
RACE ON CONSUMPTION OF FLUID MILK AND FLUID MILK SUBSTITUTES IN THE
URBAN SOUTH, (Ph.D.: Iowa State University), 1957.

A-152 Rasmussen, Ezra G., NASHVILLE, TENNESSEE, AS A WHOLESALE TRADE
CENTER, (Ph.D.: Ohio State University), 1939.

A-153 Rea, Leonard Owens, THE FINANCIAL HISTORY OF BALTIMORE, 1900-1926,
(Ph.D.: Johns Hopkins University), 1928.

A-154 Reagan, Alice E., HANIBAL I. KIMBALL: NORTHERN ENTREPRENEUR IN
RECONSTRUCTION ATLANTA, (M.A.: North Carolina State University),
1981.

A-155 Rogers, Arthur Leon Jr., MISSISSIPPI BANKING DURING DEPRESSION AND
RECOVERY, (M.A.: George Washington University), 1938.

A-156 Rogers, Ellin Lee, HISTORY OF THE PAPER MILL AT SALEM, NORTH CARO-
LINA, (M.A.: Wake Forest University), 1982.

A-157 Rupertus, John, FRANKLIN STREET: A HISTORY OF TAMPA DOWNTOWN,
1890-1980, (M.A.: University of South Florida), 1980.

A-158 Sagay, Anirejouritse, AN INQUIRY INTO THE ECONOMIC-DEMOGRAPHIC
CAUSES OF BLACK POVERTY IN THE URBAN SOUTHEAST OF THE UNITED
STATES, (Ph.D.: University of Pittsburgh), 1975.

A-159 Saussy, Gordon Anthony, AN ANALYSIS OF THE MANUFACTURING INDUSTRY
IN THE NEW ORLEANS METROPOLITAN AREA, (Ph.D.,: Yale University),
1972.

A-160 Scharre, Margaret Ellen, AN EXAMINATION OF THE CITY OF LOUISVILLE'S INDUSTRIAL DEVELOPMENT PROGRAMS, (M.A.: University of Louisiana), 1980.

A-161 Schmidt, William T., THE IMPACT OF THE CAMP SHELBY MOBILIZATION, 1940-1946, UPON CERTAIN HATTIESBURG, MISSISSIPPI, INSTITUTIONS, (M.A.: University of Southern Mississippi), 1970.

A-162 Schulz, Judith H., THE RISE AND DECLINE OF CAMDEN AS SOUTH CARO-LINA'S MAJOR INLAND TRADING CENTER, 1751-1829: A HISTORICAL GEO-GRAPHICAL STUDY, (M.A.: University of South Carolina), 1972.

A-163 Sharrer, George T., FLOUR MILLING AND THE GROWTH OF BALTIMORE, 1783-1830, (Ph.D.: University of Maryland), 1975.

A-164 Shirley, James Michael, FROM CONGREGATION TOWN TO INDUSTRIAL CITY: INDUSTRIALIZATION, CLASS, AND CULTURE IN NINETEENTH CENTURY WINSTON AND SALEM, NORTH CAROLINA, (Ph.D.: Emory University), 1986.

A-165 Siegel, Fred Fein, A NEW SOUTH IN THE OLD: SOTWEED AND SOIL IN THE DEVELOPMENT OF DANVILLE, VIRGINIA, (Ph.D.: University of Pitts-burgh), 1978.

A-166 Siener, William Harold, ECONOMIC DEVELOPMENT IN REVOLUTIONARY VIR-GINIA: FREDERICKSBURG, 1750-1810, (Ph.D.: College of William and Mary), 1982.

A-167 Sisco, Paul H., THE RETAIL FUNCTION OF MEMPHIS, (Ph.D.: University of Chicago), 1955.

A-168 Smith, Fenlon Devere, THE ECONOMIC DEVELOPMENT OF THE TEXTILE IN-DUSTRY IN THE COLUMBIA, SOUTH CAROLINA AREA FROM 1790 THROUGH 1916, (Ph.D.: University of Kentucky), 1952.

A-169 Solomon, Robert Henry, A STUDY OF THE COMPETITIVE POSITION OF SMALL TOWN DEPARTMENT STORES AND SPECIALTY APPAREL SHOPS IN CENTRAL AR-KANSAS COMPARED WITH THE LITTLE ROCK METROPOLITAN SHOPPING AREA, (Ph.D.: University of Arkansas), 1971.

A-170 Sorbet, Elizabeth Melanie, A MARKET STUDY OF A BATON ROUGE SUBURB, (Ph.D.: Louisiana State University), 1958.

A-171 Stewart, Peter Crawford, THE COMMERCIAL HISTORY OF HAMPTON ROADS, VIRGINIA, 1815-1860, (Ph.D.: University of Virginia), 1967.

A-172 Stewart, Ronald Laird, THE INFLUENCE OF THE BUSINESS COMMUNITY IN OKLAHOMA CITY POLITICS, (M.A.: Oklahoma State University), 1967.

A-173 Stuart, Alfred W., THE SUBURBANIZATION OF MANUFACTURING IN A SMALL METROPOLITAN AREA: ROANOKE, VIRGINIA, (Ph.D.: Ohio State Univer-ity), 1966.

A-174 Stumpf, Stuart Owen, THE MERCHANTS OF COLONIAL CHARLESTON, 1680-1756, (Ph.D.: Michigan State University), 1971.

A-175 Sullivan, Charles K., COAL MEN AND COAL TOWNS: DEVELOPMENT OF THE SMOKELESS COALFIELDS OF SOUTHERN WEST VIRGINIA, 1873-1923, (Ph.D.: University of Pittsburgh), 1979.

A-176 Tanney, Richard Randall, ECONOMIC EXPANSION AND URBAN DISORDER IN ANTEBELLUM NEW ORLEANS, (Ph.D.: University of Texas), 1981.

A-177 Thelin, Mark Cushman, EXECUTIVE CHARACTERISTICS AND COMMUNITY IN-VOLVEMENT: A SOCIOLOGICAL ANALYSIS OF TOP BUSINESS EXECUTIVES IN FOUR NORTH CAROLINA CITIES, (Ph.D.: University of North Carolina), 1962.

A-178 Thompson, Alan Smith, MOBILE, ALABAMA, 1850-1861: ECONOMIC, POLITICAL, PHYSICAL, AND POPULATION CHARACTERISTICS, (Ph.D.: University of Alabama), 1979.

A-179 Thibodeaux, Earl Charles, THE NEW ORLEANS-HOUSTON PORT RIVALRY, (Ph.D.: Columbia University), 1952.

A-180 Thornton, Charles Arthur, THE ROLE OF TRANSPORTATION (1790-1961): IMPLICATIONS IN THE DECENTRALIZATION AND CENTRALIZATION OF THE WHOLESALING FUNCTION IN SELECTED CITIES OF EAST TENNESSEE, (Ph.D.: University of Tennessee), 1970.

A-181 Triplette, Ralph R., ONE INDUSTRY TOWNS: THEIR LOCATION, DEVELOPMENT AND ECONOMIC CHARACTER, (Ph.D.: University of North Carolina), 1974.

A-182 Trump, Ross M., THE PORT OF NEW ORLEANS WITH SPECIAL REFERENCE TO ITS FOREIGN TRADE ZONE, (Ph.D.: Ohio State University), 1948.

A-183 Tucker, Leah B., THE HOUSTON BUSINESS COMMUNITY, 1945-1965, (Ph.D.: University of Texas), 1979.

A-184 Ullman, Edward L., MOBILE: INDUSTRIAL SEAPORT AND TRADE CENTER, (Ph.D.: University of Chicago), 1942.

A-185 Walters, Elsie M., AN ANALYSIS OF BUSINESS FLUCTUATIONS IN NEW ORLEANS, (Ph.D.: University of Texas), 1953.

A-186 Wender, Herbert, SOUTHERN COMMERCIAL CONVENTIONS, 1837-1859, (Ph.D.: Johns Hopkins University), 1927.

A-187 Westfall, L. Glenn, DON VICENTE MARTINEZ YBOR, THE MAN AND HIS EMPIRE, (Ph.D.: University of Florida), 1977.

A-188 White, Gayle Colquitt, ATLANTA MAGAZINE--MEMBER OF THE NEW BREED?, (B.A. Honors Thesis: University of Georgia), 1972.

A-189 Whites, Leeann, SOUTHERN LADIES AND MILLHANDS: THE DOMESTIC ECONOMY AND CLASS POLITICS; AUGUSTA, GEORGIA, 1870-1890, (Ph.D.: University of California), 1982.

A-190 Williams, Harry Jr., THE DEVELOPMENT OF A MARKET ECONOMY IN TEXAS: THE ESTABLISHMENT OF THE RAILWAY NETWORK, 1836-1890, (Ph.D.: University of Texas), 1957.

A-191 Wilson, Livy Thompson, FLORIDA BUSINESS CORPORATIONS, 1838-1885, (Ph.D.: University of Illinois), 1965.

A-192 Witcher, Eulis Dale, FACTORS IMFLUENCING THE LOCATION OF CHEMICAL MANUFACTURING PLANTS IN WILMINGTON, NORTH CAROLINA, (M.S.: East Carolina University), 1974.

A-193 Woody, Stephen W., BRANCH BANKING IN NORTH CAROLINA--ITS HISTORY, ECONOMIC CONTRIBUTION, AND FUTURE, (Stonier Graduate School of Banking), 1972.

A-194 Wotton, Grigsby H., THE NEW CITY OF THE SOUTH: ATLANTA, 1843-1873, (Ph.D.: Johns Hopkins University), 1973.

A-195 Yang, Ok-Hyee, LOCATIONAL FACTORS AND THE SPATIAL DISTRIBUTION OF SELECTED OFFICE INDUSTRIES IN ATLANTA, (M.A.: University of Georgia), 1982.

A-196 Yantis, Betty Louise, THE ECONOMIC IMPACT OF INDUSTRY ON COMMUNITY SERVICES IN SEVEN MUNICIPALITIES IN THE OZARKS REGION OF ARKANSAS, (Ph.D.: University of Arkansas), 1971.

Dance

A-197 Terry, Terlene Darcell, A SURVEY OF BLACK DANCE IN WASHINGTON, 1870-1945, (M.A.: American University), 1982.

Ecology and Environment

A-198 Barker, Rebecca Ann Consoul, MICROBIAL AEROSOLS GENERATED FROM AERATED POLLUTED WATERS IN URBAN AND SUBURBAN AREAS, (M.S.: University of Louisville), 1982.

A-199 Curry, Mary-Grace, LIMNOLOGY OF THE UNIVERSITY LAKE SYSTEM, BATON ROUGE, LOUISIANA, (Ph.D.: Louisiana State University), 1973.

A-200 Giaquinto, Eli Joseph, THE URBANIZATION OF NATIONAL FOREST POLICY IN THE SOUTH, (D.P.A.: University of Georgia). 1981.

A-201 Hagden, Robert S., STORM WATER RUNOFF IN A SMALL URBAN STREAM BASIN: PRESENT AND FUTURE PATTERNS IN CAMPBELL CREEK BASIN, MECKLENBURG COUNTY, NORTH CAROLINA, (M.A.: University of North Carolina), 1975.

A-202 Kung, Hsiang-Te, ASPECTS OF URBAN HYDROLOGY OF KNOXVILLE, TENNESSEE, (Ph.D.: University of Tennessee), 1980.

A-203 Massey, Joel Edward, THE APPLICATION AND VALIDATION OF THE CLIMA-TOLOGICAL DISPERSION MODEL AS APPLIED TO THE NEW ORLEANS METROPOLI-TAN AREA, (Ph.D.: University of Oklahoma), 1979.

A-204 Purvis, John Caston, THE PROBLEMS OF AIR POLUTION AND ITS RELATION-SHIP TO LAND USE IN COLUMBIA, SOUTH CAROLINA, (M.A.: University of South Carolina), 1969.

A-205 Segretto, Peter Salvatore, THE RELATIONSHIP BETWEEN URBANIZATION AND STREAM FLOW IN THE HILLSBOROUGH RIVER BASIN, 1940-1970, (Ph.D.: University of Florida), 1976.

A-206 Tarver, John Lee, AN ANALYSIS OF SELECTED TYPES OF ECONOMIC IMPACT IN THE MOBILE, ALABAMA, AREA AS RELATED TO WATER QUALITY CHANGES IN THE MOBILE RIVER SYSTEM, WITH PARTICULAR EMPHASIS UPON THE PERIOD 1960-1971, (Ph.D.: University of Arkansas), 1972.

A-207 Whitehead, Lawrence William, SOME MICROCLIMATE AND AIR QUALITY IM-PLICATIONS OF URBANIZATION IN A SOUTHERN COASTAL FOREST, (Ph.D.: University of Texas), 1976.

A-208 Wise, Robert Batey, THE EFFECT OF URBANIZATION ON WATER RESOURCES IN THE GAINESVILLE, FLORIDA, URBAN AREA, (M.A.: University of Florida), 1973.

Education

A-209 Butler, Addie L. J., THE DISTINCTIVE BLACK COLLEGE: TALLADEGA, TUSKEGEE, AND MOREHOUSE, (Ph.D.: Columbia Universtiy Teachers College), 1976.

A-210 Collins, Wellyn Fitzgerald, LOUISVILLE MUNICIPAL COLLEGE: A STUDY OF THE COLLEGE FOUNDED FOR NEGROES IN LOUISVILLE, (M.A.: University of Louisiana), 1976.

A-211 Crimmins, Timothy James, THE CRYSTAL STAIR: A STUDY OF THE EFFECTS OF CLASS, RACE, AND ETHNICITY ON SECONDARY EDUCATION IN ATLANTA, 1872-1925, (Ph.D.: Emory University), 1972.

A-212 Frascogna, Xavier M. Jr., CATHOLIC EDUCATION IN JACKSON, MISSIS-SIPPI, (M.S.: Mississippi State University), 1970.

A-213 Geisel, Paul Newton, IQ PERFORMANCE, EDUCATIONAL AND OCCUPATIONAL ASPIRATIONS OF YOUTH IN A SOUTHERN CITY: A RACIAL COMPARISON, (Ph.D.: Vanderbilt University), 1962.

A-214 Ihle, Elizabeth L., THE DEVELOPMENT OF COEDUCATION IN MAJOR SOUTHERN STATE UNIVERSITIES, (Ph.D.: University of Tennessee), 1976.

A-215 Jackson, Brenda F., THE POLICIES AND PURPOSES OF BLACK PUBLIC SCHOOLING IN LOUISVILLE, KENTUCKY, 1890-1930, (Ph.D.: Indiana University), 1976.

A-216 Jackson, McArthur, A HISTORICAL STUDY OF THE FOUNDING AND DEVELOP-MENT OF TUSKEGEE INSTITUTE, (Ph.D.: University of North Carolina), 1983.

A-217 Kazaleh, Fadwa Ann, BICULTURALISM AND ADJUSTMENT: A STUDY OF RUMALLAH-AMERICAN ADOLESCENTS IN JACKSONVILLE, FLORIDA, (Ph.D.: Florida State Universtiy), 1986.

A-218 Logsdon, Guy W., THE UNIVERSITY OF TULSA: A HISTORY FROM 1882 TO 1972, (Ph.D.: University of Oklahoma), 1975.

A-219 Montgomery, James Riley, THE UNIVERSITY OF TENNESSEE, 1887-1919, (Ph.D.: Columbia University), 1961.

A-220 Peterson, Alma H., THE ADMINISTRATION OF PUBLIC SCHOOLS IN NEW ORLEANS, 1841-1861, (Ph.D.: Louisiana State University), 1964.

A-221 Pope, Christie F., PREPARATION FOR PEDESTALS: NORTH CAROLINA ANTEBELLUM FEMALE SEMINARIES, (Ph.D.: University of Chicago), 1977.

A-222 Ramsey, Berkley Carlyle, THE PUBLIC BLACK COLLEGE IN GEORGIA: A HISTORY OF ALBANY STATE COLLEGE, 1903-1965, (Ph.D.: Florida State University), 1973.

A-223 Skelton, Phillip D., A HISTORY OF SOUTHERN ARKANSAS UNIVERSITY FROM 1909 TO 1976, (Ph.D.: University of Mississippi), 1979.

A-224 Thurman, Frances A., THE HISTORY OF SAINT PAUL'S COLLEGE, LAWRENCE-VILLE, VIRGINIA, 1888-1959, (Ph.D.: Howard University), 1978.

A-225 Williams, Ann Lawrens, IN SEARCH OF A HOME: AN HISTORICAL ANALYSIS OF THE MAJOR FACTORS CONCERNING THE LOCATION OF VIRGINIA COMMON-WEALTH UNIVERSITY, (Ed.D.: College of William and Mary), 1985.

Growth and Development

A-226 Blackbourn, Anthony, THE ROLE OF PLANNED INDUSTRIAL DISTRICTS IN THE INDUSTRIAL DEVELOPMENT OF ATLANTA, (M.A.: University of Georgia), 1961.

A-227 Buescher, Paul Allen, URBANIZATION AND REGIONAL CONVERGENCE: A COMPARATIVE STUDY OF WHEAT AND COTTON AREAS OF THE UNITED STATES, (Ph.D.: University of North Carolina), 1977.

A-228 Cigliano, Jan Elizabeth, NORRIS, TENNESSEE: AMERICA'S FORGOTTEN TVA NEW TOWN, (M.U.R.P.: George Washington University), 1982.

A-229 DeMontequia, Francois-Auguste, MAPS AND PLANS OF CITIES AND TOWNS IN COLONIAL NEW SPAIN, THE FLORIDAS AND LOUISIANA: SELECTED DOCU-MENTS FROM THE ARCHIVO GENERAL DE INDIAS OF SEVILLA, (Ph.D.: University of New Mexico), 1974.

A-230 Ernst, William J., URBAN LEADERS AND SOCIAL CHANGE: THE URBANIZA-
TION PROCESS IN RICHMOND, VIRGINIA, 1840-1880, (Ph.D.: University
of Virginia), 1978.

A-231 Gangami, Marie Elaina, TRANSITION IN ABEYANCE: URBAN GROWTH IN
RALEIGH, 1880-1900, (M.A.: University of North Carolina), 1975.

A-232 Grim, Ronald Eugene, THE ABSENCE OF TOWNS IN SEVENTEENTH-CENTURY
VIRGINIA: THE EMERGENCE OF SERVICE CENTERS IN YORK COUNTY, (PH.D.:
University of Maryland), 1977.

A-233 Grisham, Vaughn L. Jr., TUPELO, MISSISSIPPI, FROM SETTLEMENT TO
INDUSTRIAL COMMUNITY, 1860 TO 1970, (Ph.D.: University of North
Carolina), 1976.

A-234 Hargan, James, THE SEQUENCY OF DEVELOPMENT IN A TAMPA SUBURB, 1900-
1978, (M.A.: Pennsylvania State University), 1982.

A-235 Hayes, Charles, THE DISPERSED CITY: THE CASE OF PIEDMONT, NORTH
CAROLINA, (Ph.D.: University of Chicago), 1975.

A-236 Hearn, Walter Carey, TOWNS IN ANTEBELLUM MISSISSIPPI, (Ph.D.:
University of Mississippi), 1969.

A-237 Holly, John Fred, THE SOCIAL AND ECONOMIC EFFECTS PRODUCED UPON
SMALL TOWNS BY RAPID INDUSTRIALIZATION, (M.A.: University of
Tennessee), 1938.

A-238 Holly, John Fred, ELIZABETHTON, TENNESSEE: A CASE STUDY OF
SOUTHERN INDUSTRIALIZATION, (Ph.D.: Clark University), 1949.,

A-239 Howard, Etha Johannaber, THE IMPACT OF URBAN DEVELOPMENT ON ETHNIC
IDENTITY IN A TEXAS GERMAN-AMERICAN COMMUNITY, (Ph.D.: Southern
Methodist University), 1984.

A-240 Huggins, Koleen Alice Haire, THE EVALUATION OF CITY AND REGIONAL
PLANNING IN NORTH CAROLINA, 1900-1950, (Ph.D.: Duke University),
1967.

A-241 Jackson, Dorothy B., THE GROWTH OF AN INDUSTRIAL CITY, BIRMINGHAM,
1800-1851, (Ph.D.: Yale University), 1956.

A-242 Kramer, Carl Edward, THE CITY-BUILDING PROCESS: URBANIZATION IN
CENTRAL AND SOUTHERN LOUISVILLE, 1772-1932, (Ph.D.: University of
Toledo), 1980.

A-243 Lyon, Elizabeth A. M., BUSINESS BUILDINGS IN ATLANTA: A STUDY IN
URBAN GROWTH AND FORM, (Ph.D.: Emory University), 1971.

A-244 Maloney, John J., THE CHAPEL HILL-DURHAM BOULEVARD: A CASE STUDY
OF URBAN COALESCENCE, (M.A.: University of North Carolina), 1977.

A-245 Manieri, Raymond E., STREETCAR SPECULATORS: THE ROLE OF STREET
RAILWAY PROMOTERS IN THE DEVELOPMENT OF SUBURBAN NEIGHBORHOODS IN
RALEIGH AND GREENSBORO, NORTH CAROLINA, 1886-1923, (M.A.: North
Carolina State University), 1982.

A-246 Marionneaux, Ronald Lee, MONROE-WEST MONROE, LOUISIANA: AREAL
EXPANSION OF THE CORPORATE CITY, (Ph.D.: Indiana University),
1970.

A-247 Mathews, Robert C., NORTH NASHVILLE: A HISTORY OF URBAN DEVELOP-
MENT, (Thesis--Honors Certificate in Urban and Regional Studies,
University of North Carolina), 1976.

A-248 O'Mara, James J., URBANIZATION IN TIDEWATER VIRGINIA DURING THE
EIGHTEENTH CENTURY: A STUDY IN HISTORICAL GEOGRAPHY, (Ph.D.: York
University, Canada), 1979.

A-249 Oswald, Eleanor Virginia, THE DEVELOPMENT OF TOWN PLANNING IN NORTH CAROLINA, (M.A.: North Carolina State University), 1982.

A-250 Pathak, Chitteranjan, GROWTH PATTERNS OF RALEIGH, NORTH CAROLINA, Ph.D.: University of North Carolina), 1963.

A-251 Payne, James Edward, BURLINGTON-GRAHAM: A STUDY OF URBAN DEVELOP- MENT, (M.A.: University of North Carolina), 1952.,

A-252 Pile, Elsie, EXPANSION OF THE LEXINGTON URBAN AREA INTO THE RURAL AREA OF THE INNER BLUEGRASS, 1950-1958, (M.A.: University of Kentucky), 1959.

A-253 Randall, Duncan P., GEOGRAPHIC FACTORS IN THE GROWTH AND ECONOMY OF WILMINGTON, NORTH CAROLINA, (Ph.D.: University of North Carolina), 1965.

A-254 Richards, Ira Don, THE URBAN FRONTIER, LITTLE ROCK IN THE NINE- TEENTH CENTURY, (Ph.D.: Tulane University), 1964.

A-255 Russell, Kirby, URBAN GROWTH AND ECONOMIC CHANGE IN THE NINETEENTH- CENTURY SOUTH: THE HINTERLAND OF MEMPHIS, TENNESSEE, 1830-1900, (Ph.D.: University of Wisconsin), 1982.

A-256 Sears, Joan Niles, THE FIRST HUNDRED YEARS OF TOWN PLANNING IN GEORGIA, (Ph.D.: Emory University), 1977.

A-257 Sessa, Frank B., REAL ESTATE EXPANSION AND BOOM IN MIAMI AND ITS ENVIRONS DURING THE 1920s, (Ph.D.: University of Pittsburgh), 1950.

A-258 Snaden, John William, UNINCORPORATED FRINGE--CHARLESTON, WEST VIRGINIA, (Ph.D.: University of Michigan) 1958.

A-259 Stanton, James Russell, A STUDY OF PUBLIC RELATIONS IN THE MIAMI LAND BOOM OF THE 1920s, (M.A.: University of Florida), 1974.

A-260 Walker, Raul K., THE BALTIMORE COMMUNITY AND THE AMERICAN REVO- LUTION, 1763-1783: A STUDY IN URBAN DEVELOPMENT, (Ph.D.: Uni- versity of North Carolina), 1973.

A-261 Wayne, Lucy B., THE BAILEY HOUSE SITE: THE URBANIZATION OF A SOUTHERN PLANTATION, (M.S.: University of Florida), 1981.

A-262 Weiher, Kenneth Edward, SOUTHERN URBANIZATION AND URBAN GROWTH: 1880-1930. AN APPLICATION OF CENTRAL PLACE THEORY, (Ph.D.: Indiana University), 1975.

A-263 Westmeyer, Dean Paul, TAMPA, FLORIDA, A GEOGRAPHIC INTERPRETAITON OF ITS DEVELOPMENT, (M.A.: University of Florida), 1953.

A-264 Wheeler, Kenneth W., EARLY URBAN DEVELOPMENT IN TEXAS, 1836-1885, (Ph.D.: University of Rochester), 1964.

A-265 Whitley, Donna Jean, FULLER E. CALLAWAY AND TEXTILE MILL DEVELOP- MENT IN LAGRANGE, 1895-1920, (Ph.D.: Emory University), 1984.

A-266 Wiggins, James W., ATLANTA'S POSITION IN THE SOUTHEAST: AN ECOLOGICAL ANALYSIS, (Ph.D.: Duke University), 1956.

A-267 Wolton, G.H., URBANIZATION AND THE URBAN PATTERN IN THE SOUTH: ATLANTA, 1865-1881, (Ph.D.: Johns Hopkins University), 1971.

A-268 Zelinsky, Wilbur, THE SETTLEMENT PATTERNS OF GEORGIA, (Ph.D.: University of California), 1953.

A-269 Zucchetto, James John, ENERGY BASIS FOR MIAMI, FLORIDA, AND OTHER URBAN SYSTEMS, (Ph.D.: University of Florida), 1975.

Ghost Towns

A-270 Adkins, Howard Glen, THE HISTORICAL GEOGRAPHY OF EXTINCT TOWNS IN MISSISSIPPI, (Ph.D.: University of Tennessee), 1972.

Hazards and Disasters

A-271 Genessee, Jim, PERCEPTION OF THE TORNADO HAZARD IN TWO SOUTH MIS-SISSIPPI COMMUNITIES, (M.A.: University of South Mississippi), 1982.

Health

A-272 Chandler, Sue An, THE USE OF ALTERNATE HEALTH RESOURCES IN A SOUTH TEXAS TOWN, (M.A.: University of Houston), 1978.

A-273 Daley, John Michael, PARTICIPATION IN COMPREHENSIVE HEALTH PLAN-NING: THE NEW ORLEANS EXPERIENCE, 1967-1971, (D.S.W.: Tulane University School of Social Work), 1971.

A-274 Drake, Harrington Max Jr., URBAN AND RURAL PATTERNS OF FIRST ADMIS-SION RATES OF WHITE FUNCTIONAL PSYCHOTICS IN NORTH CAROLINA, 1960-1968, (Ph.D.: University of North Carolina), 1975.

A-275 Ellis, John H., YELLOW FEVER AND THE ORIGINS OF MODERN PUBLIC HEALTH IN MEMPHIS, TENNESSEE, 1970-1900, (Ph.D.: Tulane University, 1962.

A-276 Ettling, Albert J. Jr., THE GERM OF LAZINESS: THE ROCKEFELLER SANITARY COMMISSION IN THE SOUTHERN STATES, 1909-1914, (Ph.D.: Harvard University), 1978.

A-277 Galke, Warren Arthur, RELATIONSHIP OF LEAD IN HAIR AND BLOOD TO SOIL, AIR, AND PAINT LEAD EXPOSURE: A STUDY OF CHILDREN IN CHARLESTON, S.C., (Ph.D.: University of North Carolina), 1979.

A-278 Keil, Julian Eugene, HYPERTENSION: EFFECTS OF SOCIAL CLASS AND RACIAL ADMIXTURE IN A NEGRO COMMUNITY OF CHARLESTON, SOUTH CARO-LINA, (Ph.D.: University of North Carolina), 1975.

A-279 Kingsdale, Jon Michael, THE GROWTH OF HOSPITALS: AN ECONOMIC HISTORY IN BALTIMORE, (Ph.D.: University of Michigan), 1981.

A-280 Lavoie, Bonnie Britt, AN ECOLOGIC STUDY OF FAMILIES WITH DOWN'S SYNDROME CHILDREN IN THE WASHINGTON METROPOLITAN AREA: IMPLICA-TIONS FOR PREVENTION AND CARE, (Ph.D.: George Washington University), 1974.

A-281 Newhouse, Janette Kaplan, PATTERNS OF IN-HOME CARE SERVICE USE AMONG OLDER ADULTS: A RURAL-URBAN COMPARISON, (Ph.D.: Virginia Polytechnic Institute and State University), 1985.

A-282 Parrish, Theodore Roosevelt, SELECTION OF ORTHODOX VS. TRADITIONAL HEALTH CARE PRACTITIONERS: A STUDY OF FACTORS RELATED TO THE UTILIZATION BEHAVIOR OF RURAL AND URBAN BLACKS IN VANCE AND WARREN COUNTIES, N.C., (Ph.D.: University of North Carolina), 1977.

A-283 Query, Joy M. Neale, A CULTURAL COMPARISON OF SCHIZOPHRENIA IN MOUNTAIN RURAL AND METROPOLITAN KENTUCKY, (Ph.D.: University of Kentucky), 1961.

A-284 Ratigan, Marion, A SOCIOLOGICAL SURVEY OF DISEASE IN FOUR ALLEYS IN THE NATIONAL CAPITAL, (Ph.D.: Catholic University of America), 1946.

A-285 Warner, Joseph Lacy, THE JACKSONVILLE YELLOW FEVER EPIDEMIC OF
1888: A CASE STUDY OF THE EFFECT OF NATURAL DISASTER UPON GROWTH,
(M.A.: University of Florida), 1976.

A-286 Warner, Margaret Ellen, PUBLIC HEALTH IN THE NEW SOUTH: GOVERN-
MENT, MEDICINE AND SOCIETY IN THE CONTROL OF YELLOW FEVER, (Ph.D.:
Harvard University), 1983.

History and Geography

A-287 Anthony, Arthe Agnes, THE NEGRO CREOLE COMMUNITY IN NEW ORLEANS,
1880-1920: AN ORAL HISTORY, (Ph.D.: University of California),
1978.

A-288 Atkins, Emily Howard, A HISTORY OF JACKSONVILLE, FLORIDA, 1816-
1902, (M.A.: Duke University), 1941.

A-289 Autry, Willie Mae (Stowe), THE INTERNATIONAL COTTON EXPOSITION,
ATLANTA, GEORGIA, 1881, (M.A.: University of Georgia), 1938.

A-290 Bacon, H. Philip, THE HISTORICAL GEOGRAPHY OF ANTE-BELLUM NASH-
VILLE, (Ph.D.: George Peabody College for Teachers), 1955.

A-291 Barham, Betty, A HISTORY OF MERIDIAN, MISSISSIPPI, 1860-1917,
M.A.: Mississippi College), 1970.

A-292 Bergeron, Arthur William Jr., THE CONFEDERATE DEFENSE OF MOBILE,
1861-1865, (Ph.D.: Louisiana State University), 1980.

A-293 Beyer, Carolyn Holt, SOCIAL PROCESSES: A CURRICULUM APPROACH TO
LOCAL AND COMMUNITY HISTORY; JULIAN, NORTH CAROLINA: A CASE STUDY,
(Ed.D.: University of North Carolina, Greensboro), 1981.

A-294 Bigelow, Martha C. Mitchell, BIRMINGHAM: A BIOGRAPHY OF A CITY OF
THE NEW SOUTH, (Ph.D.: University of Chicago), 1946.

A-295 Boozer, Jack D., JACKSONVILLE, ALABAMA, 1833-1846, (M.A.: University of Alabama), 1951.

A-296 Briede, Kathryn C., A HISTORY OF THE CITY OF LAFAYETTE, (M.A.:
Tulane University), 1937.

A-297 Bagler, William Thomas, THE BRITISH EXPEDITION TO CHARLESTON, 1779-
1780, (Ph.D.: University of Michigan), 1957.

A-298 Burhans, Nathaniel Charles, THE GEOGRAPHY OF CHATTANOOGA, TENNES-
SEE, (Ph.D.: Ohio State University), 1932.

A-299 Case, Dale Edward, OAK RIDGE, TENNESSEE: A GEOGRAPHIC STUDY,
(Ph.D.: University of Tennessee), 1955.

A-300 Causey, Virginia E., GLEN ALLAN, MISSISSIPPI: CHANGE AND CONTINU-
ITY IN A DELTA COMMUNITY, 1900 TO 1950, (Ph.D.: Emory University),
1983.

A-301 Clark, Dennis R., BALTIMORE, 1729-1829: THE GENESIS OF A COMMUN-
ITY, (Ph.D.: Catholic University of America), 1976.

A-302 Connell, Mary A., THE HISTORY OF THE PEABODY HOTEL, (M.A.: University of Mississippi), 1971.

A-303 Cooper, Constance J., A TOWN AMONG CITIES: NEW CASTLE, DELAWARE,
1780-1840, (Ph.D.: University of Delaware), 1983.

A-304 Cornell, Charlene M., LOUISVILLE IN TRANSITION: 1870-1890, (M.A.:
University of Louisville), 1970.

A-305 Davis, Betty Robbins, VICKSBURG: THE OCCUPIED CITY, (M.A.: Stephen F. Austin State University), 1978.

A-306 Deaton, Thomas M., ATLANTA DURING THE PROGRESSIVE ERA, (Ph.D.: University of Georgia), 1969.

A-307 Demko, Donald, THE HIERARCHY OF CENTRAL PLACES IN THE BLUE GRASS REGION OF KENTUCKY, (M.A.: University of Cincinnati), 1967.

A-308 Dillman, Charles Daniel, THE FUNCTIONS OF BROWNSVILLE, TEXAS AND MATAMOROS, TAMULIPAS: TWIN CITIES OF THE LOWER RIO GRANDE, (Ph.D.: University of Michigan), 1968.

A-309 Dodd, Rebecca F., A HISTORY OF EAST POINT, GEORGIA, (M.A.: Georgia State University), 1971.

A-310 Dubose, Euba E., THE HISTORY OF MOUNT STERLING, (M.A.: University of Alabama), 1931.

A-311 Dunkle, John R., ST. AUGUSTINE, FLORIDA--A STUDY IN HISTORICAL GEOGRAPHY, (Ph.D.: Clarke University), 1955.

A-312 Durney, Michael J., TALLAHASSEE TESTIMONIAL 1905, (M.A.: Florida State University), 1974.

A-313 Dyce, Cedric, A GEOGRAPHICAL HISTORY OF THE NEGRO MIDDLE CLASS IN WEST BALTIMORE, 1880-1970, (M.A.: Syracuse University), 1973.

A-314 Eaves, Charles Dudley, POST CITY: A STUDY IN COLONIZATION ON THE TEXAS PLAINS, (Ph.D.: University of Texas), 1943.

A-315 Elliott, Mary Jane, LEXINGTON, KENTUCKY, 1792-1810: THE ATHENS OF THE WEST, (M.A.: University of Delaware), 1973.

A-316 Fisher, James Arthur, THE HISTORY OF MULBERRY AND FRONTIER FLORIDA: A MODEL FOR THE TEACHING OF LOCAL HISTORY, (D.A.: Middle Tennessee State University), 1974.

A-317 Fleming, William F., SAN ANTONIO: THE HISTORY OF A MILITARY CITY, 1865-1880, (PH.D.: University of Pennsylvania), 1963.

A-318 Gates, Grace H., THE MAKING OF A MODEL CITY: A HISTORY OF ANNIS-TON, ALABAMA, 1872-1900, (Ph.D.: Emory University), 1976.

A-319 German, Richard Henry Lee, THE QUEEN CITY OF THE SAVANNAH: AUGUSTA, GEORGIA, DURING THE URBAN PROGRESSIVE ERA, 1890-1917, (Ph.D.: University of Florida), 1971.

A-320 Gladden, James Wyman Jr., A FUNCTIONAL CLASSIFICATION OF AN INTE-GRATED URBAN COMPLEX: ALABAMA, (M.A.: University of Alabama), 1967.

A-321 Groene, Bertram Hawthorne, ANTE-BELLUM TALLAHASSEE: IT WAS A GAY TIME THEN, (Ph.D.: Florida State University), 1967.

A-322 Hagerty, Julius P., Jr., EARLY HISTORY OF THE INDUSTRIAL CITY OF ANNISTON, 1872-1889, (M.A.: Auburn University), 1960.

A-323 Hardy, Emmett L., AN INTRODUCTION TO THE STUDY OF THE NOMENCLATURE OF KENTUCKY CITIES AND TOWNS, (M.A.: University of Kentucky), 1949.

A-324 Harkins, John E., THE NEGLECTED PHASE OF LOUISIANA'S COLONIAL HIS-TORY: THE NEW ORLEANS CABILDO, 1769-1803, (Ph.D.: Memphis State University), 1976.

A-325 Hayden, Julius J., PASS CHRISTIAN, MISSISSIPPI'S FIRST RESORT TOWN, (M.S.: Mississippi State College), 1950.

A-326 Henderson, William Dalton, RECONSTRUCTION IN PETERSBURG, VIRGINIA, (M.S.: Radford College), 1966.

A-327 Hildreth, Charles Halsey, A HISTORY OF GAINESVILLE, FLORIDA, (Ph.D.: University of Florida), 1954.

A-328 Hinsley, Curtis M. Jr., THE DEVELOPMENT OF A PROFESSION: ANTHRO-POLOGY IN WASHINGTON, D. C., 1846-1903, (Ph.D.: University of Wisconsin), 1976.

A-329 Hodgson, Julia, A COMPARISON OF THREE TENNESSEE URBAN CENTERS: GOODLETTSVILLE, FRANKLIN, CLARKSVILLE, (Ph.D.: George Peabody College for Teachers), 1939.

A-330 Hofstra, Warren Raymond, THESE FINE PROSPECTS: FREDERICK COUNTY, VIRGINIA, 1738-1840, (Ph.D.: University of Virginia), 1985.

A-331 Holder, Gerald Leon, THE FALL LINE TOWNS OF GEORGIA: AN HISTORICAL GEOGRAPHY, (Ph.D.: University of Georgia), 1973.

A-332 Hussain, Farhat, GAINESVILLE, FLORIDA: A GEOGRAPHIC STUDY OF A CITY IN TRANSITION, (Ph.D.: University of Florida), 1959.

A-333 James, Dorris Clayton, ANTE-BELLUM NATCHEZ, (Ph.D.: University of Texas), 1964.

A-334 Jenkins, William T., ANTE-BELLUM MACON AND BIBB COUNTY, GEORGIA, (Ph.D.: University of Georgia), 1966.

A-335 Jones, Newton B., CHARLOTTESVILLE AND ALBEMARLE COUNTY, VIRGINIA, 1819-1860, (Ph.D.: University of Virginia), 1950.

A-336 Joyce, Allen Edward, THE ATLANTA BLACK CRACKERS, (M.A.: Emory University), 1975.

A-337 Lucas, Marion Brunson, THE BURNING OF COLUMBIA, (PH.D.: University of South Carolina), 1965.

A-338 Marvinbach, Bernard, THE GALVESTON MOVEMENT, (Ph.D.: Jewish Theo-logical Seminary of America), 1977.

A-339 Matthews, Richard Ira, THE NEW ORLEANS REVOLUTION OF 1768: A REIN-TERPRETATION, (M.A.: Northwestern State College of Louisiana), 1964.

A-340 McComb, David G., HOUSTON, THE BAYOU CITY, (Ph.D.: University of Texas), 1968.

A-341 McDonald, Patricia A., BALTIMORE WOMEN, 1870-1900, (Ph.D.: Univer-sity of Maryland), 1976.

A-342 McMillan, Lucy M., NATCHEZ, 1763-1779, (M.A.: University of Vir-ginia), 1938.

A-343 McGehee, Charles Stuart, WAKE OF THE FLOOD: A SOUTHERN CITY IN THE CIVIL WAR, CHATTANOOGA, 1838-1873, (Ph.D.: University of Virgin-ia), 1985.

A-344 Melton, Gloria Brown, BLACKS IN MEMPHIS, TENNESSEE, 1920-1955: A HISTORICAL STUDY, (Ph.D.: Washington State University), 1982.

A-345 Minton, Hubert, THE EVOLUTION OF CONWAY, ARKANSAS, (PH.D.: Univer-sity of Wisconsin), 1944.

A-346 Mitchell, Mark S., A HISTORY OF THE BLACK POPULATION OF NEW BERN, NORTH CAROLINA, 1862-1872, (M.A.: Eastern Carolina University), 1980.

A-347 Neff, Guy Charles, THE HISTORICAL GEOGRAPHY OF HATTIESBURG, MISSIS-
SIPPI, (M.A.: University of Southern Mississippi), 1968.

A-348 Owens, Harry P., APALACHICOLA BEFORE 1861, (Ph.D.: Florida State
University), 1966.

A-349 Partadiredja, Atje, HELVETIA, WEST VIRGINIA: A STUDY OF PIONEER
DEVELOPMENT AND COMMUNITY SURVIVAL IN THE APPALACHIA, (Ph.D.:
University of Wisconsin), 1966.

A-350 Peacock, Harold, MONTGOMERY, ALABAMA: A GEOGRAPHIC DESCRIPTION,
(M.A.: George Washington University), 1954.

A-351 Pendley, Barry H., SAVANNAH, GEORGIA, DURING RECONSTRUCTION 1865-
1869, (M.A.: West Georgia College), 1969.

A-352 Phillips, Coy Tatus, DURHAM, A GEOGRAPHIC STUDY, (Ph.D.: University of North Carolina), 1945.

A-353 Pinks, Helen, FERNANDIA, (M.A.: University of Florida), 1949.

A-354 Roberson, Glen R., CITY ON THE PLAINS: THE HISTORY OF TULSA,
OKLAHOMA, (Ph.D.: Oklahoma State University), 1977.

A-355 Russell, James M., ATLANTA, GATE CITY OF THE SOUTH, 1847-1885,
(Ph.D.: Princeton University), 1972.

A-356 Schaeper, Herbert R., THE HISTORICAL GEOGRAPHY OF OCEAN SPRINGS,
MISSISSIPPI, (M.A.: University of Southern Mississippi), 1965.

A-357 Scott, Andrew L., GEOGRAPHY OF FAYETTEVILLE, NORTH CAROLINA, (M.A.:
Columbia University), 1952.

A-358 Scribner, Robert Leslie, A SHORT HISTORY OF BREWTON, ALABAMA,
(M.A.: University of Alabama), 1935.

A-359 Silver, Christopher, IMMIGRATION AND THE ANTEBELLUM SOUTHERN CITY,
(M.A.: University of North Carolina), 1975.

A-360 Snyder, Perry A., SHREVEPORT, LOUISIANA, DURING THE CIVIL WAR AND
RECONSTRUCTION, (Ph.D.: Florida State University), 1979.

A-361 Staessel, John, THE PORT OF ALEXANDRIA, VIRGINIA, IN THE EIGHTEENTH
CENTURY, (M.A.: Catholic University of America), 1969.

A-362 Suhler, Samuel Aaron, SIGNIFICANT QUESTIONS RELATING TO THE HISTORY
OF AUSTIN, TEXAS, TO 1900, (Ph.D.: University of Texas), 1966.

A-363 Thomas, Emory Morton, THE CONFEDERATE STATE OF RICHMOND: A BIO-
GRAPHY OF THE CAPITAL, (Ph.D.: Rice University), 1966.

A-364 Thornbery, Jerry J., THE DEVELOPMENT OF BLACK ATLANTA, 1865-1885,
(Ph.D.: University of Maryland), 1977.

A-365 Varney, Charles B., ECONOMIC AND HISTORICAL GEOGRAPHY OF THE GULF
COAST OF FLORIDA: CEDAR KEYS TO ST. MARKS, (Ph.D.: Clark University), 1963.

A-366 Walker, Peter Franklin, CITADEL: VICKSBURG AND ITS PEOPLE, 1860-
1865, (Ph.D.: Vanderbilt University), 1858.

A-367 Walsh, Walter Richard, CHARLESTON'S SONS OF LIBERTY: A STUDY OF
THE MECHANICS, 1760-1785, (Ph.D.: University of South Carolina),
1954.

A-368 Webb, William Edward, CHARLOTTESVILLE AND ALBEMARLE COUNTY, VIR-
GINIA, 1865-1900, (Ph.D.: University of Virginia), 1955.

A-369 Williams, Clanton W., HISTORY OF MONTGOMERY, ALABAMA, 1817–1846, (Ph.D.: Vanderbilt University), 1938.

A-370 Wood, Richard Everett, PORT TOWN AT WAR: WILMINGTON, NORTH CARO-LINA, 1860–1865, (Ph.D.: Florida State University), 1976.

A-371 Worley, Lillian E., THE URBAN GEOGRAPHY OF BIRMINGHAM, ALABAMA, (Ph.D.: University of North Carolina), 1948.

Housing

A-372 Durham, Stephen, A SPATIAL ANALYSIS—SIX RESIDENTIAL NEIGHBORHOODS IN THE CENTRAL SOUTH CAROLINA URBAN AREAS, (M.A.: University of South Carolina), 1972.

A-373 Earle, Daniel William Jr., LAND SUBSIDENCE PROBLEMS AND MAINTENANCE COSTS TO HOMEOWNERS IN EAST NEW ORLEANS, LOUISIANA, (Ph.D.: Lousi-ana State University), 1975.

A-374 Evans, George Heberton, APARTMENT RENTS IN BALTIMORE, JANUARY 1917 THROUGH OCTOBER 1923, (Ph.D.: Johns Hopkins University), 1925.

A-375 Fant, Barbara G. H., SLUM RECLAMATION AND HOUSING REFORM IN THE NATION'S CAPITOL, 1890–1940, (Ph.D.: George Washington Univer-sity), 1982.

A-376 Favor, Homer E. L., THE EFFECTS OF RACIAL CHANGES IN OCCUPANCY PATTERNS UPON PROPERTY VALUES IN BALTIMORE, (Ph.D.: University of Pittsburgh), 1960.

A-377 Green, Gary Ray, GENTRIFICATION AND DISPLACEMENT: A STUDY OF RESIDENTIAL CHANGE IN A PORTION OF THE OLD LOUISVILLE NEIGHBORHOOD, (M.S.: University of Louisville), 1979.

A-378 Kronick, Jane Collier, SOCIO-ECONOMIC FACTORS AFFECTING THE CHOICE OF A NEW RESIDENCE WITHIN WILMINGTON, DELAWARE, (Ph.D.: Yale Univ-ersity), 1960.

A-379 Lapham, Victoria G., PRICE DIFFERENCES FOR BLACK AND WHITE HOUSING, (Ph.D.: Southern Methodist Universtiy), 1970.

A-380 Meyer, John Paul, HISTORY AND NEIGHBORHOOD ANALYSIS OF CAMP TAYLOR, (M.A.: University of Louisville), 1981.

A-381 O'Connor, Michael J., THE MEASUREMENT AND SIGNIFICANCE OF RACIAL RESIDENTIAL BARRIERS IN ATLANTA, 1890–1970, (Ph.D.: University of Georgia), 1977.

A-382 Smith, Robert Jesse, FAIR HOUSING IN CHARLOTTE: A SURVEY OF RECEP-TIONS AND PRACTICES OF REAL ESTATE AGENTS AND BROKERS, (M.V.A.: University of North Carolina), 1981.

A-383 Sumka, Howard J., RACIAL DISCRIMINATION IN URBAN RENTAL HOUSING: AN ANALYSIS OF SOUTHERN NONMETROPOLITAN MARKETS WITH IMPLICATIONS FOR DEMAND SIDE HOUSING ASSISTANCE, (Ph.D.: University of North Carolina). 1976.

A-384 Weatherby, Norman Lee, RACIAL SEGREGATION IN DALLAS PUBLIC HOUSING: 1970-1976, (M.A.: North Texas State University), 1978.

Journalism

A-385 Alexander, Ann F., BLACK PROTEST IN THE NEW SOUTH: JOHN MITCHELL, JR. (1863-1929) AND THE RICHMOND PLANET, (Ph.D.: Duke University),   1972.

A-386 Arnold, Thomas Brent, A CONTENT SURVEY OF TEN SUBURBAN NEWSPAPERS IN THE DALLAS-FORT WORTH METROPLEX, (M.J.: North Texas State University), 1975.

A-387 Atchison, Ray M., SOUTHERN LITERARY MAGAZINES, 1865-1887, (Ph.D.: Duke University), 1955.

A-388 Baker, Thomas Harrison III, THE MEMPHIS COMMERCIAL APPEAL, 1865-1941, (Ph.D.: University of Texas), 1965.

A-389 Baker, Thomas Harrison, THE MEMPHIS APPEAL, 1841-1865, (M.A.: University of Texas), 1962.

A-390 Bridges, Lamar Whitlow, A STUDY OF THE NEW ORLEANS DAILY PICAYUNE UNDER PUBLISHER ELIZA JANE POITERENT NICHOLSON,1876-1896, (Ph.D.: Southern Illinois University), 1974.

A-391 Britton, James C., IMAGES OF THE FUTURE IN THE CHARLESTON MERCURY, 1848-1860, (M.A.: University of Norht Carolina), 1980.

A-392 Burrage, Jack, THE OXFORD EAGLE AS SEEN FROM ITS FILES, 1883-1950, (M.A.: University of Mississippi), 1955.

A-393 Cadman, Anne Bradford, A STUDY OF WASHINGTON SUBURBAN VIRGINIA NEWSPAPERS, (M.A.: American University), 1967.

A-394 Carter, Peggy Cook, A STUDY OF PERSONS WHO WRITE LETTERS TO THE EDITOR OF THE ATLANTA CONSTITUTION, (M.A.: University of Georgia), 1973.

A-395 Cope, Neil B., A HISTORY OF THE MEMPHIS COMMERCIAL APPEAL, (Ph.D.: University of Missouri), 1969.

A-396 Dennis, Frank A., WEST TENNESSEE NEWSPAPERS DURING THE CIVIL WAR, 1860-1865, (PH.D.: University of Missouri), 1969.

A-397 De Stefano, Onofre, LA PRENSA OF SAN ANTONIO AND ITS LITERARY PAGE, 1913-1915, (Ph.D.: University of California), 1983.

A-398 Donnald, Morrill Bigby, A STUDY OF NASHVILLE NEWSPAPERS, 1850-1875, (M.A.: Vanderbilt University), 1937.

A-399 Forehand, Phyllis Hargrave, A HISTORY OF THE ARLINGTON CITIZEN-JOURNAL, (M.A.: North Texas State University), 1977.

A-400 Gilbert, Laura, RACIAL ATTITUDES EXPRESSED IN THE PENSACOLA NEWS JOURNAL, 1885-1925, (M.A.: University of West Florida), 1973.

A-402 Fudge, William G. Jr., A DESCRIPTIVE READERSHIP STUDY OF THE ATLANTA UNDERGROUND NEWSPAPER: THE GREAT SPECKLED BIRD, (Ph.D.: Florida State University), 1975.

A-401 Glaves, Robert Frederik, ESTABLISHING A SPECIAL INTEREST CITY MAGAZINE: D, THE MAGAZINE OF DALLAS, (M.J.: North Texas State University), 1975.

A-403 Graham, Hugh Davis, TENNESSEE EDITORIAL RESPONSES TO CHANGES IN THE BIRACIAL SYSTEM, 1954-1960, (Ph.D.: Stanford University), 1965.

A-404 House, Katherine Shepherd, AN HISTORICAL STUDY OF THE FIRST FORTY-FIVE YEARS OF THE HOUSTON POST, (M.A.: Stephen F. Austin State University), 1978.

A-405 Grose, Charles William, BLACK NEWSPAPERS IN TEXAS, 1868-1970, (Ph.D.: University of Texas), 1972.

A-406 Haralson, Marianne Odom, AN HISTORICAL STUDY OF THE TYLER COURIER-TIMES AND TYLER MORNING TELEGRAPH WITH EMPHASIS ON COMMUNITY LEADERSHIP, (M.S.: East Texas State University), 1975.

A-407 Harris, Robert A., THE ARKANSAS POST, 1805-1810, (M.A.: Delta State University), 1974.

A-408 Hazmark, Mary Frances, THE SOUTHERN RELIGIOUS PRESS AND THE SOCIAL GOSPEL MOVEMENT, 1910-1915, (M.A.: Lamar University), 1979.

A-409 Henderson, James B., A STUDY OF WEEKLY NEWSPAPERS IN VIRGINIA, (M.A.: American University), 1961.

A-410 Hill, Mary E., A STUDY OF THE LEADING NEWSPAPERS IN TUSCALOOSA, 1837-1865, AND THEIR POLITICAL IMPORTANCE, (M.A.: University of Alabama), 1951.

A-411 Holland, Harold E., RELIGIOUS PERIODICALS IN THE DEVELOPMENT OF NASHVILLE, TENNESSEE AS A REGIONAL PUBLISHING CENTER, 1830-1880, (Ph.D.: Columbia University), 1976.

A-412 Hooker, Robert W., RACE AND THE NEWS MEDIA IN MISSISSIPPI, (M.A.: Vanderbilt University), 1971.

A-413 Houston, Michael, EDWARD ALFRED POLLARD AND THE RICHMOND EXAMINER: A STUDY OF JOURNALISTIC OPPOSITION IN WARTIME, (M.A.: American University), 1963.

A-414 Jackson, Elaine Mikeska, A HISTORY OF THE FREE PRESS OF DIBOLL, TEXAS: 1952-1976, (M.A.: Stephen F. Austin State University), 1976.

A-415 Karst, Judith W., NEWSPAPER MEDICINE: A CULTURAL STUDY OF THE COLONIAL SOUTH, (Ph.D.: Tulane University), 1971.

A-416 Keel, Edna A., HISTORY OF THE NEWSPAPERS OF HUNTSVILLE, ALABAMA--1812 TO 1939, (M.A.: George Peabody College for Teachers), 1939.

A-417 Leavens, Finnian P., THE NEW ORLEANS TRIBUNE AND L'UNION, 1862-1870, (M.A.: Louisiana State University), 1966.

A-418 Make, Philip M., RACIAL IDEALOGY IN THE NEW ORLEANS PRESS, 1862-1877, (Ph.D.: Unbiversity of Southwestern Louisiana), 1977.

A-419 McCumber, James Byron, A HISTORY OF THE ATLANTA (GEORGIA) TIMES, (M.A.: University of Georgia), 1970.

A-420 Melton, Martha Faye, STARTING A NEW MAGAZINE: TWO CASE STUDIES, (M.A.: University of Georgia), 1982.

A-421 Miller, George Arnold, GEORGE FORT MILTON: THE FIGHT FOR TVA AND THE LOSS OF THE CHATTANOOGA NEWS, (D.A.: Middle Tennessee State University), 1983.

A-422 Morris, Robert L., THE WHEELING DAILY INTELLIGENCER AND THE CIVIL WAR, (Ph.D.: West Virginia University), 1965.

A-423 Nelson, William James, THE FREE NEGRO IN THE ANTEBELLUM NEW ORLEANS PRESS, (Ph.D.: Duke University), 1977.

A-424 O'Conner, Adrian J., CHARLOTTE AND ITS OBSERVER: DEVELOPMENT OF SPORTS COVERAGE, 1892-1925, (M.A.: University of North Carolina), 1979.

A-425 Prior, Granville T., A HISTORY OF THE CHARLESTON MERCURY, 1822-1852, (Ph.D.: Harvard University), 1946-47.

A-426 Reddick, Lawrence D., THE NEGRO IN THE NEW ORLEANS PRESS, 1850-1860: A STUDY IN ATTITUDES AND PROPAGANDA, (Ph.D.: University of Chicago), 1939.

A-427 Rhodes, Muriel Holmes, BLACK JOURNALISM IN VIRGINIA: PLUMME BERNARD YOUNG, SR. AND THE NORFOLK JOURNAL AND GUIDE--1920-1930, (D.A.: Carnegie-Mellon University), 1976.

A-428 Ritter, Charles Francis, THE PRESS IN FLORIDA, LOUISIANA, AND SOUTH CAROLINA, AND THE END OF RECONSTRUCTION, 1865-1877: SOUTHERN MEN WITH NORTHERN INTERESTS, (Ph.D.: Case Western Reserve University), 1976.

A-429 Rogers, William Curran, A COMPARISON OF THE COVERAGE OF THE LEO FRANK CASE BY THE HEARST-CONTROLLED ATLANTA GEORGIAN AND THE HOME-OWNED ATLANTA JOURNAL, APRIL 28, 1913-AUGUST 30, 1913, (M.A.: University of Georgia), 1950.

A-430 Sabin, David B., IRA A. BATTERTON AND THE VICKSBURG DAILY HERALD, 'AN UNCONDITIONAL UNION NEWSPAPER,' (M.A.: Mississippi College), 1968.

A-431 Secrest, Andrew McDowd, IN BLACK AND WHITE: PRESS OPINION AND RACE RELATIONS IN SOUTH CAROLINA, 1954-1964, (Ph.D.: Duke University), 1972.

A-432 Simms, Elizabeth L., A STUDY OF THE FLAG OF THE UNION, A TUSCA-LOOSA, ALABAMA NEWSPAPER, 1833-43: ITS IMPORTANCE AND INFLUENCE, (M.A.: University of Alabama), 1950.

A-433 Skates, John Ray Jr., A SOUTHERN EDITOR VIEWS THE NATIONAL SCENE: FREDERICK SULLERS AND THE JACKSON, MISSISSIPPI DAILY NEWS, (Ph.D.: Mississippi State University), 1965.

A-434 Suggs, Henry Lewis, P.B. YOUNG AND THE NORFOLK JOURNAL AND GUIDE, 1910-1954, (Ph.D.: University of Virginia), 1976.

A-435 Thomas, Eugene M., THE COLUMBUS, GEORGIA, ENQUIRER, 1855-1865, (M.A.: University of Georgia), 1971.

A-436 Thomas, Richard Gehman, SOUTHERN APPALACHIAN STATE NEWSPAPERS' TREATMENT OF THE ANTI-POVERTY AND APPALACHIA ACTS, (M.A.: American University), 1968.

A-437 Wardlaw, Harold Clinton, A GATEKEEPER ANALYSIS OF MINORITY AND MAJORITY NEWSPAPERS: ATLANTA INQUIRER, ATLANTA WORLD, AND ATLANTA CONSTITUTION, (M.A.: University of Georgia), 1969.

A-438 Warnock, Henry Young, THE ATLANTA CONSTITUTION AND THE GUBERNATOR-IAL CAMPAIGN OF 1942: A STUDY IN NEWS TECHNIQUE, (M.A.: University of Georgia), 1949.

A-439 Weldon, Ellen, THE ATLANTA CONSTITUTION VIEWS THE KU KLUX KLAN: 1868-1872, (M.A.: University of Missouri), 1964.

A-440 West, William Franciscus Jr., A SOUTHERN EDITOR VIEWS THE CIVIL WAR: A COLLECTION OF EDITORIALS BY HENRY TIMROD AND OTHER EDI-TORIAL MATERIALS PUBLISHED IN THE DAILY SOUTH CAROLINIAN, JANUARY 14, 1864, TO FEBRUARY 17, 1865 (2 vols), (Ph.D.: Florida State University), 1983.

A-441 Zimmer, Roxanne Marie, THE URBAN DAILY PRESS: BALTIMORE, 1797-1816, (Ph.D.: University of Iowa), 1982.

Labor and Employment

A-442 Adams, Arvil Van., A STUDY OF NEGRO EMPLOYMENT PATTERNS IN METRO-
      POLITAN MEMPHIS, TENNESSEE, (Ph.D.: University of Kentucky), 1970.

A-443 Barksdale, Oliver D., ORGANIZED LABOR IN ETOWAH COUNTY, ALABAMA,
      (M.A.: University of Alabama), 1956.

A-444 Cannon, Bernard, SOCIAL DETERRENTS TO THE UNIONIZATION OF SOUTHERN
      COTTON TEXTILE MILL WORKERS, (Ph.D.: Harvard University), 1952.

A-445 Carlton, Daniel L., MILL AND TOWN: THE COTTON MILL WORKERS AND THE
      MIDDLE CLASS IN SOUTH CAROLINA, 1880-1920, (Ph.D.: Yale Univer-
      sity), 1977.

A-446 Carpenter, Charles G., SOUTHERN LABOR AND THE SOUTHERN-URBAN CON-
      TINUUM, 1919-1929, (Ph.D.: Tulane University), 1973.

A-447 Eblen, James Horace, THE OUTMIGRATION OF WORKERS FROM SOUTHEASTERN
      METROPOLITAN AREAS, (Ph.D.: University of Tennessee), 1975.

A-448 Fishback, Price V., EMPLOYMENT CONDITIONS OF BLACKS IN THE COAL
      INDUSTRY, 1900-1930, (Ph.D.: University of Washington), 1983.

A-449 Green, Earl Jr., LABOR IN THE SOUTH: A CASE STUDY OF MEMPHIS--THE
      1968 SANITATION STRIKE AND ITS EFFECT ON AN URBAN COMMUNITY,
      (Ph.D.: New York University), 1980.

A-450 Hefner, James A., BLACK EMPLOYMENT IN A SOUTHERN "PROGRESSIVE"
      CITY: THE ATLANTA EXPERIENCE, (Ph.D.: University of Colorado),
      1971.

A-451 Holley, William Henry, EMPLOYMENT PRACTICES RELATING TO THE HARD-
      CORE JOBLESS: A STUDY OF THE METROPOLITAN BIRMINGHAM AREA, (Ph.D.:
      University of Alabama), 1970.

A-452 Hopkins, Richard Joseph, PATTERNS OF RESISTENCE AND OCCUPATIONAL
      MOBILITY IN A SOUTHERN CITY: ATLANTA, 1870-1920, (Ph.D.: Emory
      University), 1972.

A-453 Janiewski, Delores E., FROM FIELD TO FACTORY: RACE, CLASS, SEX,
      AND THE WOMAN WORKER IN DURHAM, 1880-1940, (Ph.D.: Duke Univer-
      sity), 1979.

A-454 Kearns, David T., THE SOCIAL MOBILITY OF NEW ORLEANS LABORERS,
      1870-1900, (Ph.D.: Tulane University), 1977.

A-455 Kamer, Pearl M., A CASE STUDY OF A SUBURBAN LABOR MARKET: THE
      NASSAU-SUFFOLK SMSA, (Ph.D.: New York University), 1976.

A-456 Kocolowski, Gary Paul, LOUISVILLE AT LARGE: INDUSTRIAL-URBAN
      ORGANIZATION, INTER-CITY MIGRATION AND OCCUPATIONAL MOBILITY IN THE
      CENTRAL UNITED STATES, 1865-1906, (Ph.D.: University of Cincin-
      nati, 1978.

A-457 Landolt, Robert Garland, THE MEXICAN-AMERICAN WORKERS OF SAN
      ANTONIO, TEXAS, (Ph.D.: University of Texas), 1965.

A-458 Lewis, Selma S., SOCIAL RELIGION AND THE MEMPHIS SANITATION STRIKE,
      (Ph.D.: Memphis State University), 1976.

A-459 McHugh, Cathy L., THE FAMILY LABOR SYSTEM IN THE SOUTHERN COTTON
      TEXTILE INDUSTRY, 1880-1915, (Ph.D.: Stanford University), 1981.

A-460 O'Brien, Mary Lawrence, SLAVERY IN LOUISVILLE DURING THE ANTEBELLUM
      PERIOD: 1820-1860: A STUDY OF THE EFFECTS OF URBANIZATION ON THE
      INSTITUTION OF SLAVERY AS IT EXISTED IN LOUISVILLE, KENTUCKY,
      (M.A.: University of Louisville), 1979.

A-461 Rachleff, Peter Jay, BLACK, WHITE AND GRAY: WORKING-CLASS ACTIVISM IN RICHMOND, VIRGINIA, 1865-1890, (Ph.D.: University of Pittsburgh), 1981.

A-462 Sapiro, Harold A., THE WORKERS OF SAN ANTONIO, TEXAS, 1900-1940, (Ph.D.: University of Texas), 1952.

A-463 Selby, John, INDUSTRIAL GROWTH AND WORKERS' PROTEST IN A NEW SOUTH CITY: HIGH POINT, NORTH CAROLINA, 1859-1959, (Ph.D.: Duke University), 1984.

A-464 Stafford, Hanford Dozier, SLAVERY IN A BORDER CITY: LOUISVILLE, 1790-1860, (Ph.D.: University of Kentucky), 1982.

A-465 Steffen, Charles G., BETWEEN REVOLUTIONS: THE PRE-FACTORY URBAN WORKER IN BALTIMORE, 1780-1820, (Ph.D.: Northwestern University), 1977.

A-466 Straw, Richard A., THIS IS NOT A STRIKE, IT IS SIMPLY A REVOLUTION: BIRMINGHAM MINERS' STRUGGLE FOR POWER, 1894-1908, (Ph.D.: University of Missouri), 1980.

A-467 Woessner, Herman C. III, NEW ORLEANS, 1840-1860: A STUDY IN URBAN SLAVERY, (M.A.: Louisiana State University), 1967.

Land Use

A-468 Adedibu, Afolabi, SPATIAL DIFFUSION ANALYSIS OF COMMERCIAL LAND-USE CHANGES ASSOCIATED WITH THE JACKSONVILLE, FLORIDA, INTERNATIONAL AIRPORT, 1965-1976, (Ph.D.: Unviersity of Florida), 1978.

A-469 Ainsley, William F. Jr., CHANGING LAND USE IN DOWNTOWN NORFOLK, VIRGINIA: 1860-1930, (Ph.D.: University of North Carolina), 1977.

A-470 Birchard, Ralph Edwin, THE SPATIAL STRUCTURE OF THE OKLAHOMA CITY METROPOLITAN REGION, (Ph.D.: University of Iowa), 1954.

A-471 Brown, Robert Charles, SPATIAL VARIATIONS OF IDLE LAND IN TULSA, OKLAHOMA, (Ph.D.: Michigan State University), 1967.

A-472 Clarke, Frank Joseph, DIFFERENTIAL VIEWS OF ATLANTANS TOWARD ZONING, (Ph.D.: Emory University), 1972.

A-473 Fehrenback, Joseph, THE RECONSTRUCTION OF PAST URBAN LAND USE IN ATHENS, GEORGIA, UTILIZING SANBORN FIRE INSURANCE MAPS, (M.A.: University of Georgia), 1977.

A-474 Johnson, Raburn W., LAND UTILIZATION IN MEMPHIS, (Ph.D.: University of Chicago), 1936.

A-475 Kirk, Lewis M. Jr., AN ANALYSIS OF OPPOSITION TO REZONING CASES IN LOUISVILLE AND JEFFERSON COUNTY, KENTUCKY, (M.A.: University of Louisville), 1972.

A-476 Klingman, Thomas B., THE CHARACTER AND EVOLUTION OF BLACK URBAN COMMERCIAL LAND USE IN GREENVILLE, NORTH CAROLINA, 1917-1918, (M.S.: East Carolina University), 1980.

A-477 Koos, Philip D., CHANGES IN LAND USE PATTERNS AFTER OPENING OF INTERSTATE 75 IN THE AREA OF TIFTON, GEORGIA, (M.A.: University of Georgia), 1965.

A-478 Marge, (Carter) Gail B., A FUNCTIONAL ANALYSIS OF LAND USE PATTERNS IN THE NEGRO SHOPPING AREAS OF RALEIGH AND CHARLOTTE, NORTH CAROLINA, (M.A.: University of North Carolina), 1969.

A-479 Mookherjee, Debnath, THE URBAN FRINGE OF ORLANDO, FLORIDA: A STUDY OF LAND USE PATTERNS AND CHANGES ASSOCIATED WITH URBAN GROWTH, (Ph.D.: University of Florida), 1961.

A-480 Painter, William Keith, THE ROLE OF VACANT LAND USE IN THE CONTEMPORARY ANALYSIS OF THE URBAN CORE: A CASE STUDY OF DURHAM, NORTH CAROLINA, (M.A.: Appalachian State University), 1977.

A-481 Replies, Robert W., VACANT LAND IN ATHENS, GEORGIA: ITS DISTRIBUTION AND CAUSES, (M.A.: University of Georgia), 1959.

A-482 Prior, Roger A., URBAN LAND USE ALONG MISSISSIPPI SOUND, (Ph.D.: University of Chicago), 1947.

A-483 Rayburn, Johnson W., LAND UTILIZATION IN MEMPHIS, (Ph.D.: University of Chicago), 1936.

A-484 Schwendeman, Gerald, SOME GEOGRAPHIC ASPECTS OF LAND USE IN THE CITY OF LEXINGTON, FAYETTE COUNTY, KENTUCKY; A COMPARATIVE AND ANALYTICAL STUDY, (M.A.: University of Kentucky), 1964.

A-485 Stafford, Dorothy Allen, CONTEMPORARY LAND OCCUPANCE TRAITS AT ST. HELENA, NORTH CAROLINA, (M.A.: University of Georgia), 1960.

A-486 Stephenson, Richard A., TRAFFIC-LAND USE INTERRELATIONS ALONG CHAPMAN HIGHWAY AND MARYVILLE PIKE IN METROPOLITAN KNOXVILLE, (M.A.: University of Tennessee), 1961.

Libraries

A-487 Aldrich, Willie Lee B., THE HISTORY OF PUBLIC LIBRARY SERVICE FOR NEGROES IN SALISBURY, NORTH CAROLINA, 1937-1963, (M.A.: Atlanta University), 1964.

A-488 Allman, Cora Margaret, REGIONAL LIBRARIES IN THE SOUTHEAST, (M.A.: University of North Carolina), 1953.

A-489 Baroco, John Vincent, THE LIBRARY ASSOCIATION OF PENSACOLA, 1885-1933, (M.A.: Florida State University), 1953.

A-490 Barfield, I.R., HISTORY OF THE MIAMI PUBLIC LIBRARY, (M.A.: Atlanta University), 1958.

A-491 Brant, B.S., THE ALEXANDRIA LIBRARY, ITS HISTORY, PRESENT FACILITIES AND FUTURE PROGRAM, (M.A.: Catholic University), 1950

A-492 Cooke, Addie M., A HISTORY OF THE PUBLIC LIBRARY IN MURPHY, NORTH CAROLINA, (M.A.: Florida State University), 1962.

A-493 Flener, Jane Gardner, A HISTORY OF LIBRARIES IN TENNESSEE BEFORE THE CIVIL WAR, (Ph.D.: Indiana University), 12963.

A-494 Garrison, Barbara S., A HISTORY OF THE CONCORD PUBLIC LIBRARY OF CONCORD, NORTH CAROLINA, (M.A.: University of North Carolina), 1965.

A-495 Gill, S.C., HISTORY OF THE MIAMI, FLORIDA, PUBLIC LIBRARY, (M.A.: Western Reserve University), 1954.

A-496 Hoover, Anne R., HISTORY OF THE CARNEGIE LIBRARY OF CHARLOTTE AND MECKLENBURG COUNTY, NORTH CAROLINA, (M.A.: University of North Carolina), 1968.

A-497 Hunter, Carolyn, A HISTORY OF THE OLIVIA RANEY LIBRARY, 1899-1959, (M.A.: University of North Carolina), 1964.

A-498 Moore, Bonnie L., A HISTORY OF THE PUBLIC LIBRARY SERVICE TO NEGROES IN WINSTON-SALEM, NORTH CAROLINA, 1927-1951, (M.A.: Atlanta University), 1961.

A-499 Moyers, Joyce C., HISTORY OF THE ROCKINGHAM PUBLIC LIBRARY, HAR-RISONBURG, VIRGININA, (M.A.: University of North Carolina), 1959.

A-500 Patane, Jane Seager, A HISTORY OF THE PUBLIC LIBRARY IN ST. PETERS-BURG, FLORIDA, (M.A.: Florida State University), 1960.

A-501 Perres, M.J., HISTORY AND DEVELOPMENT OF PUBLIC LIBRARY SERVICE FOR NEGROES IN PENSACOLA, FLORIDA, 1947-1961, (M.A.: Atlanta University), 1963.

A-502 Scott, Ellen, THE HISTORY AND INFLUENCE OF THE OLD LIBRARY OF TRANSYLVANIA, (M.A.: University of Kentucky), 1929.

A-503 Settlemeri, Claude L., THE TENNESSEE STATE LIBRARY, 1854-1923, (M.A.: George Peabody College for Teachers), 1951.

A-504 Smith, Patricia Christine, THE TENNESSEE VALLEY AUTHORITY AND ITS INFLUENCE IN THE DEVELOPMENT OF REGIONAL LIBRARIES IN THE SOUTH, (M.A.: University of North Carolina), 1954.

A-505 Stewart, William L. Jr., A HISTORY OF THE HIGH POINT, NORTH CARO-LINA, PUBLIC LIBRARY, (M.A.: University of North Carolina), 1963.

A-506 Tamblyn, Eldon Waldo, CENSORSHIP AND NORTH CAROLINA PUBLIC LIBRAR-IES (M.A.: University of North Carolina), 1964.

A-507 Thomas, Evelyn F., THE ORIGIN AND DEVELOPMENT OF THE SOCIETY OF THE FOUR ARTS LIBRARY, PALM BEACH, FLORIDA, (M.A.: Florida State Uni-versity), 1958.

A-508 Worley, M.M., TAMPA, FLORIDA, PUBLIC LIBRARY, (M.A.: University of Mississippi), 1961.

Life, Culture, and Social Organization

A-509 Adams, Eva D., NEGRO SOCIAL LIFE AS REFLECTED BY THE LIVES OF THE STUDENTS OF ATLANTA UNIVERSITY, 1870-1900, (M.A.: Atlanta Uni-versity), 1968.

A-510 Amos, Harriet Elizabeth, SOCIAL LIFE IN AN ANTEBELLUM COTTON PORT: MOBILE, ALABAMA, 1820-1860, (Ph.D.: Emory University), 1976.

A-511 Anders, Sarah Frances, THE SOCIAL PARTICIPATION OF MARRIED COUPLES IN TALLAHASSEE, FLORIDA, (Ph.D.: Florida State University), 1955.

A-512 Bennett, Linda A., PATTERNS OF ETHNIC IDENTITY AMONG SERBS, CROATS, AND SLOVENES IN WASHINGTON, D.C., (Ph.D.: American University), 1976.

A-513 Berkeley, Kathleen C., "LIKE A PLAGUE OF LOCUSTS": IMMIGRATION AND SOCIAL CHANGE IN MEMPHIS, TENNESSEE, 1850-1880, (Ph.D.: University of California), 1980.

A-514 Berry, Benjamin Donaldson Jr., PLYMOUTH SETTLEMENT HOUSE AND THE DEVELOPMENT OF BLACK LOUISVILLE: 1900-1930, (Ph.D.: Case Western Reserve University), 1977.

A-515 Bittinger, Bear Stanley, LEADERSHIP SYSTEMS AND SOCIAL CHANGE IN A TEXAS CITY OF 100,000, (Ph.D.: University of Texas), 1967.

A-516 Bogger, Tommy L., THE SLAVE AND FREE BLACK COMMUNITY IN NORFOLK 1775-1865, (Ph.D.: University of Virginia), 1976.

A-517 Buxbaum, Edwin Clarence, THE GREEK-AMERICAN GROUP OF TARPON
SPRINGS, FLORIDA: A STUDY OF ETHNIC IDENTIFICATION AND ACCULTURA-
TION, (Ph.D.: University of Pennsylvania), 1967.

A-518 Cade, Catherine Elise, ORIENTATIONS TOWARD SOCIAL CHANGE IN THE
NEGRO COMMUNITY OF A SOUTHERN TOWN, (Ph.D.: Tulane University),
1969.

A-519 Carballo, Manuel, A SOCIO-PSYCHOLOGICAL STUDY OF ACCULTURATION/
ASSIMILATION: CUBANS IN NEW ORLEANS, (Ph.D.: Tulane University),
1970.

A-520 Carr, Harriet G., A STUDY OF DISCRIMINATORY PRACTICES IN SEMI-
PUBLIC INSTITUTIONS RELATIVE TO JEWISH PEOPLE IN WASHINGTON, D.C.,
(Ph.D.: Catholic University of America), 1950.

A-521 Chan, Kit-Mui Leung, ASSIMILATION OF THE CHINESE-AMERICANS IN THE
MISSISSIPPI DELTA, (M.A.: Mississippi State University), 1969.

A-522 Christopherson, Susan Marie, FAMILY AND CLASS IN THE NEW INDUSTRIAL
CITY, (Ph.D.: University of California), 1983.

A-523 Conlee, Anita Clendennen, OCCUPATIONAL INFLUENCES ON THE FOLKLORE
OF GRAFORD, TEXAS, (M.A.: North Texas State University), 1975.

A-524 Deagan, Kathleen, SEX, STATUS AND ROLE IN THE MESTIZAJE OF SPANISH
COLONIAL FLORIDA, (Ph.D.: University of Florida), 1974.

A-525 Deckelbaum, Yetta, LITTLE HAITI: THE EVOLUTION OF A COMMUNITY,
(M.A.: Florida Atlantic University), 1983.

A-526 DeGroot, Dudley Edward, THE ASSIMILATION OF POSTWAR IMMIGRANTS IN
ATLANTA, GEORGIA, (Ph.D.: Ohio State University), 1959.

A-527 DeNatale, Douglas, TRADITIONAL CULTURE AND COMMUNITY IN A PIEDMONT
TEXTILE MILL VILLAGE, (M.A.: University of North Carolina), 1980.

A-528 Doyle, Elizabeth J., CIVILIAN LIFE IN OCCUPIED NEW ORLEANS, (Ph.D.:
Louisiana State University), 1955.

A-529 Earnes, Grace E., CITY LIFE IN THE OLD SOUTH: THE BRITISH TRAVEL-
ERS' IMAGE, (Ph.D.: Florida State University), 1966.

A-530 Engs, Robert Frances, THE DEVELOPMENT OF BLACK CULTURE AND COMMUN-
ITY IN THE EMANCIPATION ERA: HAMPTON ROADS, VIRGINIA, 1861-1870,
(Ph.D.: Yale University), 1972.

A-531 Everett, Donald E., THE FREE PERSONS OF COLOR IN NEW ORLEANS, 1803-
1865, (PH.D.: Tulane University), 1952.

A-532 Feibelman, Julian B., A SOCIAL AND ECONOMIC STUDY OF THE NEW
ORLEANS JEWISH COMMUNITY, (Ph.D.: University of Pennsylvania),
1939.

A-533 Fishman, Robert G., CRISIS IN IDENTITY: AN URBAN ETHNOGRAPHY OF
NEIGHBORHOOD REVITALIZATION, (Ph.D.: University of New York),
1983.

A-534 Fitchett, G. Horace, THE FREE NEGRO IN CHARLESTON, SOUTH CAROLINA,
(Ph.D.: University of Chicago), 1950.

A-535 Fleishman, Edward Jay, JEWS IN NORTH CAROLINA: IDENTIFICATION AND
COMMUNITY SATISFACTION, (M.A.: University of North Carolina),
1975.

A-536 Fowler, Anne Clarke, THE CONTEMPORARY NEGRO SUBCULTURE: AN EX-
PLORATORY STUDY OF LOWER-CLASS NEGRO WOMEN OF NEW ORLEANS, (Ph.D.:
Tulane University), 1970.

A-537 Garcia, Richard Amado, THE MAKING OF THE MEXICAN-AMERICAN MIND, SAN ANTONIO, TEXAS, 1929-1941: A SOCIAL AND INTELLECTUAL HISTORY OF AN ETHNIC COMMUNITY, (Ph.D.: University of California), 1980.

A-538 Garrison, Joseph Yates, THE AUGUSTA BLACK COMMUNITY SINCE WORLD WAR II, (M.A.: University of Miami), 1971.

A-539 Gilmore, Harlan Welsh, RACIAL DISORGANIZATION IN A SOUTHERN CITY, (Ph.D.: Vanderbilt University), 1931.

A-540 Giordano, Paul Anthony, THE ITALIANS OF LOUISIANA: THEIR CULTURAL BACKGROUND AND THEIR MANY CONTRIBUTIONS IN THE FIELDS OF LITERA- TURE, THE ARTS, EDUCATION, POLITICS, AND BUSINESS AND LABOR, (Ph.D.: Indiana University), 1978.

A-541 Gordon, Joan Louise, SOME SOCIO-ECONOMIC ASPECTS OF SELECTED NEGRO FAMILIES IN SAVANNAH, GEORGIA: WITH SPECIAL REFERENCE TO THE EF- FECTS OF OCCUPATIONAL STRATIFICATION ON CHILD REARING, (Ph.D.: University of Pennsylvania), 1955.

A-542 Hahn, Phyliss, GERMAN SETTLERS IN NASHVILLE, (M.A.: Vanderbilt University), 1935.

A-543 Hertzberg, Steven, THE JEWS OF ATLANTA, 1865-1915, (Ph.D.: Univer- sity of Chicago), 1975.

A-544 Hess, Ann Leslie, RURAL-URBAN DIFFERENCES IN QUALITY OF LIFE, (M.A.: University of Louisville), 1981.

A-545 Hess, George Montgomery, PARTICIPATION OF NEGROES IN COMMUNITY LIFE IN TWO SMALL SOUTHERN CITIES, (Ph.D.: Mississippi State Univer- sity), 1971.

A-546 Hicks, Ronald Graydon, THE PROTESTANT ETHIC AND THE GENERATION GAP IN THE MODERN URBAN SOUTHERN FAMILY, (Ph.D.: Louisiana State University), 1970.

A-547 Ho, Isabel Maria, LIFE SATISFACTION OF THE ELDERLY PEOPLE IN LOUISVILLE, (M.A.: University of Louisiana), 1978.

A-548 Hoffelder, Robert L., SOCIAL RELATIONS IN LATER MATURITY: SOCIAL INTERACTION AND LIFE SATISFACTION IN CORBIN, KENTUCKY, Ph.D.: Uni- versity of Maryland), 1974.

A-549 Jacknus, Jr., KINSHIP AND RESIDENTIAL PROPINQUITY: A CASE STUDY OF A BLACK EXTENDED FAMILY IN NEW ORLEANS, (Ph.D.: University of Pittsburgh), 1980.

A-550 Jalla, Frank L. Jr., EL PASO, TEXAS, AND JUAREZ, MEXICO: A STUDY OF A BI-ETHNIC COMMUNITY, 1846-1881, (Ph.D.: University of Texas), 1978.

A-551 Johnson, Allan John, SURVIVING FREEDOM: THE BLACK COMMUNITY OF WASHINGTON, D.C., 1860-1880, (Ph.D.: Duke University), 1980.

A-552 Johnson, James Haywood, FAMILY ORGANIZATION IN LIGHTNING: THE STUDY OF AN URBAN CULTURAL SYSTEM, (M.A.: University of Georgia), 1970.

A-553 Johnson, Paul M., THE NEGRO IN MACON, GEORGIA, 1865-1871, (M.A.: University of Georgia), 1972.

A-554 Jones, Clifton Ralph, SOCIAL STRATIFICATION IN THE NEGRO POPULA- TION: A STUDY OF SOCIAL CLASSES IN SOUTH BOSTON, VIRGINIA, (Ph.D.: University of Iowa), 1944.

A-555 Kaslow, Andrew Jonathan, OPPRESSION AND ADAPTATION: THE SOCIAL ORGANIZATION AND EXPRESSIVE CULTURE OF AN AFRO-AMERICAN COMMUNITY IN NEW ORLEANS, (Ph.D.: Columbia University), 1981.

A-556 King, Charles E., FACTORS MAKING FOR SUCCESS OR FAILURE IN MARRIAGE AMONG 466 NEGRO COUPLES IN A SOUTHERN CITY, (Ph.D.: University of Chicago), 1951.

A-557 Kipp, Samuel Millar III, URBAN GROWTH AND SOCIAL CHANGE IN THE SOUTH, 1870-1920: GREENSBORO, NORTH CAROLINA, AS A CASE STUDY, (Ph.D.: Princeton University), 1974.

A-558 Klopper Ruth, THE FAMILY'S USE OF URBAN SPACE. ELEMENTS OF FAMILY STRUCTURE AND FUNCTION AMONG ECONOMIC ELITES: ATLANTA, GEORGIA 1880-1920, (Ph.D.: Emory University), 1977.

A-559 Kich, Joan, MORTUARY BEHAVIOR PATTERNING IN COLONIAL ST. AUGUSTINE, (M.A.: Florida State University), 1977.

A-560 Kraft, Katherine A., EUROPEAN REFUGEES IN MISSISSIPPI, 1942-1952, (M.A.: Mississippi State University), 1980.

A-561 Lane, John H., VOLUNTARY ASSOCIATIONS AMONG MEXICAN AMERICANS IN SAN ANTONIO, TEXAS: ORGANIZATIONAL AND LEADERSHIP CHARACTERISTICS, (Ph.D.: University of Texas), 1968.

A-562 Lewis, Earl, AT WORK AND AT HOME: BLACKS IN NORFOLK, VIRGINIA, 1910-1945, (Ph.D.: University of Minnesota), 1984.

A-563 Lewis, Hylan G., THE SOCIAL LIFE OF THE NEGRO IN A SOUTHERN PIED-MONT TOWN, (Ph.D.: University of Chicago), 1952.

A-564 Lim, Hy Sop, SOME SOCIOLOGICAL AND PSYCHOLOGICAL DETERMINANTS OF MILITANCY AMONG THE LOWSES NEGROES IN A LARGE SOUTHERN CITY, (Ph.D.: Emory University), 1970.

A-565 Lindley, Melinda Ann, A HISTORY OF DEBUTANT PRESENTATION IN DALLAS, TEXAS, 1884-1977, (M.A.: North Texas State University), 1977.

A-566 Lilly, Samuel Alvin, THE CULTURE OF REVOLUTIONARY CHARLESTON, (Ph.D.: Miami University), 1972.

A-567 Loewen, James W., THE MISSISSIPPI CHINESE, (Ph.D.: Harvard University), 1968.

A-568 Loftin, Bernadette Kuehn, A SOCIAL HISTORY OF THE MID-GULF SOUTH (PANAMA CITY-MOBILE), 1930-1950, (Ph.D.: University of Southern Mississippi), 1971.

A-569 Lofton, Paul S. Jr., A SOCIAL AND ECONOMIC HISTORY OF COLUMBIA, SOUTH CAROLINA, DURING THE GREAT DEPRESSION, (Ph.D.: University of Texas), 1977.

A-570 Love, Ronald, COMMUNITY IN TRANSITION: A STUDY OF MOUND BAYOU, MISSISSIPPI, (Ph.D.: Boston University), 1982.

A-571 MacDonald, Lois, SOUTHERN MILL HILLS, A STUDY OF SOCIAL AND ECO-NOMIC FORCES IN CERTAIN TEXTILE MILL VILLAGES, (Ph.D.: New York University), 1929.

A-572 Macnair, Ray Hugh, SOCIAL DISTANCE AMONG KIN ORGANIZATIONS: CIVIL RIGHTS NETWORKS IN CLEVELAND AND BIRMINGHAM, (Ph.D.: University of Michigan), 1970.

A-573 Mallard, Esther R., THE JEWS OF SAVANNAH, 1733-1860, (M.A.: Georgia Southern College), 1972.

A-574 Mazey, Mary Ellen, AN ANALYSIS OF URBAN ACTIVITY SYSTEMS: THE CASE
OF NEWPORT, KENTUCKY, (Ph.D.: University of Cincinnati), 1977.

A-575 McCall, Bevode C., GEORGIA TOWN AND CRACKER CULTURE: A SOCIO-
LOGICAL STUDY, (M.A.: University of Chicago), 1954.

A-576 Megleazzo, Arlen Charles, ETHNIC DIVERSITY ON THE SOUTHERN
FRONTIER: A SOCIAL HISTORY OF PURRYSBURG, SOUTH CAROLINA, 1732-
1792, (Ph.D.: Washington State University), 1982.

A-577 Meredith, Mary Louise, THE MISSISSIPPI WOMAN'S RIGHTS MOVEMENT,
1889-1923: THE LEADERSHIP ROLE OF NELLIE NUGEHT SOMERVILLE AND
GREENVILLE IN SUFFRAGE REFORM, (M.A.: Delta State University),
1974.

A-578 Michell, Kay F., A GEOGRAPHICAL ANALYSIS OF SOCIAL AND ECONOMIC
ASPECTS OF ST. MARKS, FLORIDA, (M.A.: Florida State University),
1964.

A-579 Miller, Bertha Hampton, BLACKS IN WINSTON-SALEM, NORTH CAROLINA
1895-1920: COMMUNITY DEVELOPMENT IN AN ERA OF BENEVOLENT PATERNAL-
ISM, (Ph.D.: Duke University), 1981.

A-580 Mills, Gwen Ann, CULTURAL LIFE IN JACKSON, MISSISSIPPI, (M.A.:
University of Mississippi), 1967.

A-581 Morland, John K., MILL-VILLAGE LIFE IN A PIEDMONT TOWN, (Ph.D.:
University of North Carolina), 1951.

A-582 Mugge, Robert Herman, NEGRO MIGRANTS IN ATLANTA, (Ph.D.: University of Chicago), 1957.

A-583 Muir, Donal Ewart, THE SOCIAL DEBT: AN INVESTIGATION OF LOWER-
CLASS AND MIDDLE-CLASS NORMS OF SOCIAL OBLIGATION IN LOUISVILLE,
KENTUCKY, (Ph.D.: Vanderbilt University), 1961.

A-584 Murray, M. John, Sister, A SOCIO-CULTURAL STUDY OF 118 MEXICAN
FAMILIES LIVING IN A LOW-RENT PUBLIC PROJECT IN SAN ANTONIO, TEXAS,
(Ph.D.: Catholic University of America), 1955.

A-585 Newman, Sue Etcheson, THE CULTURAL DEVELOPMENT OF McALLEN, TEXAS,
(M.A.: Pan American University), 1976.

A-586 Niehaus, Earl, THE IRISH IN ANTE-BELLUM NEW ORLEANS, (Ph.D.:
Tulane University), 1961.

A-587 Nix, Ruth Aleman, LINGUISTIC VARIATION IN SPEECH OF WILMINGTON,
NORTH CAROLINA, (Ph.D.: Duke University), 1980.

A-588 Norris, Clarence W., A COMPARATIVE STUDY OF SELECTED WHITE AND
NEGRO YOUTH OF SAN ANTONIO, TEXAS, WITH SPECIAL REFERENCE TO
CERTAIN BASIC SOCIAL ATTITUDES, (Ph.D.: University of Southern
California), 1951.

A-589 O'Cain, Raymond, A SOCIAL DIALECT SURVEY OF CHARLESTON, SOUTH
CAROLINA, (Ph.D.: University of Chicago), 1972.

A-590 O'Connor, Michael James, THE EFFECTS OF SOCIAL CHANGE ON THE GEO-
GRAPHICAL STRUCTURE OF AN URBAN SUB-AREA: THE 10TH STREET AREA OF
ATLANTA, (M.A.: University of Georgia), 1971.

A-591 Odum, Howard W., SOCIAL AND MENTAL TRAITS OF THE NEGRO: RESEARCH
INTO THE CONDITIONS OF THE NEGRO RACE IN SOUTHERN TOWNS, (Ph.D.:
Columbia University), 1910.

A-592 Ordonez, Margaret T., A FRONTIER REFLECTED IN COSTUME: TALLAHAS-
SEE, LEON COUNTY, FLORIDA: 1824-1861, (Ph.D.: Florida State
University), 1979.

A-593 Ousley, Stanley Jr., THE IRISH IN LOUISVILLE, (M.A.: University of Louisville), 1974.

A-594 Perdue, Robert E., THE NEGRO IN SAVANNAH, 1865-1900, (Ph.D.: University of Georgia), 1971.

A-595 Phillips, Gayle Yvonne, THE QUALITY OF LIFE AMONG BLACK AND HISPANIC ELDERLY IN THREE SOUTHERN CITIES, (D.S.W.: University of Pennsylvania), 1983.

A-596 Porter, Michael L., THE EAST SIDE OF BLACK ATLANTA, (Ph.D.: Emory University), 1974.

A-597 Porter, William Henry Jr., MIDDLEVILLE MORTICIANS: SOME SOCIAL IMPLICATIONS OF CHANGE IN THE FUNERAL BUSINESS IN A SOUTHERN CITY, (Ph.D.: Louisiana State University), 1958.

A-598 Potwin, Marjorie Adeela, COTTON MILL PEOPLE OF THE PIEDMONT: A STUDY IN SOCIAL CHANGE, (Ph.D.: Columbia University), 1927.

A-599 Powers, Bernard Edward Jr., BLACK CHARLESTON: A SOCIAL HISTORY 1822-1885, (Ph.D.: Northwestern University), 1982.

A-600 Prewitt, Terry J., GERMAN-AMERICAN SETTLEMENT IN AN OKLAHOMA TOWN: ECOLOGICAL, ETHNIC, AND CULTURAL CHANGE, (Ph.D.: University of Oklahoma), 1979.

A-601 Pycior, Julie L., LA RAZA ORGANIZES: MEXICAN AMERICAN LIFE IN SAN ANTONIO, 1915-1930 AS REFLECTED IN MUTUALISTA ACTIVITIES, (Ph.D.: University of Notre Dame), 1979.

A-602 Radford, John P., CULTURE, ECONOMY AND RESIDENTIAL STRUCTURE IN CHARLESTON, SOUTH CAROLINA 1860-1880, (Ph.D.: Clark University), 1974.

A-603 Ragglund, Carol L., IRISH IMMIGRANTS IN ATLANTA, 1850-1896, (M.A.: Emory University), 1968.

A-604 Rankin, David C., THE FORGOTTEN PEOPLE: FREE PEOPLE OF COLOR IN NEW ORLEANS, 1850-1870, (Ph.D.: Johns Hopkins University), 1976.

A-605 Reed, Ruth, THE NEGRO WOMEN OF GAINESVILLE, GEORGIA, (M.A.: University of Georgia), 1921.

A-606 Richardson, Barbara Ann, A HISTORY OF BLACKS IN JACKSONVILLE, FLORIDA, 1860-1895: A SOCIOECONOMIC AND POLITICAL STUDY, (D.A.: Carnegie-Mellon University), 1975.

A-607 Ridley, May A. H., THE BLACK COMMUNITY OF NASHVILLE AND DAVIDSON COUNTY, 1860-1870, (Ph.D.: University of Pittsburgh), 1982.

A-608 Ritchey, David Anthony, THE CONSEQUENCES OF GAINING POWER: THE ARLINGTONIANS FOR BETTER COUNTY (ABC), (M.A.: University of Virginia), 1976.

A-609 Robbins, Faye W., A WORLD-WITHIN-A-WORLD: BLACK NASHVILLE, 1880-1915, (Ph.D.: University of Arkansas), 1980.

A-610 Robinson, Clayton, THE IMPACT OF THE CITY ON RURAL IMMIGRANTS TO MEMPHIS, 1880-1940, (Ph.D.: University of Minnesota), 1967.

A-611 Robinson, Leonard H., NEGRO STREET SOCIETY: A STUDY OF RACIAL ADJUSTMENT IN TWO SOUTHERN URBAN COMMUNITIES, (Ph.D.: Ohio State University), 1950.

A-612 Ross, Elmer L., ETHNICITY AND CULTURAL DIVERSITY AMONG INDIANS, NEGROES, AND WHITES IN MISSISSIPPI, (Ph.D.: University of Georgia), 1970.

A-613 Roth, Darlene Rebecca, MATRONAGE: PATTERNS IN WOMEN'S ORGANIZA-
      TIONS, ATLANTA, GEORGIA, 1890-1940, (Ph.D.: George Washington
      University), 1978.

A-614 Rouse, Jacqueline Ann, LUGENIA D. BURNS HOPE: A BLACK FEMALE
      REFORMER IN THE SOUTH, 1871-1947, (Ph.D.: Emory University), 1983.

A-615 Rummel, George Albert, THE DELTA CHINESE: AN EXPLORATORY STUDY IN
      ASSIMILATION, (M.A.: University of Mississippi), 1966.

A-616 Savage, Howard Allan, CIVIC LIFE-STYLES IN DALLAS, TEXAS, (M.A.:
      North Texas State University), 1975.

A-617 Schinkel, Peter E., THE NEGRO IN ATHENS AND CLARKE COUNTY, 1872-
      1900, (M.A.: University of Georgia), 1971.

A-618 Skrabanek, Robert L., SOCIAL ORGANIZATION AND CHANGE IN A CZECH-
      AMERICAN RURAL COMMUNITY: A SOCIOLOGICAL STUDY OF SNOOK, TEXAS,
      (Ph.D.: Louisiana State University), 1950.

A-619 Slack, Joann Pollard, A METHOD OF DELIMITATION AND IDENTIFICATION
      OF SOCIAL SECTIONS IN ATLANTA, GEORGIA BY CENSUS TRACT DATA, (M.A.:
      University of Georgia), 1968.

A-620 Smith, Glenda, NEIGHBORHOOD IDENTITY: A SOURCE OF CITIZEN PARTICI-
      PATION: A CASE STUDY OF THREE RALEIGH COMMUNITIES, (M.A.: North
      Carolina State University), 1976.

A-621 SoRelle, James M., THE DARKER SIDE OF 'HEAVEN': THE BLACK COMMUN-
      ITY IN HOUSTON TEXAS, 1917-1945, (Ph.D.: Kent State University),
      1980.

A-622 Spletstoser, Frederick Marcel, BACK DOOR TO THE LAND OF PLENTY:
      NEW ORLEANS AS AN IMMIGRANT PORT, 1820-1860, (Ph.D.: Louisiana
      State University), 1978.

A-623 Steffy, Joan Marie, THE CUBAN IMMIGRATION OF TAMPA, FLORIDA, 1886-
      1896, (M.A.: University of South Florida), 1975.

A-624 Suther, Solomon, THE JEWS OF ATLANTA: THEIR SOCIAL STRUCTURE AND
      LEADERSHIP PATTERNS, (Ph.D.: University of North carolina), 1952.

A-625 Thurber, Bert Henry, THE NEGRO AT THE NATION'S CAPITAL, 1913-1921,
      (Ph.D.: Yale University), 1973.

A-626 Torrieri, Nancy K., RESIDENTIAL DISPERSAL AND THE SURVIVAL OF THE
      ITALIAN COMMUNITY IN METROPOLITAN BALTIMORE, 1920-1980, (Ph.D.:
      University of Maryland), 1982.

A-627 Van Horn, Sharyn, THE SENSIBLE SPACE IN A PRIVATELY OWNED HOUSING
      PROJECT, (M.A.: Florida Atlantic University), 1974.

A-628 Veit, Richard John, THE GROWTH AND EFFECTS OF ANTI-GERMAN SENTIMENT
      IN WACO, TEXAS, 1914-1918, (M.A.: Baylor University), 1980.

A-629 Weisel, Jonathan Edward, THE COSMOPOLITAN-LOCAL ORIENTATION OF AGED
      BLACKS AND WHITES IN DENTON, TEXAS, (M.S.: North Texas State
      University), 1973.

A-630 West, Herbert Lee Jr., URBAN LIFE AND SPATIAL DISTRIBUTION OF
      BLACKS IN BALTIMORE, MARYLAND, (Ph.D.: University of Minnesota),
      1973.

A-631 Williams, James Howard, PRIMARY FRIENDSHIP RELATIONS OF HOUSEWIVES
      IN TWO SOCIAL STATUS AREAS: COLUMBIA, SOUTH CAROLINA, (Ph.D.:
      Vanderbilt University), 1956.

A-632 Williams, Joyce Elayne, BLACK COMMUNITY IN TRANSITION: ISSUES AND LEADERSHIP IN A TEXAS GHETTO, (Ph.D.: Washington University), 1971.

A-633 Williams, Melvin R., BLACKS IN WASHINGTON, D.C., 1860-1870, (Ph.D.: Johns Hopkins University), 1976.

A-634 Williams, Stanley B., THE FAMILY DOG AND THE FAMILY LIFE CYCLE: AN EXPLORATORY STUDY OF THE ROLE OF THE DOG IN FAMILY RELATIONS IN A SOUTHEASTERN METROPOLITAN AREA, (Ph.D.: Florida State University), 1967.

A-635 Woods, Frances J., MEXICAN ETHNIC LEADERSHIP IN SAN ANTONIO, TEXAS, (Ph.D.: Catholic University of America), 1949.

A-636 Wright, George Carlton, BLACKS IN LOUISVILLE, KENTUCKY, 1890-1930, (Ph.D.: Duke University), 1977.

A-637 Yamamoto, Kinzo, ASSIMILATION OF MIGRANT NEGROES IN THE DISTRICT OF COLUMBIA: A STUDY OF THE EFFECT OF LENGTH OF RESIDENCE ON URBAN LIFE ADJUSTMENT, (Ph.D.: Pennsylvania State University), 1971.

Literature

A-638 Bryan, Violet D.H. THE IMAGE OF NEW ORLEANS IN THE FICTION OF GEORGE WASHINGTON CABLE AND WILLIAM FAULKNER: A STUDY OF PLACE IN FICTION, (Ph.D.: Harvard University), 1981.

A-639 Cardwell, Guy A., CHARLESTON PERIODICALS, 1795-1860: A STUDY IN LITERARY INFLUENCES, (Ph.D.: University of North Carolina), 1936.

A-640 Carson, Clements, FOUR MAGAZINE CENTERS OF THE OLD SOUTH, (M.A.: Vanderbilt University), 1933.

A-641 McGinnis, Adelaide P., NEW ORLEANS IN FAULKNER'S NOVELS, (Ph.D.: Tulane University), 1984.

A-642 Wetmore, Thomas H. Jr., THE LITERARY AND CULTURAL DEVELOPMENT OF ANTE-BELLUM WILMINGTON, NORTH CAROLINA, (A.M.: Duke University, 1940.

A-643 Yeatman, Joseph Lawrence, BALTIMORE LITERARY CULTURE, 1815-1840, (Ph.D.: University of Maryland), 1983.

Music

A-644 Allen, Larry Steven, MUSICAL LIFE IN OLD TOWN ALEXANDRIA, VIRGINIA, 1749-1814, (M.A.: American University), 1979.

A-645 Bagdon, Robert Joseph, MUSICAL LIFE IN CHARLESTON, SOUTH CAROLINA, FROM 1732 TO 1776 AS RECORDED IN COLONIAL SOURCES, (Ph.D.: University of Miami), 1978.

A-646 Barello, Rudolph V., A HISTORY OF THE NEW ORLEANS ACADEMY OF MUSIC THEATRE, 1887-1893, (M.A.: Louisiana State University), 1967.

A-647 Birkhead, Carole Caudill, THE HISTORY OF THE ORCHESTRA IN LOUIS-VILLE, (M.A.: University of Louisville), 1977.

A-648 Ferguson, James S., A HISTORY OF MUSIC IN VICKSBURG, MISSISSIPPI, 1820-1900, (Ed.D.: University of Michigan), 1970.

A-649 Hindman, John J., CONCERT LIFE IN ANTE-BELLUM CHARLESTON, (Ph.D.: University of North Carolina), 1971.

A-650 Hines, James Robert, MUSICAL ACTIVITY IN NORFOLK, VIRGINIA, 1680-
      1973, (Ph.D.: University of North Carolina), 1974.

A-651 Kmen, Henryt Arnold, SINGING AND DANCING IN NEW ORLEANS; A SOCIAL
      HISTORY OF THE BIRTH AND GROWTH OF BALLS AND OPERA, 1791-1841,
      (Ph.D.: Tulane University), 1961.

A-652 Lornell, Christopher, HAPPY IN THE SERVICE OF THE LORD: AFRO-
      AMERICAN GOSPEL QUARTETS IN MEMPHIS, TENNESSEE, (Ph.D.: Memphis
      State University), 1983.

A-653 Murray, Ronald S., FROM MEMPHIS TO MOTOWN: SOME GEOGRAPHICAL IM-
      PLICATIONS OF THE ORIGIN AND DIFFUSION OF ROCK 'N' ROLL MUSIC,
      (M.A.: Oklahoma State University), 1973.

A-654 Ping, Nancy Regan, MUSIC IN ANTEBELLUM WILMINGTON AND THE LOWER
      CAPE FEAR OF NORTH CAROLINA, (Ph.D.: University of Colorado),
      1979.

A-655 Reynolds, Ina Christeen, A HISTORY OF THE NEW ORLEANS ACADEMY OF
      MUSIC THEATRE, 1861-1869, (M.A.: Louisiana State University),
      1964.

A-656 Rumble, John Woodruff, FRED ROSE AND THE DEVELOPMENT OF THE NASH-
      VILLE MUSIC INDUSTRY, 1942-54, (Ph.D.: Vanderbilt University),
      1980.

Politics and Government

A-657 Aboul-Hosn, Kamal Jamil, AN ANALYSIS OF THE SOCIOECONOMIC CONDI-
      TIONS OF THE LOUISVILLE METROPOLITAN AREA AND THEIR RELATIONS TO
      GOVERNMENT FISCAL BEHAVIOR, (M.A.: University of Louisville),
      1971.

A-658 Adkins, Walter P., BEALE STREET GOES TO THE POLLS, (M.A.: Ohio
      State University), 1935.

A-659 Aiesi, Margaret A., PARTISANSHIP IN THE URBAN SOUTH: A STUDY IN
      CHANGE, 1960-1974, (Ph.D.: University of Florida), 1976.

A-660 Ardrey, Saundra Curry, THE POLITICAL BEHAVIOR OF BLACK WOMEN IN THE
      SOUTH: A CASE STUDY OF RALEIGH, NORTH CAROLINA, (Ph.D.: Ohio
      State University), 1983.

A-661 Boldon, Willie Miller, THE POLITICAL STRUCTURE OF CHARTER REVISION
      MOVEMENTS IN ATLANTA DURING THE PROGRESSIVE ERA, (Ph.D.: Emory
      University), 1978.

A-662 Bornholdt, Laura, BALTIMORE AS A PORT OF PROPAGANDA FOR SOUTH
      AMERICAN INDEPENDENCE, ((Ph.D.: Yale University), 1945.

A-663 Calhoun, John J., SOME CONTRIBUTIONS OF NEGRO LEADERS TO THE
      PROGRESS OF ATLANTA, (M.A.: Atlanta University), 1968.

A-664 Cannon, Robert Joseph, THE ORGANIZATION AND GROWTH OF BLACK
      POLITICAL PARTICIPATION IN DURHAM, NORTH CAROLINA, 1933-1958,
      (Ph.D.: University of North Carolina), 1975.

A-665 Carey, Addison, C. Jr., BLACK POLITICAL PARTICIPATION IN NEW
      ORLEANS, (Ph.D.: Tulane University), 1971.

A-666 Carleton, Don E., A CRISIS OF RAPID CHANGE: THE RED SCARE IN
      HOUSTON, 1945-1955, (Ph.D.: University of Houston), 1978.

A-667 Carroll, George Douglas, CITY-COUNTY CONSOLIDATION: THE CHARLOTTE-
      MECKLINBURG COUNTY, NORTH CAROLINA, CASE, (Ph.D.: University of
      North Carolina), 1974.

A-668 Cobb, James Charles, POLITICS IN A NEW SOUTH CITY: AUGUSTA, GEORGIA, 1946-1971, (Ph.D.: University of Georgia), 1975.

A-669 Cosman, Bernard, REPUBLICANISM IN THE METROPOLITAN SOUTH, (Ph.D.: University of Alabama), 1960.

A-670 Coussons, John Stanford, THIRTY YEARS WITH CALHOUN, RHETT, AND THE CHARLESTON MERCURY: A CHAPTER IN SOUTH CAROLINA POLITICS, (Ph.D.: Louisiana State University), 1971.

A-671 Dearborn, Bonnie Battistula, MUNICIPAL BOUNDARIES IN BISCAYNE BAY: EVOLUTION AND CONFLICT POTENTIAL, (M.A.: University of Miami), 1983.

A-672 Denning, Carolyn Luckett, THE LOUISVILLE (KENTUCKY) DEMOCRATIC PARTY: POLITICAL TIMES OF "MISS LENNIS" McLAUGHLIN, (M.A.: University of Louisville), 1981.

A-673 Dickinson, A. J., MYTH AND MANIPULATION: THE STORY OF THE CRUSADE FOR VOTERS IN RICHMOND, A CASE STUDY OF BLACK POWER IN A SOUTHERN URBAN AREA, (Honors Thesis: Yale University), 1967.

A-674 Drew, Annette Lawrence, A STRUGGLE FOR POWER: THE INTERNAL STRAINS OF FIVE NEIGHBORHOOD ORGANIZATIONS IN NEW ORLEANS, (Ph.D.: Princeton University), 1984.

A-675 Duffy, John Joseph, CHARLESTON POLITICS IN THE PROGRESSIVE ERA, (Ph.D.: University of South Carolina), 1963.

A-676 Dunston, F. Myron, BLACK LEADERSHIP IN DURHAM, NORTH CAROLINA: A QUESTION OF DIVERSIFICATION, (M.A.: University of North Carolina), 1983.

A-677 Duruamaku, G. Chukwuemeka Emeruem, ADMINISTRATIVE COMPLICATIONS STEMMING FROM POLITICS OF URBAN MASS TRANSPORTATION: LOUISVILLE METROPOLITAN AREA, A CASE STUDY, (M.A.: University of Louisville), 1982.

A-678 Fredericks, David W., THE ROLE OF THE NEGRO MINISTER IN POLITICS IN NEW ORLEANS, (Ph.D.: Tulane University), 1967.

A-679 Gomillion, Charles Goode, CIVIC DEMOCRACY IN THE SOUTH, (Ph.D.: Ohio State University), 1959.

A-680 Grable, Stephen W., FROM PRIVATE REALTOR TO PUBLIC SLUM FIGHTER: THE TRANSFORMATION OF THE CAREER IDENTITY OF CHARLES F. PALMER, (Ph.D.: Emory University), 1983.

A-681 Harris, Carl Vernon, ECONOMIC POWER AND POLITICS: A STUDY OF BIRMINGHAM, ALABAMA, 1890-1920, (Ph.D.: University of Wisconsin), 1970.

A-682 Hast, Adele, LOYALISM IN VIRGINIA DURING THE AMERICAN REVOLUTION: THE NORFOLK AREA AND THE EASTERN SHORE, (Ph.D.: University of Iowa), 1979.

A-683 Holland, James Crawford Jr., TEXAS CITY MANAGERS: A STUDY OF PROFESSIONALISM AND ROLE ORIENTATION, (M.A.: Stephen F. Austin State University), 1975.

A-684 Huddleston, Norman Ray, ATTITUDES AND KNOWLEDGE OF FARMERS AND URBAN LEADERS CONCERNING FARMER COOPERATIVES IN MISSISSIPPI, (Ph.D.: Mississippi State University), 1968.

A-685 Hughes, Dorene, URBANIZATION AND REPUBLICAN GROWTH IN THE SOUTH, 1950-1968, (M.A.: North Texas State University), 1975.

A-686 Hughes, Dorene Linda, THE ECOLOGICAL BASIS OF POLITICAL CHANGE: URBANIZATION, INDUSTRIALIZATION AND PARTY COMPETITION IN THE AMERICAN SOUTH, (Ph.D.: North Texas State University), 1981.

A-687 Humphrey, Craig Reed, VOTING PATTERNS IN CITY-COUNTY CONSOLIDATION REFERENDA: CASE STUDIES OF MEMPHIS AND NASHVILLE, TENNESSEE, (Ph.D.: Brown University), 1971.

A-688 Jackson, Joy J., MUNICIPAL PROBLEMS IN NEW ORLEANS, 1880-1896, (Ph.D.: Tulane University), 1961.

A-689 Jalanak, James B., BEALE STREET POLITICS: A STUDY OF NEGRO POLITICAL ACTIVITY IN MEMPHIS, TENNESSEE, (Honors Thesis: Yale University), 1961.

A-690 Lee, E. L., THE HISTORY OF BRUNSWICK, NORTH CAROLINA: THE POLITI- CAL AND ECONOMIC DEVELOPMENT OF A COLONIAL TOWN, (M.A.: University of North Carolina), 1951.

A-691 Lewis, Virginia Emerson, FIFTY YEARS OF POLITICS IN MEMPHIS, 1900- 1950, (Ph.D.: New York University), 1955.

A-692 McDuffie, Jerome A., POLITICS IN WILMINGTON AND NEW HANOVER COUNTY, NORTH CAROLINA, 1865-1900: THE GENESIS OF A RACE RIOT, (Ph.D.: Kent State University), 1979.

A-693 Miley, Jerry Leon, SOCIO-ECONOMIC AND POLITICAL STRUCTURE, (Ph.D.: Florida State University), 1975.

A-694 Moye, William Transor, CHARLOTTE-MECKLINBURG CONSOLIDATION: METRO- LINA IN MOTION, (Ph.D.: University of North Carolina), 1975.

A-695 Nesbitt, Martha T., THE SOCIAL GOSPEL MOVEMENT IN ATLANTA, 1900- 1920, (Ph.D.: Georgia State University), 1978.

A-696 Parker, Beverly Deele, REFORMISM IN MUNICIPAL GOVERNMENT IN TEXAS: THE CASE OF PORT ARTHUR, (M.A.: Lamar University), 1980.

A-697 Parker, Joseph B., MACHINE AND REFORM POLITICS IN NEW ORLEANS: THE MORRISON ERA, (Ph.D.: Tulane University), 1970.

A-698 Parrish, Chas (sic), MINORITY POLITICS IN A SOUTHERN CITY, 1950-60, TAMPA, (M.A.: University of Florida), 1960.

A-699 Peacock, Robert Gary, THE ORIGINS OF COMMISSION GOVERNMENT IN DALLAS, 1902-1907, (M.A.: North Texas State University), 1975.

A-700 Remmington, Bruce Donald, TWELVE FIGHTING YEARS: HOMOSEXUALS IN HOUSTON, 1969-1981, (M.A.: University of Houston), 1983.

A-701 Rosenzweig, Allen, THE INFLUENCE OF CLASS AND RACE ON POLITICAL BEHAVIOR IN NEW ORLEANS, 1960-1967, (M.A.: University of Okla- homa), 1967.

A-702 Schneider, Andrus George, DELAWARE: THE POLITICS OF URBAN UNREST: JULY 1967-JANUARY 1969, (M.A.: Woodrow Wilson School of Public and International Affairs Scholars Program), 1971.

A-703 Schnellings, William John, TAMPA, FLORIDA: ITS ROLE IN THE SPANISH AMERICAN WAR, 1898, (M.A.: University of Miami), 1954.

A-704 Silver, Christopher, 'GREATER RICHMOND' AND THE 'GOOD CITY': POLITICS AND PLANNING IN A NEW SOUTH METROPOLIS, 1900-1976, (Ph.D.: University of North Carolina), 1981.

A-705 Staiger, Charles Carpenter, CITY REORGANIZATION: A CASE STUDY OF LOUISVILLE, KENTUCKY, (M.A.: Louisiana State University), 1977.

A-706 Sudhjeendran, Kesavan, COMMUNITY POWER STRUCTURE IN ATLANTA: A STUDY IN DECISION MAKING, 1920-1929, (Ph.D.: Georgia State University), 1982.

A-707 Turner, Robert Leonard, THE POLITICAL EFFECTS OF INTEGRATION ON SCHOOL BOARD POLITICS: A CASE STUDY OF GALVESTON, TEXAS, (M.A.: Stephen F. Austin State University), 1974.

A-708 Turner-Jones, Marcia, A POLITICAL ANALYSIS OF BLACK EDUCATIONAL HISTORY: ATLANTA, 1865-1943, (Ph.D.: University of Chicago), 1982.

A-709 Walker, Jack Lamar, PROTEST AND NEGOTIATION: A STUDY OF NEGRO POLITICAL LEADERS IN A SOUTHERN CITY, (Ph.D.: State University of Iowa), 1963.

A-710 Watts, Eugene John, CHARACTERISTICS OF CANDIDATES IN CITY POLITICS: ATLANTA, 1865-1903, (Ph.D.: Emory University), 1969.

A-711 Werner, Randolph Dennis, HEGEMONY AND CONFLICT: THE POLITICAL ECONOMY OF A SOUTHERN REGION, AUGUSTA, GEORGIA, 1865-1895, (Ph.D.: University of Virginia), 1977.

A-712 White, Dave Alan, URBANIZATION, IN-MIGRATION AND INTER-PARTY COMPETITION: THE CASE OF FLORIDA, (M.A.: Florida Atlantic University), 1978.

A-713 Whiteford, Gary Thomas, THE MUNICIPAL ENCLAVES OF OKLAHOMA CITY: AN ANALYSIS OF THEIR FUNCTIONAL RELATIONSHIP TO OKLAHOMA CITY, (Ph.D.: University of Oklahoma), 1972.

A-714 Williams, Charles Jr., TWO BLACK COMMUNITIES IN MEMPHIS, TENNES-SEE: A STUDY IN URBAN SOCIO-POLITICAL STRUCTURE, (Ph.D.: University of Illinois), 1982.

A-715 Williamson, Shelly, THE EFFECTS OF ANNEXATION ON SMALL NORTH CAROLINA CITIES AND TOWNS, (M.A.: Appalachian State University), 1978.

A-716 Wilson, Spencer, EXPERIMENT IN REUNION: THE UNION ARMY IN CIVIL WAR NORFOLK AND PORTSMOUTH, VIRGINIA, (Ph.D.: University of Maryland), 1973.

A-717 Wrenn, Lynette B., THE TAXING DISTRICT OF SHELBY COUNTY: A POLITI-CAL AND ADMINISTRATIVE HISTORY OF MEMPHIS, TENNESSEE, 1879-1893, (Ph.D.: Memphis State University), 1983.

Population

A-718 Crandell, Ralph J., NEW ENGLAND'S HAVEN PORT: CHARLESTON AND HER RESTLESS PEOPLE, A STUDY OF COLONIAL MIGRATION, 1629-1775, (Ph.D.: University of Southern California), 1975.

A-719 Darasz, Kathy Ann, CUBAN REFUGEES IN MIAMI: PATTERNS OF ECONOMIC AND POLITICAL ADJUSTMENT, (M.A.: Florida Atlantic University), 1982.

A-720 Dodson, Jack Elwood, DIFFERENTIAL FERTILITY IN HOUSTON, TEXAS, 1940-1950, (Ph.D.: University of Texas), 1956.

A-721 Ellis, John Morris, MORTALITY IN HOUSTON, TEXAS, 1949-51: A STUDY OF SOCIO-ECONOMIC DIFFERENTIALS, (Ph.D.: University of Texas), 1956.

A-722 Fraser, Leigh D., DEMOGRAPHIC ANALYSIS OF MEMPHIS AND SHELBY COUNTY, TENNESSEE, 1820-1972, (M.A.: Memphis State University), 1974.

A-723 Grigg, Charles M., DEMOGRAPHIC CHANGE AS A MEASURE OF SUBREGIONAL
ANALYSIS, 1930-1950: A STUDY IN THE EMERGING URBAN DOMINANCE IN
THE SOUTHEAST, (Ph.D.: University of North Carolina), 1952.

A-724 Grone, Beverly C., A STUDY OF AREAS OF HIGH DENSITY OF AGED PERSONS
IN THE CITY OF MIAMI, FLORIDA--1970, (M.A.: California State University), 1982.

A-725 Groth, Philip Gerald, POPULATION CHANGE AND THE URBANIZATION AND
INDUSTRIALIZATION OF THE SOUTH, 1910-1970, (Ph.D.: University of
Wisconsin), 1975.

A-726 Halley, Helen, A HISTORICAL FUNCTIONAL APPROACH TO THE STUDY OF THE
GREEK COMMUNITY OF TARPON SPRINGS, (Ph.D.: Columbia University),
1952.

A-727 Hareemski, Roman, THE UNATTACHED, AGED IMMIGRANT. A DESCRIPTIVE
ANALYSIS OF THE PROBLEMS EXPERIENCED IN OLD AGE BY THREE GROUPS OF
POLES LIVING APART FROM THEIR FAMILIES IN BALTIMORE, (Ph.D.:
Catholic University of America), 1940.

A-728 Hertz, Hilda, NEGRO ILLEGITIMACY IN DURHAM, NORTH CAROLINA, (M.A.:
Duke University), 1944.

A-729 Hillery, George A., THE NEGRO IN NEW ORLEANS: A DEMOGRAPHIC ANALY-
SIS, (Ph.D.: Louisiana State University), 1954.

A-730 Hinojosa, Gilberto M., SETTLERS AND SOJOURNERS IN THE CHAPARRAL: A
DEMOGRAPHIC STUDY OF A BORDERLANDS TOWN IN TRANSITION, LAREDO,
1755-1870, (Ph.D.: University of Texas), 1979.

A-731 Hirzel, Robert K., THE INFLUENCE OF URBAN FACTORS UPON THE FERTIL-
ITY OF THE WHITE RURAL-FARM POPULATION OF SOUTH CAROLINA, (Ph.D.:
Louisiana State University). 1955.

A-732 Hopkins, William E., A DEMOGRAPHIC ANALYSIS OF HOUSTON, TEXAS,
(Ph.D.: Louisiana State University), 1951.

A-733 Jackson, M. Susan, THE PEOPLE OF HOUSTON IN THE 1980s, (Ph.D.:
Indiana University), 1975.

A-734 Kruegel, David L., METROPOLITAN DOMINANCE AND THE DIFFUSION OF HU-
MAN FERTILITY PATTERNS, 1939-65, (Ph.D.: University of Kentucky),
1968.

A-735 Kwan, Yui-Huen, RESIDENCE AS A FACTOR IN LONGEVITY: A STUDY OF THE
LIFE SPAN OF RURAL AND URBAN LOUISIANANS, 1962-1974, (Ph.D.:
Louisiana State University), 1977.

A-736 Lief, Thomas Parish, THE DECISION TO MIGRATE: BLACK COLLEGE
GRADUATES AND THEIR TENDENCY TO LEAVE NEW ORLEANS, (Ph.D.: Tulane
University), 1970.

A-737 Margavio, Anthony Victor, RESIDENTIAL SEGREGATION IN NEW ORLEANS:
A STATISTICAL ANALYSIS OF CENSUS DATA, (Ph.D.: Louisiana State
University), 1968.

A-738 Matthews, Diller G., THE DISTRIBUTION OF THE NEGRO POPULATION OF
THE DISTRICT OF COLUMBIA, 1800-1960, (M.A.: Catholic University of
America), 1967.

A-739 Meade, Anthony Carl, THE RESIDENTIAL SEGREGATION OF POPULATION
CHARACTERISTICS IN THE ATLANTA STANDARD METROPOLITAN STATISTICAL
AREA, 1960, (Ph.D.: University of Tennessee), 1971.

A-740 Milne, Nelson Dann, A MIGRATION POLICY: NONMETROPOLITAN TO METRO-
POLITAN MIGRATION IN THE SOUTH, (Ph.D.: University of Texas),
1975.

A-741 McMahan, Chalmers A., A DEMOGRAPHIC STUDY OF THE CITY OF ATLANTA, GEORGIA, (Ph.D.: Vanderbilt University), 1949.

A-742 Rogers, Tommy W., DIFFERENTIAL NET MIGRATION PATTERNS IN SOUTHERN STANDARD METROPOLITAN STATISTICAL AREAS, 1950-1960, (Ph.D.: Mississippi State University), 1966.

A-743 Singer, Joseph Frank, THE ROLE OF MIGRATION IN THE SOCIOECONOMIC ADJUSTMENT OF HOUSEHOLDS IN AN ARKANSAS OZARK AREA, (Ph.D.: University of Arkansas), 1971.

A-744 Watson, Ora Vesta Russell, A COMPARATIVE DEMOGRAPHIC ANALYSIS OF TWO LOUISIANA CITIES: BATON ROUGE AND SHREVEPORT, (Ph.D.: Louisiana State University), 1956.

A-745 Whitney, Vincent Heath, THE PATTERN OF VILLAGE LIFE: A STUDY OF SOUTHERN PIEDMONT VILLAGES IN TERMS OF POPULATION, STRUCTURE, AND ROLE, (Ph.D.: University of North Carolina), 1945.

A-746 Woodbury, Kimball, THE SPATIAL DIFFUSION OF THE CUBAN COMMUNITY IN DADE COUNTY, FLORIDA, (M.A.: University of Florida), 1978.

A-747 Zokoski, Kimberly J., THE EFFECTS OF LENGTH OF RESIDENCE AND STAGE MIGRATION ON THE DEMOGRAPHIC CHARACTERISTICS OF A HAITIAN COMMUNITY IN MIAMI, FLORIDA, (M.A.: University of Miami), 1980.

Race Relations

A-748 Benson, A.W., RACE RELATIONS IN ATLANTA, AS SEEN IN A CRITICAL ANALYSIS OF THE CITY COUNCIL PROCEEDINGS AND OTHER RELATED WORKS, 1865-1877, (M.A.: Atlanta University), 1966.

A-749 Blalock, J.W., SOCIAL, POLITICAL AND ECONOMIC ASPECTS OF RACE RELATIONS IN ATLANTA, 1890-1908, (M.A.: Atlanta University) 1969.

A-750 Bruton, Frederic, DESEGREGATION IN SAN ANTONIO, (M.A.: Trinity University), 1971.

A-751 Chamis, George Christopher, ATTITUDE TOWARD FAMILY INTEGRATION AMONG WHITE MARRIED COUPLES IN TALLAHASSEE, FLORIDA, (Ph.D.: Florida State University), 1955.

A-752 Cobb, Jimmy G., A STUDY OF WHITE PROTESTANTS' ATTITUDES TOWARD NEGROES IN CHARLESTON, SOUTH CAROLINA, 1790-1845, (Ph.D.: Baylor University), 1976.

A-753 Corley, Robert Gaines, THE QUEST FOR RACIAL HARMONY: RACE RELATIONS IN BIRMINGHAM, ALABAMA, 1947-1963, (Ph.D.: University of Virginia), 1979.

A-754 Dunstan, Aingred G., THE BLACK STRUGGLE FOR EQUALITY IN WINSTON-SALEM, NORTH CAROLINA, 1947-1977, (Ph.D.: Duke University), 1981.

A-755 Glenn, Joanne, THE WINSTON-SALEM RIOT OF 1918, (M.A.: University of North Carolina), 1979.

A-756 Goldberg, Louis C., CORE IN TROUBLE: A SOCIAL HISTORY OF THE ORGANIZATIONAL DILEMMAS OF THE CONGRESS OF RACIAL EQUALITY TARGET CITY PROJECT IN BALTIMORE (1965-1967), (Ph.D.: Johns Hopkins University), 1970.

A-757 Graham, Leroy, ELISHA TYSON, BALTIMORE, AND THE NEGRO, (M.A.: Morgan State College), 1975.

A-758 Graves, John William, TOWN AND COUNTRY: RACE RELATIONS AND URBAN DEVELOPMENT IN ARKANSAS, 1865-1905, (Ph.D.: University of Virginia), 1979.

A-759 Howard, Mark, AN HISTORICAL STUDY OF THE DESEGREGATION OF THE ALEXANDRIA, VIRGINIA, CITY PUBLIC SCHOOLS, 1954-1973, (Ph.D.: George Washington University), 1976.

A-760 Howard, William Harry, THE RANK ORDER OF SENSITIVITY TO DISCRIMINA- TIONS OF NEGROES IN ORANGEBURG, SOUTH CAROLINA, (Ph.D.: Ohio State University), 1957.

A-761 Hudson, James B., III, THE HISTORY OF LOUISVILLE MUNICIPLE COLLEGE. EVENTS LEADING TO THE DESEGREGATION OF THE UNIVERSITY OF LOUIS- VILLE, (Ph.D.: University of Kentucky), 1981.

A-762 Jones, Douglas, R., AN ABSTRACT OF AN OPINION POLL ON ATTITUDES OF WHITE ADULTS ABOUT DESEGREGATION IN THE PUBLIC SCHOOLS OF KNOX- VILLE, TENNESSEE, (Ph.D.: George Peabody College for Teachers), 1958.

A-763 Jones, Yollette Trigg, THE BLACK COMMUNITY, POLITICS, AND RACE RELATIONS IN THE "IRIS CITY": NASHVILLE, TENNESSEE, 1870-1954, (Ph.D.: Duke University), 1985.

A-764 Leach, Damaria Etta Brown, PROGRESS UNDER PRESSURE: CHANGES IN CHARLOTTE RACE RELATIONS, 1955-1965, (M.A.: University of North Carolina), 1976.

A-765 McClure, Edward Ellis, PATTERNS OF RACIAL SEGREGATION IN SOUTHERN CITIES: IMPLICATIONS FOR PLANNING POLICY, (Ph.D.: Harvard Univer- sity), 1971.

A-766 McElhone, Patrick Shaheen, THE CIVIL RIGHTS ACTIVITIES OF THE LOUISVILLE BRANCH OF THE NAACP: 1914-1960, (M.A.: University of Louisville), 1976.

A-767 Miller, Authur Madden, DESEGREGATION AND NEGRO LEADERSHIP IN DUR- HAM, NORTH CAROLINA, 1954-1963, (M.A.: University of North Caro- ina), 1976.

A-768 Millner, Steven M., THE MONTGOMERY BUS BOYCOTT: CASE STUDY IN THE EMERGENCE AND CAREER OF A SOCIAL MOVEMENT, (Ph.D.: University of California), 1981.

A-769 Padgett, Gregg C. K. STEELE AND THE TALLAHASSEE BUS BOYCOTT, 1956- 1960, (M.A.: Florida State University), 1977.

A-770 Pate, Artie T. Jr., AN INVESTIGATION OF THE DESEGREGATION PROCESS IN THE METROPOLITAN NASHVILLE-DAVIDSON COUNTY PUBLIC SCHOOL SYSTEM, 1954-1969, (Ph.D.: George Peabody College, Vanderbilt University), 1981.

A-771 Peck, June Cary Chapman, SCHOOL DESEGREGATION IN GREENSBORO, NORTH CAROLINA, 1954-1981. A CASE STUDY OF PURPOSIVE SOCIAL CHANGE, (Ph.D.: Boston University), 1974.

A-772 Powe, Alphonso Stewart, THE ROLE OF NEGRO PRESSURE GROUPS IN INTER- RACIAL INTEGRATION IN DURHAM CITY, NORTH CAROLINA, (Ph.D.: New York University), 1954.

A-773 Rabinowitz, Howard D., THE SEARCH FOR SOCIAL CONTROL: RACE RELA- IONS IN THE URBAN SOUTH, 1865-1890, (Ph.D.: University of Chi- cago), 1973.

A-774 Reese, William Alvin II, WINDSOR VILLAGE: A SOUTHERN TEST OF THE CONTACT HYPOTHESIS, (M.A.: University of Houston), 1978.

A-775 Saxe, Allan A., PROTEST AND REFORM: THE DESEGREGATION OF OKLAHOMA CITY, (Ph.D.: University of Oklahoma), 1969.

A-776 Sheeley, Dean Lee, THE EFFECTS OF INCREASING RACISM ON THE CREOLE COLORED IN THREE GULF COAST CITIES BETWEEN 1803 AND 1860, (M.A.: University of West Florida), 1971.

A-777 Smead, Edwin Howard Jr., THE LYNCHING OF MACK CHARLES PACKER IN POPLARVILLE, MISSISSIPPI, APRIL 25, 1959, (Ph.D.: University of Maryland), 1979.

A-778 Spofford, Timothy John, LYNCH STREET: THE STORY OF MISSISSIPPI'S KENT STATE--THE MAY 1970 SLAYINGS AT JACKSON STATE COLLEGE, (D.A.: State University of New York, Albany), 1984.

A-779 Thomas, B.C., RACE QUESTIONS IN ATLANTA FROM 1877 THROUGH 1890, AS SEEN IN A CRITICAL ANALYSIS OF THE ATLANTA CITY COUNCIL PROCEEDINGS AND OTHER RELATED WORKS, (M.A.: Atlanta University), 1965.

A-780 Thomas, Larry Reni, A STUDY OF RACIAL VIOLENCE IN WILMINGTON, NORTH CAROLINA, PRIOR TO FEBRUARY 1, 1971, (M.A.: University of North Carolina), 1980.

A-781 Thompkins, George Washington Jr., RACIAL DISCRIMINATION AND THE EQUALIZATION OF NEGRO AND WHITE TEACHERS' SALARIES IN THE DALLAS PUBLIC SCHOOLS, (M.A.: North Texas State University), 1974.

A-782 Vaudal, Giles, THE NEW ORLEANS RIOT OF 1866: THE ANATOMY OF A TRAGEDY, (Ph.D.: College of William and Mary), 1978.

A-783 Verkler, Billy Duan, AN APPLICATION OF COGNITIVE DISSONANCE THEORY TO REFERENCE GROUP BEHAVIOR: A STUDY OF RACIAL ATTITUDES OF CHURCH MEMBERS IN SEARCY, ARKANSAS, (Ph.D.: Mississippi State University), 1970.

A-784 Wallace, David, THE LITTLE ROCK CENTRAL DESEGREGATION CRISIS OF 1957, (Ph.D.: University of Missouri), 1977.

A-785 Yeaky, Lamont Henry, THE MONTGOMERY, ALABAMA BUS BOYCOTT, 1955-56, (Ph.D.: Columbia University), 1979.

Radio and Television

A-786 Gibbs, George Fort, TWENTY YEARS OF NEWS AND PUBLIC AFFAIRS AT WSB-TV, (M.A.: University of Georgia), 1967.

A-787 Pellegrino, Joseph Anthony, EDITORIAL BROADCASTING IN THE METRO-POLITAN WASHINGTON, D.C. AREA, (M.A.: American University), 1967.

A-788 Sachs, Robin Leslie, A HISTORY OF STATION WRR: PIONEER IN MUNICIPALLY OWNED RADIO, (M.A.: North Texas State University), 1978.

A-789 Spencer, John Morgan, AN INTENSIVE HISTORY OF A BROADCAST STATION KBGO, WACO, TEXAS, (M.A.: MICHIGAN STATE UNIVERSITY), 1967.

Recreation and Sports

A-790 Bertalan, John J., RECREATION AS AN ISSUE OF URBAN PUBLIC POLICY IN TWELVE SOUTH FLORIDA MUNICIPALITIES, (M.A.: Florida Atlantic University), 1972.

A-791 Click, Patricka Catherine, LEISURE IN THE UPPER SOUTH IN THE NINE-TEENTH CENTURY: A STUDY OF TRENDS IN BALTIMORE, NORFOLK, AND RICH-MOND, (Ph.D.: University of Virginia), 1980.

A-792 Cole, Gerald Leon, TOWARD THE MEASUREMENT OF DEMAND FOR OUTDOOR RECREATION IN THE PHILADELPHIA-BALTIMORE-WASHINGTON METROPOLITAN REGION WITH IMPLICATIONS FOR AGRICULTURAL LAND USE, (Ph.D.: Michigan State University), 1967.

A-793 Cordell, Harold Kenneth, SUBSTITUTION BETWEEN PRIVATELY AND COLLECTIVELY SUPPLIED URBAN RECREATIONAL OPEN SPACE, (Ph.D.: North Carolina State University), 1975.

A-794 Craig, William W., WEEKEND AND VACATION RECREATIONAL BEHAVIOR OF A NEGRO COMMUNITY IN LOUISIANA--A SPATIAL STUDY, (Ph.D.: University of Michigan), 1968.

A-795 Foret, Claire Marie, LIFE SATISFACTION, LEISURE SATISFACTION, AND LEISURE PARTICIPATION AMONG YOUNG-OLD AND OLD-OLD ADULTS WITH RURAL AND URBAN RESIDENCE, (Ph.D.: Texas Woman's University), 1985.

A-796 Kirk, Christopher Cline, RECREATION DEMAND AND SUPPLY IN NACOG-DOCHES, TEXAS, (M.S.F.: Stephen F. Austin State University), 1977.

Religion

A-797 Alvirez, David, THE EFFECTS OF FORMAL CHURCH AFFILIATION AND RELIGIOSITY ON FERTILITY PATTERNS OF MEXICAN AMERICANS IN AUSTIN, TEXAS, (Ph.D.: University of Texas), 1971.

A-798 Ammerman, Nancy Tatom, LOCALISM, SOUTHERN CULTURE, AND THE ROLE OF CLERGYMEN IN THE CIVIL RIGHTS MOVEMENT IN A SOUTHERN COMMUNITY, (M.A.: University of Louisville), 1977.

A-799 Bilhartz, Terry D., URBAN RELIGION AND THE SECOND GREAT AWAKENING: A RELIGIOUS HISTORY OF BALTIMORE, MARYLAND, 1790-1830, (Ph.D.: George Washington University), 1979.

A-800 Bramkamp, Walter H., SOME ASPECTS OF THE GEOGRAPHY OF RELIGION IN KNOXVILLE, TENNESSEE, (Ph.D.: University of Tennessee), 1978.

A-801 Cowert, Mark, RABBI MORRIS NEWFIELD OF BIRMINGHAM: A STUDY IN ETHNIC LEADERSHIP, (Ph.D.: University of Cincinnati), 1982.

A-802 Lefever, Harry Groff, GHETTO RELIGION: A STUDY OF THE RELIGIOUS STRUCTURES AND STYLES OF A POOR WHITE COMMUNITY IN ATLANTA, GEORGIA, (Ph.D.: Emory University), 1971.

A-803 Piner, William David, WHEN SALEM WAS SALEM: AN ORAL HISTORY APPROACH TO COMMUNITY AMONG THE MORAVIANS, (M.A.: University of North Carolina), 1979.

A-804 Shepherd, Samuel C. Jr., CHURCHES AS WORK: RICHMOND, VIRGINIA, WHITE PROTESTANT LEADERS AND SOCIAL CHANGE IN A SOUTHERN CITY, 1900-1919, (Ph.D.: University of Wisconsin), 1980.

A-805 Weitzman, Louis Gabriel, ONE HUNDRED YEARS OF CATHOLIC CHARITIES IN THE DISTRICT OF COLUMBIA, (Ph.D.: Catholic University of America), 1931.

A-806 Salzman, Gerald, A HISTORY OF ZIONISM IN HOUSTON, 1897-1975, (M.A.: University of Houston), 1976.

Social Problems and Social Services

A-807 Armstrong, Helen P., PUBLIC WELFARE AND PRIVATE PROGRAMS ADMINISTERED IN NATCHEZ AND ADAMS COUNTY, MISSISSIPPI, 1798-1822, (M.A.: University of Chicago), 1943.

A-808 Ayers, Edward Lynn, CRIME AND SOCIETY IN THE NINETEENTH-CENTURY SOUTH, (Ph.D.: Yale University), 1980.

A-809 Barker, Robert H., A SOCIAL STUDY OF JUVENILE DELINQUENCY IN CHARLOTTESVILLE AND ALBERMARLE COUNTY, VIRGINIA, (Ph.D.: University of Virginia, 1934.

A-810 Bellows, Barbarta Lawrence, TEMPERING THE WIND: THE SOUTHERN RESPONSE TO URBAN POVERTY, 1850-1865, (Ph.D.: University of South Carolina), 1983.

A-811 Borchert, James A., AMERICAN MINI-GHETTOES: ALLEYS, ALLEY DWELLINGS AND ALLEY DWELLERS IN WASHINGTON, D.C., 1850-1970, (Ph.D.: University of Maryland), 1976.

A-812 Branch, Roosevelt, DIFFERENTIAL LAW-ENFORCEMENT IN LOUISVILLE: AN ATTITUDINAL STUDY, (M.A.: University of Louisville), 1976.

A-813 Coker, Lisabeth Margareta Lund, SPECIAL TRANSPORTATION SERVICES FOR ELDERLY AND HANDICAPPED IN ATHENS AND CLARKE COUNTY, GEORGIA, M.L.A.: University of Georgia), 1979.

A-814 Conlin, James J., AN AREA STUDY OF JUVENILE DELINQUENCY IN BALTIMORE, MARYLAND: A RETEST OF LAUDER'S THESES AND A TEST OF COHEN'S HYPOTHESES, (Ph.D.: Saint Louis University), 1961.

A-815 Fraser, Russell Edward, ECONOMIC DETERMINANTS OF URBAN CRIME RATES, (M.A.: Florida Atlantic University), 1972.

A-816 George, Paul S., CRIMINAL JUSTICE IN MIAMI, 1896-1930, (Ph.D.: Florida State University), 1975.

A-817 Helper, Mark K., COLOR, CRIME, AND THE CITY [OF NEW ORLEANS], (Ph.D.: Rice University), 1972.

A-818 Hepler, Morris K., NEGROES AND CRIME IN NEW ORLEANS, 1850-1861, (M.A.: Tulane University), 1939.

A-819 Hindman, Baker Michael, THE EMOTIONAL PROBLEMS OF NEGRO HIGH SCHOOL YOUTH WHICH ARE RELATED TO SEGREGATION AND DISCRIMINATION IN A SOUTHERN URBAN COMMUNITY, (Ph.D.: New York University), 1953.

A-820 Jackson, Kathleen Margaret, THE EMERGENCE OF WELFARE PROBLEMS IN THE CITY OF WASHINGTON WITH SPECIAL REFERENCE TO CONFRONTATIONS BETWEEN CONGRESS AND COMMUNITY, (D.S.W.: Catholic University of America), 1970.

A-821 Lauder, Bernard, A STUDY OF JUVENILE DELINQUENCY IN BALTIMORE, (Ph.D.: Columbia University), 1953.

A-822 Lindsay, Inabel B., THE PARTICIPATION OF NEGROES IN THE ESTABLISHMENT OF WELFARE SERVICES, 1865-1900, WITH SPECIAL REFERENCE TO THE DISTRICT OF COLUMBIA, MARYLAND, AND VIRGINIA, (Ph.D.: University of Pittsburgh), 1952.

A-823 Marchiafava, Louis J., INSTITUTIONAL AND LEGAL ASPECTS OF THE GROWTH OF PROFESSIONAL URBAN POLICE SERVICE: THE HOUSTON EXPERIENCE, 1878-1948, (Ph.D.: Rice University), 1976.

A-824 Meyers, Lawrence C., EVOLUTION OF THE JEWISH SERVICE AGENCY IN MEMPHIS, TENNESSEE: 1847 TO 1963, (M.A.: Memphis State University), 1965.

A-825 Modey, Yqo F., THE STRUGGLE OVER PROHIBITION IN MEMPHIS, 1880-1930, (Ph.D.: Memphis State University), 1983.

A-826 Pumphrey, Muriel Warren, MARY RICHMOND AND THE RISE OF PROFESSIONAL
      SOCIAL WORK IN BALTIMORE: THE FOUNDATIONS OF A CREATIVE CAREER,
      (D.S.W.: Columbia University), 1956.

A-827 Rhines, Charlotte C., A CITY AND ITS SOCIAL PROBLEMS: POVERTY,
      HEALTH AND CRIME IN BALTIMORE, 1865-1875, (Ph.D.: University of
      Maryland), 1975.

A-828 Rousey, Dennis Charles, THE NEW ORLEANS POLICE, 1805-1889: A
      SOCIAL HISTORY, (Ph.D.: Cornell University), 1978.

A-829 Schreider, Mariam, AN EXPLORATION OF HOW THE NEEDS OF AGING JEWS IN
      BALTIMORE ARE MET IN FOUR DIFFERENT SETTINGS: OWN HOME, FOSTER
      HOME, NURSING HOME AND OLD AGE HOME, (D.S.W.: Catholic University
      of America), 1967.

A-830 Sheldon, Randall G., RESCUED FROM EVIL: ORIGINS OF THE JUVENILE
      USTICE SYSTEM IN MEMPHIS, TENNESSEE, 1900-1917, (Ph.D.: Southern
      Illinois University), 1976.

A-831 Silverman, Edgar, THE JUVENILE COURT FOR THE DISTRICT OF COLUMBIA:
      AN HISTORICAL VIEW OF ITS DEVELOPMENT FROM 1937 TO 1957, (D.S.W.:
      Catholic University of America), 1971.

A-832 Vyhnanek, Louis Andrew, THE SEAMIER SIDE OF LIFE: CRIMINAL ACTIV-
      ITY IN NEW ORLEANS DURING THE 1920s, (Ph.D.: Louisiana State Uni-
      versity), 1979.

Theatre

A-833 Arnold, Claude Ahmed, THE DEVELOPMENT OF THE STAGE IN NASHVILLE,
      TENNESSEE, 1807-1870, (Ph.D.: University of Iowa), 1933.

A-834 Bilbo, Jack L. Jr., ECONOMY AND CULTURE: THE BOOM-AND-BUST THEA-
      TRES OF PENSACOLA, FLORIDA, 1821-1917, (Ph.D.: Texas Tech Uni-
      versity), 1982.

A-835 Boyd, Theodore E., A HISTORY OF THE NEW ORLEANS ACADEMY OF MUSIC
      THEATRE, 1869-1880, (M.A.: Louisiana State University), 1965.

A-836 Chidsey, Martha Ann, THE WEST STREET THEATRE, ANNAPOLIS, MARYLAND:
      1771-1774, (M.A.: American University), 1977.

A-837 Combs, Don Whitney, A HISTORY OF MACAULEY'S THEATRE, LOUISVILLE,
      KENTUCKY, 1873-1925, (Ph.D.: University of Illinoius), 1977.

A-838 Cook, Patricia Lynn, AGENDA-SETTING: THE POLITICS AND POLICIES OF
      GROWTH CONTROL IN BOCA RATON, FLORIDA, (M.A.: Florida Atlantic
      University), 1977.

A-839 DeMitz, Ouida Kay, THE USES OF DANCE IN THE ENGLISH LANGUAGE THEA-
      TRES OF NEW ORLEANS PRIOR TO THE CIVIL WAR, 1806-1861, (Ph.D.:
      Florida State University), 1975.

A-840 Dorman, James Hunter, THE THEATER IN THE ANTE-BELLUM SOUTH, 1815-
      1861, (Ph.D.: University of North Carolina), 1966.

A-841 Elliott, Barbara Anne, "THE PLAY'S THE THING": BOYD MARTIN AND THE
      LOUISVILLE LITTLE THEATER COMPANY, (M.A.: University of Louis-
      ville), 1974.

A-842 Epperson, James Register, THE COMBINATION TOURING COMPANY AND ITS
      INFLUENCE ON THE THEATRE IN SALISBURY, ROWN COUNTY, NORTH CAROLINA,
      (Ph.D.: Florida State University), 1977.

A-843 Green, E.M. THEATRE AND OTHER ENTERTAINMENTS IN SAVANNAH, GEORGIA
      FROM 1810 TO 1965, (Ph.D.: University of Iowa), 1971.

A-844 Groves, William McDonald Jr., A HISTORY OF THE PROFESSIONAL THEATRE IN MARSHALL, TEXAS FROM 1877 TO 1915, (M.A.: Stephen F. Austin State University), 1976.

A-845 Hadley, Richard H., THE THEATRE IN LYNCHBURG, VIRGINIA, FROM ITS BEGINNINGS IN 1822 TO THE OUTBREAK OF THE CIVIL WAR, (Ph.D.: University of Michigan), 1946-47.

A-846 Harrison, Shirley Madeline, THE GRAND OPERA HOUSE (THIRD VARIETIES THEATRE) OF NEW ORLEANS, LOUISIANA, 1871 TO 1906: A HISTORY AND ANALYSIS, (Ph.D.: Louisiana State University), 1965.

A-847 Head, Sadie Faye, A HISTORICAL STUDY OF THE TULANE AND CRESCENT THEATRES OF NEW ORLEANS, LOUISIANA: 1897-1937, (Ph.D.: Louisiana State University), 1963.

A-848 Hostetler, Paul Smith, JAMES H. CALDWELL: NEW ORLEANS THEATRICAL MANAGER, (Ph.D.: Louisiana State University), 1964.

A-849 Keeton, Guy H., THE THEATRE IN MISSISSIPPI FROM 1840 TO 1870, (Ph.D.: Louisiana State University), 1979.

A-850 Lawlor, JoAnn, THE ST. CHARLES THEATRE OF NEW ORLEANS, 1888-1899, (M.A.: Louisiana State University), 1966.

A-851 Manry, Joe E., A HISTORY OF THEATRE IN AUSTIN, TEXAS, 1839-1905: FROM MINSTRELS TO MOVING PICTURES, (Ph.D.: University of Texas), 1979.

A-852 Menefee, Larry Thomas, THE DEATH OF A ROAD SHOW TOWN: LITTLE ROCK, ARKANSAS 1899-1921, (Ph.D.: University of Denver), 1977.

A-853 O'Neal, Aaron B., THEATRE--HISTORY OF THE ST. CHARLES THEATRE OF NEW ORLEANS, 1880-1890, (M.A.: Louisiana State University), 1965.

A-854 Schmidt, Rita Jane, THE HISTORY OF THE THEATRE GUILD IN LOUISVILLE, 1956-1971, (M.A.: University of Louisville), 1972.

Theory and Models

A-855 Nicholas, Francis W., PARAMETERIZATION OF THE URBAN FABRIC: A STUDY OF SURFACE ROUGHNESS WITH APPLICATIONS TO BALTIMORE, (Ph.D.: University of Maryland), 1974.

A-856 Spar, Michael Allen, CAUSAL MODELS OF SMALL SOUTHERN CITY CHANGE, 1960-1970, (Ph.D.: University of Virginia), 1975.

Transportation

A-857 Baucom, Thomas F., THE SPATIAL DIMENSION OF PERCEIVED HIGHWAY IMPACT: AN ANALYSIS OF THE RELATIONSHIP BETWEEN PROXIMITY AND RESIDENTIAL ATTITUDES TOWARD A PROPOSED URBAN EXPRESSWAY IN ATLANTA, GEORGIA, (Ph.D.: University of Georgia), 1978.

A-858 Coffee, William David Jr., AN EMPIRICAL STUDY OF PLANT LOCATION AND URBAN TRANSPORTATION DEMAND RELATIONSHIPS IN AUSTIN, TEXAS, (Ph.D.: University of Texas), 1971.

A-859 Corbett, William P., OKLAHOMA'S HIGHWAYS: INDIAN TRAILS TO URBAN EXPRESSWAYS, (Ph.D.: Oklahomna State University), 1982.

A-860 Cranford, Sammy Orren, THE FERNWOOD, COLUMBIA AND GULF: A RAILROAD IN THE PINEY WOODS OF SOUTH MISSISSIPPI, (Ph.D.: Mississippi State University), 1983.

A-861 Fussell, James Richard, ATLANTA'S CIRCULATION: A GEOGRAPHY OF HUMAN TRANSPORT AND COMMUNICATIONS, (Ph.D.: University of Georgia), 1971.

A-862 Goldstone, Robert Lee, HISTORICAL GEOGRAPHY OF SCOTTSVILLE, VIRGINIA: THE RELATION OF CHANGING TRANSPORTATION PATTERNS TO A RIVERINE-PIEDMONT COMMUNITY, (Ph.D.: University of Virginia), 1953.

A-863 Heath, Milton S., PUBLIC COOPERATION IN RAILROAD CONSTRUCTION IN THE SOUTHERN UNITED STATES TO 1861, (Ph.D.: Harvard University), 1938.

A-864 Kithcart, Philip E., INTRA-URBAN TRAVEL PATTERNS OF THE NORTH NASHVILLE, TENNESSEE BLACK COMMUNITY 1969 AND 1975, (Ph.D.: University of Cincinnati), 1982.

A-865 Krawczyk, Raymond Douglas, THE CITY OF LOUISVILLE AND THE LOUISVILLE AND NASHVILLE RAILROAD COMPANY, 1850-1755, (M.A.: University of Louisiana), 1978

A-866 Palmer, Cecil E., RAIL DEPENDENCE OF INDUSTRY IN THE ATLANTA AREA, (M.A.: University of Georgia), 1960.

A-867 Stanley, Raymond, THE RAILROAD PATTERN OF ATLANTA, (M.A.: University of Chicago), 1947.

Urban Renewal

A-868 Andre, J. R., URBAN RENEWAL AND HOUSING IN NEW ORLEANS, 1949-1962, (M.A.: Louisiana State University), 1963.

A-869 Brown, Esther Fireston, DOWNTOWN LOUISVILLE: A STUDY OF PROBLEMS AND PROPOSALS, (M.B.A.: University of Louisville), 1969.

A-870 Friedenreich, Catherine J., DEVELOPMENT STRATEGIES FOR NORTH GRAHAM STREET AREA OF FOURTH WARD, CHARLOTTE, NORTH CAROLINA, (M.A.: University of North Carolina), 1982.

A-871 Harman, Bryan Douglas, CONGRESS AND URBAN RENEWAL IN THE DISTRICT OF COLUMBIA, (M.A.: American University), 1964.

A-872 Judge, DeAnn DeFord, THE SPATIAL STRUCTURE OF URBAN NEIGHBORHOOD REVITALIZATION: A SOUTHERN CITY'S EXPERIENCE, (M.A.: University of North Carolina), 1984.

A-873 Koehl, Frederick, INTRA-METROPOLITAN VARIATIONS IN THE PROCESS OF NEIGHBORHOOD REVITALIZATION, (Ph.D.: University of Georgia), 1984.

A-874 Krammer, Linda Sue, LOUISVILLE'S RIVERFRONT REDEVELOPMENT PROJECT: AN EXAMPLE OF COOPERATIVE DECISIONMAKING BY CIVIC AND POLITICAL LEADERS IN AN AMERICAN URBAN COMMUNITY, (M.A.: University of Louisville), 1974.

A-875 Rosenberg, Helen, AREAS OF RELOCATION OF DISPLACED LOWER GARDEN DISTRICT AND IRISH CHANNEL RESIDENTS, (M.A.: University of New Orleans), 1977.

A-876 Sasser, Robert H., MUNICIPAL SERVICE DISTRICTS: ONE APPROACH TO DOWNTOWN REVITALIZATION IN NORTH CAROLINA, (M.V.A.: University of North Carolina), 1982.

A-877 Schaffer, Daniel, GARDEN CITIES FOR AMERICA: THE RADBURN [N.C.] EXPERIENCE, (Ph.D.: Rutgers University), 1981.

A-878 Webb, Tommy Grey, AN ANALYTICAL STUDY OF URBAN RENEWAL, (M.A.: Appalachian State University), 1975.

Urbanism

A-879 Armstrong, Thomas Field, URBAN VISION IN VIRGINIA: A COMPARATIVE STUDY OF ANTE-BELLUM FREDERICKSBURG, LYNCHBURG, AND STAUNTON, (Ph.D.: University of Virginia), 1974.

A-880 Brownell, Blaine Allison, THE URBAN MIND IN THE SOUTH: THE GROWTH OF URBAN CONSCIOUSNESS IN SOUTHERN CITIES, 1920-1927, (Ph.D.: University of North Carolina), 1969.

A-881 Mochon, Marian Johnson, TOWARD URBANISM: THE CULTURAL DYNAMICS OF THE PREHISTORIC AND HISTORIC SOCIETIES OF THE AMERICAN SOUTHEAST, (Ph.D.: University of Wisconsin), 1972.

A-882 Smith, Douglas Lloyd, THE NEW DEAL AND THE URBAN SOUTH: THE ADVANCEMENT OF A SOUTHERN URBAN CONSCIOUSNESS DURING THE DEPRESSION DECADE, (Ph.D.: University of Southern Mississippi), 1978.

A-883 Wall, Carolyn Lineberger, URBAN IDEALISM: WINSTON-SALEM'S SEARCH FOR THE GOOD CITY, (M.A.: Wake Forest University), 1974.

Periodical Literature

Archaeology

B-1   Austin, Robert J. and Kenneth W. Hardin, "CONSERVING A CITY'S PRE-
       HISTORY: ST. PETERSBURG'S ARCHAEOLOGICAL SURVEY AND PLANNING
       PROJECT," Florida Anthropologist 40:4 (November 1987), 266-274.

B-2   Beaudoin, Kenneth L., "AN ADVENTURE INTO THE PREHISTORY OF THE MEM-
       PHIS AREA," Tennessee Historical Quarterly 13:4 (December 1954),
       291-296.

B-3   Bostwick, John A., "ABORIGINAL CERAMICS IN PRE-EIGHTEENTH CENTURY
       COLONIAL ST. AUGUSTINE, FLORIDA: THE DeLEON SITE," Conference on
       Historic Site Archaeology Papers (1976) 11:part 2 (April 1977),
       140-150.

B-4   Bostwick, John A., "THE PLAZA II SITE EXCAVATION OF A COLONIAL
       SPANISH WELL IN ST. AUGUSTINE," Historical Archaeology 14:(1980),
       73-81.

B-5   Brooms, Bascom McDonald, "THE COLLIER-BOONE HOUSE,", Conference on
       Historic Site Archaeology Papers (1987) 13:(1979), 180-203.

B-6   Calmes, Alan, "THE BRITISH REVOLUTIONARY FORTIFICATIONS OF CAMDEN,
       SOUTH CAROLINA," Conference on Historic Site Archaeology Papers
       (1967) 2:part 1 (September 1968), 50-61.

B-7   Carnes, Linda F., "PRELIMINARY INVESTIGATIONS OF ATLANTA'S FOLK
       POTTERIES," Conference on Historic Site Archaeology Papers (1977)
       12:(1978), 211-249.

B-8   Carrillo, Richard F., "ARCHAEOLOGICAL INVESTIGATION AT FORT DOR-
       CHESTER: AN ARCHAEOLOGICAL ASSESSMENT," Notebook 7:5 (September-
       October 1975), 137-171.

B-9   Cressey, Pamela J., "THE CITY AS A SITE: THE ALEXANDRIA MODEL FOR
       URBAN ARCHAEOLOGY," Conference on Historic Site Archaeology, Papers
       (1978) 13:(1979) 204-227.

B-10   Deagan, Kathleen, "THE ARCHAEOLOGY OF SIXTEENTH CENTURY ST. AUGUS-
       TINE," Florida Anthropologist 38:1-2, part 1 (March-June 1985),
       6-33.

B-11   Deagan, Kathleen, "THE ARCHAEOLOGY OF THE FIRST SPANISH PERIOD ST.
       AUGUSTINE, 1972-1978," El Escribano 15:(1978), 1-22.

B-12   Deagan, Kathleen, "ARCHITECTURE, ARCHAEOLOGY AND HISTORY IN SPANISH
ST. AUGUSTINE: NEW DATA FROM SEALED CONTEXTS," Conference on Historic Site Archaeology, Papers 9:13-29.

B-13   Deagan, Kathleen, "DOWNTOWN SURVEY: THE DISCOVERY OF SIXTEENTH
CENTURY ST. AUGUSTINE IN AN URBAN AREA," American Antiquity
46:(1981), 626-634.

B-14   Deagan, Kathleen, "THE MATERIAL ASSEMBLAGE OF 16TH CENTURY SPANISH
FLORIDA," Historical Archaeology 12:(1978), 25-50.

B-15   Deagan, Kathleen, "ST. AUGUSTINE: FIRST URBAN ENCLAVE IN THE
UNITED STATES," North American Archaeologist 3:3 (1981), 183-206.

B-16   Deagan, Kathleen, "THE SEARCH FOR 16H CENTURY ST. AUGUSTINE, Conference on Historic Site Archaeology, Papers 12:(1978), 266-285.

B-17   Deagan, Kathleen, "SPANISH ST. AUGUSTINE: AMERICA'S FIRST 'MELTING
POT'," Archaeology 33:5 (September-October 1980), 22-30.

B-18   Deetz, James, "HARRINGTON HISTOGRAMS VERSUS BINFORD MEAN DATES AS A
TECHNIQUE FOR ESTABLISHING THE OCCUPATIONAL SEQUENCE OF SITES AT
FLOWERDEN, VIRGINIA," American Archeology 6:1 (1987), 62-67.

B-19   Dickens, Roy S. Jr. and William R. Bowen, "PROBLEMS AND PROMISES IN
URBAN HISTORICAL ARCHAEOLOGY: THE MARTA PROJECT," Historical
Archaeology 14:(1980), 42-57.

B-20   Gilmore, Kathleen, "THE SINGLE BROTHERS' INDUSTRIAL COMPLEX: RE-
SEARCH PLAN, OLD SALEM, NORTH CAROLINA," Conference on Historic
Site Archaeology, Papers (1978) 13:(1979), 76-108.

B-21   Hardin, Kenneth W. and Robert J. Austin, "A PRELIMINARY REPORT ON
THE BAY CADILLAC SITE: A PREHISTORIC CEMETARY IN TAMPA, FLORIDA,"
Florida Anthropologist 40:3 (September 1987), 233-234.

B-22   Harper, Robert W. III, "SOUVENIRS OF THE ANCIENT CITY," El
Escribano 18:(1981), 33-44.

B-23   Harrington, J.C., "EVIDENCE OF MANUAL RECONING IN THE CITY OF RA-
LEIGH," North Carolina Historical Review 33:1 (January 1956), 1-11.

B-24   Harrington, J.C., Albert C. Manucy and John M. Goggin, "ARCHEOLO-
GICAL EXCAVATIONS IN THE COURTYARD OF CASTILLO DE SAN MARCOS, ST.
AUGUSTINE, FLORIDA," Florida Historical Quarterly 34:2 (October
1955), 99-141.

B-25   Heite, Edward F. and Louise B. Heite, "TOWN PLANS AS ARTIFACTS:
THE MID-ATLANTIC EXPERIENCE," Archeological Society of Virginia
Quarterly Bulletin 41:3 (September 1986), 142-159.

B-26   Hudson, J. Paul, "JAMESTOWN: BIRTHPLACE OF HISTORICAL ARCHEOLOGY
IN THE UNITED STATES," Archeological Society of Virginia Quarterly
Bulletin 40:1 (March 1985), 48-57.

B-27   Hume, Ivar Noel, "EXCAVATIONS AT THE AMELUNG GLASS FACTORY IN MARY-
LAND," Florida Anthropologist 18:3, Part 2 (September 1965), 2-7.

B-28   King, Julia, "CERAMIC VARIABILITY IN 17TH CENTURY ST. AUGUSTINE,
FLORIDA," Historical Archaeology 18:2 (1984), 75-82.

B-29   Ledford, Thomas G., "BRITISH MATERIAL CULTURE IN ST. AUGUSTINE:
THE ARTIFACT AS SOCIAL COMMENTARY," in Eighteenth Century Florida:
The Impact of the American Revolution. Samuel Proctor ed., Gaines-
ville University Presses of Florida, 1978.

B-30   Lewis, Kenneth E.,"INTRASITE SAMPLING IN THE ARCHAEOLOGICAL RECORD:
THE DISCOVERY PHASE AT CAMDEN," Conference on Historic Site Archaeology, Papers (1975) 10:part 3 (March 1977), 131-139.

B-31 Lewis, Kenneth E., "PATTERN AND LAYOUT ON THE SOUTH CAROLINA FRON-
      TIER: AN ARCHAEOLOGICAL INVESTIGATION OF SETTLEMENT FUNCTION,"
      North American Archaeologist 1:2 (1979-80), 177-200.

B-32 Lewis, Kenneth E., "REGIONAL MODELS AND COMPONENT ANALYSIS: CAMDEN
      ON THE CAROLINA FRONTIER," Notebook 7:4 (July-August 1975), 119-
      134.

B-33 Lewis, Kenneth E., "SETTLEMENT PATTERN AND FUNCTIONAL VARIATION ON
      THE SOUTH CAROLINA FRONTIER," Conference on Historic Site Archae-
      ology, Papers (1978) 13:(1979), 228-237.

B-34 McDaniel, John et al., "LIBERTY HALL ACADEMY: AN INTERIM REPORT,"
      Archeology Sociology of Virginia Quarterly Bulletin 31-32:4-1
      (June-September 1977), 141-167.

B-35 McMurray, Carl D., "EXCAVATIONS AT THE XIMENEZ-FATIO HOUSE, ST.
      AUGUSTINE, FLORIDA," Historical Archaeology 6(1972), 57-64.

B-36 Moore, Roger and Texas Andersen, "GUILDED AGE ARCHAEOLOGY: THE
      ASHTON VILLA," Archaeology 37:3 (May/June 1984), 44-50.

B-37 Perlman, Stephen M., "AN ARCHEOLOGICAL EXCAVATION AT THE FALLS OF
      THE JAMES RIVER: THE MAURY STREET SITE," Archeology Society of
      Virginia Quarterly Bulletin 38:2 (June 1983), 108-123.

B-38 Piper, Harry M. and Jacqueline G. Piper, "SUMMARY INTERIM REPORT OF
      EXCAVATIONS AT THE QUAD BLOCK SITE (8Hi998), TAMPA, FLORIDA,"
      Florida Anthropologist 34:4 (December 1981), 177-179.

B-39 Piper, Harry M. and Jacquelyn G. Piper, "URBAN ARCHAEOLOGY IN
      FLORIDA: THE SEARCH FOR PATTERN IN TAMPA'S HISTORIC CORE," Florida
      Anthropologist 40:4 (December 1987), 260-265.

B-40 Pogue, Dennis J., "AN ANALYSIS OF WARES SALVAGED FROM THE SWAN-
      SMITH-MILBURN POTTERY SITE (44AX29), ALEXANDRIA, VIRGINIA,"
      Archeology Society of Virginia Quarterly Bulletin 34:3 (March
      1980), 149-160.

B-41 Polhemus, Richard R., "EXPLORATORY EXCAVATION IN THE YARD OF THE
      JOHN FOX HOUSE (38LX31)," Notebook 4:1 (January-February), 97-111.

B-42 Potter, Parker B., Jr. and Mark P. Leone, "ARCHEOLOGY IN PUBLIC IN
      ANNAPOLIS . . .," American Archeology 6:1 (1987), 51-60.

B-43 Reitz, Elizabeth J., "FAUNAL EVIDENCE FOR SIXTEENTH CENTURY SPANISH
      SUBSISTANCE AT ST. AUGUSTINE, FLORIDA," Florida Anthropologist
      38:1-2 part 1 (March-June 1985), 54-69.

B-44 Reitz, Elizabeth and Nicholas Honorkamp, "BRITISH COLONIAL SUBSIS-
      TENCE STRATEGY ON THE SOUTHEASTERN COASTAL PLAIN," Historical
      Archaeology 17:2 (1983), 4-26.

B-45 Reitz, Elizabeth J. and Nicholas Honorkamp, "'HISTORICAL' VERSUS
      'ARCHAEOLOGICAL' DIETARY PATTERNS ON THE SOUTHEASTERN COASTAL
      PLAIN," South Carolina Antiquities 16:1, 2 (1984), 67-86.

B-46 Singleton, Theresa A., "THE SLAVE TAG: AN ARTEFACT OF URBAN SLAV-
      ERY," South Carolina Antiquities 16:1, 2 (1984), 41-66.

B-47 South, Stanley A., "EXCAVATING THE EIGHTEENTH CENTURY MORAVIAN TOWN
      OF BETHABARA, NORTH CAROLINA," Florida Anthropologist 18:3 (Septem-
      ber 1965),45-48.

B-48 South, Stanley A., "RESTORATION ARCHAEOLOGY AT THE PACA HOUSE,
      ANNAPOLIS, MARYLAND," Conference on Historic Site Archaeology,
      Papers (1967) 2:part 1 (September 1968), 23-32.

B-49   Stephenson, Robert L., "ARCHAEOLOGY AT CHARLES TOWNE," Notebook
       1:10 (October 1969), 9-13.

B-50   Strickland, Robert N., "CAMDEN REVOLUTIONARY WAR FORTIFICATIONS
       (38KE1): THE 1969-70 EXCAVATIONS," Notebook 3:3 (May-June 1971),
       55-71.

B-51   Sudbury, Bryan, "HISTORY OF THE PAMPLIN AREA TOBACCO PIPE
       INDUSTRY," Archeology Society of Virginia Quarterly Bulletin 32:2
       (December 1977), 1-34.

B-52   Tippitt, V. Ann, "ARCHEOLOGICAL FIELD RECONNAISSANCE OF PROPOSED
       CITY OF DENMARK WASTE TREATMENT PROJECT," Notebook 16:1 (January-
       March 1964), 1-41.

B-53   Wayne, Lucy B., "THE BAILEY HOUSE: INTERPRETATION OF TRASH DIS-
       POSAL AT AN URBAN SITE," Florida Anthropologist 36:3-4 (September-
       December 1983), 177-185.

B-54   Wienker, Curtis W., "THE HUMAN REMAINS FROM THE QUAD BLOCK SITE
       (8Hi998), TAMPA, FLORIDA," Florida Anthropologist 37:4 (December
       1984), 156-164.

B-55   Wittkofski, J. Mark, Martha W. McCartney and Beverly Bogley,
       "ARCHEOLOGICAL TEST EXCAVATIONS AT NEWTOWN, NORFOLK, VIRGINIA,"
       Archeology Society of Virginia Quarterly Bulletin 35:2 (December
       1980) 49-71.

B-56   Yentsch, Anne and Larry W. McKee, "FOOTPRINTS OF BUILDINGS IN 18TH
       CENTURY ANNAPOLIS," American Archeology 6:1 (1987), 40-58.

B-57   Zierden, Martha A., "URBAN ARCHAEOLOGY IN CHARLESTON: A MUSEUM
       INTERPRETATION," South Carolina Antiquities 16:1,2 (1984), 29-40.

B-58   Zierden, Martha A. and Jeanne A. Calhoun, "AN ARCHAEOLOGICAL RE-
       SEARCH DESIGN FOR THE CITY OF CHARLESTON, SOUTH CAROLINA," South
       Carolina Antiquities 16:1, 2 (1984), 1-28.

B-59   Zierden, Martha A. and Jeanne A. Calhoun, "URBAN ADAPTATION IN
       CHARLESTON, SOUTH CAROLINA, 1730-1820," Historical Archaeology 20:1
       (1986), 29-43.

Architecture and Historic Preservation

B-60   Adler, Emma M., "HISTORIC CHURCHES IN DOWNTOWN SAVANNAH," Georgia
       Journal 2:2 (February-March 1980), 18-20, 25.

B-61   Adler, Gale Shipman, "1785: ARCHITECT AND IMAGE-MAKER JULES HENRI
       DE SIBOUR," Historic Preservation 31:3 (July/August 1979), 12-14.

B-62   Adler, Leopold II, "ECONOMIC INCENTIVES," Historic Preservation
       23:2 (April-June 1971), 25-28.

B-63   Adler, Wendy J., "THE COLLEGE OF CHARLESTON--AN INTERVIEW WITH
       THEODORE S. STEIN," Historic Preservation 27:3 (July-September
       1975), 30-37.

B-64   Aguar, Charles E., "AN ATHENS SHOWPLACE, TUCKED INTO A CITY
       FOREST," Landscape Architecture 69:2 (March 1979), 171-175.

B-65   Alexander, Robert L., "BALTIMORE ROW HOUSES OF THE EARLY NINETEENTH
       CENTURY," American Studies 16:2 (1975), 65-76.

B-66   Alexander, Robert L., "NICHOLAS ROGERS, GENTLEMAN-ARCHITECT OF BAL-
       TIMORE," Maryland Historical Magazine 78:2 (Summer 1983), 85-105.

B-67   Anderson, Nancy, "RESTORATION IN MACON: "THE BEST KEPT SECRET IN
       GEORGIA," Georgia Journal 1:2 (January-February 1981), 21-25.

B-68 "ANNAPOLIS," American Preservation 1:1 (1977), 27-33.

B-69 Appleton, Lynn M. and Bruce London, "MIAMI BEACH'S ART DECO BUILD-
      INGS: RESOURCES FOR RECYCLING," Urban Resources 2:2 (Winter 1985),
      3-8.

B-70 Arana, Luis Rafel, "CONSERVATION AND REVITALIZATION OF THE CASTILLO
      DE SAN MARCOS AND FORT MATANZAS," Florida Historical Quarterly 65:1
      (July 1986), 72-91.

B-71 "AN ARCHITECT LOOKS AT RICHMOND," Virginia Cavalcade, 16:3 (Winter
      1967), 22-30.

B-72 Argintar, Sybil H., "ROBERT CRIDLAND GARDENS IN ATLANTA," Atlanta
      Historical Journal 27:2 (Summer 1983), 25-38.

B-73 Bailey, James H., "THE GREEK REVIVAL IN PETERSBURG," Virginia
      Cavalcade 7:3 (Winter 1957), 33-37.

B-74 Bancroft, Bill, "THE NIGHT THE HUNT BROTHERS PUSHED DALLAS TOO
      FAR," Historic Preservation 34:3 (May-June 1982), 10-15.

B-75 Bartlett, Ellen, "MIAMI BEACH BETS ON ART DECO," Historic Preserva-
      tion 33:1 (January-February 1981), 8-15.

B-76 Beasley, Ellen, "END OF THE RAINBOW," Historic Preservation 24:1
      (January-March 1972), 18-23.

B-77 Beeson, Leola Selman, "THE OLD STATE CAPITOL IN MILLEDGEVILLE AND
      ITS COST," Georgia Historical Quarterly 34:3 (September 1950), 195-
      202.

B-78 Beirne, Rosamond Randall, "TWO ANOMALOUS ANNAPOLIS ARCHITECTS:
      JOSEPH HORATIO ANDERSON AND ROBERT KEY," Maryland Historical
      Magazine 55:3 (September 1960), 183-200.

B-79 Bernstein, Alan, "PROGRESS CALLS ON POND BRANCH," Historic
      Preservation 32:4 (July-August 198), 10-13.

B-80 Bidwell, Spencer Jr., "ATLANTA'S EARLY BUILDERS," Atlanta Histori-
      cal Journal 15:4 (Winter 1970), 88-98.

B-81 Blunt, Ruth H., "LYNCHBURG'S TOBACCO WAREHOUSES," Virginia
      Cavalcade 14:3 (Winter 1964), 16-21.

B-82 Blunt, Ruth H., "POINT OF HONOR," Virginia Cavalcade 18:3 (Winter
      1969), 29-33.

B-83 Booth, Helen Sutton, "OLD CHRIST CHURCH IN THE CIVIL WAR," Virginia
      Cavalcade 11:1 (Summer 1961), 12-17.

B-84 Bowling, Francis Goodwin, "AN INDIVIDUAL APPROACH," Southern
      Accents 6:3 (Summer 1983), 108-111.

B-85 Bowman, David, "BEALE STREET BLUES," Southern Exposure 5:1 (Spring
      1977), 75-79.

B-86 Briston, Eugene K., "FROM TEMPLE TO BARN: THE GREELOW OPERA HOUSE
      IN MEMPHIS 1860-1880," West Tennessee Historical Society Papers 21:
      (1967), 5-23.

B-87 Broward, Robert C., "JACKSONVILLE: SOUTHERN HOME FOR THE PRAIRIE
      SCHOOL," Historic Preservation 30:1 (January-March 1978), 16-19.

B-88 Brower, Sidney N., "STREET FRONT & SIDEWALK: THAT'S WHERE THE
      ACTION IS, BALTIMORE STUDY SHOWS," Landscape Architecture 63:4
      (July 1973), 364-369.

B-89   Brown, Joan Sayers, "MERIDIAN HOUSE," Southern Accents 6:1 (Winter 1983), 102-110.

B-90   Brown, Joan Sayers, "TREASURE-FILLED TOWN HOUSE," Southern Accents 7:1 (January-February 1984), 70-75.

B-91   Brown, Patricia Leigh, "THE PROBLEM WITH MISS LAURA'S HOUSE," Historic Preservation 32:5 (September/October 1980), 16-19.

B-92   Brumbaugh, Thomas B., "THE ARCHITECTURE OF NASHVILLE'S UNION STATION," Tennessee Historical Quarterly 27:1 (Spring 1968), 3-12.

B-93   Bryant, Keith L. Jr., "CATHEDRALS, CASTLES, AND ROMAN BATHS: RAILWAY STATION ARCHITECTURE IN THE URBAN SOUTH," Journal of Urban History 2:2 (1976), 195-230.

B-94   Bryant, Keith L. Jr., "THE RAILROAD STATION AS A SYMBOL OF URBANIZATION IN THE SOUTH, 1890's-1920," South Atlantic Quarterly 75:4 (Spring 1976), 499-509.

B-95   Bryant, Keith L. Jr., "RAILROAD STATIONS OF TEXAS: A DISAPPEARING ARCHITECTURAL HERITAGE," Southwestern Historical Quarterly 79:4 (April 1976), 417-440.

B-96   Bultman, Bethany Ewald, "ACADIAN HERITAGE," Southern Accents 6:4 (Fall 1983), 94-104.

B-97   Bultman, Bethany Ewald, "ALLURE OF THE POOL," Southern Accents 7:4 (July-August 1984), 64-69.

B-98   Bultman, Bethany Ewald, "DRAMATIC AND DISTINCTIVE," Southern Accents 7:1 (January-February 1984), 40-51.

B-99   Bultman, Bethany Ewald, "AN ELEGANT COUNTRY HOUSE," Southern Accents 7:5 (September-October 1984), 78-87.

B-100 Bultman, Bethany Ewald, "NEW ORLEANS ELAN, "Southern Accents 8:4 (July-August 1985), 68-77.

B-101 Burrell, Deane D., "BAYOU BEND GARDENS," Southern Accents 8:4 (July-August 1985), 60-67.

B-102 Burton, Marda Kaiser, "NATCHEZ: NO LONGER YOUR TYPICAL SOUTHERN BELLE," Historic Preservation 32:6 (November-December 1980), 8-15.

B-103 Burton, Tommye S., "COURT HOUSES OF PRINCE WILLIAM COUNTY," Virginia Cavalcade 28:1 (Summer 1978), 34-47.

B-104 Bushong, Williamn B., "A.G. BAUER, NORTH CAROLINA'S NEW SOUTH ARCHITECT," North Carolina Historical Review 60:3 (July 1983), 304-332.

B-105 Bushong, William B., "WILLIAM PERCIVAL, AN ENGLISH ARCHITECT IN THE OLD NORTH STATE, 1857-1860," North Carolina Historical Review 57:3 (July 1980) 310-339.

B-106 Butcher, Lee, "HYPER-DEMAND BRINGS CRITICAL OVERHEATING IN COMMERCIAL BUILDING," South Business 7:3 (March 1980), 22-26.

B-107 Butler, Jeanne F., "COMPETITION 1792: DESIGNING A NATION'S CAPITOL," Capitol Studies 4:1 (Spring 1976), 7-96.

B-108 Caldwell-Swann, Lee Ann, "HISTORIC CHURCHES IN AUGUSTA," Georgia Journal 1:3 (March-April 1981), 22-25.

B-109 Campioli, Mario, "THE ORIGINAL EAST CENTRAL PORTICO OF THE CAPITOL," Capitol Studies 1:1 (Spring 1972), 73-86.

B-110 Capitman, Barbara Baer, "RE-DISCOVERY OF ART DECO," American Preservation 2:6 (1978), 30-41.

B-111 Cawley, Peter, "FORT WORTH RIDES AGAIN," Historic Preservation 32:1 (January-February 1980), 10-16.

B-112 Chalfant, Randolph W., "CALVERT STATION: ITS STRUCTURE AND SIG-NIFICANCE," Maryland Historical Magazine 74:1 (March 1979). 11-22.

B-113 Cheeseman, Bruce S., "THE SURVIVAL OF THE CUPOLA HOUSE: A VENER-ABLE OLD MANSION," North Carolina Historical Review 63:1 (January 1986), 40-73.

B-114 Cizek, Eugene D., "THE CREOLE ARCHITECTURE OF NINETEENTH CENTURY NEW ORLEANS," Southern Quarterly 20:2 (Winter 1982), 62-86.

B-115 Clark, James, "VICTORIAN SUMMERVILLE," Augusta Magazine 13:3 (Fall 1986), 6-10.

B-116 Coclanis, Peter A., "THE SOCIOLOGY OF ARCHITECTURE IN COLONIAL CHARLESTON: PATTERN AND PROCESS IN AN EIGHTEENTH-CENTURY SOUTHERN CITY," Journal of Social History 18:4 (Summer 1985), 607-624.

B-117 Cohen, Philip M. and Debra Dale, "A CAPITAL PLACE ON CAPITOL HILL," Landscape Architecture 71:2 (March 1981), 224-248.

B-118 Coleman, J. Winston, "EARLY LEXINGTON ARCHITECTS AND THEIR WORK," Filson Club History Quarterly 42:3 (July 1968), 222-234.

B-119 Colin, Thomas J., "REPRIEVE IN PALM BEACH," Historic Preservation 38:4 (July-August 1986), 38-41.

B-120 Condit, Carl W., "THE PIONEER CONCRETE BUILDINGS OF ST. AUGUSTINE," Progressive Architecture (July 1971), 128-133.

B-121 Conrad, Glenn R., "SHADOWS-ON-THE-LECHE," Southern Accents 7:2 (March-April 1984), 88-94, 122.

B-122 Conway, William G., "MIAMI," Progressive Architecture 61:8 (August 1980), 49-59.

B-123 Coody, A.S. "REPAIR OF AND CHANGES IN THE OLD CAPITOL," Journal of Mississippi History 11:2 (April 1949), 87-103.

B-124 Corry, John P., "THE HOUSES OF COLONIAL GEORGIA," Georgia Historical Quarterly 14:3 (September 1930) 181-201.

B-125 Cotter, John L., "ARCHITECTURE AT JAMESTOWN: SEVENTEENTH CENTURY AND BEYOND," Archaeology 29:3 (July 1976), 152-163.

B-126 Craig, Robert M., "SPLENDOR IN DALLAS," Southern Accents 6:1 (Winter 1983), 46-57.

B-127 Crawford, Charles W. and Robert M. McBride, "THE MAGEVNEY HOUSE, MEMPHIS," Tennessee Historical Quarterly 28:4 (Winter 1969), 345-355.

B-128 Crocker, Mary Wallace, "COLLECTOR'S MELANGE," Southern Accents 7:2 (March-April 1984), 82-87.

B-129 Crocker, Mary Wallace, "EVALUATION OF A WAREHOUSE," Southern Accents 6:2 (Spring 1983), 80-87.

B-130 Cullison, William R., "TULANE'S RICHARD KOCK, COLLECTION--A VISUAL SURVEY OF HISTORIC ARCHITECTURE IN THE MISSISSSIPPI DELTA," Louisiana History 18:4 (Fall 1977), 453-471.

B-131 Curtis, James R., "ART DECO ARCHITECTURE IN MIAMI BEACH," Journal of Cultural Geography 3:1 (Fall-Winter 1982), 51-64.

B-132 Daiker, Virginia, "THE CAPITOL OF JEFFERSON AND LATROBE," Quarterly Journal of the Library of Congress 32:1 (January 1975), 25-32.

B-133 Davis, Louise Littleton, "THE PARTHENON AND THE TENNESSEE CENTEN-NIAL: THE GREEK TEMPLE THAT SPARKED A BIRTHDAY PARTY," Tennessee Historical Quarterly 26:4 (Winter 1967), 335-353.

B-134 DeLaughter, Jerry, "JONESBORO," Tennessee Valley Perspective 10:1 (Fall 1979), 4-10.

B-135 Dekle, Clayton B., "THE TENNESSEE STATE CAPITOL," Tennessee Historical Quarterly 25:3 (Fall 1966), 213-238.

B-136 Dill, Alonzo Thomas Jr., "PUBLIC BUILDINGS IN CRAVEN COUNTY, 1722-1835," North Carolina Historical Review 20:4 (October 1943), 301-326.

B-137 Dill, Alonzo Thomas Jr., "TRYON'S PALACE--A NEGLECTED NICHE OF NORTH CAROLINA HISTORY," North Carolina Historical Review 19:2 (April 1942), 119-167.

B-138 Dillon, Rodney E. Jr., "FRANCIS L. ABREV AND FORT LAUDERDALE'S BOOMTIME ARCHITECTURE," New River News 20: (Spring 1982), 3-10.

B-139 Dixon, Caroline Wyche, "THE MILES BREWTON HOUSE: EZRA WAITE'S ARCHITECTURAL BOOKS AND OTHER POSSIBLE DESIGN SOURCES," South Carolina Historical Magazine 82:2 (April 1981), 118-142.

B-140 Douglas, William Lake, "ZOO GOES NATIVE," Landscape Architecture 75:2 (March-April 1985), 82-87.

B-141 Doyle, Don H., "SAVING YESTERDAY'S CITY: NASHVILLE'S WATERFRONT," Tennessee Historical Quarterly 35:4 (Winter 1976), 353-364.

B-142 Driscoll, Mark and Margaret Anne Lane, "DOWN AT THE COURTHOUSE: A PHOTOGRAPHIC ESSAY," Tampa Bay History 2:1 (Spring/Summer 1980), 34-48.

B-143 Druyvesteyn, Kent, "COURTHOUSE OF FRANKLIN COUNTY," Virginia Cavalcade 21:2 (Autumn 1971), 12-19.

B-144 Druyvesteyn, Kent, "COURTHOUSES OF HENRY AND PATRICK COUNTIES," Virginia Cavalcade 22:1 (Summer 1972), 6-13.

B-145 Druyvesteyn, Kent, "SHELTERING ARMS HOSPITAL: WHERE PATIENTS HAVE NEVER PAID," Virginia Cavalcade 22:2 (Autumn 1972), 16-27.

B-146 Dubay, Robert W., "THE GOLDEN CAP: A SAGA OF THE CAPITOL DOME," Atlanta Historical Journal 26:4 (Winter 1982-83), 47-52.

B-147 Dudar, Helen, "A KNOCKOUT MUSEUM FOR A CITY ON THE MOVE," Smithsonian 15:2 (May 1984), 58-69.

B-148 Edelson, Judy Flemming, "FRENCH INTERPRETATION," Southern Accents 7:5 (September-October 1984), 58-69.

B-149 Edelson, Judy Flemming, "PRIVATE SANCTUARY," Southern Accents 7:1 (January-February 1984) 52-59.

B-150 Edmunds, Mrs. S. Henry, "PRESERVATION IN CHARLESTON," Historic Preservation 23:1 (January-March 1971), 4-8.

B-151 Elder, William V., "THE ADAMS-KILTY HOUSE IN ANNAPOLIS," Maryland Historical Magazine 60:3 (Fall 1965), 314-324.

B-152 Falcon, Teresita and Juan Antonio Bueno, "NEATLY TUCKED INTO A LIGHT SITE," Landscape Architecture 71:2 (March 1981), 178-183.

B-153 Fasla, A.E. Bye, "THE GARDEN IN BLACK AND WHITE," Garden Design 1:1 (Spring 1982), 88-92.

B-154 Faust, Patricia L., "SAVANNAH: A CITY RECLAIMED," Early American Life 9:4 (August 1978), 20-23, 52.

B-155 Favrot, Charles A., "NEW ORLEANS CUSTOM HOUSE," Louisiana Historical Quarterly 3:4 (October 1920), 467-474.

B-156 Fazio, Michael, "ARCHITECTURAL PRESERVATION IN NATCHEZ, MISSISSIPPI: A CONCEPTION OF TIME AND PLACE," Southern Quarterly 19:1 (Fall 1980), 136-149.

B-157 Fern, Alan and Milton Kaplan, "JOHN PLUMBE, JR. AND THE FIRST ARCHITECTURAL PHOTOGRAPHS OF THE NATION'S CAPITOL," Quarterly Journal of the Library of Congress 31:1 (January 1974), 3-20.

B-158 Fitch, James Marston, "THE LAWN: AMERICA'S GREATEST ARCHITECTURAL ACHIEVEMENT," American Heritage 35:4 (June/July 1984), 49-64.

B-159 Fitzpatrick, Virginia, "FREDERICK LAW OLMSTEAD AND THE LOUISVILLE PARK SYSTEM," Filson Club History Quarterly 59:1 (January 1985), 54-63.

B-160 Flowers, John, "PEOPLE AND PLANTS: NORTH CAROLINA'S GARDEN HISTORY REVISITED," Eighteenth Century Life 8:2 (January 1983), 117-129.

B-161 Floyd, M.H. and D.B. Floyd, "OGLETHORPE'S HOME AT FREDERICA," Georgia Historical Quarterly 20:3 (September 1936), 239-249.

B-162 Forman, H.C., "THE ST. MARY'S CITY 'CASTLE,' PREDECESSOR OF THE WILLIAMSBURG 'PALACE'," William and Mary College Historical Magazine 22:2 (April 1942) 136-143.

B-163 Frank, John G., "ADOLPHUS HEIMAN: ARCHITECT AND SOLDIER," Tennessee Historical Quarterly 5:1 (March 1946), 35-57, 5:2 (June 1946), 111-140, 5:3 (September 1946), 222-233.

B-164 Frazier, Evelyn McD., "THE COLLETON COUNTY COURTHOUSE," South Carolina History Illustrated 1:2 (May 1970), 23-25, 66-68.

B-165 Freeman, Allen, "A CITY WITH A LUST FOR LIFE," AIA Journal 72:3 (March 1983), 68-77.

B-166 Frey, Susan Rademacher, "THE GARDEN LIFE: P. DUNCAN CALLICOTT OF FRANKLIN, TENNESSEE," Garden Design 1:1 (Spring 1982), 60-69.

B-167 Frey, Susan Rademacher, "SHOWERED BY FLOWER CONFETTI: A PALETTE OF SPRING PLANTS IN WASHINGTON, D.C.," Garden Design 3:1 (Spring 1984), 28-33.

B-168 Gaines, William H. Jr., "BUCKINGHAM AND APPOMATTOX COURTHOUSES," Virginia Cavalcade 17:4 (Spring 1968), 32-40.

B-1649 Gaines, William H. Jr., "COURTHOUSES OF ALLEGHANY COUNTY," Virginia Cavalcade 22:2 (Autumn 1972), 5-9.

B-170 Gaines, William H. Jr., "COURTHOUSES OF AMHERST AND NELSON COUNTIES," Virginia Cavalcade 18:2 (Autumn 1968), 5-8.

B-171 Gaines, William H. Jr., "COURTHOUSES OF AMELIA AND DINWIDDIE COUNTIES," Virginia Cavalcade 18:3 (Winter 1969), 17-28.

B-172 Gaines, William H. Jr., "COURTHOUSES OF BEDFORD AND CHARLOTTE COUNTIES," Virginia Cavalcade 21:1 (Summer 1971), 5-13.

B-173 Gaines, William H. Jr., "COURTHOUSES OF BRUNSWICK AND GREENSVILLE COUNTIES," Virginia Cavalcade 19:3 (Winter 1970), 37-41.

B-174 Gaines, William H. Jr., "COURTHOUSES OF CHARLES CITY AND PRINCE GEORGE COUNTIES," Virginia Cavalcade 18:1 (Summer 1968), 5-12.

B-175 Gaines, William H. Jr., "COURTHOUSES OF CUMBERLAND AND POWHATAN COUNTIES," Virginia Cavalcade 17:3 (Winter 1968), 38-41.

B-176 Gaines, William H. Jr., "COURTHOUSES OF GOOCHLAND AND ALBEMARLE COUNTIES," Virginia Cavalcade 17:4 (Spring 1968), 5-11.

B-177 Gaines, William H. Jr., "COURTHOUSES OF HALIFAX AND PITTSYLVANIA COUNTIES," Virginia Cavalcade 20:4 (Spring 1971), 5-12.

B-178 Gaines, William H. Jr., "COURTHOUSES OF HENRICO AND CHESTERFIELD," Virginia Cavalcade 17:3 (Winter 1968), 30-37.

B-179 Gaines, William H. Jr., "COURTHOUSES OF ISLE OF WRIGHT AND SOUTH-HAMPTON COUNTIES," Virginia Cavalcade 20:1 (Summer 1970), 5-14.

B-180 Gaines William H. Jr., "THE COURTHOUSES OF JAMES CITY COUNTY," Virginia Cavalcade 18:4 (Spring 1969), 20-30.

B-181 Gaines, William H. Jr., "COURTHOUSES OF LUNENBURG AND MECKLINBURG COUNTIES," Virginia Cavalcade 20:3 (Winter 1971), 22-33.

B-182 Gaines, William H. Jr., "COURTHOUSES OF PRINCE EDWARD AND NOTTOWAY COUNTIES," Virginia Cavalcade 20:2 (Autumn 1970), 40-47.

B-183 Gaines, William H. Jr., "COURTHOUSES OF SURRY AND SUSSEX COUNTIES," Virginia Cavalcade 19:2 (Autumn 1969), 42-47.

B-184 Gaines, William H. Jr., "COURTHOUSES OF VIRGINIA'S EASTERN SHORE," Virginia Cavalcade 14:1 (Summer 1964), 20-27.

B-185 Gaines, William H. Jr., "THE FATAL LAMP, OR, PANIC AT THE PLAY," Virginia Cavalcade 2:1 (Summer 1952), 4-8.

B-186 Gaines, William H. Jr., "THE PUBLIC HOSPITAL FOR DISORDERED MINDS," Virginia Cavalcade 3:1 (Summer 1953), 34-38.

B-187 Gaines, William H. Jr., "STUART HALL," Virginia Cavalcade 18:3 (Winter 1969), 34-40.

B-188 Gaines, William H. Jr., "WAREHOUSE AND ROMAN TEMPLE," Virginia Cavalcade 1:3 (Winter 1951), 4-8.

B-189 Gary, Joy, "PATRICK CREAGH OF ANNAPOLIS," Maryland Historical Magazine 48:4 (Decembeer 1953), 310-326.

B-190 Gaskie, Margaret, "INTELSAT HEADQUARTERS BUILDING, WASHINGTON, DC," Architectural Record 173 (October 1985), 138-147.

B-191 Gatton, John Spalding, "ONLY FOR GREAT ATTRACTIONS: LOUISVILLE'S AMPHITHEATRE AUDITORIUM," Register of the Kentucky Historical Society 78:1 (Winter 1980), 1-26.

B-192 Gilborn, Craig, "A ROMANTIC PILGRIMAGE," Virginia Cavalcade 15:2 (Autumn 1965), 44-47.

B-193 Goldberger, Paul, "THE PENSON BUILDING, HOME OF THE NATIONAL BUILDING MUSEUM," Antiques 128:4 (October 1985), 724-731.

B-194 Goode, James M., "VANISHED WASHINGTON AND ITS ARCHITECTURAL 'CAPITAL LOSSES,'" Smithsonian 10:9 (1979), 58-66.

B-195 Govan, Gilbert E., "THE CHATTANOOGA UNION STATION," Tennessee Historical Quarterly 29:4 (Winter 1970-71), 372-378.

B-196 Graham, Thomas, "FLAGLER'S MAGNIFICENT HOTEL PONCE DE LEON," Florida Historical Quarterly 54:1 (July 1975), 1-17.

B-197 Granger, Joseph E., "WINE AND VINE: THE ARCHAEOLOGY OF URBAN CORE
TO RURAL PERIPHERY TRANSITION IN AUGUSTA, KENTUCKY," North American
Archaeologist 5:1 (1984), 25-44.

B-198 Greenberg, Allan, "THE BRITISH EMBASSY IN WASHINGTON, D.C.,"
Antiques 125:6 (June 1984), 1340-1349.

B-199 Greenberg, Allan and Stephen Kieran, "THE UNITED STATES SUPREME
COURT BUILDING, WASHINGTON, D.C.," Antiques 128:4 (October 1985),
760-769.

B-200 Greenberg, Mike, "THE WATCHFUL WARRIORS," Historical Preservation
35:3 (May-June 1983), 42-47.

B-201 Greene, Melissa Fay, "THE GARDNER FROM SAVANNAH," American Preservation 3:1 (January-February 1980), 34-38.

B-202 Gregory, Geo. C., "JAMESTOWN: FIRST BRICK STATE HOUSE," Virginia
Magazine of History and Biography 43:3 (July 1935), 193-199.

B-203 Greiner, Charles W., "DESIGN SEEN: LIBERTY GREEN, BIRMINGHAM,
ALABAMA," Landscape Architecture 71:3 (May 1981), 362-369.

B-204 Grider, Sylvia Ann, "THE SHOTGUN HOUSE IN OIL BOOMTOWNS OF THE
TEXAS PANHANDLE," Pioneer America 7:2 (1975), 47-55.

B-205 Griffith, Helen C., "ALABAMA AMBIENCE," Southern Accents 6:2
(Spring 1983), 94-101.

B-206 Griffith, Helen C., "ATLANTA'S NEW HIGH MUSEUM OF ART," Southern
Accents 7:2 (March-April 1984), 112-118.

B-207 Griffith, Helen C., "SEQUESTERED TREASURES," Southern Accents 7:2
(March-April 1984), 66-71.

B-208 Griffith, Helen C., "SMALL COMPASS," Southern Accents 7:6
(November-December 1984), 60-67.

B-209 Griffith, Helen C., "A SOPHISTICATED APPROACH," Southern Accents
7:4 (July-August 1984), 56-63.

B-210 Griffith, Helen C., "THE SUBJECT IS ROSES," Southern Accents 7:5
(September-October 1984), 116-120.

B-211 Grigg, Jessie, "OLD SALEM LIVES AGAIN," Early American Life 5:1
(February 1974), 30-35.

B-212 Guide Committee, Potomac Chapter, "GUIDE TO THE LANDSCAPE ARCHI-
TECTURE OF WASHINGTON, D.C.," Landscape Architecture 60:3 (April
1970), 177-192.

B-213 Gunn, Clare A., "RIVER WALK GENERATES 'STRONG POSITIVE RESPONSE,'"
Landscape Architecture 63:3 (April 1973), 236-338.

B-214 Hagy, James William, "COURTHOUSES OF RUSSELL COUNTY," Virginia
Cavalcade 22:4 (Spring 1973) 12-18.

B-215 Hagy, James William, "COURTHOUSES OF WASHINGTON COUNTY," Virginia
Cavalcade 25:2 (Autumn 1975) 80-85.

B-216 Hammon, Stratton, "ARCHITECTS OF LOUISVILLE: FROM THE 1920s
THROUGH WORLD WAR II," Filson Club History Quarterly 61:4, (October
1987), 419-443.

B-217 Handler, Mimi, "AN EARLY ATLANTA HOUSE," Early American Life 13:3
June 1982), 16-20.

B-218 Hanny, H. Russell Jr., "COMMITTED TO THE CITY," Landscape Architecture 71:2 (March 1981), 224-229.

B-219 Hardy, Janice A. and Betty S. Snyder, "SOUTH LIBERTY STREET, A MICROCOSM OF MILLEDGEVILLE'S ARCHITECTURAL HERITAGE," Georgia Journal 1:3 (March-April 1981), 12-15.

B-220 Hardy, Roderick A., "OLD WORLD GRACE," Southern Accents 7:3 (May-June 1984), 96-105.

B-221 Harris, Sally, "COURT HOUSES OF SMYTH COUNTY, Virginia Cavalcade 30:1 (Summer 1980) 30-37.

B-222 Hart, Bertha Sheppard, "THE FIRST GARDEN OF GEORGIA," Georgia Historical Quarterly 19:4 (December 1935), 325-332.

B-223 Hatch, Charles E. Jr., "STOREHOUSE AND CUSTOMHOUSE," Virginia Cavalcade 16:2 (Autumn 1966) 12-18.

B-224 Haywood, Mary Ellen, "URBAN VERNACULAR ARCHITECTURE IN NINETEENTH-CENTURY BALTIMORE," Winterthur Portfolio 16: (Spring 1981), 33-63.

B-225 Hemphill, W. Edwin, "HALOWED BE THE PLACE . . ." Virginia Cavalcade 6:4 (Spring 1957), 22-29.

B-226 Hinkle, Mrs. C. H., "HISTORIC HOMES IN BATESVILLE," Arkansas Historical Quarterly 5:3 (Fall 1946), 283-287.

B-227 Hoffecker, Carol E., "CHURCH GOTHIC: A CASE STUDY OF REVIVAL ARCHITECTURE IN WILMINGTON, DELAWARE," Winterthur Portfolio No. 8 (1973), 215-231.

B-228 Hole, Donna C., "DANIEL PRATT AND BARACHIAS HOLT: ARCHITECTS OF THE ALABAMA STATE CAPITOL?" Alabama Review 37:2 (April 1984), 83-97.

B-229 Holley, Vivian, "THE HAY HOUSE: AN EASY SORT OF ELEGANCE," Georgia Life 4:2 (1977) 19-21.

B-230 Hollis, Jane G., "A WISE FOLLY," Southern Accents 7:4 (July-August 1984), 92-101.

B-231 Holmes, Jack D. L. "AN 1858 VIEW ON HISTORICAL PRESERVATION IN MOBILE," Alabama Historical Quarterly 44:1-2 (Spring-Summer, 1982), 123-124.

B-232 Holtzkay, Jane, "MIZNER'S EDEN," American Preservation 4:2 (March-April 1981), 35-48.

B-233 Hoobler, James A., "WILLIAM STRICKLAND, ARCHITECT," Tennessee Historical Quarterly, 45:1 (Spring 1986), 3-17.

B-234 Hopping, Michael E., "TEXTURES WEAVE A DEEP-SOUTH TAPESTRY," Landscape Architecture 71:2 (March 1981), 174-177.

B-235 Houston, Charles, "CHURCH HILL REVIVES," Virginia Cavalcade 14:1 Summer 1964), 5-10.

B-236 Howett, Catherine M., "A SOUTHERN LADY'S LEGACY: THE ITALIAN TERRRACES' OF LA GRANGE, GEORGIA," Journal of Garden History 2:4 (October-December 1982), 343-360.

B-237 Hutchinson, Albert S. Jr., "DOMESTIC ARCHITECTURE IN MIDDLE TENNESSEE," Antiques 99 (September 1971), 402-407.

B-238 Huth, Tom, "SHOULD CHARLESTON GO NEW SOUTH?" Historic Preservation 31:3 (July-August 1979), 32-38.

B-239 Hyde, Bryden Bordley, "EVESHAM, A BALTIMORE VILLA," Maryland Historical Magazine 52:3 (September 1957), 202-209.

B-240 Ivy, Robert A., "FOOD AND ARCHITECTURE IN NEW ORLEANS," AIA Journal 72:3 (March 1983), 88-95.

B-241 Ivy, Robert A. Jr., "YOUTHFUL PERSPECTIVE," Southern Accents 7:6 (November-December 1984), 86-97.

B-242 Jacobs, Bonnie Sue, "AN ARCHITECT'S INSPIRATION," Southern Accents 6:5 (Winter 1983-84), 90-95.

B-243 Jacobs, Bonnie Sue, "A SLEEPING BEAUTY AWAKENS," Southern Accents 7:6 (November-December 1984), 108-117.

B-244 Jennings, J.L. Sibley Jr., "A CAPITOL SAGA," Landscape Architecture 71:6 (November 1981), 723-726.

B-245 Johnson, Philip C., "A CHARLESTON CRITIQUE," Historic Preservation 23:1 (January-March 1971), 17-18.

B-246 Jones, H.G., "PRESERVATION PROJECTS GRANTS-IN-AID IN URBAN AREAS," Historic Preservation 23:1 (January-March 1971), 46-50.

B-247 "KAHN'S MUSEUM: AN INTERVIEW WITH RICHARD F. BROWN," Art in America 60:5 (September-October 1972), 44-48.

B-248 Kendall, John S., "OLD NEW ORLEANS HOUSES," Louisiana Historical Quarterly 17:4 (October 1934), 680-705.

B-249 Kendall, John S., "OLD NEW ORLEANS HOUSES AND SOME OF THE PEOPLE WHO LIVED IN THEM," Louisiana Historical Quarterly 20:3 (July 1937), 794-820.

B-250 Kendall, John S., "THE PONTALBA BUILDINGS," Louisiana Historical Quarterly 19:1 (January 1936), 119-149.

B-251 Kennan, Clara B., "ARKANSAS' OLD STATE HOUSE," Arkansas Historical Quarterly 9:1 (Spring 1950), 33-42.

B-252 Kernan, Michael, "WASHINGTON'S CULTURAL CROWN," Horizon 21:6 (June 1978),40-49.

B-253 Kruse, Albert, "AN IMPRESSION OF THE OLD MANNER OF BUILDING IN NEW CASTLE, DELAWARE," Delaware History 4:3 (June 1951), 171-206.

B-254 Kulik, Gary B., "BIRMINGHAM," American Preservation 1:3 (1978), 20-23.

B-255 La Farge, Fran, "ITALINATE SPLENDOR IN MIDDLE GEORGIA, THE HAY HOUSE," Georgia Journal 1:4 (May-June 1981), 24-26.

B-256 Lachs, John, "NASHVILLE: AT THE RIVER'S EDGE," Historic Preservation 19:2 (April-June 1977), 22-24.

B-257 Lafarque, Andre, "THE FOUNDING OF BILOXI," Louisiana Historical Quarterly 3:4 (October 1920), 617-623.

B-258 Lafarque, Andre, "THE LITTLE OBELISK IN THE CATHEDRAL SQUARE IN NEW ORLEANS," Louisiana Historical Quarterly 28:1 (January 1945), 326-348.

B-259 Lafarque, Andre, "THE NEW ORLEANS FRENCH OPERA HOUSE: A RETROSPECT," Louisiana Historical Quarterly 3:3 (July 1920), 368-372.

B-260 Lauder, Val, "THE BETTY SMITH HOUSE," Southern Accents 7:2 (March-April 1984), 104-111.

B-261 Lauder, Val, "THE NORTH CAROLINA MUSEUM OF ART," Southern Accents 7:1 (January-February 1984) 114-122.

B-262 Lee, R. Alton, "THE REBUILDING OF THE WHITE HOUSE," History Illustrated 12:10 (February 1978), 12-18.

B-263 Lehmann, Bill, "BICENTENNIAL OUTLOOK: GUTHRIE AWAKES," Historic Preservation 27:4 (October-December 1975), 4-9.

B-264 Leitner, Bernhard, "JOHN PORTMAN: ARCHITECTURE IS NOT A BUILDING," Art in America 61:2 (March-April 1973), 80-82.

B-265 Lentz, Lloyd C. III, "NO WILD VENTURE," Chronicles of Oklahoma 61:3 (Fall 1983), 268-287.

B-266 Lester, Nancy, "THE SWAN HOUSE," Georgia Journal 1:2 (January/February 1981), 17-20.

B-267 Lewis, Kenneth E., "ARCHAEOLOGICAL INVESTIGATIONS IN THE INTERIOR OF McCRADY'S LONGROOM, 38CH559, CHARLESTON, SOUTH CAROLINA," Notebook 15:3 and 4 (September-December 1983), 1-14.

B-268 Lewis, Kenneth E., "THE CAMDEN JAIL AND MARKET SITE: A REPORT ON PRELIMINARY INVESTIGATIONS," Notebook 16:4 (October-December 1984), 1-44.

B-269 Lewis, Kenneth E., "A FUNCTIONAL STUDY OF THE KERSHAW HOUSE SITE IN CAMDEN, SOUTH CAROLINA," Notebook 9 (January-December 1977), 1-87.

B-270 Lewis, Monnie S., "HISTORIC CHURCHES IN ALBANY," Georgia Journal 1:5 (July-August 1981), 30-32.

B-271 "THE LEXINGTON OPERA HOUSE: RESTORATION/RECONSTRUCTION," Southern Theatre 20:2 (Spring 1977), 8-11.

B-272 "LIBRARIES," Southern Architect 9 (November 1962), 8-15, 17-18, 21.

B-273 "THE LIGHTNER MUSEUM," Southern Accents 8:4 (July-August 1985), 120-123.

B-274 Lockwood, Grace S., Darwina L. Neal, and James van Sweden, "FAVORITE PLACES," Landscape Architecture 71:6 (November 1981), 728-733.

B-275 Lockwood, Grace S., Darwina L. Neal, and James van Sweden, "RECENT WORKS," Landscape Architecture 71:6 (November 1981), 734-746.

B-276 Lowrey, Janet K., "SWEET BRIAR HOUSE," Southern Accents 6:1 (Winter 1983), 90-95.

B-277 Luening, William, "CIGAR CITY RISES FROM THE ASHES," Historic Preservation 34:4 (July-August 1982), 46-51.

B-278 Lupold, John S., "REVITALIZING FOUNDARIES, HOTELS, AND GRIST MILLS IN COLUMBUS," Georgia Historical Quarterly 63:1 (Spring 1979), 138-142.

B-279 Lyle, Royster Jr., "COURTHOUSES OF ROCKBRIDGE COUNTY," Virginia Cavalcade 25:3 (Winter 1976), 118-125.

B-280 Lyon, Elizabeta A., "ATLANTA'S PIONEER SKYSCRAPER," Southern Review 19:2 (Summer 1962), 204-210.

B-281 Lyon, Helen Kilpatric, "RICHARD PETERS: ATLANTA PIONEER-GEORGIA BUILDER," Atlanta Historical Bulletin 10:38 (December 1957), 21-42.

B-282 McCartney, Martha W., "A HISTORY OF COLLEGE LANDING," Archeology Society of Virginia Quarterly Bulletin 32:3 (March 1978), 68-78.

B-283 McCue, George, "AIRPORT ARCHITECTURE: THE DALLAS-FORT WORTH SOLUTION," Art in America 62:1 (January-February 1974), 74-77.

B-284 McCue, George, "ARCHITECTURE: NEW ORLEANS' VIEUX CARRE," Art in America 59:3 (May-June 1971), 96-97.

B-285 McCue, George, "THE OCTAGON: TOWN HOUSE THAT PRECEDED THE TOWN," Historic Preservation 26:2 (April-June 1974), 27-31.

B-286 McDowell, Andrea, "THE STUART ROBINSON-JOSEPH B. MARVIN-BLAKEMORE WHEELER HOME," Filson Club History Quarterly 44:2 (April 1970), 117-132.

B-287 McDowell, Peggy, "NEW ORLEANS CEMETARIES: ARCHITECTURAL STYLES AND INFLUENCES," Southern Quarterly 20:2 (Winter 1982), 9-27.

B-288 McGee, Joseph H. Jr., LEGAL ASPECTS OF PRESERVATION," Historic Preservation 23:1 (January-March 1971), 14-16.

B-289 McMellan, George, "STAYING HOME IN SAVANNAH," Historic Preservation 32:2 (March-April 1980), 10-17.

B-290 McNabb, W.R., "THE KNOXVILLE CITY HALL," Tennessee Historical Quarterly 31:3 (Fall 1972), 256-260.

B-291 Macdonald-Millar, Donald, "THE GRUNDY-POLK HOUSES, NASHVILLE," Tennessee Historical Quarterly 25:3 (Fall 1966), 281-286.

B-292 Manarin, Louis H., " BUILDING FOR THE PRESERVATION OF THE PUBLIC RECORDS," Virginia Cavalcade 24:1 (Summer 1974), 22-30.

B-293 Manucy, Albert, "BUILDING MATERIALS IN 16-CENTURY ST. AUGUSTINE," El Escribano 20 (1983), 51-71.

B-294 Manucy, Albert, "CHANGING TRADITIONS IN ST. AUGUSTINE ARCHITEC-TURE," El Escribano 19 (1982), 1-28.

B-295 Manucy, Albert, "TOWARD RE-CREATION OF 16TH CENTURY ST. AUGUSTINE, El Escribano 14 (1977), 1-4.

B-296 Marck, Jan Van Der "HOUSTON'S 'CLEAN MACHINE': THE CONTEMPORARY ARTS MUSEUM," Art in America 60:5 (September-October 1972), 50-51.

B-297 Martin, Peter, "'LONG AND ASSIDUOUS ENDEAVORS': GARDENING IN EARLY EIGHTEENTH-CENTURY VIRGINIA," Eighteenth Century Life 8:2 (January 1983), 107-116.

B-298 Martin, Peter, "'PROMISED FRUITES OF WELL ORDERED TOWNS'--GARDENS IN EARLY 18TH CENTURY WILLIAMSBURG," Journal of Garden History 2:4 (October-December 1982), 309-324.

B-299 Marvin, Robert E. and James Paddock, "A CORPORATE HEADQUARTERS ACHIEVES MINIMUM LANDSCAPE IMPACT," Landscape Architecture 69:1 (January 1979), 70-73.

B-300 Mason, George C., "THE COURT-HOUSES OF PRINCESS ANNE AND NORFOLK COUNTIES," Virginia Magazine of History and Biography 57:4 (October 1949), 405-415.

B-301 Masten, Susannah, "AN ARCHITECTS FIRST VENTURE," Southern Accents 6:2 (Spring 1983), 56-63.

B-302 Masten, Susannah, "CONTEMPORARY DRAMA," Southern Accents 7:3 (May-June 1984), 80-87.

B-303 Masten, Susannah, "THE ELEMENT OF SURPRISE," Southern Accents 6:1 (Winter 1983), 64-71.

B-304 Masten, Susannah, "A HOUSE ON LIDO SHORES," Southern Accents 7:2 (March-April 1984), 72-81.

B-305 Masten, Susannah, "LIGHT AND NAUTICAL," Southern Accents 7:1
       (January-February 1984), 60-69.

B-306 Matlack, Carol, "EUFAULA," American Preservation 2:1 (October-
       November 1978), 9-21.

B-307 Matlack, Carol, "SAVANNAH," American Preservation 2:3 (February-
       March 1979), 9-25.

B-308 Maxa, Kathleen, "GEORGETOWN," American Preservation 3:2 (March-
       April 1980), 42-58.

B-309 Maxa, Kathleen, "KEY WEST," American Preservation 3:3 (May-June
       1980), 9-23.

B-310 Meikle, Jeffrey L, "THE MALLING OF THE MALL: CULTURAL RESONANCES
       OF THE EAST BUILDING," Southwest Review 66:3 (Summer 1981), 233-
       244.

B-311 Mellown, Robert O., "ALABAMA'S FOURTH CAPITAL: THE CONSTRUCTION OF
       THE STATE HOUSE IN TUSCALOOSA," Alabama Review 60:4 (October 1987),
       259-283.

B-312 Mitchell, William R. Jr., "A SAVANNAH LANDMARK: THE RICHARDSON-
       OWENS-THOMAS HOUSE," Southern Accents 8:1 (January-February 1985),
       48-61.

B-313 Mitchell, William Robert Jr., "THE SWAN HOUSE," Southern Accents
       8:4 (July-August 1985), 42-53.

B-314 Mobley, Anita Morrison, "HARMONIOUS DESIGN," Southern Accents 7:3
       May-June 1984), 64-71.

B-315 Mobley, Anita Morrison, "LOWNDESBORO, ALABAMA," Southern Accents
       6:5 (Winter 1983-84), 96-101.

B-316 Mobley, Anita Morrison, "PERFECT PLANNING," Southern Accents 7:4
       (July-August 1984), 102-108.

B-317 Moorehead, Singleton P., "COLONIAL WILLIAMSBURG: PROBLEMS IN
       ARCHITECTURAL RESTORATION," Art in America 43:2 (May 1955), 23-29,
       63-68.

B-318 Morrow, Sara Sprott, "ADOLPHUS HEIMAN'S LEGACY TO NASHVILLE,"
       Tennessee Historical Quarterly 33:1 (Spring 1974), 3-21.

B-319 Morrow, Sara Sprott, "THE CHURCH OF THE HOLY TRINITY: ENGLISH
       COUNTRYSIDE TRANQUILITY IN DOWNTOWN NASHVILLE," Tennessee Histori-
       cal Quarterly 34:4 (Winter 1975), 333-349.

B-320 Morrow, Sara Sprott, "ST. PAUL'S CHURCH, FRANKLIN," Tennessee His-
       torical Quarterly 34:1 (Spring 1975), 3-18.

B-321 Morse, Margaret E., "THE LUXURY OF TIME," Southern Accents 7:5
       (September-October 1984), 96-105.

B-322 Muldawer, Paul, "CRITERIA OF URBAN DESIGN RELATEDNESS," Historical
       Preservation 23:1 (January-March 1971), 29-36.

B-323 Murfee, Patty T., "HISTORY IN TOWNS," Antiques 99 (December 1971),
       914-918.

B-324 Netherton, Nan and Ross Netherton, "COURTHOUSES OF FAIRFAX COUNTY,"
       Virginia Cavalcade 27:2 (Autumn 1977), 86-95.

B-325 'NEW ORLEANS," American Preservation 1:3 (1978), 51-56.

B-326 Nichols, Ashton, "FISH IS FRESH, THE HERITAGE IS ALIVE," Historic
       Preservation 31:3 (July-August 1979), 14-20.

B-327 Nix, Dorothy, "SOME OF DECATUR'S LOVELY OLD HOMES," Georgia Life 6:4 (Spring 1980), 19-21.

B-328 Nolen, Laura Bryant, "COURTHOUSES OF GRAYSON COUNTY," Virginia Cavalcade 24:4 (Spring 1976), 158-163.

B-329 Ognibene, Peter J., "MAIN STREET OF AMERICA: EXPLORING PENNSYL-VANIA AVENUE," Horizon 28:1 (January-February 1985), 17-32.

B-330 Oldham, Sally G., "HISTORIC PRESERVATION TAX INCENTIVES," Urban Land 38:11 (December 1979), 3-10.

B-331 Olmert, Michael, "HOW ANNAPOLIS KEEPS ITS CHARM," Historic Preservation 38:3 (May-June 1986), 48-54.

B-332 Olmert, Michael, "THE NEW, NO-FRILLS WILLIAMSBURG," Historic Preservation 3:5 (October 1985), 26-33.

B-333 Orr, Henry P., "ORNAMENTAL PLANTINGS IN EUFAULA," Alabama Review 16:4 (October 1963), 260-269.

B-334 Orr-Cahall, Christina, "PALM BEACH: THE PREDICAMENT OF A RESORT," Historic Preservation 30:1 (January-March 1978), 10-15.

B-335 Osborn, Anne, "THE LAST GREAT MANSION OF ANTEBELLUM GEORGIA," Augusta Magazine 11:1 (Spring 1984), 26-35.

B-336 Paraschos, Janet N., "BALTIMORE: A MAYOR HELPS HIS CITY REGAIN ITS PRIDE THROUGH NEIGHBORHOOD POWER," American Preservation 3:4 (July/August 1980), 23-38.

B-337 Parsons, Edward Alexander, "THE LATIN CITY: A PLEA FOR ITS MONU-MENTS," Louisiana Historical Quarterly 3:3 (July 1920), 361-367.

B-338 Patrick, James, "THE ARCHITECTURE OF ADOLPHUS HEIMAN, I," Tennessee Historical Quarterly 38:2 (Summer 1979), 167-187.

B-339 Patrick, James, "THE ARCHITECTURE OF ADOLPHUS HEIMAN, II," Tennessee Historical Quarterly 38:3 (Fall 1979), 277-295.

B-340 Patton, Glenn, "THE COLLEGE OF WILLIAM AND MARY, WILLIAMSBURG, AND THE ENLIGHTENMENT," Journal of the Society of Architectural Historians 24:1 (March 1970), 24-32.

B-341 Paul, J. Gilman D'Arcy, "A BALTIMORE ESTATE: GUILFORD AND ITS THREE OWNERS," Maryland Historical Magazine 51:1 (March 1956), 14-26.

B-342 Paul, Lewis, "NEEL REID, 1885-1926," Atlanta Historical Journal 16:1 (Spring 1971), 9-30.

B-343 Perlman, Bennard B., "THE CITY HALL, BALTIMORE," Maryland Historical Magazine 47:1 (March 1952), 40-54.

B-344 Piatek, Bruce J., "NON-LOCAL ABORIGINAL CEREMAC'S FROM EARLY HIS-TORIC CONTEXTS IN ST. AUGUSTINE," Florida Anthropologist 38:1-2, art 1 (March-June 1985), 81-89.

B-345 Platt, Frederick, "NEW CASTLE: LIVING WITH HISTORY," Early American Life 8:1 (February 1977), 56-58.

B-346 Priddy, Benjamin Jr., OLD CHURCHES OF MEMPHIS," West Tennessee Historical Society Papers No. 29 (1975), 130-161.

B-347 Reece, Ray, "GALVESTON," American Preservation 1:1 (1977), 42-55.

B-348 Reeves, F. Blair, "THE ARCHITECTURE OF HISTORIC ST. AUGUSTINE: A
       PHOTOGRAPHIC ESSAY," Florida Historical Quarterly 44:1 (July 1965),
       94-96.

B-349 Reeves, Ruth P., "HONORING TRADITION," Southern Accents 7:5
       (September-October 1984), 106-115.

B-350 Reiter, Beth Lattimore and Leopold Adler II, "RESTORATION OF
       SAVANNAH'S VICTORIAN DISTRICT," Georgia Historical Quarterly 63:1
       (Spring 1979), 164-172.

B-351 Reynolds, Ann Vines, "NASHVILLE'S CUSTOM HOUSE," Tennessee His-
       torical Quarterly 37:3 (Fall 1978), 263-277.

B-352 Rhangos, Audrey Dunn, "HISTORIC SAVANNAH FOUNDATION," Georgia
       Historical Quarterly 63:1 (Spring 1979), 173-179.

B-353 Rhoads, William B., "FRANKLIN D. ROOSEVELT AND THE ARCHITECTURE OF
       WARM SPRINGS," Georgia Historical Quarterly 67:1 (Spring 1983), 70-
       87.

B-354 Ricci, James M., "THE BUNGALOW: A HISTORY OF THE MOST PREDOMINANT
       STYLE OF TAMPA BAY," Tampa Bay History 1:2 (Fall-Winter 1979), 6-
       13.

B-355 Roberts, Charles Blanton, "THE BUILDING OF MIDDLESBORO," Filson
       Club History Quarterly 7:1 (January 1933), 18-33.

B-356 Robinson, Willard B., "THE PUBLIC SQUARE AS A DETERMINANT OF COURT-
       HOUSE FORM IN TEXAS," Southwestern Historical Quarterly 75:3 (Janu-
       ary 1972), 339-372.

B-357 Rock, Maxine, "URBANE RENEWAL," Southern Accents 6:3 (Summer 1983),
       46-57.

B-358 Rogers, Evelyna K., "THOMASVILLE--ROSES AND GRAND OLD HOMES,"
       Georgia Journal 1:6 (September-October 1981), 26-28.

B-359 Roper, Bartlett, "TRAPEZIUM HOUSE," Virginia Cavalcade 15:2 (Autumn
       1965), 9-13.

B-360 Roper, James H., "EUTAW," American Preservation 2:6 (November-
       December 1979), 49-62.

B-361 Roper, James H., "NATCHITOCHES," American Preservation 3:4 (July-
       August 1980), 49-58.

B-362 Ross, Margaret, "THE HINDERLITER HOUSE: ITS PLACE IN ARKANSAS
       HISTORY," Arkansas Historical Quarterly 30:3 (Autumn 1971), 181-
       192.

B-363 Rothra, Elizabeth Ognen, "TREEHOUSE LIVING IN A SOUTH FLORIDA
       HAMMOCK," Landscape Architecture 70:2 (March 1980), 148-153.

B-364 Russell, Nadine Carter, "RESTORING ARCHITECT GALLIER'S HOUSE IN NEW
       ORLEANS," Historic Preservation 23:4 (October December 1971), 26-
       29.

B-365 Sanchez-Saavedra, E.M., "RICHMOND'S OLD BELL HOUSE," Virginia
       Cavalcade 19:2 (Autumn 1969), 5-11.

B-366 Sanders, John L., THE NORTH CAROLINA STATE CAPITOL OF 1840,"
       Antiques 128:3 (September 1985), 474-484.

B-367 Sauder, Robert A., "ARCHITECTURE AND URBAN GROWTH IN NINETEENTH
       CENTURY NEW ORLEANS," Southeastern Geographer 17:2 (November 1977),
       93-107.

B-368 Scardino, Barrie, "A LEGACY OF CITY HALLS FOR HOUSTON," Houston
       Review (Fall 1982), 155-163.

B-369 Scheets, Eleanor, "COSMOPOLITAN COMFORT," Southern Accents 6:4
       (Fall 1983), 56-61.

B-370 Schulze, Franz, "THE EAST BUILDING: TRAPEZOID TRIUMPHANT," Art in
       America 66:4 (July-August 1978), 55-63.

B-371 Schwartz, Sally, "THE OLD STATE HOUSE: A STUDY OF ITS ORIGINS AND
       CONSTRUCTION," Delaware History 17:3 (Spring-Summer 1977), 179-190.

B-372 "SCOTTSBORO REVITALIZES," Tennessee Valley Prespective 9:2 (Winter
       1978), 29-30.

B-373 Scribner, Robert L., "VIRGINIA HOUSE," Virginia Cavalcade 5:3
       Winter 1955), 20-29.

B-374 Shanshoty, Andre, "SWEET VICTORY--AT LAST," Historic Preservation
       36:1 (February 1984), 46-51.

B-375 Shepard, E. Lee, "'THE EASE AND CONVENIENCE OF THE PEOPLE': COURT-
       HOUSE LOCATIONS IN SPOTSYLVANIA COUNTY, 1720-1840," Virginia Maga-
       zine of History and Biography, 87:3 (July 1979), 279-299.

B-376 Sheppard, Peggy and Kit Corley, "A SALUTE TO COLUMBUS: ON THE OC-
       CASION OF HER SESQUICENTENNIAL," Georgia Life 5:1 (1978), 12-16.

B-377 Sherman, Philip, "BALTIMORE'S 104 THE MEDICAL REGIMENT ARMORY,"
       Maryland Historical Magazine 70:3 (Fall 1975), 275-278.

B-378 Sherwood, Dolly, "CELEBRATING AMERICAN STYLE," Southern Accents 6:2
       (Spring 1983), 46-55.

B-379 Shiras, Ginger, "EUREKA SPRINGS," American Preservation 2:4
       (April/May 1979), 44-60.

B-380 Shopes, Linda, "THE BALTIMORE NEIGHBORHOOD HERITAGE PROJECT: ORAL
       HISTORY AND COMMUNITY INVOLVEMENT," Radical History Review 25
       (October 1981), 27-44.

B-381 Simons, Harriet P. and Albert Simons, "THE WILLIAM BURROWS HOUSE OF
       CHARLESTON," South Carolina Historical Magazine 70:3 (July 1969),
       155-176.

B-382 Smith, Susan Hunter, "WOMEN ARCHITECTS IN ATLANTA, 1895-1979,"
       Atlanta Historical Journal 23:4 (Winter 1979-80), 85-107.

B-383 Snell, David, "'HUBBUB' OF HOUSTON, THE RICE HOTEL, GOES TO THE
       GREAT CONVENTION IN THE SKY," Smithsonian 6:4 (1975), 48-59.

B-384 Snow, Nan, "COLUMBUS: A COMBINATION OF HISTORIC PRESERVATION AND
       ADAPTIVE REUSE HAS TRANSFORMED THIS GEORGIA CITY," American
       Preservation 4:1 (January-February 1981), 44-58.

B-385 Somers, Dale A., Timothe J. Crimmins, and Merl E. Reed., "SURVEYING
       THE RECORDS OF A CITY: THE HISTORY OF ATLANTA PROJECT," American
       Architect 36:3 (1973), 353-359.

B-386 South, Stanley A., "'RUSSELLBOROUGH': TWO ROYAL GOVERNORS' MANSION
       AT BRUNSWICK TOWN," North Carolina Historical Review 44:4 (Autumn
       1967), 360-372.

B-387 Spalding, Phinizy, "NEIGHBORHOOD CONSERVATION, OR, GETTING IT ALL
       TOGETHER IN COBBHAM," Georgia Historical Quarterly 63:1 (Spring
       1979), 90-99.

B-388 Stagg, Brian L., "GETTING YOUNG PEOPLE INVOLVED," Historic Preser-
       vation 24:2 (April-June 1972), 16-18.

B-389 Stevens, R. Randolph, "THE RAILROAD DEPOT: A PHOTOGRAPHIC ESSAY," Tampa Bay History 6:1 (Spring-Summer 1984), 36-52.

B-390 Stevens, Sallie S., "THE BEST OF TWO WORLDS," Southern Accents 6:4 (Fall 1983), 82-87.

B-391 Stuck, Goodloe, "HISTORICAL PRESERVATION IN SHREVEPORT: SIX YEARS OF STRUGGLING AND EDUCATING," North Louisiana Historical Association Journal 9:3 (1978), 131-133.

B-392 Swartz, Mimi, "STANDING UP FOR KING WILLIAM STREET," Historic Preservation 36:5 (October 1984), 22-31.

B-393 Tazwell, William L., NORFOLK: A REMARKABLE RESURGENCE," Virginia Cavalcade 32:2 (Autumn 1982), 76-85.

B-394 Terrell, David, "LITTLE ROCK STORY," American Preservation 1:1 (1977), 62-72.

B-395 Terrell, David., "OAKLAND CEMETARY," American Preservation 2:6 (November-December 1979), 41-48.,

B-396 Thomas, William H.B., "COURTHOUSES OF MADISON COUNTY," Virginia Cavalcade 19:4 (Spring 1970), 16-21.

B-397 Thomas, William H.B., "COURTHOUSES OF ORANGE COUNTY," Virginia Cavalcade 19:1 (Summer 1969), 32-37.

B-398 Tiller, Kay, "SPECTRUM CENTER," Landscape Architecture 74:2 (March-April 1984), 65-67.

B-399 Todd, Evalyn E., "HISTORIC HALIFAX," Daughters of the American Revolution Magazine 110:2 (1976), 186-191.

B-400 Troubetzkoy, Ulrich, "THE GOVERNOR'S MANSION," Virginia Cavalcade 11:1 (Summer 1961), 23-29.

B-401 Upchurch, Mary Walton, "GIVING A SUBURBAN ALABAMA HOME MORE SPACE," Landscape Architecture 69:2 (March 1979), 161-165.

B-402 van Sweden, Frederick L., "URBANELY NATURALISTIC: A GEORGETOWN GARDEN," Landscape Architecture 71:2 (March 1981), 202-205.

B-403 van Sweden, James A. and Wolfgang Oehme, "DESIGN SEEN: VIRGINIA AVENUE GARDENS, WASHINGTON, D.C.," Landscape Architecture 71:4 (July 1981), 476-479.

B-404 Vaseff, James and Timothy J. King., "ACTION PLANS FOR HISTORIC DANVILLE," Urban Land 38:11 (December 1979), 11-18.

B-405 Vickers, Edward, "HISTORIC CHURCHES IN ATLANTA," Georgia Journal 2:5 (August-September 1982), 20-23, 26.

B-406 "THE VIEUX CARRE, 1923" AIA Journal 72:3 (March 1983), 83-87.

B-407 "THE VIEUX CARRE, 1983" AIA Journal 72:3 (March 1983), 78-82.

B-408 Vogel, Erika Farkac, "PREAMBLE TO HOSPITALITY," Garden Design 2:2 (Summer 1983), 52-55.

B-409 Waddell, Gene, "ROBERT MILLS' FIREPROOF BUILDING," South Carolina Historical Magazine 80:2 (April 1979), 105-135.

B-410 Warren, Bonnie, "NEW ORLEANS FLAIR," Southern Accents 6:2 (Spring 1983), 102-108.

B-411 Waterbury, Jean Parker, "'LONG NEGLECTED, NOW RESTORED': THE XIMENEZ-FATIO HOUSE (Ca. 1797)," El Escribano 22 (1985), 1-30.

B-412 Watson, Catherine, "BROWNSVILLE," <u>American</u> <u>Preservation</u> 2:5 (September October 1979), 7-21.

B-413 Watson, Thomas D. and Samuel Wilson, Jr., "A LOST LANDMARK REVISITED: THE PANTON HOUSE OF PENSACOLA," <u>Florida</u> <u>Historical</u> <u>Quarterly</u> 60:1 (July 1981), 42-50.

B-414 Weathers, Ed., "SELF-HELP THE MEMPHIS WAY," <u>Historic</u> <u>Preservation</u> 33:4 (July-August 1981), 34-39.

B-415 Webster, John C., "JUMP THE ALLEY WITH A GARDEN," <u>Landscape</u> <u>Architecture</u> 71:2 (March 1981), 222-223.

B-416 Weinberg, Steve., "OLA DAVIS' ONE-DOLLAR HOUSE," <u>American</u> <u>Preservation</u> 1:4 (April-May 1979), 38-43.

B-417 Welch, Cliff., "HOMETOWN BALTIMORE," <u>Historic</u> <u>Preservation</u> 36:5 (October 1984), 48-55.

B-418 Wertenbaker, Thomas Jefferson, "THE RESTORING OF COLONIAL WILLIAMS-BURG," <u>North</u> <u>Carolina</u> <u>Historical</u> <u>Review</u> 27:2 (April 1950), 218-232.

B-419 Wheeler, Nick., "LOOK WHAT'S BREWING IN SAN ANTONIO," <u>Historical</u> <u>Preservation</u> 34:5 (September-October 1982), 32-36.

B-420 White, Dana F., "LANDSCAPED ATLANTA: THE ROMANTIC TRADITION IN CEMETARY, PARK, AND SUBURBAN DEVELOPMENT." <u>Atlanta</u> <u>Historical</u> <u>Journal</u> 26:2-3 (Summer-Fall 1982), 95-112.

B-421 White, Philip A. Jr., "ARLINGTON," <u>Southern</u> <u>Accents</u> 8:5 (September October 1985), 102-107.

B-422 "WHITEHALL," <u>Southern</u> <u>Accents</u> 8:1 (January-February 1985), 112-124.

B-423 Whitehead, Thomas N., "URBAN PLANNING: HISTORICAL PRESERVATION OF THE VIEUX CARRE," <u>Louisiana</u> <u>Studies</u> 9:2 (Summer 1970), 73-87.

B-424 Whitwell, W.A., "SAINT ANDREW'S ROMAN CATHOLIC CHURCH: ROANOKE'S HIGH VICTORIAN GOTHIC LANDMARK," <u>Virginia</u> <u>Cavalcade</u> 24:3 (Winter 1975), 124-133.

B-425 Wilkins, Woodrow W., "CORAL GABLES: 1920'S NEW TOWN," <u>Historic</u> <u>Preservation</u> 30:1 (January-March 1978), 6-9.

B-426 Wolcott, Daniel F., "THE RESTORATION OF THE COURTHOUSE IN NEW CASTLE," <u>Delaware</u> <u>History</u> 7:3 (March 1957), 193-206.

B-427 Wooden, Howard E., "THE RECTORY OF ST. PAUL'S PARISH, BALTIMORE: AN ARCHITECTURAL HISTORY," <u>Maryland</u> <u>Historical</u> <u>Magazine</u> 57:3 (Fall 1962), 210-228.

B-428 Woodward, Anne, "1785: A LANDMARK FOR THE NATIONAL TRUST," <u>Historic</u> <u>Preservation</u> 31:3 (July-August 1979), 2-7.

Art

B-429 Bonner, Judith Hopkins, "GEORGE DAVID COVLON: A NINETEENTH CENTURY FRENCH LOUISIANA PAINTER," <u>Southern</u> <u>Quarterly</u> 20:2 (Winter 1982), 41-61.

B-430 Burrell, Diane D., "THE SOUTHERN ARTISTS: DALE KENNINGTON," <u>Southern</u> <u>Accents</u> 8:5 (September-October) 116-121.

B-431 Garner, Bob, "THE SOUTHERN ARTISTS: WILLIAM MAGNUM," <u>Southern</u> <u>Accents</u> 8:4 (July-August 1985).

B-432 Garrison, Gail L., "TWO EARLY ROMANTIC PAINTINGS AT THE BALTIMORE
      CO-CATHEDRAL," Maryland Historical Magazine 72:2 (Summer 1977),
      253-265.

B-433 Goode, James M., "OUTDOOR SCULPTURE--WASHINGTON'S OVERLOOKED MONU-
      MENTS," Historic Preservation 25:1 (January-March 1973), 4-14.

B-434 Grootkerk, Paul, "GEORGE OHR: THE BILOXI 'OHR-NA-MENT,'" Southern
      Quarterly 24:1-2 (Fall-Winter 1985), 138-150.

B-435 Hewitt, Susan L., "THE SOUTHERN ARTISTS: RONALD LEWIS," Southern
      Accents 6:1 (Winter 1983), 96-101.

B-436 Hoobler, James A., "T.M. SCHLEIER, PHOTOGRAPHER," Tennessee His-
      torical Quarterly 45:3 (Fall 1986), 230-243.

B-437 Horne, John C. Van., "'AMPHITHEATRE OF HILLS': LATE EIGHTEENTH-
      CENTURY RICHMOND FROM THE WATERCOLORS OF BENJAMIN HENRY LATROBE,"
      Virginia Cavalcade 35:1 (Summer 1985), 22-29.

B-438 Johnson, Sona K., "AMERICAN PAINTINGS IN THE BALTIMORE MUSEUM OF
      ART," Antiques 128:5 (November 1985), 986-995.

B-439 Kiah, Virginia, "ULYSSES DAVIS: SAVANNAH FOLK SCULPTOR," Southern
      Folklore Quarterly 42:2-3 (1978), 271-286.

B-440 Masten, Susannah, "THE SOUTHERN ARTISTS: ARTHUR WEEKS," Southern
      Accents 8:3 (May-June 1985), 116-121.

B-441 Masten, Susannah, "SOUTHERN ARTISTS: EVE AND ROBERT W. BRAGG,"
      Southern Accents 6:4 (Fall 1983), 88-93.

B-442 Masten, Susannah, "THE SOUTHERN ARTISTS: ROBERT BRUCE WILLIAMS,"
      Southern Accents 7:5 (September-October 1984), 88-95.

B-443 Mobley, Anita Morrison, "THE SOUTHERN ARTISTS: LAMAR DODD,"
      Southern Accents 7:2 (March-April 1984), 96-103.

B-444 Mobley, Anita Morrison and Susannah Masten, "THE SOUTHERN ARTISTS:
      BARBARA GALLAGHER," Southern Accents 8:6 (November-December 1985),
      104-107, 144.

B-445 Moffatt, Frederick C., "A TALE OF TWO MONUMENTS: CIVIL WAR SCULP-
      TURE IN KNOXVILLE," East Tennessee Historical Society's Publica-
      tions No. 50 (1978), 3-20.

B-446 Moore, Jack B. and Robert E. Snyder., "PIONEER COMMERCIAL PHOTO-
      GRAPHERS: THE BURGERT BROTHERS OF TAMPA, FLORIDA," Journal of
      American Culture 8:3 (Fall 1985), 11-26.

B-447 Moore, John H., "THE JEFFERSON DAVIS MONUMENT," Virginia Cavalcade
      10:4 (Spring 1961), 28-34.

B-448 Olson, Barbara and Eric Olson, "SOUTHERN ARTISTS: ARTHUR STEWART,"
      Southern Accents 7:3 (May-June 1984), 88-95.

B-449 Pleasants, J. Hall, "WILLIAM DERING: A MID-EIGHTEENTH CENTURY
      WILLIAMSBURG PORTRAIT PAINTER," Virginia Magazine of History and
      Biography 60:1 (January 1952), 56-63.

B-450 Proby, Kathryn Hall., "THE SOUTHERN ARTISTS: MARIO SANCHEZ,"
      Southern Accents 6:2 (Spring 1983), 88-93.

B-451 Ritchey, David., "ROBERT DE LAPOUYADE: THE LAST OF THE LOUISIANA
      SCENE PAINTERS," Louisiana History 14:1 (Winter 1973), 5-20.

B-452 Romeyn, Carlyn G. Crannell., "HENRY O. TANNER: ATLANTA INTERLUDE,"
      Atlanta Historical Journal 27:4 (Winter 1983-84), 27-40.

B-453 Roper, James E., "THE EARLIEST PICTURES OF MEMPHIS: CHARLES LESUEUR'S DRAWINGS, 1828-1830," West Tennessee Historical Society Papers No. 2 (1971), 5-25.

B-454 Severens, Martha R., "JEREMIAH THEUS OF CHARLESTON: PLAGIARIST OR PUNDIT," Southern Quarterly 24:1, 2 (Fall-Winter 1985), 56-70.

B-455 Shewmake, Mitzi, "RELATIONSHIPS AND IMAGES: TWO WINSTON-SALEM ARTISTS," Southern Quarterly 17:2 (Winter 1979), 16-27.

B-456 Simms. L. Moody Jr., "A VIRGINIA SCULPTOR," Virginia Cavalcade 20:1 (Summer 1970), 20-27.

B-457 Sinclair, Bruce, "TREASURES FROM THE VASTY DEEP," Delaware History 12:1 (April 1966), 6-24.

B-458 "THE SOUTH," Print 40:4 (July-August 1986), 193-218.

B-459 "THE SOUTHERN ARTISTS: RICHARD MACDONALD," Southern Accents 7:6 (November-December 1984), 118-125.

B-460 Staiti, Paul, "SAMUEL F. B. MORSE IN CHARLESTON, 1818-1821," South Carolina Historical Magazine 79:2 (April 1978), 87-112.

B-461 Troubetzkoy, Ulrich., "THE LEE MONUMENT," Virginia Cavalcade 11:4 (Spring 1962), 5-10.

B-462 Weesner, Richard W., "WILLIAM WASHINGTON GIRARD," Tennessee Historical Quarterly 45:1 (Spring 1986), 30-40.

B-463 Westfall, L. Glenn, "CIGAR LABEL ART: A PHOTOGRAPHIC ESSAY," Tampa Bay History 7:2 (Fall-Winter 1985), 106-116.

B-464 Westfall, L. Glenn, "CIGAR LABEL ART: PORTRAITS OF TAMPA'S PAST," Tampa Bay History 6:1 (Spring-Summer 1984), 5-15.

B-465 Westfall, L. Glenn, "HIDDEN TREASURES OF TAMPA HISTORY IN TOBACCO JOURNALS AND CIGAR LABEL ART," Sunland Tribune (Tampa Historical Society Publication) 8, 53-62,

B-466 Williams, Jon M., "DAGUERREOTYPISTS, AMBROTYPISTS, AND PHOTOGRAPH-ERS IN WILMINGTON, DELAWARE, 1842-1859," Delaware History 18:3 (Spring-Summer 1979), 180-193.

Artisans and Crafts

B-467 Briggs, Marth Wren, "SIGNBOARDS AND SIGN PAINTERS OF EIGHTEENTH-CENTURY WILLIAMSBURG," Virginia Cavalcade 27:2 (Autumn 1977), 68-87.

B-468 Carll-White, Allison, "SOUTH CAROLINA'S FORGOTTEN CRAFTSMEN," South Carolina Historical Magazine 86:1 (January 1985), 32-38.

B-469 Combs, Diana Williams, "ALL THAT LIVE MUST HEAR," Atlanta Historical Bulletin 20:2 (Summer 1976), 61-96.

B-470 Gould, Christopher, "ROBERT WELLS, COLONIAL CHARLESTON PRINTER," South Carolina Historical Magazine 79:1 (February 1978), 23-49.

B-471 Harrington, J.C., "SEVENTEENTH CENTURY BRICKMAKING AND TILEMAKING AT JAMESTOWN, VIRGINIA," Virginia Magazine of History and Biography 58:1 (January 1950), 16-39.

B-472 "THE HENKEL PRESS--THE FIRST SIXTY YEARS," Virginia Cavalcade 13:3 (Winter 1963-64), 16-22.

B-473 McMurtrie, Douglas, "A BIBLIOGRAPHY OF SOUTH CAROLINA IMPRINTS, 1731-1740," South Carolina Historical and Geneological Magazine 34:3 (July 1933), 117-137.

B-474 McMurtrie, Douglas C., "THE FIRST TWELVE YEARS OF PRINTING IN NORTH CAROLINA, 1749-1760," North Carolina Historical review 10:3 (July 1933), 214-234.

B-475 McMurtrie, Douglas C., "PIONEER PRINTING IN GEORGIA," Georgia Historical Quarterly 16:2 (June 1932), 77-113.

B-476 Magruder, Louise E., "JOHN SHAW, CABINETMAKER OF ANNAPOLIS," Maryland Historical Magazine 42:1 (1947), 35-40.

B-477 Peary, Charles D., "FRENCH CABINETMAKERS IN THE VIEUX CARRE," Louisiana Studies 1:2 (Summer 1962), 6-19.

B-478 Rabun, Josette Hensley and Robbie G. Blackmore, "LEWIS S. BUCKNER, BLACK ARTISAN (C 1856-1924) OF SEVIERVILLE, TENNESSEE," Tennessee Folklore Society Bulletin 48:1 (March 1982), 1-10.

B-479 Ritter, Christine, "LIFE IN EARLY AMERICA: SOUTHERN FURNITURE MAKERS," Early American Life 8:6 (December 1977).

B-480 Schmidt, Martin, "THE EARLY PRINTERS OF LOUISVILLE 1800-1860," Filson Club History Quarterly 40:4 (October 1966), 307-334.

B-481 South, Stanley, "BAKED CLAY OBJECTS FROM THE SITE OF THE 1670 SETTLEMENT AT CHARLES TOWNE, SOUTH CAROLINA," Notebook 2:1 (January 1970), 3-17.

B-482 Troubetzkoy, Ulrich, "BEADS, BOTTLES AND BULL'S-EYES," Virginia Cavalcade 9:3 (Winter 1959), 10-17.

B-483 Vlach, John Michael, "PHILIP SIMMONS, CHARLESTON BLACKSMITH," Southern Exposure 10:1 (January-February 1982), 14-19.

B-484 Walsh, Richard, "THE CHARLESTON MECHANICS: A BRIEF STUDY 1760-1776," South Carolina Historical Magazine 60:3 (July 1959), 123-144.

B-485 Weiner, A.N., "COLONIAL CRAFT APPENTICES OF WILLIAMSBURG," Early American Life 5:4 (August 1974), 46-51.

B-486 Willingham, Robert M. Jr., "CONFEDERATE PRINTING IN AUGUSTA," Richmond County History 17:2 (Summer 1985), 5-14.

Arts and Culture

B-487 Albert, Allen D. Jr., "FINE ARTS AND THE NEWLY URBAN SOUTH," Mississippi Quarterly 10:2 (Spring 1957), 59-64.

B-488 Appleton, Carolyn and Jan Huebner, "NINETEENTH-CENTURY AMERICAN ART AT THE UNIVERSITY OF TEXAS AT AUSTIN," Antiques 126:5 (November 1984), 1234-1243.

B-489 Baker, Elizabeth C., "SOUTHERN EXPOSURE," Art in America 64:4 (July-August 1976), 49-51.

B-490 Baker, Mary Lou, "BALTIMORE: STAR SPANGLED ARTS," Horizon 27:6 (July/August 1984), 25-32.

B-491 Baro, Gene., "WASHINGTON: THE CYBERNETICS OF COTTAGE INDUSTRY," Art in America 60:3 (May-June 1972), 108-110.

B-492 Bonner, Judith Hopkins, "ARTISTS' ASSOCIATIONS IN NINETEENTH-CENTURY NEW ORLEANS: 1842-1860," Southern Quarterly 24:1, 2 (Fall-Winter 1985), 119-137.

B-493 Bourdon, David, "WASHINGTON REVISITED," Art in America 66:4 (July-
      August 1978), 95-99.

B-494 Brumbaugh, Thomas B., "ART ARRIVES IN ATLANTA: A NOTE ON THE
      SOUTHERN RENAISSANCE," Georgia Review 19:3 (Fall 1965), 360-367.

B-495 Crannell, Carlyn Gaye, "THE HIGH HERITAGE," Atlanta Historical
      Journal 23:4 (Winter 1979-80), 71-84.

B-496 Crannell, Carlyn Gaye, "PUBLIC TASTE AND 'HIGH ART' IN ATLANTA,
      1870-1900," Atlanta Historical Journal 24:4 (Winter 1980), 51-74.

B-497 Daniels, William G., "THE EPWORTH JUBILEE COMMUNITY ARTS CENTER OF
      KNOXVILLE, TENNESSEE: COMMUNITY ARTS IN AN URBAN APPALACHIAN
      CENTER," Arts in Society 12:1 (1975), 24-31.

B-498 Davis, Gene, "STARTING OUT IN THE '50s," Art in America 66:4 (July-
      August 1978), 88-94.

B-499 Forgey, Benjamin, "WASHINGTON: NEW ART, NEW GALLERIES, NEW SCENE!"
      Art in America 60:1 (January-February 1972), 104-109.

B-500 Freed, Eleanor, "TEXAS ROUNDUP," Art in America 56:5 (September-
      October 1968), 102-105.

B-501 Freed, Eleanor, "WINDFALL FOR TEXAS," Art in America 57:6
      (November-December 1969), 78-85.

B-502 Geracimous, Ann and Gerald Maryorate, "THE ARTOCRATS," Art in
      America 66:4 (July-August 1978), 100-109.

B-503 Hickman, Caroline Mesrobian, "PERSPECTIVES ON ART PATRONAGE IN THE
      CAROLINA LOW COUNTRY TO 1825," Southern Quarterly 24:1, 2 (Fall-
      Winter 1985), 95-118.

B-504 Hopkins, Henry, "FORT WORTH SIBLINGS," Art in America 60:5 (Septem-
      ber-October 1972), 49.

B-505 Jack, Carolyn and Gary Schwan, "PALM BEACH: ARTS ADVENTURE IN
      PARADISE," Horizon 27:8 (October 1984), 27-34.

B-506 Kalin, Berkley, "ISAAC L. MYERS: A MAN WHO BROUGHT THE BEST IN THE
      ARTS TO MEMPHIS," West Tennessee Historical Society Papers No. 26
      (1972), 74-93.

B-507 Kutner, Janet, "THE HOUSTON-DALLAS AXIS," Art in America 60:5
      (September-October 1972), 59-61.

B-508 Lansford, Alonzo, "THE SOUTH--FOUR NEW ORLEANS ARTISTS," Art in
      America 43:1 (February 1955), 72-78.

B-509 Lunt, Dudley, "THE HOWARD PYLE SCHOOL OF ART," Delaware History 5:3
      (March 1953), 151-177.

B-510 McFadden, Sarah, "MEANWHILE, AROUND TOWN. . . ." Art in America
      66:4 (July-August 1978), 64-69.

B-511 McIntyre, Florence M., "THE HISTORY OF ART IN MEMPHIS," West
      Tennessee Historical Society Papers No. 7 (1953), 79-92.

B-512 "NEW ORLEANS/LOUISIANA: ARTS PARADISE SPECIAL TRAVEL SECTION,"
      Horizon 27:3 (April 1984), 21-44.

B-513 Northern, Mary Lou, "LOUISVILLE: GATEWAY TO THE ARTS," Horizon
      27:1 (January-February 1984), 21-28.

B-514 Peirce, Neal R. and Whitney Jones, "THE ARTS AND WINSTON-SALEM,"
      Ekistics 48:288 (May-June 1981), 228-233.

B-515 Putnam, Leslie, "ATLANTA: MORE THAN SURVIVING," Art in America 60:2 (March–April 1972), 108–109.

B-516 Ratcliff, Carter, "MODERNISM FOR THE AGES," Art in America 66:4 (July–August 1978), 50–54.

B-517 Roades, Antoinette W., "HAMPTON ROADS: CONSOLIDATING FOR THE ARTS," Horizon 17:5 (June 1984), 29–36.

B-518 Robinson, Judith Helm., "1785: WHERE THE NATIONAL GALLERY BEGAN," Historical Preservation 31:3 (July–August), 8–11.

B-519 Rutledge, Anna Wells, "ARTISTS IN THE LIFE OF CHARLESTON: THROUGH COLONY AND STATE FROM RESTORATION TO RECONSTRUCTION PHILADELPHIA," American Philosophical Society 39, part 2 (1949), 101–260.

B-520 Semmes, Raphael, "BALTIMORE DURING THE TIME OF THE OLD PEALE MUSEUM," Maryland Historical Magazine 27:2 (June 1932), 115–122.

B-521 Silberman, Robert, "OUR TOWN," Art in America 73:7 (July 1985), 110–107.

B-522 Simms, L. Moody Jr., "TOWARD NORMS: THE FINE ARTS IN THE AMERICAN SOUTH," Southern Quarterly 21:2 (Winter 1983), 39–67.

B-523 Simon, Joan, "TENDING TO ART IN WASHINGTON AND BALTIMORE: THE ITINERANT CURATOR AND THE MUSEUM," Art in America 64:4 (July–August 1976), 89–91.

B-524 Steele, Karen D., "AGECROFT HALL: AN ENGLISH COUNTRY HOUSE MUSEUM," Southern Accents 8:6 (November–December 1985), 80–89.

B-525 Tannous, David, "CAPITAL ART: IN THE MAJOR LEAGUES," Art in America 66:4 (July–August 1978), 70–77.

B-526 Tannous, David, "THOSE WHO STAY," Art in America 66:4 (July–August 1978), 78–87, 135.

B-527 "THREE NEW MUSEUMS IN TEXAS," Art in America 60:5 (September–October 1972), 52–53.

B-528 Turner, Arlin, "GEORGE W. CABLE'S BEGINNINGS AS A REFORMER," Journal of Southern History 17:2 (May 1951), 135–161.

B-529 "U.S. ARTS: STRATEGIES FOR THE 80s," Horizon 25:3 (April 1982), 16–23.

B-530 "U.S. ARTS: STRATEGIES FOR THE 80s," Horizon 25:4 (May–June, 1982), 25–32.

B-531 "U.S. ARTS: STRATEGIES FOR THE 80s," Horizon 25:5 (July–August 1982), 29–37.

B-532 "U.S. ARTS: STRATEGIES FOR THE 80s," Horizon 25:6 (September 1982), 26–33.

B-533 "U.S. ARTS: STRATEGIES FOR THE 80s," Horizon 25:8 (December 1982), 29–40.

B-534 "U.S. ARTS: STRATEGIES FOR THE 80s," Horizon 26:1 (January–February 1983), 29–36.

B-535 Vandenberg, Laura Lieberman, "SOUTHERN HISTORIES, CONTEMPORARY OPINIONS: THREE ATLANTA WOMEN ARTISTS," Southern Quarterly 27:2 (Winter 1979), 52–68.

B-536 Weston, Latrobe, "ART AND ARTISTS IN BALTIMORE," Maryland Historical Magazine 33:2 (June 1938), 213–227.

B-537 White, Chappell, "THE ARTS ARE ALIVE AND REASONABLY WELL UNDER ATLANTA'S BUSINESS-BRED ALLIANCE," Southern Voices 1:1 (1974), 71-74.

B-538 Wills, J. Robert, "CENSORSHIP OF THE ARTS: AN INCIDENT IN LEXINGTON," Southern Theatre 21:3 (Summer 1978), 17-24.

B-539 Wright, R. Lewis, "JAMES WARREEL: ARTIST AND ENTREPRENEUR," Virginia Cavalcade 22:3 (Winter 1973), 5-19.

Business and Economics

B-540 Adkins, William G., "ECONOMIC IMPACTS OF EXPRESSWAYS IN DALLAS AND SAN ANTONIO," Traffic Quarterly 13:3 (July 1959), 333-345.

B-541 Agapos, A.M., "AN ECONOMIC APPROACH TO APPALACHIAN DEVELOPMENT: THE BECKLEY, WEST VIRGINIA CASE," Land Economics 44:4 (November 1968), 518-522.

B-542 Alexander, Robert J., "NEGRO BUSINESS IN ATLANTA," Southern Economic Review 17:4 (April 1951), 451-464.

B-543 Anderson, Arthur T., "ISSUES IN MARKETING TO LOW-INCOME URBAN CONSUMERS: A CASE STUDY," Review of Regional Studies 1:3 (Spring 1971-72), 13-26.

B-544 Angel, William D. Jr., "TO MAKE A CITY: ENTREPRENEURSHIP ON THE SUNBELT FRONTIER," in D. Perry, The Rise of the Sunbelt Cities, (1978), 109-128.

B-545 Angel, William D. Jr., "ZENITH REVISITED: URBAN ENTREPRENEURSHIP AND THE SUNBELT FRONTIER," Social Science Quarterly 61:3, 4 (December 1980), 434-445.

B-546 Arena, C. Richard, "PHILADELPHIA-SPANISH NEW ORLEANS TRADE IN THE 1790's," Louisiana History 2:4 (Fall 1961), 429-445.

B-547 Arendale, Marirose, "LUPTON CITY: CHATTANOOGA'S MODEL MILL VILLAGE," Tennessee Historical Quarterly 43:1 (Spring 1984), 68-78.

B-548 Arnold, Joseph L., "BALTIMORE'S NEIGHBORHOODS, 1800-1980," Working Papers from the Regional Economic History Research Center, 4 (1981), 76-98.

B-549 Atherton, Lewis E., "JOHN McDONOGH--NEW ORLEANS MERCANTILE CAPITALIST," Journal of Southern History 7:4 (November 1941), 451-481.

B-550 Atherton, Lewis E., "MERCANTILE EDUCATION IN THE ANTE-BELLUM SOUTH," Mississippi Valley Historical Review 39:4 (March 1953), 623-640.

B-551 Atherton, Lewis E., "PREDECESSORS OF THE COMMERCIAL DRUMMER IN THE OLD SOUTH," Bulletin of the Business Historical Society 21:1 (February 1947), 17-24.

B-552 Axelrod, Bernard, "GALVESTON: DENVER'S DEEP-WATER PORT," Southwestern Historical Quarterly 70:2 (October 1966), 217-228.

B-553 Ayers, Edward L., "NORTHERN BUSINESS AND THE SHAPE OF SOUTHERN PROGRESS: THE CASE OF TENNESSEE'S 'MODEL CITY,'" Tennessee Historical Quarterly 39:2 (Summer 1980), 208-222.

B-554 Bacon, H. Philip, "NASHVILLE'S TRADE AT THE BEGINNING OF THE NINETEENTH CENTURY," Tennessee Historical Quarterly 15:1 (March 1956), 30-36.

B-555 Badger, Andrew, "RURAL SALESMANSHIP: SOME GLEANINGS FROM THIGPEN'S
      STORE NEWS," Mid-South Folklore 2:1 (Spring 1974), 19-28.

B-556 Bailey, Jennifer, "'A NEW BATTLE ON EVALUATION': THE ANTI-CHAIN
      STORE TRADE-AT-HOME AGITATION OF 1929-1930," Journal of American
      Studies 16:3 (December 1982), 407-426.

B-557 Barnes, Annie S., "THE BLACK BEAUTY PARLOR COMPLEX IN A SOUTHERN
      CITY," Phylon 36:2 (June 1975), 149-154.

B-558 Beck, Lewis Addison Jr., "THE SEAMAN AND THE SEAMAN'S BRIDE, BALTI-
      MORE CLIPPER SHIPS," Maryland Historical Magazine 51:4 (December
      1956), 302-314.

B-559 Bellenger, Danny and Ugas Yavas, "ANALYZING KEY ECONOMIC SECTORS OF
      ATLANTA," Atlanta Economic Review 23:3 (May-June 1973), 29-33.

B-560 Bentley, Marvin, "INCORPORATED BANKS AND THE ECONOMIC DEVELOPMENT
      OF MISSISSIPPI, 1829-1837," Journal of Mississippi History 35:4
      (November 1973), 361-380.

B-561 Benton, J. Edwin and Darwin Gamble, "CITY/COUNTY CONSOLIDATION AND
      ECONOMIES OF SCALE: EVIDENCE FROM A TIME-SERIES ANALYSIS IN JACK-
      SONVILLE, FLORIDA," Social Science Quarterly 65:1 (March 1984),
      190-198.

B-562 Bernard, Richard M., "OKLAHOMA CITY: BOOMING SOONER," in R.
      Barnard (ed.) Sunbelt Cities: Politics and Growth Since World War
      II (1983), 213-234.

B-563 Bernard, Richard M., "A PORTRAIT OF BALTIMORE IN 1800: ECONOMIC
      AND OCCUPATIONAL PATTERNS IN AN EARLY AMERICAN CITY," Maryland His-
      torical Magazine 69:4 (Winter 1974), 341-360.

B-564 Berry, Thomas F., "THE RISE OF FLOUR MILLING IN RICHMOND," Virginia
      Magazine of History and Biography, 78:4 (October 1970), 387-408.

B-565 Bidgood, Lee., "INDUSTRIAL ALABAMA," Annals of the American Academy
      of Political and Social Science, 153 (January 1931), 148-155.

B-566 Bigger, Jeanne Ridgway, "JACK DANIEL DISTILLERY AND LYNCHBURG: A
      VISIT TO MOORE COUNTY, TENNESSEE," Tennessee Historical Quarterly
      31:1 (Spring 1972), 3-21.

B-567 "BIRMINGHAM," Black Enterprise 2:4 (September 1971), 40-42.

B-568 Blankenhorn, Dana, "ATLANTA'S FIRST FAMILY OF BUSINESS," Business
      Atlanta 15:7 (July 1986), 76-79.

B-569 Blankenhorn, Dana, "FOUNDING FORTUNES: ATLANTA LIFE INSURES HERN-
      DON HERITAGE," Business Atlanta 15:10 (October 1986), 102-111.

B-570 Blankenhorn, Dana, "OF RAGS AND RICHE'S," Business Atlanta 54:8
      (August 1986), 54-58.

B-571 "BLAST FURNACES IN FLORENCE, ALABAMA," Journal of Muscle Shoals
      History, 3 (1975), 46-48.

B-572 Blood, Pearle, "FACTORS IN THE ECONOMIC DEVELOPMENT OF BALTIMORE,
      MARYLAND," Economic Geography 13:2 (April 1937), 187-208.

B-573 Bogett, Gene W., "MONEY AND MARITIME ACTIVITIES IN NEW ORLEANS
      DURING THE MEXICAN WAR," Louisiana History 17:4 (Fall 1976), 413-
      430.

B-574 Bolding, Gary A., "CHANGE, CONTINUITY AND COMMERCIAL IDENTITY OF A
      SOUTHERN CITY: NEW ORLEANS, 1850-1950," Louisiana Studies 14:2
      (Summer 1975), 161-178.

B-575 Bolding, Gary A., "NEW ORLEANS COMMERCE: THE ESTABLISHMENT OF THE PERMANENT WORLD TRADE MART," Louisiana History 8:4 (Fall 1967), 351-362.

B-576 Bolding, Gary A., "THE NEW ORLEANS SEAWAY MOVEMENT, Louisiana History 10:1 (Winter 1969), 49-60.

B-577 Boles, Daralice D., "ROBERT DAVIS: SMALL TOWN ENTREPRENEUR," Progressive Architecture 66 (July 1985), 111-118.

B-578 Boney, F. N., "FIRST ATLANTA AND THEN THE WORLD: A CENTURY OF COCA-COLA," Georgia Historical Quarterly 71:1 (Spring 1987), 91-105.

B-579 Bonham, Milledge L., "FINANCIAL AND ECONOMIC DISTURBANCE IN NEW ORLEANS ON THE EVE OF SECESSION," Louisiana Historical Quarterly 13:1 (January 1930), 32-36.

B-580 Born, John D. Jr., "JOHN FITZPATRICK OF MANCHE: A SCOTTISH MERCHANT IN THE LOWER MISSISSIPPI," Journal of Mississippi History 32:2 (May 1970), 117-134.

B-581 Bounds, Harvey, "WILMINGTON MATCH COMPANIES," Delaware History 5:1 (April 1962), 3-32.

B-582 Bowden, Martyn J., "GROWTH OF CENTRAL DISTRICTS IN LARGE CITIES," in L. Schnore (ed.) The New Urban History, 1975.

B-583 Bowman, Bob, "LUFKIN: A CENTURY OF LOCOMOTIVES, SAWMILLS AND INDUSTRY," East Texas Historical Journal 19:2 (1981), 3-12.

B-584 Boxerman, Burton Alan, "THE EDISON BROTHERS, SHOE MERCHANTS: THEIR GEORGIA YEARS," Georgia Historical Quarterly 57:4 (Winter 1973), 511-525.

B-585 Boyd, Julian P., "HIGH FINANCE ON THE SAVANNAH," South Atlantic Quarterly 33:1 (January 1934) 83-101.

B-586 Boyd, Mark F., " CENTURY OF CONFIDENCE AND CONSERVATISM CULMINATES IN THE LEWIS STATE BANK OF TALLAHASSEE, FLORIDA," Florida Historical Quarterly 34:4 (April 1956), (Supplement), 1-51.

B-587 Bradley, Donald S., "BACK TO THE CITY?" Atlanta Economic Review 28:2 (March-April 1978), 15-21.

B-588 Branch, Mary Emerson, "PRIME EMERSON AND STEAMBOAT BUILDING IN MEMPHIS," West Tennessee Historical Society Papers 38 (1984), 69-83.

B-589 Brasseaux, Carl A., "THE CADILLAC-DUCLOS AFFAIR: PRIVATE ENTERPRISE VERSUS MERCHANTILISM IN COLONIAL MOBILE," Alabama Review 37:4 (October 1984), 257-270.

B-590 Brophy, William J., "BLACK BUSINESS DEVELOPMENT IN TEXAS CITIES, 1900-1950," Red River Valley Historical Review 6:2 (Spring 1981), 42-55.

B-591 Brown, C. K., "INDUSTRIAL DEVELOPMENT IN NORTH CAROLINA," Annals of the American Academy of Political and Social Science, 153 (January 1931), 133-140.

B-592 Brown, Earl J., "A LOOK AT SOME OF TAMPA'S CIGAR FACTORIES INSIDE AND OUT," Sunland Tribune 8 (November 1982), 73-84.

B-593 Brown, J.A., "PANTON, LESLIE, AND COMPANY," Florida Historical Quarterly 37:3, 4 (January-April 1959), 328-336.

B-594 Browne, Gary L., "BUSINESS INNOVATION AND SOCIAL CHANGE: THE CAREER OF ALEXANDER BROWN AFTER THE WAR OF 1812," Maryland Historical Magazine 69:3 (Fall 1974), 243-255.

B-595 Browne, Gary L., "THE EVOLUTION OF BALTIMORE'S MARKETING CONTROLS OVER AGRICULTURE," Maryland Historian 11:1 (Spring 1950), 1-12.

B-596 Browning, Clyde E., "RURAL-URBAN LOCATIONAL PREFERENCES OF SOUTHERN MANUFACTURERS," Annals of the American Association of Geographers 61 (June 1971), 225-268.

B-597 Bruchey, Eleanor, "THE DEVELOPMENT OF BALTIMORE BUSINESS, 1880-1914, PART I," Maryland Historical Magazine 64:1 (Spring 1969), 18-42.

B-598 Bruckey, Eleanor, "THE DEVELOPMENT OF BALTIMORE BUSINESS, 1880-1914, PART II," Maryland Historical Magazine 64:1 (Summer 1969), 144-160.

B-599 Bruner, D., "A LARGE NUMBER OF CORPORATIONS ESTABLISHING OFFICES IN THE SOUTH," American Banker (May 6, 1976), p. 10.

B-600 Bryan, T. Conn, "THE GOLD RUSH IN GEORGIA," Georgia Review 9:4 (Winter 1955), 398-403.

B-601 Bryant, Keith L. Jr., "ARTHUR E. STILWELL AND THE FOUNDING OF PORT ARTHUR: A CASE OF ENTREPRENEURIAL ERROR," Southwestern Historical Quarterly 75:1 (July 1971), 19-40.

B-602 Bryant, Keith Jr. and Lyndon E. Dawson Jr., "AN ECONOMIC EVALUATION OF RAYVILLE, LOUISIANA AND ITS DEVELOPMENT POTENTIAL," Louisiana Studies 8:4 (Winter 1969), 312-320.

B-603 Buchanan, Patricia, "MIAMI'S BOOTLEG BOOM," Tequesta No. 30 (1970), 13-31.

B-604 Buckalew, A. R. and R. B. Buckalew, "THE DISCOVERY OF OIL IN SOUTH ARKANSAS, 1920-1924," Arkansas Historical Quarterly 33:3 (Autumn 1974), 195-238.

B-605 Buker, George E., "TAMPA'S MUNICIPAL WHARVES," Tampa Bay History 5:2 (Fall-Winter 1983), 37-46.

B-606 Bull, Jacqueline P., "THE GENERAL MERCHANT IN THE ECONOMIC HISTORY OF THE NEW SOUTH," Journal of Southern History 18:1 (February 1952), 37-59.

B-607 Burnett, Gene, "BREAKING THE MISSISSIPPI POVERTY MOLD," South Business 7:9 (September 1980), 58-64.

B-608 Burnett, Gene, "THE WATERFRONT REVOLUTION," South Business 7:4 (April 1980), 34-41.

B-609 Burns, Anna C., "THE GULF LUMBERING COMPANY, FULLERTON: A VIEW OF LUMBERING DURING LOUISIANA'S GOLDEN ERA," Louisiana History 20:2 (Spring 1979), 197-208.

B-610 Bushnell, Amy, "THE EXPENSES OF HIDALQUIA IN SEVENTEENTH-CENTURY ST. AUGUSTINE," El Escribano 15 (1978), 23-36.

B-611 Calhoun, Jeanne A., Martha A. Zierden and Elizabeth A. Paysinger, "THE GEOGRAPHIC SPREAD OF CHARLESTON'S MERCANTILE COMMUNITY, 1732-1767," South Carolina Historical Magazine 86:3 (July 1985), 182-220.

B-612 Calvert, Monte, "THE WILMINGTON BOARD OF TRADE, 1867-1875," Delaware History 12:3 (April 1967), 175-197.

B-613 Carlton, David L., "THE PIEDMONT AND WACCAMAW REGIONS: AN ECONOMIC COMPARISON," South Carolina Historical Magazine 88:1 (January 1987), 83-100.

B-614 Carpenter, Clifton C., "MORRISTOWN, TENNESSEE: A CASE STUDY IN INDUSTRIAL ADJUSTMENT TO AN AGRICULTURAL COMMUNITY," Memorandum Folio, Southeastern Division, Association of American Geographers, 13 (November 1961), 15-21.

B-615 Carson, Gerald, "CRACKER BARRELL STORE: SOUTHERN STYLE," Georgia Review 9:1 (Spring 1955), 27-36.

B-616 Carson, William J., "BANKING IN THE SOUTH: ITS RELATION TO AGRI-CULTURAL AND INDUSTRIAL DEVELOPMENT," Annals of the American Academy of Political and Social Science 153 (January 1931), 210-223.

B-617 Chambers, Henry E., "EARLY COMMERCIAL PRESTIGE OF NEW ORLEANS," Louisiana Historical Quarterly 5:4 (October 1922), 451-461.

B-618 Chambers, William T., "THE GULF PORT CITY REGION OF TEXAS," Economic Geography 7:1 (January 1931), 69-83.

B-619 Chambers, William T., "KILGORE, TEXAS: AN OIL BOOM TOWN," Economic Geography 9:1 (Janaury 1933), 72-84.

B-620 Chambers, William T., "SAN ANTONIO, TEXAS," Economic Geography 16:3 (July 1940), 291-298.

B-621 Chang, Semoon, "AN ECONOMETRIC FORECASTING MODEL BASED ON REGIONAL ECONOMIC INFORMATION SYSTEM DATA: THE CASE OF MOBILE, ALABAMA," Journal of Regional Science 19:4 (November 1979), 437-448.

B-622 Cho, Yong Hyo, "FISCAL IMPLICATIONS OF ANNEXATION: THE CASE OF METROPOLITAN CENTRAL CITIES IN TEXAS," Land Economics 45:3 (August 1969), 368-371.

B-623 Cimino, Jo Ann Haskins, "'ALEX' PHILLIPS WAS A PIONEER TAMPA MER-CHANT," Sunland Tribune 7 (November 1981), 57-58.

B-624 "CITY IN PROFILE: NEW ORLEANS," Black Enterprise 2:10 (May 1972), 77-80.

B-625 Clark, John G., "THE ANTEBELLUM GRAIN TRADE OF NEW ORLEANS: CHANG-ING PATTERNS IN THE RELATION OF NEW ORLEANS WITH THE OLD NORTH-WEST," Agricultural History 38:3 (July 1964), 131-142.

B-626 Clark, John G., "NEW ORLEANS: ITS FIRST CENTURY OF ECONOMIC DEVEL-OPMENT," Louisiana History 10:1 (Winter 1969), 35-48.

B-627 Clark, Thomas D., "THE COUNTRY STORE IN POST-CIVIL WAR TENNESSEE," East Tennessee Historical Society's Publications No. 17 (1945), 3-21.

B-628 Clark, Thomas D., "THE POST-CIVIL WAR ECONOMY IN THE SOUTH," American Jewish Historical Quarterly 55:4 (June 1966), 424-433.

B-629 Cleland, Charles E., "MERCHANTS, TRADESMEN AND TENANTS: THE ECO-NOMICS OF DIFFUSION OF MATERIAL CULTURE ON A LATE NINETEENTH CEN-TURY SITE," Geoscience and Man 23 (April 1983), 35-44.

B-630 Coddington, Edwin B., "THE ACTIVITIES AND ATTITUDES OF A CONFED-ERATE BUSINESS MAN: GAZAWAY B. LAMAR," Journal of Southern History 9:1 (February 1943), 3-36.

B-631 Coerver, Don M. and Linda B. Hall, "NEIMAN-MARCUS: INNOVATORS IN FASHION AND MERCHANDISING," American Jewish Historical Quarterly 66:1 (September 1976), 123-136.

B-632 Cohen, Robert B., "MULTINATIONAL CORPORATIONS, INTERNATIONAL FINANCE, AND THE SUNBELT," in D. Perry, (ed.) The Rise of the Sunbelt Cities, (1978) pp. 211-226.

B-633 Coleman, Elizabeth Dabney, "RICHMOND'S FLOWERING SECOND MARKET," Virginia Cavalcade 4:4 (Spring 1955), 8-13.

B-634 Coleman, J. Winston, "LEXINGTON'S SLAVE DEALERS AND THEIR SOUTHERN TRADE," Filson Club History Quarterly 12:1 (January 1938), 1-23.

B-635 Cordle, Charles G., "THE BANK OF HAMBURG, SOUTH CAROLINA," Georgia Historical Quarterly 23:2 (June 1939), 148-153.

B-636 Crabb, Alfred L., "WILKINS TANNEHILL, BUSINESS AND CULTURAL LEAD-ER," Tennessee Historical Quarterly 7:4 (December 1948), 314-321.

B-637 Cramer, M. Richard, "SCHOOL DESEGREGATION AND NEW INDUSTRY: THE SOUTHERN COMMUNITY LEADERS' VIEWPOINT," Social Forces 41:4 (May 1963), 384-390.

B-638 Crisler, Robert M., "A DELIMITATION OF MAJOR TRADE AREAS IN LOUISI-ANA, ARKANSAS, AND MISSOURI," Southwestern Louisiana Journal 1:2 (April 1957), 111-118.

B-639 Crockett, Norman L., "THE OPENING OF OKLAHOMA: A BUSINESSMAN'S FRONTIER," Chronicles of Oklahoma 56:1 (Spring 1978), 85-95.

B-640 Crouse, Maurice, "GABRIEL MANEGAULT: CHARLESTON MERCHANT," South Carolina Historical Magazine 68:4 (October 1967), 220-231.

B-641 Cubby, Edwin A., "RAILROAD BUILDING AND THE RISE OF THE PORT OF HUNTINGTON," West Virginia History 33:3 (April 1972), 234-247.

B-642 Cuter, Addison T. and James E. Hansz, "COMPARATIVE ECONOMIC CONDI-TIONS IN POVERTY AREAS OF SELECTED CITIES," Journal of Regional Science 10:2 (August 1970), 243-251.

B-643 Dare, Robert, "INVOLVEMENT OF THE POOR IN ATLANTA," Phylon 31:2 (Summer 1970), 114-128.

B-644 Davidson, Lawrence S. and William A. Schaffer, "AN ECONOMIC-BASE MULTIPLIER FOR ATLANTA," Atlanta Economic Review 23:4 (July-August 1973), 52-54.

B-645 Davies, Christopher, "LIFE AT THE EDGE: URBAN AND INDUSTRIAL EVO-LUTION OF TEXAS FRONTIER WILDERNESS-FRONTIER SPACE, 1836-1986," Southwestern Historical Quarterly 89:4 (April 1986), 443-554.

B-646 Davis, Harold E., "HENRY W. GRADY, MASTER OF THE ATLANTA RING-- 1880-1886," Georgia Historical Quarterly 69:1 (Spring 1985), 1-38.

B-647 Davis, Howard W., "A CASE STUDY IN INDUSTRIAL LOCATION," Land Eco-nomics 45:4 (November 1969), 444-452.

B-648 Davis, Sid and Truman A. Hartshorn, "HOW DOES YOUR CITY GROW? THE CHANGING PATTERN OF ACTIVITY LOCATION IN THE ATLANTA METROPOLITAN AREA," Atlanta Economic Review 23:4 (July-August 1973), 4-13.

B-649 Davis, William W., "ANTE-BELLUM SOUTHERN COMMERCIAL CONVENTIONS," Transactions of the Alabama Historical Society 5 (1904), 153-202.

B-650 Deaton, Tom M., "THE CHAMBER OF COMMERCE IN THE ECONOMIC AND POLI-TICAL DEVELOPMENT OF ATLANTA FROM 1900 TO 1916," Atlanta Historical Journal 19:3 (1975), 19-33.

B-651 Dent, Borden D., "THE CHALLENGE TO DOWNTOWN SHOPPING," Atlanta Economic Review 28:1 (January February 1975), 29-33.

B-652 Dent, Borden D., "MAPPING REGIONAL SHOPPING CENTER TRADE VOLUMES IN ATLANTA, GEORGIA," Southeastern Geographer 12:2 (November 1972), 69-77.

B-653 Dent, Tom, "NEW ORLEANS VERSUS ATLANTA: POWER TO THE PARADE," Southern Exposure 7:1 (Spring 1979), 64-68.

B-654 Derks, Scott, "THE FIGHT TO UNIFY TENNESSEE'S TRI-CITIES," South Business 7:10 (October 1980) 42-47.

B-655 Dew, Lee A., "THE BLYTHEVILLE CASE AND REGULATION OF ARKANSAS COTTON SHIPMENTS," Arkansas Historical Quarterly 38:2 (Summer 1979), 116-130.

B-656 Dew, Lee A., "THE HOPE COTTON OIL COMPANY CASES: A QUESTION OF REASONABLENESS," Arkansas Historical Quarterly 39:3 (Winter 1980), 287-300.

B-657 Dew, Lee A., "THE OWENSBORO CATTLE CASES: A STUDY IN COMMERCE REGULATION," Filson Club History Quarterly 49:2 (April 1975), 195-203.

B-658 Dilisio, James, "THE MARYLAND STATE LOTTERY IN BALTIMORE: IS IT REGRESSIVE?" South Atlantic Urban Studies 5 (1981), 276-286.

B-659 Dillman, C. Daniel, "BROWNSVILLE: BORDER PORT FOR MEXICO AND THE U.S.," Professional Geographer 21:3 (May 1969), 178-183.

B-660 Dishman, P., "MARKETPLACE USA: DALLAS," Merchandising 2 (September 977), 51-58.

B-661 Dobkin, J. B., "TRAILS TO TAMPA BAY: A PHOTO ESSAY," Tampa Bay History 1:1 (1979), 24-30.

B-662 Donald, Jud G., "THE EFFECTS OF ZONING ON SINGLE-FAMILY RESIDENTIAL PROPERTY VALUES: CHARLOTTE, NORTH CAROLINA," Land Economics 56:2 (May 1980), 142-154.

B-663 Donaldson, Loraine and Raymond S. Strangways, "CAN GHETTO GROCERIES PRICE COMPETITIVELY AND MAKE A PROFIT?" Journal of Business 46:1 (January 1973), 61-65.

B-664 Donovan, William F. Jr., "REAL ESTATE SPECULATION IN CARDIFF AND HARRIMAN, 1890-1893," Tennessee Historical Quarterly 14:3 (September 1955), 253-256.

B-665 Dorsey, Rhoda M., "THE CONDUCT OF BUSINESS IN BALTIMORE, 1783-1785," Maryland Historical Magazine 55:3 (September 1960), 230-242.

B-666 Dorsey, Rhoda M., "THE PATTERN OF BALTIMORE COMMERCE DURING THE CONFEDERATION PERIOD," Maryland Historical Magazine 62:2 (Summer 1967), 119-134.

B-667 Doster, James F., "THE CHATTANOOGA ROLLING MILL: AN INDUSTRIAL BY-PRODUCT OF THE CIVIL WAR," East Tennessee Historical Society's Publications No. 36 (1964), 45-55.

B-668 Doster, James F., "TRADE CENTERS AND RAILROAD RATES IN ALABAMA 1873-1885: THE CASES OF GREENVILLE, MONTGOMERY, AND OPELIKA," Journal of Southern History 18:2 (May 1952), 169-192.

B-669 Downs, Dorothy, "COPPINGER'S TROPICAL GARDENS: THE FIRST COMMER-CIAL INDIAN VILLAGE IN FLORIDA," Florida Anthropologist 34:4 (December 1981), 225-231.

B-670 Duryea, Charles E., "THE RETAIL BUSINESS IN ATLANTA," The Horseless Age 24 (15 December 1909), n.p.

B-671 Eaddy, Elaine Y., "BROWNTOWN: EARLY INDUSTRY ON LYNCHES RIVER,"
       South Carolina Historical Magazine 80:3 (July 1979), 236-241.

B-672 Eader, Thomas S., "BALTIMORE ORGANS AND ORGAN BUILDING," Maryland
       Historical Magazine 65:3 (Fall 1970), 263-282.

B-673 Eberstein, Isaac W. and Omer R. Galle, "THE METROPOLITAN SYSTEM IN
       THE SOUTH: FUNCTIONAL DIFFERENTIATION AND TRADE PATTERNS," Social
       Forces 62:4 (June 1984), 926-940.

B-674 Ebert, Charles H.V., "FURNITURE MAKING IN HIGH POINT, NORTH CARO-
       LINA," North Carolina Historical Review 36:3 (July 1959), 330-339.

B-675 Eisterhold, John A., "CHARLESTON LUMBER AND TRADE IN A DECLINING
       SOUTHERN PORT," South Carolina Historical Magazine 74:2 (April
       1973), 61-72.

B-676 Eisterhold, John A., "LUMBER AND TRADE IN PENSACOLA AND WEST
       FLORIDA; 1800-1860," Florida Historical Quarterly 51:3 (January
       1973), 267-280.

B-677 Eisterhold, John A., "LUMBER AND TRADE IN THE LOWER MISSISSIPPI
       VALLEY AND NEW ORLEANS, 1800-1860," Louisiana History 13:1 (Winter
       1972), 71-92.

B-678 Eisterhold, John A., "MOBILE: LUMBER CENTER OF THE GULF COAST,"
       Alabama Review 26:2 (April 1973), 83-104.

B-679 Eisterhold, John A., "SAVANNAH: LUMBER CENTER OF THE SOUTH
       ATLANTIC," Georgia Historical Quarterly 57:4 (Winter 1973), 526-
       543.

B-680 Ellis, L. Tuffly, "THE NEW ORLEANS COTTON EXCHANGE: THE FORMATIVE
       YEARS, 1870-1880," Journal of Southern History 39:4 (November
       1973), 545-564.

B-681 Ellis, L. Tuffly, "THE REVOLUTIONIZING OF THE TEXAS COTTON TRADE,"
       Southwestern Historical Quarterly 73:4 (April 1970), 478-508.

B-682 Ellsworth, Lucias F., "RAIFORD AND ABERCROMBE: PENSACOLA'S PREMIER
       ANTEBELLUM MANUFACTURER," Florida Historical Quarterly 52:3
       (January 1975), 247-260.

B-683 Engerrand, Steven W., "BLACK AND MULATTO MOBILITY AND STABILITY IN
       DALLAS, TEXAS, 1880-1910," Phylon 39:3 (September 1978), 203-215.

B-684 Evans, Harry Howard, "JAMES ROBB, BANKER AND PIONEER RAILROAD
       BUILDER OF ANTE-BELLUM LOUISIANA," Louisiana Historical Quarterly
       23:1 (January 1940), 170-258.

B-685 Everett, Donald E., "SAN ANTONIO WELCOMES THE 'SUNSET'--1877,"
       Southwestern Historical Quarterly 65:1 (July 1961), 47-60.

B-686 Fabel, Robin F., "JAMES THOMPSON, PENSACOLA'S FIRST REALTOR,"
       Florida Historical Quarterly 61:1 (July 1983), 62-72.

B-687 Fallows, James, "HOUSTON: A PERMANENT BOOMTOWN," Atlantic 256:1
       (July 1985), 16-28.

B-688 Fanelli, Doris D., "WILLIAM POLK'S GENERAL STORE IN SAINT GEORGE'S,
       DELAWARE," Delaware History 19:4 (Fall-Winter 1981), 212-228.

B-689 Farris, Sara Guertler, "WILMINGTON'S MARITIME COMMERCE, 1775-1807,"
       Delaware History 14:1 (April 1970), 1-21.

B-690 Filante, Ronald W., "REGIONAL PATTERNS OF URBAN FINANCE: 1880-
       1890," Journal of Regional Science, 14:2 (August 1974), 269-272.

B-691 Fink, Paul M., "THE BUMPASS COVE MINES AND EMBREEVILLE," East Tennessee Historical Society's Publications 16 (1944), 48-64.

B-692 Firestine, Robert E., "ECONOMIC GROWTH AND INEQUALITY, DEMOGRAPHIC CHANGE, AND THE PUBLIC SECTOR RESPONSE," in D. Perry, ed., The Rise of the Sunbelt Cities, (1977), 191-210.

B-693 Fischer, LeRoy H., "THE FAIRCHILD WINERY," Chronicles of Oklahoma 55:2 (Summer 1977), 135-156.

B-694 Fisher, James S., "MANUFACTURING ADDITIONS IN GEORGIA: METROPOLITAN-NONMETROPOLITAN DIFFERENCES FROM 1961 TO 1975," Growth and Change 10:2 (April 1979), 9-16.

B-695 Fisher, James S. and Ronald L. Mitchelson, "EXTENDED AND INTERNAL COMMUTING IN THE TRANSFORMATION OF THE INTERMETROPOLITAN PERIPHERY," Economic Geography 57:3 (July 1981), 189-207.

B-696 Fisher, James S. and Sam Ock Park, "LOCATIONAL DYNAMICS OF MANUFACTURING IN THE ATLANTA METROPOLITAN REGION, 1968-1976," Southeastern Geographer 20:2 (November 1980), 100-119.

B-697 Fisher, Susan and Thomas L. Williams, "THE ECONOMICS OF INCORPORATION: AN EMPIRICAL STUDY," American Economist 28:2 (Fall 1984), 64-68.

B-698 Fishkind, Henry H., Jerome W. Meelman and Richard W. Ellson, "A PRAGMATIC ECONOMETRIC APPROACH TO ASSESSING ECONOMIC IMPACTS OF GROWTH OR DECLINE IN URBAN AREAS," Land Economics 54:4 (November 1978), 442-460.

B-699 Ford, Lacyk, "REDNECKS AND MERCHANTS: ECONOMIC DEVELOPMENT AND SOCIAL TENSIONS IN THE SOUTH CAROLINA UPCOUNTRY, 1865-1900," Journal of American History 71:2 (September 1984), 294-318.

B-700 Foscue, Edwin J., "GATLINBURG: A MOUNTAIN COMMUNITY," Economic Geography 21:3 (July 1945), 192-205.

B-701 Friedenberg, Howard L. and Roger A. Matson, "REGIONAL DELINEATION: DESIGNATION OF A DEVELOPMENT REGION FOR THE MID-SOUTH," Growth and Change 5:3 (July 1974), 41-46.

B-702 Fries, Adelaide L., "ONE HUNDRED YEARS OF TEXTILES IN SALEM," North Carolina Historical Review 27:1 (January 1950), 1-19.

B-703 Fuller, Justin, "ALABAMA BUSINESS LEADERS: 1865-1900, PART I," Alabama Review 16:4 (October 1963), 279-286.

B-704 Fuller, Justin, "ALABAMA BUSINESS LEADERS: 1865-1900, PART II," Alabama Review 17:1 (January 1964), 63-75.

B-705 Fuller, Justin, "BOOM TOWNS AND BLAST FURNACES: TOWN PROMOTION IN ALABAMA, 1885-1893," Alabama Review 29:1 (January 1976), 37-48.

B-706 Fuller, Justin, "HENRY F. DEBARDELEBEN, INDUSTRIALIST OF THE NEW SOUTH," Alabama Review 39:1 (January 1986), 3-18.

B-707 Galpin, W. Freeman, "THE GRAIN TRADE OF ALEXANDRIA, VIRGINIA, 1801-1815," North Carolina Historical Review 4:4 (October 1927), 404-427.

B-708 Galpin, W. Freeman, "THE GRAIN TRADE OF NEW ORLEANS," Mississippi Valley Historical Review 14:4 (March 1928), 496-507.

B-709 Garofalo, Charles Paul, "THE SONS OF HENRY GRADY: ATLANTA BOOSTEES IN THE 1920s," Journal of Southern History 42:2 (May 1976), 187-204.

B-710 Garrett, Jane N., "PHILADELPHIA AND BALTIMORE, 1790-1840," Maryland Historical Magazine 55:1 (March 1960), 1-15.

B-711 Gates, Grace Hooten, "ANNISTON: MODEL CITY AND RIVAL CITY," Alabama Review 31:1 (January 1978), 33-47.

B-712 Gates, Grace Hooten, "ANNISTON: TRANSITION FROM A COMPANY TOWN TO A PUBLIC TOWN," Alabama Review 37:1 (January 1984), 34-44.

B-713 Gayle, Charles Joseph, "THE NATURE AND VOLUME OF EXPORTS FROM CHARLESTON, 1724-1774," Proceedings of the South Carolina Historical Association 7 (1937), 25-33.

B-714 Gee, Wilson, "THE EFFECTS OF URBANIZATION ON AGRICULTURE," Southern Economic Journal 2:1 (May 1935), 3-15.

B-715 George, Paul S., "BROKERS, BINDERS, AND BUILDERS: GREATER MIAMI'S BOOM OF THE MID-1920s," Florida Historical Quarterly 65:1 (July 1986), 27-51.

B-716 George, Paul S., "PASSAGE TO THE NEW EDEN: TOURISM IN MIAMI FROM FLAGLER THROUGH ENERST G. SEWELL," Florida Historical Quarterly 59:4 (April 1981), 440-463.

B-717 German, R.H.L., "THE ECONOMIC DEVELOPMENT OF AUGUSTA IN THE GILDED AGE," Richmond County History 3:1 (Winter 1971), 5-20.

B-718 Germany, Richard H. L., "AUGUSTA ENTREPRENEURES, ARTISANS AND POLITICIANS," Richmond County History 5:2 (Summer 19073), 15-22.

B-719 Gilbert, Geoffrey, "MARITIME ENTERPRISE IN THE NEW REPUBLIC: INVESTMENT IN BALTIMORE SHIPPING, 1789-1793," Business History Review 58:1 (Spring 1984), 14-29.

B-720 Gilbert, Geoffrey, "THE SHIPS OF FEDERALIST BALTIMORE: A STATISTICAL PROFILE," Maryland Historical Magazine 79:4 (Winter 1984), 314-318.

B-721 Gilbert, Jess and Steve Brown, "ALTERNATIVE LAND REFORM PROPOSALS IN THE 1930s: THE NASHVILLE AGRARIANS AND THE SOUTHERN TENANT FARMERS' UNION," Agricultural History 55:4 (October 1981), 351-369.

B-722 Giovinazzo, Vincent J., "MEASURING CONVENTION IMPACT," Atlanta Economic Review 28:1 (January-February 1975), 37-42.

B-723 Glassman, James K., "NEW ORLEANS: I HAVE SEEN THE FUTURE AND IT'S HOUSTON," Atlantic 242:1 (July 1978), 10-18.

B-724 Good, Daniel B., "INDUSTRIAL PARK OCCUPANCY AND COMMUNITY SIZE IN EAST TENNESSEE," Southeastern Geographer 14:2 (November 1974), 121-132.

B-725 Goodall, Elizabeth J., "THE CHARLESTON INDUSTRIAL AREA: DEVELOPMENT, 1797-1937," West Virginia History 30:1 (October 1968), 358-412.

B-726 Goodrich, Carter and Harvey H. Segal, "BALTIMORE'S AID TO RAILROADS," Journal of Economic History 13:1 (Winter 1953), 2-35.

B-727 Goolsby, William C., "SATELLITE ECONOMETRIC MODELS FOR METROPOLITAN AREAS," South Atlantic Urban Studies 5 (1981), 246-275.

B-728 Green, Rodney D., "INDUSTRIAL TRANSITION IN THE LAND OF CHATTEL SLAVERY: RICHMOND, VIRGINIA, 1820-60," International Journal of Urban and Regional Research 8:2 (June 1984), 238-254.

B-729 Greene, Kenneth V., William B. Neenan and Claudia D. Scott, "FISCAL INCIDENCE IN THE WASHINGTON METROPOLITAN AREA," Land Economics 52:1 (February 1976), 13-31.

B-730 Griffin, J. David, "SAVANNAH'S CITY INCOME TAX," Georgia Historical Quarterly 50:2 (June 1966), 173-176.

B-731 Griffin, Richard W., "FLORENCE, ALABAMA: A TEXTILE MANUFACTURING CENTER OF THE OLD SOUTH, 1822-1871," North Alabama Historical Association Bulletin 2 (1957), 21-24.

B-732 Griffin, Richard W., "AN ORIGIN OF THE INDUSTRIAL REVOLUTION IN MARYLAND: THE TEXTILE INDUSTRY, 1789-1826," Maryland Historical Magazine 61:1 (Spring 1966), 24-36.

B-733 Haites, Erik F. and James Mak, "STEAMBOATING ON THE MISSISSIPPI, 1810-1860: A PURELY COMPETITIVE INDUSTRY," Business History Review 45:1 (1971), 52-78.

B-734 Hall, Linda, "NEIMAN-MARCUS: THE BEGINNING," Western States Jewish Historical Quarterly 7:2 (1975), 138-150.

B-735 Halsell, Willie D., "A VICKSBURG SPECULATOR AND PLANTER WITH THE YAZOO DELTA," Journal of Mississippi History 11:4 (October 1949), 231-242.

B-736 Hamer, Andrew M., "METROPOLITAN PLANNING AND THE LOCATION BEHAVIOR OF BASIC OFFICE FIRMS: A CASE STUDY," Review of Regional Studies 4:Supplement (1973), 34-45.

B-737 Hamilton, Neil A., "TENNESSEE VILLAGER IN A MODERN WORLD: G.S. LANNOM, JR., BASEBALL AND LEATHER ENTREPRENEUR," East Tennessee Historical Society Publications 54-55 (1982-83), 47-69.

B-738 Hancock, James E., "THE BALTIMORE CLIPPER AND THE STORY OF AN OLD BALTIMORE SHIPBUILDER," Maryland Historical Magazine 30:2 (June 1935), 138-148.

B-739 Hansen, Niles, "LOCATION PREFERENCE AND OPPORTUNITY COST: A SOUTH TEXAS PERSPECTIVE," Social Science Quarterly 63:3 (September 1982), 506-516.

B-740 Hardy, James D. Jr., "A SLAVE SALE IN ANTEBELLUM NEW ORLEANS," Southern Studies 23:3 (Fall 1984), 306-314.

B-741 Harmon, J.H. Jr., THE NEGRO AS A LOCAL BUSINESS MAN," Journal of Negro History 14:2 (April 1929), 116-155.

B-742 Harris, Malcolm H., "PORT TOWNS OF THE PAMUNKEY," William and Mary College Historical Magazine 23:1 (January 1943), 493-516.

B-743 Hartman, Margaret Strebel, "COVINGTON AND THE COVINGTON COMPANY," Register of the Kentucky Historical Society 69:2 (April 1971), 128-139.

B-744 Hartshorn, Truman A., "GETTING AROUND ATLANTA: NEW APPROACHES," Atlanta Economic Review 28:1 (January-February 1975), 43-51.

B-745 Harney, Katherine A., "WILLIAM ALEXANDER: A COMMISSION MERCHANT IN A NEW ROLE, 1837-43," Maryland Historical Magazine 71:1 (Spring 1976), 26-36.

B-746 Haskins, Ralph W., "PLANTER AND COTTON FACTOR IN THE OLD SOUTH: SOME AREAS OF FRICTION," Agricultural History 29:1 (January 1955), 1-14.

B-747 Hayes, Charles R. and Norman Schul, "SOME CHARACTERISTICS OF SHOPPING CENTERS," Professional Geographer 17:6 (November 1965), 11-14.

B-748 Hayes, Charles R. and Norman W. Schul, "WHY DO MANUFACTURERS LOCATE IN THE SOUTHERN PIEDMONT?" Land Economics 44:1 (February 1968), 117-121.

B-749 Hayward, Larry R., "F.E. MADDOX: CHAPLAIN OF PROGRESS, 1908," Arkansas Historical Quarterly 38:2 (Summer 1979), 146-166.

B-750 Hearden, Patrick J., "AGRICULTURAL BUSINESSMEN IN THE NEW SOUTH," Louisiana Studies 14:2 (Summer 1975), 145-159.

B-751 Heberle, Rudolf, "SOCIAL CONSEQUENCES OF THE INDUSTRIALIZATION OF SOUTHERN CITIES," Social Forces 27:1 (October 1948), 29-37.

B-752 Heite, Edward, "MARKETS AND PORTS," Virginia Cavalcade 16:2 (Autumn 1966), 29-41.

B-753 Heleniak, Roman, "LOCAL REACTION TO THE GREAT DEPRESSION IN NEW ORLEANS, 1929-1933," Louisiana History 10:4 (Fall 1969), 289-306.

B-754 Hemphill, W. Edwin, "IT GINGERED THEM UP, BUT THEY LET IT DOWN," Virginia Cavalcade 4:1 (Summer 1954), 39-42.

B-755 Hemphill, W. Edwin, "THREE HORSE TEAM," Virginia Cavalcade 3:2 (Autumn 1953), 8-9.

B-756 Henderson, Alexa Benson, "ALONZO F. HERNDON AND BLACK INSURANCE IN ATLANTA, 1904-1915," Atlanta Historical Journal 21:1 (Spring 1977), 34-47.

B-757 Henderson, William D., "'A GREAT DEAL OF ENTERPRISE': THE PETERS-BURG COTTON MILLS IN THE NINETEENTH CENTURY," Virginia Cavalcade 30:4 (Spring 1981), 176-185.

B-758 Henderson, William D., "RAPIDS AND POWER: THE APPOMATTOX RIVER AND ELECTRICAL POWER IN PETERSBURG, VIRGINIA," Virginia Cavalcade 27:4 (Spring 1978), 148-163.

B-759 Henderson, William Wallace, "THE NIGHT RIDERS' RAID ON HOPKINS-VILLE," Filson Club History Quarterly 24:4 (October 1950), 345-358.

B-760 Hendricks, Theodore W., "BALTIMORE'S GROWTH: THE ROLE OF THE RUSSIAN JEWS," Generations 3 (June 1982), 3-9.

B-761 Herbst, Lawrence A., "PATTERNS OF AMERICAN INTERREGIONAL COMMODITY TRADE: NORTH TO SOUTH, 1824-1839," American Economist 22:2 (Fall 1978), 61-66.

B-762 Hertzberg, Steven, "MAKING IT IN ATLANTA: ECONOMIC MOBILITY IN A SOUTHERN JEWISH COMMUNITY, 1870-1911," Yivo Annals of Jewish Social Science 17 (1978), 185-216.

B-763 Hess, Earl J., "CONFISCATION AND THE NORTHERN WAR EFFORT: THE ARMY OF THE SOUTHWEST AT HELENA," Arkansas Historical Quarterly 44:1 (Spring 1985), 56-75.

B-764 Higgins, W. Robert, "CHARLES TOWN MERCHANTS AND FACTORS DEALING IN THE EXTERNAL NEGRO TRADE, 1735-1775," South Carolina Historical Magazine 65:4 (October 1964), 205-217.

B-765 Hill, Forest G., "THE SOUTH'S ROLE AND OPPORTUNITY IN PROSPECTIVE NATIONAL GROWTH--," American Journal of Economics and Sociology 22:1 (January 1963), 141-147.

B-766 Hill, T. Arnold, "NEGROES IN SOUTHERN INDUSTRY," Annals of the American Academy of Political and Social Science 153 (January 1931), 170-181.

B-767 Hodge, David C., "BUSINESS AND INDUSTRY IN URBAN GEORGIA," Georgia Business 19:12 (June 1960), 1-7.

B-768 Hodge, Jo Dent, "THE LUMBER INDUSTRY IN LAUREL, MISSISSIPPI, AT THE TURN OF THE NINETEENTH CENTURY," Journal of Mississippi History 35:4 (November 1973), 361-379.

B-769 Hofsommer, Donovan L., "RAILROADS AND RICHES: THE BURKBURNETT BOOM," Great Plains Journal 14:1 (1974), 72-86.

B-770 Holbrook, Abigail Curlee, "COTTON MARKETING IN ANTEBELLUM TEXAS," Southwestern Historical Quarterly 73:4 (April 1970), 431-455.

B-771 Holly, J. Fred, "THE CO-OPERATIVE TOWN COMPANY OF TENNESSEE: A CASE STUDY OF PLANNED ECONOMIC DEVELOPMENT," East Tennessee Historical Society's Publications No. 36 (1964), 56-69.

B-772 Hon, Ralph C., "THE MEMPHIS POWER AND LIGHT DEAL," Southern Economic Journal 6:3 (January 1940), 344-375.

B-773 Hooks, Michael Q., "THE ROLE OF PROMOTERS IN URBAN RIVALRY: THE DALLAS-FORT WORTH EXPERIENCE, 1870-1910," Red River Valley Historical Review 7:2 (Spring 1982), 4-16.

B-774 Hopkins, Evelyn H., "A PROPOSED WATER MANAGEMENT PLAN FOR METROPOLITAN ATLANTA," Southeastern Geographer 25:2 (November 1985), 105-121.

B-775 Hopkins, Fred, "FOR FLAG OR PROFIT: THE LIFE OF COMMODORE JOHN DANIELS OF BALTIMORE," Maryland Historical Magazine 80:4 (Winter 1985), 392-401.

B-776 Horner, Dennis and Kingsley E. Haynes, "THE IMPACT OF NATURAL GROWTH CENTERS: AN EMPIRICAL INVESTIGATION IN WEST TEXAS," Review of Regional Studies 5:2 (Fall 1975), 84-97.

B-777 Howard, Ian McLeod, "THE SAVING OF SAVANNAH," Atlanta Economic Review 19:7 (July 1969), 10-14.

B-778 Hoyt, Homer, "ECONOMIC AND HOUSING SURVEY OF THE ORLANDO, FLORIDA METROPOLITAN REGION," Journal of Land & Public Utility Economics 23:2 (May 1947), 219-227.

B-779 Hughes, Melvin Edward, "WILLIAM J. HOWEY AND HIS FLORIDA DREAMS," Florida Historical Quarterly 66:3 (January 1988), 243-264.

B-780 Hula, Richard C., "THE ALLOCATION OF HOME CREDIT: MARKET VERSUS NONMARKET FACTORS," Journal of Urban Affairs 6:2 (Spring 1984), 151-165.

B-781 Huntley, Francis Carroll, "THE SEABORNE TRADE OF VIRGINIA IN MID-EIGHTEENTH CENTURY: PORT HAMPTON," Virginia Magazine of History and Biography 59:3 (July 1951), 297-308.

B-782 Ideson, Julia and Sanford W. Higginbotham, "A TRADING TRIP TO NATCHEZ AND NEW ORLEANS, 1822: DIARY OF THOMAS S. TEAS," Journal of Southern History 7:3 (August 1941), 378-399.

B-783 Jackson, Joy, "BOSSES AND BUSINESSMEN IN GUILDED AGE NEW ORLEANS POLITICS," Louisiana History 5:4 (Fall 1964), 387-400.

B-784 Joel, Richard, "A BRIEF HISTORY OF RICHES," Atlanta Historical Bulletin 7:27 (January-April 1942), 5-15.

B-785 Johnson, Arthur T., "ECONOMIC AND POLICY IMPLICAITONS OF HOSTING SPORTS FRANCHISES: LESSONS FROM BALTIMORE," Urban Affairs 21:3 (March 1986) 411-434.

B-786 Johnson, Ludwell H. III, "BLOCKADE OR TRADE MONOPOLY? JOHN A. DIX AND THE UNION OCCUPATION OF NORFOLK," Virginia Magazine of History and Biography 93:1 (January 1985), 54-78.

B-787 Jones, Barclay Gibbs, "APPLICATIONS OF CENTROGRAPHIC TECHNIQUES TO THE STUDY OF URBAN PHENOMENA: ATLANTA, GEORGIA, 1940-1975," Economic Geography 56:3 (July 1980), 201-222.

B-788 Jones, Donald Wade and Kingsley E. Haynes, "THE STRUCTURE AND SPAC-
ING OF INTRA-URBAN RETAILING: AUSTIN, TEXAS," Annals of Regional
Science 6:2 (December 1972), 117-138.

B-789 Jones, William S. and Dennis D. McConnell, "REINVESTMENT IN
ATLANTA," Urban Land 36 (June 1977), 22-25.

B-790 Johnson, David R., "SAN ANTONIO: THE VICISSITUDES OF BOOSTERISM,"
in R. Bernard ed., Sunbelt Cities; Politics and Growth Since World
War II, 1983, 235-254.

B-791 Johnson, Dudley S., "THE SOUTHERN EXPRESS COMPANY: A GEORGIA COR-
PORATION," Georgia Historical Quarterly 56:2 (Spring 1972), 224-
242.

B-792 Johnson, Keach, "THE BALTIMORE COMPANY SEEKS ENGLISH MARKETS: A
STUDY OF THE ANGLO-AMERICAN IRON TRADE, 1731-1755," William and
Mary Quarterly 16:1 (January 1959), 37-60.

B-793 ohnson, Keach, "THE GENESIS OF THE BALTIMORE IRONWORKS," Journal
of Southern History 19:2 (May 1953), 157-179.

B-794 Johnson, Kenneth R., "THE TROY CASE: A FIGHT AGAINST DISCRIMINA-
TORY FREIGHT RATES," Alabama Review 22:3 (July 1969), 175-187.

B-795 Jordan, Weymouth T., "ANTE-BELLUM MOBILE: ALABAMA'S AGRICULTURAL
EMPORIUM," Alabama Review 1:3 (July 1948), 180-202.

B-796 Jordan, Weymouth T., "COTTON PLANTERS' CONVENTIONS IN THE OLD
SOUTH," Journal of Southern History 19:3 (August 1953), 321-345.

B-797 Jumper, Sidney R., "A GEOGRAPHICAL ANALYSIS OF THE ATLANTA AND
COLUMBIA FRUIT AND VEGETABLE MARKETS," Memorandum Folio, Southeastern Division, Association of American Geographers, 13 (November
1961), 72-80.

B-798 Kaplan, Barry J., "HOUSTON: THE GOLDEN BUCKLE OF THE SUNBELT," in
R. Bernard, ed., Sunbelt Cities: Politics and Growth Since World
War II, 1983.

B-799 Kerr, William T., "BUSINESS RESPONSE TO URBAN NEEDS IN LATE NINE-
TEENTH CENTURY WILMINGTON: TWO CASE STUDIES," Delaware History
13:4 (October 1969), 257-282.

B-800 Keuchel, Edward F., "MASTER OF THE ART OF CANNING: BALTIMORE,
1860-1900," Maryland Historical Magazine 67:4 (Winter 1972), 351-
362.

B-801 Killick, J. R., "THE TRANSFORMATION OF COTTON MARKETING IN THE LATE
NINETEENTH CENTURY: ALEXANDER SPRUNT AND SON OF WILMINGTON, N. C.,
1866-1956," Business History Review 55:2 (Summer 1981), 143-169.

B-802 Killick, John R., "THE COTTON OPERATIONS OF ALEXANDER BROWN AND
SONS IN THE DEEP SOUTH, 1820," Journal of Southern History 43:2
(May 1977), 169-194.

B-803 Killick, John R., "RISK, SPECIALIZATION AND PROFIT OF THE MERCAN-
TILE SECTOR OF THE NINETEENTH CENTURY COTTON TRADE: ALEXANDER
BROWN AND SONS, 1820-80," Business History 16 (1964), 1-16.

B-804 King, John O., "THE EARLY TEXAS OIL INDUSTRY: BEGINNINGS AT
CORSICANA, 1894-1901," Journal of Southern History 32:4 (November
1966), 505-515.

B-805 Kossoff, Evan D., "SHREVEPORT, LA. HOOKS GENERAL MOTORS," South
Magazine 7:2 (February 1980), 55-57.

B-806 Kuykendal, James R., "THE HEYDAY OF DRUGSTORES IN ALABAMA," Alabama
Review 60:1 (January 1987), 3-12.

B-807 Labode, Errol, "TOURISM: THE MARKETING OF NEW ORLEANS," New
Orleans 15 (January 1981), 68 ff.

B-808 LahmeyerLobo, Eulalia Maria, "O COMERCEO ATLANTICO E A COMMUNIDADE
DE MERCADORES NO RIO DE JANEIRO E EM CHARLESTON NO SECULO XVIII,"
Revistia de Historia [BRAZIL] 51:101 (1975), 49-106.

B-809 Lancaster, Jane, "PIPER AIRCRAFT'S VERO BEACH PLANT: AN ANALYSIS
OF LOCATIONAL DETERMINANTS IN LIGHT AIRCRAFT MANUFACTURING,"
Southeastern Geographer 7 (1967), 22-33.

B-810 Lander, Ernest M. Jr.,. "CHARLESTON: MANUFACTURING CENTER OF THE
OLD SOUTH," Journal of Southern History 26:3 (August 1960), 330-
351.

B-811 Landreth, Pamela Sue, "SCOTTSVILLE: EARLY TRANSSHIPMENT CENTER FOR
PIEDMONT VIRGINIA," Virginia Geographer 7:1 (Spring-Summer 1972),
3-6.

B-812 Langley, C. John Jr., "ADVERSE IMPACTS OF THE WASHINGTON BELTWAY ON
RESIDENTIAL PROPERTY VALUES," Land Economics 52:1 (February 1976),
54-65.

B-813 Larios, Brother Avila F.S.C., "BROWNSVILLE-MATAMOROS: CONFEDERATE
LIFELINE," Mid-America 40:2 (April 1958), 67-91.

B-814 Laurent, E.A. and J.C. Hite, "ECONOMIC-ECOLOGIC LINKAGES AND
REGIONAL GROWTH: A CASE STUDY," Land Economics 48:1 (February
1972), 70-72.

B-815 Le Fave, Don, "TIME OF THE WHITETAIL: THE CHARLES TOWN INDIAN
TRADE, 1690-1715," Studies in History and Society 5:1 (1973), 5-15.

B-816 Leavenworth, Geoffrey, "HOUSTON: WILL IT CHOKE ON ITS OWN SUC-
CESS?" Texas Business (December 1980), 28-36.

B-817 Lehman, Paul, "THE EDWARDS FAMILY AND BLACK ENTREPRENEURIAL
SUCCESS," Chronicles of Oklahoma 64:4 (Winter 1986-87), 88-97.

B-818 Leinbach, Thomas R. and Robert G. Cromley, "APPALACHIAN KENTUCKY:
THE ROLE OF MANUFACTURING IN MICROPOLITAN DEVELOPMENT," Growth and
Change 13:3 (July 1982), 11-20.

B-819 Lewis, W. David and Wesley P. Newton, "DELTA MOVES TO ATLANTA,"
Atlanta Historical Journal 24:2 (Summer 1980), 7-16.

B-820 Lindley, James T. and Edward B. Selby Jr., "DIFFERENCES BETWEEN
BLACKS AND WHITES IN THE USE OF SELECTED FINANCIAL SERVICES,"
American Journal of Economics and Sociology 36:4 (October 1977),
393-399.

B-821 Linebeck, Neal G., "LOW-WAGE INDUSTRIALIZATION AND TOWN SIZE IN
RURAL APPALACHIA," Southeastern Geographer 12:1 (May 1972), 1-14.

B-822 Littlefield, Daniel F. Jr. and Lonnie E. Underhill, "KILDARE,
OKLAHOMA TERRITORY: STORY OF AN AGRICULTURAL BOOM TOWN," Great
Plains Journal 15:1 (Fall 1975), 28-54.

B-823 Livingood, James W., "CHATTANOOGA, TENNESSEE: ITS ECONOMIC HISTORY
IN THE YEARS IMMEDIATELY FOLLOWING APPOMATTOX," East Tennessee Historical Society's Publications No. 15 (1943), 35-48.

B-824 Lockman, William O., "AIRPORT INDUSTRIAL PARK: MEMPHIS, TENNESSEE:
A LOCATIONAL ANALYSIS," Memorandum Folio Southeastern Division Association of American Geographers 18 (November 1966), 116-119.

B-825 Logan, Frenise, "THE COLORED INDUSTRIAL ASSOCIATION OF NORTH
CAROLINA AND ITS FAIR OF 1886," North Carolina Historical Review
34:1 (January 1957), 58-67.

B-826 Logan, Frenise A., "THE ECONOMIC STATUS OF THE TOWN NEGRO IN POST-RECONSTRUCTION NORTH CAROLINA," North Carolina Historical Review 35:4 (October 1958), 448-460.

B-827 Lonsdale, Richard E. and Clyde E. Browing, "RURAL-URBAN LOCATIONAL PREFERENCES OF SOUTHERN MANUFACTURING," Annals of the Association of American Geographers 61:2 (June 1971), 255-268.

B-828 Lord, J. Dennis, "LOCATIONAL SHIFTS IN SUPERMARKET PATRONAGE," Professional Geographer 27:3 (August 1975), 310-314.

B-829 Losse, Winifred J., "THE FOREIGN TRADE OF VIRGINIA, 1789-1809," William and Mary Quarterly 1:2, (April 1944), 161-178.

B-830 "LOUISVILLE," Black Enterprise 2:17 (February 1972), 42-46.

B-831 Lovett, Bobby L., "SOME 1871 ACCOUNTS FOR THE LITTLE ROCK, ARKANSAS FREEDMAN'S SAVINGS AND TRUST COMPANY," 66:4 (Winter 1981-1982), 322-327.

B-832 Luce, W. Ray, "THE COHEN BROTHERS OF BALTIMORE: FROM LOTTERIES TO BANKING," Maryland Historical Magazine 68:3 (Fall 1973), 288-308.

B-833 Lyle, Royster Jr., "JOHN BLAIR LYLE OF LEXINGTON AND HIS 'AUTOMATIC BOOKSTORE,'" Virginia Cavalcade 21:2 (Autumn 1971), 20-28.

B-834 Lyle, Royster Jr., "ROCKBRIDGE COUNTY'S BOOM HOTELS," Virginia Cavalcade 20:3 (Winter 1971), 5-14.

B-835 McAdoo, Harriette Pipes, "STRATEGIES USED BY BLACK SINGLE MOTHERS AGAINST STRESS," Review of Black Political Economy 14:2-3 (Fall-Winter 1985-86), 153-166.

B-836 McAlexander, Hubert H., "FLUSH TIMES IN HOLLY SPRINGS," Journal of Mississippi History 48:1 (February 1986), 1-14.

B-837 McClendon, Bruce W., "REFORMING ZONE REGULATIONS TO ENCOURAGE ECONOMIC DEVELOPMENT: BEAUMONT, TEXAS," Urban Land 40:4 (April 1981), 3-7.

B-838 McClendon, Bruce W. and Ray Quay, "TARGETED ENERGY CONSERVATION STRATEGIES IN GALVESTON, TEXAS," Urban Land 39:6 (June 1980), 19-22.

B-839 McCoy, Drew R., "THE VIRGINIA PORT BILL OF 1784," Virginia Magazine of History and Biography 83:3 (July 1975), 288-303.

B-840 McElreath, Walter, "SIDNEY ROOT: MERCHANT PRINCE AND GREAT CITIZEN," Atlanta Historical Bulletin 7:29 (October 1944), 171-183.

B-841 McGrain, John W., "ENGLEHART CRUSE AND BALTIMORE'S FIRST STEAM MILL," Maryland Historical Magazine 71:1 (Spring 1976), 65-79.

B-842 McGregor, John R. and Robert H. Maxey, "THE DALTON, GEORGIA, TUFTED TEXTILE CONCENTRATION," Southeastern Geographer 14:2 (November 1974), 133-144.

B-843 McHenry, Stewart G., "LEBANESE PEDDLERS IN THE LOWER MISSISSIPPI RIVER VALLEY," Mississippi Geographer 7:1 (Spring 1979), 35-47.

B-844 McKenzie, Robert H., Warner O. Moore, and Jerry C. Oldshue, "BUSINESS SUCCESS AND LEADERSHIP IN ALABAMA: A PRELIMINARY INQUIRY," Alabama Historical Quarterly 43:4 (Winter 1981), 259-287.

B-845 McPheters, Lee R. and William B. Stronge, "CRIME AS AN ENVIRONMENTAL EXTERNALITY OF TOURISM: MIAMI, FLORIDA," Land Economics 50:3 (August 1974), 288-292.

B-846 McWilliams, Tennant S., "PETITION FOR EXPANSION: MOBILE BUSINESS-MEN AND THE CUBAN CRISIS, 1898," Alabama Review 27:1 (January 1975), 58-63.

B-847 Melosi, Martin V., "DALLAS-FORT WORTH: MARKETING THE METROPLEX," in R. Bernard, Sunbelt Cities: Politics and Growth Since World War II, 1983, pp. 162-195.

B-848 MacCord, Howard A., "TRADE GOODS FROM THE TRIGG SITE, RADFORD, VIRGINIA," Conference on Historic Site Archaeology, Papers (1975) 10:part 1 (March 1977), 60-68.

B-849 Mackle, Eliott, "TWO WAY STRETCH: SOME DICHOTOMIES IN THE ADVERTISING OF FLORIDA AS THE BOOM COLLAPSED," Tequesta No. 33 (1973), 17-29.

B-850 Mannard, Joseph G., "BLACK COMPANY TOWN: A PECULIAR INSTITUTION IN PIERCE, FLORIDA," Tampa Bay History 1:1 (Spring-Summer 1979), 61-66.

B-851 Marable, Manning, "POWER TO THE PEOPLE? ENERGY AND ECONOMIC UNDER-DEVELOPMENT OF BLACK PEOPLE AND THE 'NEW SOUTH,'" Black Books Bulletin 7:3 (1981), 8-13.

B-852 Marburg, Theodore F., "MANUFACTURER'S DRUMMER, 1852, WITH COMMENTS ON WESTERN AND SOUTHERN MARKETS," Bulletin of the Business Historical Society 22:3 (June 1948), 106-114.

B-853 Martin, Kenneth R., "WILMINGTON'S FIRST WHALING VOYAGE," Delaware History 16:2 (October 1974), 152-170.

B-854 Martin, Thomas P., ed., "THE ADVENT OF WILLIAM GREGG AND THE GRANITVILLE COMPANY," Journal of Southern History 11:3 (August 1945), 389-423.

B-855 Massey, Mary Elizabeth, "THE FREE MARKET OF NEW ORLEANS, 1861-1862," Louisiana History 3:3 (Summer 1962), 202-220.

B-856 Meier, August, "BOOKER T. WASHINGTON AND THE TOWN OF MOUND BAYOU," Phylon 15:4 (1954), 396-401.

B-857 Mercier, Laurie, "THE BUSINESS HISTORY OF JACKSON, TENNESSEE," West Tennessee Historical Society Papers No. 35 (1981), 95-102.

B-858 Merrill, James M., "CONFEDERATE SHIPBUILDING AT NEW ORLEANS," Journal of Southern History 28:1 (February 1962), 87-93.

B-859 Meyer, David R., "CONTROL AND COORDINATION LINKS IN THE METROPOLITAN SYSTEM OF CITIES: THE SOUTH AS CASE STUDY," Social Forces 63:2 (December 1984), 349-362.

B-860 Meyer, Gary C., "THE CALVERT CITY, KENTUCKY, INDUSTRIAL COMPLEX," Memorandum Folio, Southeastern Division Association of American Geographers 18 (November 1966), 147-152.

B-861 Miller, Ira J., "RESIDENTIAL SEGREGATION PATTERNS: ECONOMIC OR RACIAL," Review of Regional Studies 4:supplement (1974), 101-109.

B-862 Milz, Barbara, "LILY-TULIP JOINS THE GARDEN CITY," Augusta Magazine 11:2 (Summer 1984), 22-29.

B-863 Min, Pyong Gap, "FROM WHITE-COLLAR OCCUPATION TO SMALL BUSINESS: KOREAN IMMIGRANTS' OCCUPATIONAL ADJUSTMENT," Sociological Quarterly 25:3 (Summer 1984), 333-352.

B-864 Min, Pyong Gap and Charles Jaret, "ETHNIC BUSINESS SUCCESS: THE CASE OF KOREAN SMALL BUSINESS IN ATLANTA," Sociology and Social Research 69:3 (April 1985), 412-435.

B-865 Mintz, Leonora Ferguson, "THE WORLD'S ONE AND ONLY ROCKMART," Georgia Life 4:4 (1978), 16-19.

B-866 Mitchell, Harry A., "THE DEVELOPMENT OF NEW ORLEANS AS A WHOLESALE CENTER," Louisiana Historical Quarterly 27:4 (October 1944), 933-963.

B-867 Mohl, Raymond A., "CHANGING ECONOMIC PATTERNS IN THE MIAMI METRO-POLITAN AREA, 1940-1948," Tequestra No. 42 (1982), 63-73.

B-868 Moke, Irene A., "CANNING IN NORTHWESTERN ARKANSAS: SPRINGDALE, ARKANSAS," Economic Geography 28:2 (April 1952), 151-159.

B-869 Moore, Jamie W., "THE LOWCOUNTRY IN ECONOMIC TRANSITION: CHARLES-TON SINCE 1865," South Carolina Historical Magazine 80:2 (April 1979), 156-171.

B-870 Moore, John Hammond, "NO ROOM, NO RICE, NO GRITS: CHARLESTON'S 'TIME OF TROUBLE,' 1942-1944," South Atlantic Quarterly 85:1 (Winter 1986), 23-31.

B-871 Moore, W.O. Jr., "THE LARGEST EXPORTERS OF DEERSKINS FROM CHARLES TOWN, 1735-1775," South Carolina Historical Magazine 74:3 (July 1973), 144-150.

B-872 Moore, William H., "PREOCCUPIED PATERNALISM: THE ROANE IRON COM-PANY IN HER COMPANY TOWN--ROCKWOOD, TENNESSEE," East Tennessee Historical Society's Publications No. 39 (1967), 56-70.

B-873 Moss, B. G., "COOPERVILLE: IRON CAPITAL OF SOUTH CAROLINA," South Carolina History Illustrated 1:2 (May 1970), 32-35, 64-65.

B-874 "MOUND BAYOU," Black Enterprise 3:5 (December 1972), 37-40.

B-875 Muller, Edward K., "SPATIAL ORDER BEFORE INDUSTRIALIZATION: BALTI-MORE'S CENTRAL DISTRICT, 1833-1860," Working Papers from the Regional Economic History Research Center 4 (1981), 100-140.

B-876 Muller, Edward K. and Paul A. Groves, "THE EMERGENCE OF INDUSTRIAL DISTRICTS IN MID-NINETEENTH CENTURY BALTIMORE," Geographical Review 69:2 (April 1979), 159-178.

B-877 Mullis, Sharon M., "EXTRAVAGANZA OF THE NEW SOUTH: THE COTTON STATES AND THE INTERNATIONAL EXPOSITION, 1895," Atlanta Historical Bulletin 20:3 (Fall 1976), 17-36.

B-878 Murphy, Raymond E., "A SOUTHERN WEST VIRGINIA MINING COMMUNITY," Economic Geography 9:1 (January 1933), 51-59.

B-879 Murray, Malcolm A., "ENERGY USE PATTERNS IN GEORGIA AS THEY RELATE TO POPULATION, URBANIZATION, AND QUALITY OF LIFE," Southeastern Geographer 22:1 (May 1982), 20-34.

B-880 Nash, William W. Jr., "GUESSING ABOUT ATLANTA'S FUTURE," Atlanta Economic Review 28:1 (January-February 1975), 22-28.

B-881 Nathan, Joseph H., "TOWN BUILDING: THE CASE OF SHEFFIELD, ALA-BAMA," Journal of Muscle Shoals History 3 (1975), 65-74.

B-882 Nelson, Irene J., "OPPORTUNITIES FOR GEOGRAPHICAL RESEARCH ON THE ROLE OF THE NEGRO IN THE SOUTHERN ECONOMY," Southeastern Geographer 11:2 (November 1971), 145-148.

B-883 Nelson, Richard Alan, "PALM TREES, PUBLIC RELATIONS, AND PROMOTERS: BOOSTING SOUTHEAST FLORIDA AS A MOTION PICTURE EMPIRE, 1910-1930," Florida Historical Quarterly 61:4 (April 1983), 383-403.

B-884 Niemi, Albert W. Jr., "STRUCTURAL SHIFTS IN SOUTHERN MANUFACTURING, 1849-1899," Business History Review 45 (1971), 78-84.

B-885 Noland, E. William, "INDUSTRY COMES OF AGE IN THE SOUTH," Social
      Forces 32:1 (October 1953), 28-35.

B-886 Ogburn, William F., "DOES IT COST LESS TO LIVE IN THE SOUTH?"
      Social Forces 14:2 (December 1935), 211-214.

B-887 Olson, James S. and Liz Byford, "OASIS IN EAST TEXAS: CONROE AND
      THE DEPRESSION, 1929-1933," Texana 12:2 (Summer 1974), 141-148.

B-888 Orr, Douglas M. Jr., "THE GILBERT AND BARKER MANUFACTURING COMPANY:
      AN INDUSTRIAL RELOCATION," Southeastern Geographer 7(1967), 13-21.

B-889 Osterbind, Carter C. and George B. Hurff, "VARIATIONS IN COSTS OF
      MORTGAGE FINANCING TO VETERANS IN JACKSONVILLE," Land Economics
      30:1 (February 1954), 64-71.

B-890 Oyebanji, Joshua O., "SUBURBAN GROWTH AND REGIONAL SHOPPING CENTER
      DEVELOPMENT IN NORTHERN VIRGINIA," Virginia Social Science Journal
      12:1 (April 1977), 1-11.

B-891 Perry, David C. and Alfred J. Watkins, "PEOPLE AND THE RISE OF THE
      SUNBELT CITIES," in R. Bernard, The Rise of the Sunbelt Cities,
      Politics and Growth Since World War II, (1983), 277-305.

B-892 Paisley, Clifton, "TALLAHASSEE THROUGH THE STOREBOOKS, 1843-1863:
      ANTEBELLUM COTTON PROSPERITY," Florida Historical Quarterly 50:2
      (October 1971), 111-127.

B-893 Paisley, Clifton, "TALLAHASSEE THROUGH THE STOREBOOKS: WAR CLOUDS
      AND WAR, 1860-1863," Florida Historical Quarterly 51:1 (July 1972),
      37-51.

B-894 Paisley, Clifton, "TALLAHASSEE THROUGH THE STOREBOOKS: ERA OF
      RADICAL RECONSTRUCTION, 1867-1877," Florida Historical Quarterly
      53:1 (July 1974), 49-65.

B-895 Paisley, Clifton L., VAN BRUNT'S STORE, IAMONIA, FLORIDA, 1902-
      1911," Florida Historical Quarterly 48:4 (April 1970), 353-367.

B-896 Pancake, John S., "BALTIMORE AND THE EMBARGO: 1807-1809," Maryland
      Historical Magazine 47:3 (September 1952), 173-187.

B-897 Parkins, A. E., "PROFILES OF THE RETAIL BUSINESS SECTION OF NASH-
      VILLE, TENN., AND THEIR INTERPRETATION," Annals of the American
      Association of Geographers 20:1 (March 1930), 164-176.

B-898 Parks, Joseph H., "A CONFEDERATE TRADE CENTER UNDER FEDERAL OCCUPA-
      TION: MEMPHIS, 1862 TO 1865," Journal of Southern History 7:3
      (August 1941), 289-314.

B-899 Parramore, Thomas C., "THE BARTONS OF BARTONSVILLE," North Carolina
      Historical Review 51:1 (Winter 1974), 22-40.

B-900 Paul, Charles L., "FACTORS IN THE ECONOMY OF COLONIAL BEAUFORT,"
      North Carolina Historical Review 44:2 (Spring 1967), 111-134.

B-901 Pelzman, Joseph, "FORECASTING WATERBORNE EXPORTS WITH ALTERNATIVE
      REGIONAL ECONOMIC MODELS: A STATISTICAL ANALYSIS BASED ON THE
      CHARLESTON PORT," Review of Regional Studies 8:1 (Spring 1978), 97-
      106.

B-902 Perkins, Edwin J., "FINANCING ANTEBELLUM IMPORTEES: THE ROLE OF
      BROWN BROS. AND CO. IN BALTIMORE," Business History Review 45:4
      (Winter 1971), 421-451.

B-903 Persky, Joseph, "THE DOMINANCE OF THE RURAL-INDUSTRIAL SOUTH, 1900-
      1930," Journal of Regional Science 13:3 (December 1973), 409-420.

B-904 Petrof, John V., "ATTITUDES OF THE URBAN POOR TOWARD THEIR NEIGH-
      BORHOOD SUPERMARKETS," Phylon 31:3 (Fall 1970), 290-301.

B-905 Petrof, John V., "READERSHIP STUDY OF THE INFLUENCE OF PRINTED
      COMMERCIAL MESSAGES ON NEGRO READERS IN ATLANTA, GEORGIA," Phylon
      28:4 (Winter 1967), 399-407.

B-906 Phillips, Horace P., "THE BONDED DEBT OF NEW ORLEANS 1822 TO 1920
      INCLUSIVE," Louisiana Historical Quarterly 3:4 (October 1920), 596-
      611.

B-907 Phillips, William H., "SOUTHERN TEXTILE MILL VILLAGES ON THE END OF
      WORLD WAR II: THE COURTENAY MILL OF SOUTH CAROLINA," Journal of
      Economic History 45:2 (June 1985), 269-276.

B-908 Powers, R. Thomas, "MIAMI/DADE MARKET CONDITIONS AND TRENDS," Urban
      Land 43:9 (September 1983), 8-11.

B-909 Preston, Howard L., "THE AUTOMOBILE BUSINESS IN ATLANTA, 1909-1920:
      A SYMBOL OF 'NEW SOUTH' PROSPERITY," Georgia Historical Quarterly
      58:2 (Summer 1974), 262-277.

B-910 Primeaux, Walter J., "THE DECLINE IN ELECTRIC UTILITY COMPETITION,"
      Land Economics 51:2 (May 1975), 144-148.

B-911 Provine, Dorothy, "THE ECONOMIC POSITION OF FREE BLACKS IN THE
      DISTRICT OF COLUMBIA, 1800-1860," Journal of Negro History 58:1
      (January 1973), 61-72.

B-912 Provine, W. A., "LARDNER CLARK, NASHVILLE'S FIRST MERCHANT AND
      FOREMOST CITIZEN," (Part 1), Tennessee Historical Magazine 3:1
      (March 1917), 28-50.

B-913 Provine, W.A., LARDNER CLARK, NASHVILLE'S FIRST MERCHANT AND
      FOREMOST CITIZEN," (Part 2), Tennessee Historical Magazine 3:2
      (June 1917), 115-133.

B-914 Prunty, Merle C. and Carl F. Ojala, "LOCATIONAL STABILITY FACTORS
      IN THE MEN'S APPAREL INDUSTRY IN THE SOUTHEAST," Southeastern
      Geographer 14:2 (November 1974), 106-120.

B-915 Purse, Thomas, "FUTURE OF THE SOUTH ATLANTIC PORTS," Annals of the
      American Academy of Political and Social Science 35:1 (January
      1910), 120-123.

B-916 Pusey, William Allen, "GRAHAMTON AND THE EARLY TEXTILE MILLS OF
      KENTUCKY," Filson Club History Quarterly 5:1 (January 1931), 123-
      135.

B-917 Quenzel, Carroll H., "THE MANUFACTURE OF LOCOMOTIVES AND CARS IN
      ALEXANDRIA IN THE 1850's," Virginia Magazine of History and Bio-
      graphy 62:2 (April 1954), 181-189.

B-918 Rachal, William M. E., "WHEN VIRGINIA OWNED A SHIPYARD," Virginia
      Cavalcade 2:2 (Autumn 1952), 31-35.

B-919 Rainard, R. Lyn, "READY CASH ON EASH TERMS: LOCAL RESPONSES TO THE
      DEPRESSION IN LEE COUNTY," Florida Historical Quarterly 64:3
      (1986), 284-300.

B-920 Ratchford, Benjamin Ulysses, "TOWARD PRELIMINARY SOCIAL ANALYSIS:
      II. ECONOMIC ASPECTS OF THE GASTONIA SITUATION," Social Forces 8:3
      (March 1930), 359-367.

B-921 Rees, John, "MANUFACTURING HEADQUARTERS IN A POST-INDUSTRIAL URBAN
      CONTEXT," Economic Geography 54:4 (October 1978), 337-354.

B-922 Reilly, John G., "TYSON & JONES BUGGY COMPANY: THE HISTORY OF A
      SOUTHERN CARRIAGE WORKS," North Carolina Historical Review 46:3
      (Summer 1969), 201-213.

B-923 Reinders, Robert C., "THE FREE NEGRO IN THE NEW ORLEANS ECONOMY,
      1850-1860," Louisiana History 6:3 (Summer 1965), 273-286.

B-924 Reinecke, John A. and Caroline Fisher, "THE ECONOMIC IMPACT OF THE
      PORT OF NEW ORLEANS," Louisiana Business Survey 12 (January 1981),
      4-7.

B-925 Ricci, James M., "BOASTERS, BOOSTERS AND BOOM: POPULAR IMAGES OF
      FLORIDA IN THE 1920's," Tampa Bay History 6:2 (Fall-Winter 1984),
      31-57.

B-926 Richter, Wendy, "THE IMPACT OF THE CIVIL WAR ON HOT SPRINGS, ARKAN-
      SAS," Arkansas Historiucal Quarterly 43:2 (Summer 1984), 125-142.

B-927 Ridgeway, Whitman H., "MARYLAND COMMUNITY LEADERS AND ECONOMIC
      DEVELOPMENT, 1793-1836," Working Papers from the Regional Economic
      History Research Center 2:2 (1978), 1-24.

B-928 Riggs, David, "CHARLES CONWAY FLOWERREE (1842-1929): VICKSBURG
      COLONEL AND ENTERPRENEUR," Journal of Mississippi History 46:3
      (August 1984), 163-178.

B-929 Roberson, Jere W., "THE MEMPHIS COMMERCIAL CONVENTION OF 1853:
      SOUTHERN DREAMS AND 'YOUNG AMERICA,'" Tennessee Historical
      Quarterly 33:3 (Fall 1974), 279-298.

B-930 Roberts, Derrell C., "JOSEPH E. BROWN AND THE FAILURE OF ATLANTA'S
      CITIZEN'S BANK," Atlanta Historical Journal 13:4 (December 1968),
      42-45.

B-931 Robertson, James I., "THE DEVELOPMENT OF THE FUNERAL BUSINESS IN
      GEORGIA, 1900-1957," Georgia Review 13:1 (Spring 1959), 86-96.

B-932 Roeder, Robert E., "MERCHANTS OF ANTE-BELLUM NEW ORLEANS,"
      Explorations in Entrepreneurial History 10 (1958), 113-122.

B-933 Rose, Warren, "CATALYST OF AN ECONOMY: THE HOUSTON SHIP CHANNEL,"
      Land Economics 43:1 (February 1967), 32-43.

B-934 Rothstein, Morton, "SUGAR AND SECESSION: A NEW YORK FIRM IN ANTE-
      BELLUM LOUISIANA," Explorations in Entrepreneurial History 5:2
      (Winter 1968), 115-131.

B-935 Rugg, Dean S., "THE COMPARATIVE ASPECTS OF THE URBAN GEOGRAPHY OF
      ALEXANDRIA, VIRGINIA, AND BAD GODESBURG, WEST GERMANY," Economic
      Geography 41:2 (April 1945), 157-181.

B-936 Rutherford, Harry, "TUPELO--FIRST TVA CITY," Tennessee Valley
      Perspective 3:3 (Spring 1973), 31-35.

B-937 Ryan, John B. Jr., "WILLARD WARNER AND THE RISE AND FALL OF THE
      IRON INDUSTRY IN TECUMSEH, ALABAMA," Alabama Review 24:4 (October
      1971), 261-279.

B-938 Ryant, Carl G., "THE SOUTH AND THE MOVEMENT AGAINST CHAIN STORES,"
      Journal of Southern History 39:2 (May 1973), 207-222.

B-939 Saltow, James H., "THE ROLE OF WILLIAMSBURG IN THE VIRGINIA ECON-
      OMY, 1750-1775," William and Mary Quarterly 4:4 (October 1958),
      467-482.

B-940 Sauder, Robert A., "MUNICIPAL MARKETS IN NEW ORLEANS," Journal of
      Cultural Geography 2:1 (Fall-Winter 1981), 82-95.

B-941 Sauder, Robert A., "THE ORIGIN AND SPREAD OF THE PUBLIC MARKET SYS-
TEM IN NEW ORLEANS," Louisiana History 22:3 (Summer 1981), 281-298.

B-942 Saunders, Robert J., "POPULATION FLOWS, SPATIAL ECONOMIC ACTIVITY,
AND URBAN AREAS IN APPALACHIA," Annals of Regional Science 5:1
(June 1971), 125-136.

B-943 Savage, V. Howard, "THE INTERDEPENDENCE OF THE SAN ANTONIO ECONOMIC
STRUCTURE AND THE DEFENSE ESTABLISHMENT," Land Economics 50:4
(November 1974), 374-379.

B-944 Schaffer, Daniel, "WAR MOBILIZATION IN MUSCLE SHOALS, ALABAMA,
1917-1918," Alabama Review 39:2 (April 1986), 110-146.

B-945 Schenker, Eric, "SOUTHERN STATE PORT AUTHORITIES AND FLORIDA," Land
Economics 35:1 (February 1959), 35-47.

B-946 Schmier, Louis E., "THE MAN FROM GEHAR," Atlanta Historical Journal
23:3 (Fall 1979), 91-106.

B-947 Schnable, Richard T., "MARYVILLE-ALCOA, BLOUNT COUNTY'S URBAN AREA
MOVES AHEAD," Tennessee Planner (Summer 1967), 114-124.

B-948 Schul, Norman W. and Charles R. Hayes, "SPATIAL ASPECTS OF THE RE-
TAIL CORE: THE CASE OF GREENSBORO, NORTH CAROLINA," Southeastern
Geographer 5 (1965), 1-14.

B-949 Schweikart, Larry, "TENNESSEE BANKS IN THE ANTEBELLUM PERIOD, PART
I," Tennessee Historical Quarterly 45:2 (Summer 1986), 119-132.

B-950 Schweikart, Larry, "TENNESSEE BANKS IN THE ANTEBELLUM PERIOD: PART
II," Tennessee Historical Quarterly 15:3 (Fall 1986), 199-209.

B-951 Scott, Carole E., "COPING WITH INFLATION: ALTANTA 1860-1865,"
Georgia Historical Quarterly 69:4 (Winter 1985), 536-556.

B-952 Seymour, Davis R. and Frederick J. Hekein, "RELATIONSHIP BETWEEN
INCOME DISTRIBUTION AND URBAN STRUCTURAL CHANGES IN DALLAS, TEXAS,"
Annals of Regional Science 6:1 (June 1972), 61-78.

B-953 Shank, George K., "MERIDIAN: A MISSISSIPPI CITY AT BIRTH DURING
THE CIVIL WAR, AND IN RECONSTRUCTION," Journal of Mississippi History 26:4 (November 1964), 275-282.

B-954 Sharrer, G. Terry, "FLOUR MILLING IN THE GROWTH OF BALTIMORE, 1750-
1830," Maryland Historical Magazine 71:3 (Fall 1976), 322-333.

B-955 Sharrer, G. Terry, "THE MERCHANT MILLERS: BALTIMORE'S FLOUR MILL-
ING INDUSTRY, 1783-1860," Agricultural History 56:1 (January 1982),
138-150.

B-956 Shepherd, Samuel C. Jr., "A GLIMMER OF HOPE: THE WORLD'S INDUS-
TRIAL AND COTTON CENTENNIAL EXPOSITION, NEW ORLEANS, 1884-1885,"
Louisiana History 26:3 (Summer 1985), 271-290.

B-957 Shick, Tom W. and Don H. Doyle, "THE SOUTH CAROLINA PHOSPHATE BOOM
AND THE STILLBIRTH OF THE NEW SOUTH, 1867-1920," South Carolina
Historical Magazine 86:1 (January 1985), 1-31.

B-958 Shipley, Ellen Compton, "THE ARKANSAS LUMBER COMPANY IN WARREN,
BRADLEY COUNTY," Arkansas Historical Quarterly 46:1 (Spring 1987),
60-68.

B-959 Short, James R., "MEET ME AT PENDEE'S," Virginia Cavalcade 3:3
(Winter 1953), 44-47.

B-960 Sibley, Marilyn McAdams, "AUSTIN'S FIRST NATIONAL AND THE ERRANT
TELLER," Southwestern Historical Quarterly 74:4 (April 1971), 478-
506.

B-961 Siener, William H., "CHARLES YATES, THE GRAIN TRADE, AND ECONOMIC DEVELOPMENT IN FREDERICKSBURG, VIRGINIA, 1750-1810," Virginia Magazine of History and Biography 73:4 (October 1985), 409-426,

B-962 Simon, Richard M., "MILL VILLAGE AND COAL TOWN COMPARED: A REVIEW ESSAY," Appalachian Journal 8:1 (Autumn 1980), 67-71.

B-963 Sisco, Paul H., "GEOGRAPHIC TRAINING AND METHOD APPLIED TO TRADE AREA ANALYSIS OF LOCAL SHOPPING CENTERS," Journal of Geography 56:5 (May 1957), 201-212.

B-964 Sisk, Glenn, "POST-WAR VIGOR AND INDUSTRY IN THE ALABAMA BLACK BELT," Mississippi Quarterly 12:2 (Spring 1959), 90-96.

B-965 Sisk, Glenn N., "TOWN BUSINESS IN THE ALABAMA BLACK BELT," Mid-America 38:1 (January 1956), 47-55.

B-966 Sitterson, J. Carlyle, "FINANCING AND MARKETING THE SUGAR CROP OF THE OLD SOUTH," Journal of Southern History 10:2 (May 1944), 188-199.

B-967 Smith, George Winston, "COTTON FROM SAVANNAH IN 1865," Journal of Southern History 21:4 (November 1955), 495-512.

B-968 Smith, Julia F., "COTTON AND THE FACTORAGE SYSTEM IN ANTEBELLUM FLORIDA," Florida Historical Quarterly 49:1 (July 1970), 36-48.

B-969 Smith, Robert S., "MILL ON THE DAN: RIVERSIDE COTTON MILLS, 1882-1901," Journal of Southern History 21:1 (February 1955), 38-66.

B-970 Sollins, Helen B. and Moses Aberbach, "THE BALTIMORE SPICE COMPANY," Generations 3 (June 1982), 10-22.

B-971 Somers, Dale, "BLACK AND WHITE IN NEW ORLEANS: A STUDY IN URBAN RACE RELATIONS, 1865-1900," Journal of Southern History 40:1 (February 1974), 19-42.

B-972 Somers, Dale A. (ed.), "NEW ORLEANS AT WAR: A MERCHANT'S VIEW," Louisiana History 14:1 (Winter 1973), 49-68.

B-973 Spencer, C.A., "BLACK BENEVOLENT SOCIETIES IN THE DEVELOPMENT OF BLACK INSURANCE COMPANIES IN NINETEENTH CENTURY ALABAMA," Phylon 46:3 (September 1985), 251-261.

B-974 Sprague, Stuart Seely, "ALABAMA AND THE APPALACHIAN AND COAL TOWN BOOM, 1889-1893," Alabama Historical Quarterly 37:2 (Summer 1975), 85-91.

B-975 Sprague, Stuart Seely, "ALABAMA TOWN PRODUCTION DURING THE ERA OF GOOD FEELINGS," Alabama Historical Quarterly 36:1 (Spring 1974), 15-20.

B-976 Sprague, Stuart Seely, "THE GREAT APPALACHIAN IRON AND COAL TOWN BOOM OF 1889-1893," Appalachian Journal 4:3, 4 (Spring-Summer 1977), 216-223.

B-977 Steel, Edward M. Jr., "FLUSH TIMES IN BRUNSWICK, GEORGIA IN THE 1830s," Georgia Historical Quarterly 39:3 (September 1955), 221-239.

B-978 Steel, William, "DISCRIMINATION IN SUPERMARKET PRICES AND LOCATION NASHVILLE," Review of Black Political Economyy 4:2 (Winter 1974), 19-34.

B-979 Steffen, Charles G., "CHANGES IN THE ORGANIZATION OF ARTESAN PRODUCTION IN BALTIMORE, 1790 TO 1820," William and Mary Quarterly 36:1 (January 1979), 101-117.

B-980 Steiner, W. H., "CHANGING COMPOSITION OF THE SAVANNAH BUSINESS COMMUNITY 1900–1940," Southern Economic Journal 10:4 (April 1944), 303–310.

B-981 Stephens, Paula, "DOWNTOWN FINALLY LOOKS UP," Business Atlanta 15:11 (November 1986), 84–92.

B-982 Stephenson, Wendell H., "ANTE-BELLUM NEW ORLEANS AS AN AGRICULTURAL FOCUS," Agricultural History 15:4 (October 1941), 161–174.

B-983 Sternberg, Irma O., "MEMPHIS MERCHANT FOR MORE THAN SIXTY YEARS: MY FATHER, "UNCLE" IKE OTTENHEIMER," West Tennessee Historical Society Papers No. 35 (1981), 122–127.

B-984 Stockham, Richard J., "ALABAMA IRON FOR THE CONFEDERACY: THE SELMA WORKS," Alabama Review 21:3 (July 1968), 163–172.

B-985 Stone, Alfred H., "THE COTTON FACTORAGE SYSTEM OF THE SOUTHERN STATES," American Historical Review 20:3 (April 1915), 557–565.

B-986 Stone, James H., "ECONOMIC CONDITIONS IN MACON, GEORGIA, IN THE 1830's," Georgia Historical Quarterly 54:2 (Summer 1970), 209–225.

B-987 Stone, James H., THE ECONOMIC DEVELOPMENT OF HOLLY SPRINGS DURING THE 1840's," Journal of Mississippi History 32:4 (November 1970), 341–362.

B-988 Stuart, Alfred W., "THE SUBURBANIZATION OF MANUFACTURING IN SMALL METROPOLITAN AREAS: A CASE STUDY OF ROANOKE, VIRGINIA," Southeastern Geographer 8 (1968), 23–38.

B-989 Stumpf, Stuart O., "A CASE OF ARRESTED DEVELOPMENT: CHARLES TOWN'S COMMERCIAL LIFE, 1670–1690," Southern Studies 20:4 (Winter 1981), 61–377.

B-990 Stumpf, Stuart O., "IMPLICATIONS OF KING GEORGE'S WAR FOR THE CHARLESTON MERCHANTILE COMMUNITY," South Carolina Historical Magazine 77:3 (July 1976), 161–188.

B-991 Stumpf, Stuart O., "TRENDS IN CHARLESTON'S INTER-REGIONAL IMPORT TRADE, 1735–1764," Southern Studies 23:3 (Fall 1984), 243–265.

B-992 Surratt, Jerry L., "THE MORAVIAN AS BUSINESSMAN: GOTTLIEB SCHOBER OF SALEM," North Carolina Historical Review 60:1 (January 1983), 1–23.

B-993 Sweat, Dan E., "DOWNTOWN ATLANTA: WHERE IT ALL COMES TOGETHER," Urban Georgia 33:4 (May 1983), 25, 27.

B-994 Tansey, Richard, "BERNARD KENDIG AND THE NEW ORLEANS SLAVE TRADE," Louisiana History 23:2 (Spring 1982), 159–178.

B-995 Tarpley, Fred A. Jr., L.S. Davidson, and D.D. Clark, "FLIGHT TO THE FRINGES: AN EMPIRICAL STUDY OF OFFICE DECENTRALIZATION IN ATLANTA, GEORGIA," Review of Regional Studies 1 (1969), 117–140.

B-996 Tarter, Brent, "'AN INFANT BOROUGH ENTIRELY SUPPORTED BY COMMERCE': THE GREAT FIRE OF 1776 AND THE REBUILDING OF NORFOLK," Virginia Cavalcade 28:2 (Autumn 1978), 52–61.

B-997 Taylor, Rosser H., "HAMBURG: AN EXPERIMENT IN TOWN PROMOTION," North Carolina Historical Review 11:1 (January 1934), 20–38.

B-998 Taylor, George Rogers, "WHOLESALE COMMODITY PRICES AT CHARLESTON, SOUTH CAROLINA [PART 1]," Journal of Economic and Business History 4:2 (February 1932), 356–377.

B-999 Taylor, George Rogers, "WHOLESALE COMMODITY PRICES AT CHARLESTON, SOUTH CAROLINA [PART 2]," Journal of Economic and Business History 4:4 (November 1932), 848-878.

B-1000 "TEXAS MERCHANTS AFTER THE CIVIL WAR-1871," American Jewish Archives 12:1 (April 1960), 71-74.

B-1001 Thomas, Bettye C., "A NINETEENTH CENTURY BLACK OPERATED SHIPYARD, 1866: REFLECTIONS UPON ITS INCEPTIONS AND OWNERSHIP," Journal of Negro History 59:1 (January 1974), 1-12.

B-1002 Thompson, Lorin A., "URBANIZATION, OCCUPATIONAL SHIFT AND ECONOMIC PROGRESS," in R. Vance, ed., The Urban South, (1954), 38-54.

B-1003 Thorn, Cecelia Jean, "THE BELL FACTORY: EARLY PRIDE OF HUNTSVILLE," Alabama Review 32:1 (January 1979), 28-37.

B-1004 Throckmorton, H. Bruce, "THE FIRST WOMAN'S BANK IN TENNESSEE, 1919-1926," Tennessee Historical Quarterly 35:4 (Winter 1976), 389-392.

B-1005 Tower, J. Allen, "THE INDUSTRIAL DEVELOPMENT OF THE BIRMINGHAM REGION," Bulletin of Birmingham-Southern College 46:4 (December 1953), 32 pp.

B-1006 Trimble, Lee S., "A CONNECTICUT YANKEE IN TALLAPOOSA," Georgia Review 6:3 (Fall 1952), 352-357.

B-1007 Tucker, Robert H., "INDUSTRIAL DEVELOPMENT IN VIRGINIA," Annals of the American Academy of Political and Social Science 153 (January 1931), 124-132.

B-1008 Turano, L.R. and S.K. Moak, "CONSUMPTION BEHAVIOR OF THE DOUGHNUTS IN RICHMOND," Virginia Social Studies Journal 8:1 (April 1973), 31-37.

B-1009 Turnbow, Long L., "NASHVILLE'S VINE STREET," Tennessee Historical Quarterly 45:1 (Spring 1986), 18-29.

B-1010 Tyler, Bruce, "THE MISSISSIPPI RIVER TRADE, 1784-1788," Louisiana History 12:3 (Summer 1971), 255-267.

B-1011 Tyler, David B., "SHIPBUILDING IN DELAWARE," Delaware History 7:3 (March 1957), 207-216.

B-1012 Tyson, Gertrude, "BALANCED GROWTH AT SCOTTSBORO," Tennessee Valley Perspective 4:3 (Spring 1974), 20-26.

B-1013 Vahaly, John Jr., "THE LOCATION OF SERVICE AND OFFICE ACTIVITIES IN NASHVILLE--DAVIDSON COUNTY, 1970," Land Economics 52:4 (November 1976), 479-492.

B-1014 Vanderhill, Burke G., "THE PORTS OF THE ST. MARKS RIVER, FLORIDA," Southeastern Geographer 5 (1965), 15-23.

B-1015 Veazey, Kay Dunlap, "CLARKSVILLE, TENN. TRIES COOPERATION," South Magazine 7:2 (February 1980), 59-61.

B-1016 Vill, Martha J., "BUILDING ENTERPRISE IN LATE NINETEENTH-CENTURY BALTIMORE," Journal of Historical Geography 12:2 (April 1986), 162-181.

B-1017 Vowels, Robert C., "ATLANTA NEGRO BUSINESS AND THE NEW BLACK BOURGEOISE," Atlanta Historical Journal 21:1 (Spring 1977), 48-63.

B-1018 Wagner, Fredrick W., "THE IMPACT OF INFLATION AND RECESSION ON URBAN LEISURE IN NEW ORLEANS," Journal of Leisure Research 8:4 (1976), 300-306.

B-1019 Walker, Paul K., "BUSINESS AND COMMERCE IN BALTIMORE ON THE EVE OF INDEPENDENCE," Maryland Historical Magazine 71:3 (Fall 1976), 296-309.

B-1020 Wall, Bennett H., "LEON GODCHAUX AND THE GODCHAUX BUSINESS ENTERPRISES," American Jewish Historical Quarterly 66:1 (September 1976), 50-66.

B-1021 Walsh, Doris L., "WITH A SCORE OF 50, THE DEMOGRAPHICS OF TEST MARKET TULSA, OKLAHOMA COME OUT ON TOP," American Demographics 7:5 (May 1985), 38-43.

B-1022 Walsh, Lorena S., "URBAN AMENITIES AND RURAL SUFFICIENCY: LIVING STANDARDS AND CONSUMER BEHAVIOR IN THE COLONIAL CHESAPEAKE, 1643-1777," Journal of Economic History 43:1 (March 1983), 109-117.

B-1023 Walsh, Walter Richard, "EDMUND EGAN: CHARLESTON'S REBEL BREWER," South Carolina Historical Magazine 56:4 (1955), 200-204.

B-1024 Walters, Billie J. and James O. Wheeler, "LOCALIZATION ECONOMIES IN THE AMERICAN CARPET INDUSTRY," Geographical Review 74:2 (April 1984), 183-191.

B-1025 Ward, Frank Bird., "THE INDUSTRIAL DEVELOPMENT OF TENNESSEE," Annals of the American Academy of Political and Social Science 153 (January 1931), 141-147.

B-1026 Waring, Thomas P., "CHARLESTON: THE CAPITAL OF THE PLANTATIONS," in Augustine T. Smythe et al., The Carolina Low Country, 1931.

B-1027 Watson, Thomas D., "STAGING THE 'CROWNING ACHIEVEMENT OF THE AGE' --MAJOR EDWARD A. BURKE, NEW ORLEANS AND THE COTTON CENTENNIAL," Louisiana History 25:3 (Summer 1984), 229-258.

B-1028 Watters, Gary, "THE RUSSIAN JEW IN OKLAHOMA: THE MAY BROTHERS," Chronicles of Oklahoma 53:4 ((Winter 1975-76), 479-491.

B-1029 Weaver, David C., "A SURVEY OF SHORT-TERM CHANGES IN THE LAND USE MIX OF THREE AMERICAN CENTRAL BUSINESS DISTRICTS," Southeastern Geographer 1:1 (April 1971), 52-61.

B-1030 Weiher, Kenneth, "THE COTTON INDUSTRY AND SOUTHERN URBANIZATION, 1880-1930," Explorations in Economic History 14:2 (April 1977), 120-140.

B-1031 Welsh, Peter C., "THE BRANDYWINE MILLS: A CHRONICLE OF AN INDUSTRY," Delaware History 7:1 (March 1956), 17-36.

B-1032 Welsh, Peter C., "MERCHANTS MILLERS, AND OCEAN SHIPS: THE COMPONENTS OF AN EARLY AMERICAN INDUSTRIAL TOWN," Delaware History 7:4 (September 1957), 319-336.

B-1033 Wennersten, John R., "THE ALMIGHTY OYSTER: A SAGE OF OLD SOMERSET AND THE EASTERN SHORE, 1850-1920," Maryland Historical Magazine 74:1 (March 1979), 80-93.

B-1034 Wesson, Kenneth R., "THE SOUTHERN COUNTRY STORE REVISITED: A TEST CASE," Alabama Historical Quarterly 42:3-4 (1980), 157-166.

B-1035 Westfall, Glenn L., "LATIN ENTREPRENEURS AND THE BIRTH OF YBOR CITY," Tampa Bay History 7:2 (Fall-Winter 1985), 5-21.

B-1036 Whaley, John W., Dexter R. Rowell, and Alan H. Y. Tsao, "SPATIAL VARIATIONS OF RETAILING IN THE SOUTHEASTERN VIRGINIA ECONOMY," Virginia Social Science Journal 13:2 (November 1978), 58-71.

B-1037 Wheeler, James O., "CENTRAL CITY VERSUS SUBURBAN LOCATIONS OF CORPORATE HEADQUARTERS: THE ATLANTA EXAMPLE," Southeastern Geographer 26 (November 1986), 75-89.

B-1038 Wheeler, James O., "EFFECTS OF GEOGRAPHICAL SCALE ON LOCATION DECISIONS IN MANUFACTURING: THE ATLANTA EXAMPLE," Economic Geography 57:2 (April 1981), 134-145.

B-1039 Wheeler, James O., "REGIONAL MANUFACTURING STRUCTURE IN THE SOUTHEASTERN UNITED STATES, 1973," Southeastern Geographer 14:2 (November 1974), 67-83.

B-1040 Wheeler, James O. and Catherine L. Brown, "THE METROPOLITAN CORPORATE HIERARCHY IN THE U.S. SOUTH, 1960-1980," Economic Geography 61:1 (January 1985), 66-78.

B-1041 Wheeler, James O. and Sam Och Park, 'INTRAMETROPOLITAN LOCATIONAL CHANGES IN MANUFACTURING: THE ATLANTA METROPOLITAN AREA, 1958 TO 1976," Southeastern Geographer 21:1 (May 1981), 10-25.

B-1042 White, Langdon, "THE IRON AND STEEL INDUSTRY OF THE BIRMINGHAM, ALABAMA, DISTRICT," Economic Geography 4:4 (October 1928), 349-365.

B-1043 White, Langdon, "IRON AND STEEL INDUSTRY OF WHEELING, WEST VIRGINIA," Economic Geography 8:3 (July 1932), 274-281.

B-1044 White, Otis, "SAVING MACON FROM ITSELF," South Business 7:8 (August 1980), 24-31.

B-1045 Whitfield, Stephen J., "COMMERCIAL PASSIONS: THE SOUTHERN JEW AS BUSINESSMAN," American Jewish History 71:3 (March 1982), 342-357.

B-1046 Williams, Bobby Joe., "LET THERE BE LIGHT: TENNESSEE VALLEY AUTHORITY COMES TO MEMPHIS," West Tennessee Historical Society Papers No. 30 (1976), 43-66.

B-1047 Williams, Edward F. III, "MEMPHIS' EARLY TRIUMPH OVER ITS RIVER RIVALS," West Tennessee Historical Society Papers No. 22 (1968), 5-27.

B-1048 Wilson, Franklin D., "ECOLOGY OF A BLACK BUSINESS DISTRICT," Review of Black Political Economy 5:4 (Summer 1975), 353-375.

B-1049 Wilson, Kenneth L. and W. Allen Martin, "ETHNIC ENCLAVES: A COMPARISON OF THE CUBAN AND BLACK ECONOMIES IN MIAMI," American Journal of Sociology 88:1 (July 1982), 135-160.

B-1050 Wilson, Thelma, "FORT VALLEY: ITS CENTURY OF PROGRESS," Georgia Review 12:3 (Fall 1958), 334-343.

B-1051 Winsberg, Morton D., "INTENSITY OF AGRICULTURAL PRODUCTION AND DISTANCE FROM THE CITY: THE CASE OF THE SOUTHEASTERN UNITED STATES," Southeastern Geographer 21:1 (May 1981), 54-63.

B-1052 Winston, James E., "NOTES ON THE ECONOMIC HISTORY OF NEW ORLEANS, 1803-1836," Journal of American History 11:2 (September 1924), 200-226.

B-1053 Wolfe, Margaret Ripley, "J. FRED JOHNSON, HIS TOWN, AND HIS PEOPLE: A CASE STUDY OF CLASS VALUES, THE WORK ETHIC, AND TECHNOLOGY IN SOUTHERN APPALACHIA, 1916-1944," Appalachian Journal 7:1-2 (Autumn-Winter 1979-80), 70-83.

B-1054 Wood, W. Kirk, "CONSERVATIVE BANKING DURING CRISIS: THE GEORGIA RAILROAD AND BANKING COMPANY, 1836-1842," Richmond County History 3:2 (Summer 1971), 37-52.

B-1055 Woodman, Harold D., "THE DECLINE OF COTTON FACTORAGE AFTER THE CIVIL WAR," American Historical Review 71:4 (July 1966), 1219-1236.

B-1056 Worley, Ted R., "THE ARKANSAS STATE BANK: ANTE-BELLUM PERIOD," Arkansas Historical Quarterly 23:1 (Spring 1964), 65-73.

B-1057 Worley, Ted R., "THE BATESVILLE BRANCH OF THE STATE BANK, 1836-1839," Arkansas Historical Quarterly 6:3 (Fall 1947), 286-299.

B-1058 Wright, Alexander S. III, "THE OFFICE MARKET: CENTRAL ATLANTA VS. SUBURBS," Atlanta Economic Review 28:1 (January-February 1975), 34-36.

B-1059 Wright, Alexander S. III, "THE OFFICE MARKET: CENTRAL ATLANTA VS. THE SUBURBS," in A. Hamer, ed., Urban Atlanta: Redefining the Role of the City, 91-96.

B-1060 Wyatt, C.J., "CHEROKEE GEORGIA--1888," Northwest Georgia Historical and Genealogical Quarterly 18:2 (Spring 1986), 2-18.

B-1061 Yates, Bowling C., "MACON, GEORGIA, INLAND TRADING CENTER, 1826-1836," Georgia Historical Quarterly 55:3 (Fall 1971), 365-377.

B-1062 Ziegler, Joseph, "THE ECONOMIC IMPACT OF THE UNIVERSITY OF ARKANSAS ON WASHINGTON COUNTY," Arkansas Business and Economic Review 11:2 (Summer 1978), 18-26.

B-1063 Ziglar, W. Larry, "SHIPBUILDING ON THE PASCAGOULA RIVER," Journal of Mississippi History 34:1 (February 1974), 1-16.

B-1064 Zweigenhaft, Richard L., "TWO CITIES IN NORTH CAROLINA: A COMPARATIVE STUDY OF JEWS IN THE UPPER CLASS," Jewish Social Studies 41 (Summer-Fall 1979), 291-200.

Ecology and Environment

B-1065 Anderson, L. M. and H. W. Schroeder, "APPLICATION OF WILDLAND SCENIC ASSESSMENT METHODS TO THE URBAN LANDSCAPE," Landscape Planning 10:3 (October 1983), 219-238.

B-1066 Andreassen, John C. L., MISSISSIPPI RIVER ICE AT NEW ORLEANS," Louisiana Historical Quarterly 21:2 (April 1938), 349-353.

B-1067 Atkins, Robert L. and Michael Higgins, "SUPERIMPOSED FOLDING AND ITS BEARING ON GEOLOGIC HISTORY OF THE ATLANTA, GEORGIA, AREA," in R. Frey (ed.) Excursions in Southeastern Geology, 1980, 19-40.

B-1068 Bell, Laura Palmer, "THE VANISHING GARDENS OF SAVANNAH," Georgia Historical Quarterly 28:3 (September 1944), 196-208.

B-1069 Bullard, Robert D., "ENDANGERED ENVIRONS: THE PRICE OF UNPLANNED GROWTH IN BOOMTOWN HOUSTON," California Sociologist 7 (Summer 1984), 84-102.

B-1070 Bullard, Robert D. and Beverly Hendrix Wright, "ENDANGERED ENVIRONS: DUMPING GROUNDS IN A SUNBELT CITY," Urban Resources 2:2 (Winter 1985), 37-39.

B-1071 Bullard, Robert D. and Beverly Hendrix Wright, "THE POLITICS OF POLUTION: IMPLICATIONS FOR THE BLACK COMMUNITY," Phylon 47:1 (March 1986), 71-78.

B-1072 Cerwinske, Laura, "RANDOM ACCENTS," Garden Design 5:3 (Autumn 1986), 48-55.

B-1073 Coppock, Paul K., "PARKS OF MEMPHIS," West Tennessee Historical Society Papers, No. 12 (1958), 120-133.

B-1074 Crocker, Mary Wallace, "DIXON GARDENS," Southern Accents 6:5 (Winter 1983-84), 58-63.

B-1075 Danadjieva, Angela, "GARDENS THAT VANISH AND RETURN: A CONCEPT FOR RICHMOND'S JAMES RIVER," Landscape Architecture 68:5 (September 1978), 408-412.

B-1076 Emory, S.T., "TOPOGRAPHY AND TOWNS OF THE CAROLINA PIEDMONT," Economic Geography 12:1 (January 1936), 91-97.

B-1077 Fallows, James, "ONE DETERMINED MAN," Southern Exposure 10:4 (JulyAugust 1982), 36-45.

B-1078 Galchutt, William H. and William John Wallis, "DISNEY'S OTHER WORLD: MICKEY-MOUSING FLORIDA'S WATER SUPPLIES," Landscape Architecture 63:1 (October 1972), 28-31.

B-1079 Harrison, J.O., "OLDER URBAN CEMETERIES AS POTENTIAL WILDLIFE SANCTUARIES," Georgia Journal of Science 39:3, 4 (June-September 1981), 117-126.

B-1080 Hendon, William S., "PARK SERVICE AREAS AND RESIDENTIAL PROPERTY VALUES," American Journal of Economics and Sociology 33:2 (April 1974), 175-183.

B-1081 Hutter, Harry K., "A CLIMATIC STUDY: LEXINGTON, KENTUCKY," Ohio Journal of Science 49:6 (November 1949), 221-229.

B-1082 Ives, Sallie M. and Owen J. Furuseth, "IMMEDIATE RESPONSE TO HEAD-WATER FLOODING IN CHARLOTTE, NORTH CAROLINA," Environment and Behavior 15:4 (July 1983), 512-525.

B-1083 Kopec, Richard J., "FURTHER OBSERVATIONS OF THE URBAN HEAT ISLAND IN A SMALL CITY," Bulletin of the American Meterological Society 51 (July 1970), 602-606.

B-1084 Krupnick, Alan J., "COSTS OF ALTERNATIVE POLICIES FOR THE CONTROL OF NITROGEN DIOXIDE IN BALTIMORE," Journal of Environmental Economics and Management 13:2 (June 1986), 189-197.

B-1085 Landsberg, H. E., "ATMOSPHERIC CHANGES IN A GROWING COMMUNITY (THE COLUMBIA, MARYLAND EXPERIENCE," Urban Ecology 4:1 (May 1979), 53-82.

B-1086 Learner, W. H. and J. Duke, "WEATHER IN METRO-ATLANTA: HIGHLIGHTS FOR THE 1970's," Georgia Journal of Science 38:1 (January 1980), 3-10.

B-1087 Liew, Chung Ja, "POLUTION-RELATED VARIABLE INPUT-OUTPUT MODEL: THE TULSA SMSA AS A CASE STUDY," Journal of Urban Economics 15:3 (May 1984), 327-349.

B-1088 Page, Lake, "WILL SUCCESS SPOIL BRIGADOON?" American Land Forum 5:3 (Summer 1985), 44-52.

B-1089 Plummer, G. L. et al., "CLIMATIC PERIODS AND TRENDS IN A RAIN-SHADOW ECOSYSTEM; INTERPRETATION OF CHANGES AT AUGUSTA, GEORGIA," Georgia Journal of Science 38:3, 4, (June-September 1980), 185-198.

B-1090 Reynolds, Barbara, "TRIANA, ALABAMA: THE UNHEALTHIEST TOWN IN AMERICA," National Wildlife 18 (August 1980).

B-1091 Richardson, Otis Dunban, "FULLERTON, LOUISIANA: AN AMERICAN MONUMENT," Journal of Forest History 27:4 (October 1983), 192-201.

B-1092 Rogers, George A., et al., "DR. THOMAS JARRAM WRAY (1781-1851): PIONEER BOTANIST OF AUGUSTA, GEORGIA," Georgia Historical Quarterly 71:1 (Spring 1987), 75-90.

B-1093 Rogers, George C. Jr., "GARDEN AND LANDSCAPES IN EIGHTEENTH-CENTURY SOUTH CAROLINA," Eighteenth Century Life 8:2 (January 1983), 148-158.

B-1094 Rowntree, Rowan A., "FOREST CANOPY COVER AND LAND USE IN FOUR EASTERN UNITED STATES CITIES," Urban Ecology 8:special issue (1984), 55-68.

B-1095 Schwendeman, Joseph R., "COLD WAVE PATTERNS OF LEXINGTON, KEN-TUCKY, AND ORLANDO, FLORIDA," Transactions of the Kentucky Academy of Science 26 (1965), 38-46.

B-1096 Share, Allen J., "RESTORATION OF A TORNADO RAVAGED PARK," Land-scape Architecture 66:5 (September 1976), 456-462.

B-1097 Slogan, Patrick J., "THE DAY THEY SHUT DOWN BIRMINGHAM," Washing-ton Monthly 4 (May 1972), 41-51.

B-1098 Smith, Frank E., "IMPROVING THE SOUTHERN ENVIRONMENT," South Atlantic Quarterly 70:4 (Autumn 1971), 507-517.

B-1099 States, Stanley J., "WEATHER AND DEATH IN BIRMINGHAM, ALABAMA," Environmental Research 12 (December 1976), 340-354.

B-1100 Sutton, Jonathan S. and Dan L. McHarg, "ECOLOGICAL PLUMING FOR THE TEXAS COASTAL PLAIN," Landscape Architecture 65:1 (January 1975), 78-89.

B-1101 "TESTING THE WATERS," Southern Exposure 14:2 (March-April 1986), 17-20.

B-1102 Thomas, Kenny, "'OUR GOVERNMENT WOULDN'T DO THIS TO US': STONE-WALLING MEMPHIS DUMPING VICTIMS," Southern Exposure 9:3 (1981), 28-33.

B-1103 Thompson, Priscilla M., "CREATION OF THE WILMINGTON PARK SYSTEM BEFORE 1896," Delaware History 18:2 (Fall-Winter 1978), 75-92.

B-1104 Williamson, R. D. and R. M. DeGraaf, "HABITAT ASSOCIATIONS OF TEN BIRD SPECIES IN WASHINGTON, D.C.," Urban Ecology 5:2 (November 1981), 125-136.

B-1105 Wundram, Ina Jane, "URBAN ETHOLOGY: AN ANTHROPOLOGICAL APPROACH TO WILDLIFE IN THE CITY," Human Organization 40:2 (Summer 1981), 168-171.

Education

B-1106 Alsobrook, David E., "MOBILE V. BIRMINGHAM: THE ALABAMA MEDICAL COLLEGE CONTROVERSY, 1912-1920," Alabama Review 36:1 (January 1983), 37-56.

B-1107 Altman, James David, "THE CHARLESTON MARINE SCHOOL," South Carolina Historical Magazine 88:1 (January 1987), 76-82.

B-1108 Andrews, Andrea R., "THE BALTIMORE SCHOOL BUILDING PROGRAM 1870 TO 1900: A STUDY OF URBAN REFORM," Maryland Historical Magazine 70:3 (Fall 1975), 260-274.

B-1109 Antone, George P., "THE Y.M.C.A. GRADUATE SCHOOL, NASHVILLE, 1919-1936," Tennessee Historical Quarterly 32:1 (Spring 1973), 67-82.

B-1110 Armistead, Margaret Beauchamp, "A HIGH SCHOOL THAT STOOD HIGH," Georgia Review 9:2 (Summer 1955), 168-177.

B-1111 Bacote, Clarence A., "JAMES WELDON JOHNSON AND ATLANTA UNIVER-SITY," Phylon 32:4 (Winter 1971), 333-343.

B-1112 Baughn, Milton L., "AN EARLY EXPERIMENT IN ADULT EDUCATION: THE
NASHVILLE LYCEUM, 1830-1832," Tennessee Historical Quarterly 11:3
(September 1952), 235-245.

B-1113 Beeler, Park L., "THE MERGER URGERS OF JACKSONVILLE ARE WINNING A
QUIET REVOLUTION," Urban Review 6:5-6 (1973), 57-61.

B-1114 Berkeley, Kathleen C., "'THE LADIES WANT TO BRING ABOUT REFORM IN
THE PUBLIC SCHOOLS': PUBLIC EDUCATION AND WOMEN'S RIGHTS IN THE
POST-CIVIL WAR SOUTH," History of Education Quarterly 24:1 (Spring
1984), 45-58.

B-1115 Birnie, C.W., "THE EDUCATION OF THE NEGRO IN CHARLESTON, SOUTH
CAROLINA, BEFORE THE CIVIL WAR," Journal of Negro History 12:1
(January 1927), 13-21.

B-1116 Black, Marian Watkins, "PRIVATE AID TO PUBLIC SCHOOLS: THE PEA-
BODY FUND IN FLORIDA, 1867-1880," History of Education Quarterly
1:3 (September 1961), 38-42.

B-1117 Blair, Marian, "CONTEMPORARY EVIDENCE--SALEM BOARDING SCHOOL,
1834-1844," North Carolina Historical Review 27:2 (April 1950),
142-161.

B-1118 Bratton, Mary Jo Jackson, "CRADLED IN CONFLICT: ORIGINS OF EAST
CAROLINA UNIVERSITY," North Carolina Historical Review 63:1
(January 1986), 74-103.

B-1119 Breeden, James O., "BODY SNATCHERS AND ANATOMY PROFESSORS:
MEDICAL EDUCATION IN NINETEENTH-CENTURY VIRGINIA," Virginia
Magazine of History and Biography 83:3 (July 1975), 321-345.

B-1120 Byrne, Ann D. and Dana F. White, "ATLANTA UNIVERSITY'S 'NORTHEAST
LOT': COMMUNITY BUILDING FOR BLACK ATLANTA'S TALENTED TENTH,"
Atlanta Historical Journal 26:2-3 (Summer-Fall 1982), 155-176.

B-1121 Camp, Paul Eugen, ed., "ST. PETERSBURG'S FIRST PUBLIC SCHOOL,"
Tampa Bay History 7:1 (Spring-Summer 1985), 76-82.

B-1122 Campbell, Daniel R., "RIGHT-WING EXTREMISTS AND THE SARASOTA
SCHOOLS, 1960-1966," Tampa Bay History 6:1 (Spring-Summer 1984),
16-26.

B-1123 Chitty, Arthur Ben, "SEWANEE: THEN AND NOW," Tennessee Historical
Quarterly 38:4 (Winter 1979), 383-400.

B-1124 Clinton, Catherine, "EQUALLY THEIR DUE: THE EDUCATION OF THE
PLANTER DAUGHTER IN THE EARLY REPUBLIC," Journal of the Early
Republic 2:2 (Spring 1982), 39-60.

B-1125 Conway, Thomas G., "JOHN A. KENNECOTT: A TEACHER IN NEW ORLEANS,"
Louisiana History 26:4 (Fall 1985), 399-415.

B-1126 Coulter, E. Merton, "THE BIRTH OF A UNIVERSITY, A TOWN, AND A
COUNTY," Georgia Historical Quarterly 46:2 (June 1962), 113-150.

B-1127 Crosthwait, D. N. Jr., "THE FIRST BLACK HIGH SCHOOL IN NASHVILLE,"
Negro History Bulletin 37:4 (1974), 266-268.

B-1128 Cunningham, George K., "NONPUBLIC SCHOOL ALTERNATIVES TO BUSING:
ATTITUDES AND CHARACTERISTICS," Urban Education 16:1 (April 1981),
3-12.

B-1129 Daniel, W. Harrison, "THE GENESIS OF RICHMOND COLLEGE, 1843-1860,"
Virginia Magazine of History and Biography 83:2 (April 1975), 131-
149.

B-1130 Daniel, W. Harrison, "OLD LYNCHBURG COLLEGE, 1855-1869," Virginia
Magazine of History and Biography 88:4 (October 1980), 446-477.

B-1131 Dart, Henry P., "PUBLIC EDUCATION IN NEW ORLEANS IN 1800," Louisiana Historical Quarterly 11:2 (April 1928), 241-252.

B-1132 Davis, T. Frederick, "A FREE PUBLIC SCHOOL IN ST. AUGUSTINE, 1832," Florida Historical Quarterly 22:4 (April 1944), 200-207.

B-1133 Dillingham, George A., "THE UNIVERSITY OF NASHVILLE, A NORTHERN EDUCATOR AND A NEW MISSION IN THE POST-RECONSTRUCTION SOUTH," Tennessee Historical Quarterly 37:3 (Fall 1978), 329-338.

B-1134 Dodd, William G., "EARLY EDUCATION IN TALLAHASSEE AND THE WEST FLORIDA SEMINARY NOW FLORIDA STATE UNIVERSITY, PART I," Florida Historical Quarterly 27:1 (July 1948), 1-27.

B-1135 Dodd, William G., "EARLY EDUCATION IN TALLAHASSEE AND THE WEST FLORIDA SEMINARY NOW FLORIDA STATE UNIVERSITY, PART II," Florida Historical Quarterly 27:2 (October 1948), 157-180.

B-1136 Dozier, Richard K., "TUSKEGEE INSTITUTE COMES OF AGE," Historic Preservation 33:1 (January-February 1981), 40-49.

B-1137 Duffy, John, "THE EVOLUTION OF MEDICAL EDUCATION, INSTITUTIONAL HISTORIES, AND THE MEDICAL COLLEGE OF GEORGIA," Georgia Historical Quarterly 71:4 (Winter 1987), 623-637.

B-1138 Durden, Robert F., "THE ORIGINS OF THE DUKE ENDOWMENT AND THE LAUNCHING OF DUKE UNIVERSITY," North Carolina Historical Review 52:2 (Spring 1975), 130-146.

B-1139 Durden, Robert F., "CRISIS IN UNIVERSITY GOVERNANCE: THE LAUNCH- ING OF DUKE UNIVERSITY, 1925-1935," North Carolina Historical Review 64:3 (July 1987), 294-319; 64:4 (October 1987), 416-437.

B-1140 Durham, Louise, "THE OLD MARKET STREET SCHOOL, 1872-1920," West Tennessee Historical Society Papers No. 7 (1953), 57-71.

B-1141 Engelman, Uriah Zevi, "JEWISH EDUCATION IN CHARLESTON, SOUTH CAROLINA, DURING THE EIGHTEENTH AND NINETEENTH CENTURIES," Publicaitons of the American Jewish Historical Society 42:1 (September 1952), 43-70.

B-1142 Engle, Fred A. Jr., "CENTRAL UNIVERSITY OF RICHMOND, KENTUCKY," Register of the Kentucky Historical Society 66:3 (July 1968), 279- 304.

B-1143 Epps, Edgar G., "CORRELATES OF ACADEMIC ACHIEVEMENT AMONG NORTHERN AND SOUTHERN URBAN NEGRO STUDENTS," Journal of Social Issues 25:3 (Summer 1969), 55-70.

B-1144 Ezell, John S., "A SOUTHERN EDUCATION FOR SOUTHRONS," Journal of Southern History 17:3 (August 1951), 303-327.

B-1145 Falk, Stanley, "THE WARRENTON FEMALE ACADEMY OF JACOB MORDECAI, 1809-1818," North Carolina Historical Review 35:3 (July 1958), 281-298.

B-1146 Fen, Sing-nan, "NOTES ON THE EDUCATION OF NEGROES AT NORFOLK AND PORTSMOUTH, VIRGINIA, DURING THE CIVIL WAR," Phylon 27:2 (Summer 1967), 197-208.

B-1147 Feuer, Lewis S., "AMERICA'S FIRST JEWISH PROFESSOR: JAMES JOSEPH SYLVESTER AT THE UNIVERSITY OF VIRGINIA," American Jewish Archives 36:2 (November 1984), 152-201.

B-1148 Fitzgerald, Michael R. and David R. Morgan, "CHANGING PATTERNS OF URBAN SCHOOL DESEGREGATION," American Political Quarterly 5:4 (1977), 437-464.

B-1149 Flemming, Cynthia Griggs, "A SURVEY OF THE BEGINNINGS OF TENNES-
SEE'S BLACK COLLEGES AND UNIVERSITIES, 1865-1920," Tennessee
Historical Quarterly 39:2 (Summer 1980), 195-207.

B-1150 Fraser, James W., "'THE BISHOPS, I PRESUME, ARE DIVIDED' METHODIST
OPPOSITION TO THE ESTABLISHMENT OF VANDERBILT UNIVERSITY," Southern Studies 24:2 (Summer 1985), 167-187.

B-1151 Friedlander, Amy, "'NOT A VENEER OR A SHAM': THE EARLY DAYS OF
AGNES SCOTT," Atlanta Historical Journal 23:4 (Winter 1979-80),
31-44.

B-1152 Gardner, Bettye, "ANTE-BELLUM BLACK EDUCATION IN BALTIMORE,"
Maryland Historical Magazine 71:3 (Fall 1976), 360-366.

B-1153 Giles, Michael W., "RACIAL STABILITY AND URBAN SCHOOL DESEGREGA-
TION," Urban Affairs Quarterly 12:4 (June 1977), 499-510.

B-1154 Griffin, Barbara J., "THOMAS RITCHIE AND THE FOUNDING OF THE RICH-
MOND LANCASTERIAN SCHOOL," Virginia Magazine of History and Biography 86:4 (October 1978), 447-460.

B-1155 Griffin, Richard W., "WESLEYAN COLLEGE: ITS GENESIS, 1835-1840,"
Georgia Historical Quarterly 50:1 (March 1966), 54-73.

B-1156 Gross, Dellvina, "A DEVELOPMENTAL PROGRAM IN THE BLACK COMMUNITY:
A CRITICAL APPRAISAL," Journal of Black Studies 6:2 (December
1975), 127-135.

B-1157 Gwinn, Frances Farley, "PATTY SMITH HILL, LOUISVILLE'S CONTRIBU-
TION TO EDUCATION," Filson Club History Quarterly 31:3 (July
1957), 203-226.

B-1158 Hardacre, Paul H., "HISTORY AND HISTORIANS AT VANDERBILT, 1875-
1918," Tennessee Historical Quarterly 25:1 (Spring 1966), 22-31.

B-1159 Hardin, J. Fair, "THE EARLY HISTORY OF THE LOUISIANA STATE UNI-
VERSITY," Louisiana Historical Quarterly 11:1 (January 1928), 5-
31.

B-1160 Hargrett, Lester, "STUDENT LIFE AT THE UNIVERSITY OF GEORGIA IN
THE 1840s," Georgia Historical Quarterly 8:1 (March 1924), 49-59.

B-1161 Harlan, Louis R., "DESEGREGATION IN NEW ORLEANS PUBLIC SCHOOLS
DURING RECONSTRUCTION," American Historical Quarterly 67:3 (April
1962), 663-675.

B-1162 Harris, Carl V., "STABILITY AND CHANGE IN DISCRIMINATION AGAINST
BLACK PUBLIC SCHOOLS: BIRMINGHAM, ALABAMA, 1871-1931," Journal of
Southern History 51:3 (August 1985), 375-396.

B-1163 Harrison, Lowell, "BEREA COLLEGE: AN EXPERIMENT IN EDUCATION,"
American History Illustrated 15:10 (February 1981), 8-17.

B-1164 Harrison, Lowell, "JACKSON . . . IS A RUINED TOWN," Civil War
Times Illustrated 15:10 (February 1977), 4-7.

B-1165 Hein, David, "THE FOUNDING OF THE BOY'S SCHOOL OF ST. PAUL'S
PARISH, BALTIMORE," Maryland Historical Magazine 81:2 (Summer
1986), 149-159.

B-1166 Holley, Howard L., "MEDICAL EDUCATION IN ALABAMA," Alabama Review
7:4 (October 1954), 245-264.

B-1167 Hollow, Elizabeth Patton, "DEVELOPMENT OF THE BROWNSVILLE BAPTIST
FEMALE COLLEGE: AN EXAMPLE OF FEMALE EDUCATION IN THE SOUTH,
1850-1910," West Tennessee Historical Society Papers No. 32
(1978), 48-59.

B-1168 Holmes, Dwight O., "FIFTY YEARS OF HOWARD UNIVERSITY, PART I," Journal of Negro History 3:2 (April 1918), 128-138.

B-1169 Holmes, Dwight O., "FIFTY YEARS OF HOWARD UNIVERSITY, PART II," Journal of Negro History 3:4 (October 1918), 368-380.

B-1170 Holmes, Robert A., "THE UNIVERSITY AND POLITICS IN ATLANTA: A CASE STUDY OF THE ATLANTA UNIVERSITY CENTER," Atlanta Historical Journal 25:1 (Spring 1981), 49-68.

B-1171 Hooker, Robert, "SCHOOL CRISIS IN ST. PETERSBURG," New South 27:1 (Winter 1972), 48-52.

B-1172 Horine, Emmet F., "HISTORY OF THE LOUISVILLE MEDICAL INSTITUTE," Filson Club History Quarterly 7:3 (July 1933), 133-147.

B-1173 Howard, Victor B., "SECTIONALISM, SLAVERY AND EDUCATION: NEW ALBANY, INDIANA, VERSUS DANVILLE, KENTUCKY," Register of the Kentucky Historical Society 68:4 (October 1970), 292-310.

B-1174 Jackson, L. P., "THE ORIGIN OF HAMPTON INSTITUTE," Journal of Negro History 10:2 (April 1925), 131-149.

B-1175 January, Alan F., "THE SOUTH CAROLINA ASSOCIATION: AN AGENCY FOR RACE CONTROL IN ANTEBELLUM CHARLESTON," South Carolina Historical Magazine 78:3 (July 1977), 191-201.

B-1176 Johnson, Kenneth R., "URBAN BOOSTERISM AND HIGHER EDUCATION IN THE NEW SOUTH: A CASE STUDY," Alabama Historical Quarterly 42:1, 2 (Spring & Summer 1980), 40-58.

B-1177 Jordan, Laylon Wayne, "EDUCATION FOR A COMMUNITY: C. G. MEMMINGER AND THE ORIGINATION OF COMMON SCHOOLS IN ANTEBELLUM CHARLESTON," South Carolina Historical Magazine 83:2 (April 1982), 99-115.

B-1178 Kennan, Clara B., "THE FIRST NEGRO TEACHER IN LITTLE ROCK," Arkansas Historical Quarterly 9:3 (Autumn 1950), 194-204.

B-1179 Lamon, Lester C., "THE BLACK COMMUNITY IN NASHVILLE AND THE FISK UNIVERSITY STUDENT STRIKE OF 1924-1925," Journal of Southern History 40:2 (May 1974), 225-244.

B-1180 Lamon, Lester C., "THE TENNESSEE AGRICULTURAL AND INDUSTRIAL NORMAL SCHOOL: PUBLIC EDUCATION FOR BLACK TENNESSEANS," Tennessee Historical Quarterly 32:1 (Spring 1973), 42-58.

B-1181 Levin, Alexandra Lee, "HENRIETTA SZOLD AND THE RUSSIAN IMMIGRANT SCHOOL," Maryland Historical Magazine 57:1 (Spring 1962), 1-15.

B-1182 Lewis, Frank G., "EDUCATION IN ST. AUGUSTINE 1821-1845," Florida Historical Quarterly 30:3 (January 1952), 237-260.

B-1183 McBride, Mary G., "SENATOR RANDALL LEE GIBSON AND THE ESTABLISH-MENT OF TULANE UNIVERSITY," Louisiana History 28:3 (Summer 1987), 245-262.

B-1184 McGinnis, Clyde, "ARKANSAS COLLEGE," Arkansas Historical Quarterly 31:3 (Autumn 1972), 234-245.

B-1185 McHugh, Cathy L., "SCHOOLING IN THE POST-BELLUM SOUTHERN COTTON MILL VILLAGES," Journal of Social History 20:1 (Fall 1986), 149-162.

B-1186 McMillan, Neil R., "THE WHITE CITIZENS COUNCIL AND RESISTANCE TO SCHOOL DESEGREGATOIN IN ARKANSAS," Arkansas Historical Quarterly 30:2 (Summer 1971), 95-122.

B-1187 McMurry, Linda O., "A BLACK INTELLECTUAL IN THE NEW SOUTH: MONROE NATHAN WORK, 1866-1945," Phylon 41:4 (December 1980), 333-344.

B-1188 Macintosh, Douglas et al., "SEX EDUCATION IN NEW ORLEANS: THE BIRCHERS WIN A VICTORY," New South 25:3 (Summer 1970), 46-56.

B-1189 Marable, Manning, "TUSKEGEE AND THE POLITICS OF ILLUSION," from M. Mirable, ed., The Grassroots: Social and Political Essays Towards Afro-American Liberation, Boston: South End Press, 1980, 159-177.

B-1190 Marks, Bayly Ellen, "LIBERAL EDUCATION IN THE GILDED AGE: BALTI-MORE AND THE CREATION OF THE MANUAL TRAINING SCHOOL," Maryland Historical Magazine 74:3 (September 1979), 238-252.

B-1191 Mathis, Ray, ed., "'UNCLE TOM' REED AND THE ATLANTA PUBLIC SCHOOLS," Atlanta Historical Journal 15:4 (Winter 1970), 97-101.

B-1192 Mauldin, W. Parker, "A SAMPLE STUDY OF MIGRATION TO KNOXVILLE, TENNESSEE," Social Forces 18:3 (March 1940), 360-364.

B-1193 Meriwether, Robert W., "GALLOWAY COLLEGE: THE EARLY YEARS, 1889-1907," Arkansas Historical Quarterly 40:4 (Winter 1981), 291-337.

B-1194 Moffatt, Walter, "ARKANSAS SCHOOLS, 1819-1840," Arkansas Historical Quarterly 12:2 (Summer 1953), 91-105.

B-1195 Montgomery, James R., "JOHN R. NEAL AND THE UNIVERSITY OF TENNES-SEE: A FIVE-PART TRAGEDY," Tennessee Historical Quarterly 38:2 (Summer 1979), 214-234.

B-1196 Montgomery, James R., "THE SUMMER SCHOOL OF THE SOUTH," Tennessee Historical Quarterly 22:4 (December 1963), 361-381.

B-1197 Morland, J. Kenneth, "EDUCATIONAL AND OCCUPATIONAL ASPIRATIONS OF MILL AND TOWN SCHOOL CHILDREN IN A SOUTHERN COMMUNITY," Social Forces 39:2 (December 1960), 169-175.

B-1198 Nagy, J. Emerick, "THE SOUTH NASHVILLE INSTITUTE," Tennessee His-torical Quarterly 36:2 (Summer 1977), 180-196.

B-1199 Nagy, J. Emerick, "WANTED: A TEACHER FOR THE NASHVILLE ENGLISH SCHOOL," Tennessee Historical Quarterly 21:2 (June 1962), 171-186.

B-1200 Nelms, Jack, "THE DALLAS ACADEMY: BACKBONE OF THE PERMANENT SCHOOL SYSTEM IN SELMA," Alabama Review 29:2 (April 1976), 113-123.

B-1201 Newberry, Farrar, "THE YANKEE SCHOOLMARM WHO 'CAPTURED' POST-WAR ARKADELPHIA," Arkansas Historical Quarterly 17:3 (Autumn 1958), 265-271.

B-1202 Nichols, Guerdon D., "BREAKING THE COLOR BARRIER AT THE UNIVERSITY OF ARKANSAS," Arkansas Historical Quarterly 27:1 (Spring 1968), 3-21.

B-1203 Niemi, Albert W. Jr., "RACIAL DIFFERENCES IN RETURNS TO EDUCATION-AL INVESTMENT IN THE SOUTH," American Journal of Economics and Sociology 34:1 (January 1975), 87-94.

B-1204 Noble, Stuart Grayson, "SCHOOLS OF NEW ORLEANS DURING THE FIRST QUARTER OF THE NINETEENTH CENTURY," Louisiana Historical Quarterly 14:1 (January 1931), 65-80.

B-1205 Noblit, George W. and Thomas W. Collins, "SCHOOL FLIGHT AND SCHOOL POLICY: DESGREGATION AND RESEGREGATION IN THE MEMPHIS CITY SCHOOLS," Urban Review 10:3 (1978), 203-212.

B-1206 Osborne, Irene and Richard K. Bennett, "ELEMENTARY EDUCATIONAL SEGREGATION IN THE NATION'S CAPITAL, 1951-1955," Annals of the American Academy of Political and Social Science 304 (March 1956), 98-108.

B-1207 O'Steen, Neal, "THE UNIVERSITY OF TENNESSEE: EVOLUTION OF A CAMPUS," Tennessee Historical Quarterly 39:3 (Fall 1980), 257-281.

B-1208 Parker, Harold M. Jr., "A SCHOOL OF THE PROPHETS AT MARYVILLE," Tennessee Historical Quarterly 34:1 (Spring 1975), 72-90.

B-1209 Pedea, Creighton, "A PIONEER MODEL: LAWTON B. EVANS," Richmond County History 9:2 (Summer 1977), 5-13.

B-1210 Penton, Emily, "TYPICAL WOMEN'S SCHOOLS IN ARKANSAS BEFORE THE WAR OF 1861-65," Arkansas Historical Quarterly 4:4 (Winter 1945), 325-339.

B-1211 Perry, B. L. Jr., "BLACK COLLEGES AND UNIVERSITIES IN FLORIDA: PAST, PRESENT, AND FUTURE," Journal of Black Studies 6:1 (September 1975), 69-78.

B-1212 Pinsky, Mark, "FINANCES: DOUBLE DEALING IN PLAINS, GA.," Southern Exposure 7:2 (Summer 1979), 98-102.

B-1213 Plank, David N. and Paul E. Peterson, "DOES URBAN REFORM IMPLY CLASS CONFLICT? THE CASE OF ATLANTA'S SCHOOLS," History of Education Quarterly 23:2 (Summer 1983), 151-174.

B-1214 Prestor, E. Delorus Jr., "WILLIAM SYPHAX, A PIONEER IN NEGRO EDUCATION IN THE DISTRICT OF COLUMBIA," Journal of Negro History 20:4 (October 1935), 448-476.

B-1215 Pusey, William Webb III, "LEXINGTON'S FEMALE ACADEMY," Virginia Cavalcade 32:1 (Summer 1982), 40-47.

B-1216 Putney, Martha S., "THE BALTIMORE NORMAL SCHOOL FOR THE EDUCATION OF COLORED TEACHERS: ITS FOUNDERS AND ITS FOUNDING," Maryland Historical Magazine 72:2 (Summer 1977), 238-252.

B-1217 Pyburn, Nita K., "THE PUBLIC SCHOOL SYSTEM OF CHARLESTON BEFORE 1860," South Carolina Historical Magazine 61:2 (April 1960), 86-97.

B-1218 Pyburn, Nita Katharine, "MOBILE PUBLIC SCHOOLS BEFORE 1860," Alabama Review 11:3 (July 1958), 177-188.

B-1219 Rabinowitz, Howard N., "HALF A LOAF: THE SHIFT FROM WHITE TO BLACK TEACHERS IN THE NEGRO SCHOOLS OF THE URBAN SOUTH, 1865-1890," Journal of Southern History 40:4 (November 1974), 565-594.

B-1220 Racine, Philip N., "A PROGRESSIVE FIGHTS EFFICIENCY: THE SURVIVAL OF WILLIS SUTTON, SCHOOL SUPERINTENDENT," South Atlantic Quarterly 76:1 (Winter 1977), 103-116.

B-1221 Racine, Philip N., "TEACHERS, STUDENTS AND CURRICULA IN ATLANTA SCHOOLS, 1871-1879," Atlanta Historical Journal 15:1 (Spring 1970), 43-58.

B-1222 Racine, Philip N., "WILLIS ANDERSON SUTTON AND PROGRESSIVE EDUCATION, 1921-1943," Atlanta Historical Bulletin 20:1 (Spring 1976), 9-23.

B-1223 Reinders, Robert C., "NEW ENGLAND INFLUENCES ON THE FORMATION OF PUBLIC SCHOOLS IN NEW ORLEANS," Journal of Southern History 30:2 (May 1964), 181-195.

B-1224 Rembert, Sarah H., "BARHAMVILLE: A COLUMBIA ANTEBELLUM GIRLS SCHOOL," South Carolina History Illustrated 1:1 (February 1970), 44-48.

B-1225 Richardson, Joe M., "FISK UNIVERSITY: THE FIRST CRITICAL YEARS," Tennessee Historical Quarterly 29:1 (Spring 1970), 24-41.

B-1226 Ritterbrand, Paul, "ETHNICITY AND SCHOOL DISORDER," Education and Urban Society 8:4 (1976), 383-400.

B-1227 Roberson, Jere W., "EDWARD P. McCABE AND THE LANGSTON EXPERIMENT," Chronicles of Oklahoma 51:3 (Fall 1973), 343-355.

B-1228 Robinson, Walter J., "NEW ORLEANS AS A CENTER IN THE DEVELOPMENT OF INDUSTRIAL EDUCATION IN LOUISIANA," Louisiana Studies 3:2 (Summer 1964), 210-218.

B-1229 Rogers, George C., "THE COLLEGE OF CHARLESTON AND THE YEAR 1785," South Carolina Historical Magazine 86:4 (October 1985), 282-296.

B-1230 Rogers, George C. Jr., AEDENUS BURKE, NATHANAEL GREEN, ANTHONY WAYNE, AND THE BRITISH MERCHANTS OF CHARLESTON," South Carolina Historical Magazine 67:2 (April 1967), 75-83.

B-1231 Rogers, Tommy Wayne, "THE SCHOOLS OF HIGHER LEARNING AT SHARON, MISSISSIPPI," Journal of Mississippi History 28:1 (February 1966), 40-55.

B-1232 Rogers, William Warren, "THE FOUNDING OF ALABAMA'S LAND GRANT COLLEGE AT AUBURN," Alabama Review 60:1 (January 1987), 14-37.

B-1233 Roper, James E., "SOUTHWESTERN AT MEMPHIS, 1848-1981," Tennessee Historical Quarterly 41:3 (Fall 1982), 207-224.

B-1234 Rosentraub, Mark S. and Lyke Thompson, "REPRESENTATIVE BUREAU-CRACIES AND STUDENT DISCIPLINE IN AN URBAN SCHOOL DISTRICT," Journal of Urban Affairs 4:3 (Summer 1982), 65-78.

B-1235 Rothrock, Thomas, "JOSEPH CARTER CORBIN AND NEGRO EDUCATION AT THE UNIVERSITY OF ARKANSAS," Arkansas Historical Quarterly 30:4 (Winter 1971), 277-214.

B-1236 Rothrock, Thomas, "THE UNIVERSITY OF ARKANSAS 'OLD MAIN,'" Arkansas Historical Quarterly 30:1 (Spring 1971), 1-52.

B-1237 Scott, Charlotte H., "COLLEGE DESEGREGATION: VIRGINIA'S SAD EXPERIENCE," Virginia Quarterly Review 58:2 (Spring 1982), 221-235.

B-1238 Scribner, Robert L., "THE MEDICAL COLLEGE OF VIRGINIA," Virginia Cavalcade 2:3 (Winter 1952), 43-47.

B-1239 Shannon, Samuel H., "LAND-GRANT COLLEGE LEGISLATION AND BLACK TEN-NESSEANS: A CASE STUDY IN THE POLITICS OF EDUCATION," History of Education Quarterly 22:2 (Summer 1982), 139-158.

B-1240 Shaw, Arthur Marvin, "RAMPANT INDIVIDUALISM IN AN ANTE-BELLUM SOUTHERN COLLEGE," Louisiana Historical Quarterly 31:4 (October 1948), 877-897.

B-1241 Sheeler, Tina H., "THE ORIGINS OF PUBLIC EDUCATION IN BALTIMORE, 1825-1829," History of Education Quarterly 22:1 (Spring 1982), 23-44.

B-1242 Sills, James H., "EQUALIZING TEACHERS SALARIES: RACIAL AND POLICY IMPLICATIONS IN A NEW METROPOLITAN PUBLIC SCHOOL DISTRICT," Urban Education 17:3 (October 1982), 351-374.

B-1243 Smith, Herschel Kennon, "ANTE-BELLUM SCHOOLS AT TULIP, ARKANSAS," Arkansas Historical Quarterly 18:3 (Autumn 1959), 280-286.

B-1244 Sowell, Thomas, "BLACK EXCELLENCE: THE CASE OF DUNBAR HIGH SCHOOL," Public Interest No. 35 (1974), 3-21.

B-1245 Spivey, Donald, "CRISIS ON A BLACK CAMPUS: LANGSTON UNIVERSITY AND ITS STRUGGLE FOR SURVIVAL," Chronicles of Oklahoma 59:4 (Winter 1981-1982),430-447.

B-1246 Starke, Aubrey, "RICHARD HENRY WILDE IN NEW ORLEANS AND THE ESTABLISHMENT OF THE UNIVERSITY OF LOUISIANA," Louisiana Historical Quarterly 17:4 (October 1934), 605-624.

B-1247 Stetar, Joseph M., "IN SEARCH OF A DIRECTION: SOUTHERN HIGHER EDUCATION AFTER THE CIVIL WAR," History of Education Quarterly 25:3 (Fall 1985), 341-368.

B-1248 Stuart, Reginald, "BUSING AND THE MEDIA IN NASHVILLE," New South 28:2 (Spring 1973), 79-87.

B-1249 Taylor, Alrutheus A., "FISK UNIVERSITY AND THE NASHVILLE COMMUNITY, 1866-1900," Journal of Negro History 39:2 (April 1954), 111-126.

B-1250 Terrell, Mary Church, "THE HISTORY OF THE HIGH SCHOOL FOR NEGROES IN WASHINGTON [D.C.]," Journal of Negro History 2:3 (July 1917), 252-266.

B-1251 Terrell, Robert L., "BLACK AWARENESS VERSUS NEGRO TRADITIONS: AT THE ATLANTA UNIVERSITY CENTER," New South 24:1 (Winter 1969), 29-40.

B-1252 TeSelle, Eugene, "THE NASHVILLE INSTITUTE AND ROGER WILLIAMS UNIVERSITY: BENEVALENCE, PATERNALISM, AND BLACK CONSCIOUSNESS, 1867-1910," Tennessee Historical Quarterly 41:4 (Winter 1982), 360-379.

B-1253 Thomas, Bettye C., "PUBLIC EDUCATION AND BLACK PROTEST IN BALTIMORE, 1865-1900," Maryland Historical Magazine 71:3 (Fall 1976), 381-391.

B-1254 Thomsen, Roszel C., "THE INTEGRATION OF BALTIMORE'S POLYTECHNIC INSTITUTE: A REMINISCENCE," Maryland Historical Magazine 79:3 (Fall 1984), 235-238.

B-1255 Toppin, Edgar A., "WALTER WHITE AND THE ATLANTA NAACP'S FIGHT FOR EQUAL SCHOOLS," History of Education Quarterly 7:1 (Spring 1967), 3-21.

B-1256 Townsend, Sara Bertha, "THE ADMISSION OF WOMEN TO THE UNIVERSITY OF GEORGIA," Georgia Historical Quarterly 43:2 (June 1959), 156-169.

B-1257 Wall, Bennett H., "ACADEMIC REQUIREMENTS OF SALEM COLLEGE, 1854-1909," North Carolina Historical Review 27:4 (October 1950), 419-429.

B-1258 Wallace, David, "ORVAL FAUBUS: THE CENTRAL FIGURE AT LITTLE ROCK CENTRAL HIGH SCHOOL," Arkansas Historical Quarterly 39:4 (Winter 1980), 314-329.

B-1259 Waring, Martha Gallaudet, "SAVANNAH'S EARLIEST PRIVATE SCHOOLS, 1733 TO 1800," Georgia Historical Quarterly 14:4 (December 1930), 324-334.

B-1260 Wenhold, Lucy Leinback, "THE SALEM BOARDING SCHOOL BETWEEN 1801 AND 1822," North Carolina Historical Review 27:1 (January 1950), 32-45.

B-1261 White, Kate, "KNOXVILLE'S OLD EDUCATIONAL INSTITUTIONS," Tennessee Historical Magazine 9:1 (April 1924), 4-6.

B-1262 White, Forrest P., "TUITION GRANTS: STRANGE FRUIT OF SOUTHERN SCHOOL INTEGRATION," South Atlantic Quarterly 60:2 (Spring 1961), 226-229.

B-1263 Wills, Ridley II, "THE MONTEAGLE SUNDAY SCHOOL ASSEMBLY--A BRIEF ACCOUNT OF ITS ORIGIN AND HISTORY," Tennessee Historical Quarterly 44:1 (Spring 1985), 3-26.

B-1264 Woolard, Annette, "PARKER V. THE UNIVERSITY OF DELAWARE: THE DESEGREGATION OF HIGHER EDUCATION IN DELAWARE," Delaware History 22:2 (Fall-Winter 1986), 111-123.

B-1265 Wormley, G. Smith, "EDUCATORS OF THE FIRST HALF CENTURY OF THE PUBLIC SCHOOLS OF THE DISTRICT OF COLUMBIA," Journal of Negro History 17:2 (April 1932), 124-140.

B-1266 Wormley, G. Smith, "MYRTILLA MINER," Journal of Negro History 5:4 (October 1920), 448-457.

B-1267 Wright, C.T., "THE DEVELOPMENT OF PUBLIC SCHOOLS FOR BLACKS IN ATLANTA, 1872-1900," Atlanta Historical Journal 21:1 (Spring 1977), 115-128.

Ghost Towns

B-1268 Adkins, Howard G., "THE HISTORICAL GEOGRAPHY OF EXTINCT TOWNS," Southern Quarterly 17:3, 4 (Spring-Summer 1979), 123-152.

B-1269 Bennett, Cheryl Ann, "LORANGER, 1900-1920: A NORTHERN COLONY IN LOUISIANA," Louisiana Studies 9:2 (Summer 1970), 88-99.

B-1270 Bennett, Mary Louise, "RUSKIN: WARE COUNTY'S VANISHED CITY," Georgia Review 5:2 (Summer 1951), 193-199.

B-1271 Burgess, Martha, "VANISHING TOWNS OF GEORGIA: OLD CLINTON," Georgia Journal 2:2 (February-March 1982), 7-9.

B-1272 Cawthon, John Ardis, "GHOST TOWNS OF OLD CLAIBORNE," Louisiana Historical Quarterly 39:4 (October 1956), 391-415.

B-1273 Crittenden, H. Temple, "LOST: TWO TOWNS," Virginia Cavalcade 10:3 (Winter 1960-61), 29-34.

B-1274 Hamer, Marguerite Bartlett, "EDMUND GRAY AND HIS SETTLEMENT AT NEW HANOVER," Georgia Historical Quarterly 13:1 (March 1929), 1-12.

B-1275 Hayden, Ethel Roby, "PORT TOBACCO, LOST TOWN OF MARYLAND," Maryland Historical Magazine 40:4 (December 1945), 261-276.

B-1276 Hollis, J.H. IV., "VANISHING TOWNS OF GEORGIA: AURARIA," Georgia Journal 2:2 (February-March), 10-11.

B-1277 Houchens, Miriam S., "THREE KENTUCKY TOWNS THAT NEVER WERE," Filson Club History Quarterly 40:1 (January 1966), 17-21.

B-1278 House, Boyce, "RECOLLECTIONS OF COLDWATER, A VANISHED TOWN," Journal of Mississippi History 21:1 (January 1959), 40-55.

B-1279 Hurst, Robert R. Jr., "MAPPING OLD ST. JOSEPH, ITS RAILROAD, AND ENVIRONS," Florida Historical Quarterly 37:4 (April 1961), 354-365.

B-1280 Janta, Alexander, "THE VIRGINIA VENTURE: A PROPOSED POLISH COLONY WHICH WENT WRONG [DOCUMENT]," Polish Review 19:2 (1974), 3-19.

B-1281 Jenkins, William H., "SOME ALABAMA 'DEAD' TOWNS," Alabama Review 12:4 (October 1959), 281-285.

B-1282 Madden, Robert R., "OLD BAY SPRINGS, MISSISSIPPI," Journal of Mississippi History 31:2 (May 1969), 116-120.

B-1283 Mitcham, Howard, "OLD RODNEY: A MISSISSIPPI GHOST TOWN," Journal of Mississippi History 15:4 (October 1953), 242-251.

B-1284 Mooney, Charles W., "GHOST TOWN: McGEE, INDIAN TERRITORY," Chronicles of Oklahoma 47:2 (Summer 1969), 160-167.

B-1285 Phillips, Randolph, "VANISHING TOWNS OF GEORGIA: TALBOTTON,"
Georgia Journal 2:2 (February-March), 12-13, 26.

B-1286 Pierce, Rita S. and Gorden Moore, "FROM DUST TO DUST: GIBBON, AN
OKLAHOMA TOWN," Chronicles of Oklahoma 61:2 (Summer 1983), 116-
129.

B-1287 Pogue, Dennis J., "CALVERTON, CALVERT COUNTY, MARYLAND: 1668-
1725," Maryland Historical Magazine 80:4 (Winter 1985), 371-376.

B-1288 Pond, Neil, "TENNESSEE'S TYREE SPRINGS: 'THE MOST CELEBRATED
WATERING PLACE IN THE STATE,'" Kentucky Folklore Record 24:3-4
(July-December 1978), 64-73.

B-1289 Riley, Franklin L., "EXTINCT TOWNS AND VILLAGES OF MISSISSIPPI,"
Publications of the Mississippi Historical Society 5 (1902), 311-
383.

B-1290 Ross, Margaret Smith, "CADRON: AN EARLY TOWN THAT FAILED,"
Arkansas Historical Quarterly 16:1 (Spring 1957), 3-27.

B-1291 "ST. JOSEPH, FLORIDA," Florida Historical Society Quarterly 2:2
(July 1909), 23-25.

B-1292 Shankman, Arnold, "HAPPYVILLE, THE FORGOTTEN COLONY," American
Jewish Archives 30:1 (April 1978), 3-19.

B-1293 Shappee, Nathan D., "THE CELESTIAL RAILROAD TO JUNO," Florida
Historical Quarterly 40:4 (April 1962), 329-349.

B-1294 Smith, Henry A. M., "THE TOWN OF DORCHESTER IN SOUTH CAROLINA --A
SKETCH OF ITS HISTORY," South Carolina Historical and Genealogical
Magazine 6:2 (April 1905), 62-95.

B-1295 Stabler, Esther B., "TRIADELPHIA: FORGOTTEN MARYLAND TOWN,"
Maryland Historical Magazine 43:2 (June 1948), 108-120.

B-1296 Summers, Marie, "NICHOLSON SPRINGS RESORT HOTEL: A NINETEENTH
CENTURY SPA," Tennessee Historical Quarterly 45:3 (Fall 1986),
244-255.

B-1297 Wesler, Kit W., "AN ARCHAEOLOGIST'S PERSPECTIVE ON THE ANCIENT
TOWN OF DONCASTER," Maryland Historical Magazine 80:4 (Winter
1985), 383-391.

B-1298 Wharton, James, "VIRGINIA'S DROWNED VILLAGE," Virginia Cavalcade
7:3 (Winter 1957), 6-12.

B-1299 Williams, Samuel C., "THE SOUTH'S FIRST COTTON FACTORY," Tennessee
Historical Quarterly 5:3 (September 1946), 212-221.

B-1300 Yelton, Susan, "NEWNANSVILLE: A LOST FLORIDA SETTLEMENT," Florida
Historical Quarterly 53:3 (January 1975), 319-331.

Growth, Development and Land Use

B-1301 Abbott, Carl, "NORFOLK IN THE NEW CENTURY: THE JAMESTOWN EXPOSI-
TION AND URBAN BOOSTERISM," Virginia Magazine of History and Biography 85:1 (January 1977), 86-96.

B-1302 Adkins, Howard G., "THE GEOGRAPHIC BASE OF URBAN RETARDATION IN
MISSISSIPPI, 1800-1840," West Georgia College Studies in the
Social Sciences 12 (June 1973), 35-49.

B-1303 Armstrong, Thomas F., "ANTEBELLUM URBAN PROMOTION IN FREDERICKS-
BERG, VIRGINIA," Southeastern Geographer 20:1 (May 1980), 58-74.

B-1304 Armstrong, Thomas F., "IN PURSUIT OF PEOPLE: THE ANTE-BELLUM TOWN
       PROMOTION OF STAUNTON, VIRGINIA," Virginia Geographer 12:1
       (Spring-Summer 1977), 15-20.

B-1305 Bacon, H. Philip, "SOME PROBLEMS OF ADJUSTMENT TO NASHVILLE'S SITE
       AND SITUATION 1780-1860," Tennessee Historical Quarterly 15:4
       (December 1956), 322-329.

B-1306 Barbour, Kirol, "SLUM CLEARANCE IN SHREVEPORT DURING THE GARDNER
       ADMINISTRATION: 1954-1958," North Louisiana Historical Associa-
       tion Journal 10:2 (1979), 1-6.

B-1307 Barker, James F., "DESIGNING FOR A SENSE OF PLACE IN MISSISSIPPI
       SMALL TOWNS," Southern Quarterly 17:3, 4 (Spring-Summer 1979),
       162-178.

B-1308 Beatty, Richmond Croom, "FUGITIVE AND AGRARIAN WRITERS AT VANDER-
       BILT," Tennessee Historical Quarterly 3:1 (March 1944), 3-23.

B-1309 Bell, Laura Palmer, "A NEW THEORY ON THE PLAN OF SAVANNAH,"
       Georgia Historical Quarterly 48:2 (June 1964), 147-165.

B-1310 Biles, Roger, "EPITAPH FOR DOWNTOWN: THE FAILURE OF CITY PLANNING
       IN POST-WORLD WAR TWO MEMPHIS," Tennessee Historical Quarterly
       44:3 (Fall 1985), 267-284.

B-1311 Bjornseth, Dick, "HOUSTON DEFIES THE PLANNERS . . . AND THRIVES,"
       Reason 9:10 (1978), 16-22.

B-1312 Bodenstein, William G., "ST. MICHAELS, MARYLAND: AN 18TH CENTURY
       SPECULATIVE DEVELOPMENT," Maryland Historical Magazine 80:3 (Fall
       1985), 228-239.

B-1313 Bowman, David, "MEMPHIS, TENNESSEE: HOW TO STOP DEVELOPERS,"
       Southern Exposure 3:4 (Winter 1976), 18-24.

B-1314 Brechenfeld, Gurney, "REFILLING THE METROPOLITAN DOUGHNUT," in D.
       Perry, ed., The Rise of the Sunbelt Cities, 1978, 231-258.

B-1315 Brown, Nancy Benzinger, "THE PRACTICAL PERSPECTIVE OF PLANNING,"
       Historic Preservation 28:1 (January-March 1976), 38-40.

B-1316 Brownell, Blaine A., "THE COMMERCIAL-CIVIC ELITE AND CITY PLANNING
       IN ATLANTA, MEMPHIS, AND NEW ORLEANS IN THE 1920's," Journal of
       Southern History 41:3 (August 1975), 339-368.

B-1317 Brownell, Blaine A., "THE IDEA OF THE CITY IN THE AMERICAN SOUTH,"
       in D. Fraser et al., eds., The Pursuit of Urban History, 1983,
       138-150.

B-1318 Brownell, Blaine A., "URBAN THEMES IN THE AMERICAN SOUTH," Journal
       of Urban History 2:2 (1976), 139-145.

B-1319 Brownell, Blaine A., "URBANIZATION IN THE SOUTH: A UNIQUE
       EXPERIENCE?" Mississippi Quarterly 26:2 (Spring 1973), 105-120.

B-1320 Burnet, Gene, "SURVIVING URBANIZATION: A TALE OF TWO CITIES,"
       South Magazine 7:2 (February 1980), 14-22.

B-1321 Capers, Gerald M., "THE RURAL LAG ON SOUTHERN CITIES," Mississippi
       Quarterly 21:4 (Fall 1968), 253-262.

B-1322 Carr, Louis Green, "'THE METROPOLES OF MARYLAND': A COMMENT ON
       TOWN DEVELOPMENT ALONG THE TOBACCO COAST," Maryland Historical
       Magazine 69:2 (Summer 1974), 124-145.

B-1323 Carter, Luther J., "THE DADE MASTER PLAN: FILLING THE METROPOLI-
       TAN POLICY VACUUM," Habitat International 2:1/2 (1977), 337-338.

B-1324 Cassity, Michael J., "THE PAST FORSAKEN: THE CRISES OF AN OKLA-
HOMA COMMUNITY," Southwest Review 61:4 (Autumn 1976), 396-408.

B-1325 Chapin, F. Stuart Jr., "CITY PLANNING: ADJUSTING PEOPLE AND
PLACE," in R. Vance, The Urban South, (1954), 268-282.

B-1326 Cobb, James C., "URBANIZATION AND THE CHANGING SOUTH: A REVIEW OF
LITERATURE," South Atlantic Urban Studies 1 (1977), 253-266.

B-1327 Cole, William E., "URBAN DEVELOPMENT IN THE TENNESSEE VALLEY,"
Social Forces 26:1 (October 1947), 67-75.

B-1328 Connelly, Thomas Lawrence, "THE VANDERBILT AGRARIANS: TIME AND
PLACE IN SOUTHERN TRADITION," Tennessee Historical Quarterly 22:1
(March 1963), 22-37.

B-1329 Cook, Charles Orson and Barry J. Kaplan, "CIVIC ELITES AND URBAN
PLANNING: HOUSTON'S RIVER OAKS," East Texas Historical Journal
15:2 (1977), 29-37.

B-1330 Coomer, James C. and Kim Quaile Hill, "THE POLICY MAPS OF URBAN
DECISION MAKERS: ATTITUDE TOWARD LONG-RANGE PLANNING," Journal of
Political Science 10:1 (Fall 1982), 31-42.

B-1331 Cosgrove, Michael H., "MEASURING METROPOLITAN DEVELOPMENT," Land
Economics 50:1 (February 1974), 82-84.

B-1332 Cox, Richard J., "TROUBLE ON THE CHAIN GANG: CITY SURVEYING,
MAPS, AND THE ABSENCE OF URBAN PLANNING IN BALTIMORE, 1730-1823;
WITH A CHECKLIST OF MAPS OF THE PERIODS," Maryland Historical
Magazine 8:1 (Spring 1986), 8-49.

B-1333 Cruzat, Heloise H. (trans.), "ALLOTMENT OF BUILDING SITES IN NEW
ORLEANS, 1722," Louisiana Historical Quarterly 7:4 (October 1924),
564-566.

B-1334 Cummings, Steve, "FLORIDA: LOVE IT OR SELL IT," Southern Exposure
1:2 (Summer-Fall 1973), 23-28.

B-1335 Curry, Leonard P., "URBANIZATION AND URBANISM IN THE OLD SOUTH: A
COMPARATIVE VIEW," Journal of Southern History 40:1 (February
1974), 43-60.

B-1336 DeVine, Jerry W., "TOWN DEVELOPMENT IN WIREGRASS GEORGIA, 1870-
1900," Journal of Southwest Georgia History (Fall 1983), 1-22.

B-1337 Diettrich, Sigismond DeR., "FLORIDA'S NON-METROPOLITAN URBAN
GROWTH, 1930 TO 1950," Quarterly Journal of the Florida Academy of
Sciences 16:4 (December 1953), 209-216.

B-1338 Dorsett, Lyle W. and Arthur H. Shaffer, "WAS THE ANTEBELLUM SOUTH
ANTIURBAN? A SUGGESTION," Journal of Southern History 38:1 (February 1972), 93-100.

B-1339 Doyle, Don H., "THE URBANIZATION OF DIXIE," Journal of Urban
History 7:1 (November 1980), 83-92.

B-1340 Draper, E. S., "URBAN DEVELOPMENT IN THE SOUTHEAST: WHAT OF THE
FUTURE," Social Forces 19:1 (October 1940), 17-22.

B-1341 Dyer, Donald R., "URBAN GROWTH IN FLORIDA; EXEMPLIFIED BY LAKE-
LAND," Journal of Geography 55:6 (September 1956), 278-286.

B-1342 Earle, Carville and Ronald Hoffman, "URBAN DEVELOPMENT IN THE 18TH
CENTURY SOUTH," Perspectives in American History 10 (1976), 7-78.

B-1343 Elliott, Harold, "CARDINAL PLACE GEOMETRY IN THE AMERICAN SOUTH,"
Southeastern Geographer 24:2 (November 1984), 65-77.

B-1344 Epperson, Terry E. Jr., "SELECTED UNIQUE URBAN NODULES ON ROUTE-WAYS," Memorandum Folio: Southeastern Division Association of American Geographers 15 (November 1963), 33-40.

B-1345 Epperson, Terry E. Jr., "STAGES OF URBAN EVALUATION USING KINGS-PORT, TENNESSEE, AS AN EXAMPLE," Memorandum Folio: Southeastern Division Association of American Geographers 14 (November 1962), 33-40.

B-1346 Ernst, Joseph A. and H. Roy Merrens, "'CAMDEN'S TURRETS PIERCE THE SKIES!': THE URBAN PROCESS IN THE SOUTHERN COLONIES DURING THE EIGHTEENTH CENTURY," William and Mary Quarterly 30:4 (October 1973), 549-574.

B-1347 Ervin, Osbin L., "THE EFFECTIVENESS OF COMMUNITY INDUSTRIAL DEVELOPMENT PROGRAMS: A STUDY OF A DEVELOPMENT DISTRICT IN SOUTHERN APPALACHIA," Review of Regional Studies 6:1 (Spring 1976), 75-97.

B-1348 Feagin, J. R., "THE ROLE OF THE STATE IN URBAN DEVELOPMENT," Society and Space 2:4 (December 1984), 447-460.

B-1349 Furlong, William Barry, "FERMENT IN GEORGETOWN," Horizon 19:4 (July 1977), 4-13.

B-1350 Galehouse, Richard F., "LAND PLANNING FOR LARGE-SCALE RESIDENTIAL DEVELOPMENT," Urban Land 40:9 (October 1981), 12-18.

B-1351 Galle, O. R. and R. N. Stern, "THE METROPOLITAN SYSTEM IN THE SOUTH: CONTINUITY AND CHANGE," in D. Poston, ed., The Population of the South, (1981), 155-174.

B-1352 Garofallo, Charles, "THE ATLANTA SPIRIT: A STUDY IN URBAN IDEOLOGY," South Atlantic Quarterly 74:1 (Winter 1975), 34-44.

B-1353 Garren, Robert Earl, "URBANISM: A NEW WAY OF LIFE FOR THE SOUTH," Mississippi Quarterly 10:2 (Spring 1957), 65-72.

B-1354 Garrett, Franklin M., "A SHORT HISTORY OF LAND LOT 49 OF THE FOURTEENTH DISTRICT OF ORIGINALLY HENRY, NOW FULTON COUNTY IN GEORGIA," Atlanta Historical Journal 25:1 (Spring 1981), 17-40.

B-1355 Garrett, Franklin M., "A SHORT HISTORY OF LAND LOTS 105 AND 106 OF THE 17TH DISTRICT OF FULTON COUNTY, GEORGIA. PART 1, LAND LOT 106," Atlanta Historical Journal 27:1 (Spring 1983), 51-70.

B-1356 Garrett, Franklin M., "A SHORT HISTORY OF LAND LOTS 205 AND 106 OF THE 17TH DISTRICT OF FULTON COUNTY, GEORGIA. PART II, LAND LOT 105," Atlanta Historical Journal 27:2 (Summer 1983), 39-54.

B-1357 Goldfield, David R., "PLANNING FOR URBAN GROWTH IN THE OLD SOUTH," South Atlantic Urban Studies, 4 (1980), 234-256.

B-1358 Gordon, David M., "CLASS STRUGGLE AND THE STAGES OF AMERICAN URBAN DEVELOPMENT," in D. Perry, ed., The Rise of the Sunbelt Cities (1978), 55-82.

B-1359 Greene, David L., "URBAN SUBCENTERS: RECENT TRENDS IN URBAN SPATIAL STRUCTURE," Growth and Change 11:1 (January 1980), 29-40.

B-1360 Groth, Philip, "PLANTATION AGRICULTURE AND THE URBANIZATION OF THE SOUTH," Rural Sociology 42:2 (Summer 1977), 206-219.

B-1361 Hamer, Andrew M., "METROPOLITAN PLANNING AND THE LOCATION BEHAVIOR OF BASIC OFFICE FIRMS: A CASE STUDY," Review of Regional Studies 4:supplement (1974), 34-45.

B-1362 Hampton, Ellen, "LITTLE HAITI: THE CITY WITHIN," Miami Herald Tropic Magazine (July 3, 1983), 7-26.

B-1363 Heberle, Rudolf, "THE MAINSPRINGS OF SOUTHERN URBANISM," in R. Vance, The Urban South, (1954), 6-23.

B-1364 Hinds, Dudley S., "NEW CITIES FOR GEORGIA," Atlanta Economic Review 21:10 (October 1971), 8-15.

B-1365 Hinkley, Katherine A., "THE BANG AND THE WIMPER: MODEL CITIES AND GHETTO OPINION," Urban Affairs Quarterly 13:2 (December 1977), 131-150.

B-1366 Hofsommer, Donovan L., "TOWNSITE DEVELOPMENT ON THE WICHITA FALLS AND NORTHWESTERN RAILWAY," Great Plains Journal 16:2 (Spring 1977), 107-122.

B-1367 Holland, Robert B., "THE AGRARIAN MANIFESTO--A GENERATION LATER," Mississippi Quarterly 10:2 (Spring 1957), 73-78.

B-1368 Holmes, Jack D. C., "VIDAL AND ZONING IN SPANISH NEW ORLEANS, 1797," Louisiana History 14:3 (Summer 1973), 271-282.

B-1369 Horwatt, Michael S. and John E. Lynch, "FAIRFAX CENTER URBAN VILLAGE PLAN," Urban Land 44:5 (May 1985), 15-19.

B-1370 Hourihan, J. Kevin and Curtis C. Roseman, "URBAN STRUCTURE AND THE SPACING OF CITIES: AN EMPIRICAL INVESTIGATION," Review of Regional Studies 5:3 (Winter 1975), 68-81.

B-1371 Huggins, Kay Haire, "CITY PLANNING IN NORTH CAROLINA, 1900-1929: PART 1," North Carolina Historical Review 46:4 (Autumn 1969), 377-397.

B-1372 Hultquist, Nancy B., "A SPATIAL PERSPECTIVE ON URBAN PROBLEMS: A VIEW FROM ATLANTA, GEORGIA," Southeastern Geographer 12:2 (November 1972), 78-90.

B-1373 Inge, M. Thomas, "THE GREAT DEBATE IN RICHMOND," Prospects 3 (1977), 521-530.

B-1374 Jacobs, Sam, "MIAMI: MANHATTAN OF THE SOUTH," Planning 45 (February 1979), 10-13.

B-1375 Jones, George F., "PETER GORDON'S (?) PLAN OF SAVANNAH," Georgia Historical Quarterly 60:1 (Spring 1986), 97-101.

B-1376 Jones, Kenneth J. and Wyatt C. Jones, "TOWARD A TYPOLOGY OF AMERICAN CITIES," Journal of Regional Science 10:2 (August 1970), 217-224.

B-1377 Kaplan, Barry J., "URBAN DEVELOPMENT, ECONOMIC GROWTH, AND PER-SONAL LIBERTY: THE RHETORIC OF THE HOUSTON ANTI-ZONING MOVEMENTS, 1947-1962," Southwestern Historical Quarterly 84:2 (October 1980), 133-168.

B-1378 Keeley, Artheel, "SEQUENT OCCUPANCY OF THE YAZOO BASIN, MISSIS-SIPPI: 1830 TO 1976," The Mississippi Geographer 4:1 (Spring 1978), 3-18.

B-1379 Kennedy, G. W., "DISCOVERING SHOCK CITY: HOUSTON AND THE PUBLIC MEDIA," Journal of Popular Culture 15:4 (Spring 1982), 157-162.

B-1380 Kenzie, Roy, "MIAMI: A CITY SEEKS AN IMAGE," Urban Design International 2 (March-April 1981), 12-17.

B-1381 Koch, Walter F., "REGIONAL COMPARISONS OF URBANIZATION IN ALABAMA, 1900-1960," Memorandum Folio Southeast Division, Association of American Geographers 18 (November 1966), 100-111.

B-1382 Kurtz, Wilbur G., "THE STORY OF LAND LOT 77-ATLANTA," Atlanta Historical Bulletin 8:32 (1947), 41-67.

B-1383 LaBorde, Rene, "A FOOTNOTE THAT CHANGED THE CHARLESTON SKYLINE,"
       Georgia Review 19:3 (Fall 1965), 332-336.

B-1384 Lemon, James T., "URBANIZATION AND THE DEVELOPMENT OF EIGHTEENTH-
       CENTURY SOUTHEASTERN PENNSYLVANIA AND ADJACENT DELAWARE," William
       and Mary Quarterly 24:4 (October 1967), 502-542.

B-1385 Leverette, William E. Jr. and David E. Shi, "AGRARIANISM FOR
       COMMUTEES," South Atlantic Quarterly 79:2 (Spring 1980), 204-218.

B-1386 Levitt, Rachelle L., "LOUISVILLE, KENTUCKY: A COMMITMENT TO
       DEVELOPMENT," Urban Land 44:6 (June 1985), 2-6.

B-1387 Lindsay, Suzanne A., "IS THEIR GROWTH OUTSIDE ATLANTA?" Georgia
       Business and Economic Conditions 45:4 (September-October 1985),
       3-12.

B-1388 Lloyd, Robert B. Jr., "DEVELOPMENT OF THE PLAN OF PENSACOLA DURING
       THE COLONIAL ERA, 1559-1821," Florida Historical Quarterly 64:3
       (January 1986), 253-272.

B-1389 London, Bruce and Richard P. Palmieri, "TOWARDS AN HISTORICAL
       URBAN ECOLOGY: TESTING ASPECTS OF SCHNAIE'S EVOLUTIONARY SEQUENCE
       HYPOTHESIS," South Atlantic Urban Studies 5 (1981), 198-211.

B-1390 Markham, Wayne, "WELCOME TO THE FRONTIER," Urban Land 42:9
       (September 1983), 2-6.

B-1391 Matherly, Walter J., "THE URBAN DEVELOPMENT OF THE SOUTH,"
       Southern Economic Journal 1:4 (February 1935), 3-26.

B-1392 Meeks, Ann McDonald, "WHITEHAVEN AND LEVI: THE EVOLUTION OF RURAL
       COMMUNITIES IN WEST TENNESSEE, 1819-1865," West Tennessee Histori-
       cal Society Papers 39 (1985), 10-25.

B-1393 Meredith, Howard L. and Shirk, George H., "OKLAHOMA CITY: GROWTH
       AND RECONSTRUCTION, 1889-1939," Chronicles of Oklahoma 55:3 (Fall
       1977), 293-308.

B-1394 Millas, Aristides, "PLANNING FOR THE ELDERLY WITHIN THE CONTEXT OF
       A NEIGHBORHOOD," Ekistics 47:283 (July-August 1980), 264-272.

B-1395 Miller, Harold V., "THE GROWTH AND DEVELOPMENT OF THE MORRISTOWN,
       TENNESSEE COMMUNITY," Professional Geographer 8 (December 1948),
       28-40.

B-1396 Miller, Harold V., "MEETING PROBLEMS OF URBAN GROWTH (TENNESSEE
       EXAMPLES)," Tennessee Planner 17:2 (October 1957), 47-55.

B-1397 Miller, Randall, "DANIEL PRATT'S INDUSTRIAL URBANISM: THE COTTON
       MILL TOWN IN ANTEBELLUM ALABAMA," Alabama Historical Quarterly
       34:1 (Spring 1972), 5-36.

B-1398 Miller, William D., "RURAL VALUES AND URBAN PROGRESS: MEMPHIS,"
       Mississippi Quarterly 21:4 (Fall 1968), 263-274.

B-1399 Miller, Zane L., "URBAN GROWTH IN THE SOUTH: GENERAL PATTERNS,"
       Houston Review (Fall 1981), 276-287.

B-1400 Millet, Donald J., "TOWN DEVELOPMENT IN SOUTHWEST LOUISIANA,"
       Louisiana History 13:2 (Spring 1972), 139-168.

B-1401 Mitchell, Robert D., "THE SHENANDOAH VALLEY FRONTIER," Annals of
       the Association of American Geographers 62:3 (September 1972),
       461-486.

B-1402 Moger, Allen W., "INDUSTRIAL AND URBAN PROGRESS IN VIRGINIA FROM
       1880 TO 1900," Virginia Magazine of History and Biography 66:3
       (July 1958), 307-336.

B-1403 Mookerjie, Debrath, "THE CONCEPT OF URBAN FRINGE AND ITS DELINEA-
TION (THE CASE OF ORLANDO, FLORIDA)," Geographical Review of India
25:1 (March 1963), 44-57.

B-1404 Mookerjie, Debrath, "THE IMPACT OF URBAN GROWTH ON LAND USE IN THE
URBAN FRINGE OF ORLANDO, FLORIDA," Southeastern Geographer 2
(1962), 7-18.

B-1405 Moxley, Robert L., "VERTICAL ASSISTANCE, POPULATION SIZE, AND
GROWTH IN THE CONTEXT AND RESULTS OF COMMUNITY CIVIL ACTION,"
Journal of the Community Development Society 16:1 (1985), 57-74.

B-1406 Munn, Robert F., "THE DEVELOPMENT OF MODEL TOWNS IN THE BITUMINOUS
COAL FIELDS," West Virginia History 40:3 (Spring 1979), 243-253.

B-1407 Nichols, Cheryl Griffith, "PULASKI HEIGHTS: EARLY SUBURBAN DEVEL-
OPMENT IN LITTLE ROCK, ARKANSAS," Arkansas Historical Quarterly
41:2 (Summer 1982), 129-145.

B-1408 Olson, Sherry H., "BALTIMORE IMITATES THE SPIDER," Annals of the
Association of American Geographers 69:4 (December 1979), 557-574.

B-1409 Owens, Michael S. and Wayne R. Thirsk, "LAND TAXES AND IDLE LAND:
A CASE STUDY OF HOUSTON," Land Economics 50:3 (August 1974), 251-
260.

B-1410 Padgett, James A., "SOME DOCUMENTS RELATING TO THE BATTURE CONTRO-
VERSY IN NEW ORLEANS," Louisiana Historical Quartyerly 23:3 (July
1940), 679-732.

B-1411 Pannell, Clifton W., "THE RECENT METROPOLITAN GROWTH IN THE
SOUTHERN UNITED STATES," Southeastern Geographer 14:1 (May 1974),
7-16.

B-1412 Pathak, Chittaranjan, "THE GROWTH AND DEVELOPMENT OF RALEIGH,
NORTH CAROLINA," Southeastern Geographer 15 (November 1963), 77-
81.

B-1413 Paul, Charles L., "BEAUFORT, NORTH CAROLINA: ITS DEVELOPMENT AS A
COLONIAL TOWN," North Carolina Historical Review 47:4 (Autumn
1970), 370-387.

B-1414 Peck, Dennis L., "URBAN DEVELOPMENT PROGRAMMING: THE PROBLEM OF
FEDERAL INVOLVEMENT AND SELF-EVALUATION," Sociological Spectrum
2:3/4 (July-December 1982), 387-406.

B-1415 Phillips, Coy T., "CITY PATTERNS OF DURHAM, N. C.," Economic
Geography 23:4 (October 1947), 233-247.

B-1416 Phillips, Phillip D., "NEWSPAPER CIRCULATION AS A MEASURE OF
METROPOLITAN INFLUENCE AND DOMINANCE," Southeastern Geographer
14:1 (May 1974), 17-25.

B-1417 Piene, Nan R., "PAUL RUDOLPH DESIGNS A TOWN," Art in America 55:
(July-August 1967), 58-63.

B-1418 Pine, W. Morton, "HISTORY RIDES THE WINDS TO COLONIAL CHARLESTON,"
South Carolina Historical Magazine 87:3 (July 1986), 162-175.

B-1419 Power, Garrett, "HIGH SOCIETY: THE BUILDING HEIGHT LIMITATION ON
BALTIMORE'S MT. VERNON PLACE," Maryland Historical Magazine 79:3
(Fall 1984), 197-219.

B-1420 Quinn, Jane, "REID V. BARRY: THE LEGAL BATTLE OVER THE 'BEST
LOCATION IN ORLANDO,'" Florida Historical Quarterly 64:3 (January
1986), 273-283.

B-1421 Rabinowitz, Howard N., "CONTINUITY AND CHANGE: SOUTHERN URBAN DEVELOPMENT, 1860-1900," in B. Brownell, ed., The City in Southern History (1977), 92-122.

B-1422 Rainbolt, John C., "THE ABSENCE OF TOWNS IN SEVENTEENTH-CENTURY VIRGINIA," Journal of Southern History 35:3 (August 1969), 343-360.

B-1423 Randall, Duncan P., "WILMINGTON, NORTH CAROLINA: THE HISTORICAL DEVELOPMENT OF A PORT CITY," Annals of the Association of American Geographers 58:3 (September 1968), 441-451.

B-1424 Ratajczak, Donald, "CAN WE COUNT ON CONTINUED GROWTH," Atlanta Economic Review 28:1 (January-February 1975), 16-21.

B-1425 Ratner, James, "CHARLESTON TOWN CENTER," Urban Land 44:6 (June 1985), 16-17.

B-1426 Redman, Carl, "ALEXANDRIA, LA. REORGANIZES FOR GROWTH," South Magazine 7:2 (February 1980), 57-58.

B-1427 Reid, Ird De A., 'METHODOLOGICAL NOTES FOR STUDYING THE SOUTHERN CITY," Social Forces 19:2 (December 1940), 228-235.

B-1428 Reid, John D., "BLACK URBANIZATION IN THE SOUTH, Phylon 35:3 (Fall 1974), 259-267.

B-1429 Reynolds, John E. and Devin L. Tower, "FACTORS AFFECTING RURAL LAND PRICES IN AN URBANIZING AREA," Review of Regional Studies 8:3 (Winter 1978), 23-34.

B-1430 Rice, Bradley R., "THE BATTLE OF BUCKHEAD: THE PLAN OF IMPROVEMENT AND ATLANTA'S LAST BIG ANNEXATION," Atlanta Historical Journal 25:4 (Winter 1981), 5-22.

B-1431 Rice, Bradley R., "URBANIZATION, 'ATLANTA-IZATION,' AND SUBURBANIZATION: THREE THEMES FOR THE URBAN HISTORY OF TWENTIETH-CENTURY GEORGIA," Georgia Historical Quarterly 68:1 (Spring 1984), 40-59.

B-1432 Richelton, Jeffery P. and Henry E. Moon Jr., "RURAL-URBAN LAND USE CONVERSION IN THE SOUTH'S BLACK-BELT: A CASE STUDY OF MONTGOMERY COUNTY, AL," Journal of the Alabama Academy of Science 57:1 (January 1986), 24-38.

B-1433 Rivers, David E., "ATLANTA'S PLANNING PROCESS: COMPREHENSIVE, COORDINATED," National Civic Review 68:3 (March 1979), 136-141.

B-1434 Roberts, Frances, "DR. DAVID MOORE, URBAN PIONEER OF THE OLD SOUTHWEST," Alabama Review 18:1 (January 1965), 37-46.

B-1435 Rodabaugh, Karl, "AGRARIAN IDEOLOGY AND THE FARMERS' REVOLT IN ALABAMA," Alabama Review 36:3 (July 1983), 195-219.

B-1436 Rogers, Tom, "NASHVILLE--BUILDING FOR ITS THIRD CENTURY," Tennessee Valley Perspective 9:4 (Summer 1979), 21-27.

B-1437 Rohe, William M. and Lauren B. Gates, "NEIGHBORHOOD PLANNING: PROMISE AND PRODUCT," Urban and Social Change Review 14:1 (Winter 1981), 26-32.

B-1438 Romsa, Gerald H. and Wayne L. Hoffman, "SOME TEMPORAL CONSIDERATIONS OF BASIC URBAN DIMENSIONS IN THE SOUTHEAST: A FACTOR ANALYSIS SOLUTION," Southeastern Geographer 9:1 (April 1969), 1-12.

B-1439 Rubin, Louis D., "THE BOLL WEEVIL, THE IRON HORSE, AND THE END OF THE LINE: THOUGHTS ON THE SOUTH," Virginia Quarterly Review 55:2 (Spring 1979), 193-221.

B-1440 Russell, Judith F. and William H. Berentsen, "URBAN REGIONS IN GEORGIA: 1964-1979," Southeastern Geographer 21:2 (November 1981), 84-107.

B-1441 Rutlan, Vernon W., "THE IMPACT OF URBAN-INDUSTRIAL DEVELOPMENT ON AGRICULTURE IN THE TENNESSEE VALLEY AND THE SOUTHEAST," Regional Science Association Papers and Proceedings 1 (1955), R. I-R. 23.

B-1442 Salmop, Myrene, "L'ENFANT AND THE PLANNING OF WASHINGTON, D. C.," History Today [Great Britain] 26:11 (1976), 699-706.

B-1443 Saunders, Robert, "MODERNIZATION AND THE FREE PEOPLES OF RICHMOND IN THE 1780s AND THE 1850s," Southern Studies 24:3 (Fall 1985), 237-272.

B-1444 Schalck, Harry G., "PLANNING ROLAND PARK, 1891-1910," Maryland Historical Magazine 67:4 (Winter 1972), 419-428.

B-1445 Schretter, Howard A., "ROUND TOWNS," Southeastern Geographer 3 (1963), 46-52.

B-1446 Schul, Norman W. and Charles B. Hayes, "INTRA-URBAN MANUFACTURING LAND USE PATTERNS: AN EXAMINATION OF GREENSBORO, NORTH CAROLINA," Southeastern Geographer 8 (1968), 39-45.

B-1447 Schulz, Judith, "THE HINTERLAND OF REVOLUTIONARY CAMDEN, SOUTH CAROLINA," Southeastern Geographer 16:2 (November 1976), 91-97.

B-1448 Scott, Anne Firor, "THE STYE OF SOUTHERN URBANIZATION," Urban Affairs Quarterly 1:3 (March 1966), 5-14.

B-1449 Sears, Joan N., "TOWN PLANNING IN WHITE AND HAVERSHAM COUNTIES, GEORGIA," Georgia Historical Quarterly 54:1 (Spring 1970), 20-40.

N-1450 Sessa, Frank B., "MIAMI ON THE EVE OF THE BOOM: 1923," Tequesta 11 (1951), 3-26.

B-1451 Shapi, Edward, "THE SOUTHERN AGRARIANS AND THE TENNESSEE VALLEY AUTHORITY," American Quarterly 22:4 (Winter 1970), 792-806.

B-1452 Shappee, Nathan D., "FLAGLER'S UNDERTAKINGS IN MIAMI IN 1897," Tequesta 19 (1959), 3-14.

B-1453 Sharp, Helen R., "SAMUEL A. SWANN AND THE DEVELOPMENT OF FLORIDA, 1855-1900," Florida Historical Quarterly 20:2 (October 1941), 169-196.

B-1454 Sharpe, Mollie Hawkins, "TEXAS: THE URBAN FRONTIER," American Demographics 3:10 (November 1981), 21-23.

B-1455 Silver, Christopher, "THE ORDEAL OF CITY PLANNING IN POSTWAR RICHMOND, VIRGINIA: A QUEST FOR GREATNESS," Journal of Urban History 10:1 (November 1983), 33-60.

B-1456 Sledge, John S., "CORDELE, 1887-1917: THIRTY YEARS OF GROWTH AND BOOSTER SPIRIT," Journal of Southwest Georgia History (Fall 1983), 49-54.

B-1457 Smith, T. Lynn, "THE EMERGENCE OF CITIES," in R. Vance, The Urban South (1954), 24-37.

B-1458 Smith, T. Lynn, "THE EMERGENCE OF URBAN CENTERS IN THE SOUTH," in T. Smith, ed., The Sociology of Urban Life (1951).

B-1459 Soniat, Meloncy C., "THE FAUBOURGS FORMING THE UPPER SECTION OF THE CITY OF NEW ORLEANS," Louisiana Historical Quarterly 20:1 (January 1937), 192-211.

B-1460 Sorant, Peter, Robert Whelan and Alma Young, "CITY PROFILE: NEW ORLEANS," Cities 1:4 (May 1984), 314-321.

B-1461 Sprague, Stuart S., "INVESTING IN APPALACHIA: THE VIRGINIA VALLEY BOOM OF 1889-1893," Virginia Cavalcade 24:3 (Winter 1975), 134-143.

B-1462 Sprague, Stuart S., "TOWN MAKING IN THE ERA OF GOOD FEELINGS: KENTUCKY 1814-1820," Register of the Kentucky Historical Society 72:4 (October 1978), 337-341.

B-1463 Stanton, Dietrich T., "NATURE AND DIRECTIONS OF SUBURBANIZATION IN THE SOUTH," Social Forces 39:2 (December 1960), 181-186.

B-1464 Starling, Robert B., "THE PLANK ROAD MOVEMENT IN NORTH CAROLINA, PART I," North Carolina Historical Review 16:1 (January 1939), 1-22.

B-1465 Steller, Joseph D. Jr., ed., "A MXD TAKES OFF: BALTIMORE'S INNER HARBOR," Urban Land 41:3 (March 1982), 10-20.

B-1466 Stephenson, Richard A., "IMPACT OF URBAN GROWTH ON WATER RESOURCES IN SOUTHEASTERN UNITED STATES," Southeastern Geographer 12:2 (November 1972), 155-161.

B-1467 Stuart, Alfred W., "METROLINA: A SOUTHERN DISPERSED URBAN REGION," Southeastern Geographer 12:2 (November 1972, 101-112.

B-1468 Sugg, John, "DOWNTOWN MIAMI: FEUDING OVER ITS FUTURE," Florida Trend 24 (May 1981), 34-37.

B-1469 Sullivan, Walter, "THE CITY AND THE OLD VISION," in L. Rubin Jr., ed., The Lasting South: Fourteen Southerners Look at Their Home 1957.

B-1470 Sussman, Carl, "MOVING THE CITY SLICKERS OUT," Southern Exposure 2:2-3 (Fall 1974), 99-107.

B-1471 Tanner, Ralph M., "SOME CHARACTERISTICS OF EIGHT LAND COMPANIES IN NORTH ALABAMA, 1863-1900," Alabama Review 29:2 (April 1976), 124-134.

B-1472 Tata, Robert J., "THE EFFECT OF LAND FRAGMENTATION IN INTERNAL URBAN CIRCULATION IN BOCA RATON, FLORIDA," Southeastern Geographer 12:2 (November 1972), 112-120.

B-1473 Thomas, Mary Martha, "ROSIE THE ALABAMA RIVITER," Alabama Review 39:3 (July 1986), 196-212.

B-1474 Thomason, Philip, "THE MEN'S QUARTER OF DOWNTOWN NASHVILLE," Tennessee Historical Quarterly 41:1 (Spring 1982), 48-66.

B-1475 Thompson, Daniel C., "THE NEW SOUTH," Journal of Social Issues 22:1 (January 1966), 7-19.

B-1476 Thorp, Daniel B., "THE CITY THAT NEVER WAS: COUNT VON ZINZEN-DORF'S ORIGINAL PLAN FOR SALEM," North Carolina Historical Review 61:1 (January 1984), 36-58.

B-1477 "TOWNS IN THE ALABAMA TERRITORY [1817]," Alabama Historical Quarterly 3:1 (Spring 1941), 74-82.

B-1478 Tsao, Alan H. Y. and John W. Whaley, "CHANGES IN URBAN LAND USE IN TIDEWATER, VIRGINIA, 1970-75," Virginia Social Science Journal 12:2 (November 1977), 33-43.

B-1479 Turner, Julie, "HARLEM, GA.: INFLUENCES ON EARLY DEVELOPMENT AND GROWTH," Richmond County History 16:2 (Summer 1984), 11-20.

B-1480 Veenendaal, Augustus J. Jr., "RAILROADS, OIL AND DUTCHMEN,"
Chronicles of Oklahoma 63:1 (Spring 1985), 28-47.

B-1481 Watkins, Alfred J. and David C. Perry, "REGIONAL CHANGE AND THE
IMPACT OF UNEVEN URBAN DEVELOPMENT," in D. Perry, ed., The Rise of
the Sunbelt Cities (1978), 19-54.

B-1482 Watkins, Edgar, "GEOGRAPHY, RAILROADS AND MEN MADE ATLANTA,"
Atlanta Historical Bulletin 8:33 (October 1948), 71-81.

B-1483 Watts, Ann DeWitt, "CITIES AND THEIR PLACE IN SOUTHERN APPALA-
CHIA," Appalachian Journal 8:2 (Winter 1981), 105-118.

B-1484 Weems, John Edward, "THE GALVESTON STORM OF 1900," Southwestern
Historical Quarterly 61:4 (April 1958), 494-507.

B-1485 Weiher, Kenneth, "CENTRAL PLACE THEORY AND SOUTHERN URBANIZATION,"
Review of Regional Studies 6:2 (Fall 1976), 62-77.

B-1486 Weiss, Shirley, Thomas G. Donnelly, and Edward J. Kaiser, "LAND
VALUE AND LAND DEVELOPMENT INFLUENCE FACTORS: AN ANALYTICAL
APPROACH FOR EXAMINING POLICY ALTERNATIVES," Land Economics 42:2
(May 1966), 230-233.

B-1487 Wellenruther, Hermann, "URBANIZATION IN THE COLONIAL SOUTH: A CRI-
TIQUE," William and Mary Quarterly 31:4 (October 1974), 653-671.

B-1488 White, Dana F. and Timothy J. Crimmins, "HOW ATLANTA GREW,"
Atlanta Economic Review 28:1 (January-February 1978), 7-15.

B-1489 White, Otis, "CHARLOTTE'S NEW GOAL," South Business 7:6 (June
1980), 22-27.

B-1490 Wilbur, George L., "GROWTH OF METROPOLITAN AREAS IN THE SOUTH,"
Social Forces 42:4 (May 1964), 489-500.

B-1491 Wilson, Bobby M., "USING VACANT URBAN LAND IN BIRMINGHAM," Urban
Land 40:6 (June 1981), 8-13.

B-1492 Withington, William A., "APPROACHES TO THE DIFFUSION OF URBANI-
ZATION IN KENTUCKY, 1790-1970," Proceedings, Kentucky Academy of
Sciences (Nov. 2-3, 1973), 35-42.

B-1493 Wood, W. K., "A NOTE ON PRO-URBANISM AND URBANIZATION IN THE
ANTEBELLUM SOUTH: AUGUSTA, GEORGIA, 1820-1860," Richmond County
History 6:1 (Winter 1974), 23-31.

Hazards and Disasters

B-1494 Bailey, Mrs. Hugh C., "MOBILE'S TRAGEDY: THE GREAT MAGAZINE
EXPLOSION OF 1865," Alabama Review 21:1 (January 1968), 40-52.

B-1495 Billman, Calvin J., "THE 1916 AUGUSTA FIRE: AN UNNECESSARY
TRAGEDY," Richmond County History 7:2 (Summer 1975), 77-100.

B-1496 Black, Henry, "A SPEAR OF HELL: THE TUPELO TORNADO OF 1936,"
Journal of Mississippi History 37:3 (August 1976), 263-278.

B-1497 Breaux, Gustave A., "1937 FLOOD AT LOUISVILLE," Filson Club
History Quarterly 11:2 (April 1937), 109-119.

B-1498 Callahan, Helen, "THE FLOOD THREATENS AUGUSTA'S EFFORTS TO BECOME
'THE LOWELL OF THE SOUTH,'" Richmond County History 7:2 (Summer
1975), 47-60.

B-1499 Campbell, Steve B., "THE GREAT FIRE OF ATLANTA, MAY 21, 1917,"
Atlanta Historical Journal 13:2 (June 1968), 9-48.

B-1500 Campbell, Steve B., "HOLOCAUST ON PEACHTREE," Atlanta Historical
        Journal 14:4 (December 1969), 9-28.

B-1501 Carlton, LaNey, "FISK SOCIAL WORK STUDENTS' EMERGENCY RELIEF WORK
        FOLLOWING THE EAST NASHVILLE FIRE OF 1916," Tennessee Historical
        Quarterly 44:4 (Winter 1985), 371-379.

B-1502 Coulter, E. Merton, "THE GREAT SAVANNAH FIRE OF 1820," Georgia
        Historical Quarterly 23:1 (March 1939), 1-27.

B-1503 Crooks, James B., "THE BALTIMORE FIRE AND BALTIMORE REFORM,"
        Maryland Historical Magazine 65:1 (Spring 1970), 1-17.

B-1504 Davis, R. Bruce, "THE TORNADO OF 1840 HITS MISSISSIPPI," Journal
        of Mississippi History 34:1 (February 1974), 43-52.

B-1505 de Rojas, Lauro A., "THE GREAT FIRE OF 1788 IN NEW ORLEANS,"
        Louisiana Historical Quarterly 20:3 (July 1937), 578-589.

B-1506 Gaby, Donald C., "MIAMI'S EARLIEST KNOWN GREAT HURRICANE,"
        Tequesta No. 34 (1974), 65-67.

B-1507 "GAINESVILLE'S 1936 TORNADO," North Georgia Journal 2:1 (Spring
        1985), 7-15.

B-1508 "THE GREAT STORM, TALLAHASSEE, AUGUST, 1851," Florida Historical
        Quarterly 18:4 (April 1940), 270-273.

B-1509 Hammon, Stratton, "'SEND A BOAT'! IMAGES OF LOUISVILLE'S 1937
        FLOOD," Register of the Kentucky Historical Society 81:2 (Spring
        1983), 154-167.

B-1510 Hebel, Louis J., "TRAGIC INCIDENT ON BROADWAY, LOUISVILLE, 1895,"
        Filson Club History Quarterly 42:4 (October 1968), 316-322.

B-1511 Heite, Edward, "THE TUNNELS OF RICHMOND," Virginia Cavalcade 14:3
        (Winter 1964), 42-47.

B-1512 Hickin, Patricia, "THE LOSS OF AN OLD FRIEND," Virginia Cavalcade
        21:3 (Winter 1972), 5-13.

B-1513 Holmes, Jack D. L., "MOBILE'S GREAT HURRICANE OF 1819," Alabama
        Historical Quarterly 43:4 (Winter 1981), 322-332.

B-1514 Holmes, Jack D. L., "THE 1794 NEW ORLEANS FIRE: A CASE STUDY OF
        SPANISH NOBLESSE OBLIGE," Louisiana Studies 15:1 (Spring 1976),
        21-44.

B-1515 Huff, Millicent and H. Bailey Carroll, "HURRICANE CARLA AT GALVES-
        TON, 1961," Southwestern Historical Quarterly 65:3 (January 1962),
        293-309.

B-1516 Jones, V. C., "THE GREAT BALTIMORE FIRE," American History Illus-
        trated 7:6 (October 1972), 4-9.

B-1517 Kutak, Robert I., "THE SOCIOLOGY OF CRISIS: THE LOUISVILLE FLOOD
        OF 1937," Social Forces 17:1 (October 1938), 66-72.

B-1518 Lewis, Donald W., "THE GREAT CHARLESTON EARTHQUAKE," American
        History Illustrated 1:4 (July 1966), 25-28.

B-1519 Marszalek, John F. Jr., "THE CHARLESTON FIRE OF 1861 AS DESCRIBED
        IN THE EMMA E. HOLMES DIARY," South Carolina Historical Magazine
        76:2 (April 1975), 60-67.

B-1520 Nurnberger, Ralph D., "THE GREAT BALTIMORE DELUGE OF 1817," Mary-
        land Historical Magazine 69:4 (Winter 1974), 405-408.

B-1521 Pease, Jane H. and William H. Pease, "THE BLOOD-THIRSTY TIGER: CHARLESTON AND THE PSYCHOLOGY OF FIRE," South Carolina Historical Magazine 79:4 (October 1978), 281-295.

B-1522 Preston, Robert M., "THE GREAT FIRE OF EMMETSBURG, MARYLAND: DOES A CATASTROPHIC EVENT CAUSE MOBILITY?" Maryland Historical Magazine 77:2 (June 1982), 172-182.

B-1523 Richter, William L., "THE BRENHAM FIRE OF 1866: A TEXAS RECON- STRUCTION ATROCITY," Louisiana Studies 14:3 (Fall 1975), 287-314.

B-1524 Robbins, Peggy, "GALVESTON'S 'HURRICANE HELL,'" American History Illustrated 10:7 (November 1975), 4-9, 49-52.

B-1525 Robbins, Peggy, "TOWN IN FLAME," American History Illustrated 13:9 (January 1979), 20-29.

B-1526 Rumore, Samuel A., Jr., "NOTEWORTHY BIRMINGHAM FIRES," Alabama Review 31:1 (January 1978), 65-71.

B-1527 Sale, Marian Marsh, "DISASTER AT THE SPOTSWOOD," Virginia Caval- cade 12:2 (Autumn 1962), 13-19.

B-1528 Scott, Kenneth, "SUFFERERS IN THE CHARLESTON FIRE OF 1740," South Carolina Historical Magazine 64:4 (October 1963), 203-211.

B-1529 Smith, John Robert, "THE DAY OF ATLANTA'S BIG FIRE," Atlanta His- torical Journal , 24:3 (Fall 1980), 57-66.

B-1530 Tilly, Bette B., "MEMPHIS AND THE MISSISSIPPI VALLEY FLOOD OF 1927," West Tennessee Historical Society Papers No. 24 (1970), 41-56.

B-1531 Underhill, David, "HURRICANE FREDERIC VS. MOBILE," South Atlantic Quarterly 80:1 (Winter 1981), 16-35.

B-1532 Wright, Mrs. Anton (ed.), "THE EARTHQUAKE IN CHARLESTON, 1886," South Carolina Historical and Genealogical Magazine 50:2 (April 1948), 69-75.

Health

B-1533 Baird, Nancy D., "ASIATIC CHOLERA: KENTUCKY'S FIRST PUBLIC HEALTH INSTRUCTOR." Filson Club History Quarterly 48:4 (October 1974), 327-341.

B-1534 Baird, Nancy D., "ASIATIC CHOLERA'S FIRST VISIT TO KENTUCKY: A STUDY IN PANIC AND FEAR," Filson Club History Quarterly 48:3 (July 1974), 228-240.

B-1535 Baird, Nancy D., "A KENTUCKY PHYSICIAN EXAMINES MEMPHIS," Tennessee Historical Quarterly 37:2 (Summer 1978), 190-202.

B-1536 Balsamo, James J. and Harold George Scott, "THE URBAN SCENE: NEW ORLEANS," Journal of Environmental Health 44:3 (November-December 1981).

B-1537 Bauer, Mary, "GULFPORT'S AND BILOXI'S HOSPITALS: THEIR FIRST FIFTY YEARS," Journal of Mississippi History 39:4 (November 1977), 317-338.

B-1538 Bellows, Barbara, "'INSANITY IS THE DISEASE OF CIVILIZATION': THE FOUNDING OF THE SOUTH CAROLINA LUNATIC ASYLUM," South Carolina Historical Magazine 82:3 (July 1981), 263-272.

B-1539 Blok, Jack H., "THE GEOGRAPHY OF SUDDEN INFANT DEATH SYNDROME IN NORTH CAROLINA," Southeastern Geographer 18:1 (May 1978), 37-53.

B-1540 Brown, Russell W. and James H. M. Henderson, "THE MASS PRODUCTION AND DISTRIBUTION OF HeLa CELLS AT TUSKEGEE INSTITUTE, 1953-55," Journal of the History of Medicine and Allied Sciences 38:4 (October 1983), 415-431.

B-1541 Bruesch, S. R., "EARLY MEDICAL HISTORY OF MEMPHIS (1819-1861)," West Tennessee Historical Society Papers, No. 2 (1948), 33-94.

B-1542 Capers, Gerald M., "YELLOW FEVER IN MEMPHIS IN THE 1870's," Mississippi Valley Historical Review 24:4 (March 1938), 483-502.

B-1543 Carbo, Terry M., "THE FAITH HEALING BELIEFS OF A NEW ORLEANS FAMILY," Louisiana Folklore Miscellaney 2:4 (August 1968), 91-100.

B-1544 Carrigan, Jo Ann, "PRIVILEGE, PREJUDICE AND THE STRANGER'S DISEASE IN NINETEENTH-CENTURY NEW ORLEANS," Journal of Southern History 36:4 (November 1970), 568-578.

B-1545 Carrigan, Jo Ann, "YELLOW FEVER IN NEW ORLEANS, 1853: ABSTRACTIONS AND REALITIES," Journal of Southern History 25:3 (August 1959), 339-355.

B-1546 Carrigan, Jo Ann, "THE YELLOW FEVER PANIC OF 1897 IN LOUISIANA," Louisiana Studies 6:1 (Spring 1967), 7-26.

B-1547 Coleman, James C., "THE 'FLU' EPIDEMIC IN PENSACOLA," Echo 2 (Winter 1981), 25-28.

B-1548 Couto, Richard A. et al., "HEALTH CARE AND THE HOMELESS OF NASHVILLE: DEALING WITH A PROBLEM WITHOUT DEFINITION," Urban Resources 2:2 (Winter 1985), 17-24.

B-1549 Crockett, Bernice, "'NO JOB FOR A WOMAN,'" Chronocles of Oklahoma 61:2 (Summer 1983), 148-167.

B-1550 Crutcher, Charlotte, "ASIATIC CHOLERA IN JONESBORO, 1873," Tennessee Historical Quarterly 31:1 (Spring 1972), 74-79.

B-1551 Dever, G. E. Alan, "LEUKEMIA IN ATLANTA, GEORGIA," Southeastern Geographer 12:2 (November 1972), 91-100.

B-1552 Dial, Timothy, "REFUSE DISPOSAL AND PUBLIC HEALTH IN ATLANTA DURING THE PROGRESSIVE ERA: A CONTINUING CRISIS," Atlanta Historical Journal 17:3-4 (Fall-Winter), 31-40.

B-1553 Duffy, John, "NINETEENTH CENTURY PUBLIC HEALTH IN NEW YORK AND NEW ORLEANS: A COMPARISON," Louisiana History 15:4 (Fall 1974), 325-338.

B-1554 Duffy, John, "ONE HUNDRED YEARS OF THE NEW ORLEANS MEDICAL AND SURGICAL JOURNAL," Louisiana Historical Quarterly 40:1 (January 1957), 3-24.

B-1555 Duffy, John, "YELLOW FEVER IN COLONIAL CHARLESTON," South Carolina Historical and Genealogical Magazine 52:4 (October 1951), 189-197.

B-1556 Earle, Carville, "ENVIRONMENT, DISEASE AND MORTALITY IN VIRGINIA," Journal of Historical Geography 5:4 (October 1979), 365-390.

B-1557 East, Dennis II, "HEALTH AND WEALTH: GOALS OF THE NEW ORLEANS PUBLIC HEALTH MOVEMENT, 1879-84," Louisiana History 9:3 (Fall 1968), 245-275.

B-1558 Ellis, John H., "BUSINESSMEN AND PUBLIC HEALTH IN THE URBAN SOUTH DURING THE NINETEENTH CENTURY: NEW ORLEANS, MEMPHIS, AND ATLANTA," Bulletin of the History of Medicine 54 (May-June and July-August 1970), 197-212, 346-371.

B-1559 Ellis, John H., "DISEASE AND THE DESTINY OF A CITY: THE 1878
        YELLOW FEVER EPIDEMIC IN MEMPHIS," West Tennessee Historical
        Society Papers No. 28 (1974), 75-89.

B-1560 Ellis, John H. "MEMPHIS' SANITARY REVOLUTION," Tennessee Histori-
        cal Quarterly 23:1 (March 1964), 59-72.

B-1561 Ellis, John H., "THE NEW ORLEANS YELLOW FEVER EPIDEMIC IN 1878: A
        NOTE ON THE AFFECTIVE HISTORY OF SOCIETIES AND COMMUNITIES," Clio
        Medica [Netherlands] 12:2-3 (1977), 189-216.

B-1562 Engelhardt, H. Tristram Jr., "THE DISEASE OF MASTERBATION: VALUES
        AND THE CONCEPT OF DISEASE," Bulletin of the History of Medicine
        48:2 (1974), 234-248.

B-1563 Everett, Donald E., "THE NEW ORLEANS YELLOW FEVER EPIDEMIC OF
        1853," Louisiana Historical Quarterly 33:4 (October 1950), 380-
        405.

B-1564 Ewing, C. LeRoy and George W. Schucher, "ENDEMIC TYPHUS IN BALTI-
        MORE," Southern Medical Journal 41:1 (January 1948), 21-26.

B-1565 Fairlie, Margaret C., "THE YELLOW FEVER EPIDEMIC OF 1888 IN JACK-
        SONVILLE," Florida Historical Quarterly 19:2 (October 1940), 95-
        108.

B-1566 Farley, M. Foster, "THE MIGHTY MONARCH OF THE SOUTH: YELLOW FEVER
        IN CHARLESTON AND SAVANNAH," Georgia Review 27:1 (Spring 1973),
        56-70.

B-1567 Farley, M. Foster, "STRANGER'S FEVER," South Carolina Histor
        Illustrated 1:1 (February 1970), 54-61.

B-1568 Fonaroff, Arlene, "THE AESTHETIC NEW TOWN ENVIRONMENT AND ITS
        EFFECT ON COMMUNITY HEALTH," Sociological Symposium No. 12 (Fall
        1974), 83-98.

B-1569 Fossier, A. E., "CHARLES ALOYSIUS LUZENBERG, 1805-1848: A HISTORY
        OF MEDICINE IN NEW ORLEANS DURING THE YEARS 1830 TO 1848,"
        Louisiana Historical Quarterly 26:1 (January 1943), 49-137.

B-1570 Fossier, A. E., "HISTORY OF YELLOW FEVER IN NEW ORLEANS," Louisi-
        ana Historical Quarterly 34:3 (1951), 205-216.

B-1571 Gillson, Gordon, "NINETEENTH CENTURY NEW ORLEANS: ITS PUBLIC
        HEALTH ORDEAL," Louisiana Studies 4:2 (Summer 1965), 87-100.

B-1572 Goldfield, David R., "THE BUSINESS OF HEALTH PLANNING: DISEASE
        PREVENTION IN THE OLD SOUTH," Journal of Southern History 42:4
        (November 1976), 557-570.

B-1573 Goldfield, David R., "DISEASE AND URBAN IMAGE: YELLOW FEVER IN
        NORFOLK, 1855," Virginia Cavalcade 23:2 (Autumn 1973), 34-41.

B-1574 Griffin, J. David, "MEDICAL ASSISTANCE FOR THE SICK POOR IN ANTE-
        BELLUM SAVANNAH," Georgia Historical Quarterly 53:4 (December
        1969), 463-469.

B-1575 Hamlin, Percy G., "AESCULAPIUS IN CHARLOTTESVILLE: ROBLEY
        DUNGLISON, M.D.," Virginia Cavalcade 22:1 (Summer 1972), 14-21.

B-1576 Hammond, E. L., Kenneth Redman and J. G. Wickstrom Jr., "DRUG AND
        MEDICAL ADVERTISING IN WOODVILLE, MISSISSIPPI, 1823-1843," Journal
        of the American Pharmaceutical Association 9:2 (March 1948), 160-
        165.

B-1577 Harris, Collier C., "'FOR PERSONS OF INSANE AND DISORDERED MINDS':
        THE TREATMENT OF MENTAL DEFICIENCY IN COLONIAL VIRGINIA," Virginia
        Cavalcade 21:1 (Summer 1971), 34-41.

B-1578 Harvey, Katherine A., "PRACTICING MEDICINE AT THE BALTIMORE ALMSHOUSE, 1828-1850," Maryland Historical Magazine 74:3 (September 1979), 223-237.

B-1579 "HEALTH CARE ON A SHOE STRING," Tennessee Valley Perspective 3:1 (Fall 1972), 15-19.

B-1580 Hertz, Hilda, "NOTES ON CLAY AND STARCH EATING AMONG NEGROES IN A SOUTHERN URBAN COMMUNITY," Social Forces 25:1 (October 1946), 343-344.

B-1581 Hildreth, Peggy, "EARLY RED CROSS: THE HOWARD ASSOCIATION OF NEW ORLEANS, 1837-1878," Louisiana History 20:1 (Winter 1979), 77-92.

B-1582 Hildreth, Peggy, "THE HOWARD ASSOCIATION OF GALVESTON: THE 1850s, THEIR PEAK YEARS," East Texas Historical Journal 17:2 (1979), 33-44.

B-1583 Hirschman, Jim C. and Eugene L. Nagel, "PREHOSPITAL MOBILE EMER-GENCY CARE IN MIAMI, FLORIDA, AN HISTORICAL COMMENTARY," Journal of the Florida Medical Association 68 (August 1981), 624-634.

B-1584 Holahan, Charles J., John F. Betak, James L. Spearly, and Barbara J. Chance, "SOCIAL INTEGRATION AND MENTAL HEALTH IN A BIRACIAL COMMUNITY," American Journal of Community Psychology 11:3 (June 1983), 301-312.

B-1585 Hopkins, Richard J., "PUBLIC HEALTH IN ATLANTA: THE FORMATIVE YEARS, 1865-1879," Georgia Historical Quarterly 53:3 (September 1969), 287-304.

B-1586 Jones, James Boyd Jr., "A TALE OF TWO CITIES: THE HIDDEN BATTLE AGAINST VENEREAL DISEASE IN CIVIL WAR NASHVILLE AND MEMPHIS," Civil War History 31:3 (September 1985), 270-276.

B-1587 Kerson, Toba Schwaber, "ALMSHOUSE TO MUNICIPAL HOSPITAL: THE BALTIMORE EXPERIENCE," Bulletin of the History of Medicine 55 (Summer 1981), 203-220.

B-1588 Kiple, Kenneth L. and Virginia H. Kiple, "BLACK YELLOW FEVER IMMUNITIES, INATE AND ACQUIRED, AS REVEALED IN THE AMERICAN SOUTH," Social Science History 1:4 (Summer 1977), 419-436.

B-1589 Kupperman, Karen Ordahl, "APATHY AND DEATH IN EARLY JAMESTOWN," Journal of American History 66:1 (June 1979), 24-40.

B-1590 LaPointe, Patricia M., "THE DISRUPTED YEARS: MEMPHIS CITY HOS-PITALS, 1860-1867," West Tennessee Historical Society Papers No. 37 (1983), 9-29.

B-1591 LaPointe, Patricia M., "MILITARY HOSPITALS IN MEMPHIS, 1861-1865," Tennessee Historical Quarterly 42:4 (Winter 1983), 325-342.

B-1592 Lee, Anne S. and Evertt S. Lee, "THE HEALTH OF SLAVES AND THE HEALTH OF FREEDMAN: A SAVANNAH STUDY," Phylon 38:2 (June 1977), 170-180.

B-1593 Legan, Marshall Scott, "MISSISSIPPI AND THE YELLOW FEVER EPIDEMICS OF 1878-1879," Journal of Mississippi History 33:3 (August 1971), 199-218.

B-1594 Lewis, Carl P. Jr., "THE BALTIMORE COLLEGE OF DENTAL SURGERY AND THE BIRTH OF PROFESSIONAL DENTISTRY, 1840," Maryland Historical Magazine 59:3 (Fall 1964), 268-285.

B-1595 Long, Durward, "AN IMMIGRANT CO-OPERATIVE MEDICINE PROGRAM IN THE SOUTH, 1887-1963," Journal of Southern History 31:4 (November 1965), 417-434.

B-1596 McClary, Ben H., "INTRODUCING A CLASSIC: 'GUNN'S DOMESTIC MEDI-
CINE,'" Tennessee Historical Quarterly 45:3 (Fall 1986), 210-216.

B-1597 Marshall, John, "THE MADSTONE: ITS ORIGINS AND APPLICATIONS IN
BARLOW, BALLARD COUNTY, KENTUCKY," Kentucky Folklore Record 24:2
(April-June 1978), 42-48.

B-1598 Matas, Rudolph, "A YELLOW FEVER RETROSPECT AND PROSPECT," Louisiana Historical Quarterly 8:3 (July 1925), 454-473.

B-1599 Maxwell, William Quentin, "A TRUE STATE OF THE SMALLPOX IN
WILLIAMSBURG, FEBRUARY 22, 1748," Virginia Magazine of History and
Biography 63:3 (July 1955), 269-274.

B-1600 Merritt, Webster, "PHYSICIANS AND MEDICINE IN EARLY JACKSONVILLE,"
Florida Historical Quarterly 24:4 (April 1946), 266-286.

B-1601 Mitchell, Memory F., "A HALF-CENTURY OF HEALTH CARE: RALEIGH'S
REX HOSPITAL, 1894-1944," North Carolina Historical Review 64:2
(April 1987), 162-198.

B-1602 Morris, James P., "AN AMERICAN FIRST: BLOOD TRANSFUSION IN NEW
ORLEANS IN THE 1850S," Louisiana History 16:4 (Fall 1975), 341-
360.

B-1603 Morson, Donald, Frank Reuter, and Wayne Viitanen, "NEGRO FOLK
REMEDIES COLLECTED IN EUDORA, ARKANSAS, 1974-75," Mid-South Folklore 4:1 (Spring 1976), 11-24.

B-1604 Moss, Genevieve, "BOOMER WITH A 'HATFUL OF PILLS,'" Chronicles of
Oklahoma 63:2 (Summer 1985), 192-203.

B-1605 Ochsner, Alton, "THE HISTORY OF THORACTIC AND VASCULAR SURGERY IN
THE NEW ORLEANS AREA DURING THE FIRST HALF OF THE TWENTIETH CEN-
TURY," Bulletin of the History of Medicine 51:2 (1977), 169-187.

B-1606 O'Conner, Sheila, "THE CHARITY HOSPITAL AT NEW ORLEANS: AN
ADMINISTRATION AND FINANCIAL HISTORY, 1736-1941," Louisiana
Historical Quarterly 31:1 (January 1948), 1-109.

B-1607 Overholser, Winfred, "JACKSONVILLE 1847--PSYCHIATRY THEN AND NOW,"
Journal of the History of Medicine and Allied Science 3:3 (Summer
1948), 381-394.

B-1608 Partin, Robert, "ALABAMA'S YELLOW FEVER EPIDEMIC OF 1878," Alabama
Review 10:1 (January 1957), 31-51.

B-1609 Pearce, George F., "TORMENT OF PESTILENCE: YELLOW FEVER EPIDEMICS
IN PENSACOLA," Florida Historical Quarterly 56:4 (April 1978),
448-472.

B-1610 Plaisance, Aloysius and Leo F. Schelver III, "FEDERAL MILITARY
HOSPITALS IN NASHVILLE, MAY AND JUNE, 1863," Tennessee Historical
Quarterly 29:2 (Summer 1970), 166-175.

B-1611 Rea, Robert R., "'GRAVEYARD FOR BRITONS,' WEST FLORIDA, 1763-
1781," Florida Historical Quarterly 47:4 (April 1969), 345-364.

B-1612 Ready, Timothy, "ANTHROPOLOGY AND THE STUDY OF CHRONIC DISEASE:
ADOLESCENT BLOOD PRESSURE IN CORPUS CHRISTI, TEXAS," Social
Science and Medicine 21:4 (1985), 443-450.

B-1613 Roberts, William C., "TOMLINSON FORT OF MILLEDGEVILLE, GEORGIA:
PHYSICIAN AND STATESMAN," Journal of the History of Medicine and
Allied Science 23:2 (April 1968), 131-152.

B-1614 Rooney, William E., "THE FIRST 'INCIDENT' OF SECESSION: SEIZURE
OF THE NEW ORLEANS MARINE HOSPITAL," Louisiana Historical
Quarterly 34:2 (April 1951), 135-146.

B-1615 Rooney, William E., "THOMAS JEFFERSON AND THE NEW ORLEANS MARINE HOSPITAL," Journal of Southern History 22:2 (May 1956), 167-182.

B-1616 Rousey, Dennis C., "YELLOW FEVER AND BLACK POLICEMEN IN MEMPHIS: A POST-RECONSTRUCTION ANOMALY," Journal of Southern History 51:3 (August 1985), 357-374.

B-1617 Savitt, Todd L., "FILARIASIS IN THE UNITED STATES," Journal of the History of Medicine and Allied Science 32:2 (January 1977), 140-150.

B-1618 Scarry, C. Margaret, "THE USE OF PLANT FOODS IN SIXTEENTH CENTURY ST. AUGUSTINE," Florida Anthropologist 38:1-2, part 1 (March-June 1985), 70-80.

B-1619 Stickle, Douglas F., "DEATH AND CLASS IN BALTIMORE: THE YELLOW FEVER EPIDEMIC OF 1800," Maryland Historical Magazine 74:3 (September 1979), 282-299.

B-1620 Strader, Clifton, "A WINSTON-SALEM FOLK HERBALIST," North Carolina Folklore Journal 27:1 (May 1979), 20-25.

B-1621 Straight, William M., "JAMES M. JACKSON, JR., MIAMI'S FIRST PHYSICIAN," Tequesta No. 33 (1973), 75-86.

B-1622 Trevino-Richard, Terry, "DEATH TIMING AMONG DECEASED MARRIED COUPLES IN A SOUTHERN CEMETARY," Phylon 45:4 (December 1984), 323-330.

B-1623 Usinger, Robert L., "YELLOW FEVER FROM THE VIEWPOINT OF SAVANNAH," Georgia Historical Quarterly 28:3 (September 1944), 143-156.

B-1624 Walls, Edwina, "OBSERVATIONS ON THE NEW ORLEANS YELLOW-FEVER EPIDEMIC, 1878," Louisiana History 23:1 (Winter 1982), 60-67.

B-1625 Waring, Joseph I., "CHARLESTON MEDICINE 1800-1860," Journal of the History of Medicine and Allied Sciences 31:3 (July 1976), 320-342.

B-1626 Waring, Joseph Ioor, "THE YELLOW FEVER EPIDEMIC OF SAVANNAH IN 1820, WITH A SKETCH OF WILLIAM COFFEE DANIEL," Georgia Historical Quarterly 52:4 (December 1968), 398-404.

B-1627 Weisberger, Bernard A., "EPIDEMIC," American Heritage 35:6 (October-November 1984), 57-64.

B-1628 Wienker, Curtis W., "ABNORMAL HEMOGLOBINS IN TARPON SPRINGS IN BLACKS AND GREEKS," Florida Scientist 49:2 (Spring 1986), 98-103.

B-1629 Wright, R. Lewis, "MEDICINE IN THE COLONIAL CAPITAL," Virginia Cavalcade 8:2 (Autumn 1958), 4-6.

B-1630 "YELLOW FEVER IN CHARLESTON IN 1852," Southern Quarterly Review 7:13 (January 1853), 140-178.

History and Geography

B-1631 Abbott, Martin and Elmer L. Puryear, eds., "BELEAGUERED CHARLESTON: LETTERS FROM THE CITY, 1860-1864 (1)," South Carolina Historical Magazine 61:2 (April 1960), 61-74.

B-1632 Abbott, Martin and Elmer L. Puryear, eds., "BELEAGUERED CHARLESTON: LETTERS FROM THE CITY, 1860-1864, (2)," South Carolina Historical Magazine 61:3 (July 1960), 164-175.

B-1633 Abbott, Martin and Elmer L. Puryear, eds., "BELEAGUERED CHARLESTON: LETTERS FROM THE CITY, 1860-1864 (3)," South Carolina Historical Magazine 61:4 (October 1960), 210-218.

B-1634 Adamoli, Guilio, NEW ORLEANS IN 1867," Louisiana Historical Quarterly 6:2 (April 1923), 271-279.

B-1635 Adams, J. Lewis, "OLD PURDY," West Tennessee Historical Society Papers No. 6 (1952), 5-33.

B-1636 Adams, Reed McC., "NEW ORLEANS AND THE WAR OF 1812, I," Louisiana Historical Quarterly 16:2 (April 1933 (221-235.

B-1637 Adams, Reed McC., "NEW ORLEANS AND THE WAR OF 1812, II," Louisiana Historical Quarterly 16:3 (July 1933), 479-503.

B-1638 Adams, Reed McC., "NEW ORLEANS AND THE WAR OF 1812, III," Louisiana Historical Quarterly 16:4 (October 1933), 681-703.

B-1639 Adams, Reed McC., "NEW ORLEANS AND THE WAR OF 1812, IV," Louisiana Historical Quarterly 17:1 (January 1934), 169-182.

B-1640 Adams, Reed McC., "NEW ORLEANS AND THE WAR OF 1812, V," Louisiana Historical Quarterly 17:2 (April 1934), 349-363.

B-1641 Adams, Reed McC., "NEW ORLEANS AND THE WAR OF 1812, VI," Louisiana Historical Quarterly 17:3 (July 1934), 502-523.

B-1642 Agenw, Brad, "WAGNER, I. T., QUEEN CITY OF THE PRAIRIES," Chronicles of Oklahoma, 64:4 (Winter 1986-87), 16-47.

B-1643 Albrecht, Andrew C., "THE ORIGIN AND EARLY SETTLEMENT OF BATON ROUGE, LOUISIANA," Louisiana Historical Quarterly 28:1 (January 1945), 5-67.

B-1644 Allred, Fred J. and Alonzo T. Dill, eds., "THE FOUNDING OF NEW BERN: A FOOTNOTE," North Carolina Historical Review 40:3 (Summer 1963), 361-374.

B-1645 Anderson, E.H., "A MEMOIR ON RECONSTRUCTION IN YAZOO CITY," Journal of Mississippi History 4:1 (January 1942), 187-194.

B-1646 Anthony, Allen, "A LINK WITH THE OUTSIDE WORLD: THE LINTON MAIL-BOAT ON THE CUMBERLAND RIVER," Filson Club History Quarterly 59:1 (January 1985), 5-39.

B-1647 Arana, Louis Rafael, "THE EXPLORATION OF FLORIDA AND SOURCES ON THE FOUNDING OF ST. AUGUSTINE," Florida Historical Quarterly 44:1 (July 1965), 1-16.

B-1648 Arndt, Karl J. R., "THE GENESIS OF GERMANTOWN, LOUISIANA: OR THE MYSTERIOUS PAST OF LOUISIANA'S MYSTIC COUNT DE LEON," Louisiana Historical Quarterly 24:2 (April 1941), 378-433.

B-1649 Ash, Stephen V., "A COMMUNITY AT WAR: MONTGOMERY COUNTY, 1861-65," Tennessee Historical Quarterly 36:1 (Spring 1977), 30-43.

B-1650 Ash, Stephen V., "POSTWAR RECOVERY: MONTGOMERY COUNTY, 1865-70," Tennessee Historical Quarterly 36:2 (Summer 1977), 208-221.

B-1651 Ash, Steven V., "SHARKS IN AN ANGRY SEA: CIVILIAN RESISTANCE AND GUERRILLA WARFARE IN OCCUPIED MIDDLE TENNESSEE, 1862-1865," Tennessee Historical Quarterly 45:3 (Fall 1986), 217-229.

B-1652 Asplin, Ray, "HISTORY OF COUNCIL GROVE, OKLAHOMA," Chronicles of Oklahoma 45:4 (Winter 1967-1968), 433-450.

B-1653 Austerman, Wayne R., "BATON ROUGE AND THE BLACK REGULARS," Louisiana History 21:3 (Summer 1980), 277-286.

B-1654 Bachus, Gordon, "BACKGROUND AND EARLY HISTORY OF A COMPANY TOWN: BAUXITE, ARKANSAS," Arkansas Historical Quarterly 27:4 (Winter 1968), 330-357.

B-1655 Bacon, H. Phillip, "THE TOWNSCAPE OF NASHVILLE, TENNESSEE ON THE EVE OF THE CIVIL WAR," Journal of Geography 56:8 (November 1957), 353-363.

B-1656 Ball, Bruce W., "SAMUEL HODGMAN, HAINES CITY, FLORIDA, PIONEER," Tequesta No. 30 (1970), 53-63.

B-1657 Balogh, George Walter, "CROSSETT: THE COMMUNITY, THE COMPANY, AND CHANGE," Arkansas Historical Quarterly 44:2 (Summer 1985), 156-176.

B-1658 Banks, William Nathaniel, "WASHINGTON, NEW HAMPSHIRE, AND WASHINGTON, GEORGIA," Antiques 126:6 (December 1984), 1398-1421.

B-1659 Bardsley, Virginia O., ed., "A VISIT TO SAVANNAH, 1892," Georgia Historical Quarterly 50:1 (March 1966), 100-104.

B-1660 Barnett, Mrs. I. N. Sr., "EARLY DAYS OF BATESVILLE," Arkansas Historical Quarterly 11:1 (Spring 1952), 15-23.

B-1661 Barnwell, Joseph H., "THE EVACUATION OF CHARLESTON BY THE BRITISH IN 1782," South Carolina Historical and Genealogical Magazine 11:1 (January 1910), 1-26.

B-1662 Barrow, Elfrida DeRenne, "ON THE BAY ONE HUNDRED YEARS AGO," Georgia Historical Quarterly 14:1 (March 1930), 1-16.

B-1663 Bauer, Craig A., "FROM BURNT CANES TO BUDDING CITY: A HISTORY OF THE CITY OF KENNER, LOUISIANA," Louisiana History 23:4 (Fall 1982), 353-382.

B-1664 Beck, Lewis H., "GRIFFIN: EARLY CULTURAL AND MILITARY CENTER OF GEORGIA," Georgia Review 4:4 (Winter 1950), 331-339.

B-1665 Beeth, Howard, "HOUSTON AND HISTORY, PAST AND PRESENT: A LOOK AT BLACK HOUSTON IN THE 1920's," Southern Studies 25:2 (Summer 1986), 172-186.

B-1666 Bejack, Judge Lois D., "THE SEVEN CITIES ABSORBED BY MEMPHIS," West Tennessee Historical Society Papers No. 8 (1954), 95-104.

B-1667 Berry, Evalena, "SUGAR LOAF: THE MOUNTAIN, THE SPRINGS, THE TOWN," Arkansas Historical Quarterly 42:1 (Spring 1983), 27-36.

B-1668 Bigge, A. E., "OTTERBEIM, KENTUCKY, A PLANNED SETTLEMENT," Filson Club History Quarterly 30:4 (October 1956) 299-314.

B-1669 Biles, Roger, "THE PERSISTENCE OF THE PAST: MEMPHIS IN THE GREAT DEPRESSION," Journal of Southern History 62:2 (May 1986), 183-212.

B-1670 Bingham, Millicent Todd (ed.), "KEY WEST IN THE SUMMER OF 1864," Florida Historical Quarterly 43:3 (January 1965), 262-265.

B-1671 Bingham, Millicent Todd, "MIAMI: A STUDY IN URBAN GEOGRAPHY," Tequesta No. 8 (1948), 73-107.

B-1672 Bissell, A. K., "A REMINISCENCE OF OAK RIDGE," East Tennessee Historical Society's Publications No. 39 (1967), 71-86.

B-1673 Blue, Mathew P., "THE STATE CAPITAL IN MONTGOMERY," Alabama Historical Quarterly 25:3, 4 (Fall-Winter 1963), 242-245.

B-1674 Bocock, Pamela S., "CAMP GUTHRIE: URBAN OUTPOST IN THE TERRITORY, 1889-1891," Chronicles of Oklahoma 62:2 (Summer 1984), 166-189.

B-1675 Bohannan, A. W., "THE OLD TOWN OF COBHAM," Virginia Magazine of
       History and Biography 57:3 (July 1949), 252-268.

B-1676 Bonner, James C., "PROFILE OF A LATE ANTE-BELLUM COMMUNITY,"
       American Historical Review 49:4 (July 1944), 663-680.

B-1677 Bonner, James C., "SHERMAN AT MILLEDGEVILLE IN 1864," Journal of
       Southern History 22:3 (August 1956), 273-291.

B-1678 Book J. David, "AUDUBON IN LOUISVILLE, 1807-1810," Filson Club
       History Quarterly 45:2 (April 1971), 186-226.

B-1679 Borden, Elizabeth, "BLACKSMITH LORE: JOE HANSBERRY, MASTER BLACK-
       SMITH," Tennessee Folklore Society Bulletin 50:1 (Spring 1985),
       10-21.

B-1680 Bowden, Jesse Earle, "PENSACOLA: A 1781 PERSPECTIVE," Echo 11
       (Spring-Summer 1981), 5-11.

B-1681 Bowman, Martha, "A CITY OF THE OLD SOUTH: JACKSON, MISSISSIPPI,
       1850-1860," Journal of Mississippi History 15:1 (January 1953),
       1-32.

B-1682 Bradberry, David, "ROGER LACY, THE FOUNDER OF AUGUSTA," Richmond
       County History 16:1 (Winter 1984), 30-35.

B-1683 Braden, Guy B., "A JEFFERSONIAN VILLAGE: WASHINGTON, MISSIS-
       SIPPI," Journal of Mississippi History 30:2 (May 1968), 135-142.

B-1684 Brannon, Peter A., "DEXTER AVENUE," Alabama Historical Quarterly
       19:3, 4 (Fall-Winter 1957), 466-470.

B-1685 Brantley, William H. Jr., "HENRY HITCHCOCK OF MOBILE, 1816-1839,"
       Alabama Review 5:1 (January 1952), 3-39.

B-1686 Brewer, Alberta, "NORRIS--FIRST PLANNED CITY," Tennessee Valley
       Perspective 4:1 (Fall 1973), 16-21.

B-1687 Bridges, Katherine, "'ALL WELL IN NATCHITOCHES': A LOUISIANA CITY
       ON THE STAGE," Louisiana Studies 10:2 (Summer 1971), 85-91.

B-1688 Bridges, Katherine and Winston DeVille, "NATCHITOCHES IN 1766,"
       Louisiana History 4:2 (Spring 1963), 145-160.

B-1689 Briede, Kathryn C., "A HISTORY OF THE CITY OF LAFAYETTE," Louisi-
       ana Historical Quarterly 20:4 (October 1937), 895-964.

B-1690 Briney, Melville O., "SOME GLIMPSES OF EARLY LOUISVILLE," Filson
       Club History Quarterly 34:2 (April 1960), 105-114.

B-1691 Bristoll, William Merrick, "ESCAPE FROM CHARLESTON," American
       Heritage 26:3 (April 1975), 25-27, 82-88.

B-1692 Bronner, Edwin B., ed., "A PHILADELPHIA QUAKER VISITS NATCHEZ,
       1847," Journal of Southern History 27:4 (November 1961), 513-520.

B-1693 Brown, Dorothy, "ANCESTORYS: EIGHTEENTH CENTURY PENSACOLIANS,"
       Echo 2 (Spring-Summer 1981), 73-78.

B-1694 Brown, Jane Lightcap, "FROM AUGUSTA TO COLUMBUS: THACKERAY'S
       EXPERIENCES IN GEORGIA, 1853 AND 1856," Georgia Historical
       Quarterly 67:3 (Fall 1983), 305-320.

B-1695 Brown, Virginia Pounds and Jane Porter Nabers, "THE ORIGIN OF
       CERTAIN PLACE NAMES IN JEFFERSON COUNTY, ALABAMA," Alabama Review
       5:3 (July 1952), 177-202.

B-1696 Brownell, Blain A., "BIRMINGHAM, ALABAMA: NEW SOUTH CITY IN THE 1920s," Journal of Southern History 38:1 (February 1972), 21-48.

B-1697 Brownell, Blaine A. and David R. Goldfield, "SOUTHERN URBAN HIS-TORY," in B. Brownell (ed.,) The City in Southern History, 1977, 5-22.

B-1698 Bullitt, Cuthbert, "REMEMBRANCES OF NEW ORLEANS AND THE OLD ST. LOUIS HOTEL," Louisiana Historical Quarterly 4:1 (January 1921), 128-129.

B-1699 Burkhardt, Sue Pope, "THE PORT OF PALM BEACH: THE BREAKERS PIER," Tequesta No. 33 (1973), 69-74.

B-1700 Burns, Francis P., "THE GRAVIERS AND THE FAUBOURG STE. MARIE," Louisiana Historical Quarterly 22:2 (April 1939), 385-427.

B-1701 Burns, Francis P., "HENRY CLAY VISITS NEW ORLEANS," Louisiana Historical Quarterly 27:3 (July 1944), 717-782.

B-1702 Butler, Mann, "AN OUTLINE OF THE ORIGIN AND SETTLEMENT OF LOUIS-VILLE," Filson Club History Quarterly 4:2 (April 1930), 51-76.

B-1703 Caldwell-Swann, Lee Ann, "OLD TOWNE AUGUSTA," Georgia Journal 2:4 (June-July 1982), 29-31.

B-1704 Cappon, Lester J., "THE PROVINCIAL SOUTH," Journal of Southern History 16:1 (February 1950), 5-24.

B-1705 Carson, Ruby Leach, "FORTY YEARS OF MIAMI BEACH," Tequesta No. 15 (1955), 3-28.

B-1706 Carson, Ruby Leach, "MIAMI BEACH REACHES THE HALF CENTURY MARK," Tequesta No. 24 (1964), 3-20.

B-1707 Carson, Ruby Leach, "MIAMI: 1896-1900," Tequesta No. 16 (1956), 3-14

B-1708 Cash, W. T. ed., "TALLAHASSEE AND ST. MARKS IN 1841: A LETTER OF JOHN S. TAPPAN," Florida Historical Quarterly 24:2 (October 1945), 108-112.

B-1709 Cashin, Edward J., "AUGUSTA'S REVOLUTION OF 1779," Richmond County History 7:2 (Summer 1975), 5-14.

B-1710 Cashin, Edward J., "SUMMERVILLE, RETREAT OF THE OLD SOUTH," Richmond County History 5:2 (Summer 1973), 44-59.

B-1711 Cassell, Frank A., "BALTIMORE IN 1813: A STUDY OF URBAN DEFENSE IN THE WAR OF 1812," Military Affairs 33:3 (December 1969), 349-360.

B-1712 Cassell, Frank A., "THE GREAT BALTIMORE RIOT OF 1812," Maryland Historical Magazine 70:3 (Fall 1975), 241-259.

B-1713 Cassell, Frank A., "RESPONSE TO CRISIS: BALTIMORE IN 1814," Maryland Historical Magazine 66:3 (Fall 1971), 261-287.

B-1714 Cawthon, John Ardis, "A BRIEF HISTORY OF SHREVEPORT, CADDO PAR-RISH, BASED ON A SAMPLING OF DESCRIPTIONS ON TOMBSTONES," North Louisiana Historical Association Journal 6:4 (1975), 165-173.

B-1715 Chadick, Mrs. W. D., "CIVIL WAR DAYS IN HUNTSVILLE, A DIARY BY MRS. W. D. CHADICK," Alabama Historical Quarterly 9:2 (Summer 1947), 196-333.

B-1716 Chamberlain, Donald L., "FORT BROOKE: FRONTIER OUTPOSTS 1824-42," Tampa Bay History 7:1 (Spring-Summer 1985), 5-29.

B-1717 Chambers, Ruth H., "HILTON VILLAGE," Virginia Cavalcade 16:4
(Spring 1967) 41-47.

B-1718 Chandler, Walter, "THE MEMPHIS NAVY YARD: AN ADVENTURE IN IN-
TERNAL IMPROVEMENT," West Tennessee Historical Society Papers No.
1 (1947), 68-72.

B-1719 Chandler, Walter, "PERSONAL RECOLLECITONS OF MEMPHIS," West Tennessee Historical Society Papers No. 22 (1968), 86-92.

B-1720 Chestnutt, E. F., ed., "LITTLE ROCK GETS ELECTRIC LIGHTS,"
Arkansas Historical Quarterly 42:3 (Autumn 1983), 239-253.

B-1721 Chumney, James R., "THE PINK PALACE: CLARENCE SAUNDERS AND THE
MEMPHIS MUSEUM," Tennessee Historical Quarterly 32:1 (Spring
1973), 3-21.

B-1722 Church, Randolph W., "HORSE FORD TO GLASS MEMORIAL," Virginia
Cavalcade 4:2 (Autumn 1954), 13-19, 48.

B-1723 Church, Randolph W. and W. Edwin Hemphil, "VIEW AT LITTLE YORK IN
VIRGINIA," Virginia Cavalcade 1:2 (Autumn 1951), 44-47.

B-1724 [CLAIBORNE, ALABAMA] Alabama Historical Quarterly 19:2 (Summer
1957), 213-255.

B-1725 Clark, George P., "THE ROLE OF THE HAITIAN VOLUNTEERS AT SAVANNAH
IN 1779: AN ATTEMPT AT AN OBJECTIVE VIEW," Phylon 41:4 (December
1980), 356-366.

B-1726 Clark, John C., "NEW ORLEANS AND THE RIVER: A STUDY IN ATTITUDES
AND RESPONSES," Louisiana History 8:2 (Spring 1967), 117-136.

B-1727 Clarke, Caroline McKinney, "DAYS OF OLD DECATUR," Georgia Life 6:4
(Spring 1980), 15-18.

B-1728 Clarke, James N., "HISTORY OF ALLARDT," Tennessee Historical Magazine 9:3 (October 1925). 185-189.

B-1729 Clayton, Claude F., "THE DEDICATION OF THE LAST COURTHOUSE OF OLD
TISHOMINGO COUNTY AT JACINTO, MISSISSIPPI," Journal of Mississippi
History 31:3 (August 1969), 172-186.

B-1730 Clinton, Charles A., "CONTINUITY AND CHANGE IN A SMALL SOUTHERN
TOWN," Southern Quarterly 19:1 (Fall 1980), 62-70.

B-1731 Clinton, Thomas P., "EARLY HISTORY OF TUSCALOOSA (1), Alabama
Historical Quarterly 1:1 (Spring 1930), 139-147.

B-1732 Clinton, Thomas P., "EARLY HISTORY OF TUSCALOOSA (2)," Alabama
Historical Quarterly 1:2 (Summer 1930), 169-179.

B-1733 Clower, George W., "THE SHEEHAN FAMILY--ATLANTA PIONEERS,"
Atlanta Historical Journal 13:4 (December 1968), 38-41.

B-1734 Clubbs, Occie, "PENSACOLA IN RETROSPECT, 1870-1890," Florida
Historical Quarterly 37:3-4 (January-April 1959), 377-396.

B-1735 Cohn, David I., "NEW ORLEANS--THE CITY THAT CARE FORGOT," Atlantic
Monthly 165:4 (April 1940), 484-491.

B-1736 Coker, Robert Ervin, "SPRINGVILLE: A SUMMER VILLAGE OF OLD DAR-
LINGTON DISTRICT," South Carolina Historical and Genealogical
Magazine 53:4 (1952), 190-211.

B-1737 Cole, Houston, "GLIMPSES OF EARLY ANNISTON," Alabama Review 20:2
(April 1967), 131-141.

B-1738 Coleman, Elizabeth Dabney, "GUNS FOR INDEPENDENCE," Virginia
Cavalcade 13:1 (Summer 1963), 40-47.

B-1739 Coleman, Elizabeth Dabney, "A LIGHTHOUSE FOR THE STREETS OF RICH-
MOND," Virginia Cavalcade 5:4 (Spring 1956), 4-8.

B-1740 Coleman, Elizabeth Dabney, "PERAMBULATORY PROCESSION," Virginia
Cavalcade 3:4 (Spring 1954), 44-47.

B-1741 Coleman, J. Winston Jr., "LEXINGTON AS SEEN BY TRAVELLERS, 1810-
1835," Filson Club History Quarterly 29:3 (July 1955), 267-282.

B-1742 Colville, Derek, "HISTORY AND HUMOR: THE TALL TALE IN NEW
ORLEANS," Louisiana Historical Quarterly 39:2 (April 1956), 153-
168.

B-1743 Colwill, Stiles Tuttle, "TOWN & COUNTRY: THE SMALLER GREENER
BALTIMORE OF FRANCIS GREY," American Heritage 32:2 (February-March
1981), 18-27.

B-1744 Connell, Mary Ann Strong, "THE FIRST PEABODY HOTEL: 1869-1923,"
West Tennessee Historical Society Papers No. 29 (1975), 38-54.

B-1745 Connelly, John Lawrence, "OLD NORTH NASHVILLE AND GERMANTOWN,"
Tennessee Historical Quarterly 39:2 (Summer 1980), 115-148.

B-1746 Conway, Alan, "NEW ORLEANS AS A PORT OF IMMIGRATION, 1820-1860,"
Louisiana Studies 1:3 (Fall 1962), 1-22.

B-1747 Coomes, Charles S., "THE BASILICA-CATHEDRAL OF ST. AUGUSTINE, ST.
AUGUSTINE, FLORIDA AND ITS HISTORY," El Escribano 20 (1983), 32-
44.

B-1748 Cooper, Kirk, and Carolyn G. Kayne, "GROWING UP IN EARLY POMPANO:
AN ORAL HISTORY INTERVIEW WITH ELIZABETH H. WARREN," Broward
Legacy 4 (Summer/Fall 1981), 30-44.

B-1749 Cooper, W. Raymond, "FOUR FATEFUL YEARS--MEMPHIS 1858-1861," West
Tennessee Historical Society Papers No. 11 (1957), 36-75.

B-1750 Coppock, Paul R., "HISTORY IN MEMPHIS STREET NAMES," West Tennessee Historical Society Papers No. 11 (1957), 93-111.

B-1751 Coppock, Paul R., "THE MEMPHIS AND CHARLESTON DEPOT," West Tennessee Historical Society Papers No. 21 (1967), 48-59.

B-1752 Cordell, Anna H., "CHAMPAGNOLLE A PIONEER RIVER TOWN," Arkansas
Historical Quarterly 10:1 (Spring 1951) 37-45.

B-1753 Corley, Florence Fleming, "THE OLD MEDICAL COLLEGE AND THE OLD
GONUNEIS MANSION," Richmond County History 8:2 (Summer 1976), 5-
22.

B-1754 Coulter, E. Merton, "THE CONFEDERATE MONUMENT IN ATHENS," Georgia
Review 10:1 (Spring 1956), 56-68.

B-1755 Coulter, E. Merton, "THE CONFEDERATE MONUMENT IN ATHENS, GEORGIA,"
Georgia Historical Quarterly 40:3 (September 1956), 230-248.

B-1756 Coulter, E. Merton, "THE STORY OF THE TREE THAT OWNED ITSELF,"
Georgia Historical Quarterly 46:3 (September 1962), 237-249.

B-1757 Coulter, E. Merton, "WILLIAM HOWARD TAFT'S VISIT TO ATHENS,"
Georgia Historical Quarterly 52:4 (Decembert 1968), 338-397.

B-1758 Covington, James W., "DRAKE DESTROYS ST. AUGUSTINE: 1586,"
Florida Historical Quarterly 44:1 (July 1965), 81-93.

B-1759 Covington, James W., "THE ROUGH RIDERS IN TAMPA," Sunland Tribune 3 (November 1977), 2-5.

B-1760 Covington, James W., "THE TAMPA BAY HOTEL," Tequesta No. 26 (1966), 3-20.

B-1761 Cox, Richard J., "UNDERSTANDING THE MONUMENTAL CITY: A BIBLIO-GRAPHICAL ESSAY ON BALTIMORE HISTORY," Maryland Historical Magazine 77:1 (March 1982), 70-111.

B-1762 Crabb, Alfred Leland, "THE TWILIGHT OF THE NASHVILLE GODS," Tennessee Historical Quarterly 15:4 (December 1956), 291-305.

B-1763 Craig, Alberta Ratliffe, "OLD WENTWORTH SKETCHES," North Carolina Historical Review 11:3 (July 1934), 185-204.

B-1764 Crane, Sophie and Paul Crane, "HISTORIC JAILS OF TENNESSEE," Tennessee Historical Quarterly 39:1 (Spring 1980), 3-10.

B-1765 Crenshaw, May V., "PUBLIC LIBRARIES IN THE SOUTH," Library Journal 42 (1917), 163-174.

B-1766 Crews, Clyde F., "PERSONAGES: EMINENT VISITORS IN 20TH CENTURY LOUISVILLE," Filson Club History Quarterly 54:4 (October 1980), 346-359.

B-1767 Crimmins, Timothy J., "THE ATLANTA PALIMPSEST: STRIPPING AWAY THE LAYERS OF THE PAST," Atlanta Historical Journal 26:2-3 (Summer-Fall 1982), 13-32.

B-1768 Crimmins, Timothy J., "THE PAST IN THE PRESENT: AN URBAN HIS-TORIAN'S AGENDA FOR PUBLIC HISTORY AND HISTORIC PRESERVATON," Georgia Historical Quarterly 63:1 (Spring 1979), 53-59.

B-1769 Crooks, James B., "CHANGING FACE OF JACKSONVILLE, FLORIDA: 1900-1910," Florida Historical Quarterly 62:4 (April 1984), 439-463.

B-1770 Crooks, James B., "JACKSONVILLE IN THE PROGRESSIVE ERA: RESPONSES TO URBAN GROWTH," Florida Historical Quarterly 65:1 (July 1986), 52-71.

B-1771 Crutchfield, James A., "THE SETTLEMENT OF NASHVILLE," Early American Life 8:2 (April 1977), 50-52.

B-1772 Cuelen, Joseph P., "RICHMOND FALLS," American History Illustrated 8:9 (January 1974), 10-21.

B-1773 Cumming, Inez Parker, "MADISON: MIDDLE GEORGIA MINERVA," Georgia Review 5:1 (Spring 1951), 121-136.

B-1774 Cunningham, Noble E. Jr., "THE DIARY OF FRANCES FEW, 1808-1809," Journal of Southern History 29:3 (August 1963), 345-362.

B-1775 Curry, Leonard P., "SUMMING UP SOUTHERN URBAN HISTORY," Journal of Urban History 5 (February 1979), 255-263.

B-1776 Cushman, Joseph D. Jr., "THE BLOCKADE AND FALL OF APALACHICOLA, 1861-1862," Florida Historical Quarterly 41:1 (July 1962), 38-46.

B-1777 Damaris, Gypsy, "THE COLUMBIA RESTAURANT," North Louisiana Historical Association Journal 9:1 (1978), 43-46.

B-1778 Daniel, Larry, "THE QUINBY AND ROBINSON CANNON FOUNDRY AT MEM-PHIS," West Tennessee Historical Society Papers No. 27 (1973), 18-32.

B-1779 Dart, Henry P., "THE CIBILDO OF NEW ORLEANS," Louisiana Historical Quarterly 5:2 (April 1922), 279-281.

B-1780 Dart, Henry P. ed., "NEW ORLEANS IN 1758," Louisiana Historical Quarterly 5:1 (January 1922), 53-57.

B-1781 Dart, Henry P., "A TWELVE YEAR LAWSUIT IN NEW ORLEANS DURING THE SPANISH REGIME, 1781-1792," Louisiana Historical Quarterly 17:2 (April 1934), 294-305.

B-1782 Dart, Sally (trans.), "FRENCH INCERTITUDE IN 1718 AS TO A SITE FOR NEW ORLEANS (1)," Louisiana Historical Quarterly 15:1 (January 1932), 37-43.

B-1783 Dart, Sally (trans.), "FRENCH INCERTITUDE IN 1718 AS TO A SITE FOR NEW ORLEANS (2)," Louisiana Historical Quarterly 15:3 (July 1932), 417-427.

B-1784 Davenport, Will, "GROWING UP, SORT OF, IN MIAMI, 1909-1915," Tequesta No. 40 (1980), 5-30.

B-1785 Davidson, Chalmers G., "INDEPENDENT MECKLENBURG," North Carolina Historical Review 46:2 (Spring 1969), 122-129.

B-1786 Davidson, Donald, "SOME DAY IN OLD CHARLESTON," Georgia Review 3:2 (Summer 1949), 150-161.

B-1787 Davis, Kathleen, "YEAR OF CRUCIFIXION: GALVESTON, TEXAS," Texana 8:2 (Summer 1970), 140-153.

B-1788 Davis, Stephen, "CONFEDERATE MEMORIAL DAY IN ATLANTA: OLD TIMES HERE ARE NEARLY FORGOTTEN," Atlanta Historical Journal 27:1 (Spring 1983), 71-86.

B-1789 Davis, T. Frederica, "SIDELIGHTS ON EARLY AMERICAN ST. AUGUSTINE," Florida Historical Quarterly 23:2 (October 1944), 116-121.

B-1790 Dehler, Katherine B., "MT. VERNON PLACE AT THE TURN OF THE CEN- TURY: A VIGNETTE OF THE GARRETT FAMILY," Maryland Historical Magazine 69:3 (Fall 1974), 279-292.

B-1791 Demerath, Nicholas J. and Harlan W. Gilmore, "THE ECOLOGY OF SOUTHERN CITIES," in R. Vance, ed., The Urban South, 1954, 135- 164.

B-1792 Demuth, David O., "THE BURNING OF HOPEFIELD," Arkansas Historical Quarterly 36:2 (Summer 1977), 123-129.

B-1793 Derr, Marjorie Holmes, "REMOVAL OF THE CAPITAL OF WEST VIRGINIA FROM CHARLESTON TO WHEELING, 1875," West Virginia History 7:4 (July 1946), 312-331.

B-1794 Deskins, Donald R. Jr. and John D. Nystven, "DIRECT OBSERVATIONS AS A LEARNING STRATEGY IN GEOGRAPHY: PEDESTRIAN DENSITY AND FUNC- TIONAL AREAS IN ATLANTA," Southeastern Geographer 13:2 (November 1973), 105-126.

B-1795 Dew, Lee A., "FROM TRAILS TO RAILS IN EUREKA SPRINGS," Arkansas Historical Quarterly 41:3 (Autumn 1982), 203-214.

B-1796 Dill, Alonzo Thomas Jr., "EIGHTEENTH CENTURY NEW BERN. A HISTORY OF THE TOWN AND CRAVEN COUNTY, 1700-1800, PART I, COLONIZATION OF THE NEUSE," North Carolina Historical Review 21:1 (January 1944), 1-21.

B-1797 Dill, Alonzo Thomas Jr., "EIGHTEENTH CENTURY NEW BERN. A HISTORY OF THE TOWN AND CRAVEN COUNTY, 1700-1800, PART II, THE FOUNDING OF NEW BERN," North Carolina Historical Review 22:2 (April 1945), 152-175.

B-1798 Dill, Alonzo Thomas Jr., "EIGHTEENTH CENTURY NEW BERN. A HISTORY
OF THE TOWN AND CRAVEN COUNTY, 1700-1800, PART III, REBELLION AND
INDIAN WARFARE," North Carolina Historical Review 22:3 (July
1945), 293-319.

B-1799 Dill, Alonzo Thomas Jr., "EIGHTEENTH CENTURY NEW BERN. A HISTORY
OF THE TOWN AND CRAVEN COUNTY 1700-1800, PART IV, YEARS OF SLOW
DEVELOPMENT," North Carolina Historical Review 22:4 (October
1945), 460-489.

B-1800 Dill, Alonzo Thomas Jr., "EIGHTEENTH CENTURY NEW BERN. A HISTORY
OF THE TOWN AND CRAVEN COUNTY, 1700-1800, PART V, POLITICAL AND
COMMERCIAL RISE OF NEW BERN," North Carolina Historical Review
23:1 (January 1946), 47-78.

B-1801 Dill, Alonzo Thomas Jr., "EIGHTEENTH CENTURY NEW BERN. A HISTORY
OF THE TOWN AND CRAVEN COUNTY, 1700-1800, PART VI, NEW BERN AS A
COLONIAL CAPITAL," North Carolina Historical Review 23:2 (April
1946), 142-171.

B-1802 Dill, Alonzo Thomas Jr., "EIGHTEENTH CENTURY NEW BERN. A HISTORY
OF THE TOWN AND CRAVEN COUNTY, 1700-1800, PART VII, NEW BERN
DURING THE REVOLUTION," North Carolina Historical Review 23:3
(July 1946), 325-359.

B-1803 Dill, Alonzo Thomas Jr., "EIGHTEENTH CENTURY NEW BERN. A HISTORY
OF THE TOWN AND CRAVEN COUNTY 1700-1800, PART VIII, NEW BERN AT
THE CENTURY'S END," North Carolina Historical Review 23:4 (October
1946), 495-535.

B-1804 Dill, Alonzo T. and Brent Tarter, "THE 'HELLISH SCHEME' TO MOVE
THE CAPITAL," Virginia Cavalcade 30:1 (Summer 1980), 4-11.

B-1805 Dillon, Rodney E. Jr., and Daniel T. Hobby, "FORT LAUDERDALE: A
BRIEF HISTORY," Florida History Newsletter 8 (March 1982), 3-10.

B-1806 Dimick, Howard T., "MOTIVES FOR THE BURNING OF OXFORD, MISSIS-
SIPPI," Journal of Mississippi History 8:3 (July 1946), 111-120.

B-1807 Dimitry, Charles Patton, "THE OLD 'MOBILE LANDING,' HEAD OF THE
BASIN IN NEW ORLEANS," Louisiana Historical Quarterly 3:1 (January
1920), 131-135.

B-1808 Doherty, Herbert J., "ANTE-BELLUM PENSACOLA: 1821-1860," Florida
Historical Quarterly 37:3-4 (January-April 1959), 337-356.

B-1809 D'Olive, Annie Louise, "REMINISCENCES OF TEN MILE: A SOUTH MIS-
SISSIPPI SAW MILL TOWN," Journal of Mississippi History 39:2 (May
1977), 173-184.

B-1810 Dorn, J. K., "RECOLLECTIONS OF EARLY MIAMI," Tequesta 9 (1949),
43-60.

B-1811 Doster, James F., "PEOPLE VS. RAILROAD AT ASHVILLE: A COMMUNITY
SQUABBLE OF 1881," Alabama Review 9:1 (January 1956), 46-53.

B-1812 Douglas, William Lake, "AN EVENT OF PLACE," Landscape Architecture
74:4 (July-August 1984), 48-55.

B-1813 Drago, Edmund and Ralph Melnick, "THE OLD SLAVE MART MUSEUM,
CHARLESTON, SOUTH CAROLINA: REDISCOVERING THE PAST," Civil War
History 27:2 (June 1981), 138-154.

B-1814 Drewry, Jones M., "THE DOUBLE-BARRELLED CANNON OF ATHENS,
GEORGIA," Georgia Historical Quarterly 48:4 (December 1964), 442-
450.

B-1815 Druzhinnina, E. I., "THE EMERGENCE OF TOWNS IN THE SOUTH OF THE UKRAINE AND IN THE SOUTH OF THE UNITED STATES," Novaia: Noveishaia Istoriia (USSR), No. 2 (1976), 69-76.

B-1816 DuBose, Beverly M. Jr., "VININGS," Atlanta Historical Journal 16:1 (Spring 1971), 60-67.

B-1817 Duke, Basil W., "OLD LOUISIVILLE," Filson Club History Quarterly 44:2 (April 1970), 140-155.

B-1818 Dunn, Milton, "HISTORY OF NATCHITOCHES," Louisiana Historical Quarterly 3:1 (January 1920), 26-56.

B-1819 Dyer, Donald R., "JACKSONVILLE AND MIAMI: URBAN CONTRASTS IN FLORIDA," Quarterly Journal of the Florida Academy of Sciences 18:4 (December 1955), 233-238.

B-1820 Dyer, John P., "NORTHERN RELIEF FOR SAVANNAH DURING SHERMAN'S OCCUPATION," Journal of Southern History 19:4 (November 1953), 457-472.

B-1821 Dykstra, Robert, "THE LAST DAYS OF 'TEXAN' ABILENE: A STUDY IN COMMUNITY CONFLICT ON THE FARMER'S FRONTIER," Agricultural History 34:3 (July 1960), 107-118.

B-1822 Earle, Carville V., "THE FIRST ENGLISH TOWNS OF NORTH AMERICA," Geographical Review 67:1 (January 1977), 34-50.

B-1823 Earle, Carville and Ronald Hoffman, "THE URBAN SOUTH: THE FIRST TWO CENTURIES," in B. Brownell, ed., The City in Southern History 1977, 23-51.

B-1824 East, Omega G., "ST. AUGUSTINE DURING THE CIVIL WAR," Florida Historical Quarterly 31:2 (October 1952), 75-91.

B-1825 Edmonson, James H., "DENMARK, TENNESSEE--THE FIRST 150 YEARS," West Tennessee Historical Society Papers No. 34 (1980), 88-95.

B-1826 Edson, Andrew S., "HOW NINETEENTH CENTURY TRAVELERS VIEWED MEMPHIS BEFORE THE CIVIL WAR," West Tennessee Historical Society Papers No. 24 (1970), 30-40.

B-1827 Edwards, John Carver, "RADICAL RECONSTRUCTION AND THE NEW ORLEANS RIOT OF 1866," International Review of History and Political Science [India], 10:3 (August 1973), 48-64.

B-1828 Eidson, William G., "LOUISVILLE, KENTUCKY, DURING THE FIRST YEAR OF THE CIVIL WAR," Filson Club History Quarterly 38:3 (July 1964), 224-238.

B-1829 "An 1870 ITINERARY FROM ST. AUGUSTINE TO MIAMI," Florida Historical Quarterly 18:3 (January 1940), 204-215.

B-1830 Ellis, Mary Louise, "A LYNCHING AVERTED: THE ORDEAL OF JOHN MILLER," Georgia Historical Quarterly 70:2 (Summer 1986), 306-316.

B-1831 Eltzroth, Elsbeth Lee, "ATLANTA VIGNETTES," Atlanta Historical Journal 24:4 (Winter 1980), 75-82.

B-1832 Eltzroth, Elsbeth Lee, "ATLANTA VIGNETTES," Atlanta Historical Journal 25:2 (Summer 1981), 39-44.

B-1833 Emory, Samuel T., "THE GEOGRAPHY OF FREDERICKSBURG, VIRGINIA," Memorandum Folio: Southeastern Division Association of American Geographers 15 (November 1963), 22-32.

B-1834 Eno, Clara B., "OLD AND NEW CAPITOLS OF ARKANSAS," Arkansas Historical Quarterly 4:3 (Fall 1945), 241-249.

B-1835 Enright, Brian J. (contrib.), "AN ACCOUNT OF CHARLES TOWN IN
       1725," South Carolina Historical Magazine 61:1 (February 1960),
       13-17.

B-1836 Erlick, David P., "THE PEALES AND GAS LIGHTS IN BALTIMORE,"
       Maryland Historical Magazine 80:1 (Spring 1875), 9-18.

B-1837 Ernst, William, "THOMAS HICKS WYNNE: HORATIO ALGER IN NINETEENTH-
       CENTURY RICHMOND," Virginia Cavalcade 27:4 (Spring 178), 186-191.

B-1838 Eubank, Wayne C., "BENJAMIN MORGAN PALMER'S LOTTERY SPEECH, NEW
       ORLEANS, 1891," Southern Speech Journal 24:1 (Fall 1958), 2-15.

B-1839 Evans, C. W., "NEWPORT NEWS; ORIGIN OF THE NAME," Virginia Maga-
       zine of History and Biography 55:1 (January 1947), 31-44.

B-1840 Fabel, Robin F. A., "ORDEAL BY SIEGE: JAMES BRUCE IN PENSACOLA
       1780-1781," Florida Historical Quarterly 66:3 (January 1988), 280-
       297.

B-1841 Fakes, Turner J. Jr., "MEMPHIS AND THE MEXICAN WAR," West Tennes-
       see Historical Society Papers No. 2 (1948), 119-144.

B-1842 Faucette, Shirley, "CLINTON--YESTERDAY," Journal of Mississippi
       History 40:3 (August 1978), 215-230.

B-1843 Favrot, J. St. Clair, "BATON ROUGE THE HISTORICAL CAPITAL OF
       LOUISIANA," Louisiana Historical Quarterly 12:4 (October 1929),
       611-629.

B-1844 Fink, Paul M., "JONESBORO'S CHESTER INN," East Tennessee Histori-
       cal Society's Publications No. 27 (1955), 19-38.

B-1845 Fink, Paul M., "THE RAILROAD COMES TO JONESBORO," Tennessee His-
       torical Quarterly 36:2 (Summer 1977), 161-179.

B-1846 Fink, Paul M., "THE REBIRTH OF JONESBORO," Tennessee Historical
       Quarterly 31:3 (Fall 1972), 223-239.

B-1847 Fischer, LeRoy H. and Robert E. Smith, "OKLAHOMA AND THE PARKING
       METER," Chronicles of Oklahoma 47:2 (Summer 1969), 168-208.

B-1848 Fishman, Joshua A., "SOUTHERN CITY," Midstream 7 (September 1961),
       39-56.

B-1849 Fleischman, Joel L., "THE SOUTHERN CITY: NORTHERN MISTAKES IN
       SOUTHERN SETTINGS," in H. Ayers, ed., You Can't Eat Magnolias,
       (1972), 169-194.

B-1850 Fleming, Berry, "AUTOBIOGRAPHY OF A CITY IN ARMS: AUGUSTA,
       GEORGIA, 1861-1865," Richmond County History 7:1 (Winter 1975),
       1-90.

B-1851 Fletcher, Mary P., "EARLY DAYS OF LITTLE ROCK UP TO 1828,"
       Arkansas Historical Quarterly 5:2 (Summer 1946), 179-181.

B-1852 Flexner, James Thomas, "THE GREAT COLUMBIAN FEDERAL CITY,"
       American Art Journal 2:1 (Spring 1970), 30-45.

B-1853 "A FLORIDA SETTLER OF 1877: THE DIARY OF ERASTUS G. HILL,"
       Florida Historical Quarterly 28:4 (April 1950), 271-294.

B-1854 Folmsbee, S. J., "THE BEGINNINGS OF THE RAILROAD MOVEMENT IN EAST
       TENNESSEE," East Tennessee Historical Society's Publications No. 5
       (January 1933), 81-104.

B-1855 Folmsbee, Stanley J. and Lucile Deadrick, "THE FOUNDING OF KNOX-
       VILLE," East Tennessee Historical Society's Publications No. 13
       (1941), 3-20.

B-1856 Folmsbee, Stanley J. and Susan Hill Dillon, "THE BLOUNT MANSION, TENNESSEE'S HISTORICAL CAPITAL," Tennessee Historical Quarterly 22:2 (June 1963), 103-122.

B-1857 Fonseca, James W., "THE GROWTH OF TYSONS CORNER, VIRGINIA," in Virginia Historical Society, The Word, 1977.

B-1858 Forman, William HJ. Jr., "WILLIAM P. HARPER AND THE EARLY NEW ORLEANS CARNIVAL," Louisiana History 14:1 (Winter 1973), 41-48.

B-1859 Formwalt, Lee W., "A CONVERSATION BETWEEN TWO RIVERS: A DEBATE ON THE LOCATION OF THE U.S. CAPITAL IN MARYLAND," Maryland Historical Magazine 71:3 (Fall 1976), 310-321.

B-1860 Fornell, Earl W., "A CARGO OF CAMELS IN GALVESTON," Southwestern Historical Quarterly 59:1 (July 1955), 40-45.

B-1861 Fornell, Earl W., "THE CIVIL WAR COMES TO SAVANNAH," Georgia Historical Quarterly 43:3 (September 1959), 248-260.

B-1862 Foster, M. I., "THE MOVE TO URBAN LIVING," Tennessee Valley Perspective 4:1 (Fall 1973), 4-9.

B-1863 Frank, Beryl, "LEXINGTON ON THE HOOKSTOWN ROAD," History Trails 17 (Autumn 1982), 1-3.

B-1864 Frazer, Mary Reece, "EARLY HISTORY OF AUBURN," Alabama Historical Quarterly 7:3 (Fall 1945), 434-445.

B-1865 Frazier, Evelyn McD., "FIFTY-DAY STATE CAPITAL ON THE EDISTON," South Carolina History Illustrated 1:1 (February 1970), 34-39.

B-1866 Frisbie, Louise K., "'COME IN AND BE OUR GUESTS': HISTORIC HOTELS ALONG THE SUNCOAST," Tampa Bay History 5:1 (Spring/Summer 1983), 42-55.

B-1867 Frost, Margaret Fullerton, "SMALL GIRL IN A NEW TOWN," Great Plains Journal 19, 20, 21 (1980, 81, 82), 1-73, 1-71, 1-78.

B-1868 Fuermann, George M., "HOUSTON, 1880-1910," Southwestern Historical Quarterly 71:2 (October 1967), 226-246.

B-1869 Gage, Larry Jay, "THE CITY OF AUSTIN ON THE EVE OF THE CIVIL WAR," Southwestern Historical Quarterly 63:3 (January 1960), 428-438.

B-1870 Galphin, Bruce, "ATLANTA: CITY OF TRADITION AND PROGRESS," Americas 26:3 (March 1974), 50-55.

B-1871 Gantzhorn, Alan, "THE BRITISH IN PENSACOLA," Echo 2 (Spring-Summer 1981), 13-21.

B-1872 Garner, John S., "THE SAGA OF A RAILROAD TOWN: CALVERT, TEXAS (1868-1918,) Southwestern Historical Quarterly 85:2 (October 1981), 139-160.

B-1873 Garnett, Angelica, "LIFE AT CHARLESTON," Southwest Review 70:2 (Spring 1985), 160-172.

B-1874 Garrett, Franklin M., "ATLANTA AND ENVIRONS (I)," Atlanta Historical Bulletin 10:39 (September 1965), 15-41.

B-1875 Garrett, Franklin M., "ATLANTA AND ENVIRONS (II)," Atlanta Historical Bulletin 10:40 (December 1965), 56-82.

B-1876 Garrett, Franklin M., "ATLANTA AND ENVIRONS (III)," Atlanta Historical Bulletin 11:1 (March 1966), 55-113.

B-1877 Garrett, Franklin M., "ATLANTA AND ENVIRONS (IV)," Atlanta Historical Bulletin 11:2 (June 1966), 39–94.

B-1878 Garrett, Franklin M., "ATLANTA AND ENVIRONS (V)," Atlanta Historical Bulletin 11:3 (September 1966), 51–117.

B-1879 Garrett, Franklin M., "ATLANTA AND ENVIRONS (VI)," Atlanta Historical Bulletin 11:4 (December 1966), 53–99.

B-1880 Garrett, Franklin M., "ATLANTA AND ENVIRONS (VII)," Atlanta Historical Bulletin 12:1 (March 1967), 50–105.

B-1881 Garrett, Franklin M., "ATLANTA AND ENVIRONS (VIII)," Atlanta Historical Bulletin 12:2 (June 1967), 72–115.

B-1882 Garrett, Franklin M., "ATLANTA AND ENVIRONS (IX)," Atlanta Historical Bulletin 12:3 (September 1967), 65–102.

B-1883 Garrett, Franklin M., "ATLANTA AND ENVIRONS (X)," Atlanta Historical Bulletin 12:4 (December 1967), 67–117.

B-1884 Garrett, Franklin M., "ATLANTA AND ENVIRONS (XI)," Atlanta Historical Bulletin 13:1 (March 1968), 64–102.

B-1885 Garrett, Franklin M., "ATLANTA AND ENVIRONS (XIII)," Atlanta Historical Bulletin 13:3 (September 1968), 81–120.

B-1886 Garrett, Franklin M., "ATLANTA AND ENVIRONS (XIV)," Atlanta Historical Bulletin 13:4 (December 1968), 46–126.

B-1887 Garrett, Franklin M., "ATLANTA AND ENVIRONS (XV)," Atlanta Historical Bulletin 14:1 (March 1969), 59–101.

B-1888 Garrett, Franklin M., "ATLANTA AND ENVIRONS (XVI)," Atlanta Historical Journal 14:2 (June 1969), 66–122.

B-1889 Garrett, Franklin M., "ATLANTA AND ENVIRONS (XVII)," Atlanta Historical Journal 14:3 (September 1969), 130–153.

B-1890 Garrett, Franklin M., "ATLANTA AND ENVIRONS (XVIII)," Atlanta Historical Journal 14:4 (December 1969), 100–144.

B-1891 Garrett, Franklin M., "ATLANTA AND ENVIRONS (XIX)," Atlanta Historical Journal 15:1 (Spring 1970), 87–118.

B-1892 Garrett, Franklin M., "ATLANTA AND ENVIRONS (XX)," Atlanta Historical Journal 15:2 (Summer 1970), 85–113.

B-1893 Garrett, Franklin M., "ATLANTA AND ENVIRONS (XXI)," Atlanta Historical Journal 15:3 (Fall 1970), 95–132.

B-1894 Garrett, Franklin M., "ATLANTA AND ENVIRONS, CHAPTER 44 (1866)," Atlanta Historical Journal 5:4 (Winter 1970), 102–141.

B-1895 Garrett, Franklin M., "ATLANTA AND ENVIRONS, CHAPTER 45 (1867)," Atlanta Historical Journal 16:1 (Spring 1971), 68–113.

B-1896 Garrett, Franklin M., "ATLANTA AND ENVIRONS, CHAPTER 46 (1868)," Atlanta Historical Journal 16:2 (Summer 1971), 68–103.

B-1897 Garrett, Franklin M., "ATLANTA AND ENVIRONS, CHAPTER 47 (1869)," Atlanta Historical Journal 17:1, 2 (Spring–Summer 1972), 64–94.

B-1898 Garrett, Franklin M., "ATLANTA AND ENVIRONS, CHAPTER 48 (1870)," Atlanta Historical Journal 17:3, 4 (Fall–Winter 1972), 59–95.

B-1899 Garrett, Franklin M., "ATLANTA AND ENVIRONS," Atlanta Historical
       Journal 18:1, 2 (Spring-Summer 1973), 60-77.

B-1900 Garrett, Franklin M., "ATLANTA AND ENVIRONS, CHAPTER 50 (1872),"
       Atlanta Historical Journal 18:3, 4 (Fall-Winter 1973), 82-101.

B-1901 Garrett, Franklin M., "A SHORT ACCOUNT OF THE ATLANTA HISTORICAL
       SOCIETY," Georgia Historical Quarterly 63:1 (Spring 1979), 100-
       108.

B-1902 Gaston, Kay Baker, "CHATTANOOGA'S WALNUT STREET BRIDGE," Tennessee
       Historical Quarterly, 46:2 (Summer 1987), 110-119.

B-1903 Gatewood, Willard B. Jr., ed., "ARKANSAS NEGROES IN THE 1890S:
       DOCUMENTS," Arkansas Historical Quarterly 33:4 (Winter 1974), 293-
       325.

B-1904 Gaughan, J. E., "HISTORIC CAMDEN," Arkansas Historical Quarterly
       20:3 (Autumn 1961), 245-255.

B-1905 Gelders, Maud and Isidor Gelders, "FITZGERALD, GEORGIA: A SOL-
       DIERS' COLONY," Georgia Review 7:2 (Summer 1953), 165-173.

B-1906 Gifford, George E. Jr. and Florence B. Smallwood, "AUDUBON'S 'VIEW
       OF BALTIMORE,'" Maryland Historical Magazine 72:2 (Summer 1977),
       266-271.

B-1907 Giles, Albert S., "THE INLAND PRAIRIE TOWN," Chronicles of Okla-
       homa 43:3 (Autumn 1965), 284-288.

B-1908 Gillaspie, William R., "SURVIVAL OF A FRONTIER PRESIDO: ST.
       AUGUSTINE AND THE SUBSIDY AND PRIVATE CONTRACT SYSTEMS, 1680-
       1702," Florida Historical Quarterly 62:3 (January 1984), 273-295.

B-1909 Gilmore, Harlan W., "THE OLD NEW ORLEANS AND THE NEW: A CASE FOR
       ECOLOGY," American Sociological Review 9:4 (August 1944), 385-394.

B-1910 Giltner, Helen Fairleigh, "EARLY DAYS OF EMINENCE, KENTUCKY,"
       Filson Club History Quarterly 32:1 (January 1958), 25-29.

B-1911 Goff, John H., "THE SANDTOWN TRAIL," Atlanta Historical Bulletin
       11:4 (December 1966), 34-52.

B-1912 Goldfield, David R., "THE LIMITS OF SUBURBAN GROWTH: THE WASH-
       INGTON, D. C. SMSA," Urban Affairs Quarterly 12:1 (September
       1976), 83-102.

B-1913 Goldfield, David R., "RESCUING THE AMERICAN DREAM: CITIES IN THE
       OLD SOUTH," in B. Brownell (ed.), The City in Southern History,
       1977, 52-91.

B-1914 Goldfield, David R., "THE URBAN SOUTH: A REGIONAL FRAMEWORK,"
       American Historical Review 86:5 (December 1981), 1009-1034.

B-1915 Goldfield, David R., "URBAN-RURAL RELATIONS IN THE OLD SOUTH: THE
       EXAMPLE OF VIRGINIA," Journal of Urban History 2 (1976), 146-168.

B-1916 Gonzalez, Mrs. S.J., "PENSACOLA: ITS EARLY HISTORY," Florida
       Historical Society Quarterly 2:1 (April 1909), 9-25.

B-1917 Goodstein, Anita S., "BLACK HISTORY ON THE NASHVILLE FRONTIER,
       1780-1810," Tennessee Historical Quarterly 38:4 (Winter 1979),
       401-420.

B-1918 Govan, Gilbert E., "SOME SIDELIGHTS ON THE HISTORY OF CHATTA-
       NOOGA," Tennessee Historical Quarterly 6:2 (June 1947), 148-194.

B-1919 Govan, Gilbert E. and James W. Livingood, "CHATTANOOGA, TENNESSEE-
       GEORGIA," Georgia Review 2:2 (Summer 1948), 236-247.

B-1920 Graham, Thomas, "ST. AUGUSTINE HISTORICAL SOCIETY," Florida Historical Quarterly 64:1 (July 1985), 1-31.

B-1921 Gravley, Ernestine, "EARLY TWIN CITIES OF ARKANSAS: DARDANELLE AND NORRISTOWN," Arkansas Historical Quarterly 10:2 (Summer 1957), 177-181.

B-1922 Gray, Ralph D., "WASHINGTON IN 1825: OBSERVATIONS BY HENRY D. GILPIN," Delaware History 11:3 (April 1965), 240-250.

B-1923 Green, Mary Fulton, "A PROFILE OF COLUMBIA IN 1850," South Carolina Historical Magazine 70:2 (April 1969), 104-138.

B-1924 Greenberg, Evelyn Levow, "ISAAC POLOCK: EARLY SETTLER IN WASHINGTON, D. C.," Publications of the American Jewish Historical Society 48:1 (September 1958), 1-18.

B-1925 Greene, A. C., "THE DURABLE SOCIETY: AUSTIN IN THE RECONSTRUCTION," Southwestern Historical Quarterly 721:4 (April 1969), 492-518.

B-1926 Greene, Harlan, "CHARLESTON CHILDHOOD: THE FIRST YEAR OF DUBOSE HEWARD," South Carolina Historical Magazine 83:2 (April 1982), 154-167.

B-1927 Griffin, John W., "ST. AUGUSTINE IN 1822," El Escribano 14 (1977), 45-55.

B-1928 Griffin, William B., SPANISH PENSACOLA, 1700-1763," Florida Historical Quarterly 37:3, 4 (January-April 1959), 242-262.

B-1929 Griffith, Louis, "EATONTON," Georgia Journal 2:5 (August/September 1982), 10-13, 36.

B-1930 Groene, Bertram H., "LIZZIE BROWN'S TALLAHASSEE," Florida Historical Quarterly 48:2 (October 1969), 155-175.

B-1931 Gwaltney, Francis Irby, "A SURVEY OF HISTORIC WASHINGTON, ARKANSAS," Arkansas Historical Quarterly 17:4 (Winter 1958), 337-396.

B-1932 Hass, Edward F., "THE SOUTHERN METROPOLIS, 1940-1976," in B. Brownell, ed., The City in Southern History 1977, 159-191.

B-1933 Hager, Jean, "ON THE BANKS OF THE ARKANSAS: BLACKBURN, AN OKLAHOMA TOWN," Chronicles of Oklahoma 58:4 (Winter 1980-1981), 421-439.

B-1934 Hair, Velma Lea, "THE HISTORY OF CROWLEY, LOUISIANA," Louisiana Historical Quarterly 27:4 (October 1944), 1119-1225.

B-1935 Hall, Betty Jean and Richard Allen Heckman, "BEREA'S FIRST DECADE," Filson Club History Quarterly 42:4 (October 1968), 323-339.

B-1936 Hall, Eliza Calvert, "BOWLING GREEN AND THE CIVIL WAR," Filson Club History Quarterly 11:4 (October 1937), 241-251.

B-1937 Hamer, Collin Bradfield Jr., "RECORDS OF THE CITY OF JEFFERSON (1850-1870) IN THE CITY ARCHIVES DEPARTMENT OF THE NEW ORLEANS PUBLIC LIBRARY," Louisiana History 17:1 (Winter 1976), 51-68.

B-1938 Hamer, Marguerite B., "THE CORRESPONDENCE OF THOMAS HUGHES CONCERNING HIS TENNESSEE RUGBY," North Carolina Historical Review 21:3 (July 1944), 203-214.

B-1939 Hamilton, Kenneth G., "THE MORAVIANS AND WACHOVIA," North Carolina Historical Review 44:2 (Spring 1967), 144-153.

B-1940 Hamilton, Kenneth Marvin, "THE ORIGIN AND EARLY DEVELOPMENTS OF LANGSTON, OKLAHOMA," Journal of Negro History 62:3 (July 1977), 270-287.

B-1941 Hamilton, Kenneth Marvin, "TOWNSITE SPECULATION AND THE ORIGINS OF BOLEY, OKLAHOMA," Chronicles of Oklahoma 55:2 (Summer 1977), 180-189.

B-1942 Handley, Lawrence R., "SETTLEMENT ACROSS NORTHERN ARKANSAS AS IN-FLUENCED BY THE MISSOURI AND NORTH ARKANSAS RAILROAD," Arkansas Historical Quarterly 33:4 (Winter 1974), 273-292.

B-1943 Hankinson, Christine Park, "INDIAN SPRINGS," Georgia Review 1:4 (Winter 1947), 500-510.

N-1944 Hardaway, Sylvia Jean, "CAPITAL REMOVAL," Florida Historical Quarterly 36:1 (July 1957), 77-83.

B-1945 Hardin, J. Fair, "AN OUTLINE OF SHREVEPORT AND CADDO PARISH HIS-TORY," Louisiana Historical Quarterly 18:4 (October 1935), 759-871.

B-1946 Harlow, Alvin F., "TWO LONG-AGO YEARS IN COVINGTON," Filson Club History Quarterly 16:1 (January 1942), 27-54.

B-1947 Harper, Roland M., "SOME SAVANNAH VITAL STATISTICS OF A CENTURY AGO," Georgia Historical Quarterly 15:3 (September 1931), 252-271.

B-1948 Harrigan, Anthony, "THE CHARLESTON TRADITION," American Heritage 9:2 (February 1958), 48-61, 88-93.

B-1949 Harris, Walter A., "OLD OCMULGEE FIELDS. THE CAPITAL TOWN OF THE CREEK CONFEDERACY," Georgia Historical Quarterly 19:4 (December 1935), 273-290.

B-1950 Hart, Donald S., "THE MOOD OF ATLANTA--1850-1861," Atlanta His-torical Journal 15:1 (Summer 1970), 22-42.

B-1951 Hart, John Fraser, "FUNCTIONS AND OCCUPATIONAL STRUCTURES OF CITIES OF THE AMERICAN SOUTH," Annals of the American Association of Geographers 45:3 (September 1955), 267-286.

B-1952 Harwell, Richard Barksdale, "OUR CONFEDERATE DEAD," Atlanta His-torical Bulletin 20:2 (Summer 1976), 97-111.

B-1953 Hatch, Charles E. Jr., "JAMESTOWN AND THE REVOLUTION," William and Mary College Historical Magazine 22:1 (January 1942), 30-38.

B-1954 Hecht, Arthur, "ABRAHAM COHEN: DEPUTY POSTMASTER AT GEORGETOWN, SOUTH CAROLINA (1789-1800)," Publications of the American Jewish Historical Society 48:3 (March 1959), 177-193.

B-1955 Heiss, M. W., "THE SOUTHERN COTTON MILL VILLAGE: A VIEWPOINT," Social Forces 2:3 (March 1924), 345-350.

B-1956 Heite, Edward F., "RICHMOND CITY HALLS," Virginia Cavalcade 17:2 (Autumn 1967), 19-22.

B-1957 Henderson, Alexa Benson, "PAUPERS, PASTORS AND POLITICIANS: REFLECTIONS UPON AFRO-AMERICANS BURIED IN OAKLAND CEMETERY," Atlanta Historical Bulletin 20:2 (Summer 1976), 42-60.

B-1958 Henry, Robert S., "CHATTANOOGA AND THE WAR," Tennessee Historical Quarterly 19:3 (September 1960), 222-230.

B-1959 Henson, Edward L. Jr., "GLADEVILLE AND THE MOUNTAIN STEREOTYPE, 1856-1860," Virginia Cavalcade 21:4 (Spring 1972), 30-35.

B-1960 Hershberg, Theodore, "NINETEENTH-CENTURY BALTIMORE: HISTORICAL AND GEOGRAPHICAL PERSPECTIVES: A COMMENTARY," Working Papers from the Regional Economic History Research Center 4 (1981), 141-155.

B-1961 Hertzberg, Steven, "THE JEWISH COMMUNITY OF ATLANTA FROM THE END OF THE CIVIL WAR UNTIL THE EVE OF THE FRANK CASE," American Jewish Historical Society Quarterly 62:3 (March 1973), 250-285.

B-1962 Hesseltine, William B., "ANDERSONVILLE," Georgia Review 3:1 (Spring 1949-50), 103-114.

B-1963 Hessler, Marilyn S., "MARCUS CHRISTIAN: THE MAN AND HIS COLLEC-TION," Louisiana History, 28:1 (Winter 1987), 37-56.

B-1964 Highsaw, Mary Wagner, "A HISTORY OF ZION COMMUNITY IN MAURY COUNTY, 1806-1860 (1)," Tennessee Historical Quarterly 5:1 (March 1946), 3-34.

B-1965 Highsaw, Mary Wagner, "A HISTORY OF ZION COMMUNITY IN MAURY COUNTY, 1806-1860 (2)," Tennessee Historical Quarterly 5:2 (June 1946), 111-140.

B-1966 Highsaw, Mary Wagner, "A HISTORY OF ZION COMMUNITY IN MAURY COUNTY, 1806-1860 (3)," Tennessee Historical Quarterly 5:3 (September 1946), 222-233.

B-1967 Hill, Henry Butram and Larry Gara, eds., "A FRENCH FRANELEIS VIEW OF ANTE-BELLUM NEW ORLEANS," Louisiana History 1:4 (Fall 1960), 335-341.

B-1968 Hipp, Joseph, "WHAT HAPPENED IN TAMPA ON JULY 15, 1887 OR THERE-ABOUTS," Sunland Tribune 6 (November 1980), 82-94.

B-1969 Hirsch, Arnold R., "NEW ORLEANS: SUNBELT IN THE SWAMP," in R. Bernard, ed., Sunbelt Cities, 1983, 100-137.

B-1970 Hitch, Robert M., "MODERN SAVANNAH," Georgia Historical Quarterly 13:3 (September 1929), 285-341.

B-1971 Hobbs, Sam Earle, "HISTORY OF EARLY CAHABA: ALABAMA'S FIRST STATE CAPITAL," Alabama Historical Quarterly 31:3-4 (Fall-Winter 1969), 155-182.

B-1972 Hobson, Fred, "THE SAVAGE SOUTH: AN INQUIRY INTO THE ORIGINS, ENDURANCE, AND PRESUMED DEMISE OF AN IMAGE," Virginia Quarterly Review 61:3 (Summer 1985), 377-395.

B-1973 Hoffecker, Carol E., "NINETEENTH CENTURY WILMINGTON: SATELLITE OR INDEPENDENT CITY," Delaware History 15:1 (April 1972), 1-18.

B-1974 Hoffman, Paul E., "LEGEND, RELIGIOUS IDEALISM, AND COLONIES: THE POINT OF SANTA ELENA IN HISTORY, 1552-1566," South Carolina His-torical Magazine 84:2 (April 1983) 59-71.

B-1975 Hoffman, Paul E., ST. AUGUSTINE 1580: THE RESEARCH PROJECT," El Escribano 14 (1977), 5-19.

B-1976 Hoffman, Philip, "CREATING UNDERGROUND ATLANTA, 1898-1932," Atlanta Historical Journal 13:3 (September 1968), 55-66.

B-1977 Hoffman, Ronald, "THE URBAN SOUTH: THE FIRST TWO CENTURIES," in B. Brownell, ed., The City in Southern History 1977.

B-1978 Holmes, Helen F., "'HE WAS INTO EVERYTHING,'" Chronicles of Okla-homa 61:4 (Winter 1983), 364-386.

B-1979 Holmes, Nicholas H. Jr., "THE CAPITOLS OF THE STATE OF ALABAMA," Alabama Review 32:3 (July 1979), 163-171.

B-1980 Hoole, W. Stanley, "THE CONFEDERATE ARMORY AT TALLASSEE, ALABAMA, 1864-1865," Alabama Review 25:1 (January 1972), 3-29.

B-1981 Hopkins, Richard J., "ARE SOUTHERN CITIES UNIQUE? RESISTENCE AS A CLUE," Mississippi Quarterly 26:2 (Spring 1973), 121-142.

B-1982 Horn, Stanley F., "NASHVILLE DURING THE CIVIL WAR," Tennessee Historical Quarterly 4:1 (March 1945), 3-22.

B-1983 Horn, Stanley F., "DR. JOHN RALFE HUDSON AND THE CONFEDERATE UNDERGROUND IN NASHVILLE," Tennessee Historical Quarterly 22:1 (March 1963), 38-52.

B-1984 House, Boyce, "ARKANSAS BOYHOOD, LONG AGO," Arkansas Historical Quarterly 20:2 (Summer 1961), 172-181.

B-1985 House, Boyce, "IN A LITTLE TOWN, LONG AGO," Arkansas Historical Quarterly 19:2 (Summer 1960), 151-159.

B-1986 House, Boyce, "A SMALL ARKANSAS TOWN 50 YEARS AGO," Arkansas Historical Quarterly 18:3 (Autumn 1959), 291-307.

B-1987 Howard, C. N., "COLONIAL NATCHEZ: THE EARLY BRITISH PERIOD," Journal of Mississippi History 7:3 (July 1945), 156-170.

B-1988 Howard, Clinton N., "COLONIAL PENSACOLA: THE BRITISH PERIOD. PART I," Florida Historical Quarterly 19:2 (October 1940), 109-127.

B-1989 Howard, Clinton N., "COLONIAL PENSACOLA: THE BRITISH PERIOD. PART II," Florida Historical Quarterly 19:3 (January 1941), 246-269.

B-1990 Howard, Clinton N., "COLONIAL PENSACOLA: THE BRITISH PERIOD. PART III," Florida Historical Quarterly 19:2 (April 1941), 368-401.

B-1991 Howell, R. B. C., "EARLY CORPORATE LIMITS OF NASHVILLE," Tennessee Historical Magazine 2:2 (June 1916), 110-118.

B-1992 Hudson, Charles, Marvin Smith, David Holly, Richard Pothemus and Chester DePratter, "COOSA: A CHIEFTOM IN THE SIXTEENTH-CENTURY SOUTHEASTERN UNITED STATES," American Antiquity 50:4 (October 1985), 723-737.

B-1993 Humphries, Jack W., "THE OLD TOWN OF HUNTSVILLE: THE PERSPECTIVES OF ESTILL AND THOMASON," East Texas Historical Journal 23:2 (1985), 40-46.

B-1994 Humphries, John D., "THE TERRITORY THAT IS NOW ATLANTA," Atlanta Historical Journal 18:3-4 (Fall-Winter 1973), 66-81.

B-1995 Hunter, Leslie Gene, "GREENBELT, MARYLAND: A CITY ON A HILL," Maryland Historical Magazine 63:2 (June 1968), 105-136.

B-1996 Hunter, Tom, "THE HARRISBURG STORY," Augusta Magazine 11:3 (Fall 1984), 23-27, 37.

B-1997 Hurst, Harold W., "THE NORTHERNMOST SOUTHERN TOWN: A SKETCH OF PRE-CIVIL WAR ANNAPOLIS," Maryland Historical Magazine 76:3 (September 1981), 240-249.

B-1998 Hutchins, Fred L., "BEALE STREET AS IT WAS," West Tennessee Historical Society Papers No. 26 (1972), 56-63.

B-1999 Isaac, Erich, "JAMESTOWN AND THE MID-ATLANTIC COAST: A GEOGRAPHIC RECONSIDERATION," Journal of Geography 57:1 (January 1958), 17-29.

B-2000 Jager, Ronald B., "HOUSTON, TEXAS FIGHTS THE CIVIL WAR," Texana 11:1 (Spring 1973), 30-51.

B-2001 James, Harlean, "SEVEN SOUTHERN STATE CAPITALS," Social Forces 4:2 (December 1925), 386-394.

B-2002 Jarrett, Walter, "DOWN THE RIVER TO NEW ORLEANS, PART II: UNDER AMERICAN AND CONFEDERATE FLAGS," Mankind 4:8 (1974), 18-25, 58-59.

B-2003 Jarrett, Walter, "NEW ORLEANS: THE CITY THAT CARE FORGOT: PART I UNDER FRENCH AND SPANISH FLAGS," Mankind 4:7 (1974), 16-23, 48-51.

B-2004 Jarzombeck, Michelle, "MEMPHIS-SOUTH MEMPHIS CONFLICT, 1826-1850," Tennessee Historical Quarterly 41:1 (Spring 1982), 23-36.

B-2005 Javersak, David T., "OUR PLACE ON THIS GREEN PLANET WHERE ANDREW CARNEGIE CAN'T GET A MONUMENT WITH HIS MONEY," West Virginia History 41:1 (Fall 1979), 7-19.

B-2006 Jefferson, Pat, "THE MAGNIFICENT BARBARIAN AT NASHVILLE," Southern Speech Journal 33:2 (Winter 1967), 77-87.

B-2007 Jenkins, B. Wheeler, "THE SHOTS THAT SAVED BALTIMORE," Maryland Historical Magazine 77:4 (December 1982), 362-364.

B-2008 Jillson, Willard Rouse, "THE FIRST LANDOWNERS OF FRANKFORT, KENTUCKY, 1774-1790," Register of the Kentucky Historical Society 43:143 (April 1945), 107-120.

B-2009 Jillson, Willard Rouse, "THE FOUNDING OF LEXINGTON, KENTUCKY," Filson Club History Quarterly 3:5 (October 1929), 237-242.

B-2010 Joel, Joseph, ed., "MY RECOLLECTIONS AND EXPERIENCES OF RICHMOND, VIRGINIA, U.S.A., 1884-1892," Virginia Magazine of History and Biography 87:3 (July 1979), 344-356.

B-2011 Johns, John, "WILMINGTON DURING THE BLOCKADE," Civil War Times Illustrated 13:3 (June 1974), 34-49.

B-2012 Johnson, Cecil, "PENSACOLA IN THE BRITISH PERIOD: SUMMARY AND SIGNIFICANCE," Florida Historical Quarterly 37:3-4 (January-April 1959), 263-280.

B-2013 Johnson, Gerald W., "THE SOUTH TAKES THE OFFENSIVE," American Mercury 2:5 (May 1924), 70-78.

B-2014 Johnson, Guion Griffis, "THE ANTE-BELLUM TOWN IN NORTH CAROLINA," North Carolina Historical Review 5:4 (October 1928), 372-389.

B-2015 Jones, George Fenwick, "JOHN MARTIN BOLTZIUS' TRIP TO CHARLESTON, OCTOBER 1742," South Carolina Historical Magazine 82:2 (April 1981), 87-110.

B-2016 Jones, George Fenwick, "THE 1780 SEIGE OF CHARLESTON AS EXPERIENCED BY A HESSIAN OFFICER," South Carolina Historical Magazine 88:1 (January 1987), 23-32; 88:2 (April 1987), 63-75.

B-2017 Jones, James P. and William Warren Rogers, eds., "MONTGOMERY AS THE CONEDERATE CAPITAL: VIEW OF A NEW NATION," Alabama Historical Quarterly 26:1 (Spring 1964), 1-125.

B-2018 Jones, V. C., "THE SACK OF HAMPTON, VIRGINIA," American History Illustrated 9:2 (May 1974), 36-44.

B-2019 Joshi, Manoj K. and Joseph P. Riedy, "'TO COME FORWARD AND AID IN PUTTING DOWN THIS UNHOLY REBELLION': THE OFFICERS OF LOUISIANA'S FREE BLACK NATIVE GUARD DURING THE CIVIL WAR ERA," Southern Studies 21:3 (Fall 1982), 326-347.

B-2020 Julian, Allen Phelps, "ATLANTA'S LAST DAYS IN THE CONFEDERACY," Atlanta Historical Bulletin 11:2 (June 1966), 9-18.

B-2021 Jupiter, Clare, "NEW ORLEANS, 1979: 'IT WAS WORTH IT,'" Southern Exposure 7:2 (Summer 1979), 61-62.

B-2022 Karp, Walter, "MY GAWD, THEY'VE SOLD THE TOWN," American Heritage 32:5 (August-September) 84-95.

B-2023 Kaufman, Burton I., "NEW ORLEANS AND THE PANAMA CANAL, 1900-1914," Louisiana History 14:4 (Fall 1973), 333-346.

B-2024 Keene, Jessee L., "GAVINO GUTIERREZ AND HIS CONTRIBUTIONS TO TAMPA," Florida Historical Quarterly 36:1 (July 1957), 33-41.

B-2025 Keene, Otis L., "JACKSONVILLE, FIFTY-THREE YEARS AGO," Florida Historical Society Quarterly 1:4 (January 1909), 9-15.

B-2026 Keister, Albert S., "A CITY IN DEPRESSION--GREENSBORO, NORTH CAROLINA," Social Forces 13:1 (October 1934), 91-99.

B-2027 Kelemen, Thomas A., "A HISTORY OF LYNCH, KENTUCKY, 1917-1930," Filson Club History Quarterly 48:2 (April 1974), 156-176.

B-2028 Kellar, Herbert A. ed., "A JOURNEY THROUGH THE SOUTH IN 1836: DIARY OF JAMES D. DAVIDSON," Journal of Southern History 1:3 (August 1935), 345-377.

B-2029 Kelley, William J., "BALTIMORE STEAMBOATS IN THE CIVIL WAR," Maryland Historical Magazine 37:1 (March 1942), 42-52.

B-2030 Kemper, R. A., "THE HISTORY OF GERMANTOWN," Fauquier Historical Society Bulletin 2 (1922), n p.

B-2031 Kendall, John Smith, "THE FRENCH QUARTER SIXTY YEARS AGO," Louisiana Historical Quarterly 34:2 (April 1951) 91-102.

B-2032 Kendall, John Smith, "NEW ORLEANS' MISER PHILANTHROPIST, JOHN McDONOGH," Louisiana Historical Quarterly 26:1 (January 1943), 138-161.

B-2033 Kilbourne, Annie Sanderson, "WAR TIMES IN AND AROUND OLD CLINTON, LA." Louisiana Historical Quarterly 13:1 (January 1930), 64-66.

B-2034 Kilgore, Dan E., "CORPUS CHRISTI: A QUARTER CENTURY OF DEVELOP- MENT 1900-1925," Southwestern Historical Quarterly 75:4 (April 1972), 434-460.

B-2035 Kimball, William J., "RICHMOND BEGINS THE WORK OF WAR," Virginia Cavalcade 10:4 (Spring 1961), 13-18.

B-2036 Kimball, William J., "RICHMOND 1865: THE FINAL THREE MONTHS," Virginia Cavalcade 19:1 (Summer 1969), 38-47.

B-2037 Kimball, William J., "WAR-TIME RICHMOND," Virginia Cavalcade 11:4 (Spring 1962), 33-40.

B-2038 Kincaid, Mary Elizabeth, "FAYETTEVILLE, WEST VIRGINIA, DURING THE CIVIL WAR," West Virginia History 14:4 (July 1953), 339-365.

B-2039 King, G. Wayne, "THE EMERGENCE OF FLORENCE, SOUTH CAROLINA, 1853- 1890," South Carolina Historical Magazine 82:3 (July 1981), 197- 209.

B-2040 King, Sara Singleton, "WAYCROSS: GATEWAY TO THE OKEFENOKEE," Georgia Review 4:3 (Fall 1950), 217-223.

B-2041 King, Spencer Bidwell Jr., "APRIL IN MACON," Georgia Review 14:2 (Summer 1960), 143-154.

B-2042 Kinsland, William S., "THE DAHLONEGA MINT: A CIVIL WAR MYSTERY," North Georgia Journal 1 (Summer 1984), 39-51.

B-2043 Kmen, Henry, "NEW ORLEANS' FORTY DAYS IN '49," Louisiana Historical Quarterly 40:1 (January 1957), 25-45.

B-2044 Knox, Paul L., "THE WASHINGTON METROPOLITAN AREA," Cities 4:4 (November 1987), 290-298.

B-2045 Kovacik, Charles F., "THE DECLINING SMALL SOUTHERN TOWN," West Georgia College Studies in the Social Sciences 16 (June 1977), 39-48.

B-2046 Kovacik, Charles and Lawrence S. Rowland, "IMAGES OF COLONIAL PORT ROYAL, SOUTH CAROLINA," Annals of the Association of American Geographers 63:3 (September 1973), 331-340.

B-2047 Kramer, Carl E., "IMAGES OF A DEVELOPING CITY: LOUISVILLE, 1800-1830," Filson Club History Quarterly 52:2 (April 1978), 166-190.

B-2048 Krieger, Lisa M., "A BIG BANG AND A WHIMPER," Southern Exposure 10:4 (July-August 1982), 30-34.

B-2049 Kurtz, Michael L., LEE HARVEY OSWALD IN NEW ORLEANS," Louisiana History 21:1 (Winter 1980), 7-22.

B-2050 Kurtz, Wilbur G., "A FEDERAL SPY IN ATLANTA," Atlanta Historical Bulletin 10:38 (December 1957), 13-20.

B-2051 Kurtz, Wilbur G., "MY ADVENTURES WITH ATLANTA HISTORY," Atlanta Historical Bulletin 12:1 (March 1967), 9-21.

B-2052 Kurtz, Wilbur G. and Annie Laurie Kurtz with John F. Stegeman ed., "THE KURTZ CHRONICLES OF EARLY ATLANTA," Atlanta Historical Journal 26:1 (Spring 1982), 5-32.

B-2053 Kuykendall, James R. and Elizabeth S. Havard, "TURKEY TROT DAYS AT OLIVER HALL'S STORE," Alabama Review 38:2 (April 1985), 105-118.

B-2054 Kyser, John L., "THE DEPOSITION OF BISHOP WILLIAM MONTGOMERY BROWN IN NEW ORLEANS, 1925," Louisiana History 8:1 (Winter 1967), 35-52.

B-2055 LaFar, Margaret Freeman, "LOWELL MASON'S VARIED ACTIVITIES IN SAVANNAH," Georgia Historical Quarterly 28:3 (September 1944), 113-137.

B-2056 Lamoreaux, David with Gerson G. Eisenberg, "BALTIMORE VIEWS THE GREAT DEPRESSION, 1929-33," Maryland Historical Magazine 71:3 (Fall 1976), 428-442.

B-2057 Lane, Mary, "MACON: AN HISTORICAL RETROSPECT," Georgia Historical Quarterly 5:3 (September 1921), 20-34.

B-2058 Lang, James O., "GLOOM ENVELOPS NEW ORLEANS, APRIL 24 TO MAY 2, 1862," Louisiana History 1:4 (Fall 1960), 281-299.

B-2059 Larson, Chiles T., "A PORTFOLIO OF JAMESTOWN PICTURES," Virginia Cavalcade 9:4 (Spring 1960), 23-29.

B-2060 Laughlin, Virginia (contrib.), "PARKERSBURG: HISTORY OF THE CITY FROM TIME OF ITS SETTLEMENT TO PRESENT IN GRIPPING NARRATIVE FROM THE PEN OF THE LATE MISS KATE HARRIS, FROM THE PARKERSBURG DISPATCH-NEWS OF FEBRUARY 16, 1913," West Virginia History 25:4 (July 1964) 241-264.

B-2061 Lawlor, Richard D., "THE IRON HORSE COMES TO LEBANON," Tennessee Historical Quarterly 31:4 (Winter 1972), 360-371.

B-2062 Laws, Kevin, "THE ORIGIN OF THE STREET GRID IN ATLANTA'S URBAN CORE," Southeastern Geographer, 19:2 (November 1979), 69-79.

B-2063 Ledet, Wilton P., "THE HISTORY OF THE CITY OF CARROLLTON," Louisiana Historical Quarterly 21:1 (January 1938), 220-281.

B-2064 Lee, E. Lawrence, "OLD BRUNSWICK, THE STORY OF A COLONIAL TOWN," North Carolina Historical Review 29:2 (April 1952), 230-245.

B-2065 Lee, George W., "POETIC MEMORIES OF BEALE STREET," West Tennessee Historical Society Papers No. 26 (1972), 64-73.

B-2066 Lee, W. D., "A HISTORICAL SKETCH OF CENTER POINT," Arkansas Historical Quarterly 12:3 (Autumn 1953), 262-272.

B-2067 Lefurgy, William G., "BALTIMORE'S WARDS, 1797-1978: A GUIDE," Maryland Historical Magazine 75:2 (June 1980), 145-153.

B-2068 Leighton, George R., "BIRMINGHAM, ALABAMA--THE CITY OF PERPETUAL PROMISE," Harpers Magazine 175 (August 1937), 225-242.

B-2069 Lemmon, Sarah McCullok, "RALEIGH--AN EXAMPLE OF THE 'NEW SOUTH'?" North Carolina Historical Review 43:3 (Summer 1966), 261-285.

B-2070 Levy, B. H., "SAVANNAH'S BULL STREET: THE MAN BEHIND ITS NAME," Georgia Historical Quarterly 71:2 (Summr 1987), 286-296.

B-2071 Lewis, Beasie Mary, "DARIEN, A SYMBOL OF DEFIANCE AND ACHIEVE-MENT," Georgia Historical Quarterly 20:3 (September 1936), 185-198.

B-2072 Lewis, H. H. Walker, "THE LAWYERS' ROUND TABLE OF BALTIMORE," Maryland Historical Magazine 70:3 (Fall 1975), 279-285.

B-2073 Lewis, James E., "MAJOR FUNCTIONAL REGIONS OF THE UNITED STATES SOUTH," Southeastern Geographer 7 (1967), 1-5.

B-2074 Lightfoot, Mrs. William B., "THE EVACUATION OF RICHMOND," Virginia Magazine of History and Biography 41:3 (July 1933), 215-222.

B-2075 Link, Eugene P., "THE REPUBLICAN SOCIETY OF CHARLESTON," Proceedings of the South Carolina Historical Association 13 (1943), 23-34.

B-2076 Livingood, James , "A FEW DAYS IN THE HISTORY OF CHATTANOOGA," Tennessee Historical Quarterly 32:1 (Spring 1973), 83-91.

B-2077 Livingood, James , "THE CHATTANOOGA COUNTRY IN 1860," Tennessee Historical Quarterly 20:2 (June 1961), 159-166.

B-2078 Locke, Raymond Fridiz, "MEMPHIS ON THE MISSISSIPPI," Mankind 5:2 (1975), 12-17, 52-55.

B-2079 Long, Durwood, "THE HISTORICAL BEGINNINGS OF YBOR CITY AND MODERN TAMPA," Florida Historical Quarterly 45:1 (July 1966), 31-44.

B-2080 Long, Durwood, "THE MAKING OF MODERN TAMPA: A CITY OF THE NEW SOUTH, 1885-1911," Florida Historical Quarterly 49:4 (April 1971), 333-345.

B-2081 "LOUISVILLE SCENES: THE AUTOBIOGRAPHY OF FR. RICHARD J. MEANEY," Filson Club History Quarterly 56:2 (April 1982), 170-180.

B-2082 "LOUISVILLE SCENES: THE AUTOBIOGRAPHY OF FR. RICHARD J. MEANEY," Filson Club History Quarterly 57:1 (January 1983), 7-19.

B-2083 "LOUISVILLE SCENES: THE AUTOBIOGRAPHY OF FR. RICHARD J. MEANEY," Filson Club History Quarterly 58:1 (January 1984), 5-49.

B-2084 Lovett, Bobby L., "NASHVILLE'S FORT NEGLEY: A SYMBOL OF BLACKS' INVOLVEMENT WITH THE UNION ARMY," Tennessee Historical Quarterly 41:1 (Spring 1982) 3-22.

B-2085 Luehrs, Karen and Timothy J. Crimmins, "IN THE MIND'S EYE: THE DOWNTOWN AS VISUAL METAPHOR FOR THE METROPOLIS," Atlanta Historical Journal 26:2-3 (Summer-Fall 1982), 177-198.

B-2086 Lyon, Eugene, "ST. AUGUSTINE, 1580: THE LIVING COMMUNITY," El Escribano 14 (1977), 20-33.

B-2087 McAllister, Lyle N., "PENSACOLA DURING THE SECOND SPANISH PERIOD," Florida Historical Quarterly 37:3, 4 (January-April 1959), 281-327.

B-2088 McCabe, Carol, "GEORGE WASHINGTON'S ALEXANDRIA," Early American Life 13:1 (February 1982), 74-79.

B-2089 McCallie, Elizabeth Hanleiter, "ATLANTA IN THE 1850's," Atlanta Historical Bulletin 8:33 (October 1948), 92-106.

B-2090 McCarthy, Joe, "THE MAN WHO INVENTED MIAMI BEACH," American Heritage 27:1 (December 1975), 64-71, 100-101.

B-2091 McCurdy, Mary Burton Derrickson, "MORE ON THE HISTORY OF FREDER- ICA, DELAWARE," Delaware History 15:2 (October 1972), 118-123.

B-2092 McDaniel, G. A., "MEMPHIS' PAST BECOMES A LINK TO ITS FUTURE," Place 3:2 (February 1983), 1-4.

B-2093 McGalliard, Mac, "PIONEER SPIRIT: THE CENTENNIAL HISTORY OF ARDMORE," Chronicles of Oklahoma, 65:1 (Spring 1987), 76-89.

B-2094 McGovern, James R., "PENSACOLA, FLORIDA: A MILITARY CITY IN THE NEW SOUTH," Florida Historical Quarterly 59:1 (July 1980), 24-41.

B-2095 McInvale, Morton R., "'THAT THING OF INFAMY,' MACON'S CAMP OGLE- THORPE," Georgia Historical Quarterly 63:2 (Summer 1970), 279-291.

B-2096 McKinney, John C. and Linda Brookover Bourque, "THE CHANGING SOUTH: NATIONAL INCORPORATION OF A REGION," American Sociological Review 36:3 (June 1971), 399-412.

B-2097 McLean, Malcolm D., "TENOXTITLAN, DREAM CAPITAL OF TEXAS," Southwestern Historical Quarterly 70:1 (July 1966), 23-43.

B-2098 McMillan, Malcolm Cook, "THE SELECTION OF MONTGOMERY AS ALABAMA'S CAPITAL," Alabama Review 1:2 (April 1948), 79-90.

B-2099 McNicoll, Robert E., "THE CALOOSA VILLAGE TEQUESTA: A MIAMI OF THE SIXTEENTH CENTURY," Tequesta 1:1 (March 1941), 11-20.

B-2100 McNinch, Marjorie, "THE CHANGING FACE OF RODNEY SQUARE," Delaware History 21:3 (Spring Summer 1985), 139-163.

B-2101 McReynolds, James M., "FRONTIER TOWNS IN ANTEBELLUM EAST TEXAS: JASPER COUNTY," East Texas Historical Journal 16:1 (1978), 3-14.

B-2102 Mackin, Sister Aloysius O. P., "WARTIME SCENES FROM CONVENT WINDOWS: ST. CECILIA, 1860 THROUGH 1865," Tennessee Historical Quarterly 39:4 (Winter 1980), 401-422.

B-2103 Mahoney, Nell Savage, "WILLIAM STRICKLAND AND THE BUILDING OF TENNESSEE'S CAPITOL, 1845-1854," Tennessee Historical Quarterly 4:2 (June 1945), 99-153.

B-2104 Mahoney, Nell Savage, "WILLIAM STRICKLAND'S INTRODUCTION TO NASH- VILLE," Tennessee Historical Quarterly 9:1 (March 1950), 46-63.

B-2105 Mallard, Daisy O. and Virginia M. Culpepper, "AMERICUS," Georgia Review 4:2 (Summer 1950), 115-124.

B-2106 Maness, Lonnie E., "A WEST TENNESSEE TOWN AND WORLD WAR II," West Tennessee Historical Society Papers No. 32 (1978), 110-119.

B-2107 Mann, George R., "APPENDIX: GEORGE R. MANN'S COMMENTS ON GEORGE W. DONAGHEY'S BUILDING A STATE CAPITOL," Arkansas Historical Quarterly 31:2 (Summer 1972), 134-149.

B-2108 Marks, Henry S., "EARLIEST LAND GRANTS IN THE MIAMI AREA," Tequesta No. 18 (1958), 15-22.

B-2109 Markus, Daniel, "MIAMI 1941-1945," Update 8 (November 1981), 3-7.

B-2110 Marse, W. Eugene, "'JUDGE' WILLIAM HEMINGWAY, 1869-1937," Journal of Mississippi History, 36:4 (1974), 338-351.

B-2111 Marshall, Park, "THE TOPOGRAPHICAL BEGINNINGS OF NASHVILLE," Tennessee Historical Magazine 2:1 (March 1916), 31-39.

B-2112 Martin, Richard A., "DEFEAT IN VICTORY: YANKEE EXPERIENCE IN EARLY CIVIL WAR JACKSONVILLE," Florida Historical Quarterly 53:1 (July 1974),1-32.

B-2113 Martin, Richard A., "FROM HAMLET TO CITY IN 4 YEARS," Jacksonville 18 (September-October 1981), 79-86.

B-2114 Martin, Richard A., "IT WAS A TOUGH TOWN IN 1850," Jacksonville 18 (March-April 1981), 46-48.

B-2115 Martin, Sidney Walter ed., "EDENEZER KELLOGG'S VISIT TO CHARLESTON, 1817," South Carolina Historical and Genealogical Magazine 50:1 (February 1948), 1-14.

B-2116 Marye, William B., "BALTIMORE CITY PLACE NAMES (1)," Maryland Historical Magazine 54:1 (March 1959), 15-35.

B-2117 Marye, William B., "BALTIMORE CITY PLACE NAMES (2)," Maryland Historical Magazine 54:4 (December 1959), 353-364.

B-2118 Marye, William B., "BALTIMORE CITY PLACE NAMES (3)," Maryland Historical Magazine 58:4 (Winter 1963), 211-232.

B-2119 Marye, William B., "BALTIMORE CITY PLACE NAMES (4)," Maryland Historical Magazine 59:1 (Spring 1964), 15-33.

B-2120 Marye, William B., "THE HISTORIC MULBERRY TREE OF ST. MARY'S CITY," Maryland Historical Magazine 39:1 (March 1944), 73-80.

B-2121 Matthews, James S., "SEQUENT OCCUPANCE IN MEMPHIS, TENNESSEE," West Tennessee Historical Society Papers No. 11 (1957), 112-134.

B-2122 Matthias, Virginia Park, "NATCHEZ-UNDER-THE-HILL AS IT DEVELOPED UNDER THE INFLUENCE OF THE MISSISSIPPI RIVER AND THE NATCHEZ TRACE," Journal of Mississippi History 7:4 (October 1945), 201-221.

B-2123 Mauncy, Albert C., "THE FOUNDING OF PENSACOLA--REASONS AND REALITY," Florida Historical Quarterly 37:3, 4 (January-April 1959), 223-241.

B-2124 Mayo, Bernard, "LEXINGTON: FRONTIER METROPOLIS" in E. Goldman (ed.) in Historiography and Urbanization: Essays in American History in Honor of W. Stull Holt, 1941.

B-2125 Meaney, Fr. Richard J., "LOUISVILLE SCENES: THE AUTOBIOGRAPHY OF FR. RICHARD J. MEANEY," Filson Club History Quarterly 56:2 (April 1982) 170-180.

B-2126 Messmer, Charles K., "THE END OF AN ERA: LOUISVILLE IN 1865," Filson Club History Quarterly 54:3 (July 1980) 239-271.

B-2127 Messmer, Charles K., "LOUISVILLE ON THE EVE OF THE CIVIL WAR," Filson Club History Quarterly 50:3 (July 1976), 249-289.

B-2128 Messmer, Charles K., "LOUISVILLE DURING THE CIVIL WAR," Filson Club History Quarterly 52:2 (April 1978), 206-233.

B-2129 Miller, Mary Emily, "PORT TOWN ON THE STARBOARD, A HISTORY OF FREDERICA, DELAWARE," Delaware History 14:2 (October 1970), 111-134.

B-2130 Mitchell, Stephens, "A TENTATIVE RECONSTRUCTION OF THE DECATUR TOWN MAP OF 1823," Atlanta Historical Bulletin 10:39 (September 1965), 8-14.

B-2131 Mobley, Joe A., "THE SIEGE OF MOBILE, AUGUST, 1864-APRIL, 1865," Alabama Historical Quarterly 38:4 (Winter 1976), 250-270.

B-2132 Moffatt, L. G. and J. M. Carriere, "A FRENCHMAN VISITS NORFOLK, FREDERICKSBURG AND ORANGE COUNTY, 1816," Virginia Magazine of History and Biography 53:2 (April 1945), 101-123.

B-2133 Moffatt, J. G. and J. M. Carriere, "A FRENCHMAN VISITS NORFOLK, FREDERICKSBURG, AND ORANGE COUNTY, 1816," Virginia Magazine of History and Biography 53:3 (July 1945), 197-214.

B-2134 Moffatt, Lucius Caston and Joseph Medard Carriere, "A FRENCHMAN VISITS CHARLESTON, 1817," South Carolina Historical and Geneaological Magazine 49:3 (1948), 131-154.

B-2135 Moore, John Hammond, ed., "THE ABIEL ABBOT JOURNALS, A YANKEE PREACHER IN CHARLESTON SOCIETY, 1818-1827," South Carolina Historical Magazine 68:2, 3, 4, (April, July, October 1969), 51-73, 115-139, 232-247.

B-2136 Moore, John Hammond, "CHARLESTON IN WORLD WAR I: SEEDS OF CHANGE," South Carolina Historical Magazine 86:1 (January 1985), 39-49.

B-2137 Morison, Elting E., "WHAT WENT WRONG WITH A DISNEY'S WORLD'S FAIR," American Heritage 35:1 (December 1983), 70-80.

B-2138 Mormino, Gary R., "TAMPA: FROM HELL HOLE TO THE GOOD LIFE," in R. Bernard, Sunbelt Cities: Politics and Growth Since World War II, 1983, 138-161.

B-2139 Mormino, Gary R., "TAMPA'S SPLENDID LITTLE WAR: A PHOTO ESSAY," Tampa Bay History 4:2 (Fall Winter 1982), 45-60.

B-2140 Morris, Jan, "LETTER FROM CHATTANOOGA: VIEWS FROM LOOKOUT MOUNTAIN," Encounter [Great Britain] 44:6 (1975), 42-48.

B-2141 Moyers, Bill, "THE ATLANTA QUESTION," Atlanta Historical Bulletin 21:3 (Fall 1977), 7-23.

B-2142 Mulder, Kenneth W., "TAMPA FROM SHELL MOUNT TO MODERN TOWN," Sunland Tribune 6 (November 1980), 16-31.

B-2143 Murray, Dorothy Hagnie, "WILLIAM JOHN HENNING, THE MAN--THE PUBLISHER," Richmond County History 2:1 (Winter 1970), 7-12.

B-2144 Myers, Raymond E., "THE STORY OF GERMANNA," Filson Club History Quarterly 48:1 (January 1974), 27-42.

B-2145 Myres, Sandra L., "FORT WORTH, 1870-1900," Southwestern Historical Quarterly 72:2 (October 1968), 200-222.

B-2146 Myrick, Susan, "MACON," Georgia Review 3:4 (Winter 1949), 413-423.

B-2147 Nash, Charles H. and Rodney Gates Jr., "CHUCALISSA INDIAN TOWN," Tennessee Historical Quarterly 21:2 (June 1962), 103-121.

B-2148 "NATCHEZ YESTERDAYS: A TIRELESS PHOTOGRAPHER'S RECORD OF A RIVER TOWN," American Heritage 29:4 (June-July 1978), 18-35.

B-2149 Neeley, Mary Ann, "MONTGOMERY, 1885-1887: THE YEARS OF JUBILEE," Alabama Review 32:2 (April 1979), 108-118.

B-2150 Newton, Wesley Phillips, "LINDBERGH COMES TO BIRMINGHAM,: Alabama Review 26:2 (April 1973), 105-121.

B-2151 Nichols, Woodrow W. Jr., "THE EVOLUTION OF AN ALL-BLACK TOWN: THE CASE OF ROOSEVELT CITY, ALABAMA," Professional Geographer 26:3 (August 1974), 298-302.

B-2152 Niederer, Frances J., "EARLY FINCASTLE," Virginia Cavalcade 13:1 (Summer 1963), 12-20.

B-2153 Nixon, H. C., "FAREWELL TO 'POSSUM TROT'?" in R. Vance, ed., The Urban South, 1954, 283-292.

B-2154 Nodyne, Kenneth Robert, "A VIGNETTE OF WHEELING DURING THE EARLY REPUBLIC, 1783-1840," West Virginia History 40:1 (Fall 1978), 47-54.

B-2155 Norfleet, Fillmore, ed., "BALTIMORE AS SEEN BY MOREAR DE SAINT-MERY IN 1794," Maryland Historical Magazine 35:3 (September 1940), 221-240.

B-2156 Nunn, J. B., "EARLY DAYS OF CAMDEN, ARKANSAS," Arkansas Historical Quarterly 5:4 (Winter 1946), 330-340.

B-2157 Oates, Stephen B., "NASA'S MANNED SPACECRAFT CENTER AT HOUSTON, TEXAS," Southwestern Historical Quarterly 67:3 (January 1964), 350-375.

B-2158 Ogburn, W. F. "IDEOLOGIES OF THE SOUTH IN TRANSITION," in H. Odun, ed., In Search of the Regional Balance of America, 1945.

B-2159 Oliphant, Mary C. Simms, "THE GENESIS OF AN UP-COUNTRY TOWN," Proceedings of the South Carolina Historical Association 3 (1933), 50-62.

B-2160 O'Mara, James, "TOWN FOUNDING IN SEVENTEENTH-CENTURY NORTH AMERICA: JAMESTOWN IN VIRGINIA," Journal of Historical Geography 8:1 (January 1982), 1-11.

B-2161 Oneal, Marion, "GROWING UP IN NEW ORLEANS--MEMORIES OF THE 1890's," Louisiana History 5:1 (Winter 1964), 75-86.

B-2162 Oneal, Marion Sherrard, "NEW ORLEANS SCENES," Louisiana History 6:2 (Spring 1965), 189-210.

B-2163 Osgood, H. L., "THE COLONIAL CORPORATION, PART I," Political Science Quarterly 2 (1896), 259-277.

B-2164 Osgood, H. L., "THE COLONIAL CORPORATION, PART II," Political Science Quarterly 8 (1896), 502-533.

B-2165 Osgood, H. L., "THE COLONIAL CORPORATION, PART III," Political Science Quarterly 8 (1896), 694-715.

B-2166 Otto, John Soloman, "HILLSBORO COUNTY (1850): A COMMUNITY IN THE SOUTH FLORIDA FLATWOODS," Florida Historical Quarterly 62:2 (October 1983), 180-193.

B-2167 Owens, Harry P., "APALACHICOLA: THE BEGINNING," Florida Historical Quarterly 47:3 (January 1969), 276-291.

B-2168 Owens, Harry P., "PORT OF APALACHICOLA," Florida Historical
Quarterly 48:1 (July 1969), 1-25.

B-2169 Page, Anne N. (Anne Page Brydonb, ed.), "DIARY OF A YOUNG GIRL OF
ALBEMARLE," Papers of the Albemarle County Historical Society 20
(1961-62), entire issue.

B-2170 Parham, Groesbeck and Gwen Robinson, eds., "IF I COULD GO BACK
. . ." Southern Exposure 4:1-2 (Spring-Summer 1976), 16-20.

B-2171 Parker, James C., "BLAKELEY: A FRONTIER SEAPORT," Alabama Review
27:1 (January 1974), 39-51.

B-2172 Parker, Russell D., "ALCOA, TENNESSEE: THE YEARS OF CHANGE, 1940-
1960," East Tennessee Historical Society's Publications 49 (1977),
99-116.

B-2173 Parker, Russell D., ALCOA, TENNESSEE; THE EARLY YEARS, 1919-1939,"
East Tennessee Historical Society's Publications 48 (1976), 84-
103.

B-2174 Parks, Arva Moore, "MIAMI IN 1876," Tequesta No. 35 (1975), 89-
145.

B-2175 Parks, Edd Winfield, "SOUTHERN TOWNS AND CITIES," in W. Couch,
ed., Culture in the South (1935), 501-518.

B-2176 Parks, Virginia, "THE SIEGE OF PENSACOLA," Echo 2 (Spring-Summer
1981), 57-66.

B-2177 Parlow, Anita, "PIKEVILLE: MILLIONNAIRES AND MOBILE HOMES,"
Southern Exposure 3:4 (Winter 1976), 25-30.

B-2178 Parramore, Thomas C., "THE BURNING OF WINTON IN 1862," North
Carolina Historical Review 39:1 (Winter 1962), 18-31.

B-2179 Parson, William H., "A SOVIET VIEW OF ST. PETERSBURG, FLORIDA,"
Tampa Bay History 3 (Spring-Summer 1981), 74-78.

B-2180 Parsons, Richard, comp., "TOURS FOR FAMILIES OR GROUPS IN METRO-
POLITAL BALTIMORE," Maryland Historical Magazine 72:1 (Spring
1977), 1-58.

B-2181 Partridge, Croom, "REMEMBER? - OR - ATLANTA DURING THE SPANISH-
AMERICAN WAR," Atlanta Historical Bulletin 9:35 (October 1951),
39-64.

B-2182 Paul, Charles L., "COLONIAL BEAUFORT," North Carolina Historical
Review 42:2 (Spring 1965), 139-152.

B-2183 Pecor, Charles J., "THE SOUTHERN TOUR OF SIGNOR BLITZ," Southern
Theatre 22:1 (Winter 1978), 3-10.

B-2184 Perez, Louis A. Jr., "YBOR CITY REMEMBERED," Tampa Bay History 7:2
(FallWinter), 170-173.

B-2185 Perry, Margaret, "AMERICA'S OLDEST CITY: ST. AUGUSTINE, FLORIDA,"
Early American Life 5:2 (April 1974), 26-29.

B-2186 Pfadenhauer, Ruby Mabry McCrary, "HISTORY OF AUGUSTA ARSENAL,"
Richmond County History 2:2 (Summer 1970), 5-32.

B-2187 Pinkley-Call, Cora, "STORIES ABOUT THE ORIGIN OF EUREKA SPRINGS,"
Arkansas Historical Quarterly 5:3 (Fall 1946), 297-307.

B-2188 Pittman, Carolyn, "MEMPHIS IN THE MID-1840's," West Tennessee Historical Society Papers No. 23 (1969), 30-44.

B-2189 Plaisance, Aloysius, ed., "PENSACOLA IN 1810," Florida Historical Quarterly 32:1 (July 1953), 44-48.

B-2190 Preddy, Jane A., "PORT ARTHUR IN 1923," East Texas Historical Journal 24:1 (1986), 39-57.

B-2191 Price, Virginia Polhill, "LOUISVILLE: GEORGIA'S FIRST CAPITAL," Georgia Review 6:1 (Spring 1952), 31-38.

B-2192 Proctor, Samuel, "JACKSONVILLE DURING THE CIVIL WAR," Florida Historical Quarterly 41:4 (April 1963), 343-355.

B-2193 Proefrock, Vicki, "HARRISBURG: INFLUENCES ON AUGUSTA," Richmond County History 17:1 (Winter 1985), 9-16.

B-2194 Prunty, Merle C., "TWO AMERICAN SOUTHS: THE PAST AND THE FUTURE," Southern Geographer 17:1 (May 1977), 1-24.

B-2195 Pulinka, Steven M., "SUCCESS AND FAILURE IN CANTWELL'S BRIDGE, DELAWARE: DAVID WILSON, JR.'S LIFESTYLE, STATUS, BUSINESS, AND ASSIGNMENT," Delaware History 21:1 (Spring-Summer 1984), 53-72.

B-2196 Quynn, Dorothy M., "RECRUITING IN OLD ORLEANS FOR NEW ORLEANS," American Historical Review 46:4 (July 1941), 832-836.

B-2197 Rachal, William M. E., "THE BURNING OF RICHMOND," Virginia Cavalcade 1:4 (Spring 1952), 23-28.

B-2198 Ralph, Julian, "A WASHINGTON ALBUM," American History Illustrated 14:2 (May 1979), 36-39.

B-2199 Rauchle, Robert, "BIOGRAPHICAL SKETCHES OF PROMINENT GERMANS IN MEMPHIS, TENNESSEE IN THE NINETEENTH CENTURY," West Tennessee Historical Society Papers No. 22 (1968), 73-85.

B-2200 Ravenel, Virginia, "FLORENCE, FLORENCE," South Carolina History Illustrated 1:1 (February 1970), 40-42, 62-65.

B-2201 Reinders, Robert C., "MILITIA IN NEW ORLEANS, 1853-1861," Louisiana History 3:1 (Winter 1962), 33-42.

B-2202 Reinders, Robert C., "ORESTES A. BROWNSON'S VISIT TO NEW ORLEANS, 1855," Louisiana Historical Quarterly 38:3 (July 1955), 1-19.

B-2203 Rennick, Robert M., "TRADITIONAL ACCOUNTS OF SOME EASTERN KENTUCKY PLACE NAMES," Appalachian Notes 13:4 (1985), 2-16.

B-2204 Renshaw, James A., "LIBERTY MONUMENT," Louisiana Historical Quarterly 3:3 (July 1920), 259-278.

B-2205 Rhodes, James Ford, "WHO BURNED COLUMBIA," American Historical Review 7:3 (April 1902), 485-493.

B-2206 Rice, Bradley R., "ATLANTA: IF DIXIE WERE ATLANTA," in R. Bernard, ed., Sunbelt Cities: Politics and Growth Since World War II, 1983, 31-57.

B-2207 Rice, Bradley R., "HOW DIFFERENT IS THE SOUTHERN CITY?" Journal of Urban History 11:1 (November 1984), 115-122.

B-2208 Rice, Bradley R., "MOUNTAIN VIEW, GEORGIA: THE ROUGH AND NOT THE READY SUBURB," Atlanta Historical Journal 24:4 (Winter 1980), 27-40.

B-2209 Rice, Thomas E., "FREDERICKSBURG: ALL THE IMPS OF HELL LET
       LOOSE," Civil War Times Illustrated 22:4 (June 1983), 8-15.

B-2210 Richards, Ira Don, "LITTLE ROCK ON THE ROAD TO REUNION, 1865-
       1880," Arkansas Historical Quarterly 25:4 (Winter 1966), 312-335.

B-2211 Riley, Edward M., "SUBURBAN DEVELOPMENT OF YORKTOWN, VIRGINIA,
       DURING THE COLONIAL PERIOD," Virginia Magazine of History and
       Biography 60:4 (October 1952), 522-536.

B-2212 Robertson, James I. Jr., "HOUSES OF HORROR: DANVILLE'S CIVIL WAR
       PRISONS," Virginia Magazine of History and Biography 69:3 (July
       1961), 329-345.

B-2213 Robertson, William J., "SAVANNAH," Georgia Review 2:4 (Winter
       1948), 487-496.

B-2214 Robinson, Willard B., "MARITIME FRONTIER ENGINEERING: THE DEFENSE
       OF NEW ORLEANS," Louisiana History 18:1 (Winter 1977), 5-62.

B-2215 Rochelle, John R., "THE FOUNDING OF A PORT CITY: PORT ARTHUR,
       TEXAS," East Texas Historical Journal 13:2 (Fall 1975), 25-35.

B-2216 Roeber, A. G., ed., "A NEW ENGLAND WOMAN'S PERSPECTIVE ON NORFOLK,
       VIRGINIA, 1801-1802: EXCERPTS FROM THE DIARY OF RUTH HENSHAW
       BASCOM," Proceedings of the American Antiquarian Society 88, part
       2 (October 1978), 277-326.

B-2217 Rogers, George C. Jr., "HISTORY AND CULTURAL DEVELOPMENT,"
       Historic Preservation 23:1 (January-March 1971), 9-13.

B-2218 Rogers, William Warren, ed., "ANDREW DEXTER: FOUNDER OF MONT-
       GOMERY," Alabama Historical Quarterly 43:3 (Fall 1981), 161-170.

B-2219 Rogers, William Warren, "A GREAT STIRRING IN THE LAND: TALLA-
       HASSEE AND LEON COUNTY IN 1860," Florida Historical Quarterly 64:2
       (October 1985), 148-160.

B-2220 Roper, James E., "THE FOUNDING OF MEMPHIS, AUGUST, 1818 THROUGH
       DECEMBER, 1820), West Tennessee Historical Society Papers No. 23
       (1969), 5-29.

B-2221 Roper, James E., "MARCUS WINCHESTER AND THE EARLIEST YEARS OF
       MEMPHIS," Tennessee Historical Quarterly 21:4 (December 1962),
       326-351.

B-2222 Rorer, Michael Arthur, "VANISHING VOICES OF NORFOLK HARBOR,"
       Virginia Cavalcade 11:1 (Summer 1961), 35-47.

B-2223 Rouse, Parker Jr., "MOVING DAY AT WILLIAMSBURG," Early American
       Life 9:2 (April 1978), 14, 16-18, 20.

B-2224 Rowland, A. Ray, "THE AUGUSTA CITY DIRECTORY," Richmond County
       History 5:1 (Winter 1973), 5-28.

B-2225 Rowland, A. R., "PICTURE POSTCARDS: GLIMPSES OF AUGUSTA'S PAST,"
       Richmond County History 65:1 (Winter 1983), 5-8.

B-2226 Ruffin, Thomas F., "IT ALMOST BECAME SHREVEPORT, TEXAS," North
       Louisiana Historical Association Journal 5:2 (1974), 50-55.

B-2227 Ryon, Roderick N., "OLD WEST BALTIMORE," Maryland Historical
       Magazine 77:1 (March 1982), 54-69.

B-2228 Saggus, Charles D., "1865--YEAR OF DESPAIR, YEAR OF HOPE; AUGUSTA
       RECOVERS FROM THE WAR," Richmond County History 7:2 (Summer 1975),
       21-42.

B-2229 Sale, Marian Marsh, "OLD WATERFORD," _Virginia Cavalcade_ 18:4 (Spring 1969), 13-19.

B-2230 Salley, A. S., ed., "DIARY OF WILLIAM DILLWYN DURING A VISIT TO CHARLES TOWN IN 1772," _South Carolina Historical and Genealogical Magazine_ 36 (January 1935), 1-6.

B-2231 Salley, A. S., ed., "DIARY OF WILLIAM DILLWYN DURING A VISIT TO CHARLES TOWN IN 1772," _South Carolina Historical and Genealogical Magazine_ 36 (April 1935), 28-35.

B-2232 Salley, A. S., ed., "DIARY OF WILLIAM DILLWYN DURING A VISIT TO CHARLES TOWN IN 1772," _South Carolina Historical and Genealogical Magazine_ 36 (July 1935), 73-78.

B-2233 Salley, A. S., ed., "DIARY OF WILLIAM DILLWYN DURING A VISIT TO CHARLES TOWN IN 1772," _South Carolina Historical and Genealogical Magazine_ 36 (October 1935), 107-110.

B-2234 Salley, Coleen Cole, "NINETEENTH CENTURY NEW ORLEANS IN BOOKS," _Southern Quarterly_ 20:2 (Winter 1982), 178-186.

B-2235 Saunders, Harold R., "THE EARLY HISTORY AND DEVELOPMENT OF PRINCE-TON, WEST VIRGINIA," _West Virginia History_ 20:2 (January 1959), 80-119.

B-2236 Schaleman, Harry J. Jr., "CASSADAGA: JUST A MEDIUM PLACE," _Florida Geographer_ 18:1 (September 1984), 11-15.

B-2237 Schmidt, William T., "THE IMPACT OF CAMP SHELBY IN WORLD WAR II ON HATTIESBURG, MISSISSIPPI," _Journal of Mississippi History_ 39:1 (February 1977), 41-50.

B-2238 Schweninger, Loren, "A NEGRO SOJOURNER IN ANTEBELLUM NEW ORLEANS," _Louisiana History_ 20:3 (Summer 1979), 305-314.

B-2239 Scott, Kenneth, "'THE CITY OF WRECKERS': TWO KEY WEST LETTERS OF 1838," _Florida Historical Quarterly_ 25:2 (October 1946), 191-201.

B-2240 Scramuzza, V. M., "GALVESTOWN, A SPANISH SETTLEMENT OF COLONIAL LOUISIANA," _Louisiana Historical Quarterly_ 13:4 (October 1930), 553-609.

B-2241 Scribner, Robert L., "DIGGING INTO JAMESTOWN PAST," _Virginia Cavalcade_ 7:1 (Summer 1957), 40-48.

B-2242 Scribner, Robert L., "FREDERICKSBURG, 1862: THE ASSAULT," _Virginia Cavalcade_ 6:3 (Winter 1956), 29-35.

B-2243 Scribner, Robert L., "FREDERICKSBURG, 1862: THE CROSSING," _Virginia Cavalcade_ 6:3 (Winter 1956), 20-28.

B-2244 Scribner, Robert L., "PETERSBURG NIGHTMARE, 1864-1865," _Virginia Cavalcade_ 6:2 (Autumn 1956), 5-9.

B-2245 Scribner, Robert L., "RECONNAISSANCE THROUGH FAIRFAX," _Virginia Cavalcade_ 6:1 (Summer 1956), 18-22.

B-2246 Scribner, Robert Leslie, "A SHORT HISTORY OF BREWTON, ALABAMA," _Alabama Historical Quarterly_ 11:1-4 (1949), 7-131.

B-2247 Scura, Dorothy, "GLASGON AND THE SOUTHERN RENAISSANCE: THE CON-FERENCE AT CHARLOTTESVILLE," _Mississippi Quarterly_ 26:4 (Fall 1974), 415-434.

B-2248 Sellers, Charles, "OLD MECKLENBURG AND THE MEANING OF THE AMERICAN EXPERIENCE," _North Carolina Historical Review_ 46:2 (Spring 1969), 142-156.

B-2249 Sessa, Frank B., "MIAMI IN 1926," Tequesta No. 16 (1956), 15-36.

B-2250 Seymour, Arthur B. (trans); Mark F. Boyd (foreword), "ESSAY ON MIDDLE FLORIDA 1837-1838" [Part 1], Florida Historical Quarterly 26:3 (January 1948), 199-255.

B-2251 Seymour, Arthur B. (trans.) and Mark F. Boyd (foreword), 'ESSAY ON MIDDLE FLORIDA 1837-1838," [Part 2], Florida Historical Quarterly 26:4 (April 1948), 300-324.

B-2252 Shaffer, Janet, "NEW LONDON," Virginia Cavalcade 15:3 (Winter 1966), 22-29.

B-2253 Shea, William L., "THE CAMDEN FORTIFICATIONS," Arkansas Historical Quarterly 41:4 (Winter 1982), 318-326.

B-2254 Sheppard, Peggy, "MARSHALLVILLE--HISTORIC AND BEAUTIFUL," Georgia Life 6 (Autumn 1979), 22-25.

B-2255 Shipley, Ellen Compton, "THE PLEASURES OF PROSPERITY, BELLA VISTA, ARKANSAS, 1917-1929," Arkansas Historical Quarterly 37:2 (Summer 1978), 99-129.

B-2256 Shofner, Jerrell H. and William Warren Rogers, ed., "HOT SPRINGS IN THE 'SEVENTIES," Arkansas Historical Quarterly 22:1 (Spring 1963), 24-48.

B-2257 Shores, David L., PORCHMOUTH FOR PORTSMOUTH," American Speech 61:2 (Summer 1986), 147-152.

B-2258 Shuler, Sam A., "STEPHEN F. AUSTIN AND THE CITY OF AUSTIN: AN ANOMALY," Southwestern Historical Quarterly 69:3 (January 1966), 265-286.

B-2259 Smith, David R., "THE BEAST OF NEW ORLEANS," Manuscripts 31:1 (Winter 1979), 11-21.

B-2260 Smith, Henry A. M., "BEAUFORT--THE ORIGINAL PLAN AND THE EARLIEST SETTLERS," South Carolina Historical and Genealogical Magazine 9:3 (July 1908), 143-160.

B-2261 Smith, Henry A. M., "CHARLESTON AND CHARLESTON NECK," South Carolina Historical and Genealogical Magazine 19:1 (January 1918), 3-76.

B-2262 Smith, Henry A. M., "CHARLESTON--THE ORIGINAL PLAN AND THE EARLIEST SETTLERS," South Carolina Historical and Genealogical Magazine 9:1 (January 1908), 12-27.

B-2263 Smith, Henry A. M., "CHILDSBURG," South Carolina Historical and Genealogical Magazine 15:2 (April 1914), 107-112.

B-2264 Smith, Henry A. M., "FRENCH JAMES TOWN," South Carolina Historical and Genealogical Magazine 9:4 (October 1908), 220-227.

B-2265 Smith, Henry A. M., "GEORGETOWN--THE ORIGINAL PLAN AND THE EARLIEST SETTLERS," South Carolina Historical and Genealogical Magazine 9:2 (April 1908), 85-101.

B-2266 Smith, Henry A. M., "OLD CHARLES TOWN AND ITS VICINITY, PART I," South Carolina Historicla and Genealogical Magazine 10:1 (January 1915), 1-15.

B-2267 Smith, Henry A. M., "OLD CHARLES TOWN AND ITS VICINITY, PART II," South Carolina Historical and Genealogical Magazine 16:2 (April 1915), 49-67.

B-2268 Smith, Henry A. M., "PURRYSBURGH," South Carolina Historical and Genealogical Magazine 10:4 (October 1909), 187-219.

B-2269 Smith, Henry A. M., "WILLTOWN OR NEW LONDON," South Carolina Historical and Genealogical Magazine 10:1 (January 1909), 20-32.

B-2270 Smith, Henry A. M., "RADNOR, EDMUNDSBURY AND JACKSONBORO," South Carolina Historical and Genealogical Magazine 11:1 (January 1910), 39-49.

B-2271 Smith, Herschel Kennon, "TULIP IN HER GLORY," Arkansas Historical Quarterly 17:1 (Spring 1958), 68-72.

B-2272 Smith, James M., "THOMAS HENRY HUXLEY IN NASHVILLE, PART 1," Tennessee Historical Quarterly 33:2 (Summer 1974), 191-203.

B-2273 Smith, James M., "THOMAS HENRY HUXLEY IN NASHVILLE, PART 2," Tennessee Historical Quarterly 33:3 (Fall 1974), 322-341.

B-2274 Smith, Loran, "MAKESHIFT METROPOLIS," South Carolina History Illustrated 1:4 (November 1970), 36-41.

B-2275 Smith, Miriam Jane, "THE FORGOTTEN VIRGINIAN--FROM BRITISH MERCHANT TO PROMINENT CITIZEN: THOMAS RUTHERFORD, 1755-1852," West Virginia History 36:1 (Fall 1974), 50-62.

B-2276 Smith, Winston, "EARLY HISTORY OF DEMOPOLIS," Alabama Review 18:2 (April 1965), 83-91.

B-2277 Snyder, Perry A., "CIVIL WAR SHREVEPORT," North Louisiana Historical Association Journal 6:1 (1974), 1-8.

B-2278 Snyder, Perry A., "SHREVEPORT, LOUISIANA 1861-1865; FROM SUCCESSION TO SURRENDER," Louisiana Studies 11:1 (Spring 1972), 50-70.

B-2279 Sonnichsen, C. L. "EL PASO--FROM WAR TO DEPRESSION," Southwestern Historical Quarterly 74:3 (January 1971), 357-384.

B-2280 Spencer, Warren F., "A FRENCH VIEW OF THE FALL OF RICHMOND: ALFRED PAUL'S REPORT TO DROUYN DE LLYS, APRIL 11, 1865," Virginia Magazine of History and Biography 73:2 (April 1965), 178-188.

B-2281 Stagg, Brian L., "TENNESSEE'S RUGBY COLONY," Tennessee Historical Quarterly 27:3 (Fall 1968), 209-224.

B-2282 Standard, Janet Harvill, "HISTORIC WASHINGTON-WILKES," Georgia Review 5:4 (Winter 1951), 455-471.

B-2283 Steed, Hal, "ATLANTA," Georgia Review 2:1 (Spring 1948), 98-108.

B-2284 Steen, Ivan D., "CHARLESTON IN THE 1850'S: AS DESCRIBED BY BRITISH TRAVELERS," South Carolina Historical Magazine 71:1 (January 1970), 36-45.

B-2285 Stephens, Pauline Tyson, "ALBANY," Georgia Review 3:1 (Spring 1950), 30-42.

B-2286 Sterling, Davie Lee, ed., "NEW ORLEANS, 1801: AN ACCOUNT BY JOHN PINTARD," Louisiana Historical Quarterly 34:3 (1951), 217-233.

B-2287 Stevens, M. James, "BILOXI'S FIRST LADY LIGHT HOUSE KEEPER," Journal of Mississippi History 34:1 (February 1974), 39-42.

B-2288 Strong, Mrs. Paschal N. Sr., "GLIMPSES OF SAVANNAH, 1780-1825," Georgia Historical Quarterly 33:1 (March 1949), 26-35.

B-2289 Swann, Lee Ann Caldwell and Lisa Abbot, "EZEKIEL HARRIS OF HARRISBURG, Richmond County History 12:2 (Winter 1980), 5-12.

B-2290 Swem, E. G., "VIEWS OF YORKTOWN AND GLOUCESTER TOWN, 1755," Virginia Magazine of History and Biography 54:2 (April 1946), 99-105.

B-2291 Talmadge, John E. and William Wallace Davidson, "GROWING UP IN GEORGIA AND TENNESSEE. PT. I," Georgia Review 27:1 (Spring 1973), 5-32.

B-2292 Talmadge, John E. and William Wallace Davidson, "GROWING UP IN GEORGIA AND TENNESSEE. PT. II," Georgia Review 27:2 (Summer 1973), 194-219.

B-2293 Tanner, Helen Hornbeck, "THE 1789 SAINT AUGUSTINE CELEBRATION," Florida Historical Quarterly 38:4 (April 1959), 280-293.

B-2294 Taylor, Rhea A., "THE SELECTION OF KENTUCKY'S PERMANENT CAPITAL SITE," Filson Club History Quarterly 23:4 (October 1949), 267-277.

B-2295 Teja, Jesus F. de la and John Wheat, "BEXAR: PROFILE OF A TEJANO COMMUNITY," Southwestern Historical Quarterly 89:1 (July 1985), 7-36.

B-2296 terBraake, Alex L., "WHAT'S IN A NAME: THE THREE CHARLESTOWNS," West Virginia History 30:1 (October 1968), 351-357.

B-2297 Theard, Delvaille, "THE FOUNDING OF NEW ORLEANS," Louisiana Historical Quarterly 3:1 (January 1920), 68-70.

B-2298 Thomas, Ronald, "THE FOUNDING OF A HAPPY TOWN: MARTIN, TENNES- SEE," West Tennessee Historical Society Papers No. 27 (1973), 5-17.

B-2299 Thomas, William H. B., "GORDONSVILLE," Virginia Cavalcade 19:2 (Autumn 1969), 36-41.

B-2300 Thomas, Emory M., "WARTIME RICHMOND," Civil War Times Illustrated 16: (June 1977), 3-50.

B-2301 Thorne, Charles G., "THE WATERING SPAS OF MIDDLE TENNESSEE," Tennessee Historical Quarterly 29:4 (Winter 1970-71), 321-359.

B-2302 Thrall, Price A., "JAMES H. HARKRIDER AND EARLY DAYS IN CONWAY," Arkansas Historical Quarterly 13:2 (Summer 1954), 164-171.

B-2303 Thurmond, Walter R., "THE TOWN OF THURMOND, 1884-1961," West Virginia History 22:4 (July 1961), 240-254.

B-2304 Timmons, W. H., "AMERICAN EL PASO: THE FORMATIVE YEARS, 1848-1854," Southwestern Historical Quarterly 87:1 (July 1983), 1-36.

B-2305 Tinker, Edward Larocque, "A PAEAN OF APPRECIATION OF NEW ORLEANS AND HER PEOPLE," Louisiana Historical Quarterly 54:1 (Winter 1971), 27-40.

B-2306 Tobias, Thomas J. ed., "CHARLES TOWN IN 1764," South Carolina Historical Magazine 67:2 (April 1967), 63-74.

B-2307 Tobias, Thomas J., "JOSEPH TOBIAS OF CHARLES TOWN: 'LINGUISTER," Publication of the American Jewish Historical Society 49:1 (September 1959), 33-38.

B-2308 "TOWNS OF THE ALABAMA BLACK BELT," Mid-America 39:2 (April 1957), 85-95.

B-2309 Trautmann, Frederick, "NEW ORLEANS, THE MISSISSIPPI, AND THE DELTA THROUGH A GERMAN'S EYES: THE TRAVELS OF EMIL DECHERT, 1885-1886," Louisiana History 25:1 (Winter 1984), 79-98.

B-2310 Trautmann, Frederick, "SOUTH CAROLINA THROUGH A GERMAN'S EYES: THE TRAVELS OF CLARA VON GERSTNER, 1839," South Carolina Historical Magazine 85:3 (July 1984), 220-232.

B-2311 Treanor, Sapelo, "THE STORY OF VALDOSTA," Georgia Review 9:1
(Spring 1955), 92-104.

B-2312 Trotter, Margret G., "A GLIMPSE OF CHARLESTON IN THE 1890s FROM A
CONTEMPORARY DIARY," West Virginia History 35:2 (January 1974),
131-144.

B-2313 Trumbull, Marian, "HIRAM F. HAMMON, PIONEER OF PALM BEACH,"
Florida Historical Quarterly 19:2 (October 1940), 140-144.

B-2314 Turner, Charles W., ed., "GENERAL DAVID HUNTER'S SACK OF LEXING-
TON, VIRGINIA JUNE 10-14, 1864: AN ACCOUNT BY ROSE PAGE PENDLE-
TON," Virginia Magazine of History and Biography 83:2 (April
1975), 173-183.

B-2315 Utz, Dora Doster, "WEST PALM BEACH," Tequesta No. 33 (1973), 51-
67.

B-2316 Vandiver, Wellington, "PIONEER TALLADEGA, ITS MINUTES AND MEMO-
RIES," [Part 1], Alabama Historical Quarterly 16:1 (Spring 1954),
9-155.

B-2317 Vandiver, Wellington, "PIONEER TALLADEGA, ITS MINUTES AND MEM-
OIRS," [Part 2], Alabama Historical Quarterly 16:2 (Summer 1954),
163-297.

B-2318 Van West, Carroll and Mary S. Hoffschwelle, "'SLUMBERING ON ITS
OLD FOUNDATIONS': INTERPRETATION AT COLONIAL WILLIAMSBURG," South
Atlantic Quarterly 83:2 (Spring 1984), 157-175.

B-2319 Vanstory, Burnette, "MARIETTA," Georgia Review 12:1 (Spring 1958),
41-49.

B-2320 Villiers, Baron Marc de., "A HISTORY OF THE FOUNDATION OF NEW
ORLEANS, 1717-1722," Louisiana Historical Quarterly 3:2 (April
1920), 157-250.

B-2321 Vitz, Robert, "GENERAL JAMES TAYLOR AND THE BEGINNINGS OF NEWPORT,
KENTUCKY," Filson Club History Quarterly 50:4 (October 1976), 353-
368.

B-2322 Voight, Gilbert P., "EBENEZER, GEORGIA: AN EIGHTEENTH-CENTURY
UTOPIA," Georgia Review 9:2 (Summer 1955), 209-215.

B-2323 ya Sallam, Kalamer, "NEW ORLEANS: NOTES FROM A BANANNA REPUBLIC,"
Black Books Bulletin 7:3 (1981), 14-17, 21.

B-2324 Yonge, Julian, "PENSACOLA IN THE WAR FOR SOUTHERN INDEPENDENCE,"
Florida Historical Quarterly 37:3-4 (January-April 1959), 357-371.

B-2325 Young, J. P., "CENTENNIAL HISTORY OF MEMPHIS," Tennessee Historical Magazine 8:4 (January 1925), 277-298.

B-2326 Wallace, David Duncan, "THE FOUNDING OF GRANITVILLE," Cotton
History Review 1 (1960), 19-25.

B-2327 Wallace, Mike, "MICKEY MOUSE HISTORY: PORTRAYING THE PAST AT
DISNEY WORLD," Radical History Review No. 32 (1985), 33-58.

B-2328 Walton, Sarah L., "RUGBY IN AMERICA," Georgia Review 10:4 (Winter
1956), 395-403.

B-2329 Ware, John D., "ST. AUGUSTINE, 1784: DECADENCE AND REPAIRS,"
Florida Historical Quarterly 48:2 (October 1969), 180-187.

B-2330 Waring, Martha Gallaudet, ed., "CHARLES SETON HENRY HARDEE'S
RECOLLECTIONS OF OLD SAVANNAH," Georgia Historical Quarterly 12:4
(December 1928), 353-388.

B-2331 Waring, Martha Gallaudet, ed., "CHARLES SETON HENRY HARDEE'S RECOLLECTIONS OF OLD SAVANNAH," Georgia Historical Quarterly 13:1 (March 1929),13-49.

B-2332 Waring, Martha Gallaudet, "THE STRIVING SEVENTIES IN SAVANNAH," Georgia Historical Quarterly 20:2 (June 1936), 154-171.

B-2333 Waring, Thomas Pickney, "SAVANNAH OF THE 1870's," Georgia Historical Quarterly 20:1 (March 1936), 52-64.

B-2334 Waterbury, Jean Parker, "THE OLDEST HOUSE, ITS SITE AND ITS OCCUPANTS, 1650 (?)-1984," El Escribano 21 (1984), 1-36.

B-2335 Watt, Frank H., "THE WACO INDIAN VILLAGE AND ITS PEOPLE," Texana 6:3 (Fall 1968), 195-244.

B-2336 Webb, Bernice Larson, "COMPANY TOWN--LOUISIANA STYLE," Louisiana History 9:4 (Fall 1968), 325-340.

B-2337 Weinbery, Amelia, "TROY, ALABAMA," Alabama Historical Quarterly 8:1 (Spring 1946), 105-115.

B-2338 West, Mabel, "JACKSONPORT, ARKANSAS; ITS RISE AND DECLINE," Arkansas Historical Quarterly 9:4 (Winter 1950), 231-258.

B-2339 West, Marvin, "OAK RIDGE--THE ATOMIC CITY," Tennessee Valley Perspective 4:4 (Summer 1974), 14-20.

B-2340 Westwood, Howard C., "CAPTIVE BLACK UNION SOLDIERS IN CHARLESTON-- WHAT TO DO?" Civil War History 28:1 (March 1982), 28-44.

B-2341 Westwood, Howard C., "BENJAMIN BUTLER'S ENLISTMENT OF BLACK TROOPS IN NEW ORLEANS IN 1862," Louisiana History 26:1 (Winter 1985), 5-22.

B-2342 White, Robert H., "TENNESSEE'S FOUR CAPITALS," East Tennessee Historical Society's Publications No. 6 (1934), 29-43.

B-2343 White, William W., "A COMMUNITY PORTRAIT FROM POSTAL RECORDS," Journal of Mississippi History 25:1 (January 1963), 33-37.

B-2344 Whitehill, Melford H. and Robert L. Weinberg, "GREIF--ONE OF BALTIMORE'S GREAT NAMES IN THE CLOTHING INDUSTRY," Generations 3 (June 1982), 47-51.

B-2345 Wilkins, Barratt, "A VIEW OF SAVANNAH ON THE EVE OF THE REVOLU- TION," Georgia Historical Quarterly 54:4 (Winter 1970), 577-584.

B-2346 Williams, Ames W., "THE OCCUPATION OF ALEXANDRIA," Virginia Cavalcade 11:3 (Winter 1961-62), 33-39.

B-2347 Williams, Gordon L., "THE WEST PALM BEACH THAT I REMEMBER," Tequesta No. 39 (1979), 54-69.

B-2348 Williams, Leonard, "LINGERING IN LOUISVILLE: IMPRESSIONS OF AN EARLY VISITOR," Filson Club History Quarterly 52:2 (April 1978), 191-205.

B-2349 Williams, Richard J., "IN DALLAS, AS IN MOST AMERICAN CITIES, THE CONTRAST OF GLITTER AND SQUALOR," Smithsonian 9 (November 1978), 60-69.

B-2350 Williams, Samuel C., "THE CLARKSVILLE COMPACT OF 1785," Tennessee Historical Quarterly 3:3 (September 1944), 237-247.

B-2351 Williams, William H., "THE HISTORY OF CARROLLTON," Louisiana His- torical Quarterly 22:1 (January 1939), 181-215.

B-2352 Wilson, F. Page, "MIAMI: FROM FRONTIER TO METROPOLIS: AN
        APPRAISAL," Tequesta No. 14 (1954), 25-50,

B-2353 Wilson, L. W., "A HISTORY OF WAGONER, OKLAHOMA," Chronicles of
        Oklahoma 50:4 (Winter 1972-1973), 486-496.

B-2354 Wilson, Samuel Jr., "CLIFTON--AN ILL-FATED NATCHEZ MANSION,"
        Journal of Mississippi History 46:3 (August 1984), 179-190.

B-2355 Withers, Marianne McKee, "'COMPLETE IN EVERY PART': SELECTED MAPS
        OF THE CITY OF RICHMOND," Virginia Cavalcade 35:4 (Spring 1986),
        162-171.

B-2356 Wood, Kirk, "FROM TOWN TO CITY," Richmond County History 15:2
        (Summer 1983), 8-12.

B-2357 Woodruff, Hale, "SOUTHERN SCENES, II--NATCHITOCHES, LOUISIANA,"
        Phylon 7:3 (1946), 254.

B-2358 Woods, H. Ted., "COLUMBIA ESTABLISHED AS A PORT IN EARLY 1800's,
        North Louisiana Historical Association Journal 5:2 (1974), 73-76.

B-2359 Worley, Ted R., "EARLY DAYS IN OSCEOLA," Arkansas Historical
        Quarterly 24:2 (Summer 1965), 120-126.

B-2360 Worley, Ted R., "GLIMPSES OF AN OLD SOUTHWESTERN TOWN," Arkansas
        Historical Quarterly 8:2 (Summer 1949), 133-159.

B-2361 Worley, Ted R., "HELENA ON THE MISSISSIPPI," Arkansas Historical
        Quarterly 13:1 (Spring 1954), 1-15.

B-2362 Worsley, Etta Blanchard, "COLUMBUS," Georgia Review 1:3 (Fall
        1947), 366-377.

B-2363 Worsley, Etta Blanchard, "WARM SPRINGS," Georgia Review 3:2
        (Summer 1949), 233-244.

B-2364 Wright, Henry, "AUGUSTA," Georgia Review 3:2 (Fall 1949), 329-340.

B-2365 Wright, John D., "A LEXINGTON SCIENTIST DURING THE CIVIL WAR,"
        Filson Club History Quarterly 38:1 (January 1964), 9-16.

B-2366 Wrong, Charles, "A FRENCHMAN IN BROOKSVILLE," Tampa Bay History
        5:1 (Spring-Summer 1983), 71-81.

B-2367 Wyatt, C. J. ed., "CHEROKEE, GEORGIA--1888," Northwest Georgia
        Historical and Genealogical Quarterly 18:1 (Winter 1986), 2-22.

Housing and Neighborhoods

B-2368 Arnold, Peter E, "PUBLIC HOUSING IN ATLANTA, A NATIONAL FIRST,"
        Atlanta Historical Journal 13:3 (September 1968), 9-18.

B-2369 Beard, Rick, "FROM SUBURB TO DEFENDED NEIGHBORHOOD: THE EVOLUTION
        OF INMAN PARK AND ANSLEY PARK, 1890-1980," Atlanta Historical
        Journal 26:2-3 (Summer-Fall 1982), 113-140.

B-2370 Beirne, D. Randall, "HAMPDEN-WOODBERRY: THE MILL VILLAGE IN AN
        URBAN SETTING," Maryland Historical Magazine 77:1 (March 1982), 6-
        16.

B-2371 Beirne, D. Randall, "LATE NINETEENTH CENTURY INDUSTRIAL COMMUNI-
        TIES IN BALTIMORE," Maryland Historian 11:1 (Spring 1980), 39-50.

B-2372 Beirne, Randall, "RESIDENTIAL GROWTH AND STABILITY IN THE BALTI-
        MORE INDUSTRIAL COMMUNITY OF CANTON DURING THE LATE NINETEENTH
        CENTURY," Maryland Historical Magazine 74:1 (March 1979), 39-51.

B-2373 Borchert, Jamers, "ALLEY LANDSCAPES IN WASHINGTON," Landscape 23:3 (1979), 3-10.

B-2374 Brodsky, Harold, "RESIDENTIAL LAND AND IMPROVEMENT VALUES IN A CENTRAL CITY," Land Economics 46:3 (August 1970), 229-247.

B-2375 Bullard, Robert D. and Donald Tryman, "COMPETITION FOR DECENT HOUSING: A FOCUS ON HOUSING DISCRIMINATION COMPLAINTS IN A SUNBELT CITY," Journal of Ethnic Studies 7:4 (Winter 1980), 51-64.

B-2376 Carter R. W. G., "CONDOMINIUMS IN FLORIDA," Geography 68, Part I:298 (January 1983), 41-43.

B-2377 Conn, W. Clark, "WAVERLY PLACE: THE STUDY OF A NASHVILLE STREET-CAR SUBURB ALONG THE FRANKLIN PIKE," Tennessee Historical Quarterly 43:1 (Spring 1984), 3-24.

B-2378 Cooke, Timothy W. and Bruce W. Hamilton, "EVALUATION OF URBAN HOUSING STOCKS. A MODEL APPLIED TO BALTIMORE AND HOUSTON," Journal of Urban Economics 16:3 (November 1984), 317-338.

B-2379 Cooper, Cornelia, "HISTORY OF THE WEST END 1830-1910," Atlanta Historical Bulletin 8:31 (1945), 45-94.

B-2380 Crimmins, Timothy J., "BUNGALOW SUBURBS EAST AND WEST," Atlanta Historical Journal 26:2-3 (Summer-Fall 1982), 83-94.

B-2381 Crimmins, Timothy J., "WEST END: METAMORPHOSIS FROM SUBURBAN TOWN TO INTOWN NEIGHBORHOOD," Atlanta Historical Journal 26:2-3 (Summer-Fall 1982), 33-50.

B-2382 Darling, Philip, "A SHORT-CUT METHOD FOR EVALUATING HOUSING QUALITY," Land Economics 25:2 (May 1949), 184-192.

B-2383 DeGiovanni, Frank F. and Nancy A. Paulson, "HOUSEHOLD DIVERSITY IN REVITALIZING NEIGHBORHOODS," Urban Affairs Quarterly 20:2 (December 1984), 211-232.

B-2384 Fickett, Laura J., "WOODDALE: AN INDUSTRIAL COMMUNITY," Delaware History 19:4 (Fall-Winter 1981), 229-242.

B-2385 Forman, H.C., "THE BYGONE 'SUBBERBS OF JAMES CITTIE,'" William and Mary College Historical Magazine 20:4 (October 1940), 475-486.

B-2386 Grable, Stephen W., "THE OTHER SIDE OF THE TRACKS: CABBAGETOWN--A WORKING-CLASS NEIGHBORHOOD IN TRANSITION DURING THE EARLY TWENTI-ETH CENTURY," Atlanta Historical Journal 26:2-3 (Summer-Fall 1982), 51-66.

B-2387 Hammon, Stratton O., "PHOENIX HILL PARK: LOUISVILLE, KENTUCKY," Filson Club History Quarterly 44:2 (April 1970), 156-163.

B-2388 Harvey, Diane, "THE TERRI, AUGUSTA'S BLACK ENCLAVE," Richmond County History 5:2 (Summer 1973), 60-75.

B-2389 Hirschman, Joseph, "HOUSING PATTERNS OF BALTIMORE JEWS," Generations 2 (December 1981), 30-43.

B-2390 Hula, Richard C., "HOUSING MARKET EFFECTS OF PUBLIC SCHOOL DESEG-REGATION: THE CASE OF DALLAS, TEXAS," Urban Affairs Quarterly 19:3 (March 1984), 409-423.

B-2391 Jacobs, Harvey E. and Jon S. Bailey, "EVALUATING PARTICIPATION IN A RESIDENTIAL RECYCLING PROGRAM," Journal of Environmental Systems 12:2 (1982-83), 141-152.

B-2392 Jaeger, Robert and Dale Jaeger, "LANDING AN AIRPARK DEVELOPMENT," Urban Land 41:4 (April 1982), 11-17.

B-2393 Johnson, Ronald M., "FROM ROMANTIC SUBURB TO RACIAL ENCLAVE: LEDROIT PARK, WASHINGTON, D. C., 1880-1920," Phylon 45:4 (December 1984), 264-270.

B-2394 Jones, Clifton R., "INVASION AND RACIAL ATTITUDES: A STUDY OF HOUSING IN A BORDER CITY," Social Forces 27:3 (March 1949), 285-290.

B-2395 Kane, Kevin David and Thomas L. Bell, "SUBURBS FOR A LABOR ELITE," Geographical Review 75:3 (July 1985), 319-334.

B-2396 Kellogg, John, "THE EVALUATION OF BLACK RESIDENTIAL AREAS IN LEX-INGTON, KENTUCKY, 1865-1887," Journal of Southern History 48:1 (February 1982), 21-52.

B-2397 Leonard, Marston C., "TAMPA HEIGHTS: TAMPA'S FIRST RESIDENTIAL SUBURB," Sunland Tribune (November 1978), 6-10.

B-2398 Lucas, Ernesto C., "THE EFFECTS OF NEIGHBORHOOD QUALITY, INCOME, AND RACE ON THE VALUE OF SINGLE-FAMILY HOMES IN NEW ORLEANS," Review of Black Political Economy 7:2 (Winter 1977), 183-189.

B-2399 McTigue, Geraldine, "PATTERNS OF RESIDENCE: HOUSING DISTRIBUTION BY COLOR IN TWO LOUISIANA TOWNS, 1860-1880," Louisiana Studies 15:4 (Winter 1976), 345-388.

B-2400 Mace, Ruth L., Clarles L. Weill Jr., and Gustav M. Ulrich, "TRENDS IN THE MARKET VALUE OF REAL PROPERTY IN THE CENTRAL AREAS OF TWO NORTH CAROLINA CITIES," Land Economics 42:1 (February 1966), 85-94.

B-2401 Marak, Robert J. and Ralph E. Thayer, "THE NEW ORLEANS SECTION 8 RENTAL ASSISTANCE PAYMENTS PROGRAM: AN ANALYSIS OF SUBSIDY PAY-MENTS," South Atlantic Urban Studies 5 (1981), 320-336.

B-2402 Mullendore, Walter E. and Kathleen M. Cooper, "EFFECTS OF RACE ON PROPERTY VALUES: THE CASE OF DALLAS," Annals of Regional Science 6:2 (December 1972), 61-72.

B-2403 Nichols, Woodrow D., "SPATIAL DIMENSIONS AND DYNAMICS OF RESIDEN-TIAL SEGREGATION IN DURHAM, NORTH CAROLINA," in D. Deskins, Black Americans and Urban Society.

B-2404 O'Loughlin, John and Douglas C. Munski, "HOUSING REHABILITATION IN THE INNER CITY: A COMPARISON OF TWO NEIGHBORHOODS IN NEW ORLEANS," Economic Geography 55:1 (January 1979), 52-70.

B-2405 Palmer, Charles F., 'HOUSING, THE SOUTH'S NUMBER ONE ECONOMIC OPPORTUNITY," Social Forces 25:2 (December 1946), 189-191.

B-2406 Palmore, Erdman, "INTEGRATION AND PROPERTY VALUES IN WASHINGTON, D. C.," Phylon 27:1 (Spring 1966), 15-19.

B-2407 Radford, John P., "RACE, RESIDENCE AND IDEALOGY: CHARLESTON, SOUTH CAROLINA IN THE MID-NINETEENTH CENTURY," Journal of Historical Geography 2:4 (October 1976), 329-346.

B-2408 Raine, Jesse E., "VARIATION IN PROPERTY TAXATION IN TULSA," Annals of Regional Science 6:1 (June 1972), 135-144.

B-2409 Raines, Leonora, "PRYOR STREET IN ITS YOUNG DAYS," Atlanta Historical Bulletin 8:31 (1946), 105-117.

B-2410 Reese, Bill and Marc Matre, "PROPERTY MAINTENANCE AND RESIDENTIAL INTEGRATION," Sociological Spectrum 4:4 (1984), 443-460.

B-2411 Rent, George S. and J. Dennis Lord, "NEIGHBORHOOD RACIAL TENSION AND PROPERTY VALUE TRENDS IN A SOUTHERN COMMUNITY," Social Science Quarterly 59:1 (June 1978), 51-59.

B-2412 Riley, Mark B., "EDGEFIELD: A STUDY OF AN EARLY NASHVILLE SUBURB," Tennessee Historical Quarterly 37:2 (Summer 1978), 133-154.

B-2413 Rogers, Tommy W., "RACIAL AND GEOGRAPHIC DIFFERENTIALS IN MISSIS-SIPPI HOUSING CHARACTERISTICS [1960-1970]." Mississippi Geographer 6:1 (Spring 1978), 19-31.

B-2414 Routh, Frederick B., "PEOPLE CAN LIVE IN DIGNITY IN A PLACE LIKE THIS," City 5:4 (Summer 1971), 22-29.

B-2415 St. John, Craig and Frieda Clark, "RACIAL DIFFERENCES IN DIMEN-SIONS OF NEIGHBORHOOD SATISFACTION," Social Indicators Research 15:1 (July 1984), 43-60.

B-2416 Segrest, Eileen, "INMAN PARK: A CASE STUDY IN NEIGHBORHOOD RE-VITALIZATION," Georgia Historical Quarterly 63:1 (Spring 1979), 109-117.

B-2417 Summerville, James, "THE CITY AND THE SLUM: 'BLACK BOTTOM' IN THE DEVELOPMENT OF SOUTH NASHVILLE," Tennessee Historical Quarterly 40:2 (Summer 1981), 182-192.

B-2418 Thomas, Emma Wormly, "BLACK HOUSING: A GAME OF FRUSTRATION," Crisis 86:5 (May 1979), 169-171.

B-2419 Thomas, Robert H., "BLACK SUBURBANIZATION AND HOUSING QUALITY IN ATLANTA," Journal of Urban Affairs 6:1 (Winter 1984), 17-28.

B-2420 Vill, Martha J., "RESIDENTIAL DEVELOPMENT ON A LANDED ESTATE: THE CASE OF BALTIMORE'S HARLEM," Maryland Historical Magazine 77:3 (Fall 1982), 266-278.

B-2421 Weaver, Blanche Henry Clark, "SHIFTING RESIDENTIAL PATTERNS OF NASHVILLE," Tennessee Historical Quarterly 18:1 (March 1959), 20-34.

B-2422 Wilson, Bobby M., "BLACK HOUSING OPPORTUNITIES IN BIRMINGHAM, ALABAMA," Southeastern Geographer 17:1 (May 1977), 49-57.

B-2423 Winsberg, Morton D., "ETHNIC COMPETITION FOR RESIDENTIAL SPACE IN MIAMI, FLORIDA, 1970-80," American Journal of Economics and Soci-ology 42:3 (July 1983), 305-314.

B-2424 Winsberg, Morton D., "HOUSING SEGREGATION OF A PREDOMINATELY MIDDLE CLASS POPULATION: RESIDENTIAL PATTERNS DEVELOPED BY THE CUBAN IMMIGRATION INTO MIAMI, 1950-74," American Journal of Economics and Sociology 38:4 (October 1979), 403-418.

B-2425 Wright, George C., "THE NAACP AND RESIDENTIAL SEGREGATION IN LOUISVILLE, KENTUCKY, 1914-1917," Register of the Kentucky Historical Society 78:1 (Winter 1980), 39-54.

B-2426 Wyatt, Donald W., "BETTER HOMES FOR NEGRO FAMILIES IN THE SOUTH," Social Forces 28:3 (March 1950), 297-303.

Journalism

B-2427 Abbott, Frank, "THE TEXAS PRESS AND THE COVENANT," Red River Valley Historical Review 4:1 (Winter 1979), 32-41.

B-2428 Adamson, June, "FROM BULLETIN TO BROADSIDE: A HISTORY OF BY-AUTHORITY JOURNALISM IN OAK RIDGE, TENNESSEE," Tennessee Histori-cal Quarterly 38:4 (Winter 1979), 479-493.

B-2429 Alsobrook, David E., "MOBILE'S FORGOTTEN PROGRESSIVE--A. N. JOHNSON, EDITOR AND ENTREPRENEUER," Alabama Review 32:3 (July 1979), 188-202.

B-2430 Anderson, John Q., "THE RICHMOND COMPILER," Louisiana Historical Quarterly 39:4 (October 1956), 416-442.

B-2431 Andrews, J. Cutler, "THE CONFEDERATE PRESS AND PUBLIC MORALE," Journal of Southern History 32:4 (November 1966), 445-465.

B-2432 Antunes, George E. and Patricia A. Hurley," THE REPRESENTATION OF CRIMINAL EVENTS IN HOUSTON'S TWO DAILY NEWSPAPERS," Journalism Quarterly 54:4 (Winter 1977), 756-760.

B-2433 Aptheker, Bettina, "THE SUPPRESSION OF THE FREE SPEECH: IDA B. WELLS AND THE MEMPHIS LYNCHING, 1892," San Jose Studies 3:3 (1977), 34-40.

B-2434 Armytage, W. H. G., "THE EDITORIAL EXPERIENCE OF JOSEPH GALES, 1786-1794," North Carolina Historical Review 28:3 (July 1951), 332-361.

B-2435 Bailey, Robert, "THE 'BOGUS' MEMPHIS UNION APPEAL: A UNION NEWS-PAPER IN OCCUPIED CONFEDERATE TERRITORY," West Tennessee Histori-cal Society Papers No. 32 (1978), 32-37.

B-2436 Baker, Thomas H., "REFUGEE NEWSPAPER: THE MEMPHIS DAILY APPEAL, 1862-1865," Journal of Southern History 29:3 (August 1963), 326-344.

B-2437 Bakker, Jan, "CAROLINE GILMAN AND THE ISSUE OF SLAVERY IN THE ROSE MAGAZINES, 1832-1839," Southern Studies 24:3 (Fall 1985), 273-283.

B-2438 Baldasy, Gerald J., "THE CHARLESTON, SOUTH CAROLINA, PRESS AND NATIONAL NEWS, 1804-47," Journalism Quarterly 55:3 (Autumn 1978), 519-526.

B-2439 Barnett, Stephen R., "FAST SHUFFLE IN CHATTANOOGA," Columbia Journalism Review 19:4 (November-Decembetr 1980), 65-69.

B-2440 Bissett, James S., "THE ASHEVILLE CITIZEN STRIKE: AN EXAMPLE OF THE INEFFECTIVENESS OF APPALACHIAN LABOR," Appalachian Labor 11:4 (Summer 1984), 403-409.

B-2441 Blankenship, Gary R., "THE COMMERCIAL APPEAL'S ATTACK ON THE KU KLUX KLAN," West Tennessee Historical Society Papers No. 31 (1977), 44-58.

B-2442 Bond, Donovan, "HOW THE WHEELING INTELLIGENCER BECAME A REPUBLICAN ORGAN," West Virginia History 11:3 (April 1950), 160-184.

B-2443 Bowen, Frances Jean, "THE NEW ORLEANS DOUBLE DEALER, 1921-1926," Louisiana Historical Quarterly 39:4 (October 1956), 443-456.

B-2444 Brewer, James H., "EDITORIALS FROM THE DAMNED," Journal of Southern History 28:2 (May 1962), 225-233.

B-2445 Bridges, Lamar W., "THE MEMPHIS DAILY APPEAL'S 'DIXIE': CIVIL WAR CAPITAL CORRESPONDENT," Tennessee Historical Quarterly 28:4 (Winter 1969), 377-387.

B-2446 Callahan, Helen, "PATRICK WALSH: JOURNALIST, POLITICIAN, STATES-MAN," Richmond County History 9:2 (Summer 1977), 14-29.

B-2447 Cashin, Edward J. Jr., "THE BANNER OF THE SOUTH, A JOURNAL OF THE RECONSTRUCTION ERA," Richmond County History 6:1 (Winter 1974), 13-22.

B-2448 Cashin, Edward J. Jr., "THOMAS W. LOYLESS, RESPONSIBLE JOURNAL-IST," Richmond County History 9:1 (Winter 1977), 18-28.

B-2449 Chesson, Michael B., "EDITORS INDULGING IN DOUBLE-LEADED MATTER: THE SHOOT-OUT AT THE CAPITAL IN 1866," Virginia Cavalcade 30:3 (Winter 1981), 100-109.

B-2450 Clark, E. Culpepper, "FRANCIS WARRINGTON DAWSON: THE NEW SOUTH REVISITED," American Journalism 3:1 (1986), 5-23.

B-2451 Clark, E. Culpepper, "HENRY GRADY'S NEW SOUTH: A REBUTTAL FROM CHARLESTON," Southern Speech Communication Journal 41:4 (Summer 1976), 346-358.

B-2452 Clark, Thomas D., "THE COUNTRY NEWSPAPER: A FACTOR IN SOUTHERN OPINION, 1865-1930," Journal of Southern History 14:1 (February 1948), 3-5.

B-2453 Cobbs, Nicholas H. Jr., "HAMMER COBBS AS EDITOR OF THE GREENSBORO WATCHMAN," Alabama Review 39:4 (October 1986), 261-270.

B-2454 Cohen, Henig, "LITERARY REFLECTIONS OF SLAVERY FROM THE SOUTH CAROLINA GAZETTE," Journal of Negro History 37:2 (April 1952), 188-193.

B-2455 Cohen, Shari, "A COMPARISON OF CRIME COVERAGE IN DETROIT AND ATLANTA NEWSPAPERS," Journalism Quarterly 52:4 (Winter 1975), 726-730.

B-2456 Congleton, Betty Carolyn, "GEORGE D. PRENTICE: NINETEENTH CENTURY SOUTHERN EDITOR," Register of the Kentucky Historical Society 65:2 (April 1967), 94-119.

B-2457 Congleton, Betty Carolyn, "THE LOUISVILLE JOURNAL: ITS ORIGINS AND EARLY YEARS," Register of the Kentucky Historical Society 62:2 (April 1964), 87-103.

B-2458 Connor, William P., "RECONSTRUCTION REBELS; THE NEW ORLEANS TRIBUNE IN POST-WAR LOUISIANA," Louisiana History 21:2 (Spring 1980), 159-182.

B-2459 Copeland, Fayette, "THE NEW ORLEANS PRESS AND RECONSTRUCTION," Louisiana Historical Quarterly 30:1 (January 1947), 144-337.

B-2460 Cramton, Willa G., "SELLECK OSBORN: A REPUBLICAN EDITOR IN WILMINGTON, DELAWARE," Delaware History 12:3 (April 1967), 198-217.

B-2461 Current-Garcia, Eugene, "NEWSPAPER HUMOR IN THE OLD SOUTH, 1835-1855," Alabama Review 2:2 (April 1949), 102-121.

B-2462 Cutler, Bill and Mitchell Shields, "IS JACKSONVILLE JINXED?" Columbia Journalism Review 22:6 (March-April 1984), 32-35.

B-2463 Davis, J. G. Jr., "NEWSPAPERS OF PENSACOLA, 1821-1900," Florida Historical Quarterly 37:3-4 (January-April 1959), 418-445.

B-2464 Delp, Robert W., "THE SOUTHERN PRESS AND THE RISE OF AMERICAN SPIRITUALISM, 1847-1860," Journal of American Culture 7:3 (Fall 1984), 88-95.

B-2465 Doggett, David, "THE KUDZU STORY: UNDERGROUND IN MISSISSIPPI," Southern Exposure 2:4 (1975), 86-95.

B-2466 Dougan, Michael, "THE LITTLE ROCK PRESS GOES TO WAR, 1861-1863," Arkansas Historical Quarterly 28:1 (Spring 1969), 14-27.

B-2467 Dunn, Hampton, "THOSE HELL RAISIN' TAMPA NEWSPAPERS," Sunland Tribune 6 (November 1980), 36-53.

B-2468 Dupre, Huntley, "THE KENTUCKY GAZETTE REPORTS THE FRENCH REVO-
LUTION," Mississippi Valley Historical Review 26:2 (September
1939), 163-181.

B-2469 English, John, "ST. PETERSBURG TIMES: REPORTING FOR THE
CONSUMER," Southern Exposure 2:4 (1975), 44-50.

B-2470 Ellison, George R., "WILLIAM TAPPAN THOMPSON AND THE SOUTHERN
MISCELLANY, 1842-1844," Mississippi Quarterly 23:2 (Spring 1970),
155-168.

B-2471 Ericson, Eston Everett, "FOLKLORE AND FOLKWAY IN THE TARBORO
(N.C.) FREE PRESS (1824-1850)," Southern Folklore Quarterly 5:2
(June 1941), 107-125.

B-2472 Ethridge, Mark, "THE SOUTH'S NEW INDUSTRIALISM AND THE PRESS,"
Annals of the American Academy of Political and Social Science 153
(January 1931), 251-256.

B-2473 Fink, Paul M., "THE EARLY PRESS OF JONESBORO," East Tennessee
Historical Society's Publications No. 10 (1938), 57-70.

B-2474 Folmar, John Kent, "REACTION TO RECONSTRUCTION: JOHN FORSYTH AND
THE MOBILE ADVERTISER AND REGISTER, 1865-1867," Alabama Historical
Quarterly 37:4 (Winter 1975), 245-264.

B-2475 "GETTING ANGRY SIX TIMES A WEEK: A HUGH HAYNIE ALBUM," Civil
Liberties Review 4:1 (May-June 1977), 62-69.

B-2476 Gordon, Douglas E., "THE GREAT SPECKLED BIRD: HARRASSMENT OF AN
UNDERGROUND NEWSPAPER," Journalism Quarterly 56:2 (Summer 1979),
289-295.

B-2477 Govan, G. E. and J. W. Lovingood, "ADOLPH S. OCHS: THE BOY
PUBLISHER," East Tennessee Historical Society's Publications No.
17 (1945), 84-104.

B-2478 Gray, Daniel Savage, "FRONTIER JOURNALISM: NEWSPAPERS IN ANTE-
BELLUM ALABAMA," Alabama Historical Quarterly 37:3 (Fall 1975),
183-191.

B-2479 Guertler, John Thomas, "HEZEKIAH NILES: WILMINGTON PRINTER AND
EDITOR," Delaware History 17:1 (Spring-Summer 1976), 37-53.

B-2480 Harrison, M. Clifford, "MURDER IN THE COURTROOM," Virginia Cavalcade 17:1 (Summer 1967), 43-47.

B-2481 Harrison, M. Clifford, "PETERSBURG'S NINTH OF JUNE," Virginia
Cavalcade 8:1 (Summer 1958), 10-15.

B-2482 Hart, W. O., "THE NEW ORLEANS TIMES AND THE NEW ORLEANS DEMOCRAT,"
Louisiana Historical Quarterly 8:4 (October 1925), 574-584.

B-2483 Havard, William C., "THE JOURNALIST AS INTERPRETER OF THE SOUTH,"
Virginia Quarterly Review 59:1 (Winter 1983), 1-21.

B-2484 Headley, Bernard, "THE ATLANTA ESTABLISHMENT AND THE ATLANTA
TRAGEDY," Phylon 46:4 (December 1985), 333-340.

B-2485 Helmbold, F. Wilbur, "EARLY ALABAMA NEWSPAPERMEN, 1810-1820,"
Alabama Review 11:1 (January 1959), 53-68.

B-2486 Henderson, Archibald, "RICHARD HENDERSON: THE AUTHORSHIP OF THE
CUMBERLAND COMPACT AND THE FOUNDING OF NASHVILLE," Tennessee
Historical Magazine 2:3 (September 1916), 155-174.

B-2487 Hollingsworth, J. R., "TRIAL AND TRAVAIL OF AN EDITOR OR 'I'LL DO ANYTHING FOR A BLOCK,'" Panhandle-Plains Historical Review 48 (1975), 27-41.

B-2488 Holmes, Jack D. L., "THE MOBILE GAZETTE AND THE AMERICAN OCCUPA-TION OF MOBILE IN 1813: A LESSON IN HISTORICAL DETECTIVE WORK," Journal of the Alabama Academy of Science 47:2 (April 1976), 79-86.

B-2489 Hooker, Robert, "RACE AND THE MISSISSIPPI PRESS," New South 26:1 (Winter 1971), 55-62.

B-2490 Howell, Sarah M., "THE EDITORIALS OF AUTHUR S. COLYAR, NASHVILLE PROPHET OF THE NEW SOUTH," Tennessee Historical Quarterly 27:3 (Fall 1968), 262-276.

B-2491 Jarrard, Mary W., "EMERGING E.R.A. PATTERNS IN EDITORIALS IN SOUTHERN DAILY NEWSPAPERS," Journalism Quarterly 57:4 (Winter 1980), 606-617.

B-2492 Jones, Allen W., "VOICES FOR IMPROVING RURAL LIFE: ALABAMA'S BLACK AGRICULTURAL PRESS, 1890-1965," Agricultural History 58:3 (July 1984), 209-220.

B-2493 Karlin, Alexander, "NEW ORLEANS LYNCHINGS OF 1891 AND THE AMERICAN PRESS," Louisiana Historical Quarterly 24:1 (January 1941), 187-204.

B-2494 Kelley, Leo, "PRINT THE NEWS AND RAISE HELL," Chronicles of Okla-homa, 65:3 (Fall 1987), 282-293.

B-2495 Kendall, John Smith, "EARLY NEW ORLEANS NEWSPAPERS," Louisiana Historical Quarterly 10:3 (July 1927), 383-401.

B-2496 Kendall, John Smith, "THE FOREIGN LANGUAGE PRESS OF NEW ORLEANS," Louisiana Historical Quarterly 12:3 (July 1929), 363-380.

B-2497 Kendall, John Smith, "GEORGE WILKINS KENDALL AND THE FOUNDING OF THE NEW ORLEANS PICAYUNE," Louisiana Historical Quarterly 11:2 (April 1928), 261-285.

B-2498 Kendall, John Smith, "JOURNALISM IN NEW ORLEANS BETWEEN 1880 AND 1900," Louisiana Historical Quarterly 8:4 (October 1925), 557-573.

B-2499 Kendall, John Smith, "JOURNALISM IN NEW ORLEANS FIFTY YEARS AGO," Louisiana Historical Quarterly 34:1 (January 1951), 5-24.

B-2500 Kendall, John Smith, "OLD DAYS ON THE NEW ORLEANS PICAYUNE," Louisiana Historical Quarterly 33:3 (July 1950), 317-342.

B-2501 Kennedy, R. Evan, "BALTIMORE DOWNTOWN REVIVED THROUGH PRIVATE/ PUBLIC COOPERATION," National Civic Review 65:10 (November 1976), 503-505.

B-2502 Kiplinger, John Lewis, "THE PRESS IN THE MAKING OF WEST VIRGINIA," West Virginia History 6:2 (January 1945), 127-176.

B-2503 Littlefield, Daniel F. Jr. and Patricia Washington McGraw," THE ARKANSAS FREEMAN, 1869-1870--THE BIRTH OF THE BLACK PRESS IN ARKANSAS," Phylon 40:1 (March 1979), 75-85.

B-2504 Littlefield, Mary Ann, "JOHN FOSTER WHEELER OF FORT SMITH: PIONEER PRINTER AND PUBLISHER," Arkansas Historical Quarterly 44:3 (Autumn 1985), 260-283.

B-2505 Livingood, James W., "THE CHATTANOOGA REBEL," East Tennessee Historical Society's Publications No. 39 (1967), 42-55.

B-2506 Loftin, Bernadette K., "A WOMAN LIBERATED: LILLIAN C. WEST, EDITOR," Florida Historical Quarterly 52:4 (April 1974), 396-410.

B-2507 Logue, Cal M., "RACIST REPORTING DURING RECONSTRUCTION," Journal of Black Studies 9:3 (March 1979), 335-350.

B-2508 McFarland, Daniel Miles, "NORTH CAROLINA NEWSPAPERS, EDITORS, AND JOURNALISTIC POLITICS, 1815-1835," North Carolina Historical Review 30:3 (July 1953), 376-414.

B-2509 McKenzie, Robert H., "NEWSPAPERS AND NEWSPAPER MEN DURING TUSCA-LOOSA'S CAPITAL PERIOD, 1826-1846," Alabama Historical Quarterly 44:3-4 (Fall-Winter 1982), 187-202.

B-2510 McKinney, Gary, "OKLAHOMA GHOST TOWN JOURNALISM," Chronicles of Oklahoma 46:4 (Winter 1968-1969), 387-408.

B-2511 Malone, Henry T., "ATLANTA JOURNALISM DURING THE CONFEDERACY," Georgia Historical Quarterly 37:3 (September 1953), 210-219.

B-2512 Malone, Henry T., "THE WEEKLY ATLANTA INTELLIGENCER AS A SECES-SIONIST JOURNAL," Georgia Historical Quarterly 37:4 (December 1953), 278-286.

B-2513 Margavio, Anthony V., "THE REACTION OF THE PRESS TO THE ITALIAN AMERICAN IN NEW ORLEANS, 1880 TO 1920," Italian American 4:1 (1978), 72-83.

B-2514 Marino, Samuel J., "EARLY FRENCH-LANGUAGE NEWSPAPERS IN NEW ORLEANS," Louisiana History 7:4 (Fall 1966), 309-322.

B-2515 Martin, Harold, "ABOUT RALPH McGILL," New South 28:2 (Spring 1973), 24-33.

B-2516 Martin, Richard A., "THE NEW YORK TIMES VIEWS CIVIL WAR JACKSON-VILLE," Florida Historical Quarterly 53:4 (April 1975), 409-427.

B-2517 Mathew, W. M., 'EDMUND RUFFIN AND THE DEMISE OF THE FARMER'S REGISTER," Virginia Magazine of History and Biography 94:1 (January 1986), 3-24.

B-2518 Matthews, John M., "BLACK NEWSPAPERMEN IN THE BLACK COMMUNITY IN GEORGIA, 1890-1930," Georgia Historical Quarterly 68:3 (Fall 1984), 356-381.

B-2519 Matthews, W. Bird, "CONTROL OF THE BALTIMORE PRESS DURING THE CIVIL WAR," Maryland Historical Magazine 36:2 (June 1941), 150-170.

B-2520 Mayo, Edward L., "REPUBLICANISM, ANTIPARTYISM, AND JACKSONIAN PARTY POLITICS: A VEIW FROM THE NATION'S CAPITAL," American Quarterly 31:1 (Spring 1979), 3-20.

B-2521 Miles, Edwin A., "THE MISSISSIPPI PRESS IN THE JACKSON ERA, 1824-1841," Journal of Mississippi History 19:1 (January 1957), 1-20.

B-2522 Moore, Arthur K., "SPECIMENS OF THE FOLKTALES FROM SOME ANTEBELLUM NEWSPAPERS OF LOUISIANA," Louisiana Historical Quarterly 32:4 (October 1949), 723-758.

B-2523 Morgan, William, "LOUISVILLE: CITY OF PARADOXES," Historic Preservation 34:3 (May-June 1982), 38-45.

B-2524 Mugleston, William F., "JULIAN HARRIS, THE GEORGIA PRESS, AND THE KU KLUX KLAN," Georgia Historical Quarterly 59:3 (Fall 1975), 284-295.

B-2525 Norrell, R. Jefferson, "REPORTERS AND REFORMERS: THE STORY OF THE SOUTHERN COURIER," South Atlantic Quarterly 79:1 (Winter 1980), 93-104.

B-2526 Olasky, Marvin N., "WHEN WORLD VIEWS COLLIDE: JOURNALISTS AND THE GREAT MONEKY TRIAL," American Journalism 4:3 (1987), 133-146.

B-2527 Oney, Steve, "THE SILENCING OF A SOUTHERN VOICE: ATLANTA WEEKLY, 1912-1986, R. I. P.," Columbia Journalism Review 24:4 (November-December 1985), 50-52.

B-2528 Osthaus, Carl R., "FROM OLD SOUTH TO THE NEW SOUTH: THE EDITORIAL CAREER OF WILLIAM TAPPAN THOMPSON OF THE SAVANNAH MORNING NEWS," Southern Quarterly 14:3 (April 1976), 237-260.

B-2529 Ott, Eloise Robinson, "EARLY NEWSPAPERS OF OCALA," Florida Historical Quarterly 35:4 (April 1957), 303-311.

B-2530 Pappas, Paul C., "THE WHEELING GAZETTE AND THE QUESTION OF GREEK INDEPENDENCE IN WESTERN VIRGINIA 1821-1828," West Virginia History 35:1 (October 1973), 40-55.

B-2531 Partin, Robert, "ALABAMA NEWSPAPER HUMOR: A POST-BELLUM CASE STUDY," Alabama Review 9:2 (April 1956), 83-99.

B-2532 Partin, Robert, "NEWSPAPER HUMOR IN SELMA DURING THE GAY NINETIES," Alabama Review 22:2 (April 1969), 117-134.

B-2533 Pearce, John Ed., "HELLZAPOPPIN' IN MARTIN COUNTY," Columbia Journalism Review 20:2 (July-August 1981), 62-66.

B-2534 Pease, William H. and Jane H. Pease, "WALKER'S APPEAL COMES TO CHARLESTON: A NOTE AND DOCUMENTS," Journal of Negro History 59:3 (July 1974), 287-292.

B-2535 Pfenning, Dennis Joseph, "THE CAPTAIN RETIRES: CLARK HOWELL TAKES THE HELM," Atlanta Historical Journal 25:2 (Summer 1981), 5-20.

B-2536 Porter, David L., "THE MISSISSIPPI PRESS AND THE ELECTION OF 1860," Journal of Mississippi History 34:3 (August 1972), 247-252.

B-2537 Rogers, William Warren, "ALABAMA'S REFORM PRESS: MILITANT SPOKESMAN FOR AGRARIAN REVOLT," Agricultural History 34:2 (April 1960), 62-70.

B-2538 Ross, Margaret, "THE BEGINNING OF THE ARKANSAS GAZETTE," Arkansas Historical Quarterly 28:1 (Spring 1969), 3-5.

B-2539 Ross, Margaret, "THE HOMES OF THE ARKANSAS GAZETTE AT LITTLE ROCK, 1821-1866," Arkansas Historical Quarterly 25:2 (Summer 1966), 128-144.

B-2540 Ross, Margaret, "RETALIATION AGAINST ARKANSAS NEWSPAPER EDITORS DURING RECONSTRUCTION," Arkansas Historical Quarterly 31:2 (Summer 1972), 150-165.

B-2541 Rothchild, John, "LETTER FROM MIAMI: THE CUBAN CONNECTION AND THE GRINGO PRESS," Columbia Journalism Review 23:3 (October 1984), 48-51.

B-2542 Rouen, Bussiere, "L'ABEILLE DE LA NOUVELLE ORLEANS," Louisiana Historical Quarterly 8:4 (October 1925), 585-588.

B-2543 Sanford, Bruce W., "RICHMOND NEWSPAPERS: END OF A ZIGZAG TRAIL?" Columbia Journalism Review 19:3 (September-October 1980), 46-47.

B-2544 Sederberg, Nancy B., "ANTEBELLUM SOUTHERN HUMOR IN THE CAMDEN JOURNAL: 1826-1840," Mississippi Quarterly 26:1 (Winter 1973-74), 41-74.

B-2545 Shields, Mitchell J., "THE ATLANTA STORY," Columbia Journalism Review 20:3 (September–October 1981), 29–35.

B-2546 Short, James R., "THE INCREDIBLE NEWS OF POWERED FLIGHT," Virginia Cavalcade 3:2 (Autumn 1953), 38–42.

B-2547 Simonds, Willard B., "THE SEA BREEZE: THE FIRST NEWSPAPER OF THE LOWER PINELLAS PENINSULA," Tampa Bay History 5:2 (Fall–Winter 1983), 75–80.

B-2548 Skaggs, David C., "EDITORIAL POLICIES OF THE MARYLAND GAZETTE, 1765–1783," Maryland Historical Magazine 59:4 (Winter 1964), 341–349.

B-2549 Sloan, Kathleen L., "OPERATION FREEDOM OF THE PRESS," South Carolina History Illustrated 1:3 (August 1970), 4–7, 66–67.

B-2550 Snorgrass, J. William, "THE BALTIMORE AFRO-AMERICAN AND THE ELECTION CAMPAIGNS OF FDR," American Journalism 1:2 (Winter 1984), 35–50.

B-2551 Staudenraus, P. J., "OCCUPIED BEAUFORT, 1863: A WAR CORRESPONDENT'S VIEW," South Carolina Historical Magazine 64:3 (July 1963), 136–144.

B-2552 Staudenraus, P. J. ed., "A WAR CORRESPONDENT'S VIEW OF ST. AUGUSTINE AND FERNANDIA: 1863," Florida Historical Quarterly 41:1 (July 1962), 60–65.

B-2553 Stokes, Durward T., "CHARLES NAPOLEON BONAPARTE EVANS AND THE MILTON CHRONICLE," North Carolina Historical Review 46:3 (Summer 1969), 239–270.

B-2554 Suggs, Henry Lewis, "P. B. YOUNG OF THE NORFOLK JOURNAL AND GUIDE: A BOOKER T. WASHINGTON MILITANT, 1904–1928," Journal of Negro History 64:4 (Fall 1979), 365–376.

B-2555 Summerville, James, "ALBERT ROBERTS, JOURNALIST OF THE NEW SOUTH, PART I," Tennessee Historical Quarterly 42:1 (Spring 1983), 18–38.

B-2556 Summerville, James, "ALBERT ROBERTS, JOURNALIST OF THE NEW SOUTH, PART II," Tennessee Historical Quarterly 42:2 (Summer 1983), 179–202.

B-2557 Talmadge, John E., "BEN: PERLEY POORE'S STAY IN ATHENS," Georgia Historical Quarterly 41:3 (September 1957), 247–254.

B-2558 Talmadge, John E., "SAVANNAH'S YANKEE NEWSPAPERS," Georgia Review 12:1 (Spring 1959), 66–73.

B-2559 Taylor, Heber and Forrest Martin, "THE SUNDAY TIMES: A MEMPHIS PAPER THAT FAILED," West Tennessee Historical Society Papers No. 24 (1970), 74–96.

B-2560 Taylor, Lenette Sengel, "POLEMICS AND PARTISANSHIP: THE ARKANSAS PRESS IN THE 1860 ELECTION," Arkansas Historical Quarterly 44:4 (Winter 1985), 314–335.

B-2561 Thomas, Diane, "DIARY OF A WOMAN REPORTER," Southern Exposure 2:4 (1975), 72–81.

B-2562 Tobin, Sidney, "THE EARLY NEW DEAL IN BATON ROUGE AS VIEWED BY THE DAILY PRESS," Louisiana History 10:4 (Fall 1969), 307–338.

B-2563 Trexler, Harrison A., "THE DAVIS ADMINISTRATION AND THE RICHMOND PRESS, 1861–1865," Journal of Southern History 16:2 (May 1950), 177–195.

B-2564 Tucker, David M., "MISS IDA B. WELLS AND MEMPHIS LYNCHING," Phylon 32:2 (Summer 1971), 112-122.

B-2565 Turner, Arlin, "JOAQUIN MILLER IN NEW ORLEANS," Louisiana Historical Quarterly 22:1 (January 1939), 216-225.

B-2566 Upton, Pam, "'THE FOLLOWING VERACIOUS ANECDOTE . . .' FOLKLORE IN THE ASHEVILLE NEWS, 1845-55," North Carolina Folklore Journal 30:1 (Spring-Summer 1982), 18-33.

B-2567 Watson, Charles S., "STEPHEN CULLEN CARPENTER, FIRST DRAMA CRITIC OF THE CHARLESTON COURIER," South Carolina Historical Magazine 69:4 (October 1968), 243-252.

B-2568 West, James L. W. III, "EARLY BACKWOODS HUMOR IN THE GREENVILLE MOUNTAINEER," Mississippi Quarterly 25:1 (Winter 1971-72), 69-82.

B-2569 Williams, Nudie, "THE BLACK PRESS IN OKLAHOMA," Chronicles of Oklahoma 61:3 (Fall 1983), 308-319.

B-2570 Wingfield, Marie Gregson, "MEMPHIS AS SEEN THROUGH MEREWETHER'S WEEKLY," West Tennessee Historical Society Papers No. 5 (1951), 31-61.

B-2571 Wyche, Billy H., "SOUTHERN NEWSPAPERS VIEW ORGANIZED LABOR IN THE NEW DEAL YEARS," South Atlantic Quarterly 74:2 (Spring 1975), 178-196.

Labor and Employment

B-2572 Angel, William D. Jr., "CONTROLLING THE WORKERS: THE GALVESTON DOCK WORKERS' STRIKE OF 1920 AND ITS IMPACT ON LABOR RELATIONS IN TEXAS," East Texas Historical Journal 23:2 (1985), 14-27.

B-2573 Ansley, Fran and Brenda Bell, "MINERS INSURRECTIONS/CONVICT LABOR," Southern Exposure 1:3-4 (Winter 1974), 144-159.

B-2574 Appel, J. C., "THE UNIONIZATION OF FLORIDA CIGARMAKERS AND THE COMING OF THE WAR WITH SPAIN," Hispanic American Historical Review 56:1 (February 1956), 38-49.

B-2575 Argersinger, Jo Ann E., "ASSISTING THE 'LOAFERS': TRANSIENT RELIEF IN BALTIMORE, 1933-1937," Labor History 23:2 (Spring 1982), 226-245.

B-2576 Argersinger, Jo Anne E., "'THE RIGHT TO STRIKE': LABOR ORGANIZA-TION AND THE NEW DEAL IN BALTIMORE," Maryland Historical Magazine 78:4 (Winter 1983), 299-318.

B-2577 Ashbaugh, Carolyn and Dan McCurry, "ON THE LINE AT ONEITA," Southern Exposure 4:1-2 (Spring-Summer 1976), 30-37.

B-2578 Bailey, Richard, "THE STARR COUNTY STRIKE," Red River Valley Historical Review 4:1 (Winter 1979), 42-61.

B-2579 Bass, Jack, "STRIKE AT CHARLESTON," New South 24:3 (Summer 1969), 35-44.

B-2580 Bellamy, Donnie D., "MACON, GEORGIA, 1823-1860: A STUDY IN URBAN SLAVERY," Phylon 45:4 (December 1984), 298-310.

B-2581 Bennett, Sari, "LABOR ORGANIZING IN THE SOUTH, 1975-1979: THE CASE OF THE INTERNATIONAL BROTHERHOOD OF TEAMSTERS," Southeastern Geographer 24:1 (May 1984), 1-13.

B-2582 Berlin, Ira and Herbert G. Gutman, "NATIVES AND IMMIGRANTS, FREE MEN AND SLAVES: URBAN WORKINGMEN IN THE ANTEBELLUM SOUTH," American Historical Review 88:5 (December 1983), 1175-2000.

B-2583 Berry, Brian J. L., "COMMUTING PATTERNS: LABOR MARKET PARFTICIPA-
TION AND REGIONAL POTENTIAL," Growth and Change 1:4 (October
1970), 3-10.

B-2584 Blackwelder, Julia Kirk, "MOP AND TYPEWRITER: WOMEN'S WORK IN
EARLY TWENTIETH-CENTURY ATLANTA," Atlanta Historical Journal 27:3
(Fall 1983), 21-30.

B-2585 Blackwelder, Julia Kirk, "WOMEN IN THE WORK FORCE: ATLANTA, NEW
ORLEANS, AND SAN ANTONIO, 1930-1940," Journal of Urban History 5:3
(May 1978), 331-358.

B-2586 Bokemeier, Janet L., Carolyn Sachs, and Verna Keith, "LABOR FORCE
PARTICIPATION OF METROPOLITAN, NONMETROPOLITAN, AND FARM WOMEN: A
COMPARATIVE STUDY," Rural Sociology 48:4 (Winter 1983), 515-539.

B-2587 Bopp, William J. and Michael Wiatrowski, "POLICE STRIKE IN NEW
ORLEANS: A CITY ABANDONED BY ITS POLICE," Police Journal 55:2
(April-July 1982), 125-135.

B-2588 Born, Kate, "MEMPHIS NEGRO WORKINGMEN AND THE NAACP," West Tennessee Historical Society Papers No. 28 (1974), 90-107.

B-2589 Born, Kate, "ORGANIZED LABOR IN MEMPHIS, TENNESSEE, 1826-1901,"
West Tennessee Historical Society Papers No. 21 (1967), 60-79.

B-2590 Braden, Anne, "SHOULDER TO SHOULDER," Southern Exposure 9:4
(Winter 1981), 88-93.

B-2591 Brewer, James Howard, "LEGISLATION DESIGNED TO CONTROL SLAVERY IN
WILMINGTON AND FAYETTEVILLE," North Carolina Historical Review
30:2 (April 1953), 155-166.

B-2592 Brewer, Thomas B., "STATE ANTI-LABOR LEGISLATION: TEXAS--A CASE
STUDY," Labor History 11:1 (Winter 1970), 58-76.

B-2593 Bryant, Keith L., "LABOR IN POLITICS: THE OKLAHOMA STATE FEDERA-
TION OF LABOR DURING THE AGE OF REFORM," Labor History 11:3 (Summer 1970), 259-276.

B-2594 Burrau, James A., "LABOR CONFLICT IN URBAN APPALACHIA: THE KNOX-
VILLE STREETCAR STRIKE OF 1919," Tennessee Historical Quarterly
38:1 (Spring 1979), 62-78.

B-2595 Button, James, "THE QUEST FOR ECONOMIC EQUALITY: FACTORS RELATED
TO BLACK EMPLOYMENT IN THE SOUTH," Social Science Quarterly 62:3
(September 1981), 461-474.

B-2596 Calderhead, William, "THE PROFESSIONAL SLAVE TRADER IN A SLAVE
ECONOMY: AUSTIN WOOLFOLK, A CASE STUDY," Civil War History 23:3
(September 1977), 195-211.

B-2597 Carpenter, Gerald, "PUBLIC OPINION IN THE NEW ORLEANS STREET RAIL-
WAY STRIKE OF 1919-1930," in Fink, G., ed., Essays in Southern
Labor History: Selected Papers, Southern Labor History Confer-
ence, 1976, 191-207.

B-2598 Ciscel, David and Tom Collins, "THE MEMPHIS RUNAWAY BLUES,"
Southern Exposure 4:1-2 (Winter 1976), 143-149.

B-2599 Coffin, Tom, "BUSTED BY LAW: CONSTRUCTION ORGANIZING IN ATLANTA,"
Southern Exposure 8:1 (Spring 1980), 26-34.

B-2600 Cook, Bernard A., "SELECTION 15 OF THE I.W.A.: THE FIRST INTER-
NATIONAL IN NEW ORLEANS," Louisiana History 14:3 (Summer 1973),
297-304.

B-2601 Cook, Bernard A., "THE TYPOGRAPHICAL UNION AND THE NEW ORLEANS
GENERAL STRIKE OF 1892," Louisiana History 24:4 (Fall 1983), 377–
388.

B-2602 Cook, Bernard A. and James R. Watson, "THE SAILORS AND MARINE
TRANSPORT WORKERS' 1913 STRIKE IN NEW ORLEANS: THE AFL AND THE
IWW," Southern Studies 17:1 (Spring 1979), 111–122.

B-2603 Cook, Sylvia, "GASTONIA: THE LITERARY REVERBERATIONS OF THE
STRIKE," Southern Literary Journal 7:1 (Fall 1974), 49–66.

B-2604 Coulter, E. Merton, "SLAVERY AND FREEDOM IN ATHENS, GEORGIA, 1860–
1866," Georgia Historical Quarterly 49:3 (September 1965), 264–
293.

B-2605 Cramer, M. Richard, "RACE AND SOUTHERN WHITE WORKERS' SUPPORT FOR
UNIONS," Phylon 39:4 (December 1978), 311–321.

B-2606 Cribbs, Lennie Austin, "THE MEMPHIS CHINESE LABOR CONVENTION,
1869," West Tennessee Historical Society Papers No. 37 (1983),
74–81.

B-2607 Doherty, William T. Jr., "BERKELEY'S NON-REVOLUTION: LAW AND
ORDER AND THE GREAT RAILWAY STRIKE OF 1877," West Virginia History
35:4 (July 1974), 271–289.

B-2608 Donnan, Elizabeth, "THE SLAVE TRADE INTO SOUTH CAROLINA BEFORE THE
REVOLUTION," American Historical Review 33:4 (July 1928), 804–828.

B-2609 Douty, H. M., "EARLY LABOR ORGANIZATION IN NORTH CAROLINA, 1880–
1900," South Atlantic Quarterly 34:3 (July 1935), 260–268.

B-2610 Douty, H. M., "LABOR UNREST IN NORTH CAROLINA, 1932," Social
Forces 11:4 (May 1933), 579–590.

B-2611 Dowty, Alan, "URBAN SLAVERY IN PRO-SOUTHERN FICTION OF THE
1850's," Journal of Southern History 32:1 (February 1966), 25–41.

B-2612 Dye, Nancy Schrom, "THE LOUISVILLE WOOLEN MILLS STRIKE OF 1887: A
CASE STUDY OF WORKING WOMEN, THE KNIGHTS OF LABOR, AND UNION
ORGANIZATION IN THE NEW SOUTH," Register of the Kentucky
Historical Society 82:2 (Spring 1984), 136–150.

B-2613 Eaton, Clement, "SLAVE-HIRING IN THE UPPER SOUTH: A STEP TOWARD
FREEDOM," Mississippi Valley Historical Review 46:4 (March 1960),
663–678.

B-2614 Ellis, Leonora Beck, "A STUDY OF SOUTHERN COTTON-MILL COMMUNI-
TIES," American Journal of Sociology 8:5 (March 1903), 623–630.

B-2615 Ellis, William E., "LABOR-MANAGEMENT RELATIONS IN THE PROGRESSIVE
ERA: A PROFIT SHARING EXPERIENCE IN LOUISVILLE," Register of the
Kentucky Historical Society 78:2 (Spring 1980), 140–156.

B-2616 Enstam, Elizabeth York, "THE FRONTIER WOMAN AS A CITY WORKER:
WOMEN'S OCCUPATIONS IN DALLAS, TEXAS, 1856–1880," East Texas
Historical Journal 18:1 (1980), 12–28.

B-2617 Evans, Mercer G., "SOUTHERN LABOR SUPPLY AND WORKING CONDITIONS IN
INDUSTRY," Annals of the American Academy of Political and Social
Science 153 (January 1931), 156–162.

B-2618 Finger, Bill, "TEXTILE MEN: LOOMS, LOANS, AND LOCKOUTS," Southern
Exposure 3:4 (Winter 1976), 54–65.

B-2619 Fink, Leon, "'IRRESPECTIVE OF PARTY, COLOR OR SOCIAL STANDING':
THE KNIGHTS OF LABOR AND OPPOSITION POLITICS IN RICHMOND, VIR-
GINIA," Labor History 19:3 (Summer 1978), 325–349.

B-2620 Flynt, Wayne, "FLORIDA LABOR AND POLITICAL 'RADICALISM,' 1919-1920," Labor History 9:1 (Winter 1968), 73-90.

B-2621 Flynt, Wayne, "PENSACOLA LABOR PROBLEMS AND POLITICAL RADICALISM, 1908," Florida Historical Quarterly 43:4 (April 1965), 315-332.

B-2622 "FREE NEGRO OWNERS OF SLAVES IN THE UNITED STATES IN 1830," Journal of Negro History 9:1 (January 1924), 41-85.

B-2623 Fry, Joseph A., "RAYON, RIOT, AND REPRESSION: THE COVINGTON SIT-DOWN STRIKE OF 1937," Virginia Magazine of History and Biography 84:1 (January 1976), 3-18.

B-2624 Garcia, Mario T., "RACIAL DUALISM IN THE EL PASO LABOR MARKET, 1880-1920," Aztlan 6:2 (1975), 197-217.

B-2625 German, Richard H. C., "THE AUGUSTA TEXTILE STRIKE OF 1898-1899," Richmond County History 4:1 (Winter 1972), 35-50.

B-2626 Gilmore, Harlan and Logan Wilson, "THE EMPLOYMENT OF NEGRO WOMEN AS DOMESTIC SERVANTS IN NEW ORLEANS," Social Forces 22:3 (March 1944), 318-331.

B-2627 Gittler, J. B. and R. R. Giffin, "CHANGING PATTERNS OF EMPLOYMENT IN FIVE SOUTHEASTERN STATES," Southern Economic Journal 11:2 (October 1944), 169-182.

B-2628 Goodstein, Marvin E., "A NOTE ON URBAN AND NONURBAN EMPLOYMENT GROWTH IN THE SOUTH, 1940-1960," Journal of Regional Science 10:3 (December 1970), 397-401.

B-2629 Gutman, Herbert G., "BLACK COAL MINERS AND THE GREENBACK-LABOR PARTY IN REDEEMER, ALABAMA, 1878-1879," Labor History 10:3 (Summer 1969), 506-535.

B-2630 Hale, Carl W., "EMPLOYMENT SPREAD EFFECTS IN APPALACHIA AND THE SOUTH," Growth and Change 3:1 (January 1972), 10-14.

B-2631 Hall, Grace, and Alan Saltzstein, "EQUAL EMPLOYMENT OPPORTUNITY FOR MINORITIES IN MUNICIPAL GOVERNMENT," Social Science Quarterly 57:4 (1977), 864-872.

B-2632 Hall, Jacquelyn Dowd, "DISORDERLY WOMEN: GENDER AND LABOR MILI-TANCY IN THE APPALACHIAN SOUTH," Journal of American History 73:2 (September 1986), 354-382.

B-2633 Harvey, Katherine A., "THE KNIGHTS OF LABOR IN THE MARYLAND COAL FIELDS, 1878-1882," Labor History 10:4 (Fall 1969), 555-583.

B-2634 Headlee, Thomas J. Jr., "THE RICHMOND STREETCAR STRIKE OF 1903," Virginia Cavalcade 25:4 (Spring 1976), 176-183.

B-2635 Heberle, Rudolf, "WAR-TIME CHANGES IN THE LABOR FORCE IN LOUISI-ANA," Social Forces 24:3 (March 1946), 290-299.

B-2636 Herring, Harriet L., "THE OUTSIDE EMPLOYER IN THE SOUTHERN INDUS-TRIAL PATTERN," Social Forces 18:1 (October 1939), 115-126.

B-2637 Herring, Neill and Sue Thrasher, "UAW SITDOWN STRIKE: ATLANTA, 1936," Southern Exposure 1:3-4 (Winter 1974), 63-83.

B-2638 Hewitt, Nancy A., "WOMEN IN YBOR CITY: AN INTERVIEW WITH A WOMAN CIGARWORKER," Tampa Bay History 7:2 (Fall-Winter 1985), 161-165.

B-2639 Hodges, James A., "CHALLENGE TO THE NEW SOUTH: THE GREAT TEXTILE STRIKE IN ELIZABETHTON, TENNESSEE, 1928," Tennessee Historical Quarterly 23:4 (December 1924), 343-357.

B-2640 Ingalls, Robert, "THE MURDER OF JOSEPH SHOEMAKER," Southern Exposure 8:2 (Summer 1980), 64-68.

B-2641 Ingalls, Robert, "STRIKES AND VIGILANTE VIOLENCE IN TAMPA'S CIGAR INDUSTRY," Tampa Bay History 7:2 (Fall-Winter 1985), 117-134.

B-2642 Ingalls, Robert, "VANQUISHED BUT NOT CONVINCED," Southern Exposure 14:1 (January-February 1986), 51-58.

B-2643 Jones, Beverly W., "RACE, SEX, AND CLASS: BLACK FEMALE TOBACCO WORKERS IN DURHAM, NORTH CAROLINA, 1920-1940, AND THE DEVELOPMENT OF FEMALE CONSCIOUSNESS," Feminist Studies 10:3 (Fall 1984), 441-452.

B-2644 Jones, James Boyd Jr., "THE MEMPHIS FIREFIGHTERS' STRIKES, 1858 AND 1860," East Tennessee Historical Society's Publications No. 49 (1977), 37-60.

B-2645 Joyner, Charles W., "UP IN OLD LORAY: FOLKWAYS OF VIOLENCE IN THE GASTONIA STRIKE," North Carolina Folklore 12:2 (December 1964), 20-24.

B-2646 Kahn, Kathy, "HARD TIMES IN THE MILL," New South 25:4 (Fall 1970), 54-62.

B-2647 Kann, Kenneth, "THE KNIGHTS OF LABOR AND THE SOUTHERN BLACK WORKER," Labor History 18:1 (Winter 1977), 49-70.

B-2648 Keig, Norman G., "THE OCCUPATIONAL ASPIRATIONS AND LABOR FORCE EXPERIENCE OF A NEGRO YOUTH," American Journal of Economics and Sociology 28:2 (April 1969), 113-130.

B-2649 Kendall, John S., "NEW ORLEANS 'PECULIAR INSTITUTION,'" Louisiana Historical Quarterly 23:3 (July 1940), 864-886.

B-2650 Kendall, John S., "SHADOW OVER THE CITY," Louisiana Historical Quarterly 22:1 (January 1939), 142-165.

B-2651 Laing, James T., "THE NEGRO MINER IN WEST VIRGINIA," Social Forces 14:3 (March 1936), 416-422.

B-2652 Lander, Marylee, Hollis Price, and Lanny Streeter, "INCOME, LABOR FORCE PARTICIPATION, AND RACE IN THE MIAMI SMSA," Review of Black Political Economy 5:3 (Spring 1975), 250-258.

B-2653 Laprade, William T., "THE DOMESTIC SLAVE TRADE IN THE DISTRICT OF COLUMBIA," Journal of Negro History 11:1 (January 1926), 17-34.

B-2654 Leiter, Jeffrey, "CONTINUITY AND CHANGE IN THE LEGITIMATION OF AUTHORITY IN SOUTHERN MILL TOWNS," Social Problems 29:5 (June 1982), 540-550.

B-2655 Leiter, Jeffrey, "REACTIONS TO SUBORDINATION: ATTITUDES OF SOUTHERN TEXTILE WORKERS," Social Forces 64:4 (June 1986), 948-974.

B-2656 Lewis, Ronald L., "JOB CONTROL AND RACE RELATIONS IN COAL FIELDS, 1870-1920," Journal of Ethnic Studies 12:4 (Winter 1985), 36-64.

B-2657 Lewis, Ronald L., "THE USE AND EXTENT OF SLAVE LABOR IN THE VIRGINIA IRON INDUSTRY: THE ANTE-BELLUM ERA," West Virginia History 38:2 (January 1977), 141-156.

B-2658 Lippin, Tobi and Debby Warren, "ACCOUNTS OVERDUE," Southern Exposure 9:4 (Winter 1981), 12-15.

B-2659 Long, Durward, "LABOR RELATIONS IN THE TAMPA CIGAR INDUSTRY, 1885-1911," Labor History 12:4 (Fall 1971), 551-559.

B-2660 Long, Durward, "THE OPEN-CLOSED SHOP BATTLE IN TAMPA'S CIGAR INDUSTRY, 1919-1921," Florida Historical Quarterly 47:2 (October 1968), 101-121.

B-2661 Long, Durward, "LA RESISTENCIA: TAMPA'S IMMIGRANT LABOR UNION," Labor History 6:3 (Fall 1965), 193-213.

B-2662 Lowry, Charles B., "THE PWA IN TAMPA: A CASE STUDY," Florida Historical Quarterly 52:4 (April 1975), 363-380.

B-2663 McDonald, Joseph A. and Donald A. Clelland, "TEXTILE WORKERS AND UNION SENTIMENT," Social Forces 63:2 (December 1984), 502-521.

B-2664 McKelway, A. J., "CHILD LABOR IN THE SOUTH," Annals of the American Academy of Political and Social Science 35:1 (January 1910), 156-164.

B-2665 McKnight, Gerald D., "THE 1968 MEMPHIS SANITATION STRIKE AND THE FBI: A CASE STUDY IN URBAN SURVEILLANCE," South Atlantic Quarterly 83:2 (Spring 1984), 138-156.

B-2666 McLaurin, Melton A., "EARLY LABOR UNION ORGANIZATIONAL EFFORTS IN SOUTH CAROLINA COTTON MILLS," South Carolina Historical Magazine 72:1 (February 1971), 44-59.

B-2667 Marks, George P. III, "THE NEW ORLEANS SCREWMEN'S BENEVOLENT ASSO-CIATION, 1850-1861," Labor History 14:2 (Spring 1973), 259-263.

B-2668 Maroney, James C., "THE GALVESTON LONGSHOREMEN'S STRIKE OF 1920," East Texas Historical Journal 16:1 (1978), 34-38.

B-2669 Maroney, James C., "THE UNIONIZATION OF THURBER, 1903," Red River Valley Historical Review 4:2 (Spring 1979), 27-32.

B-2670 Martin, Charles H., "SOUTHERN LABOR RELATIONS IN TRANSITION: GADSDEN, ALABAMA, 1930-1943," Journal of Southern History 47:4 (November 1981), 545-568.

B-2671 Martin, Charles H., "WHITE SUPREMACY AND BLACK WORKERS: GEORGIA'S 'BLACK SHIRTS' COMBAT THE GREAT DEPRESSION," Labor History 18:3 (Summer 1977), 366-381.

B-2672 Miller, M. Sammy, "SLAVERY IN AN URBAN AREA--DISTRICT OF COLUM-BIA," Negro History Bulletin 37:5 (1974), 293-295.

B-2673 Miller, Randall M., "THE FABRIC OF CONTROL: SLAVERY IN ANTEBELLUM SOUTHERN TEXTILE MILLS," Business History Review 53:4 (Winter 1981), 471-490.

B-2674 Mindiola, Tatcho, "THE COST OF BEING A MEXICAN FEMALE WORKER IN THE 1970 HOUSTON LABOR MARKET," Aztlan 11:2 (Fall 1980), 231-248.

B-2675 Moriarty, Barry M., "A NOTE ON UNEXPLAINED RESIDUALS IN NORTH-SOUTH WAGE DIFFERENTIAL MODELS," Journal of Regional Science 18:1 (April 1978), 105-108.

B-2676 Mormino, Gary R., "TAMPA AND THE NEW URBAN SOUTH: THE WEIGHT STRIKE OF 1899," Florida Historical Quarterly 60:3 (January 1982), 337-356.

B-2677 Nelson, Daniel, "THE RUBBER WORKERS' SOUTHERN STRATEGY: LABOR ORGANIZING IN THE NEW DEAL SOUTH, 1933-1943," Historian 47:3 (May 1984), 319-338.

B-2678 Newsom, Robert T., "METROPOLITAN AND NONMETROPOLITAN EMPLOYMENT CHANGES: THE CASE OF TEXAS," Social Science Quarterly 50:2 (September 1969), 354-368.

B-2679 Nord, Stephen and Hollis Price, "REFINED DISCRIMINATION: A CASE STUDY OF PUBLIC EMPLOYMENT IN A SOUTHEASTERN CITY," Review of Black Political Economy 9:3 (Spring 9179), 300-306.

B-2680 Northrup, Herbert R., "THE NEGRO AND UNIONISM IN THE BIRMINGHAM, ALA. IRON AND STEEL INDUSTRY," Southern Economic Journal 10:1 (July 1943), 27-40.

B-2681 Paliakoff, Phayne, "TRYING TO MAKE A LIVING," Southern Exposure 11:4 (July-August 1983), 14-18.

B-2682 Paulson, Darryl and Janet Stiff, "AN EMPTY VICTORY: THE ST. PETERSBURG SANITATION STRIKE, 1968," Florida Historical Quarterly 57:4 (April 1979), 421-433.

B-2683 Perez, Louis A. Jr., "REMINISCENCES OF A LECTOR: CUBAN CIGAR WORKERS IN TAMPA," Florida Historical Quarterly 53:4 (April 1975), 443-449.

B-2684 Phillips, William H., "THE LABOR MARKET OF SOUTHERN TEXTILE MILL VILLAGES: SOME MICRO EVIDENCE," Explorations in Economic History 23:2 (April 1986), 103-123.

B-2685 Poston, Dudley L. Jr. and Gordon C. Johnson, "INDUSTRIALIZATION AND PROFESSIONAL DIFFERENTIATION BY SEX IN THE METROPOLITAN SOUTH-WEST," Social Science Quarterly 52:2 (September 1971), 331-348.

B-2686 Poyo, Gerald E., "THE IMPACT OF CUBAN AND SPANISH WORKERS ON LABOR ORGANIZING IN FLORIDA, 1870-1900," Journal of American Ethnic History 5:2 (Spring 1986), 46-63.

B-2687 Quinney, Valerie, "TEXTILE WOMEN: THREE GENERATIONS IN THE MILL," Southern Exposure 3:4 (Winter 1976), 66-72.

B-2688 Reed, Merl E., "THE AUGUSTA TEXTILE MILLS AND THE STRIKE OF 1886," Labor History 14:2 (Spring 1973), 228-246.

B-2689 Reed, Merl E., "LUMBERJACKS AND LONGSHOREMEN: THE I.W.W. IN LOUISIANA," Labor History 13:1 (Winter 1972), 41-59.

B-2690 Reese, James V., "THE EVOLUTION OF AN EARLY TEXAS UNION: THE SCREWMEN'S BENEVOLENT ASSOCIATION OF GALVESTON, 1866-1891," Southwestern Historical Quarterly 75:2 (October 1971), 158-185.

B-2691 Reilly, John M., "IMAGES OF GASTONIA: A REVOLUTIONARY CHAPTER IN AMERICAN SOCIAL FICTION," Georgia Review 28:3 (Fall 1974), 498-517.

B-2692 Reinders, Robert C., "SLAVERY IN NEW ORLEANS IN THE DECADE BEFORE THE CIVIL WAR," Mid-America 44:4 (October 1962), 211-221.

B-2693 Rhinehart, Marilyn D., "A LESSON IN UNITY: THE HOUSTON MUNICIPAL WORKERS STRIKE OF 1946," Houston Review (Fall 1982), 137-153.

B-2694 Riches, W. T. M., "INDUSTRIALIZATION AND CLASS CONFLICT IN A SLAVE SOCIETY," Amerika Studien 30:3 (1985), 353-362.

B-2695 Richter, William L., "SLAVERY IN BATON ROUGE, 1820-1860," Louisiana History 10:2 (Spring 1969), 125-148.

B-2696 Ross, David F., "PUBLIC EMPLOYMENT AND THE NEW SEGREGATION IN THE SOUTH," Growth and Change 2:1 (January 1971), 29-33.

B-2697 Russell, Michael B., "GREENVILLE'S EXPERIMENT: THE NON-UNION CULTURE," Southern Exposure 7:1 (Spring 1979), 94-97, 100.

B-2698 Ryon, Roderick N., "BALTIMORE WORKERS AND INDUSTRIAL DECISION-MAKING," Journal of Southern History 51:4 (November 1985), 565-580.

B-2699 Saussy, Gordon A., "THE DYNAMICS OF MANUFACTURING EMPLOYMENT LOCA-
TION WITHIN THE NEW ORLEANS METROPOLITAN AREA," Review of Regional
Studies 3:1 (Fall 1972-73), 35-46.

B-2700 Schafer, Judith Kelleher, "NEW ORLEANS SLAVERY IN 1850 AS SEEN IN
ADVERTISEMENTS," Journal of Southern History 47:2 (February 1981),
33-56.

B-2701 Schulman, Michael D., Rhonda Zingraff and Linda Reif, "RACE,
GENDER, CLASS CONSCIOUSNESS AND UNION SUPPORT: AN ANALYSIS OF
SOUTHERN TEXTILE WORKERS," Sociological Quarterly 26:2 (Summer
1985), 187-204.

B-2702 Seip, Terry L., "SLAVES AND FREE NEGROES IN ALEXANDRIA, 1850-
1860," Louisiana History 10:2 (Spring 1969), 147-165.

B-2703 Selby, John G., "'BETTER TO STARVE IN THE SHADE THAN IN THE FAC-
TORY,' LABOR PROTEST IN HIGH POINT, NORTH CAROLINA, IN THE EARLY
1930s," North Carolina Historical Review 64:1 (January 1987), 43-
64.

B-2704 Shea, William L. and Merrill R. Pritchett, "THE WEHRMACHT IN
LOUISIANA," Louisiana Studies 23:1 (Winter 1982), 5-20.

B-2705 Shofner, Jerrell H., "THE LABOR LEAGUE OF JACKSONVILLE: A NEGRO
UNION AND WHITE STRIKEBREAKERS," Florida Historical Quarterly 50:3
(January 1972), 278-282.

B-2706 Shofner, Jerrell H., "MILITANT NEGRO LABORERS IN RECONSTRUCTION
FLORIDA," Journal of Southern History 39:3 (August 1973), 397-408.

B-2707 Shugg, Roger Wallace, "THE NEW ORLEANS GENERAL STRIKE OF 1892,"
Louisiana Historical Quarterly 21:2 (April 1938), 547-560.

B-2708 Siegel, Fred, "ARTISANS AND IMMIGRANTS IN THE POLITICS OF LATE
ANTEBELLUM GEORGIA," Civil War History 27:3 (September 1981), 221-
230.

B-2709 Silver, Christopher, "A NEW LOOK AT OLD SOUTH URBANIZATION: THE
IRISH WORKER IN CHARLESTON, SOUTH CAROLINA," South Atlantic Urban
Studies 3 (1979), 141-172.

B-2710 Sloan, Cliff and Bob Hall, "'IT'S GOOD TO BE HOME IN GREENVILLE'
. . . BUT IT'S BETTER IF YOU HATE UNIONS," Southern Exposure 7:1
(Spring 1979), 82-83.

B-2711 Stavisky, Leonard Price, "INDUSTRIALISM IN ANTE BELLUM CHARLES-
TON," Journal of Negro History 36:3 (July 1951), 302-322.

B-2712 Stillman, Don, "RUNAWAYS: A CALL TO ACTION," Southern Exposure
4:1-2 (Spring-Summer 1926), 50-59.

B-2713 Stuart, Meriwether, "OF SPIES AND BORROWED NAMES: THE IDENTITY OF
UNION OPERATIVES IN RICHMOND KNOWN AS 'THE PHILLIPSES' DESCRIBED,"
Virginia Magazine of History and Biography 89:3 (July 1981), 308-
327.

B-2714 Sturdivant, Joanna Farrell, "EMPLOYEE REPRESENTATION PLAN OF THE
DURHAM HOSIERY MILLS," Social Forces 4:3 (March 1926), 625-628.

B-2715 Taylor, Paul F., "LONDON: FOCAL POINT OF KENTUCKY TURBULENCE,"
Filson Club History Quarterly 49:3 (July 1975), 256-265.

B-2716 Terrill, Tom E., "EAGER HANDS: LABOR FOR SOUTHERN TEXTILES, 1850-
1860," Journal of Economic History 36:1 (March 1976), 84-99.

B-2717 Till, Thomas, "THE EXTENT OF INDUSTRIALIZATION IN SOUTHERN
NONMETRO LABOR MARKETS IN THE 1960's," Journal of Regional Science
13:3 (December 1973), 453-462.

B-2718 Tornquist, Elizabeth, "ORGANIZING LABOR IN NORTH CAROLINA," New
        South 25:2 (Spring 1970), 57-69.

B-2719 Turner, Ralph and William Rogers, "ARKANSAS LABOR IN REVOLT:
        LITTLE ROCK AND THE GREAT SOUTHWESTERN STRIKE," Arkansas Histori-
        cal Quarterly 24:1 (Spring 1965), 29-46.

B-2720 Walker, Kenneth P., "THE PECAN SHELLERS OF SAN ANTONIO," South-
        western Historical Quarterly 69:1 (July 1965), 44-58.

B-2721 Weaner, Bill L., "LOUISVILLE'S LABOR DISTURBANCES JULY, 1877,"
        Filson Club History Quarterly 4:2 (April 1974), 177-186.

B-2722 Weisbord, Vera Buch, "GASTONIA 1929: STRIKE AT THE LORAY MILL,"
        Southern Exposure 1:3-4 (Winter 1974), 185-203.

B-2723 Wells, Dave and Jim Sodder, "A SHORT HISTORY OF NEW ORLEANS
        DOCKWORKERS," Radical America 10:1 (January-February 1976), 43-69.

B-2724 Wilson, Kenneth L. and Alejandro Portes, "IMMIGRANT ENCLAVES: AN
        ANALYSIS OF THE LABOR MARKET EXPERIENCES OF CUBANS IN MIAMI,"
        American Journal of Sociology 86:2 (September 1980), 295-319.

B-2725 Wilson, Margaret Gibbons with Kim Kirkpatrick," ORGANIZING
        ACTIVITY AMONG HOUSEHOLD WORKERS: THE GREATER MIAMI HOUSEHOLD
        TECHNICIANS," Urban Resources 3:2 (Winter 1986), 53-54.

B-2726 Worthman, Paul B., "BLACK WORKERS AND LABOR UNIONS IN BIRMINGHAM,
        ALABAMA, 1897-1904," Labor History 10:3 (Summer 1969), 375-407.

B-2727 Zeigler, Robert E., "THE LIMITS OF POWER: THE AMALGAMATED ASSO-
        CIATION OF STREET RAILWAY EMPLOYEES IN HOUSTON, TEXAS, 1897-1905,"
        Labor History 18:1 (Winter 1977), 71-90.

B-2728 Zingraff, Rhonda and Michael D. Schulman, "SOCIAL BASES OF CLASS
        CONSCIOUSNESS: A STUDY OF SOUTHERN TEXTILE WORKERS WITH A COM-
        PARISON BY RACE," Social Forces 63:1 (September 1984), 98-116.

Life, Culture and Social Organization

B-2729 Abbott, Carl, "NORFOLK, VIRGINIA: FROM HONKY TONK TO HONKY
        GLITTER," Southern Exposure 3:4 (Winter 1976), 31-34.

B-2730 Abboud, Elaine J., "THE EVIL EYE AMONG THE SYRIAN-LEBANESE OF NEW
        ORLEANS," Louisiana Folklore Miscellaney, 2:4 (August 1968), 56-
        61.

B-2731 Abram, Morris B., "ORAL INTERVIEW," American Jewish History 73:1
        (September 1983), 7-19.

B-2732 Africa, Philipi, "SLAVE HOLDINGS IN THE SALEM COMMUNITY, 1771-
        1851," North Carolina Historical Review 54:3 (Summer 1977), 271-
        307.

B-2733 Alvarez, Eugene, "SOUTHERN HOSPITALITY AS SEEN BY TRAVELERS, 1820-
        1860," Studies in Popular Culture 2:1 (Spring 1979), 23-35.

B-2734 Ambrose, Andrew M., "THE TIES THAT BIND: WORK AND FAMILY PATTERNS
        IN THE OAKDALE ROAD SECTION OF DRUID HILLS, 1910-1940," Atlanta
        Historical Journal 26:2-3 (Summer-Fall 1982), 242-254.

B-2735 Amos, Harriet E., "'ALL-ABSORBING TOPICS': FOOD AND CLOTHING IN
        CONFEDERATE MOBILE," Atlanta Historical Journal 22:3-4 (Fall-
        Winter 1978), 17-28.

B-2736 Amos, Harriet E., "'CITY BELLES': IMAGES AND REALITIES OF THE
        LIVES OF WHITE WOMEN IN ANTEBELLUM MOBILE," Alabama Review 34:1
        (January 1981), 3-19.

B-2737 Anderson, John Q., "THE NEW ORLEANS VOODOO RITUAL DANCE AND ITS TWENTIETH-CENTURY SURVIVALS," Southern Folklore Quarterly 24:2 (June 1960), 135-143.

B-2738 Anderson, Russell H., "THE SHAKER COMMUNITIES IN SOUTHEAST GEORGIA," Georgia Historical Quarterly 50:2 (June 1966), 162-172.

B-2739 Arcenlaux, Pamela D., 'GUIDEBOOKS TO SIN: THE BLUE BOOKS OF STORYVILLE," Louisiana History, 28:4 (Fall 1987), 397-406.

B-2740 Arsenault, Raymond, "THE END OF THE LONG HOT SUMMER: THE AIR CONDITIONER AND SOUTHERN CULTURE," Journal of Southern History 50:4 (November 1984), 597-628.

B-2741 Bacote, Clarence A., "SOME ASPECTS OF NEGRO LIFE IN GEORGIA 1880-1908," Journal of Negro History 43:3 (July 1958), 186-213.

B-2742 Baer, Robert and Barry Mishkin, "THE SEMINOLE POLICE DEPARTMENT," Broward Legacy 5 (Summer-Fall 1982), 2-9.

B-2743 Baldwin, Lewis V., "FESTIVITY AND CELEBRATION: A PROFILE OF WILMINGTON'S BIG QUARTERLY," Delaware History 19:4 (Fall-Winter 1981), 197-211.

B-2744 Ball, Donald B., "NOTE ON THE SLANG AND FOLK SPEECH OF KNOXVILLE, KNOX COUNTY, TENNESSEE," Tennessee Folklore Society Bulletin 44:3 (September 1978), 134-142.

B-2745 Barnes, Annie S., "THE BLACK KINSHIP SYSTEM," Phylon 42:4 (December 1981), 369-380.

B-2746 Barnes, Annie S., "AN URBAN BLACK VOLUNTARY ASSOCIATION," Phylon 40:3 (September 1979), 264-269.

B-2747 Barnett, Bernice McNair, et al., "THE STATUS OF HUSBAND/FATHER AS PERCEIVED BY THE WIFE/MOTHER IN THE INTACT LOWER-CLASS URBAN BLACK FAMILY," Sociological Spectrum 4:4 (1984), 421-442.

B-2748 Basile, Leon, "LIFE IN KOSCIUSKO DURING THE 1850s," Journal of Mississippi History 42:4 (November 1980), 336-347.

B-2749 Bauman, Mark K., "THE EMERGENCE OF JEWISH SOCIAL SERVICE AGENCIES IN ATLANTA,' Georgia Historical Quarterly 69:4 (Winter 1985), 488-508.

B-2750 Beadenkopf, Anne, "THE BALTIMORE PUBLIC BATHS AND THEIR FOUNDER, THE REV. THOMAS M. BEADENKOPF," Maryland Historical Magazine 45:3 (September 1950), 201-214.

B-2751 Bean, Douglas O., "A SMALL CITY ADOPTS THE PUBLIC SAFETY CONCEPT: MORGANTOWN, NORTH CAROLINA--A CASE STUDY," Popular Government 45:1 (Summer 1979), 13-19.

B-2752 Bederman, Sanford H., "THE STRATIFICATION OF 'QUALITY OF LIFE' IN THE BLACK COMMUNITY OF ATLANTA, GEORGIA," Southeastern Geographer 14:1 (May 1974), 26-38.

B-2753 Belissary, Constantine G., "BEHAVIOR PATTERNS AND ASPIRATIONS OF THE URBAN WORKING CLASSES IN TENNESSEE IN THE IMMEDIATE POST-CIVIL WAR ERA," Tennessee Historical Quarterly 14:1 (March 1955), 24-42.

B-2754 Binder, Mory, "CARNEGIE OR COMMUNITY LIBRARY," Richmond County History 4:2 (Summer 1972), 21-32.

B-2755 Blackburn, George and Sherman L. Ricards, "THE MOTHER-HEADED FAMILY AMONG FREE NEGROES IN CHARLESTON, SOUTH CAROLINA," Phylon 42:1 (March 1981), 11-25.

B-2756 Blazek, Ron, "THE DEVELOPMENT OF LIBRARY SCIENCE IN THE NATION'S OLDEST CITY: THE ST. AUGUSTINE LIBRARY ASSOCIATION, 1874-1880," Journal of Library History 14:2 (1979), 160-182.

B-2757 Blazek, Ron, "LIBRARY IN A PIONEER COMMUNITY: LEMON CITY, FLORIDA," Tequesta No. 42 (1982), 39-55.

B-2758 Bloomer, John W., "'THE LOAFERS' IN BIRMINGHAM IN THE TWENTIES," Alabama Review 30:2 (April 1977), 101-107.

B-2759 Bobbitt, Charles A., "THE NORTH MEMPHIS DRIVING PARK, 1901-1905: THE PASSING OF AN ERA," West Tennessee Historical Society Papers No. 26 (1972), 40-55.

B-2760 Boggs, Ralph Steele, "SPANISH FOLKLORE FROM TAMPA, FLORIDA," Southern Folklore Quarterly 1:3 (September 1937), 1-12.

B-2761 Boggs, Ralph Steele, ed., "SPANISH FOLKLORE FORM TAMPA, FLORIDA (NO. III) UNA LEDI DE NASO," Southern Folklore Quarterly 1:4 (December 1937), 9-13.

B-2762 Boggs, Ralph Steele, ed., "SPANISH FOLKLORE FROM TAMPA, FLORIDA: (NO. V) FOLKTALES," Southern Folklore Quarterly 2:2 (June 1938), 87-106.

B-2763 Boles, Jacqueline and Albeno P. Garbin, "THE STRIP CLUB AND STRIPPER--CUSTOMER PATTERNS OF INTERACTION," Sociology and Social Research 58:2 (January 1974), 136-144.

B-2764 Boskoff, Alvin, "SOCIAL AND CULTURAL PATTERNS IN A SUBUBAN AREA: THEIR SIGNIFICANCE FOR CHANGE IN THE SOUTH," Journal of Social Issues 22:1 (JANUARY 1966), 85-100.

B-2765 Boswell, Thomas D. and Afolabe A. Adedebu, "THE SOCIAL STRUCTURE OF NINE FLORIDA SMSA's FOR 1970," Florida Geographer 12 (January 1978), 1-8.

B-2766 Braden, Waldo W., "LECTURING IN NEW ORLEANS, 1840-1850," Southern Studies 17:4 (Winter 1978), 433-446.

B-2767 Bradfield, Cecil D. and R. Ann Myers, "RELUCTANT ALLIES: CLERGY AND FUNERAL DIRECTORS," Virginia Social Science Journal 18:1 (April 1983), 15-21.

B-2768 Branch, Anne L., "ATLANTA AND THE AMERICAN SETTLEMENT HOUSE MOVEMENT," Atlanta Historical Bulletin 12:2 (June 1967), 37-51.

B-2769 Brannon, Peter A., "OLD GLENNVILLE: AN EARLY CENTER OF EAST ALABAMA CULTURE," Alabama Review 11:4 (October 1958), 255-266.

B-2770 Brasseaux, Carl A., "THE MORAL CLIMATE OF FRENCH COLONIAL LOUISI-ANA 1699-1763," Louisiana History 27:1 (Winter 1986), 27-42.

B-2771 Brown, David J., "THE WINDSOR HOTEL IN AMERICUS," Georgia Historical Quarterly 64:1 (Spring 1980), 35-49.

B-2772 Browne, Gary L., "CULTURAL CONSERVATION AND THE INDUSTRIAL REVOLU-TION: THE CASE OF BALTIMORE, 1776-1860," Continuity 2 (Spring 1981).

B-2773 Bruns, Roger and William Fraley, "'OLD GUNNY': ABOLITIONIST IN A SLAVE CITY," Maryland Historical Magazine 68:4 (Winter 1973), 369-382.

B-2774 Bryant, Beverly B., "ORIENTATIONS OF CORE CITY BLACKS TOWARD GOVERNMENTAL SERVICES," Virginia Social Studies Journal 10:1 (April 1975), 1-11.

B-2775 Bugler, Peggy A., "LITTLE HAVANA: FOLK TRADIITONS OF AN IMMIGRANT ENCLAVE," Kentucky Folklore Record 29:1-2 (January-June 1983), 15-23.

B-2776 Burran, James A., "THE WPA IN NASHVILLE, 1935-1943," Tennessee Historical Quarterly 34:3 (Fall 1975), 293-306.

B-2777 Caldwell, Morris G., "THE ADJUSTMENTS OF MOUNTAIN FAMILIES IN AN URBAN ENVIRONMENT," Social Forces 16:3 (March 1938), 389-395.

B-2778 Campbell, Steve B., "BIRTH OF THE ATLANTA FIRE DEPARTMENT," Atlanta Historical Journal 18:3-4 (Fall-Winter 1973), 35-65.

B-2779 Carroll, Douglas G. Jr. and Blanche D. Coll, "THE BALTIMORE ALMSHOUSE: AN EARLY HISTORY," Maryland Historical Magazine 66:2 (Summer 1971), 135-152.

B-2780 Chambers, Lenoir, "NOTES ON LIFE IN OCCUPIED NORFOLK, 1862-1865," Virginia Magazine of History and Biography 73:2 (April 1965), 131-144.

B-2781 Chandler, Charles R., "VALUE ORIENTATIONS AMONG MEXICAN AMERICANS IN A SOUTHWESTERN CITY," Sociology and Social Research 58:3 (April 1974), 262-271.

B-2782 Charmichael, James V. Jr., "ATLANTA'S FEMALE LIBRARIANS, 1883-1915," Journal of Library History 21:2 (Spring 1986), 376-399.

B-2783 Chatelain, Verne E., "SPANISH CONTRIBUTIONS IN FLORIDA TO AMERICAN CULTURE,' Florida Historical Journal 19:3 (January 1941), 213-245.

B-2784 Chenault, William W. and Robert C. Reinders, "THE NORTHERN-BORN COMMUNITY OF NEW ORLEANS IN THE 1850's," Journal of American History 51:2 (September 1964), 232-247.

B-2785 Chesson, Michael B., "HARLOTS OR HEROINES? A NEW LOOK AT THE RICHMOND BREAD RIOT," Virginia Magazine of History and Biography 92:2 (April 1984), 131-175.

B-2786 Christopherson, Merrill G., "THE CHARLESTON CONVERSATIONALISTS," Southern Speech Journal 20:2 (Winter 1954), 99-108.

B-2787 Clarke, Kenneth, "FOLKLORE OF NEGRO CHILDREN IN GREATER LOUISVILLE REFLECTING ATTITUDES TOWARD RACE," Kentucky Folklore Record 10:1 (January-March 1964), 1-11.

B-2788 Clements, William M., "THE JONESBORO TORNADO: A CASE STUDY IN FOLKLORE, POPULAR RELIGION, AND GRASSROOTS HISTORY," Red River Valley Historical Review 2:2 (Summer 1975), 273-286.

B-2789 Coll, Blanche D., "THE BALTIMORE SOCIETY FOR THE PREVENTION OF PAUPERISM, 1820-1822," American Historical Review 61:1 (October 1955), 77-87.

B-2790 Collins, Yandell Jr., "SUPERSTITIONS AND BELIEF TALES FROM LOUIS-VILLE," Kentucky Folklore Record 4 (1958), 71-78.

B-2791 Colson, John Calvin, "THE FIRE COMPANY LIBRARY ASSOCIATIONS OF BALTIMORE, 1838-1858," Journal of Library History 21:1 (Winter 1986), 158-176.

B-2792 Conger, Roger N., "WACO: COTTON AND CULTURE ON THE BRAZOS," Southwestern Historical Quarterly 75:1 (July 1971), 54-76.

B-2793 Cook, James R., "CITIZEN RESPONSE IN A NEIGHBORHOOD UNDER THREAT," American Journal of Community Psychology 11:4 (August 1983), 459-471.

B-2794 Coulter, E. Merton, "A GEORGIA LAWYER AND HIS NEGRO CLIENT: A
       STUDY IN BLACK AND WHITE," Georgia Historical Quarterly 53:3
       (September 1969), 305-320.

B-2795 Craft, Betty, "SUPERSTITIONS FROM FRENCHBURG, KENTUCKY," Kentucky
       Folklore Record 10:1964 (January-March 1964), 12-17.

B-2796 Crawley, Donald W., "THE NEW YEAR'S SHOOT AT CHERRYVILLE," North
       Carolina Folklore 10:2 (December 1962), 21-27.

B-2797 Cumming, Inez Parker, "EATONTON'S SOUTHERN ACCENT," Georgia Review
       13:2 (Summer 1959), 206-216.

B-2798 Cummings, Scott and Charles Wellford Pinnell III, "RACIAL DOUBLE
       STANDARDS OF MORALITY IN A SMALL SOUTHERN COMMUNITY: ANOTHER LOOK
       AT MYRDAL'S AMERICAN DILEMMA," Journal of Black Studies 9:1 (Sep-
       tember 1978) 67-86.

B-2799 Curtis, James R., "MIAMI'S LITTLE HAVANA: YARD SHRINES, CULT
       RELIGION AND LANDSCAPE," Journal of Cultural Geography 1:1 (Fall-
       Winter 1980), 1-15.

B-2800 Cuthbert, Nancy Bergmann, "A SOCIAL MOVEMENT: THE NORFOLK KLAN IN
       THE TWENTIES," Virginia Social Science Journal 2:2 (April 1968),
       101-118.

B-2801 Dakan, A. William and Janet R. Dakan, "VARIATIONS IN THE QUALITY
       OF LIFE AMONG FIFTEEN MEDIUM-SIZED SOUTHERN CITIES," South
       Atlantic Urban Studies 3 (1979), 210-235.

B-2802 Darkis, Fred R. Jr., "MADAME LALAURIE OF NEW ORLEANS," Louisiana
       History 23:4 (Fall 1982), 383-399.

B-2803 Dart, Henry P., ed., "A MURDER CASE TRIED IN NEW ORLEANS IN 1773,"
       Louisiana Historical Quarterly 22:3 (July 1939), 623-641.

B-2804 Dart, Henry P., ed., "SANITARY CONDITIONS IN NEW ORLEANS UNDER THE
       SPANISH REGIME, 1799-1800," Louisiana Historical Quarterly 15:4
       (October 1932), 610-617.

B-2805 Davenport, F. Garvin, "CULTURAL LIFE IN NASHVILLE ON THE EVE OF
       THE CIVIL WAR," Journal of Southern History 3:3 (August 1937),
       326-347.

B-2806 Davenport, F. Garvin, "CULTURE VERSUS FRONTIER IN TENNESSEE, 1825-
       1850," Journal of Southern History 5:1 (February 1939), 18-33.

B-2807 Davidson, Chandler and Charles M. Gaitz, "'ARE THE POOR DIFFER-
       ENT?' A COMPARISON OF WORK BEHAVIOR AND ATTITUDES AMONG THE URBAN
       POOR AND NONPOOR," Social Problems 22:2 (December 1974), 229-245.

B-2808 Davidson, Chandler and Charles M. Gaitz, "ETHNIC ATTITUDES AS A
       BASIS FOR MINORITY COOPERATION IN A SOUTHWESTERN METROPOLIS,"
       Social Science Quarterly 53:4 (March 1973), 738-748.

B-2809 Davis, Stephen, "EMPTY EYES, MARBLE HAND: THE CONFEDERATE MONU-
       MENT IN THE SOUTH," Journal of Popular Culture 16:3 (Winter 1982),
       2-21.

B-2810 Davis-Root, Brenda and Ernestine Houston Thompson, "THE FEMALE
       COMPONENT: A STUDY OF THE LIFE SATISFACTION OF ELDERLY WOMEN IN
       TWO NEIGHBORHOODS," Sociological Spectrum 2:2 (April-June 1982),
       173-186.

B-2811 Delaney, Paul, "BLACK COPS IN THE SOUTH," Nation 223 (July 31,
       1976), 78-82.

B-2812 Denis, J. W., "THE NASHVILLE CITY CEMETARY," Tennessee Historical
       Quarterly 2:1 (March 1943), 30-42.

B-2813 Deutsch, Martin and Kay Steele, "ATTITUDE DISSONANCE AMONG SOUTH-VILLE'S 'INFLUENTIALS,'" Journal of Social Issues 15:4 (1959), 44-52.

B-2814 Dickinson, Joshua C. III, Robert J. Gray, and Davis M. Smith, "THE 'QUALITY OF LIFE' IN GAINESVILLE, FLORIDA: AN APPLICATION OF TER-RITORIAL SOCIAL INDICATORS," Southeastern Geographer 12:2 (November 1972), 121-132.

B-2815 Dinnerstein, Leonard, "A NOTE ON SOUTHERN ATTITUDES TOWARDS JEWS," Jewish Social Studies 32:1 (January 1970), 43-49.

B-2816 Doyle, Don H., "URBANIZATION AND SOUTHERN CULTURE: ECONOMIC ELITES IN FOUR NEW SOUTH CITIES (ATLANTA, NASHVILLE, CHARLESTON, MOBILE) 1865-1910," in V. Burton, Toward a New South? Studies in Post Civil War Southern Communities, 1982.

B-2817 Duke, Maurice, "CABELL'S AND GLASGLOW'S RICHMOND: THE INTELLEC-TUAL BACKGROUND OF THE CITY," Mississippi Quarterly 26:4 (Fall 1974), 393-414.

B-2818 Easterby, J. H., "PUBLIC POOR RELIEF IN COLONIAL CHARLESTON," South Carolina Historical and Genealogical Magazine 42:2 (1941), 83-86.

B-2819 Eaton, Clement, "MOB VIOLENCE IN THE OLD SOUTH," Mississippi Valley Historical Review 29:3 (December 1942), 351-370.

B-2820 Ecton, Henry G., "'A MOMENTARY SENSATION IN OUR MIDST': THE PRINCE OF WALES' VISIT TO ANTEBELLUM RICHMOND," Virginia Cavalcade 30:3 (Winter 1981), 134-143.

B-2821 Elder, Harris J., "HENRY KEMP AND CULTURAL PLURALISM IN OKLAHOMA CITY," Chronicles of Oklahoma 55:1 (Spring 1977), 78-92.

B-2822 Elgie, Robert A. and Alex Rees Clark, "SOCIAL CLASS SEGREGATION IN SOUTHERN METROPOLITAN AREAS," Urban Affairs Quarterly 16:3 (March 1981), 299-316.

B-2823 Eyerdam, Rick, "DADE COUNTY: A NEW CULTURAL VISION," Horizon 28:1 (January-February 1985), 41-48.

B-2824 Fair, John D., "HATCHERT CHANDLER AND THE QUEST FOR NATIVE TRADI-TION AT FORT MORGAN," Alabama Review 60:3 (July 1987), 163-198.

B-2825 Fallows, James, "THE SEDUCTION OF WASHINGTON SOCIETY," Washington Monthly 8:7 (July 1976), 18-24.

B-2826 Feagin, Joe R., "THE SOCIAL COSTS OF HOUSTON'S GROWTH: A SUNBELT BOOMTOWN REEXAMINED," International Journal of Urban and Regional Research 9:2 (June 1985), 164-185.

B-2827 Fee, Elizabeth, Sylvia Gillette, Linda Shopes, and Linda Zeidman, "BALTIMORE BY BUS: STEERING A NEW COURSE THROUGH THE CITY'S HISTORY," Radical History Review no. 28-30 (1984), 206-216.

B-2828 Fernandez, Juan Marchena, "ST. AUGUSTINE'S MILITARY SOCIETY, 1700-1820," El Escribano 22 (1985), 43-78.

B-2829 Fielding, Lawrence W. and Clark F. Wood, "FROM RELIGIOUS OUTREACH TO SOCIAL ENTERTAINMENT: THE LOUISVILLE YWCA'S FIRST GYMNASIUM, 1876-1880," Filson Club History Quarterly 60:2 (April 1986), 239-256.

B-2830 Fielding, Lawrence W. and Clark F. Wood, "THE SOCIAL CONTROL OF INDOLENCE AND IRRELIGION: LOUISVILLE'S FIRST YMCA MOVEMENT, 1853-1871," Filson Club History Quarterly 58:2 (April 1984), 219-236.

B-2831 Fishman, Walda Katz and Richard L. Zweigenhaft, "JEWS AND THE NEW ORLEANS ECONOMIC AND SOCIAL ELITES," Jewish Social Studies 44:3-4 (Summer Fall 1982), 291-298.

B-2832 Fitchett, E. Horace, "THE TRADITIONS OF THE FREE NEGRO IN CHARLES-TON, SOUTH CAROLINA, IN SEARCH OF THE PROMISED LAND," Kennikat (1981), 44-57.

B-2833 Fitchett, E. Horace, 'THE TRADITIONS OF THE FREE NEGRO IN CHARLES-TON, SOUTH CAROLINA," Journal of Negro History 25:2 (April 1940), 139-151.

B-2834 Forderhase, Nancy, "'LIMITED ONLY BY EARTH AND SKY': THE LOUIS-VILLE WOMAN'S CLUB AND PROGRESSIVE REFORM," Filson Club History Quarterly 59:1 (July 1985), 327-343.

B-2835 Forsyth, Craig, "RAG LADY AND HER KIND: A SOCIO-NARRATIVE OF NEW ORLEANS STREET SOCIETY," Perspectives on Ethnicity in New Orleans (1981), 46-55.

B-2836 Frankland, A. E., "KRONIKALS OF THE TIMES--MEMPHIS, 1862," American Jewish Archives 9:2 (October 1957), 83-127.

B-2837 Freeman, Howard E. and Gene G. Kassebaum, "EXOGAMOUS DATING IN A SOUTHERN CITY," Jewish Social Studies 18:1 (January 1956), 55-60.

B-2838 Fuke, Richard Paul, 'THE BALTIMORE ASSOCIATION FOR THE MORAL AND EDUCATIONAL IMPROVEMENT OF THE COLORED PEOPLE, 1864-1870," Maryland Historical Magazine 66:4 (Winter 1971), 369-404.

B-2839 Garst, Ronald D., "INFLUENCES OF SOCIAL STRUCURE AND ACTION SPACE ON COGNITIVE MAPS: IMAGES OF LOUISVILLE, KENTUCKY," Southeastern Geographer 16:2 (November 1976), 113-126.

B-2840 Gay, Dorothy A., "CRISIS OF IDENTITY: THE NEGRO COMMUNITY IN RALEIGH, 1890-1900," North Carolina Historical Review 50:2 (Spring 1973), 121-140.

B-2841 Geffen, Alice and Carole Berglie, "FOOD FESTIVALS: EATING YOUR WAY AROUND THE SOUTH," Southern Exposure 14:1 (January-February 1986), 44-49.

B-2842 George, Paul S., "BOOTLEGGERS, PROHIBITIONISTS AND POLICE: THE TEMPERANCE MOVEMENT IN MIAMI, 1896-1920," Tequesta No. 39 (1979), 34-41.

B-2843 George, Paul S., "A CYCLONE HITS MIAMI: CARRIE NATION'S VISIT TO 'THE WICKED CITY,'" Florida Historical Quarterly 58:2 (October 1979), 150-159.

B-2844 Gibbono, Robert, "LIFE AT THE CROSSROADS OF THE CONFEDERACY: ATLANTA, 1861-1865," Atlanta Historicla Journal 23:2 (Summer 1979), 11-72.

B-2845 Gibbs, Samuel Jr., "VOODOO PRACTICES IN MODERN NEW ORLEANS," Louisiana Folklore Miscellaney 3:2 (April 1971), 12-16.

B-2846 Gibson, Gail, "COSTUME AND FASHION IN CHARLESTON, 1769-1782," South Carolina Historical Magazine 82:3 (July 1981), 225-247.

B-2847 Gilje, Paul A., "THE BALTIMORE RIOTS OF 1812 AND THE BREAKDOWN OF THE ANGLO-AMERICAN MOB TRADITION," Journal of Social History 13:4 (Summer 1980), 547-564.

B-2848 Goldfield, David R., "FRIENDS AND NEIGHBORS: URBAN-RURAL RELA-TIONS IN ANTEBELLUM VIRGINIA," Virginia Cavalcade 25:1 (Summer 1975), 14-27.

B-2849 Gray, Ralph D. and Gerald E. Hartdagen, "A GLIMPSE OF BALTIMORE SOCIETY IN 1827," Maryland Historical Magazine 69:3 (Fall 1974), 256-270.

B-2850 Green, Paul, "WITCHCRAFT IN CHAPEL HILL," North Carolina Folklore 4:1 (July 1956), 6-10.

B-2851 Griffin, J. David, "BENEVOLENCE AND MALEVOLENCE IN CONFEDERATE SAVANNAH," Georgia Historical Quarterly 49:4 (December 1965), 347-368.

B-2852 Griffith, Benjamin W., "CSARDAS AT SALT SPRINGS: SOUTHERN CULTURE IN 1888," Georgia Review 26:1 (Spring 1972), 53-59.

B-2853 Grinstead, Mary Jo and Sandra Schaltz, "POVERTY, RACE AND CULTURE IN A RURAL ARKANSAS COMMUNITY," Human Organization 35:1 (Spring 1976), 33-44.

B-2854 Guethlein, Carol, "WOMEN IN LOUISVILLE: MOVING TOWARD EQUAL RIGHTS," Filson Club History Quarterly 55:2 (April 1981), 151-178.

B-2855 Halle, A. Arthur, "HISTORY OF THE MEMPHIS COTTON CARNIVAL," West Tennessee Historical Society Papers No. 6 (1952), 34-63.

B-2856 Halpert, Violetta Maloney, "PLACE NAME STORIES ABOUT WEST KENTUCKY TOWNS," Kentucky Folklore Record 7:3 (July-September 1961), 103-116.

B-2857 Harlan, William H., "COMMUNITY ADAPTATION TO THE PRESENCE OF AGED PERSONS: ST. PETERSBURG, FLORIDA," American Journal of Sociology 59:4 (January 1954), 332-339.

B-2858 Harling, Kristie, "THE GRUNCH: AN EXAMPLE OF NEW ORLEANS TEEN-AGE FOLKLORE," Louisiana Folklore Miscellaney 3:2 (April 1971), 15-20.

B-2859 Harris, Robert L. Jr., "CHARLESTON'S FREE AFRO-AMERICAN ELITE: THE BROWN FELLOWSHIP SOCIETY AND THE HUMANE BROTHERHOOD," South Carolina Historical Magazine 82:4 (October 1981), 289-310.

B-2860 Harris, William, "WORK AND THE FAMILY IN BLACK ATLANTA, 1880," Journal of Social History 9:3 (Spring 1976), 319-330.

B-2861 Harris, William D., "IMPROVING FIRE SERVICE PRODUCTIVITY WITH REDUCED RESOURCES: HOW OAK RIDGE, TENNESSEE, DID IT," Urban Resources 2:1 (Fall 1984), 27-33.

B-2862 Harris, William M. and Diana Gray, "BLACK COMMUNITY DEVELOPMENT IN CHARLOTTESVILLE, VIRGINIA," Urban League Review 6:2 (Summer 1982), 25-33.

B-2863 Harwell, Richard Barksdale, "CIVILIAN LIFE IN ATLANTA IN 1862," Atlanta Historical Bulletin 7:29 (October 1944), 212-219.

B-2864 Hauptmann, O. H., "SPANISH FOLKLORE FROM TAMPA, FLORIDA (NO. VII) WITCHCRAFT," Southern Folklore Quarterly 3:4 (December 1939), 197-200.

B-2865 Hauptmann, O. H., "SPANISH FOLKLORE FROM TAMPA, FLORIDA (NO. IV) SUPERSTITIONS," Southern Folklore Quarterly 2:1 (March 1938), 11-30.

B-2866 Hawk, Alan, "DELAWARE BIRDMEN: THE WILMINGTON AERO CLUB AND THE DELTAPLANE, 1910-1912," Delaware History 21:2 (Fall-Winter 1984), 117-126.

B-2867 Hay, Robert, "FREEDOM'S JUBILEE: THE FOURTH OF JULY IN CHARLES-TON, 1826-1876," West Virginia History 26:4 (July 1965), 207-219.

B-2868 Hazelip, Pauline, "TALES OF GLASGOW JUNCTION," Kentucky Folklore Record 6:1 (January–March 1960), 1–8.

B-2869 Herring, Harriet L., "SOCIAL DEVELOPMENT IN THE MILL VILLAGE: A CHALLENGE TO THE MILL WELFARE WORKER," Social Forces 10:2 (December 1931), 264–271.

B-2870 Hesselbart, Susan, "A COMPARISON OF ATTITUDES TOWARD WOMEN AND ATTITUDES TOWARD BLACKS IN A SOUTHERN CITY," Sociological Symposium No. 17 (Fall 1976), 45–68.

B-2871 Hill, Mozell C., "THE ALL-NEGRO COMMUNITIES OF OKLAHOMA: THE NATURAL HISTORY OF A SOCIAL MOVEMENT," Journal of Negro History 31:3 (July 1946), 254–268.

B-2872 Hines, Linda O. and Allen W. Jones, "A VOICE OF BLACK PROTEST: THE SAVANNAH MEN'S SUNDAY CLUB, 1905–1911," Phylon 35:2 (Summer 1974), 193–202.

B-2873 Holland, Reid, "THE CIVILIAN CONSERVATION CORPS IN THE CITY: TULSA AND OKLAHOMA CITY IN THE 1930s," Chronicles of Oklahoma 53:3 (Fall 1975), 367–375.

B-2874 Hopkins, Richard J., "STATUS, MOBILITY, AND THE DEMENSIONS OF CHANGE IN A SOUTHERN CITY: ATLANTA, 1870–1910," in Jackson, ed., Cities in American History New York: Alfred A. Knopf, 1972, 216–231.

B-2875 Howard, Perry H. and Joseph L. Brent III, "SOCIAL CHANGE, URBANIZATION, AND TYPES OF SOCIETY," Journal of Social Issues 22:1 (January 1966), 73–84.

B-2876 Huber, Leonard V., "REFLECTIONS ON THE COLORFUL CUSTOMS OF LATTER-DAY NEW ORLEANS CREOLES," Louisiana History 21:3 (Summer 1980), 223–235.

B-2877 Huffman, Frank J. Jr., "TOWN AND COUNTRY IN THE SOUTH, 1850–1880: A COMPARISON OF URBAN AND RURAL SOCIAL STRUCTURES," South Atlantic Quarterly 76:3 (Summer 1977), 366–381.

B-2878 Hull, Jacquelyn Dowd, Robert Korstad and James Lelondis, "COTTON MILL PEOPLE: WORK, COMMUNITY, AND PROTEST IN THE TEXTILE SOUTH, 1880–1940," American Historical Review 91:2 (April 1986), 245–286.

B-2879 Hurst, Harold W., "THE MARYLAND GENTRY IN OLD GEORGE TOWN: 1783–1861," Maryland Historical Magazine 73:1 (Spring 1978), 1–12.

B-2880 Hutchenson, John D. Jr., "FIGHT, FLEE OR ACQUIESCE? RESPONSES TO URBAN DISCONTENT," Journal of Urban Affairs 4:3 (Summer 1982), 1–18.

B-2881 Hyland, Stanley and Bridget Ciarametaro, "DEVELOPING NEW MODES OF COMMUNICATION IN LOW-TO-MODERATE INCOME NEIGHBORHOODS: ISSUES IN ENERGY CONSERVATION AND FOLK BELIEFS," Journal of Voluntary Action Review 13:4 (October–December), 31–41.

B-2882 Inglesby, Charlotte, "SAVANNAH AND THE CAROLINA PLANTERS," Georgia Historical Quarterly 62:1 (Spring 1978), 24–31.

B-2883 "JACKSBORO GHOST TALES FROM THE WPA ARCHIVES," Tennessee Folklore Society Bulletin 50:2 (Summer 1984), 68–74.

B-2884 Jackson, Charles O. and Charles W. Johnson, "THE SUMMER OF '44: OBSERVATIONS ON LIFE IN THE OAK RIDGE COMMUNITY," Tennessee Historical Quarterly 32:3 (Fall 1973), 233–248.

B-2885 Jackson, Pauline P., "LIFE AND SOCIETY IN SAPULPA," Chronicles of Oklahoma 43:3 (Autumn 1965), 297–318.

B-2886 Jacob, Kathryn A., "THE WOMEN'S LOT IN BALTIMORE TOWN: 1729-97," Maryland Historical Magazine 71:3 (Fall 1976), 283-295.

B-2887 Jacques, Jeffrey M., "SELF-ESTEEM AMONG SOUTHEASTERN BLACK-AMERICAN COUPLES," Journal of Black Studies 7:1 (September 1976), 11-28.

B-2888 Jaret, Charles and Paul Dressel, "SUBURBAN SYMBOLIC COMMUNITY: A TEST OF AN URBAN MODEL," South Atlantic Urban Studies 5 (1981), 212-245.

B-2889 Johnson, David M., "DISNEY WORLD AS STRUCTURE AND SYMBOL: RE-CREATION OF THE AMERICAN EXPERIENCE," Journal of Popular Culture 15:1 (Summer 1981), 157-165.

B-2890 Johnson, Michael P., "PLANTER AND PATRIARCHY: CHARLESTON, 1800-1860," Journal of Southern History 46:1 (February 1980), 45-72.

B-2891 Johnson, Michael P. and James L. Roark, "'A MIDDLE GROUND': FREE MULATTOES AND THE FRIENDLY MORALIST SOCIETY OF ANTEBELLUM CHARLESTON," Southern Studies 21:3 (Fall 1982), 246-265.

B-2892 Jones, James Boyd Jr., "MOSE THE BOWERY B'HOY AND THE NASHVILLE VOLUNTEER FIRE DEPARTMENT," Tennessee Historical Quarterly 40:2 (September 1981), 170-181.

B-2893 Jones, James Boyd Jr., "THE SOCIAL ASPECTS OF THE MEMPHIS VOLUNTEER FIRE DEPARTMENT," West Tennessee Historical Society Papers No. 37 (1983), 62-73.

B-2894 Kaplan, Ben, "A STUDY OF JEWISH COMMUNITY LIFE IN THREE LOUISIANA TOWNS," Southwestern Louisiana Journal 2:1 (January 1958), 50-64.

B-2895 Katz, Elaine S., "VARIATION AS RELATIVE PERCEPTION IN THE LEGEND OF HAZEL FARRIS," Mid-South Folklore 6:3 (Winter 1978), 55-64.

B-2896 Kaufman, Harold F., "SOCIAL CLASS IN THE URBAN SOUTH," in R. Vance, ed., The Urban South, (1954), 165-179.

B-2897 Kay, Donald, "BRITISH INFLUENCE ON KENTUCKY MUNICIPAL PLACE NAMES, Kentucky Folklore Record 20:1 (January-March 1974), 9-13.

B-2898 Kelly, John R., "LIVING REALITIES IN RESTON," Sociological Symposium No. 13 (Spring 1975), 93-97.

B-2899 Kemp, Kathryn W., "JEAN AND KATE GORDON: NEW ORLEANS SOCIAL REFORMERS, 1898-1933," Louisiana History 24:4 (Fall 1983), 389-401.

B-2900 Kenan, Sarah, "GHOSTS AT SEVEN HEARTHS," North Carolina Folklore 19:3 (May 1971), 123-130.

B-2901 Kennedy, Renwick C., "BLACK BELT ARISTOCRATS," Social Forces 13:1 (October 1934), 80-85.

B-2902 Kilh, Kim R., "PORT TOBACCO, MARYLAND," Virginia Social Science Journal 13:2 (November 1978), 7-15.

B-2903 King, Arden R., "STATUS PERSONALITY CHANGE IN NORTHERN NEGROES IN SOUTHERN UNITED STATES," Social Forces 26:2 (December 1947), 153-166.

B-2904 King, Charles E., "THE PROCESS OF SOCIAL STRATIFICATION AMONG AN URBAN SOUTHERN MINORITY POPULATION," Social Forces 31:4 (May 1953), 352-355.

B-2905 King, Doris Elizabeth, "THE FIRST-CLASS HOTEL AND THE AGE OF THE COMMON MAN," Journal of Southern History 23:2 (May 1957), 173-188.

B-2906 Kipp, Samuel M. III, "OLD NOTABLES AND NEWCOMERS: THE ECONOMIC AND POLITICAL ELITE OF GREENSBORO, NORTH CAROLINA, 1880-1920," Journal of Southern History 43:3 (August 1977), 373-394.

B-2907 Koch, Adrienne, "TWO CHARLESTONIANS IN PURSUIT OF TRUTH: THE BRIMBE BROTHERS," South Carolina Historical Magazine 69:3 (July 1968), 159-170.

B-2908 Korte, Charles, "INDIVIDUAL AND SOCIAL DETERMINANTS OF SOCIAL SUPPORT IN AN URBAN SETTING," Journal of the Community Development Society 15:2 (1984), 31-46.

B-2909 Krech, Shepard III, "BLACK FAMILY ORGANIZATION IN THE NINETEENTH CENTURY: AN ETHNOLOGICAL PERSPECTIVE," Journal of Interdisciplinary History 12:3 (Winter 1982), 429-452.

B-2910 Lancaster, Kent, "GREEN MOUNT: THE INTRODUCITON OF THE RURAL CEMETARY INTO BALTIMORE," Maryland Historical Magazine 74:1 (March 1979), 62-79.

B-2911 Lancaster, Kent, "ON THE DRAMA OF DYING IN EARLY NINETEENTH CEN-TURY BALTIMORE," Maryland Historical Magazine 81:1 (Summer 1986), 103-116.

B-2912 Lancaster, R. Kent, "OLD ST. PAUL'S CEMETARY, BALTIMORE," Maryland Historical Magazine 78:2 (Summer 1983), 129-142.

B-2913 Koch, Joan K., "MORTUARY BEHAVIOR PATTERNING IN FIRST SPANISH PERIOD AND BRITISH PERIOD ST. AUGUSTINE," Conference on Historic Site Archaeology, Papers (1977), 12 (1978), 286-304.

B-2914 Konrad, William Robinson, "THE DIMINISHING INFLUENCES OF GERMAN CULTURE IN NEW ORLEANS LIFE SINCE 1865," Louisiana Historical Quarterly 24:1 (January 1941), 127-167.

B-2915 Lawther, Dennis E., "ONCE IN A LIFETIME--WHEELING CELEBRATES THE UNITED STATES CENTENNIAL: 1876," West Virginia History 38:4 (July 1977), 304-311.

B-2916 Lebeau, James, "PROFILE OF A SOUTHERN JEWISH COMMUNITY: WAYCROSS, GEORGIA," American Jewish Historical Quarterly 55:4 (June 1969), 429-444.

B-3917 Lebsock, Suzanne, "FREE BLACK WOMEN AND THE QUESTION OF MATRI-ARCHY: PETERSBURG, VIRGINIA," Feminist Studies 8:2 (Summer 1982), 271-292.

B-2918 Lebsock, Suzanne, "'WE HAVE NOT LIVED FOR OURSELVES ALONE': WOMEN AND DOMESTICITY IN ANTEBELLUM PETERSBURG," Virginia Cavalcade 33:2 (Autumn 1983), 53-63.

B-2919 Lemmon, Sarah McCulloh, "ENTERTAINMENT IN RALEIGH IN 1890," North Carolina Historical Review 40:3 (Summer 1963), 321-387.

B-2920 Levy, B. H., "SAVANNAH'S OLD JEWISH CEMETARIES," Georgia Historical Quarterly 66:1 (Spring 1982), 1-20.

B-2921 Levy, Marion Abrahams, "SAVANNAH'S OLD JEWISH BURIAL GROUND," Georgia Historical Quarterly 34:4 (December 1950), 265-270.

B-2922 Lewis, Eulalie M., "TIFTON: LIFE IN A SMALL GEORGIA TOWN," Georgia Historical Quarterly 42:4 (December 1958), 427-439.

B-2923 Lewis, Hylan, "INNOVATIONS AND TRENDS IN THE CONTEMPORARY SOUTHERN NEGRO COMMUNITY," Journal of Social Issues 10:1 (1954), 19-27.

B-2924 Littleton, Tucker R., "LEGENDS FROM BEAUFORT, NORTH CAROLINA," North Carolina Folklore 12:1 (July 1959), 14-16.

B-2925 Luebke, Paul, "ACTIVISTS AND ASPHALT: A SUCCESSFUL ANTI-
EXPRESSWAY MOVEMENT IN A 'NEW SOUTH CITY,'" Human Organization
40:3 (Fall 1981), 256-263.

B-2926 Lupsha, Peter A. and William J. Siembieda, "THE POVERTY OF PUBLIC
SERVICES IN THE LAND OF PLENTY: AN ANALYSIS AND INTERPRETATION,"
in D. Perry, ed., The Rise of the Sunbelt Cities (1977), 169-190.

B-2927 McCain, John Walker Jr., "SOME SMALL-TOWN FOLK BELIEFS OF THE
CAROLINA PIEDMONT," Social Forces 12:3 (March 1933), 418-420.

B-2928 McCutcheon, Roger Philip, "LIBRARIES IN NEW ORLEANS, 1771-1833,"
Louisiana Historical Quarterly 20:1 (January 1937), 152-158.

B-2929 McDonald, Archie P., "JOHN BREWER, PHARMACIST, AND THE SOCIAL AND
ECONOMIC LIFE IN HAMMOND IN THE 1890's," Louisiana Studies 10:2
(Summer 1971), 77-84.

B-2930 McGhee, Jerrilynn, "GROWING UP IN LIGHTING," New South 21:4 (Fall
1966), 51-70.

B-2931 McGovern, James R., "'SPORTING LIFE ON THE LINE': PROSTITUTION IN
PROGRESSIVE ERA PENSACOLA," Florida Historical Quarterly 54:2
(October 1975), 131-144.

B-2932 McKenney, Carlton Norris, "THE RICHMOND FREE STREET FAIRS AND CAR-
NIVALS," Virginia Cavalcade 32:2 (Autumn 1982), 86-95.

B-2933 Mallalieu, William Cassell, "ORIGINS OF LOUISVILLE CULTURE,"
Filson Club History Quarterly 38:2 (April 1964), 149-156.

B-2934 Mallalieu, William Cassell, "ORIGINS OF THE UNIVERSITY OF LOUIS-
VILLE," Filson Club History Quarterly 12:1 (January 1938), 24-41.

B-2935 Margavio, Anthony and Jerome Salomone, "NOTES ON THE AMERICANI-
ZATION OF THE ITALIAN FAMILY IN NEW ORLEANS," Perspectives on
Ethnicity in New Orleans, (1981), 76-83.

B-2936 Marshall, Elizabeth, "THE ATLANTA PEACE JUBILEE OF 1898," Georgia
Historical Quarterly 50:3 (September 1966), 276-282.

B-2937 Martin, James, "A WEARYING EXISTENCE: TEXAS REFUGEES IN NEW
ORLEANS," Louisiana History 28:4 (Fall 1987), 343-356.

B-2938 Martin, Joan M., "MARDI GRAS INDIANS, PAST AND PRESENT," Louisiana
Folklore Miscellaney 3:3 (1973 for 1972), 51-55.

B-2939 Matherly, Walter J., "THE EMERGENCE OF THE METROPOLITAN COMMUNITY
IN THE SOUTH," Social Forces 14:3 (March 1936), 311-325.

B-2940 Matthews, Linda M., "THE DILEMMA OF NEGRO LEADERSHIP IN THE NEW
SOUTH: THE CASE OF THE NEGRO YOUNG PEOPLE'S CONGRESS OF 1902,"
South Atlantic Quarterly 73:1 (Winter 1974), 130-144.

B-2941 Meaders, Margaret Inman, "LONG-AGO CHRISTMAS IN DAHLONEGA,"
Georgia Review 18:4 (Winter 1964), 385-391.

B-2942 Miller, Michael V., "CHICANO COMMUNITY CONTROL IN SOUTH TEXAS:
PROBLEMS AND PROSPECTS," Journal of Ethnic Studies 3:3 (Fall
1975), 70-89.

B-2943 Miller, Michael V. and James D. Preston, "VERTICAL TIES AND THE
REDISTRIBUTION OF POWER IN CRYSTAL CITY," Social Science Quarterly
53:4 (March 1973), 772-784.

B-2944 Miller, William D., "RURAL IDEALS IN MEMPHIS LIFE AT THE TURN OF
THE CENTURY," West Tennessee Historical Society Papers No. 4
(1950), 41-49.

B-2945 Mills, Gary B., "ALEXANDRIA, LOUISIANA: A 'CONFEDERATE CITY' AT WAR WITH ITSELF," Red River Valley Historical Review 5:1 (Winter 1980), 23-36.

B-2946 Miner, Alison, "THE MARDI GRAS INDIANS," Louisiana Folklore Miscellaney 3:3 (1973 for 1972), 48-50.

B-2947 Mishler, Craig, "THE TEXAS CHILI COOK-OFF: AN EMERGENT FOODWAY FESTIVAL," Journal of Popular Culture 17:3 (Winter 1983), 22-31.

B-2948 Mobley, Joe A., "IN THE SHADOW OF WHITE SOCIETY: PRINCEVILLE, A BLACK TOWN IN NORTH CAROLINA, 1865-1915," North Carolina Historical Review 63:3 (July 1986), 340-384.

B-2949 Mookherjee, Harsha N., George M. Hess, and Wayne Hogan, "BLACK LEADERSHIP STRUCTURE IN A SOUTHERN TOWN," Human Organization 39:3 (Fall 1980), 267-271.

B-2950 Moore, John Hammond, "THE NEGRO AND PROHIBITION IN ATLANTA, 1885-1887," South Atlantic Quarterly 69:1 (Winter 1970), 38-57.

B-2951 Moore, Mrs. John Trotwood, "THE TENNESSEE STATE LIBRARY IN THE CAPITAL," Tennessee Historical Quarterly 12:1 (March 1953), 3-22.

B-2952 Moore, Kent, "ATLANTA'S PRIDE AND PROBLEM," Atlanta Historical Bulletin 20:2 (Summer 1976), 19-41.

B-2953 Morgan, Philip D., "BLACK LIFE IN EIGHTEENTH-CENTURY CHARLESTON," Perspectives in American History v. 1 (1984), 187-232.

B-2954 Mormino, Gary R. and George E. Pozzetta, "THE CRADLE OF MUTUAL AID: IMMIGRANT COOPERATIVE SOCIETIES IN YBOR CITY," Tampa Bay History 7:2 (Fall-Winter 1985), 36-58.

B-2955 Muir, Andrew Forest, "INTELLECTUAL CLIMATE OF HOUSTON DURING THE PERIOD OF THE REPUBLIC," Southwestern Historical Quarterly 62:3 (January 1959), 312-321.

B-2956 Muller, Edward K. and Paul A. Groves, "THE CHANGING LOCATION OF THE CLOTHING INDUSTRY: A LOOK TO THE SOCIAL GEOGRAPHY OF BALTIMORE IN THE NINETEENTH CENTURY," Maryland Historical Magazine 71:3 (Fall 1976), 403-420.

B-2957 Murphy, Owen F. Jr., "7TH WARD IMAGES," Perspectives on Ethnicity in New Orleans, (1981), 38-45.

B-2958 Nash, Jeff, "BUS RIDING: COMMUNITY ON WHEELS," Urban Life 4:1 (April 1975), 99-124.

B-2959 Neary, Margaret R., "SOME ASPECTS OF NEGRO SOCIAL LIFE IN RICHMOND, VIRGINIA, 1865-1880," Maryland Historian 1:2 (Fall 1970), 105-120.

B-2960 Neff, Merry, "FINDING EARLY AMERICA IN NORTH CAROLINA," Early American Life 14:1 (February 1983), 44-47, 58-59.

B-2961 Nelson, Harold, "PUTTING TOGETHER A COALITION IN HOUSTON," New South 25:4 (Fall 1970), 46-53.

B-2962 Nelson, Michael, "THE WASHINGTON COMMUNITY REVISITED," Virginia Quarterly Review 61:2 (Spring 1985), 189-210.

B-2963 Newman, Dale, "WORK AND COMMUNITY LIFE IN A SOUTHERN TEXTILE TOWN," Labor History 19:2 (Spring 1978), 204-225.

B-2964 O'Brien, John T., "FACTORY, CHURCH, AND COMMUNITY: BLACKS IN ANTEBELLUM RICHMOND," Journal of Southern History 44:4 (November 1978), 509-536.

B-2965 Orser, W. Edward, "THE MAKING OF A BALTIMORE ROWHOUSE COMMUNITY: THE EDMONDSON AVENUE AREA, 1915-1945," Maryland Historical Magazine 80:3 (Fall 1985), 203-227.

B-2966 Orthner, Dennis, "PATTERNS OF LEISURE AND MARITAL INTERACTION," Journal of Leisure Research 8:2 (1976), 98-111.

B-2967 Painter, George, "JAMES SMITHSON'S BEQUEST TO THE UNITED STATES," American History Illustrated 17:1 (March 1982), 30-35.

B-2968 Parenton, Vernon J. and Roland I. Pellegrin, "SOCIAL STRUCTURE AND THE LEADERSHIP FACTOR IN A NEGRO COMMUNITY IN SOUTH LOUISIANA," Phylon 17:1 (1956), 74-78.

B-2969 Parko, Joseph E. Jr., "RE-DISCOVERY OF COMMUNITY NEIGHBORHOOD MOVEMENT IN ATLANTA," Journal of the Community Development Society 6:1 (Spring 1975), 46-50.

B-2970 Patterson, Daniel W., "WITCHCRAFT IN DURHAM," North Carolina Folklore 11:2 (December 1958), 32-33.

B-2971 Pease, Jane H. and William H. Pease, "SOCIAL STRUCTURE AND THE POTENTIAL FOR URBAN CHANGE: BOSTON AND CHARLESTON IN THE 1830s," Journal of Urban History 8:2 (February 1982), 171-196.

B-2972 Peden, Creighton, "BEYOND THE FOLKLORE OF INDIVIDUALISM," Richmond County History 5:2 (Summer 1973), 76-85.

B-2973 Peters, Martha Ann, "THE ST. CHARLES HOTEL: NEW ORLEANS SOCIAL CENTER, 1837-1860," Louisiana History 1:1 (Winter 1960), 191-211.

B-2974 Petrof, John V., "THE EFFECT OF STUDENT BOYCOTTS UPON THE PURCHASING HABITS OF NEGRO FAMILIES IN ATLANTA, GEORGIA," Phylon 24:3 (1963), 266-270.

B-2975 Phifer, Elizabeth Flory and Dencil R. Taylor, "CHARMICHAEL IN TALLAHASSEE," Southern Speech Journal 33:2 (Winter 1967), 88-92.

B-2976 Phillips, W. M. Jr., "THE BOYCOTT: A NEGRO COMMUNITY IN CONFLICT," Phylon 22:1 (1961), 24-30.

B-2977 Pinsky, Mark, "ASSIMILATED IN MILLTOWN," Present Tense 5:3 (1978), 35-39.

B-2978 "PORTFOLIO: THE SMITHSONIAN TODAY," American History Illustrated 17:1 (March 1982), 36-40.

B-2979 Prior, G. T., "CHARLESTON PASTIME AND CULTURE IN THE NULLIFICATION DECADE," Proceedings of the South Carolina Historical Association 10 (1940), 36-44.

B-2980 Quinney, Valerie, "CHILDHOOD IN A SOUTHERN MILL VILLAGE," International Journal of Oral History 3 (1982), 167-192.

B-2981 Radford, John, "THE CHARLESTON PLANTERS IN 1860," South Carolina Historical Magazine 77:4 (October 1976), 227-235.

B-2982 Radford, John P., "DELICATE SPACE: RACE AND RESIDENCE IN CHARLESTON, SOUTH CAROLINA, 1860-1880," West Georgia College Studies in the Social Sciences 16 (June 1977).

B-2983 Raines, Leonora, "ATLANTA'S DREAM OF FAIR WOMEN," Atlanta Historical Bulletin 9:35 (October 1951), 26-38.

B-2984 Ramirez, Manuel D., "ITALIAN FOLKLORE FROM TAMPA, FLORIDA: INTRODUCTION," Southern Folklore Quarterly 5:2 (June 1941), 101-106.

B-2985 Ramirez, Manuel D., "ITALIAN FOLKLORE FROM TAMPA, FLORIDA, SERIES NO. 11: PROVERBS," Southern Folklore Quarterly 13:3 (June 1949), 121-132.

B-2986 Rasico, Philip D., "THE SPANISH AND MINORCAN LINGUISTIC HERITAGE OF ST. AUGUSTINE, FLORIDA," El Escribano 20 (1983), 1-25.

B-2987 Reiff, Janice, Michael R. Dahlen, and Daniel Scott Smith, "RURAL PUSH AND URBAN PULL: WORK AND FAMILY EXPERIENCES OF OLDER BLACK WOMEN IN SOUTHERN CITIES, 1880-1900," Journal of Social History 16:4 (Summer 1983), 39-48.

B-2988 Reisman, Leonard, "SOCIAL DEVELOPMENT AND THE AMERICAN SOUTH," Journal of Social Issues 22:1 (January 1966), 101-116.

B-2989 Reitzes, Donald C., "DOWNTOWN ORIENTATIONS: AN URBAN IDENTIFICA-TION APPROACH," Journal of Urban Affairs 7:2 (Spring 1985), 29-46.

B-2990 Reitzes, Donald C., "URBAN IMAGES: A SOCIAL PSYCHOLOGICAL AP-PROACH," Sociological Inquiry 53:2-3 (Spring 1983), 314-332.

B-2991 Rennecke, George F., "THE NEW ORLEANS TWELFTH NIGHT CAKE," Louisiana Folklore Miscellaney 2:2 (April 1965), 45-54.

B-2992 Rennick, Robert M., "THE TRAGEDY OF THE ALLEN FAMILY OF HILLS-VILLE VIRGINIA," North Carolina Folklore 12:2 (December 1959), 1-17.

B-2993 Rights, Douglas LeTeel, "SALEM IN THE WAR BETWEEN THE STATES," North Carolina Historical Review 27:3 (July 1950), 277-288.

B-2994 Riley, Edward M., "YORKTOWN DURING THE REVOLUTION, I," Virginia Magazine of History and Biography 57:1 (January 1949), 22-43.

B-2995 Riley, Edward M., "YORKTOWN DURING THE REVOLUTION, II," Virginia Magazine of History and Biography 57:2 (April 1949), 176-188.

B-2996 Rives, Ralph Hardee, "THE JAMESTOWN CELEBRATION OF 1857," Virginia Magazine of History and Biography 66:3 (July 1958), 259-271.

B-2997 Robbins, Peggy, "WHEN THE YANKEES OCCUPIED MEMPHIS," Civil War Times Illustrated 16:9 (January 1978), 26-43.

B-2998 Robbins, Peggy, "WHERE CARNIVAL IS KING," American History Illus-trated 13:10 (February 1979), 4-11.

B-2999 Robinson, Jerry W. Jr. and James D. Preston, "CLOSE AND CASTLE IN 'OLD CITY,'" Phylon 31:3 (Fall 1970), 244-255.

B-3000 Rosebery, Marguerite, "THE GALT HOUSE," Filson Club History Quarterly 35:4 (October 1961), 353-356.

B-3001 Rostenberg, Leona, "MY GRANDMOTHER'S ACCOUNT BOOK: NEW ORLEANS 1873-1875," Manuscripts 36:1 (Winter 1984), 17-30.

B-3002 Rouse, Parke Jr., "YORKTOWN CENTENIAL CELEBRATION: 1881 EXTRAVA-GANZA," Virginia Cavalcade 24:2 (Autumn 1974), 80-87.

B-3003 Rubin, Morton, "LOCALISM AND RELATED VALUES AMONG NEGROES IN A SOUTHERN RURAL COMMUNITY," Social Forces 36:3 (March 1958), 263-267.

B-3004 Sapper, Neil, "BLACK CULTURE IN URBAN TEXAS: A LONE STAR RENAIS-SANCE," Red River Valley Historical Review 6:2 (Spring 1981), 56-77.

B-3005 Scarpaci, J. Vincenza, "LOUIS H. LEVIN OF BALTIMORE: A PIONEER IN CULTURAL PLURALISM," Maryland Historical Magazine 77:2 (June 1982), 183-192.

B-3006 Scarpaci, Jean, "A TALE OF SELECTIVE ACCOMMODATION: SICILIANS AND NATIVE WHITES IN LOUISIANA," Journal of Ethnic Studies 5:3 (Fall 1977), 37-50.

B-3007 Schinhan, Jan Philip, "SPANISH FOLKLORE FROM TAMPA, FLORIDA: (NO. VI) FOLKSONGS," Southern Folklore Quarterly 3:2 (September 1939), 129-163.

B-3008 Schmier, Louis, "A JEWISH PEDDLER AND HIS BLACK CUSTOMERS LOOK AT EACH OTHER," American Jewish History 73:1 (September 1983), 39-55.

B-3009 Schmier, Louis, "JEWS AND GENTILES IN A SOUTH GEORGIA TOWN," in Proctor, S., ed., Jews of the South, 1-16.

B-3010 Schmier, Louis, "NOTES AND DOCUMENTS ON THE 1862 EXPULSION OF JEWS FROM THOMASVILLE, GEORGIA," American Jewish Archives 32:1 (April 1980), 9-22.

B-3011 Schnare, Leo F. and Phillip C. Enenson,, "SEGREGATION IN SOUTHERN CITIES," American Journal of Sociology 72:1 (July 1966), 58-67.

B-3012 Schweninger, Loren, "THE FREE-SLAVE PHENOMENON: JAMES P. THOMAS AND THE BLACK COMMUNITY IN ANTE-BELLUM NASHVILLE," Civil War History 22:4 (December 1976), 293-307.

B-3013 Scott, Robert W., "THE GOVERNOR FOWLE GHOST AT THE EXECUTIVE MANSION," North Carolina Folklore 18:3 (November 1970), 115-116.

B-3014 Seals, Alvin M. and Jiri Kolaja, "A STUDY OF NEGRO VOLUNTARY ORGANIZATIONS IN LEXINGTON, KENTUCKY," Phylon 25:1 (Spring 1965), 27-32.

B-3015 Shankman, Arnold, "A TEMPLE IS BOMBED--ATLANTA, 1958," Atlanta Historical Journal 23:2 (November 1971), 125-153.

B-3016 Sheldon, Marianne Buroff, "BLACK-WHITE RELATIONS IN RICHMOND, VIRGINIA, 1782-1820," Journal of Southern History 45:1 (February 1979), 27-46.

B-3017 Sheldon, Marianne Buroff, "SOCIAL STRATIFICATION IN RICHMOND, VIRGINIA, 1798-1817," South Atlantic Urban Studies 4 (1980), 177-197.

B-3018 Sherman, Stuart C., "THE LIBRARY COMPANY OF BALTIMORE, 1795-1854," Maryland Historical Magazine 39:1 (March 1944), 6-24.

B-3019 Silverman, Irwin and Marnia E. Shaw, "EFFECTS OF SUDDEN MASS DESEGREGATION ON INTERRACIAL INTERACTION AND ATTITUDES IN ONE SOUTHERN CITY," Journal of Social Issues 29:4 (1973), 133-142.

B-3020 Sisk, Glenn N., "SOCIAL LIFE IN THE ALABAMA BLACK BELT, 1875-1917," Alabama Review 8:2 (April 1955), 83-103.

B-3021 Smart, George K., "THE CITY IN SOUTHERN LIFE: INTRODUCTION," Mississippi Quarterly 10:2 (Spring 1957), 51-52.

B-3022 Smith, John M. Jr., "THE RIOT OF MAY 1970: A HUMANISTIC PERSPEC-TIVE," Richmond County History 7:2 (Summer 1975), 103-116.

B-3023 Snell, William R., "FIERY CROSSES IN THE ROARING TWENTIES: ACTIVITIES OF THE REVISED KLAN IN ALABAMA, 1915-1930," Alabama Review 23:4 (October 1970), 256-276.

B-3024 Snell, William R., "MASKED MEN IN THE MAGIC CITY: ACTIVITIES OF THE REVISED KLAN IN BIRMINGHAM, 1916-1940," Alabama Historical Quarterly 34:3-4 (Fall-Winter 1972), 206-227.

B-3025 Sobel, Machal, "'THEY CAN NEVER BOTH PROSPER TOGETHER': BLACK AND
        WHITE BAPTISTS IN NASHVILLE, TENNESSEE," Tennessee Historical
        Quarterly 38:3 (Fall 1979), 296-307.

B-3026 Soileau, Jeanne Pitre, "JEAN SOT IN ST. MARTINVILLE," Louisiana
        Folklore Miscellaney 3:3 (1973 for 1972), 43-47.

B-3027 Sokolow, Jayme A. and Mary Ann Lamanna, "WOMEN AND UTOPIA: THE
        WOMEN'S COMMONWEALTH OF BELTON, TEXAS," Southwestern Historical
        Quarterly 87:4 (April 1984), 371-392.

B-3028 SoRelle, James J., "THE 'WACO HORROR': THE LYNCHING OF JESSE
        WASHINGTON," Southwestern Historical Quarterly 86:4 (April 1983),
        517-536.

B-3029 South, Stanley, "A CEREMONIAL CENTER AT THE CHARLES TOWN SITE,"
        Notebook 2:6-7 (June-July 1970), 3-5.

B-3030 South, Stanley, "CONTEMPORARY PATTERNS OF MATERIAL CULTURE OR
        HANSEL AND GRETEL IN THE MODERN WORLD: FOLLOWING THE TRAIL OF
        PULL TABS TO 'THE PAUSE THAT REFRESHES,'" Conference on Historic
        Site Archaeology, Papers (1977), 12 (1978), 87-106.

B-3031 Spain, Daphne, "RACE RELATIONS AND RESIDENTIAL SEGREGATION IN NEW
        ORLEANS: TWO CENTURIES OF PARADOX," Annals of the American
        Academy of Political and Social Science 441 (January 1979), 82-
        96.

B-3032 Spencer, Margaret Beale, "RISK AND RESILIENCE: HOW BLACK CHILDREN
        COPE WITH STRESS," Social Science 71:1 (Spring 1986), 22-26.

B-3033 Stanislow, Gail, "DOMESTIC FEMINISM IN WILMINGTON: THE NEW CEN-
        TURY CLUB, 1889-1917," Delaware History 22:3 (Spring-Summer 1987),
        158-185.

B-3034 Stephens, Lester P., "THE MERMAID HOAX: INDICATIONS OF SCIENTIFIC
        THOUGHT IN CHARLESTON, SOUTH CAROLINA, IN THE 1948s," Proceedings
        of the South Carolina Historical Association 53 (1983), 45-55.

B-3035 Stopp, G. Harry Jr., "THE DISTRIBUTION OF MASSAGE PARLORS IN THE
        NATION'S CAPITAL," Journal of Popular Culture 11:4 (Spring 1978),
        989-997.

B-3036 Sullivan, Larry E., "THE READING HABITS OF THE NINETEENTH CENTURY
        BALTIMORE BOURGEOISIE: A CROSS-CULTURAL ANALYSIS," Journal of
        Library History 16:2 (Summer 1981), 227-240.

B-3037 Swift, Lucie, "'WHO'D A THOUGHT IT' AND OTHER PADUCAH PLACE
        NAMES," Kentucky Folklore Record 7:3 (July-September 1961), 117-
        119.

B-3038 Tata, Robert J., Sharyn Van Horn and David Lee, "DEFENSIBLE SPACE
        IN A HOUSING PROJECT: A CASE STUDY FROM A SOUTH FLORIDA GHETTO,"
        Professional Geographer 27:3 (August 1975), 297-303.

B-3039 Taub, Diane E., "PUBLIC SOCIABILITY OF COLLEGE-AGED MALE HOMO-
        SEXUALS: THE GAY BAR AND THE CRUISE BLOCK," Sociological Spectrum
        1:3-4 (July-December 1982), 291-306.

B-3040 Taylor, John M., "WILLARD'S OF WASHINGTON [D. C.]: AN INSIDE VIEW
        OF A GREAT HOTEL," American History Illustrated 14:6 (October
        1979), 10-15.

B-3041 Taylor, Robert T., "THE JAMESTOWN TERCENTENNIAL EXPOSITION OF
        1907," Virginia Magazine of History and Biography 65:2 (April
        1957), 169-208.

B-3042 TePaske, John J., "FUNERALS AND FIESTAS IN EARLY EIGHTEENTH-
       CENTURY ST. AUGUSTINE," Florida Historical Quarterly 44:1 (July
       1965), 97-104.

B-3043 Terranova, Joachim, "SOME ARBRESHE FOLKLORE," Louisiana Folklore
       Miscellaney 3:2 (April 1971), 39-43.
B-3044 Thomason, Philip, "THE MEN'S QUARTER OF DOWNTOWN NASHVILLE,"
       Tennessee Historical Quarterly 41:1 (Spring 1982), 48-66.

B-3045 Thornbery, Jerry, "NORTHERNERS AND THE ATLANTA FREEDMEN, 1865-69,"
       Prologue 6:4 (1974), 236-251.

B-3046 Thornton, J. Mills III, "CHALLENGE AND RESPONSE IN THE MONTGOMERY
       BUS BOYCOTT OF 1955-1956," Alabama Review 33:3 (July 1980), 163-
       235.

B-3047 Touchstone, Blake, "VOODOO IN NEW ORLEANS," Louisiana History
       13:34 (Fall 1972), 371-386.

B-3048 Tregle, Joseph G. Jr., "EARLY NEW ORLEANS SOCIETY: A REAPPRAIS-
       AL," Journal of Southern History 18:1 (February 1952), 20-36.

B-3049 Unger, Donald G. and Abraham Wandersman, "NEIGHBORING AND ITS ROLE
       IN BLOCK ORGANIZATIONS: AN EXPLORATORY REPORT," American Journal
       of Community Psychology 11:3 (June 1983), 291-300.

B-3050 Unger, Donald G. and Abraham Wandersman, "NEIGHBORING IN AN URBAN
       ENVIRONMENT," American Journal of Community Psychology 10:5
       (October 1982), 493-510.

B-3051 Vandal, Gilles, "THE ORIGIN OF THE NEW ORLEANS RIOT OF 1866,
       REVISITED," Louisiana History 22:2 (Spring 1981), 135-166.

B-3052 Vicchio, Stephen J., "BALTIMORE'S BURIAL PRACTICES, MORTUARY ART
       AND NOTIONS OF GRIEF AND BEREAVEMENT, 1780-1900," Maryland His-
       torical Magazine 81:2 (Summer 1986), 134-148.

B-3053 Vyhnanek, Louis, "'MUGGLES,' 'INCHY,' AND 'MUD': ILLEGAL DRUGS IN
       NEW ORLEANS DURING THE 1920s," Louisiana History 22:3 (Summer
       1981), 253-280.

B-3054 Wachenheim, Maxine T., "THE STYLISTIC DEVELOPMENT OF TOMBS IN THE
       CEMETARIES OF NEW ORLEANS," Southwester Louisiana Journal 3:4
       (Fall 1956), 258-281.

B-3055 Wade, Richard C., "THE VESEY PLOT: A RECONSIDERATION," Journal of
       Southern History 30:2 (May 1964), 143-161.

B-3056 Walser, Richard, "JEMMY CRITUS, FOLK HUMORIST OF CHARLOTTE," North
       Carolina Folklore 18:2 (May 1970), 95-100.

B-3057 Waring, Martha Gallaudet, "THE GAY NINETIES IN SAVANNAH: NOTES ON
       THE 'FIN DE SECLE' AND ITS WAYS," Georgia Historical Quarterly
       18:4 (December 1934), 364-375.

B-3058 Watts, An DeWitt and Patricia Klobus Edwards, "RECRUITING AND
       RETAINING HUMAN SERVICE VOLUNTEERS: AN EMPIRICAL ANALYSIS,"
       Journal of Voluntary Action Review 12:3 (July-September 1983),
       9-22.

B-3059 Webber, Irving L., "THE ORGANIZED SOCIAL LIFE OF THE RETIRED: TWO
       FLORIDA COMMUNITIES," American Journal of Sociology 59:4 (January
       1954), 340-346.

B-3060 Weegar, W. A., "VOLUNTEERISM WORKS IN HURST, TEXAS," Small Town
       13:5 (March-April 1983), 4-7.

B-3061 Welford, T. Win, "THE CIRCUIT CHAUTAUQUA IN PONCHATOULA, LOUISI-
ANA: A SHORT ROMANCE," Louisiana History 26:3 (Summer 1985), 291-
300.

B-3062 Wells, Carol, "AGNES MORRIS," Louisiana History 27:3 (Summer
1986), 261-272.

B-3063 Western, John, "SOCIAL GROUPS AND ACTIVITY PATTERNS IN HOUMA,
LOUISIANA," Geographical Review 63:3 (July 1973), 301-321.

B-3064 White, Harry, "FOLKLORE OF THE NASHVILLE FIRE DEPARTMENT,"
Tennessee Folklore Society Bulletin 41:4 (December 1975), 153-169.

B-3065 Whiting, B. J., "WILLIAM JOHNSON OF NATCHEZ: FREE NEGRO,"
Southern Folklore Quarterly 16:2 (June 1952), 145.

B-3066 Wiedman, Dennis and J. Bryan Page, "DRUG USE ON THE STREET AND ON
THE BEACH: CUBANS AND ANGLOS IN MIAMI, FLORIDA," Urban Anthropology 11:2 (Summer 1982), 213-236.

B-3067 Wiggins, Sarah Woodfolk, "THE 'PIG IRON' KELLEY RIOT IN MOBILE,
MAY 14, 1867," Alabama Review 23:1 (January 1970), 45-55.

B-3068 Williams, Brett, "THE SOUTH IN THE CITY," Journal of Popular
Culture 16:3 (Winter 1982), 30-41.

B-3069 Williamson, Joel, "THE ONENESS OF SOUTHERN LIFE," South Atlantic
Urban Studies 1 (1977), 78-92.

B-3070 Wilson, Charles R., "THE SOUTHERN FUNERAL DIRECTOR: MANAGING
DEATH IN THE NEW SOUTH," Georgia Historical Quarterly 67:1 (Spring
1983), 49-69.

B-3071 Wilson, Samuel Jr., "THE HOWARD MEMORIAL LIBRARY AND MEMORIAL
HALL," Louisiana History 28:3 (Summer 1987), 229-244.

B-3072 Winberry, John J., "'LEST WE FORGET': THE CONFEDERATE MONUMENT
AND THE SOUTHERN TOWNSCAPE," Southeastern Geographer 23:2
(November 1983), 107-121.

B-3073 Wood, Minter, "LIFE IN NEW ORLEANS IN THE SPANISH PERIOD,"
Louisiana Historical Quarterly 22:3 (July 1939), 642-709.

B-3074 Yanich, Beverly, "URBAN COMMUNITY PARTNERSHIPS: SYMBOLS THAT
SUCCEED AND STRATEGIES THAT FAIL," Journal of Voluntary Action
Review 13:1 (January-March 1984), 23-37.

B-3075 Yeatman, Joseph Lawrence, "LITERARY CULTURE AND THE ROLE OF
LIBRARIES IN DEMOCRATIC AMERICA, 1815-1840," Journal of Library
History 20:4 (Fall 1985), 345-367.

B-3076 Zanden, James W. Vander, "DESEGREGATION AND SOCIAL STRAINS IN THE
SOUTH," Journal of Social Issues 15:4 (1959), 53-60.

B-3077 Zehner, Robert B., "PARTICIPATION IN PERSPECTIVE: A LOOK AT NEW
TOWN INVOLVEMENT," Sociological Symposium 12: (Fall 1974), 65-82.

Literature

B-3078 Adams, Holmes, "WRITERS OF GREENVILLE, MISSISSIPPI, 1915-1950,"
Journal of Mississippi History 32:3 (August 1970), 229-244.

B-3079 Aiken, Charles S., "THE TRANSFORMATION OF JAMES AGEE'S KNOXVILLE,"
Geographical Review 73:2 (April 1983), 150-165.

B-3080 "AMERICAN LITERATURE AND CHARLESTON SOCIETY," Southern Quarterly
Review 7:14 (April 1853), 380-421.

B-3081 Arner, Robert D., "THE ROMANCE OF ROANOKE: VIRGINIA DARE AND THE
LOST COLONY IN AMERICAN LITERATURE," Southern Literary Journal
10:2 (Spring 1978), 5-45.

B-3082 Bolditch, W. Kenneth, "THE LAST FRONTIER OF BOHEMIA: TENNESSEE
WILLIAMS IN NEW ORLEANS, 1938-1983," Southern Quarterly 23:2
(Winter 1985), 1-37.

B-3083 Bottner, Charles H., "THE RED BOOK, 1819-1821, A SATIRE ON BALTI-
MORE SOCIETY," Maryland Historical Magazine 51:3 (September 1956),
188-211.

B-3084 Bonner, Thomas Jr., "CHRISTIANITY AND CATHOLICISM IN THE FICTION
OF KATE CHOPIN," Southern Quarterly 20:2 (Winter 1982), 118-125.

B-3085 Briebart, Solomon, "PENINA MOISE, SOUTHERN JEWISH POETESS," in
Samuel Proctor, ed., Jews of the South (1984), 31-44.

B-3086 Brooks, Carlton P., "THE MAGNOLIA: A LITERARY MAGAZINE FOR THE
CONFEDERACY," Virginia Cavalcade 32:4 (Spring 1983), 150-157.

B-3087 Buckler, Patricia, "MARK TWAIN 'ON THE ROCKS' AT LOUISVILLE,"
Filson Club History Quarterly 60:2 (April 1986), 257-263.

B-3088 Bullock, Penelope L., "PROFILE OF A PERIODICAL: THE VOICE OF THE
NEGRO," Atlanta Historical Journal 21:1 (Spring 1977), 95-114.

B-3089 Calhoun, Richard J., "SOUTHERN LITERARY MAGAZINES, III: THE ANTE-
BELLUM LITERARY TWILIGHT: RUSSELL'S MAGAZINE," Southern Literary
Journal 3:1 (Fall 1970), 89-110.

B-3090 Carroll, Karen C., "STERLING, CAMPBELL, AND ALBRIGHT: TEXTBOOK
PUBLISHERS," North Carolina Historical Review 63:2 (April 1986),
169-198.

B-3091 Coleman, Elizabeth Dabney, "WILLIAM PARKS," Virginia Cavalcade 4:3
(Winter 1954), 38-42.

B-3092 "A COLONIAL CULTURAL ECONOMY," Southern Literary Journal 15:2
(Spring 1983), 3-6.

B-3093 "EATONVILLE'S ZORA NEALE HURSTON: A PROFILE," Black Review 2
(1972), 11-?

B-3094 Ellis, Mary Louise, "IMPROBABLE VISITOR: OSCAR WILDE IN ALABAMA,
1882," Alabama Review 39:4 (October 1986), 243-260.

B-3095 Fanning, Michael, "NEW ORLEANS AND SHERWOOD ANDERSON," Southern
Studies 17:2 (Summer 1978), 199-208.

B-3096 Geffen, David, "THE LITERARY LEGACY OF RABBI TOBIAS GEFFEN IN
ATLANTA," Atlanta Historical Journal 23:3 (Fall 1979), 85-90.

B-3097 Goudeau, John M., "BOOKSELLERS AND PRINTERS IN NEW ORLEANS, 1764-
1885," Journal of Library History 5:1 (January 1970), 5-19.

B-3098 Green, J. Lee, "ANNE SPENCER OF LYNCHBURG," Virginia Cavalcade
27:4 (Spring 1978), 178-185.

B-3099 Griffin, Max L., "A BIBLIOGRAPHY OF NEW ORLEANS MAGAZINES,"
Louisiana Historical Quarterly 18:3 (July 1935), 491-556.

B-3100 Groover, Robert L., "MARGARET MITCHELL, THE LADY FROM ATLANTA,"
Georgia Historical Quarterly 52:1 (March 1968), 53-69.

B-3101 Guilds, John C., "SOUTHERN LITERARY MAGAZINES, V: SIMMS AS EDITOR
AND PROPHET: THE FLOWERING AND EARLY DEATH OF THE SOUTHERN
MAGNOLIA," Southern Literary Journal 9:2 (Spring 1972), 69-92.

B-3102 Guillaume, Alfred J. Jr., "LOVE, DEATH, AND FAITH IN THE NEW ORLEANS POETS OF COLOR," Southern Quarterly 20:2 (Winter 1982), 126–144.

B-3103 Gulliver, Harold S., "THACKERAY IN GEORGIA," Georgia Review 1:1 (Spring 1947), 35–43.

B-3104 Hahn, H. George, "TWILIGHT REFLECTIONS: THE HOLD OF VICTORIAN BALTIMORE ON LIZETTE WOODWORTH REESE AND H. L. MECKEN," Maryland Historian 11:1 (Spring 1980), 29–38.

B-3105 Hobson, Fred, "GERALD W. JOHNSON: THE SOUTHERNER AS REALIST," Virginia Quarterly Review 58:1 (Winter 1982), 1–25.

B-3106 Hogan, Patrick G., "FAULKNER'S NEW ORLEANS IDIOM: A STYLE IN EMBRYO," Louisiana Studies 5:3 (Fall 1966), 171–181.

B-3107 Holditch, W. Kenneth, "LUST AND LANGUOR IN THE BIG EASY: THE LITERARY MYSTIQUE OF NEW ORLEANS," Perspectives on Ethnicity in New Orleans, (1981), 4–15.

B-3108 Howell, Elmo, "THE GREENVILLE WRITERS AND THE MISSISSIPPI COUNTRY PEOPLE," Louisiana Studies 8:4 (Winter 1969), 348–360.

B-3109 Howell, Elmo, "WILLIAM FAULKNER'S NEW ORLEANS," Louisiana History 7:3 (Summer 1966), 229–240.

B-3110 Hunter, Anna C., "HARRY HERNEY, SAVANNAH NOVELIST," Georgia Review 8:2 (Summer 1954), 151–155.

B-3111 Inge, M. Thomas, "RICHMOND VIRGINIA, AND SOUTHERN WRITING: INTRO-DUCTION," Mississippi Quarterly 27:4 (Fall 1974), 371–373.

B-3112 Jacobs, Robert D., "SOUTHERN LITERARY MAGAZINES, I: CAMPAIGN FOR A SOUTHERN LITERATURE: THE SOUTHERN LITERARY MESSENGER," Southern Literary Journal 2:1 (Fall 1969), 66–98.

B-3113 Johnson, Kenneth R., "THE EARLY LIBRARY MOVEMENTS IN ALABAMA," Journal of Library History 6:2 (April 1971), 120–132.

B-3114 Kendall, John Smith, "THE LAST DAYS OF CHARLES GAYARRE," Louisiana Historical Quarterly 15:3 (July 1932), 359–375.

B-3115 Kendall, John Smith, "A NEW ORLEANS LADY OF LETTERS," Louisiana Historical Quarterly 19:2 (April 1936), 436–465.

B-3116 Kett, Joseph F. and Patricia A. McClung, "BOOK CULTURE IN POST-REVOLUTIONARY VIRGINIA," Proceedings of the American Antequarian Society 94:pt. 1 (April 1984), 97–147.

B-3117 Kilson, Marion, "THE TRANSFORMATION OF EATONVILLE'S ETHNOGRAPHER," Phylon 33:2 (Summer 1972), 112–119.

B-3118 Kinney, Arthur F., "IN SEARCH OF FLANNERY O'CONNER," Virginia Quarterly Review 59:2 (Spring 1983), 271–288.

B-3119 Lefler, Hugh T., "PROMOTIONAL LITERATURE OF THE SOUTHERN COLO-NIES," Journal of Southern History 33:1 (February 1967), 3–25.

B-3120 McCoy, George W., "ASHEVILLE AND THOMAS WOLFE," North Carolina Historical Review 30:2 (April 1953), 200–217.

B-3121 McCutcheon, Roger Philip, "BOOKS AND BOOK SELLERS IN NEW ORLEANS, 1730–1830," Louisiana Historical Quarterly 20:3 (July 1937), 606–617.

B-3122 MacDonald, Edgar, "CABELL'S RICHMOND TRIAL," Southern Literary Journal 3:1 (Fall 1970), 47–71.

B-3123 MacDonald, Edgar, "GLASGOW, CABELL, AND RICHMOND," Mississippi
Quarterly 27:4 (Fall 1974), 393-414.

B-3124 Moore, Rayburn S., "SOUTHERN LITERARY MAGAZINES, II: 'A DIS-
TINCTIVELY SOUTHERN MAGAZINE': THE SOUTHERN BIVOUAC," Southern
Literary Journal 2:2 (Spring 1970), 51-67.

B-3125 Moss, William M., "VINDICATOR OF SOUTHERN INTELLECT AND INSTITU-
TIONS: THE SOUTHERN QUARTERLY REVIEW," Southern Literary Journal
13:1 (Fall 1980), 72-108.

B-3126 Mugleston, William F., "THE PERILS OF SOUTHERN PUBLISHING: A
HISTORY OF UNCLE REMUS'S MAGAZINE," Journalism Quarterly 52:3
(Autumn 1975), 515-521, 608.

B-3127 Nuhrah, Arthur G., "JOHN McDONOGH: MAN OF MANY FACETS," Louisiana
Historical Quarterly 33:1 (January 1950), 5-144.

B-3128 O'Brian, Matthew C., "WILLIAM FAULKNER AND THE CIVIL WAR IN
OXFORD, MISSISSIPPI," Journal of Mississippi History 35:2 (May
1973), 167-174.

B-3129 Parks, Edd Winfield, "LITERATURE AND SOUTHERN CITIES," Mississippi
Quarterly 10:2 (Spring 1957), 53-58.

B-3130 Pridgen, Allen, "GOING HOME: JAMES DICKEY'S SOUTH," Studies in
Popular Culture 1:1 (Winter 1977), 16-25.

B-3131 Putzel, Max, "FAULKNER'S MEMPHIS STORIES," Virginia Quarterly
Review 59:2 (Spring 1983), 254-270.

B-3132 Reinecke, George, "ALFRED MERCIER, FRENCH NOVELIST OF NEW
ORLEANS," Southern Quarterly 20:2 (Winter 1982), 145-177.

B-3133 Reitt, Barbara B., "WOMEN AUTHORS OF ATLANTA: A SELECTION OF
REPRESENTATIVE WORKS WITH AN ANALYTIC COMMENTARY," Atlanta
Historical Journal 23:4 (Winter 1979-80), 55-70.

B-3134 Ribblett, David L., "FROM CROSS CREEK TO RICHMOND: MARJORIE
KINNAN RAWLINGS RESEARCHES ELLEN CELARGON," Virginia Cavalcade
36:1 (Summer 1986), 4-15.

B-3135 Richmond, Mrs. Henry L., "RALPH WALDO EMERSON IN FLORIDA AND
EMERSON'S LITTLE JOURNAL AT ST. AUGUSTINE," Florida Historical
Quarterly 18:2 (October 1939), 75-93.

B-3136 Riley, Sam G., "SPECIALIZED MAGAZINES OF THE SOUTH," Journalism
Quarterly 59:3 (Autumn 1982), 447-450, 455.

B-3137 Roach, Abby Meguire, "THE AUTHORS' CLUB OF LOUISVILLE," Filson
Club History Quarterly 31:1 (January 1957), 28-37.

B-3138 Roach, Abby Meguire, "LOUISVILLE POETS OF EARLY NINETEEN-HUNDRED,"
Filson Club History Quarterly 33:1 (January 1959), 26-31.

B-3139 Rubin, Louis D. Jr., "SOUTHERN LITERATURE: A PIEDMONT ART,"
Mississippi Quarterly 23:1 (Winter 1969-70), 1-18.

B-3140 Rubin, Louis D. Jr., "THE SOUTHERN MUSE: TWO POETRY SOCIETIES,"
American Quarterly 13:3 (Fall 1961), 365-375.

B-3141 Scott, Elizabeth S., "'IN FAME, NOT SPECIE': THE REVIEWER, RICH-
MOND'S OASIS IN 'THE SAHARA OF THE BOZART,'" Virginia Cavalcade
27:3 (Winter 1978), 128-143.

B-3142 Shillengsburg, Miriam J., "ATLANTA'S HARD-BOILED NOVELIST,"
Atlanta Historical Journal 25:4 (Winter 1981), 67-80.

B-3143 Stearns, Bertha-Monica, "SOUTHERN MAGAZINES FOR LADIES (1819-1860)," South Atlantic Quarterly 31 (January 1932), 70-87.

B-3144 Stern, Madeleine B., "JOHN RUSSELL: 'LORD JOHN' OF CHARLESTON," North Carolina Historical Review 26:3 (July 1949), 286-299.

B-3145 Stewart, David Marshall, "WILLIAM T. BERRY AND HIS FABULOUS BOOK-STORE: NASHVILLE'S LITERARY EMPORIUM WITHOUT PARALLEL," Tennessee Historical Quarterly 37:1 (Spring 1978), 36-48.

B-3146 Tomlinson, David, "SOUTHERN LITERARY MAGAZINES, VI: SIMM'S MONTHLY MAGAZINE: THE SOUTHERN AND WESTERN MONTHLY MAGAZINE AND REVIEW," Southern Literary Journal 8:1 (Fall 1975), 95-125.

B-3147 Tucker, Edward L., "'A RASH AND PERILOUS ENTERPRISE': THE SOUTHERN LITERARY MESSENGER AND THE MEN WHO MADE IT," Virginia Cavalcade 21:1 (Summer 1971), 14-21.

B-3148 Tucker, Edward L., "SOUTHERN LITERARY MAGAZINES, VII; TWO YOUNG BROTHERS AND THEIR ORION," Southern Literary Journal 11:1 (Fall 1978), 64-80.

B-3149 Watkins, Floyd C., "THOMAS WOLFE AND ASHEVILLE AGAIN AND AGAIN AND AGAIN," Southern Literary Journal 10:1 (Fall 1977), 31-55.

B-3150 Weddell, Alexander W., "SAMUEL MORDECAI, CHRONICLER OF RICHMOND, 1786-1865," Virginia Magazine of History and Biography 53:4 (October 1945), 265-287.

B-3151 Welsh, John R., "SOUTHERN LITERARY MAGAZINES, IV: AN EARLY PIONEER: LEGARE'S SOUTHERN REVIEW," Southern Literary Journal 3:2 (Spring 1971), 79-97.

B-3152 Williams, Benjamin B., "NINETEENTH CENTURY MONTGOMERY AUTHORS," Alabama Historical Quarterly 39:2 (Summer 1975), 136-145.

B-3153 Wilson, Janice Crabtree, "THE GENERAL MAGAZINE AND IMPARTIAL REVIEW: A SOUTHERN MAGAZINE IN THE EIGHTEENTH CENTURY," Southern Literary Journal 11:2 (Spring 1979), 66-77.

B-3154 Baron, John H., "MUSIC IN NEW ORLEANS, 1718-1792," American Music 5:3 (Fall 1987), 282-290.

Music

B-3155 Bastin, Bruce, "FROM THE MEDICINE SHOW TO THE STAGE: SOME IN-FLUENCES UPON THE DEVELOPMENT OF A BLUES TRADITION IN THE SOUTHEASTERN UNITED STATES," American Music 2:1 (Spring 1984), 29-42.

B-3156 Blaustein, Richard, "WOPI--THE PIONEER VOICE OF THE APPALACHIANS," Journal of Country Music 6:3 (Fall 1975), 122-129.

B-3157 Brown, Robert L., "CLASSICAL INFLUENCES ON JAZZ," Journal of Jazz Studies 3:2 (1976), 19-35.

B-3158 Cavin, Susan, "MISSING WOMEN: ON THE VOODOO TRAIL TO JAZZ," Journal of Jazz Studies 3:1 (1975), 4-27.

B-3159 Chance, Elbert, "THE GREAT DAYS OF WILMINGTON'S GRAND OPERA HOUSE," Delaware History 8:2 (September 1958), 185-199.

B-3160 Christian, Garna L., "IT BEATS PICKING COTTON: THE ORIGINS OF HOUSTON COUNTRY MUSIC," Red River Valley Historical Review 7:3 (Summer 1982), 37-50.

B-3161 Cohen, Blanche Klasmer, "BENJAMIN KLASMER'S CONTRIBUTION TO
BALTIMORE'S MUSICAL HISTORY," Maryland Historical Magazine 72:2
(Summer 1977), 272-276.

B-3162 Crawford, Portia Naomi, "A STUDY OF NEGRO FOLK SONGS FROM GREENS-
BORO, NORTH CAROLINA AND SURROUNDING TOWNS," North Carolina Folklore 16:2 (October 1968), 67-139.

B-3163 Crews, E. Katherine, "EARLY MUSICAL ACTIVITIES IN KNOXVILLE,
TENNESSEE, 1791-1861," East Tennessee Historical Society's
Publications No. 32 (1960), 3-17.

B-3164 Crews, E. Katherine, "THE GOLDEN AGE OF MUSIC IN KNOXVILLE,
TENNESSEE, 1891-1910," East Tennessee Historical Society's
Publications No. 37 (1965), 49-76.

B-3165 Crews, E. Katherine, "MUSICAL ACTIVITIES IN KNOXVILLE, TENNESSEE,
1861-1891," East Tennessee Historical Society's Publications No.
34 (1962), 58-85.

B-3166 Curtis, James R. and Richard F. Rose, "'THE MIAMI SOUND': A
CONTEMPORARY LATIN FORM OF PLACE-SPECIFIED MUSIC," Journal of
Cultural Geography 4:1 (Fall-Winter 1983), 110-118.

B-3167 Davis, Ronald L., "EARLY JAZZ: ANOTHER LOOK (1)," Southwest
Review 58:1 (Winter 1978), 1-13.

B-3168 Davis, Ronald L., "EARLY JAZZ: ANOTHER LOOK (2)," Southwest
Review 58:2 (Spring 1978), 144-154.

B-3169 Drimmer, Melvin, "JOPKIN'S TREEMONISHA IN ATLANTA," Phylon 34:2
(June 1973), 197-202.

B-3170 Edwall, Harry R., "THE GOLDEN ERA OF MINSTRELS IN MEMPHIS—A
RECONSTRUCTION," West Tennessee Historical Society Papers No. 9
(1955), 29-47.

B-3171 Edwall, Harry R., "SOME FAMOUS MUSICIANS ON THE MEMPHIS CONCERT
STAGE PRIOR TO 1860," West Tennessee Historical Society Papers No.
5 (1951), 90-105.

B-3172 Frangiamore, Catherine Lynn and Pam Durban, "'NOT JUST WHISTLIN'
DIXIE': ATLANTA'S MUSIC 1837-1977," Atlanta Historical Bulletin
21:2 (Summer 1977), 15-36.

B-3173 French, Warren, "BLUE NOTE: WHERE IS OUR DIXIELAND EPIC,"
Southern Quarterly 23:1 (Fall 1984), 32-39.

B-3174 Gant, Alice M., "THE MUSICIANS IN NASHVILLE," Journal of Country
Music 3:2 (Summer 1972), 24-44.

B-3175 Gillespie, John, "CHARLES GROBE, THE BARD OF WILMINGTON," Delaware
History 21:1 (Spring-Summer 1984), 22-30.

B-3176 Goertzen, Chris and Alan Jabbour, "GEORGE P. KNAUFF'S VIRGINIA
REELS AND FIDDLING IN THE ANTEHBELLUM SOUTH," American Music 5:2
(Summer 1987), 121-144.

B-3177 Goodey, Brian R., "NEW ORLEANS TO LONDON: TWENTY YEARS OF THE NEW
ORLEANS JAZZ REVIVAL IN BRITAIN," Journal of Popular Culture 2:2
(Fall 1968), 173-194.

B-3178 Gusher, Lawrence, "A PRELIMINARY CHRONOLOGY OF THE EARLY CAREER OF
FRED 'JELLY ROLL' MORTON," American Music 3:4 (Winter 1985), 389-
428.

B-3179 Gwinn, Erna Ottl, "THE LIEDERKRANZ IN LOUISVILLE, 1848-1877,"
Filson Club History Quarterly 49:3 (July 1975), 276-290.

B-3180 Gwinn, Erna Ottl, "THE LIEDERKRANZ IN LOUISVILLE, 1877-1959," Filson Club History Quarterly 55:1 (January 1981), 40-59.

B-3181 Hale, Tony, "GRASSROOTS BLUEGRASS IN MEMPHIS: THE LUCY OPRY," Tennessee Folklore Society Bulletin 49:2 (Summer 1983), 51-64.

B-3182 Hambrick, Kieth S., "THE SWEDISH NIGHTINGALE IN NEW ORLEANS: JENNY LIND'S VISIT OF 1851," Louisiana History 22:4 (Fall 1981), 387-418.

B-3183 Hayse, Joseph M., "LEXINGTON'S EARLY AMATURE ACTORS," Register of the Kentucky Historical Society 76:4 (October 1978), 167-184.

B-3184 Head, Faye E., "THE BIRTH AND DEATH OF THE TULANE AND THE CRESCENT TWIN THEATRES OF NEW ORLEANS, LOUISIANA," Louisiana Studies 15:3 (Fall 1976), 294-202.

B-3185 Holditch, W. Kenneth, "THE SINGING HEART: A STUDY OF THE LIFE AND WORK OF PEARL RIVERS," Southern Quarterly 20:2 (Winter 1982), 87-117.

B-3186 Kendall, John Smith, "THE FRIEND OF CHOPIN, AND SOME OTHER NEW ORLEANS MUSICAL CELEBRITIES," Louisiana Historical Quarterly 31:4 (October 1948), 856-876.

B-3187 Kendall, John Smith, "NEW ORLEANS MUSICIANS OF LONG AGO," Louisiana Historical Quarterly 31:1 (January 1948), 130-149.

B-3188 Kendall, John Smith, "NEW ORLEANS NEGRO MINSTRALS," Louisiana Historical Quarterly 30:1 (January 1947), 128-143.

B-3189 Kirkland, Edwin Capers and Mary Neal Kirkland, "POPULAR BALLADS RECORDED IN KNOXVILLE, TENN." Southern Folklore Quarterly 2:2 (June 1938), 65-80.

B-3190 Lipscomb, Mance and A. Glenn Myers, ed., Don Gardner, "OUT OF THE BOTTOMS AND INTO THE BIG CITY," Southern Exposure 8:2 (Summer 1980), 4-11.

B-3191 Lornell, Kip, "EARLY COUNTRY MUSIC AND THE MASS MEDIA IN ROANOKE, VIRGINIA," American Music 5:4 (Winter 1987), 403-416.

B-3192 McCorkle, Donald M., "THE COLLEGIUM MUSICUM SALEM: ITS MUSIC, MUSICIANS, AND IMPORTANCE," North Carolina Historical Review 33:4 (October 1956), 483-498.

B-3193 MacCurdy, Raymond R. and Daniel D. Stanley, "JUDAEO-SPANISH BALLADS FROM ATLANTA, GEORGIA," Southern Folklore Quarterly 15:4 (December 1951), 221-235.

B-3194 Mason, Wilton, "THE MUSIC OF THE WALDENSIANS IN VALDESE, NORTH CAROLINA," North Carolina Folklore 13:1 (July 1960), 1-5.

B-3195 "NASHVILLE'S MONEY MACHINE," South Business 7:5 (May 1980), 40-49.

B-3196 Newberger, Eli H., "THE DEVELOPMENT OF NEW ORLEANS AND STRIDE PIANO STYLES," Journal of Jazz Studies 4:2 (1977), 43-71.

B-3197 Orr, N. Lee, "ALFREDO BARILI: ATLANTA MUSICIAN, 1880-1935," American Music 2:1 (Spring 1984), 43-60.

B-3198 Peterson, Richard A. and Paul Di Maggio, "THE EARLY OPRY: ITS HILLBILLY IMAGE IN FACT AND FANCY," Journal of Country Music 4:2 (Summer 1973), 39-51.

B-3199 Prophit, Willie, "THE CRESCENT CITY'S CHARISMATIC CELEBRITH: LOUI MOREAU GOTTSCHALK'S NEW ORLEANS CONCERTS, SPRING 1853," Louisiana History 12:3 (Summer 1971), 243-254.

B-3200 Rainer, Olivia, "THE EARLY HISTORY OF MUSIC OF TROY, ALABAMA," Alabama Historical Quarterly 24:1 (Spring 1962), 68-96.

B-3201 Raines, Leonora, "ATLANTA KNEW GOOD MUSIC," Atlanta Historical Bulletin 7:29 (October 1944), 184-195.

B-3202 Reagon, Bernice, "LADY STREET SINGER," Southern Exposure 2:1 (Spring-Summer 1974), 38-41.

B-3203 Reddick, L. D., "PERSONS AND PLACES: DIZZY GILLESPIE IN ATLANTA," Phylon 10:1 (1949), 44-49.

B-3204 Richey, David, "THE PHILADELPHIA COMPANY PERFORMS IN BALTIMORE," Maryland Historical Magazine 71:1 (Spring 1976), 80-85.

B-3205 Rinne, Henry Q., "A SHORT HISTORY OF THE ALPHONSO TRENT ORCHES- TRA," Arkansas Historical Quarterly 45:3 (Autumn 1986), 228-249.

B-3206 Rose, Kenneth, "A NASHVILLE MUSICAL DECADE, 1830-1840," Tennessee Historical Quarterly 2:3 (September 1943), 216-231.

B-3207 Rulfs, Donald J., "THE ERA OF THE OPERA HOUSE IN PIEDMONT NORTH CAROLINA," North Carolina Historical Review 35:3 (July 1958), 328- 346.

B-3208 Rumble, John W., "THE EMERGENCE OF NASHVILLE AS A RECORDING CENTER: LOGBOOKS FROM THE CASTLE STUDIO, 1952-1953," Journal of Country Music 7:3 (December 1978), 22-41.

B-3209 Simpson, Joel, "NEW ORLEANS' NEW JAZZMEN," Horizon 25:6 (September 1982), 34-40.

B-3210 Stolee, Marilyn S., "THE FEDERAL MUSIC PROJECT IN MIAMI," Tequesta No. 30 (1970), 3-12.

B-3211 Sutro, Ottilie, "THE WEDNESDAY CLUB," Maryland Historical Magazine 38:1 (March 1943), 60-68.

B-3212 Tarshish, Allan, "THE CHARLESTON ORGAN CASE," American Jewish Historical Quarterly 54:4 (June 1965), 411-449.

B-3213 Tosches, Nick, "BEHOLD A SHAKING: JERRY LEE LEWIS, 1953-1956," Journal of Country Music 9:1 (1981), 4-11.

B-3214 Tosches, Nick, "HARDROCK GANTER: THE MYSTERIOUS PIG-IRON MAN," Journal of Country Music 10:1 (1985), 36-39.

B-3215 Wagner, John W., "SOME EARLY MUSICAL MOMENTS IN AUGUSTA," Georgia Historical Quarterly 56:4 (Winter 1972), 529-534.

B-3216 Wiley, Stephen R., "SONGS OF THE GASTONIA TEXTILE STRIKE OF 1929: MODELS OF AND FOR SOUTHERN WORKING-CLASS WOMAN'S MILITANCY," North Carolina Folklore Journal 30:2 (Fall-Winter 1982), 87-98.

B-3217 Wilhelmsen, Finn, "CREATIVITY IN THE SONGS OF THE MARDI GRAS INDIANS OF NEW ORLEANS, LOUISIANA," Louisiana Folklore Miscellaney 3:3 (1973 for 1972), 56-74.

B-3218 Wolf, Edward C., "TWO DIVERGENT TRADITIONS OF GERMAN-AMERICAN HYMNODY IN MARYLAND CIRCA 1800," American Music 3:3 (Fall 1985), 299-312.

B-3219 Wolf, Edward C., "WHEELING'S GERMAN SINGING SOCIETIES," West Virginia History 42:1 and 2 (Fall 1980-Winter 1981), 1-56.

B-3220 Wolfe, Charles K., "FRANK SMITH, ANDREW JENKINS AND EARLY COMMER- CIAL GOSPEL MUSIC," American Music 1:1 (Spring 1983), 49-59.

B-3221 Wolfe, Charles K., "HONKY-TONK STARTS HERE: THE JIM BECK DALLAS STUDIO," Journal of Country Music 11:1 (1986), 25-30.

B-3222 Wolfe, Charles K., "NASHVILLE AND COUNTRY MUSIC, 1926-1930: NOTES ON EARLY NASHVILLE MEDIA AND ITS RESPONSE TO OLD-TIME MUSIC," Journal of Country Music 4:1 (Spring 1973), 2-16.

B-3223 Yale, Andrew, "OUR PLACE WAS BEALE STREET," Southern Exposure 6:3 (Fall 1978), 26-38.

B-3224 Yerbury, Grace H., "CONCERT MUSIC IN NEW ORLEANS, 1718-1860," Louisiana Historical Quarterly 40:2 (April 1957), 95-109.

Politics and Government

B-3225 Abbott, Margery P., "THE ADMINISTRATION OF COMPREHENSIVE PLANNING AND ZONING: THE EXPERIENCE OF NORFOLK, VIRGINIA," Virginia Social Science Journal 12:2 (November 1977), 44-52.

B-3226 Akin, Edward N., "WHEN A MINORITY BECOMES THE MAJORITY: BLACKS IN JACKSONVILLE POLITICS, 1887-1907," Florida Historical Quarterly 53:2 (October 1974), 123-145.

B-3227 Alexander, Henry M., "THE ORGANIZATION OF ARKANSAS MUNICIPALI-TIES," Arkansas Historical Quarterly 1:1 (March 1942), 10-27.

B-3228 Ammon, Harry, "THE RICHMOND JUNTO, 1800-1824," Virginia Magazine of History and Biography 61:4 (October 1953), 395-418.

B-3229 Ardoin, Birthney, "A CONTENT ANALYSIS OF MISSISSIPPI DAILY NEWS-PAPER COVERAGE OF THE WALLER-EVERS POLITICAL CAMPAIGN," Southern Quarterly 11:3 (April 1973), 207-220.

B-3230 Arnold, Joseph L., "THE LAST OF THE GOOD OLD DAYS: POLITICS IN BALTIMORE, 1920-1950," Maryland Historical Magazine 71:3 (Fall 1976), 443-448.

B-3231 Arnold, Joseph L., "THE NEIGHBORHOOD AND CITY HALL: THE ORIGIN OF NEIGHBORHOOD ASSOCIATIONS IN BALTIMORE, 1880-1911," Journal of Urban History 6:1 (November 1979), 3-30.

B-3232 Arnold, Joseph L., "SUBURBAN GROWTH AND MUNICIPAL ANNEXATION IN BALTIMORE, 1745-1918," Maryland Historical Magazine 73:2 (Summer 1978), 109-128.

B-3233 Arrington, Theodore S., "PARTISAN CAMPAIGNS, BALLOTS AND VOTING PATTERNS: THE CASE OF CHARLOTTE," Urban Affairs Quarterly 14:2 (December 1978), 253-261.

B-3234 Atkins, Leah Rawls, "SENATOR JAMES A. SIMPSON AND BIRMINGHAM POLITICS OF THE 1930's: HIS FIGHT AGAINST THE SPOILSMEN AND THE PIE-MEN," Alabama Review 1:1 (January 1988), 3-29.

B-3235 Bacote, C. A., "THE NEGRO IN ATLANTA POLITICS," Phylon 16:4 (1955), 333-350.

B-3236 Bacote, Clarence, "WILLIAM FINCH, NEGRO COUNCILMAN AND POLITICAL ACTIVITIES IN ATLANTA DURING EARLY RECONSTRUCTION," Journal of Negro History 40:4 (October 1955), 341-364.

B-3237 "BALTIMORE," Black Enterprise 2:16 (November 1971), 40-48.

B-3238 Barnard, William D., "GEORGE HUDDLESTON, SR., AND THE POLITICAL TRADITION OF BIRMINGHAM," Alabama Review 36:4 (October 1983), 243-259.

B-3239 Bartley, N. V., "ATLANTA ELECTIONS AND GEORGIA POLITICAL TRENDS," New South 15:1 (Winter 1970), 22-30.

B-3240 Beach, Rex, "SPENCER ROANE AND THE RICHMOND JUNTO," William and Mary College Historical Magazine 22:1 (January 1942), 1-17.

B-3241 Berkeley, Edmund and Dorothy Smith Berkeley, "RICHMOND'S THREE-TIME MAYOR," Virginia Cavalcade 14:4 (Spring 1975), 178-183.

B-3242 Bettersworth, John K., "THE URBANE BOURBON," Mississippi Quarterly 10:2 (Spring 1957), 79-87.

B-3243 Biles, Roger, "ROBERT R. CHURCH, JR. OF MEMPHIS: BLACK REPUBLICAN LEADER IN THE AGE OF DEMOCRATIC ASCENDANCY, 1928-1940," Tennessee Historical Quarterly 42:4 (Winter 1983), 362-382.

B-3244 Bobbitt, Charles A., "HUEY P. LONG: THE MEMPHIS YEARS," West Tennessee Historical Society Papers No. 32 (1978), 133-139.

B-3245 Boggs, Doyle W., "CHARLESTON POLITICS, 1900-1930," Proceedings of the South Carolina Historical Association 49 (1979), 1-13.

B-3246 Breslaw, Elaine G., "WIT, WHIMSY, AND POLITICS: THE USES OF SATIRE BY THE TUESDAY CLUB OF ANNAPOLIS: 1744 TO 1756," William and Mary Quarterly 32:2 (April 1975), 295-306.

B-3247 Browder, Glen and Dennis S. Ippolito, "THE SUBURBAN PARTY ACTI-VIST: THE CASE OF SOUTHERN AMATEURS," Social Science Quarterly 53:1 (June 1972), 168-175.

B-3248 Brunn, Stanley D. and Gerald L. Ingalls, "THE EMERGENCE OF REPUB-LICANISM IN THE URBAN SOUTH," Southeastern Geographer 12:2 (November 1972), 133-144.

B-3249 Bullock, Charles S., "THE ELECTION OF BLACKS IN THE SOUTH: PRE-CONDITIONS AND CONSEQUENCES," American Journal of Political Science 19:4 (November 1975), 727-739.

B-3250 Bullock, Charles S. III, "RACIAL CROSSOVER VOTING AND THE ELECTION OF BLACK OFFICIALS," Journal of Politics 46:1 (February 1984), 238-251.

B-3251 Bullock, Charles S. III and Bruce A. Campbell, "RACIST OR RACIAL VOTING IN THE 1981 ATLANTA MUNICIPAL ELECTIONS," Urban Affairs Quarterly 20:2 (December 1984), 149-164.

B-3252 Burd, Gene, "THE SELLING OF THE SUNBELT: CIVIC BOOSTERISM IN THE MEDIA," in D. Perry, ed., The Rise of the Sunbelt Cities, (1977), 129-149.

B-3253 Burman, Stephen, "THE ILLUSION OF PROGRESS: RACE AND POLITICS IN ATLANTA, GEORGIA," Ethnic and Racial Studies, 2:4 (October 1979), 441-454.

B-3254 Burns, Francis P., "CHARLES M. WATERMAN, MAYOR OF NEW ORLEANS," Louisiana Historical Quarterly 7:3 (July 1924), 466-479,

B-3255 Burns, Francis P., "WHITE SUPREMACY IN THE SOUTH: THE BATTLE FOR CONSTITUTIONAL GOVERNMENT IN NEW ORLEANS, JULY 30, 1866," Louisiana Historical Quarterly 18:3 (July 1935), 581-616.

B-3256 Button, James, "SOUTHERN BLACK ELECTED OFFICIALS: IMPACT ON SOCIOECONOMIC CHANGE," Review of Black Political Economy 12:1 (Fall 1982), 29-46.

B-3257 Button, James and Richard Scher, "IMPACT OF THE CIVIL RIGHTS MOVEMENT: PERCEPTIONS OF BLACK MUNICIPAL SERVICES CHANGES," Social Science Quarterly 60:3 (December 1979), 497-510.

B-3258 Campbell, David and Joe R. Feagin, "BLACK POLITICS IN THE SOUTH: A DESCRIPTIVE ANALYSIS," Journal of Politics 37:1 (February 1975), 129-162.

B-3259 Cann, Marvin, "BERNET MAYBANK AND CHARLESTON POLITICS IN THE NEW DEAL ERA," Proceedings of the South Carolina Historical Association 40 (1970), 39-48.

B-3260 Capers, Gerald M. Jr., "CONFEDERATES AND YANKEES IN OCCUPIED NEW ORLEANS, 1862-1865," Journal of Southern History 30:4 (November 1964), 405-426.

B-3261 Carleton, Don E., "McCARTHYISM IN HOUSTON: THE GEORGE EBEY AFFAIR," Southwestern Historical Quarterly 80:2 (October 1976), 163-176.

B-3262 Carver, Joan, "RESPONSIVENESS AND CONSOLIDATION: A CASE STUDY," Urban Affairs Quarterly 9:2 (December 1973), 211-247.

B-3263 Cassimere, Raphael Jr., "POLARITY, POLITICS, AND RACE RELATIONS IN NEW ORLEANS," Perspectives on Ethnicity in New Orleans (1981), 56-60.

B-3264 Catlin, Robert A., "AN ANALYSIS OF THE COMMUNITY DEVELOPMENT BLOCK GRANT PROGRAM IN NINE FLORIDA CITIES 1975-1979," Urban and Social Change Review 14:1 (Winter 1981), 3-10.

B-3265 Chalker, Fussell M., "FITZGERALD: PLACE OF RECONCILIATION," Georgia Historical Quarterly 55:3 (Fall 1971), 397-405.

B-3266 Chester, William Wayne, "NEW JOHNSONVILLE, TENNESSEE: A POTENTIAL INDUSTRIAL AREA," Memorandum Folio, Southeastern Division, Association of American Geographers 18 (November 1966), 23-27.

B-3267 Chubbuck, James, Edwin Renwick and Jae E. Walker, "THE EMERGENCE OF COALITION POLITICS IN NEW ORLEANS," New South 26:1 (Winter 1971), 16-25.

B-3268 "CITY OF ROME EXPERIENCES SUCCESSFUL ANNEXATION PROGRAM," Urban Georgia 35:5 (June 1985), 15-20.

B-3269 Clark, John B., "FROM BUCKET BRIGADE TO STEAM FIRE ENGINE; FIRE FIGHTING IN OLD LOUISVILLE THROUGH 1865," Filson Club History Quarterly 27:2 (April 1953), 103-118.

B-3270 Clark, John B. Jr., "FIRE PROTECTION IN OLD KNOXVILLE," East Tennessee Historical Society's Publications No. 31 (1959), 32-42.

B-3271 Clotfelter, Charles, "MEMPHIS BUSINESS LEADERSHIP AND THE POLITICS OF FISCAL CRISIS," West Tennessee Historical Society Papers No. 27 (1973), 33-49.

B-3272 Cobb, James C., "COLONEL EFFINGHAM CRUSHES THE CRACKERS: POLITICAL REFORM IN POSTWAR AUGUSTA," South Atlantic Quarterly 78:4 (Autumn 1979), 507-519.

B-3273 Collins, William P., "RACE AND POLITICAL CLEAVAGE: TEN POSITIONS IN A LOCAL ELECTION," Journal of Black Studies 11:1 (September 1980), 121-126.

B-3274 Cooper, Weldon, "TRENDS IN MUNICIPAL GOVERNMENT IN THE SOUTH," Journal of Politics 10:1 (February 1948), 490-509.

B-3275 Corty, Floyd L. and William C. Havard, Jr., "RURAL-URBAN CONSOLIDATION: THE BATON ROUGE EXPERIMENT," Louisiana Studies 3:2 (Summer 1964), 196-209.

B-3276 Craig, John M., "REDBAITING, PACIFISM, AND FREE SPEECH: LUCIA AMES MEAD AND HER 1929 LECTURE TOUR IN ATLANTA AND THE SOUTHEAST," Georgia Historical Quarterly 71:4 (Winter 1987), 601-622.

B-3277 Crooks, James B., "POLITICS AND REFORM: THE DIMENSIONS OF BALTI-
       MORE PROGRESSIVISM," Maryland Historical Magazine 71:3 (Fall
       1976), 421-427.

B-3278 Crouch, Barry A., "SELF-DETERMINATION AND LOCAL BLACK LEADERS IN
       TEXAS," Phylon 39:4 (December 1978), 344-355.

B-3279 Cumming, Inez Parker, "THE EDENTON LADIES' TEA-PARTY," Georgia
       Review 8:4 (Winter 1954), 389-396.

B-3280 Dart, Henry P., ed., "FIRE PROTECTION IN NEW ORLEANS IN UNZAGA'S
       TIME, Louiana Historical Quarterly 4:2 (April 1921), 201-204.

B-3281 Daver, Manning J., "MULTI-MEMBER DISTRICTS IN DADE COUNTY: STUDY
       OF A PROBLEM AND A DELEGATION," Journal of Polotics 28:3 (August
       1966), 617-639.

B-3282 Davis, Abraham L., "AN ANALYSIS OF THE NOVEMBER 9, 1971 REFERENDUM
       VOTE ON RAPID TRANSIT IN FULTON COUNTY," Journal of Political
       Science 2:1 (Fall 1974), 1-20.

B-3283 Davis, Harold E., "HENRY GRADY, THE ATLANTA CONSTITUTION, AND THE
       POLITICS OF FARMING IN THE 1880's," Georgia Historical Quarterly
       71:4 (Winter 1987), 571-600.

B-3284 "DESPATCHES FROM THE UNITED STATES CONSULATE IN NEW ORLEANS, 1801-
       1803, I," American Historical Review 32:4 (July 1927), 801-824.

B-3285 Deusner, Charles E., "THE KNOW NOTHING RIOTS IN LOUISVILLE,"
       Register of the Kentucky Historical Society 61:2 (April 1963),
       122-147.

B-3286 deVerges, Mrs. Edwin X., "HONORABLE JOHN T. MONROE--CONFEDERATE
       MAYOR OF NEW ORLEANS," Louisiana Historical Quarterly 34:1 (Janu-
       ary 1951), 25-34.

B-3287 Dodd, Pauly M., "BLUEPRINT FOR AN ALL-AMERICAN CITY," Popular
       Government 46:4 (Spring 1981), 16-22.

B-3288 Donaldson, Gary A., "BRINGING WATER TO THE CRESCENT CITY:
       BENJAMIN LATROBE AND THE NEW ORLEANS WATERWORKS SYSTEM," Louisiana
       History 28:4 (Fall 1987), 381-396.

B-3289 Doyle, Elizabeth Joan, "NEW ORLEANS COURTS UNDER MILITARY OCCUPA-
       TION 1861-1865," Mid-America 42:3 (July 1960), 185-192.

B-3290 Doyle, Judith Kaaz, "MAURY MAVERICK AND RADICAL POLITICS IN SAN
       ANTONIO," Journal of Southern History, 53:2 (May 1987), 194-224.

B-3291 Ducker, Richard D., "OFF-STREET PARKING PROGRAMS IN NORTH CAROLINA
       MUNICIPALITIES," Popular Government 46:1 (Summer 1980), 39-42.

B-3292 Dunn, Larry W., "KNOXVILLE NEGRO VOTING AND THE ROOSEVELT REVOLU-
       TION, 1928-1936," East Tennessee Historical Society's Publications
       No. 43 (1971), 71-93.

B-3293 Durrill, Wayne K., "PRODUCING POVERTY: LOCAL GOVERNMENT AND ECO-
       NOMIC DEVELOPMENT IN A NEW SOUTH COUNTY, 1874-1884," Journal of
       American History 71:4 (March 1985), 764-781.

B-3294 Edgmon, Terry Davis, "THE INTERORGANIZATIONAL BASIS OF METROPOLI-
       TAN AFFAIRS: EXCHANGE, POWER, AND AREAWIDE WATER SUPPLY STRATE-
       GIES," Journal of Urban Affairs 6:3 (Summer 1984), 83-96.

B-3295 Egan, Clifford L., "FRICTION IN NEW ORLEANS: GENERAL BUTLER
       VERSUS THE SPANISH CONSUL," Louisiana History 9:1 (Winter 1968),
       43-52.

B-3296 Eichelburger, Pierce, "THE CITY OF MIAMI'S URBAN INFORMATION SYSTEM (U.I.S.), THE ACCENT IS ON PLANNING-MANAGEMENT APPLICA-TIONS," Papers from the Fifteenth Annual Conference of the Urban and Regional Information Systems Association, (August 1977), 83-92.

B-3297 Ellis, Ann Wells, "A CRUSADE AGAINST 'WRETCHED ATTITUDES': THE COMMISSION ON INTERRACIAL COOPERATION'S ACTIVITIES IN ATLANTA," Atlanta Historical Journal 23:1 (Spring 1979), 21-44.

B-3298 Ellis, John and Stuart Gailishoff, "ATLANTA'S WATER SUPPLY, 1865-1918," Maryland Historian 13:1 (Spring 1977), 5-22.

B-3299 Ellis, William E., "ROBERT WORTH BINGHAM AND LOUISVILLE PROGRES-SIVISM, 1905-1910," Filson Club History Quarterly 54:2 (April 1980), 169-195.

B-3300 Erwin, Nancy, "UNIQUE SHAPES IN MISSISSIPPI'S POLITICAL DISTRICTS AND THE POSSIBILITY OF GERRYMANDERING," Mississippi Geographer 7:1 (Spring 1979), 20-34.

B-3301 Ettinger, Brian Gary, "JOHN FITZPATRICK AND THE LIMITS OF WORKING-CLASS POLITICS IN NEW ORLEANS, 1892-1896," Louisiana History 26:4 (Fall 1985), 341-368.

B-3302 Evans, Diana Yiannakis, "SUNBELT VERSUS FROSTBELT: THE EVOLUTION OF REGIONAL CONFLICT OVER FEDERAL AID TO CITIES IN THE HOUSE OF REPRESENTATIVES," Social Science Quarterly 67:1 (March 1986), 108-117.

B-3303 Everard, Wayne M., "BOURBON CITY: NEW ORLEANS, 1878-1900," Louisiana Studies 11:3 (Fall 1972), 240-251.

B-3304 Everett, Donald E., "DEMANDS OF THE NEW ORLEANS FREE COLORED POPU-LATION FOR POLITICAL EQUALITY, 1862-1865," Louisiana Historical Quarterly 38:2 (April 1955), 43-64.

B-3305 Ewing, Cortez A. M. and James E. Titus, "URBANISM AND SOUTHERN POLITICS," in R. Vance, ed., The Urban South, (1954), 230-251.

B-3306 Eyre, John, "CITY-COUNTY TERRITORIAL COMPETITON: THE PORTSMOUTH, VIRGINIA CASE," Southeastern Geographer 9:2 (November 1969), 26-38.

B-3307 Fairclough, Adam, "THE PUBLIC UTILITIES INDUSTRY IN NEW ORLEANS: A STUDY IN CAPITAL, LABOR AND GOVERNMENT, 1894-1929," Louisiana History 22:1 (Winter 1981), 45-66.

B-3308 Farley, M. Foster, "JOHN ELLIOTT WARD, MAYOR OF SAVANNAH, 1853-1854," Georgia Historical Quarterly 53:1 (March 1969), 68-77.

B-3309 Feld, Richard D. and Donald S. Lutz, "RECRUITMENT TO THE HOUSTON CITY COUNCIL," 34:3 Journal of Politics (August 1972), 924-933.

B-3310 Fifer, J. Valerie, "WASHINGTON D. C.: THE POLITICAL GEOGRAPHY OF A FEDERAL CAPITAL," Journal of American Studies 15:1 (April 1981), 5-26.

B-3311 Fleischmann, Arnold, "SUNBELT BOOSTERISM: THE POLITICS OF POSTWAR GROWTH AND ANNEXATION IN SAN ANTONIO," in D. Perry, ed., The Rise of the Sunbelt Cities, (1977), 151-168.

B-3312 Forman, William H. Jr., "THE CONFLICT OVER FEDERAL URBAN RENEWAL ENABLING LEGISLATION IN LOUISIANA," Louisiana Studies 8:3 (Fall 1969), 251-267.

B-3313 Gantt, Harvey, "WE'RE BECOMING THE MAYORS," Southern Exposure 14:2 (March-April 1986), 44-51.

B-3314 Godoy, Gustavo J., "JOSE ALEJANDRO HUAU: A CUBAN PATRIOT IN JACK-
       SONVILLE POLITICS," Florida Historical Quarterly 54:2 (October
       1975), 196-206.

B-3315 Goodall, Cecile R., "DEVELOPMENT OF MUNICIPAL GOVERNMENT, CHARLES-
       TON, WEST VIRGINIA, 1794-1936," West Virginia History 9:2 (January
       1968), 97-137.

B-3316 Goode, Victor L., "THE BLACKEST DIET, THE WHITEST PEOPLE: AN EAST
       TEXAS MUNICIPAL ELECTION SCHEME," Journal of Ethnic Studies 11:4
       (Winter 1984), 11-27.

B-3317 Goodstein, Anita S., "LEADERSHIP ON THE NASHVILLE FRONTIER, 1780-
       1800," Tennessee Historical Quarterly 35:2 (Summer 1976), 175-198.

B-3318 Govan, Gilbert and James W. Livingood, "CHATTANOOGA UNDER MILITARY
       OCCUPATION, 1863-1865," Journal of Southern History 17:1 (February
       1951), 23-47.

B-3319 Graham, Thomas S., "FLORIDA POLITICS AND THE TALLAHASSEE PRESS,
       1845-1861," Florida Historical Quarterly 46:3 (January 1968), 234-
       242.

B-3320 Grant, D., "URBAN AND SUBURBAN NASHVILLE--A CASE STUDY IN METRO-
       POLITANISM," Journal of Politics 17:1 (February 1955), 82-99.

B-3321 Grantham, Dewey W., "THE CONTOURS OF SOUTHERN PROGRESSIVISM,"
       American Historical Review 86:5 (December 1981), 1035-1059.

B-3322 Grantham, Dewey W. Jr., "GOEBEL, GONZALES, CARMAK: THREE VIOLENT
       SCENES IN SOUTHERN POLITICS," Mississippi Quarterly 11:1 (Winter
       1958), 29-37.

B-3323 Green, Constance McLaughlin, "THE JACKSONIAN 'REVOLUTION' IN THE
       DISTRICT OF COLUMBIA," Mississippi Valley Historical Review 45:4
       (March 1959), 591-605.

B-3324 Greene, Suzanne E., "BLACK REPUBLICANS ON THE BALTIMORE CITY
       COUNCIL, 1890-1931," Maryland Historical Magazine 74:3 (September
       1979), 203-222.

B-3325 Griese, Arthur A., "A LOUISVILLE TRAGEDY--1862," Filson Club
       History Quarterly 26:2 (April 1952), 133-154.

B-3326 Griffith, Louis T., "CRACKER BARRELS AND PUBLIC LIBRARIES,"
       Georgia Review 8:1 (Spring 1954), 97-107.

B-3327 Guillory, Ferrel, "NEW MOON OVER OLD NEW ORLEANS," City 5:2
       (March-April 1971), 55-59.

B-3328 Gunlicks, Arthur B., "CITY-COUNTY SEPARATION AND LOCAL GOVERNMENT
       REFORM IN VIRGINIA," Virginia Social Science Journal 8:2 (July
       1973), 47-61.

B-3329 Gustely, Richard D., "THE ALLOCATIONAL AND DISTRIBUTIONAL IMPACTS
       OF GOVERNMENTAL CONSOLIDATION: THE DADE COUNTY EXPERIENCE," Urban
       Affairs Quarterly 12:3 (March 1977), 349-364.

B-3330 Harris, Carl V., "ANNEXATION STRUGGLES AND POLITICAL POWER IN BIR-
       MINGHAM, ALABAMA, 1890-1910," Alabama Review 27:3 (July 1974),
       163-184.

B-3331 Hart, W. O., "AN INTERESTING INCIDENT IN CONNECTION WITH NEW
       ORLEANS PREMIUM BONDS," Louisiana Historical Quarterly 8:2 (April
       1925), 248-251.

B-3332 Hartsock, Nancy, "COMMENT AND DEBATE: FEMINISTS, BLACK CANDI-
       DATES, AND LOCAL POLITICS: A REPORT FROM BALTIMORE," Feminist
       Studies 10:2 (Summer 1984), 339-352.

B-3333 Hass, Edward F., "JOHN FITZPATRICK AND POLITICAL CONTINUITY IN NEW ORLEANS, 1896-1899," Louisiana History 22:1 (Winter 1981), 7-30.

B-3334 Hass, Edward F., "NEW ORLEANS ON THE HALF SHELL: THE MAESTRI ERA, 1936-1946," Louisiana History 13:3 (Summer 1972), 283-310.

B-3335 Hawkins, Brett, "PUBLIC OPINION AND METROPOLITAN REORGANIZATION IN NASHVILLE," Journal of Politics 28:2 (May 1966), 408-418.

B-3336 Hawkins, Brett W. and Cheryl Whelchel, "REAPPORTIONMENT AND URBAN REPRESENTATION IN LEGISLATIVE INFLUENCE POSITIONS: THE CASE OF GEORGIA," Urban Affairs Quarterly 3:3 (March 1968), 69-80.

B-3337 Hearn, Carey, "FIRE CONTROL IN ANTEBELLUM MISSISSIPPI," Journal of Mississippi History 40:4 (November 1978), 319-328.

B-3338 Heleniak, Roman, "LYNDON JOHNSON IN NEW ORLEANS," Louisiana History 21:3 (Summer 1980), 263-275.

B-3339 Hendricks, J. Edwin, "THE LOCAL OPTION ACT OF 1886," Virginia Cavalcade 18:2 (Autumn 1968), 31-38.

B-3340 Hennessey, Melinda, "POLITICAL TERRORISM IN THE BLACK BELT: THE EUTAW RIOT," Alabama Review 33:1 (January 1980). 35-48.

B-3341 Hennessey, Melinda M., "RECONSTRUCTION POLITICS AND THE MILITARY: THE EUFAULA RIOT OF 1874," Alabama Historical Quarterly 38:2 (Summer 1976), 112-125.

B-3342 Henrikson, Alan J., "WASHINGTON: A SMALL COZY TOWN, GLOBAL IN SCOPE," Ekistics 50:299 (March-April 1983).

B-3343 Hickey, Donald R., "THE DARKER SIDE OF DEMOCRACY: THE BALTIMORE RIOTS OF 1812," Maryland Historian 12:2 (Fall 1976), 1-20.

B-3344 Hienton, Louise Joyner, "CHARLES TOWN, PRINCE GEORGE'S FIRST COUNTY SEAT," Maryland Historical Magazine 63:4 (December 1968), 401-411.

B-3345 Highsaw, Robert B., "CITY AND COUNTY MANAGER PLANS IN THE SOUTH," Journal of Politics 11:3 (August 1949), 497-517.

B-3346 Hine, William C., "BLACK POLITICIANS IN RECONSTRUCTION CHARLESTON, SOUTH CAROLINA: A COLLECTIVE STUDY," Journal of Southern History 49:4 (November 1983), 555-584.

B-3347 Hines, Ralph H. and James E. Pierce, "NEGRO LEADERSHIP AFTER THE SOCIAL CRISIS: AN ANALYSIS OF LEADERSHIP CHANGES IN MONTGOMERY, ALABAMA," Phylon 26:2 (Summer 1965), 162-172.

B-3348 Hoffecker, Carol E., "THE POLITICS OF EXCLUSION: BLACKS IN LATE NINETEENTH-CENTURY WILMINGTON, DELAWARE," Delaware History 16:1 (April 1974), 60-72.

B-3349 Hoffman, Morton, "THE ROLE OF GOVERNMENT IN INFLUENCING CHANGES IN HOUSING IN BALTIMORE: 1940-1950," Land Economics 30:2 (May 1954), 125-140.

B-3350 Holmes, Robert A., "REAPPORTIONMENT POLITICS IN GEORGIA: A CASE STUDY," Phylon 45:3 (September 1984), 179-187.

B-3352 Holmes, William F., "ELLEN DORTCH AND THE FARMER'S ALLIANCE," Georgia Historical Quarterly 69L2 (Summer 1985), 149-172.

B-3352 Hopkins, G. W., "FROM NAVAL PAUPER TO NAVAL POWER: THE DEVELOPMENT OF CHARLESTON'S METROPOLITAN MILITARY COMPLEX," in R. W. Lotchin, ed., The Martial Metropoles: U.S. Cities in War and Peace, New York: Praeger, 1984, 1-34.

B-3353 Hornsby, Alton Jr., "THE NEGRO IN ATLANTA POLITICS, 1961-1973," Atlanta Historical Journal 21:1 (Spring 1977), 7-33.

B-3354 Howard, Perry H., William J. Long, and Gene A. Zdrazil, "AN ECO- LOGICAL ANALYSIS OF VOTING BEHAVIOR IN BATON ROUGE: FROM STROM THURMOND TO GEORGE WALLACE," Social Forces 50:1 (September 1971), 45-52.

B-3355 Huff, A. V. Jr., "THE EAGLE AND THE VULTURE: CHANGING ATTITUDES TOWARD NATIONALISM IN FOURTH OF JULY ORATIONS DELIVERED IN CHARLESTON, 1778-1860," South Atlantic Quarterly 73:1 (Winter 1974), 10-22.

B-3356 Hutchinson, C. A., "MEXICAN FEDERALISTS IN NEW ORLEANS AND THE TEXAS REVOLUTION," Louisiana Historical Quarterly 39:1 (January 1956), 1-47.

B-3357 Ippolito, Dennis S., William S. Donaldson, and Lewis Bowman, "POLITICAL ORIENTATIONS AMONG NEGROES AND WHITES," Social Science Quarterly 49:3 (December 1968), 548-556.

B-3358 Isaac, Paul E., "MUNICIPAL REFORM IN BEAUMONT, TEXAS, 1902-1909," Southwestern Historical Quarterly 78:4 (April 1975), 413-430.

B-3359 Jackson, Charles O. and Charles W. Johnson, "THE URBANE FRONTIER: THE ARMY AND THE COMMUNITY OF OAK RIDGE, TENNESSEE, 1942-1947," Military Affairs 41:1 (1977), 8-14.

B-3360 Jackson, John S. III, "ALIENATION AND BLACK POLITICAL PARTICIPA- TION," Journal of Politics 35:4 (November 1973), 849-885.

B-3361 James, D. Clayton, "MUNICIPAL GOVERNMENT IN TERRITORIAL NATCHEZ," Journal of Mississippi History 27:2 (1965), 148-167.

B-3362 Jamison, Duncan R., "MAYNARD JACKSON'S 1973 ELECTION AS MAYOR OF ATLANTA," Midwest Quarterly 18:1 (October 1976), 7-26.

B-3363 Jeansonne, Glen, "DE LESSEPS MORRISON: WHY HE COULDN'T BECOME GOVERNOR OF LOUISIANA," Louisiana History 14:3 (Summer 1973), 255- 270.

B-3364 Jennings, M. Kent and Harmon Ziegler, "CLASS, PARTY, AND RACE IN FOUR TYPES OF ELECTIONS: THE CASE OF ATLANTA," Journal of Poli- tics 28:2 (May 1966), 391-407.

B-3365 Johnson, Howard Palmer, "NEW ORLEANS UNDER GENERAL BUTLER," Louisiana Historical Quarterly 24:2 (April 1941), 434-536.

B-3366 Jones, Mack H., "BLACK POLITICAL EMPOWERMENT IN ATLANTA: MYTH AND REALITY," Annals of the American Academy of Political and Social Science 439 (September 1978), 90-117.

B-3367 Jordan, Layton Wayne, "POLICE AND POLITICS: CHARLESTON IN THE GILDED AGE, 1880-1900," South Carolina Historical Magazine 81:1 (January 1980), 35-50.

B-3368 Kendall, John S., "THE MUNICIPAL ELECTIONS OF 1858," Louisiana Historical Quarterly 5:3 (July 1922), 357-376.

B-3369 Kirkpatrick, Samuel A. and David R. Morgan, "POLICY SUPPORT AND ORIENTATIONS TOWARD METROPOLITAN POLITICAL INTEGRATION AMONG URBAN OFFICIALS," Social Science Quarterly 52:3 (December 1971), 656- 671.

B-3370 Kitchens, Joseph, "THE 'WAYCROSS WAR': PUGILISM AND POLITICS IN THE GAY NINETIES," Atlanta Historical Journal 25:1 (Spring 1981), 41-48.

B-3371 Kmen, Henry A., "REMEMBER THE VIRGINIUS: NEW ORLEANS AND CUBA IN 1873," Louisiana History 11:4 (Fall 1970), 313-332.

B-3372 Knight, Richard Jr., "PERSPECTIVES OF A BLACK CITY MANAGER," Popular Government 45:2 (Fall 1979), 27-29.

B-3373 Koch, Walter F., "POLITICAL GEOGRAPHY OF URBAN PLACES: THE PROBLEM OF THE FRAGMENTED METROPOLIS IN ALABAMA," Alabama Academy of Science Journal 40:3 (July 1969).

B-3374 Kurtz, Michael L., "DE LESSEPS S. MORRISON, POLITICAL REFORMER," Louisiana History 17:1 (Winter 1976), 19-39.

B-3375 Kurtz, Michael L., "EARL LONG'S POLITICAL RELATIONS WITH THE CITY OF NEW ORLEANS: 1948-1960," Louisiana History 10:3 (Summer 1969), 241-254.

B-3376 Latimer, Margaret K., "BLACK POLITICAL REPRESENTATION IN SOUTHERN CITIES: ELECTION SYSTEMS AND OTHER CAUSAL VARIABLES," Urban Affairs Quarterly 15:1 (September 1979), 65-86.

B-3377 Lefever, Harry G., "PROSTITUTION, POLITICS AND RELIGION: THE CRUSADE AGAINST VICE IN ATLANTA IN 1912," Atlanta Historical Journal 24:1 (Spring 1980), 7-30.

B-3378 LeFurgy, William G., "PRUDENT LAWS AND WISE REGULATIONS: THREE EARLY BALTIMORE MAYORS' MESSAGES, 1797-1799," Maryland Historical Magazine 78:4 (Winter 1983), 278-286.

B-3379 Levett, Ella Pettit, "LOYALISM IN CHARLESTON, 1761-1784," Proceedings of the South Carolina Historical Association 6 (1936), 3-17.

B-3380 Lewis, Arthur J., "PROBLEMS OF THE SELMA POST OFFICE," Alabama Review 19:4 (October 1966), 277-282.

B-3381 Littlefield, Douglas R., "MARYLAND SECTIONALISM AND THE DEVELOPMENT OF THE POTOMAC ROUTE TO THE WEST," Maryland Historian 14:2 (Fall-Winter 1983), 31-52.

B-3382 Long, Durwood, "KEY WEST AND THE NEW DEAL, 1934-1936," Florida Historical Quarterly 46:3 (January 1968), 209-218.

B-3383 Losi, Jan Joseph, "THE VALLANDIGHAMS OF NEWARK: A DELAWARE COPPERHEAD FAMILY," Delaware History 18:4 (Fall-Winter 1979), 219-225.

B-3384 Lowry, Robert E., "MUNICIPAL SUBSIDIES TO INDUSTRIES IN TENNESSEE," Southern Economic Journal 7:3 (January 1941), 317-329.

B-3385 Lu, Weiming, "WHO CAN DRIVE DOWN LEAMONE AVENUE AND SING 'AMERICA THE BEAUTIFUL'? HOW DALLAS PASSED A STRONG SIGN ORDINANCE," Urban Resources 1:1 (Summer 1983), 12-21.

B-3386 Lusting, Norman I., "THE RELATIONSHIPS BETWEEN DEMOGRAPHIC CHARACTERISTICS AND PRO-INTEGRATION VOTE OF WHITE PRECINCTS IN A METROPOLITAN SOUTHERN COUNTY," Social Forces 40:3 (March 1962), 205-209.

B-3387 Lyons, W. E. and Richard E. Engstrom, "SOCIO-POLITICAL CROSS PRESSURES AND ATTITUDES TOWARD POLITICAL INTEGRATION OF URBAN GOVERNMENTS," Journal of Politics 35:3 (August 1973), 682-711.

B-3388 McBride, Robert M., "'NORTHERN MILITARY, CORRUPT, AND TRANSITORY,' AUGUSTUS E. ALDEN, NASHVILLE'S CARPETBAGGER MAYOR," Tennessee Historical Quarterly 37:1 (Spring 1978), 63-67.

B-3389 Maier, Pauline, "THE CHARLESTON MOB AND THE EVOLUTION OF POPULAR POLITICS IN REVOLUTIONARY SOUTH CAROLINA," Perspectives in American History 4 (1970), 173-198.

B-3390 Marable, Manning, "TUSKEGEE, ALABAMA: THE POLITICS OF ILLUSTION
IN THE NEW SOUTH," Black Scholar 8 (May 1977), 13-24.

B-3391 Marlin, Matthew R., "INDUSTRIAL DEVEOPMENT BONDS: REVIEWING THE
EVIDENCE IN THE NORFOLK-VIRGINIA BEACH SMSA," Review of Regional
Studies 14:1 (Winter 1984), 45-53.

B-3392 Martin, William C. and Karin Hopkins, "ATLANTA: POLITICAL TRANS-
FER AND SUCCESSION IN A SOUTHERN METROPOLIS," Journal of Intergroup Relations 4:3 (Summer 1975), 22-32.

B-3393 Menefee, Larry T., "THE SINDICATE WAR IN LITTLE ROCK," Arkansas
Historical Quarterly 46:1 (Spring 1987), 27-45.

B-3394 Middleton, Russell, "THE CIVIL RIGHTS ISSUE AND PRESIDENTIAL
VOTING AMONG SOUTHERN NEGROES AND WHITES," Social Forces 40:3
(March 1962), 209-215.

B-3395 Miller, William D., "J. J. WILLIAMS AND THE GREATER MEMPHIS
MOVEMENT," West Tennessee Historical Society Papers No. 5 (1951),
14-30.

B-3396 Miller, William D., "THE PROGRESSIVE MOVEMENT IN MEMPHIS,"
Tennessee Historical Quarterly 15:1 (March 1956), 3-16.

B-3397 Mladenka, Kenneth R. and Kim Quaile Hill, "THE DISTRIBUTION OF
BENEFITS IN AN URBAN ENVIRONMENT: PARKS AND LIBRARIES IN
HOUSTON," Urban Affairs Quarterly 13:1 (September 1977), 73-94.

B-3398 Mladenka, Kenneth R. and Kim Quaile Hill, "THE DISTRIBUTION OF
URBAN POLICE SERVICES," 40:1 (February 1978), 112-133.

B-3399 Moeser, John F., "ADMINISTRATION ROLE ORIENTATIONS OF COUNCILMEN
AND OVERT LEGISLATIVE BEHAVIOR OF MANAGERS: THE CASE OF RICH-
MOND, VIRGINIA," Virginia Social Science Journal 11:1 (April
1976), 26-34.

B-3400 Mohl, Raymond A., "RACE, ETHNICITY AND URBAN POLITICS IN THE MIAMI
METROPOLITAN AREA," Florida Environmental and Urban Issues 9
(April 1982), 1-6, 23-25.

B-3401 Monroe, John A., "SENATOR NICHOLAS VAN DYKE OF NEW CASTLE,"
Delaware History 4:3 (June 1951), 207-227.

B-3402 Moore, Charles H., "THE POLITICS OF URBAN VIOLENCE: POLICY
OUTCOMES IN WINSTON-SALEM," Social Science Quarterly 51:2
(September 1970), 374-388.

B-3403 Moore, John Hammond, "COMMUNISTS AND FASCISTS IN A SOUTHERN CITY:
ATLANTA, 1930," South Atlantic Quarterly 67:3 (Summer 1968), 437-
454.

B-3404 Morgan, Daniel C. Jr., "FISCAL NEGLECT OF URBAN AREAS BY A STATE
GOVERNMENT," Land Economics 50:2 (May 1974), 137-144.

B-3405 Morizan, Ronald R., "THE CABILDO OF SPANISH NEW ORLEANS, 1769-
1803: THE COLLAPSE OF LOCAL GOVERNMENT," Louisiana Studies 12:4
(Winter 1973), 591-606.

B-3406 Morris, Bear, "THE POLITICAL ORIGINS OF BARKSDALE AIR FORCE BASE,"
North Louisiana Historical Association Journal 8:3 (1977), 131-
136.

B-3407 Morrison, K. C. and Joe C. Huang, "RACIAL POLITICS: THE TRANSFER
OF POWER IN A MISSISSIPPI TOWN," Growth and Change 4:2 (April
1973), 25-29.

B-3408 Mowat, Charles L., "ST. AUGUSTINE UNDER THE BRITISH FLAG, 1763-
1775," Florida Historical Quarterly 20:2 (October 1941), 131-150.

B-3409 Mundt, Robert and Peggy Herlig, "DISTRICT REPRESENTATION: DEMANDS AND EFFECTS IN THE URBAN SOUTH," Journal of Politics 44:4 (November 1982), 1035-1048.

B-3410 Murrah, Bill, "LLANO COOPERATIVE COLONY," Southern Exposure 1:3-4 (Winter 1974), 105-111.

B-3411 Murray, Hugh T. Jr., "THE NAACP VERSUS THE COMMUNIST PARTY: THE SCOTTSBORO RAPE CASES, 1931," Phylon 28:3 (Fall 1967), 276-287.

B-3412 Murray, Richard and Arnold Vedlitz, "RACE, SOCIOECONOMIC STATUS, AND VOTING PARTICIPATION IN LARGE SOUTHERN CITIES," Journal of Politics 39:4 (1977), 1064-1072.

B-3413 Murray, Richard and Arnold Vedlitz, "RACIAL VOTING PATTERNS IN THE SOUTH: AN ANALYSIS OF MAJOR ELECTIONS FROM 1960 TO 1977 IN FIVE CITIES," Annals of the American Academy of Political and Social Science 439 (September 1978), 29-39.

B-3414 Nelms, Wilie, "A DIVIDED CITY: BRISTOL'S BORDER DISPUTES AND THE WATER WORKS WAR OF 1889," Virginia Cavalcade 28:4 (Spring 1979), 172-179.

B-3415 Newby, Idus A., "THE SOUTHERN AGRARIANS: A VIEW AFTER THIRTY YEARS," Agricultural History 37:3 (July 1963), 143-155.

B-3416 Nimmo, Dan and Clifton McCleskey, "IMPACT OF THE POLL TAX ON VOTER PARTICIPATION: THE HOUSTON METROPOLITAN AREA IN 1966," Journal of Politics 31:3 (August 1969), 682-699.

B-3417 Nussbaum, Raymond O., "'THE RING IS SMASHED!': THE NEW ORLEANS MUNICIPAL ELECTION OF 1896," Louisiana History 17:3 (Summer 1976), 283-297.

B-3418 O'Brien, Gail, "POWER AND INFLUENCE IN MECKLENBURG COUNTY, 1850-1880," North Carolina Historical Review 54:2 (Spring 1977), 120-144.

B-3419 O'Brien, John T., "RECONSTRUCTION IN RICHMOND: WHITE RESTORATION AND BLACK PROTEST, APRIL-JUNE 1865," Virginia Magazine of History and Biography 89:3 (July 1981), 259-281.

B-3420 Orum, Anthony M., "RELIGION AND THE RISE OF THE RADICAL WHITE: THE CASE OF SOUTHERN WALLACE SUPPORT IN 1968," Social Science Quarterly 51:3 (December 1970), 674-688.

B-3421 Orum, Anthony M. and Edward W. McCranie, "CLASS, TRADITION, AND PARTISAN ALIGNMENTS IN A SOUTHERN URBAN ELECTORATE," Journal of Politics 32:1 (February 1970), 156-176.

B-3422 Padgett, James A., "THE DIFFICULTIES OF ANDREW JACKSON IN NEW ORLEANS," Louisiana Historical Quarterly 21:2 (April 1938), 367-419.

B-3423 Parks, Joseph, "MEMPHIS UNDER MILITARY RULE, 1862 TO 1865," East Tennessee Historical Society's Publications No. 14 (1942), 31-58.

B-3424 Patterson, S. S. P., "MUNICIPAL PRIMARIES IN THE SOUTH," Sewanee Review 2:4 (August 1894), 449-458.

B-3425 Pearson, Ralph L., "THE NATIONAL URBAN LEAGUE COMES TO BALTIMORE," Maryland Historical Magazine 72:4 (Winter 1977), 523-533.

B-3426 Perkins, Jerry, "BASES OF PARTISAN CLEVAGE IN A SOUTHERN URBAN COUNTY," Journal of Politics 36:1 (February 1974), 208-217.

B-3427 Piliawsky, Monte, "THE IMPACT OF BLACK MAYORS ON THE BLACK COMMUNITY: THE CASE OF NEW ORLEANS' ERNEST MORIAL," Review of Black Political Economy 13:4 (Spring 1985), 5-24.

B-3428 Pillsbury, Richard, "THE MORPHOLOGY OF THE PIEDMONT GEORGIA COUNTY
        SEAT BEFORE 1860," Southeastern Geographer 18:2 (November 1978),
        115-124.

B-3429 Pittman, Karen H., "RICHARD KENT: AUGUSTA'S FIRST CONSERVATOR OF
        THE PEACE," Richmond County History 18:1 (Winter 1986), 16-21.

B-3430 Platt, Harold L., "THE STILLBIRTH OF URBAN POLITICS IN THE
        RECONSTRUCTION SOUTH: HOUSTON, TEXAS AS A TEST CASE," Houston
        Review (Summer 1982), 55-74.

B-3431 Poyo, Gerald E., "CUBAN PATRIOTS IN KEY WEST, 1878-1886: GUARDI-
        ANS AT THE SEPARATIST IDEAL," Florida Historical Quarterly 61:1
        (July 1982), 20-36.

B-3432 Poyo, Gerald E., "KEY WEST AND THE CUBAN TEN YEARS WAR," Florida
        Historical Quarterly 57:3 (January 1979), 289-307.

B-3433 Poyo, Gerald E., "TAMPA CIGAR WORKERS AND THE STRUGGLE FOR CUBAN
        INDEPENDENCE," Tampa Bay History 7:2 (Fall-Winter 1985), 94-105.

B-3434 Pozzetta, George E., " 'ALETTA TABAQUEROS!', TAMPA'S STRIKING
        CIGARWORKERS," Tampa Bay History 3:2 (Fall-Winter 1981), 19-29.

B-3435 Pozzetta, George E., "IMMIGRANTS AND RADICALS IN TAMPA, FLORIDA,"
        Florida Historical Quarterly 57:3 (January 1979), 337-348.

B-3436 Price, David E. and Michael Lupfer, "VOLUNTEERS FOR GORE: THE
        IMPACT OF A PRECINCT-LEVEL CANVASS IN THREE TENNESSEE CITIES,"
        Journal of Politics 35:2 (May 1973), 410-438.

B-3437 Prichard, Walter, ed., "THE ORIGIN AND ACTIVITIES OF THE 'WHITE
        LEAGUE' IN NEW ORLEANS," Louisiana Historical Quarterly 23:2
        (April 1940), 525-543.

B-3438 Rachal, William M. E., "STAUNTON STEPS OUT OF THE MUD," Virginia
        Cavalcade 1:4 (Spring 1952), 9-11.

B-3439 Rankin, David C., "THE ORIGINS OF BLACK LEADERSHIP IN NEW ORLEANS
        DURING RECONSTRUCTION," Journal of Southern History 40:3 (August
        1974), 417-440.

B-3440 Rauchle, Bob Cyrus, "ONE POLITICAL LIFE OF THE GERMANS IN MEMPHIS,
        1848-1880," Tennessee Historical Society 27:2 (Summer 1968), 165-
        175.

B-3441 Reagan, Alice E., "PROMOTING THE NEW SOUTH: HANNIBAL I. KIMBALL
        AND HENRY W. GRADY," Atlanta Historical Journal 27:3 (Fall 1983),
        5-20.

B-3442 Reynolds, Donald E., "THE NEW ORLEANS RIOT OF 1866, RECONSIDERED,"
        Louisiana History 5:1 (Winter 1964), 5-28.

B-3443 Rice, Bradley R., "THE GALVESTON PLAN OF CITY GOVERNMENT BY COM-
        MISSION: THE BIRTH OF A PROGRESSIVE IDEA," Southwestern Histori-
        cal Quarterly 78:4 (April 1975), 365-408.

B-3444 Ridgeway, Whitman H., "COMMUNITY LEADERSHIP: BALTIMORE DURING THE
        FIRST AND SECOND PARTY SYSTEMS," Maryland Historical Magazine 71:3
        (Fall 1976), 334-348.

B-3445 Riley, Edward M., "THE TOWN ACTS OF COLONIAL VIRGINIA," Journal of
        Southern History 16:3 (August 1950), 306-323.

B-3446 Robertson, Heard, "A REVISED, OR LOYALIST PERSPECTIVE OF AUGUSTA
        DURING THE AMERICAN REVOLUTION," Richmond County History 1:2 (Sum-
        mer 1969), 5-24.

B-3447 Robinson, Lori and Bill DeYoung, "SOCIALISM IN THE SUNSHINE: THE
       ROOTS OF RUSKIN, FLORIDA," Tampa Bay History 4:1 (Spring-Summer
       1982), 5-20.

B-3448 Rodabaugh, Karl, "THE DOTHAN POST OFFICE FIGHT: A CASE STUDY OF
       THE CONFLICT OF LOCAL AND TRANSLOCAL FORCES DURING THE PROGRESSIVE
       ERA," Southern Studies 19:1 (Spring 1980), 65-80.

B-3449 Rogers, Bruce D. and C. McCurdy Lipsey, "METROPOLITAN REFORM:
       CITIZEN EVALUATIONS OF PERFORMANCES IN NASHVILLE-DAVIDSON COUNTY,
       TENNESSEE," Publius 4:4 (1974), 19-34.

B-3450 Rogers, William Warren, "THE 'NATION'S GUEST' IN LOUISIANA:
       KOSSUTH VISITS NEW ORLEANS," Louisiana History 9:4 (Fall 1968),
       355-364.

B-3451 Rojas, F. de Borja Medina, "JOSE DE EZPELETA, GOBERNADOR DE LA
       MOBILIA 1780-1781," Publicaciones de la Escuela de Estudios
       Hispano-Americanos de Sevilla, No. 264 (1980).

B-3452 Roper, James E., "PADDY MEAGHER, TOM HULING, AND THE BELL TAVERN,"
       West Tennessee Historical Society Papers No. 31 (1977), 5-32.

B-3453 Rose, Winfield H., "BLACK BALANCE OF POWER IN A METROPOLITAN
       SOUTHERN COUNTY: FACT OR FANCY," Journal of Political Science 3:2
       (Spring 1975), 121-138.

B-3454 Roseboom, Eugene H., "BALTIMORE AS A NATIONAL NOMINATING CONVEN-
       TION CITY," Maryland Historical Magazine 67:3 (Fall 1972), 215-
       224.

B-3455 Rosenbaum, Walter A. and Thomas A. Henderson, "EXPLAINING THE
       ATTITUDE OF COMMUNITY INFLUENTIALS TOWARD GOVERNMENT CONSOLIDA-
       TION: A REAPPRAISAL OF FOUR HYPOTHESES," Urban Affairs Quarterly
       9:2 (December 1973), 251-275.

B-3456 Roth, Clayton D. Jr., "150 YEARS OF DEFENSE ACTIVITY IN KEY WEST,
       1820-1970," Tequesta No. 30 (1970), 33-51.

B-3457 Rushton, Bill, "NEW ORLEANS ELECTS BLACK MAYOR (DUTCH MORIAL),"
       Southern Exposure 6:1 (Spring 1978), 5-7.

B-3458 Sajgo, Gloria, "NORTH CAROLINA'S SEAPORTS AND THE STATE PORTS
       AUTHORITY," Popular Government 50:3 (Winter 1985), 1-9.

B-3459 Salter, Paul S. and Robert C. Mings, "THE PROJECTED IMPACT OF
       CUBAN SETTLEMENT ON VOTING PATTERNS IN METROPOLITAN MIAMI,
       FLORIDA," Professional Geographer 24:2 (May 1972), 123-131.

B-3460 Saunders, Robert M., "MODERNIZATION AND THE POLITICAL PROCESS:
       GOVERNMENTAL PRINCIPLES AND PRACTICES IN RICHMOND, VIRGINIA, FROM
       THE REVOLUTION TO THE CIVIL WAR," Southern Studies 24:2 (Summer
       1985), 117-142.

B-3461 Schewel, Michael J., "LOCAL POLITICS IN LYNCHBURG, VIRGINIA, IN
       THE 1880's," Virginia Magazine of History and Biography 89:2
       (April 1981), 170-180.

B-3462 Schlozman, Kay Lehman and John T. Tierney, "MORE OF THE SAME:
       WASHINGTON PRESSURE GROUP ACTIVITY IN A DECADE OF CHANGE," Journal
       of Politics 45:2 (May 1983), 351-377.

B-3463 Schott, Matthew J., "HUEY LONG: PROGRESSIVE BACKLASH," Louisiana
       History 27:2 (Spring 1986), 133-146.

B-3464 Schott, Matthew J., "THE NEW ORLEANS MACHINE AND PROGRESSIVISM,"
       Louisiana History 24:2 (Spring 1983), 141-154.

B-3465 Scribner, Robert L., "IN AND OUT OF VIRGINIA," Virginia Cavalcade 15:2 (Autumn 1965) 4-8.

B-3466 Seale, William, "SAN AUGUSTINE, IN THE TEXAS REPUBLIC," Southwestern Historical Quarterly 72:4 (January 1969), 347-358.

B-3467 Seiber, Lones, "THE BATTLE OF ATHENS," American Heritage 36:2 (February-March 1985), 72-80.

B-3468 Simons, Theodore B. Fitz Jr., "THE CAMILLA RIOT," Georgia Historical Quarterly 35:2 (June 1951), 116-125.

B-3469 Sioussat, St. George L., "TENNESSEE, THE COMPROMISE OF 1850, AND THE NASHVILLE CONVENTION," Tennessee Historicla Magazine 4:4 (December 1918), 215-247.

B-3470 Soden, Dale, "THE NEW DEAL COMES TO SHAWNEE," Chronicles of Oklahoma 63:2 (Summer 1985), 116-127.

B-3471 Soule, Leon C., "THE CREOLE-AMERICAN STRUGGLE IN NEW ORLEANS POLITICS, 1850-1862," Louisiana Historical Quarterly 40:1 (January 1957), 54-83.

B-3472 Stabem, Karen A., "HANS FROELICHER, JR., CIVIC EDUCATOR," Maryland Historical Magazine 77:2 (June 1982), 193-201.

B-3473 Starr, J. Barton, "BIRMINGHAM AND THE 'DIXICRAT' CONVENTION OF 1948," Alabama Historical Quarterly 32:1-2 (Spring and Summer 1970), 23-50.

B-3474 Stoesen, Alexander R., "THE BRITISH OCCUPATION OF CHARLESTON, 1780-1782," South Carolina Historical Magazine 63:1 (February 1966), 71-82.

B-3475 Surratt, Jerry L., "THE ROLE OF DISSENT IN COMMUNITY EVALUATION AMONG MORAVIANS IN SALEM, 1772-1860," North Carolina Historical Review 52:3 (Summer 1975), 235-255.

B-3476 Svara, James E., "CITIZEN PREFERENCE FOR URBAN ELECTION INSTITUTIONS: DISCARDING OLD MODELS OF CITY GOVERNMENT," Urban Affairs Quarterly 12:4 (June 1977), 511-522.

B-3477 Swint, Charles Gary, "AUGUSTA ANNEXATION ATTEMPT OF 1966," Richmond County History 3:2 (Summer 1971), 23-36.

B-3478 Sykes, Leonard Jr., "JIM CROW, LYNCHINGS AND A RETURN TO BUSINESS AS USUAL IN MOBILE," Black Books Bulletin 7:3 (1981), 18-20.

B-3479 Sylvers, Malcolm, "SICILIAN SOCIALISTS IN HOUSTON, TEXAS, 1896-98," Labor History 11:1 (Winter 1970), 77-81.

B-3480 Taebel, Delbert A. and Richard L. Cole, "A COMPARATIVE ANALYSIS OF URBAN ISSUES: PERCEPTIONS BY MUNICIPAL OFFICIALS IN A SUNBELT AND FROSTBELT STATE," Journal of Urban Affairs 5:4 (Fall 1983), 349-354.

B-3481 Tansey, Richard, "PROSTITUTION AND POLITICS IN ANTEBELLUM NEW ORLEANS," Southern Studies 17:4 (Winter 1979), 449-479.

B-3482 Tarver, Jerry L., "THE POLITICAL CLUBS OF NEW ORLEANS IN THE PRESIDENTIAL ELECTION OF 1860," Louisiana History 4:2 (Spring 1963), 119-130.

B-3483 Taylor, A. Elizabeth, "WOMAN SUFFRAGE ACTIVITIES IN ATLANTA," Atlanta Historical Review 23:4 (Winter 1979-80), 45-54.

B-3484 Taylor, A. Elizabeth, "THE WOMAN SUFFRAGE MOVEMENT IN TEXAS," Journal of Southern History 17:2 (May 1951), 194-215.

B-3485 Taylor, Joe Gray, "NEW ORLEANS AND RECONSTRUCTION," Louisiana History 9:3 (Fall 1968), 189-208.

B-3486 Thakkar, Haribhai K., "'ATTENTIVE URBANITES': A THEORETICAL CONSTRUCT," Virginia Social Science Journal 11:1 (April 1976), 70-76.

B-3487 Thompson, Alan S., "SOUTHERN RIGHTS AND NATIVISM AS ISSUES IN MOBILE POLITICS, 1850-1861," Alabama Review 35:2 (April 1982), 127-141.

B-3488 Thornbrough, Emma Lou, "THE BROWNSVILLE EPISODE AND THE NEGRO VOTE," Mississippi Valley Historical Review 44:3 (December 1957), 469-493.

B-3489 Tickamyer, Ann R., "RURAL-URBAN INFLUENCES ON LEGISLATIVE POWER AND DECISION MAKING," Rural Sociology 48:1 (Spring 1983), 133-147.

B-3490 Tipton, Leonard, Roger D. Haney and John R. Baseheart, "MEDIA AGENDA-SETTING IN A CITY AND STATE ELECTION CAMPAIGNS," Journalism Quarterly 52:1 (Spring 1975), 15-22.

B-3491 Trafzer, Clifford, "HARMONY AND COOPERATION," Chronicles of Oklahoma 62:1 (Spring 1984), 70-85.

B-3492 Traver, Jerry L., "POLITICAL ORATORY AND THE NEW ORLEANS CAMPAIGN CLUBS OF 1860," Southern Speech Journal 27:4 (Summer 1962), 322-9.

B-3493 Treadway, Sandra Gioia, "SARAH LEE FAIN: NORFOLK'S FIRST WOMAN LEGISLATOR," Virginia Cavalcade 30:3 (Winter 1981), 124-133.

B-3494 Tregle, Joseph G. Jr., "ANDREW JACKSON AND THE CONTINUING BATTLE OF NEW ORLEANS," Journal of the Early Republic 1:4 (Winter 1981), 373-394.

B-3495 Treon, John A., "POLITICS AND CONCRETE: THE BUILDING OF THE ARKANSAS STATE CAPITOL, 1899-1917," Arkansas Historical Quarterly 31:2 (Summer 1972), 99-133.

B-3496 Tucker, David M., "BLACK POLITICS IN MEMPHIS, 1865-1875," West Tennessee Historical Society Papers No. 26 (1972), 13-19.

B-3497 Tucker, Leah Brooke, "THE FIRST ADMINISTRATION OF MAYOR LEWIS CUTRER OF HOUSTON, 1958-1960," East Texas Historical Journal 12:1 (Spring 1974), 39-50.

B-3498 Tunnell, Ted, "FREE NEGROES AND THE FREEDMEN: BLACK POLITICS IN NEW ORLEANS DURING THE CIVIL WAR," Southern Studies 19:1 (Spring 1980), 5-28.

B-3499 Urban, C. Stanley, "THE IDEOLOGY OF SOUTHERN IMPERIALISM: NEW ORLEANS AND THE CARIBBEAN, 1845-1860," Louisiana Historical Quarterly 39:1 (Janaury 1956), 48-74.

B-3500 Urban, Chester Stanley, "NEW ORLEANS AND THE CUBAN QUESTION DURING LOPEZ EXPEDITIONS OF 1849-1851: A LOCAL STUDY IN 'MANIFEST DES-TINY," Louisiana Historical Quarterly 22:4 (October 1939), 1095-1167.

B-3501 Vance, W. Silas, "THE MARION RIOT," Mississippi Quarterly 26:4 (Fall 1974), 447-466.

B-3502 Vedlitz, Arnold, Jon P. Alston, and Carl Pinkele, "POLITICS AND THE BLACK CHURCH IN A SOUTHERN COMMUNITY," Journal of Black Studies 10:3 (March 1980) 367-375.

B-3503 Vedlitz, Arnold and Eric P. Veblen, "VOTING AND CONTACTING: TWO FORMS OF POLITICAL PARTICIPATION IN A SUBURBAN COMMUNITY," Urban Affairs Quarterly 16:1 (September 1980), 31-48.

B-3504 Walker, Jack, "NEGRO VOTING IN ATLANTA: 1953-1961," Phylon 24:4 (Winter 1963), 379-387.

B-3505 Walker, Jack L., "PROTEST AND NEGOTIATION: A CASE STUDY OF NEGRO LEADERSHIP IN ATLANTA, GEORGIA," Midwest Journal of Political Science 7 (May 1963), 99-124.

B-3506 Walker, Leola O., "OFFICIALS IN THE CITY GOVERNMENT OF COLONIAL WILLIAMSBURG," Virginia Magazine of History and Biography 75:1 (January 1967), 35-51.

B-3507 Wall, Forrest, "RICHMOND, VIRGINIA: A CASE STUDY OF ANNEXATION IN THE SOUTH," Virginia Social Science Journal 13:2 (November 1978), 16-22.

B-3508 Ward, Judson C. Jr. 'THE ELECTION OF 1880 AND ITS IMPACT ON ATLANTA," Atlanta Historical Journal 25:1 (Spring 1981), 5-16.

B-3509 Watkins, Floyd C., "THOMAS WOLFE AND THE NASHVILLE AGRARIANS," Georgia Review 7:4 (Winter 1953), 410-423.

B-3510 Watson, Robert M. Jr., "THE MEMPHIS SOUND, 1913-1925, AS PLAYED BY THE EGYPTIANS: LEADERSHIP PROFILES AND ATTITUDES IN A SOUTHERN CITY," West Tennessee Historical Society Papers No. 25 (1971), 63-89.

B-3511 Watts, Eugene J., "BLACK POLITICAL PROGRESS IN ATLANTA, 1865-1895," Journal of Negro History 59:3 (July 1974), 268-286.

B-3512 Watts, Eugene J., "PROPERTY AND POLITICS IN ATLANTA 1865-1903," Journal of Urban History 3:3 (May 1977), 295-322.

B-3513 Wax, Jonathan I., "PROGRAM OF PROGRESS: THE RECENT CHANGE IN THE FORM OF GOVERNMENT OF MEMPHIS," West Tennessee Historical Society Papers No. 23 (1969), 81-109.

B-3514 Wax, Jonathan I., "PROGRAM OF PROGRESS: THE RECENT CHANGE IN THE FORM OF GOVERNMENT OF MEMPHIS PART II," West Tennessee Historical Society Papers No. 24 (1970), 74-96.

B-3515 Webster, Gerald and Roberta Haven Webster, "ETHNICITY AND VOTING IN THE MIAMI-DADE COUNTY SMSA," Urban Geography 8:1 (January 1987), 14-30.

B-3516 Weinstein, James, "ORGANIZED BUSINESS AND CITY COMMISSION AND MANAGER MOVEMENTS," Journal of Southern History 28:2 (May 1962), 166-182.

B-3517 Wellborn, Alfred Toledano, "THE RELATIONS BETWEEN NEW ORLEANS AND LATIN AMERICA, 1810-1824," Louisiana Historical Quarterly 22:3 (July 1939), 710-799.

B-3518 Wheeler, Harvey, "YESTERDAY'S ROBIN HOOD: THE RISE AND FALL OF BALTIMORE'S TRENTON DEMOCRATIC CLUB," American Quarterly 7:4 (Winter 1955), 332-344.

B-3519 Wheeler, William Bruce, "THE BALTIMORE JEFFERSONIANS, 1788-1800: A PROFILE OF INTRA-FACTIONAL CONFLICT," Maryland Historical Magazine 66:2 (Summer 1971), 153-168.

B-3520 White, Louise G., "FUNCTIONS OF NEIGHBORHOOD ADVISORY GROUPS," Journal of Voluntary Action Review 10:2 (April-June 1981), 27-39.

B-3521 Whiteman, Maxwell, ed., "EQUAL SUFFRAGE," Afro-American History Series Collection 3, Part 3, i-28, n.d.

B-3522 Whiteman, Maxwell, ed., "POST RECONSTRUCTION AND THE TENNESSEE CONFERENCE, 1879," Afro-American History Series Collection 5, Part 3, i-107, n.d.

B-3523 Wicker, Warren J., "MUNICIPAL ANNEXATION IN NORTH CAROLINA" Popular Government 47:3 (Winter 1982), 31-35.

B-3524 Williams, Clanton W., "CONSERVATISM IN OLD MONTGOMERY, 1817-1861," Alabama Review 10:2 (April 1957), 96-110.

B-3525 Williams, Clanton W. "EARLY ANTE-BELLUM MONTGOMERY: A BLACK-BELT CONSTITUENCY," Journal of Southern History 7:4 (November 1941), 495-525.

B-3526 Williams, Robert W., "MARTIN BEHRMAN AND NEW ORLEANS CIVIC DEVELOPMENT, 1904-1920," Louisiana History 2:4 (Fall 1961), 373-400.

B-3527 Williams, Thomas J., "URBAN AND RURAL DIFFERENCES IN SOUTHERN CHILDREN'S ATTITUDES TOWARD THE PRESIDENT AND THE U. S. GOVERNMENT," Journal of Political Science 2:2 (Spring 1975), 75-96,

B-3528 Winokur, Herbert S., "EXPENDITURE EQUALIZATION IN THE WASHINGTON, D. C. ELEMENTARY SCHOOLS," Public Policy 24:3 (1976), 309-335.

B-3529 Winston, James E., "NEW ORLEANS AND THE TEXAS REVOLUTION," Louisiana Historical Quarterly 10:3 (July 1927), 317-354.

B-3530 Winston, James E., ed., "A FAITHFUL PICTURE OF THE POLITICAL SITUATION IN NEW ORLEANS AT THE CLOSE OF THE LAST BEGINNING OF THE PRESENT YEAR," Louisiana Historical Quarterly 11:3 (July 1928), 359-433.

B-3531 Wood, Peter H., "'TAKING CARE OF BUSINESS' IN REVOLUTIONARY SOUTH CAROLINA: REPUBLICANISM AND THE SLAVE SOCIETY," South Atlantic Urban Studies 2 (1978), 49-72.

B-3532 Wood, W. Kirk, "HENRY HARFORD CUMMING: CIVIC VIRTUE IN THE OLD SOUTH," Richmond County History 9:1 (Winter 1977), 5-9.

B-3533 Woods, Randall B., "GEORGE T. RUBY, A BLACK MILITANT IN THE WHITE BUSINESS COMMUNITY," Red River Valley Historical Review 1:3 (Autumn 1974), 269-280.

B-3534 Worthen, William B., "MUNICIPAL IMPROVEMENT IN LITTLE ROCK--A CASE HISTORY," Arkansas Historical Quarterly 46:4 (Winter 1987), 317-347.

B-3535 Wrenn, Lynette B., "THE MEMPHIS SEWER EXPERIMENT," Tennessee Historical Quarterly 44:3 (Fall 1985), 340-349.

B-3536 Wright, George C., "THE BILLY CLUB AND THE BALLOT: POLICE INTIMIDATION OF BLACKS IN LOUISVILLE, KENTUCKY, 1880-1930," Southern Studies 23:1 (Spring 1984), 20-41.

B-3537 Wright, George C., "BLACK POLITICAL INSURGENCY IN LOUISVILLE, KENTUCKY: THE LINCOLN INDEPENDENT PARTY OF 1921," Journal of Negro History 68:1 (Winter 1983), 8-23.

B-3538 Wright, Gerald C., "COMMUNITY STRUCTURES AND VOTING IN THE SOUTH," Public Opinion Quarterly 40 (Summer 1976), 201-215.

B-3539 Wynne, Lewis N., "NEW SOUTH RIVALRY IN THE 1880s: GORDON VERSUS MACON," Atlanta Historical Journal 27:4 (Winter 1983), 4-56.

B-3540 Yates, Sarah R. and Karen R. Gray, "BUSINESS CONFLICTS IN THE MAYORALITY OF PAUL BOOKER REED," Filson Club History Quarterly 61:3 (July 1987), 295-314.

B-3541 Yglesias, Jose, "THE RADICAL LATINO ISLAND IN THE DEEP SOUTH," Tampa Bay History 7:2 (Fall-Winter 1985), 166-169.

B-3542 Zald, Mayer N. and Thomas A. Anderson, "SECULAR TRENDS AND HIS-
TORICAL CONTINGENCIES IN THE RECRUITMENT OF MAYORS: NASHVILLE AS
COMPARED TO NEW HAVEN AND CHICAGO," Urban Affairs Quarterly 3:4
(June 1968), 53–68.

Population

B-3543 Agresti, Barbara F., "TOWN AND COUNTRY IN A FLORIDA RURAL COUNTY
IN THE LATE NINETEENTH CENTURY: SOME POPULATION AND HOUSEHOLD
COMPARISONS," Rural Sociology 42 (Winter 1977), 555–568.

B-3544 Aguirre, Benigno, Kent P. Schwirian and Anthony J. LaGreca, "THE
RESIDENTIAL PATTERNING OF LATIN AMERICAN AND OTHER ETHNIC POPULA-
TIONS IN METROPOLITAN MIAMI," Latin American Research Review 15:1
(1980), 35–63.

B-3545 Arcury, Thomas A. and Julia D. Porter, "HOUSEHOLD COMPOSITION IN
APPALACHIAN KENTUCKY IN 1900," Journal of Family History 10:2
(Summer 1985), 183–195.

B-3546 Back, Robert L. and Joel Smith, "COMMUNITY SATISFACTION, EXPECTA-
TIONS OF MOVING, AND MIGRATION,." Demography 14:2 (May 1972), 147–
167.

B-3547 Banner, Warren M., "SOUTHERN NEGRO COMMUNITIES," Phylon 7:3
(1946), 255–259.

B-3548 Barr, Alwyn, "BLACKS IN SOUTHWESTERN CITIES," Red River Valley
Historical Review 6:2 (Spring 1981), 5–7.

B-3549 Barr, Alwyn, "OCCUPATIONAL AND GEOGRAPHIC MOBILITY IN SAN ANTONIO,
1870–1900," Social Science Quarterly 51:2 (September 1970), 396–
403.

B-3550 Barr, Ruth B. and Modeste Hargis, "THE VOLUNTARY EXILE OF FREE
NEGROES OF PENSACOLA," Florida Historical Quarterly 17:1 (July
1938), 3–14.

B-3551 Bauman, Mark, "RATE THEORY AND HISTORY: THE ILLUSTRATION OF
ETHNIC BROKERAGE IN THE ATLANTA JEWISH COMMUNITY IN AN ERA OF
TRANSITION AND CONFLICT," American Jewish History 73:1 (September
1983), 71–95.

B-3552 Bauman, Mark K., "CENTRIPETAL AND CENTRIFUGAL FORCES FACING THE
PEOPLE OF MANY COMMUNITIES: ATLANTA JEWRY FROM THE FRANK CASE TO
THE GREAT DEPRESSION," Atlanta Historical Journal 23:3 (Fall
1979), 25–54.

B-3553 Baylor, Ronald H., "ETHNIC RESIDENTIAL PATTERNS IN ATLANTA, 1880–
1940," Georgia Historical Quarterly 63:4 (Winter 1979), 435–446.

B-3554 Beasley, Jonathan, "BLACKS--SLAVE AND FREE--VICKSBURG, 1850-1860,"
Journal of Mississippi History 37:1 (February 1976), 1–32.

B-3555 Beatty, Bess, "THE LOO CHANG CASE IN WAYNESBORO: A CASE STUDY OF
SINOPHOBIA IN GEORGIA," Georgia Historical Quarterly 67:1 (Spring
1983) 35–48.

B-3556 Beckner, Lucien, "ESKIPPAKITHIKI: THE LAST INDIAN TOWN IN KEN-
TUCKY," Filson Club History Quarterly 6:4 (October 1932), 355–382.

B-3557 Bederman, Sanford H. and Truman A. Hartshorn, "QUALITY OF LIFE IN
GEORGIA: THE 1980 EXPERIENCE," Southeastern Geographer 24:2
(November 1984), 78–98.

B-3558 Bederman, Sanford H., Frank V. Keeler and Truman A. Hartshorn,
"MIGRATION PATTERNS OF ATLANTA'S INNER CITY DISPLACED RESIDENTS,"
West Georgia Studies in the Social Sciences 16 (June 1977), 49–58.

B-3559 Beers, Howard W. and Catherine Heflin, "THE URBAN STATUS OF RURAL MIGRANTS," Social Forces 23:1 (October 1944), 32-37.

B-3560 Berthoff, Rowland T., "SOUTHERN ATTITUDES TOWARD IMMIGRATION, 1865-1914," Journal of Southern History 17:3 (August 1951), 328-360.

B-3561 Best, Gary Dean, "JACOB H. SCHIFF'S GALVESTON MOVEMENT: AN EXPERIMENT IN IMMIGRANT DEFLECTION, 1907-1914," American Jewish Archives 30:1 (April 1978), 43-79.

B-3562 Biggar, Jeanne C. and Francis C. Biasiolli, "METROPOLITAN DECON-CENTRATION: SUBAREAL IN-MIGRATION AND CENTRAL CITY TO RING MOBIL-ITY PATTERNS AMONG SOUTHERN SMSAS," Demography 15:4 (November 1978), 589-604.

B-3563 Bigger, Jeanne C. and Julia H. Martin, "ECOLOGICAL DETERMINANTS OF WHITE AND BLACK IMMIGRATION TO SMALL AREAS IN CENTRAL CITIES, 1965 TO 1970," Social Forces 55:1 (September 1976), 72-84.

B-3564 Bittle, William E. and Gelbert L. Geis, "RACIAL SELF-FULFILLMENT AND THE RISE OF AN ALL-NEGRO COMMUNITY IN OKLAHOMA," Phylon 18:3 (1957), 247-260.

B-3565 Blackwelder, Julia Kirk, "QUIET SUFFERING: ATLANTA WOMEN IN THE 1930s," Georgia Historical Quarterly 61:2 (Summer 1977), 112-124.

B-3566 Blassingame, John W., "BEFORE THE GHETTO: THE MAKING OF THE BLACK COMMUNITY IN SAVANNAH, GEORGIA, 1865-1880," Journal of Social History 6:4 (Summer 1973), 463-488.

B-3567 Blevins, Audie L., "MIGRATION RATES IN TWELVE SOUTHERN METROPOLI-TAN AREAS: A 'PUSH-PULL' ANALYSIS," Social Science Quarterly 50:2 (September 1969), 337-353.

B-3568 Block, W. T., "TULIP TRANSPLANTS TO EAST TEXAS: THE DUTCH MIGRA-TION TO NEDERLAND, PORT ARTHUR, AND WINNIE, 1895-1915," East Texas Historical Journal 13:2 (Fall 1975), 36-50.

B-3569 Bogger, Tommy L., "REVOLUTIONARY SENTIMENT AND THE GROWTH OF NORFOLK'S FREE BLACK POPULATION," Virginia Social Science Journal 12:1 (April 1977), 51-60.

B-3570 Boswell, Thomas D., "IN THE EYE OF THE STORM: THE CONTEXT OF HATIAN MIGRATION TO MIAMI, FLORIDA," Southeastern Geographer 23:2 (November 1983), 57-77.

B-3571 Bragaw, Donald H., "LOSS OF IDENTITY ON PENSACOLA'S PAST: A CREOLE FOOTNOTE," Florida Historical Quarterly 50:4 (April 1972), 414-418.

B-3572 Bragaw, Donald H., "STATUS OF NEGROES IN A SOUTHERN PORT CITY IN THE PROGRESSIVE ERA," Florida Historical Quarterly 51:3 (January 1973), 287-302.

B-3573 Bratton, Mary J., "JOHN JASPER OF RICHMOND: FROM SLAVE PREACHER TO COMMUNITY LEADER," Virginia Cavalcade 29:1 (Summer 1979), 32-39.

B-3574 Breed, Warren, "SUICIDE, MIGRATION, AND RACE: A STUDY OF CASES IN NEW ORLEANS," Journal of Social Issues 22:1 (January 1966), 30-43.

B-3575 Brown, Catherine L. and Thomas Ganshaw, "THE AUGUSTA, GEORGIA CHINESE: 1865-1980," West Georgia College Studies in the Social Sciences 22 (June 1983), 27-41.

B-3576 Brown, David L. and Glenn V. Fuguitt, "PERCENT NONWHITE AND RACIAL DISPARITY IN NONMETROPOLITAN CITIES IN THE SOUTH," Social Science Quarterly 53:3 (December 1972), 573-582.

B-3577 Brown, Kenny L., "PEACEFUL PROGRESS: THE ITALIANS OF KREBS," Chronicles of Oklahoma 53:3 (Fall 1975), 332-352.

B-3578 Brunn, Stanley D., "WHERE HAVE ALL THE MISSISSIPPIANS GONE?" Mississippi Geographer 5:1 (Spring 1977), 5-10.

B-3579 Bugg, James L., "THE FRENCH HUGUENOT FRONTIER SETTLEMENT OF MANAKIN TOWN," Virginia Magazine of History and Biography 61:4 (October 1953), 359-394.

B-3580 Burnett, Robert A., "LOUISVILLE'S FRENCH PAST," Filson Club History Quarterly 50:2 (April 1976), 5-27.

B-3581 Cahil, Edward E. and Urmil Salvja, "DE-POPULATION AND RE-POPULA-TION: A DEMOGRAPHIC ANALYSES OF TURN-AROUND COUNTIES OF THE SOUTH," Review of Regional Studies 5:3 (Winter 1975), 1-13.

B-3582 Callahan, Helen, "A STUDY OF DUBLIN: THE IRISH IN AUGUSTA," Richmond County History 5:2 (Summer 1973), 5-14.

B-3583 Carey, George W., Lenore Macomber and Michael Greenberg, "EDUCA-TIONAL AND DEMOGRAPHIC FACTORS IN THE URBAN GEOGRAPHY OF WASHING-TON, D. C.," Geographical Review 59:4 (October 1968), 515-537.

B-3584 Carney, James J., "POPULATION GROWTH IN MIAMI AND DADE COUNTY, FLORIDA," Tequesta No. 6 (1946), 50-55.

B-3585 Chaikin, Ellen, "THE JEWISH SECTIONS OF OAKLAND CEMETARY," Atlanta Historical Journal 23:3 (Fall 1979), 55-64.

B-3586 Chan, Lit Mui L., "THE CHINESE AMERICANS IN THE MISSISSIPPI DEL-TA," Journal of Mississippi History 35:1 (February 1973), 29-36.

B-3587 Chapman, Anne W., "INADEQUACIES OF THE 1848 CHARLESTON CENSUS," South Carolina Historical Magazine 81:1 (January 1980), 24-34.

B-3588 Chiu, S. M., "THE CHINESE OF AUGUSTA, GEORGIA," Bulletin: Chinese Historical Society of America, 13:2 (February 1978), 1-14.

B-3589 Chyet, Stanley F., "LUDWIG LEWISOHN IN CHARLESTON (1892-1903)," American Jewish Historical Quarterly 54:3 (March 1965), 296-322.

B-3590 Chyet, Stanley F., "MOSES JACOB EZEKIEL: A CHILDHOOD IN RICH-MOND," American Jewish Historical Quarterly 62:3 (March 1973), 286-294.

B-3591 Clark, Robert T. Jr., "THE GERMAN LIBERALS IN NEW ORLEANS (1840-1860)," Louisiana Historical Quarterly 20:1 (January 1937), 137-151.

B-3592 Clark, Robert T. Jr., "THE NEW ORLEANS GERMAN COLONY IN THE CIVIL WAR," Louisiana Historical Quarterly 20:4 (October 1937), 990-1015.

B-3593 Clark, Robert T. Jr., "RECONSTRUCTION AND THE NEW ORLEANS GERMAN COLONY," Louisiana Historical Quarterly 23:2 (April 1940), 501-524.

B-3594 Coclanis, Peter A., "DEATH IN EARLY CHARLESTON: AN ESTIMATE OF THE CRUDE DEATH RATE FOR THE WHITE POPULATION OF CHARLESTON, 1722-32," South Carolina Historical Magazine 85:4 (October 1984), 280-291.

B-3595 Cohen, Rev. Henry, "THE JEWS IN TEXAS," Publications of the American Jewish Historical Society 4 (1896), 9-21.

B-3596 Coony, Rosemary Santana and Maria Aliva Contreras, "RESIDENCE PATTERNS OF SOCIAL REGISTER CUBANS: A STUDY OF MIAMI, SAN JUAN, AND NEW YORK SMSAS," Cuban Studies 8:2 (1978), 33-50.

B-3597 Corbett, Theodore G., "POPULATION STRUCTURE IN HISPANIC ST. AUGUSTINE, 1629-1763," Florida Historical Quarterly 54:3 (January 1976), 263-284.

B-3598 Corbitt, Duvon C., "THE LAST SPANISH CENSUS OF PENSACOLA," Florida Historical Quarterly 24:1 (July 1945), 30-38.

B-3599 Crimmins, Eileen and Gretchen A. Condran, "MORTALITY VARIATION IN U.S. CITIES IN 1900: A TWO-LEVEL EXPLANATION BY CAUSE OF DEATH AND UNDERLYING FACTORS," Social Science History 7:1 (Winter 1983), 31-60.

B-3600 Davis, Nettie Vans, "HELVETIA--WEST VIRGINIA'S SWISS VILLAGE," West Virginia Review 12:3 (December 1934), 80-81.

B-3601 Della, M. Ray Jr., "AN ANALYSIS OF BALTIMORE'S POPULATION IN THE 1850'S," Maryland Historical Magazine 68:1 (Spring 1973), 20-35.

B-3602 Deskins, Donald R. Jr., "RACE AS AN ELEMENT IN THE INTRA-CITY REGIONALIZATION OF ATLANTA'S POPULATION," Southeastern Geographer 11:2 (November 1971), 90-100.

B-3603 Dinkel, Robert, "PEOPLING THE CITY: FERTILITY," in R. Vance, ed., The Urban South, (1954), 78-110.

B-3604 Dinnerstein, Leonard, "LEO FRANK AND THE AMERICAN JEWISH COMMUN- ITY," American Jewish Archives 20:2 (November 1968), 107-126.

B-3605 Dinnerstein, Leonard, "NEGLECTED ASPECT OF SOUTHERN JEWISH HISTORY," American Jewish Historical Quarterly 61:1 (September 1971), 52-68.

B-3606 Dunkle, John R., "POPULATION CHANGE AS AN ELEMENT IN THE HISTORI- CAL GEOGRAPHY OF ST. AUGUSTINE," Florida Historical Quarterly 37:1 (July 1958), 3-32.

B-3607 Durel, Lionel C., "CREOLE CIVILIZATION IN DONALDSVILLE, 1850, ACCORDING TO 'LE VIGILANT,'" Louisiana Historical Quarterly 31:4 (October 1948), 981-994.

B-3608 Durr, W. Theodore, "PEOPLE OF THE PENINSULA," Maryland Historical Magazine 77:1 (March 1982), 27-53.

B-3609 Dysart, Jane, "ANOTHER ROAD TO DISAPPEARANCE: ASSIMILATION OF CREEK INDIANS IN PENSACOLA, FLORIDA, DURING THE NINETEENTH CENTURY," Florida Historical Quarterly 61:1 (July 1982), 37-48.

B-3610 Dysart, Jane, "MEXICAN WOMEN IN SAN ANTONIO, 1830-1860: THE ASSI- MILATION PROCESS," Western Historical Quarterly 7:4 (1976), 365-375.

B-3611 Eckman, Jeannette, "LIFE AMONG THE EARLY DUTCH AT NEW CASTLE," Delaware History 4:3 (June 1951), 246-302.

B-3612 Eitcher, Edward, "MARYLAND'S 'JEW BILL,'" American Jewish Histori- cal Quarterly 60 (March 1971), 258-279.

B-3613 Ellis, Ann W., "THE GREEK COMMUNITY IN ATLANTA DURING THE ERA OF WORLD WAR II, 1939-1947," Atlanta Historical Bulletin 20:1 (Spring 1976), 33-42.

B-3614 Ellis, Ann W., "THE GREEK COMMUNITY IN ATLANTA, 1900-1923," Georgia Historical Quarterly 58:4 (Winter 1974), 400-408.

B-3615 Engleman, Uriah Zevi, "THE JEWISH POPULATION OF CHARLESTON: WHAT STUNTED ITS GROWTH AND PREVENTED ITS DECLINE," Jewish Social Studies 13:3 (July 1951), 195-210.

B-3616 Espina, Marina, "A BRIEF SKETCH OF FILIPINO VOLUNTARY ASSOCIATIONS IN SOUTHERN LOUISIANA," Perspectives on Ethnicity in New Orleans (1981), 84-87.

B-3617 Evans, V. J. and W. J. Serow, "POTENTIAL ECONOMIC COSTS OF MIGRA-TION: A CASE STUDY OF A SOUTH ATLANTIC METROPOLITAN AREA," Review of Regional Studies 3:1 (Fall 1972-1973), 109-118.

B-3618 Everett, Donald E., "EMIGRES AND MILITIAMEN: FREE PERSONS OF COLOR IN NEW ORLEANS 1803-1815," Journal of Negro History 38:4 (October 1953), 377-402.

B-3619 Everett, George A. Jr., "THE HISTORY OF THE GERMAN-AMERICAN COMMUNITY OF GLUCHSTADT, MISSISSIPPI: A STUDY IN PERSISTENCE," Journal of Mississippi History 37:4 (November 1976), 361-370.

B-3620 Ezekiel, Jacob, "THE JEWS OF RICHMOND," Publications of the American Jewish Historical Society 4 (1896), 22-28.

B-3621 Fabricio, Roberto, "MIAMI GOES LATIN AND LIKES IT," Florida Trend 18 (April 1976), 140-146.

B-3622 Fein, Isaac M., "BALTIMORE JEWS DURING THE CIVIL WAR," American Jewish Historical Quarterly 51:2 (December 1961), 67-96.

B-3623 Fischer, Reynolds, "THE URBANIZATION OF NEGROES IN THE UNITED STATES," Journal of Social History 1:3 (Spring 1968), 241-258.

B-3624 Fischer, Robert, "HISPANICS IN ATLANTA," Atlanta Historical Journal 24:2 (Summer 1980), 31-38.

B-3625 Fitchett, E. Horace, "THE ORIGIN AND GROWTH OF THE FREE NEGRO POPULATION OF CHARLESTON, SOUTH CAROLINA," Journal of Negro History 26:4 (October 1941), 421-437.

B-3626 Fitchett, E. Horace, "THE STATUS OF THE FREE NEGRO IN CHARLESTON, SOUTH CAROLINA," Journal of Negro History 32:4 (October 1947), 430-451.

B-3627 Fjellman, Stephen M. and Hugh Gladwin, "HAITIAN FAMILY PATTERNS OF MIGRATION TO SOUTH FLORIDA," Human Organization 44:4 (Winter 1985), 301-312.

B-3628 Flowerdew, Robin, "SPATIAL PATTERNS OF RESIDENTIAL SEGREGATION IN A SOUTHERN CITY," Journal of American Studies 13:1 (April 1979), 93-108.

B-3629 Folger, John and John Rowan, "MIGRATION AND MARITAL STATUS IN TEN SOUTHEASTERN CITIES," Social Forces 32:2 (December 1953), 178-185.

B-3630 Frank, Fedora Small, "NASHVILLE JEWRY DURING THE CIVIL WAR," Tennessee Historical Quarterly 39:3 (Fall 1980), 310-322.

B-3631 Garonzik, Joseph, "THE RACIAL AND ETHNIC MAKE-UP OF BALTIMORE NEIGHBORHOODS, 1850-1870," Maryland Historical Magazine 71:3 (Fall 1976), 392-402.

B-3632 Geffen, M. David, "DELAWARE JEWRY: THE FORMATIVE YEARS, 1872-1889," Delaware History 16:4 (October 1975), 269-297.

B-3633 George, Paul S., "COLORED TOWN: MIAMI'S BLACK COMMUNITY, 1896-1930," Florida Historical Quarterly 56:4 (April 1978), 432-447.

B-3634 Georges, Roger A., "THE GREEKS OF TARPON SPRINGS," Southern Folklore Quarterly 29:2 (June 1965), 129-141.

B-3635 Gilmore, Harlan W., "DIFFERENTIAL SEX RATIOS OF YOUNG CHILDREN IN NEW ORLEANS," Social Forces 38:3 (March 1960), 230-240.

B-3636 Ginsberg, Louis, "TWO STREAMS BECOME ONE," Virginia Cavalcade 7:4 (Spring 1958), 23-29.

B-3637 Glaser, Richard, "THE GREEK JEWS IN BALTIMORE," Jewish Social Studies 38:3-4 (1976), 321-336.

B-3638 Goldberg, Irving L., "THE CHANGING JEWISH COMMUNITY OF DALLAS," American Jewish Archives 11:1 (April 1959), 82-97.

B-3639 Goldberg, Robert A., "RACIAL CHANGE ON THE SOUTHERN PERIPHERY: THE CASE OF SAN ANTONIO, TEXAS, 1960-1965," Journal of Southern History 49:3 (August 1983), 349-374.

B-3640 Gorden, G. Arthur, "THE ARRIVAL OF THE SCOTCH HIGHLANDERS AT DARIEN," Georgia Historical Quarterly 20:3 (September 1936), 199-209.

B-3641 Greenbaum, Susan D., "AFRO-CUBANS IN EXILE: TAMPA, FLORIDA, 1886-1984," Tampa Bay History 7:2 (Fall-Winter 1985), 77-93.

B-3642 Hadden, Kenneth P., "MIGRATION ATTRACTIVENESS OF SOUTHERN METRO-POLITAN AREAS: A CRITIQUE AND REANALYSIS," Social Science Quarterly 51:4 (March 1971), 975-982.

B-3643 Hamilton, C. Horace, "POPULATION PRESSURE AND OTHER FACTORS AFFECTING NET RURAL-URBAN MIGRATION," Social Forces 30:2 (December 1951), 209-215.

B-3644 Hamilton, C. Horace, "RURAL-URBAN MIGRATION IN THE TENNESSEE VAL-LEY BETWEEN 1920 AND 1930," Social Forces 13:1 (October 1934), 57-64.

B-3645 Hammer, Andrew Marshall, "THE BACK-TO-THE-CITY MOVEMENT," Atlanta Economic Review 28:2 (March-April 1978), 4-6.

B-3646 Haney, C. Allen, et al., "THE VALUE STRETCH HYPOTHESIS: FAMILY SIZE PREFERENCE IN A BLACK POPULATION," Social Problems 21:2 (Fall 1973), 206-219.

B-3647 Harris, William, 'RESEARCH NOTE ON MOBILITY IN ATLANTA," South Atlantic Urban Studies 1 (1977), 267-272.

B-3648 Harrison, John M., "THE IRISH INFLUENCE IN EARLY ATLANTA," Atlanta Historical Bulletin 7:29 (October 1944), 196-211.

B-3649 Hawkes, Roland K., "SPATIAL PATTERNING OF URBAN POPULATION CHARAC-TERISTICS," American Journal of Sociology 78:5 (March 1973), 1216-1234.

B-3650 Hawkins, Homer C., "TRENDS IN BLACK MIGRATION FROM 1863 TO 1960," Phylon 34:2 (Summer 1973), 140-152.

B-3651 Hays, Steele, "BUTCHERTOWN," American Preservation 2:2 (1978), 58-63.

B-3652 Heatwole, Charles A., "MENNONITES' CHANGING ATTITUDES TOWARD THE CITY: A VIRGINIA EXAMPLE," Southeastern Geographer 19:1 (May 1979), 1-12.

B-3653 Hertzberg, Steven, "UNSETTLED JEWS: GEOGRAPHIC MOBILITY IN A NINETEENTH CENTURY CITY," American Jewish Historical Quarterly 67:2 (December 1977), 125-139.

B-3654 Hewes, Leslie, "TONTITOWN: OZARK VINEYARD CENTER," Economic Geography 29:2 (April 1953), 125-143.

B-3655 Hinds, Dudley S. and Nicholas Ordway," THE INFLUENCE OF RACE ON
REZONING DECISIONS: EQUALITY OF TREATMENT IN BLACK AND WHITE
CENSUS TRACTS, 1955-1980, Review of Black Political Economy 14:4
(Spring 1986), 51-64.

B-3656 Hitt, Homer L., "PEOPLING THE CITY: MIGRATION," in R. Vance, ed.,
The Urban South, (1954), 54-77.

B-3657 Hitt, Homer L. and T. Lynn Smith, "POPULATION REDISTRIBUTION IN
LOUISIANA," Social Forces 20:4 (May 1942), 437-444.

B-3658 Holmes, Jack D. L., "THE ROLE OF BLACKS IN SPANISH ALABAMA: THE
MOBILE DISTRICT, 1780-1813," Alabama Historical Quarterly 39:1
(Spring 1975), 5-18.

B-3659 Hopkins, Richard J., "OCCUPATIONAL AND GEOGRAPHIC MOBILITY IN
ATLANTA, 1870-1896," Journal of Southern History 34:2 (May 1968),
200-213.

B-3660 Howell, Isabel, "JOHN ARMFIELD OF BEERSHEBA SPRINGS [1]" Tennessee
Historical Quarterly 3:1 (March 1944), 46-64.

B-3661 Howell, Isabel, "JOHN ARMFIELD OF BEERSHEBA SPRINGS [2],"
Tennessee Historical Quarterly 3:2 (June 1944), 156-167.

B-3662 Hutcheson, John D. Jr. and Elizabeth T. Beer, "IN-MIGRATION AND
ATLANTA'S NEIGHBORHOODS," Atlanta Economic Review 28:2 (March-
April 1978), 7-14.

B-3663 Iden, George, "ALTERNATIVE MIGRATION STRATEGIES FOR THE SOUTHERN
POOR," Review of Regional Studies 5:1 (Spring 1975), 29-36.

B-3664 "THE IRISH IN ATLANTA, GEORGIA," Journal of the American Irish
Historical Society 30 (1932), 164-172.

B-3665 Jackson, L. P., "FREE NEGROES OF PETERSBURG, VIRGINIA," Journal of
Negro History 12:3 (July 1927), 365-388.

B-3666 Jackson, Susan, "MOVIN' ON: MOBILITY THROUGH HOUSTON IN THE
1850s," Southwestern Historical Quarterly 81:3 (January 1978),
257-282.

B-3667 Johnson, Michael P., "RUNAWAY SLAVES AND THE SLAVE COMMUNITIES IN
SOUTH CAROLINA, 1799 TO 1830," William and Mary Quarterly 38:3
(July 1981), 418-441.

B-3668 Johnson, Whittington B., "FREE BLACKS IN ANTEBELLUM AUGUSTA,
GEORGIA," Richmond County History 14:1 (Winter 1982), 10-22.

B-3669 Johnson, Whittington B., "FREE BLACKS IN ANTEBELLUM SAVANNAH,"
Georgia Historical Quarterly 64:4 (Winter 1980), 418-431.

B-3670 Kaplan, Barry J., "RACE, INCOME, AND ETHNICITY: RESIDENTIAL
CHANGE IN A HOUSTON COMMUNITY, 1920-1970," Houston Review 3
(Winter 1981), 178-202.

B-3671 Kartman, Laurraine Levy, "THE JEWISH BOARD OF ARBITRATION IN
BALTIMORE, THE EARLY YEARS,' Maryland Historical Magazine 79:4
(Winter 1984), 332-338.

B-3672 Kau, James B. and Charles F. Floyd, "A MULTIVARIATE ANALYSIS OF
PUBLIC HOUSING RESIDENTS," Review of Regional Studies 4:1 (Spring
1974), 42-49.

B-3673 Keeth, Kent, "SANKT ANTONIUS: GERMANS IN THE ALAMO CITY IN THE
1850's," Southwestern Historical Quarterly 76:2 (October 1972),
183-201.

B-3674 Keller, Frank V. Stanford H. Bederman, and Freeman A. Hartshorn, "MIGRATION PATTERNS OF ATLANTA'S INNER CITY DISPLACED RESIDENTS," West Georgia College Studies in the Social Sciences 16 (June 1977), 49-58.

B-3675 Kellogg, John, "NEGRO URBAN CLUSTERS IN THE POSTBELLUM SOUTH," Geographical Review 67:3 (July 1977), 310-321.

B-3676 Ken, Sally, "THE CHINESE COMMUNITY OF AUGUSTA, GEORGIA, 1873 TO 1971," Richmond County History 4:1 (Winter 1972), 51-60.

B-3677 Kendall, John Smith, "SOME DISTINGUISHED HISPANO-ORLEANIANS," Louisiana Historical Quarterly 18:1 (January 1935), 40-55.

B-3678 Kenyon, James B., "SPATIAL ASSOCIATIONS IN THE INTEGRATION OF THE AMERICAN CITY," Economic Geography 52:4 (October 1976), 287-303.

B-3679 Kocolowski, Gary P., "STABILIZING MIGRATION TO LOUISVILLE AND CINCINNATI, 1865-1901," Cincinnati Historical Society Bulletin 37:1 (1979), 23-47.

B-3680 Kuo, Wen H. and Nan Lin, "ASSIMILATION OF CHINESE-AMERICANS IN WASHINGTON, D. C.," Sociological Quarterly 18:3 (Summer 1977), 340-352.

B-3681 Lack, Paul D., "AN URBAN SLAVE COMMUNITY: LITTLE ROCK, 1831-1862," Arkansas Historical Quarterly 41-43 (Autumn 1982), 258-287.

B-3682 Law, Eileen and Sally Ken, "A STUDY OF THE CHINESE COMMUNITY," Richmond County History 5:2 (Summer 1973), 23-43.

B-3683 Lewellen, Jeffrey, "'SHEEP AMONG THE WOLVES': FATHER BAUDINI AND THE COLONY AT TONTITOWN, 1898-1917," Arkansas Historical Quarterly 45:1 (Spring 1986), 19-40.

B-3684 Littlefield, Daniel, "CHARLESTON AND INTERNAL SLAVE REDISTRIBU-TION," South Carolina Historical Magazine 87:2 (April 1986), 93-105.

B-3685 Lockey, Joseph B., "THE ST. AUGUSTINE CENSUS OF 1786," Florida Historical Quarterly 18:1 (July 1939), 11-31.

B-3686 Long, Larry H., "SELECTIVITY OF BLACK RETURN MIGRATION TO THE SOUTH," Rural Sociology 42:3 (Fall 1977), 317-331.

B-3687 Lovrich, Frank M., "THE DALMATION YUGOSLAVS IN LOUISIANA," Louisiana History 8:2 (Spring 1967), 149-164.

B-3688 Lowry, Mark II, "POPULATION AND RACE IN MISSISSIPPI, 1940-1960," Annals of the Association of American Geographers 61:3 (September 1971), 576-588.

B-3689 Luebke, B. H. and John Fraser Hart, "MIGRATION FROM A SOUTHERN APPALACHIAN COMMUNITY," Land Economics 34:1 (February 1958), 44-53.

B-3690 MacDonell, Alexander R., "THE SETTLEMENT OF THE SCOTCH HIGHLANDERS AT DARIEN," Georgia Historical Quarterly 20:3 (September 1936), 250-262.

B-3691 Magarian, Horen Henry, "THE FOUNDING AND ESTABLISHMENT OF THE ARMENIAN COMMUNITY OF RICHMOND, VIRGINIA," Armenian Review 28:3 (1975), 265-271.

B-3692 Magnaghi, Russell M., "LOUISIANA'S ITALIAN IMMIGRANTS," Louisiana History 27:1 (Winter 1986), 43-68.

B-3693 Makofsky, Abraham, "DEMOGRAPHICS AND CULTURE: THE 1980 CENSUS REPORT ON LUMBEE INDIANS OF THE BALTIMORE METROPOLITAN AREA," Maryland Historical Magazine 79:3 (Fall 1984), 239-248.

B-3694 Makofsky, Abraham, "TRADITION AND CHANGE IN THE LUMBEE INDIAN COMMUNITY OF BALTIMORE," Maryland Historical Magazine 75:1 (March 1980), 55-71.

B-3695 Margario, Anthony V. and J. Lambert Molyneaux, "RESIDENTIAL SEGREGATION OF ITALIANS IN NEW ORLEANS AND SELECTED AMERICAN CITIES," Louisiana Studies 12:4 (Winter 1973), 639-648.

B-3696 Margavio, A. V. and Jerry Salomone, "THE PASSAGE, SETTLEMENT AND OCCUPATIONAL CHARACTERISTICS OF LOUISIANA'S ITALIAN IMMIGRANTS," Sociological Spectrum 1:4 (October-December 1981), 345-360.

B-3697 Martin, John M., "THE PEOPLE OF NEW ORLEANS AS SEEN BY HER VISITORS, 1803-1860," Louisiana Studies 6:4 (Winter 1967), 357-372.

B-3698 Meade, Anthony, "THE DISTRIBUTION OF SEGREGATION IN ATLANTA," Social Forces 51:2 (December 1972), 182-191.

B-3699 Meigs, Peveril III, "AN ETHNO-TELEPHONIC SURVEY OF FRENCH LOUISIANA," Annals of the American Association of Geographers 31:1 (March 1941), 243-250.

B-3700 Melnick, Ralph, "BILLY SIMONS: THE BLACK JEW OF CHARLESTON," American Jewish Archives 32:1 (April 1980), 3-8.

B-3701 Miller, Randall M., "THE ENEMY WITHIN: SOME EFFECTS OF FOREIGN IMMIGRANTS ON ANTEBELLUM SOUTHERN CITIES," Southern Studies 24:1 (Spring 1985), 30-54.

B-3702 Miller, Zane L., "URBAN BLACKS IN THE SOUTH, 1865-1920: AN ANALYSIS OF SOME QUANTITATIVE DATA ON RICHMOND, SAVANNAH, NEW ORLEANS, LOUISVILLE, AND BIRMINGHAM," in Schnore, L., ed., The New Urban History: Quantitative Exploration by American Historians, (1975), 184-204.

B-3703 Mitchelson, Ronald L. and James S. Fisher, "SPATIAL PERSPECTIVE OF POPULATION DYNAMICS IN GEORGIA, 1960-1980," Southeastern Geographer 23:1 (May 1983), 35-50.

B-3704 Mohl, Raymond A., "AN ETHNIC 'BOILING POT': CUBANS AND HAITIANS IN MIAMI," Journal of Ethnic Studies 13:2 (Summer 1985), 51-74.

B-3705 Mohl, Raymond A., "MIAMI: THE ETHNIC CALDRON," in R. Bernard, ed., Sunbelt Cities, Politics and Growth Since World War II, (1983), 58-99.

B-3706 Molyneaux, J. Lambert and Anthony V. Margavio, "POPULATION CHANGE IN NEW ORLEANS FROM 1940 TO 1960," Louisiana Studies 9:4 (Winter 1970), 228-242.

B-3707 Morgan, David T., "THE SHEFTAILS OF SAVANNAH," American Jewish History 62:4 (June 1973), 348-361.

B-3708 Mormino, Gary, "'WE WORKED HARD AND TOOK CARE OF OUR OWN': ORAL HISTORY AND ITALIANS IN TAMPA," Labor History 23:3 (Summer 1982), 395-415.

B-3709 Mormino, Gary R. and George E. Pozzetta, "IMMIGRANT WOMEN IN TAMPA: THE ITALIAN EXPERIENCE, 1890-1930," Florida Historical Quarterly 61:3 (January 1983), 296-313.

B-3710 Nau, John F., "THE GERMAN PEOPLE OF NEW ORLEANS, 1850-1900," Louisiana Historical Quarterly 54:2 (Spring 1971), 30-45.

B-3711 Nesbitt, George B., "DISPERSION OF NONWHITE RESIDENCE IN WASH-
INGTON, D. C.: SOME OF ITS IMPLICATIONS," Land Economics 32:3
(August 1956), 202-212.

B-3712 Nichols, Jeannette Paddoch, "DOES THE MILL VILLAGE FOSTER ANY
SOCIAL TYPES," Social Forces 2:3 (March 1924), 350-357.

B-3713 Obermiller, Phillip," "APPALACHIANS AS AN URBAN ETHNIC GROUP:
ROMANTICISM, RENAISSANCE, OR REVOLUTION? AND A BRIEF BIBLIOGRAPH-
ICAL ESSAY ON URBAN APPALACHIANS," Appalachian Journal 5:1 (Autumn
1977), 145-152.

B-3714 O'Brien, Michael J., "THE IRISH IN CHARLESTON, SOUTH CAROLINA,"
Journal of the American Irish Historical Society 25 (1926), 134-
146.

B-3715 O'Hare, William, "THE BEST METROS FOR BLACKS," American Demographics 8:7 (July 1986), 26-29, 32-33.

B-3716 "OLD BILLY," American Jewish Archives 15:1 (April 1963), 3-5.

B-3717 Owen, Polly, "IS IT TRUE WHAT THEY SAY ABOUT THE IRISH?" West
Tennessee Historical Society Papers No. 32 (1978), 120-132.

B-3718 Owen, Thomas M., "INDIAN TRIBES AND TOWNS IN ALABAMA," Alabama
Historical Quarterly 12:1-4 (1950), 118-241.

B-3719 Owsley, Harriet C., "THE RUGBY PAPERS: A BIBLIOGRAPHIC NOTE,"
Tennessee Historical Quarterly 27:3 (Fall 1968), 225-228.

B-3720 Pantazes, William N., "THE GREEKS OF TARPON SPRINGS: AN AMERICAN
ODYSSEY," Tampa Bay History 1:2 (Fall-Winter 1979), 24-31.

B-3721 Pathak, Chittarajan, "SPATIAL ANALYSIS OF URBAN POPULATION
DISTRIBUTION IN RALEIGH, NORTH CAROLINA," Southeastern Geographer
4 (1964), 41-50.

B-3722 Percal, Raul Moncary, "THE GOLDEN CAGE: CUBANS IN MIAMI,"
International Migration [Netherlands] 16:3-4 (1978), 160-173.

B-3723 Perez, Lisandro and Maisy L. Cheng, "THE REVIVAL OF POPULATION
GROWTH IN NONMETROPOLITAN AMERICA: THE EXCEPTION OF LOUISIANA,"
Southern Studies 19:2 (Summer 1980), 193-210.

B-3724 Perez, Louis A. Jr., "CUBANS IN TAMPA: FROM EXILES TO IMMIGRANTS,
1892-1901," Florida Historical Quarterly 57:2 (October 1978), 129-
140.

B-3725 Perez, Louis A. Jr., "CUBANS IN TAMPA: FROM EXILES TO IMMIGRANTS,
1892-1901," Tampa Bay History 7:2 (Fall-Winter 1985), 22-35.

B-3726 Petrusak, Frank and Steven Steinert, "THE JEWS OF CHARLESTON:
SOME OLD WINE IN NEW BOTTLES," Jewish Social Studies 38:3-4
(1976), 337-346.

B-3727 Pettigrew, Thomas F. and M. Richard Cramer, "THE DEMOGRAPHY OF
DESEGREGATION," Journal of Social Issues 15:4 (1959), 61-71.

B-3728 Pizzo, Tony, "THE ITALIAN HERITAGE IN TAMPA," Sunland Tribune 3
(November 1977), 24-33.

B-3729 Portes, Alejandro, "THE RISE OF ETHNICITY: DETERMINANTS OF ETHNIC
PERCEPTIONS AMONG CUBAN EXILES IN MIAMI," American Sociological
Review 49:3 (June 1984), 383-397.

B-3730 Proctor, Samuel, "JEWISH LIFE IN NEW ORLEANS, 1718-1860,"
Louisiana Historical Quarterly 40:2 (April 1957), 110-132.

B-3731 Rankin, David C., "THE IMPACT OF THE CIVIL WAR ON THE FREE COLORED COMMUNITY OF NEW ORLEANS," Perspectives in American History 11 (1977-78), 379-416.

B-3732 Rasico, Philip D., "MINORCAN POPULATION OF ST. AUGUSTINE IN THE SPANISH CENSUS OF 1768," Florida Historical Quarterly 66:2 (October 1987), 160-184.

B-3733 Reckless, Walter C., "THE INITIAL EXPERIENCE WITH CENSUS TRACTS IN A SOUTHERN CITY," Social Forces 15:1 (October 1936), 47-54.

B-3734 Reed, John Shelton, "THE HEART OF DIXIE: AN ESSAY IN FOLK GEOGRAPHY," Social Forces 54:4 (June 1976), 925-939.

B-3735 Reissman, Leonard, "THE NEW ORLEANS JEWISH COMMUNITY," Jewish Journal of Sociology 9:1 (June 1962), 110-123.

B-3736 Remy, Caroline, "HISPANIC-MEXICAN SAN ANTONIO: 1836-1861," Southwestern Historical Quarterly 71:4 (April 1968), 564-582.

B-3737 Rhoads, Edward J. M., "THE CHINESE IN TEXAS," Southwestern Historical Quarterly 81:1 (July 1977), 1-36.

B-3738 Robinson, Henry S., "SOME ASPECTS OF THE FREE NEGRO POPULATION OF WASHINGTON, D. C.," Maryland Historical Magazine 64:1 (Spring 1969), 43-64.

B-3739 Rogers, Tommy W., "MIGRATION ATTRACTIVENESS OF SOUTHERN METROPOLI-TAN AREAS," Social Science Quarterly 50:2 (September 1969), 325-336.

B-3740 Rogers, Tommy W., "NET MIGRATION RATES OF THE EIGHTY STANDARD METROPOLITAN STATISTICAL AREAS OF THE CENSUS SOUTH, 1950-1960," Louisiana Studies 6:2 (Summer 1967), 135-148.

B-3741 Roof, Wade Clark; Thomas L. Van Valey and Daphne Spain, "RESI-DENTIAL SEGREGATION IN SOUTHERN CITIES: 1970," Social Forces 55:1 (September 1976), 59-71.

B-3342 Rose, Harold M., "METROPOLITAN MIAMI'S CHANGING NEGRO POPULATION, 1950-1960," Economic Geography 40:3 (July 1964), 221-238.

B-3743 Rosenwaike, Ira, "ESTIMATING JEWISH POPULATION DISTRIBUTION IN U. S. METROPOLITAN AREAS IN 1970," Jewish Social Studies 36:2 (April 1974), 106-117.

B-3744 Rosenwaike, Ira, "THE FIRST JEWISH SETTLERS IN LOUISVILLE," Filson Club History Quarterly 53:1 (January 1979), 37-44.

B-3745 Rosenwaike, Ira, "THE JEWS OF BALTIMORE TO 1810," American Jewish Historical Quarterly 64:4 (June 1975), 291-320.

B-3746 Rosenwaike, Ira, "THE JEWS OF BALTIMORE: 1810 TO 1820," American Jewish Historical Quarterly 67:2 (December 1977), 101-124.

B-3747 Rosenwaike, Ira, "THE JEWS OF BALTIMORE: 1820 TO 1830," American Jewish Historical Quarterly 67:3 (March 1978), 246-259.

B-3748 Rothrock, Thomas, "THE STORY OF TONTITOWN, ARKANSAS," Arkansas Historical Quarterly 16:1 (Spring 1957), 84-88.

B-3749 Rothschild, Janice, "PRE-1867 ATLANTA JEWRY," American Jewish Historical Quarterly 62:3 (March 1973), 242-249.,

B-3750 Sarna, Jan, ed., "MARCHE, ARKANSAS: A PERSONAL REMINISCENCE OF LIFE AND CUSTOMS," Arkansas Historical Quarterly 36:1 (Spring 1977), 31-50.

B-3751 Savage, William W. Jr., "MONOLOGUES IN RED AND WHITE: CONTEMPO-
       RARY ATTITUDES IN TWO SOUTHERN PLAINS COMMUNITIES," Journal of
       Ethnic Studies 2:3 (Fall 1974), 24-31.

B-3752 Schmier, Louis, "THE FIRST JEWS OF VALDOSTA," Georgia Historical
       Quarterly 62:1 (Spring 1978), 32-49.

B-3753 Schroeder, Larry D., "AN ANALYSIS OF INCOME CONCENTRATION IN SMALL
       AREAS," Review of Regional Studies 6:3 (Winter 1976), 1-10.

B-3754 Schroeder, Larry D., "GEOGRAPHICAL MOBILITY IN THE ATLANTA AREA,
       1965-1970," Atlanta Economic Review 25:4 (July-August 1975), 28-
       30.

B-3755 Schroeder, Larry D. and David L. Sjoquist, "INVESTIGATION OF
       POPULATION DENSITY GRADIENTS USING TREND SURFACE ANALYSIS," Land
       Economics 52:3 (August 1976), 382-392.

B-3756 Schuster, Ruth, "MIGRATION OF JEWISH REFUGEES TO ATLANTA," Atlanta
       Historical Journal 23:3 (Fall 1979), 65-76.

B-3757 Scribner, Robert L., "THE 'PEANUT KING,'" Virginia Cavalcade 8:1
       (Summer 1958), 16-31.

B-3758 Sean-Shong Hwany and Steve H. Murdock, "RESIDENTIAL SEGREGATION IN
       TEXAS IN 1980," Social Science Quarterly 63:4 (December 1982),
       737-748.

B-3759 Semyonou, M. and R. I. Scott, "PERCENT BLACK, COMMUNITY CHARACTER-
       ISTICS AND RACE-LINKED OCCUPATIONAL DIFFERENTIATION IN THE RURAL
       SOUTH," Rural Sociology 48:2 (Summer 1983), 240-252.

B-3760 Serow, William J., "THE ROLE OF LONG DISTANCE MIGRATION IN THE
       RURAL RENAISSANCE, IN GENTRIFICATION, AND IN GROWTH OF THE SUN-
       BELT," Review of Regional Studies 10:3 (Winter 1980), 23-31.

B-3761 Serow, William J., Julia H. Martin, and Michael A. Spar, "AN
       ANALYSIS OF POPULATION GROWTH RATES WITHIN TYPOLOGICAL CATEGORIES
       OF SMALL SOUTHERN CITIES," Review of Regional Studies 10:1
       (Spring 1980), 29-47.

B-3762 Shankman, Arnold, "THE GALVESTON MOVEMENT: THE LETTERS OF ANNIE
       E. JOHNSON AND JACOB SCHIFF," Atlanta Historical Journal 23:3
       (Fall 1979), 77-84.

B-3763 Sherman, Philip, "BALTIMORE JEW ALLEY," Generations 2 (December
       1981), 43-46.

B-3764 Shosteck, Robert, "THE JEWISH COMMUNITY OF WASHINGTON, D. C.
       DURING THE CIVIL WAR," American Jewish Historical Quarterly 56:3
       (March 1967), 319-347.

B-3765 Sirmans, C. F., "THE JOURNEY TO WORK: A CROSS-SECTIONAL ANALY-
       SIS," Review of Regional Studies 4:1 (Spring 1974), 73-81.

B-3766 Sisco, Paul H., "POPULATION CHANGES IN MEMPHIS, 1950-1958,"
       Memorandum Folio, Southeastern Division, Association of American
       Geographers 12 (November 1960), 91-97.

B-3767 Sisco, Paul H., "POPULATION CHANGES IN MEMPHIS, 1950-1958," South-
       eastern Geographer 1 (1961), 24-38.

B-3768 Skinner, Woodward B., "ETHNIC GROUPS INFLUENCE THE HISTORY OF
       PENSACOLA," Echo 2 (Spring-Summer 1981), 67-72.

B-3769 Smith, Helen, "WHITE BLUFF: A COMMUNITY OF COMMUTERS," Economic
       Geography 19:2 (April 1943), 143-147.

B-3770 Spriggs, William, "MEASURING RESIDENTIAL SEGREGATION: AN APPLI-
CATION OF TREND SURFACE ANALYSIS," Phylon 45:4 (1984), 249-263.

B-3771 Stanton, William M., "THE IRISH OF MEMPHIS," West Tennessee
Historical Society Papers No. 6 (1952), 87-118.

B-3772 Stephanides, Marios, "THE GREEK COMMUNITY IN LOUISVILLE," Filson
Club History Quarterly 55:1 (January 1981), 5-26.,

B-3773 Stepick, Alex and Alejandro Portes, "FLIGHT INTO DESPAIR: A
PROFILE OF RECENT HAITIAN REFUGEES IN SOUTH FLORIDA," International Migration Review 20:2 (Summer 1986), 329-350.

B-3774 Stern, Malcolm H., "NEW LIGHT ON THE JEWISH SETTLEMENT OF
SAVANNAH," American Jewish Historical Quarterly 52:3 (March 1963),
169-199.

B-3775 Stern, Malcolm H., "THE SHEFTALL DIARIES: VITAL RECORDS OF
SAVANNAH JEWRY (1733-1808)," American Jewish Historical Quarterly
54:3 (March 1965), 243-277.

B-3776 Stern, Malcolm H., "SOME NOTES ON THE HISTORY OF THE ORGANIZED
JEWISH COMMUNITY OF NORFOLK, VIRGINIA," Journal of the Southern
Jewish Historical Society 3:1 (November 1963), 12-36.

B-3777 Stowers, Dewey M. Jr. and Harry J. Scholeman Jr., "MASARYKTOWN: A
SUCCESSFUL ETHNIC EXPERIMENT," Florida Geographer 16:1 (August
1982),13-16.

B-3778 Stowers, Dewey M. Jr. and Harry J. Scholeman Jr., "TARPON SPRINGS,
FLORIDA--A STUDY IN CULTURAL TRANSFERENCE," Mississippi Geographer
4 (Spring 1976), 43-49.

B-3779 Sumka, Howard J., "RACIAL SEGREGATION IN SMALL NORTH CAROLINA
CITIES," Southeastern Geographer 17:1 (May 1977), 58-75.

B-3780 Sutker, Solomon, "THE JEWISH ORGANIZATIONAL ELITE OF ATLANTA,
GEORGIA," Social Forces 31:2 (December 1952), 136-143.

B-3781 Sweat, Edward F., "FREE BLACKS IN ANTEBELLUM ATLANTA," Atlanta
Historical Journal 21:1 (Spring 1977), 64-71.

B-3782 Tansey, Richard, "OUT-OF-STATE FREE BLACKS IN LATE ANTEBELLUM NEW
ORLEANS," Louisiana History 22:4 (Fall 1981), 369-386.

B-3783 Tarver, James D., "MIGRATION DIFFERENTIALS IN SOUTHERN CITIES AND
SUBURBS," Social Science Quarterly 50:2 (September 1969), 298-234.

B-3784 Taylor, Joe, "ATLANTA MORTALITY TRENDS: 1853-1873," Atlanta
Historical Bulletin 20:2 (Summer 1976), 112-119.

B-3785 Teske, Robert, "GREEK IMMIGRATION TO NASHVILLE, TENNESSEE: AN
ORAL HISTORY," Kentucky Folklore Record 29:3-4 (July-December
1983), 102-110.

B-3786 Thomas, Herbert A. Jr., "VICTIMS OF CIRCUMSTANCES: NEGROES IN A
SOUTHERN TOWN, 1865-1880," Register of the Kentucky Historical
Society 71:3 (July 1973), 253-271.

B-3787 "TONY PIZZO'S YBOR CITY," Tampa Bay History 2:1 (Spring-Summer
1980), 49-64.

B-3788 TONY PIZZO'S YBOR CITY: AN INTERVIEW WITH TONY PIZZO," Tampa Bay
History 7:2 (Fall-Winter 1985), 142-160.

B-3789 Tracy, Sterling, "THE IMMIGRANT POPULATION OF MEMPHIS," West
Tennessee Historical Society Papers No. 4 (1950), 72-82.

B-3790 Tsong, Peter Z. W., "THE IMPACT OF HIGHWAYS ON RURAL POPULATION
DENSITY," Review of Regional Studies 4:1 (Spring 1974), 82-87.

B-3791 Vujnovich, Milos M., "CROATIANS IN SOUTHERN LOUISIANA: IMMIGRA-
TION, SETTLEMENT, AND CULTURAL DEFINITION," Perspectives on
Ethnicity in New Orleans (1981), 71-75.

B-3792 Ward, Martha C. and Zahary Gusson, "THE VIETNAMESE IN NEW ORLEANS:
A PRELIMINARY REPORT," Perspectives on Ethnicity in New Orleans
(1980), 53-62.

B-3793 Watkins, Alfred J., "INTERMETROPOLITAN MIGRATION AND THE RISE OF
THE SUNBELT," Social Science Quarterly 59:3 (December 1978), 553-
561.

B-3794 Wax, James A., "THE JEWS OF MEMPHIS: 1860-1865," West Tennessee
Historical Society Papers No. 3 (1949), 39-89.

B-3795 Weaver, Herbert, "FOREIGNERS IN ANTE-BELLUM SAVANNAH," Georgia
Historical Quarterly 37:1 (March 1953), 1-17.

B-3796 Weaver, Herbert, "FOREIGNERS IN ANTE-BELLUM TOWNS OF THE LOWER
SOUTH," Journal of Southern History 13:1 (February 1947), 62-73.

B-3797 Weissbach, Lee Shai, "THE PEOPLING OF LEXINGTON, KENTUCKY: GROWTH
AND MOBILITY IN A FRONTIER TOWN," Register of the Kentucky
Historical Society 81:2 (Spring 1983), 115-133.

B-3798 West, Patty, "THE MIAMI INDIAN TOURIST ATTRACTIONS: A HISTORY AND
ANALYSIS OF A TRANSITIONAL MAKASUKI SEMINOLE ENVIRONMENT," Florida
Anthropologist 34:4 (December 1981), 200-224.

B-3799 Wheeler, James O. and Barry W. Davis, "INTRAMETROPOLITAN MIGRATION
IN ATLANTA: DECONCENTRATION OR BACK TO THE CITY?" Southeastern
Geographer 22:1 (May 1982), 35-51.

B-3800 Wheeler, James O. and Barry W. Davis, "MIGRATION OF BLACKS IN THE
ATLANTA METROPOLITAN AREA, 1973 TO 1977," Southeastern Geographer
24:2 (November 1984), 99-114.

B-3801 White, Dana F., "THE BLACK SIDES OF ATLANTA: A GEOGRAPHY OF
EXPANSION AND CONTAINMENT, 1970-1870," Atlanta Historical Journal
216:2-3 (Summer-Fall 1982), 199-225.

B-3802 Wilhelm, Gene Jr., "APPALACHIA: IN-MIGRATION IN THE TWENTIETH
CENTURY," Appalachian Journal 1:4 (Spring 1974), 301-306.

B-3803 Wilkie, Jane Riblett, "THE BLACK URBAN POPULATION OF THE PRE-CIVIL
WAR SOUTH," Phylon 37:3 (September 1976), 250-262.

B-3804 Williams, Beverly S., "ANTI-SEMITISM AND SHREVEPORT, LOUISIANA:
THE SITUATION IN THE 1920s," Louisiana History 21:4 (Fall 1980),
387-398.

B-3805 Williams, L. A., "THE INTELLECTUAL STATUS OF CHILDREN IN COTTON
MILL VILLAGES," Social Forces 4:1 (September 1925), 183-188.

B-3806 Williams, Roger, "THE NEGRO IN ATLANTA," Atlanta 6 (June 1966),
25-30.

B-3807 Wilson, Bobby M., "RACIAL SEGREGATION TRENDS IN BIRMINGHAM,
ALABAMA," Southeastern Geographer 25:1 (May 1985), 30-43.

B-3808 Winsberg, Morton D., "CHANGING DISTRIBUTION OF THE BLACK POPULA-
TION: FLORIDA CITIES, 1970-1980," Urban Affairs Quarterly 18:3
(March 1983), 361-370.

B-3809 Winsberg, Morton D., "RELATIVE GROWTH AND DISTRIBUTION OF FLORIDA'S EUROPEAN BORN," Florida Geographer 18:1 (September 1984), 16-21.

B-3810 Winston, James E., "THE FREE NEGRO IN NEW ORLEANS, 1803-1860," Louisiana Historical Quarterly 21:4 (October 1938), 1075-1085.

B-3811 Woodrow, Karen, Donald W. Hastings, and Edward J. Lu, "RURAL-URBAN PATTERN OF MARRIAGE, DIVORCE, AND MORTALITY: TENNESSEE, 1970," Rural Sociology 43:1 (Spring 1978), 70-84.

B-3812 Wooster, Ralph A., "FOREIGNERS IN THE PRINCIPAL TOWNS OF ANTE-BELLUM TEXAS," Southwestern Historical Quarterly 66:2 (October 1962), 208-220.

Race Relations

B-3813 Adams, Samuel L., "BLUEPRINT FOR SEGREGATION: A SURVEY OF ATLANTA HOUSING," New South 22:2 (Spring 1967), 73-84.

B-3814 Alvis, Joel L. Jr., "RACIAL TURMOIL AND RELIGIOUS REACTION: THE RT. REV. JOHN M. ALLEN," Historical Magazine 50:1 (March 1981), 83-96.

B-3815 Amprich, John, "THE BEGINNING OF THE BLACK SUFFRAGE MOVEMENT IN TENNESSEE, 1864-65," Journal of Negro History 65:3 (Summer 1980), 185-195.

B-3816 Badger, Tony, "REVIEW ESSAY: SEGREGATION AND THE SOUTHERN BUSINESS ELITE," Journal of American Studies 18:1 (April 1984), 105-109.

B-3817 Bambara, Lon Cade, "WHAT'S HAPPENING IN ATLANTA," Southern Exposure 11:4 (July-August 1983), 25-35.

B-3818 Barksdale, Marcellus, "CIVIL RIGHTS ORGANIZATION AND THE INDI-GENOUS MOVEMENT IN CHAPEL HILL, N. C., 1960-1965," Phylon 37:1 (March 1986), 29-42.

B-3819 Barnes, Brooks Miles, "THE ONANCOCK RACE RIOT OF 1907," Virginia Magazine of History and Biography 92:3 (July 1984), 336-352.

B-3820 Bartley, N. V., "LOOKING BACK AT LITTLE ROCK," Arkansas Historical Quarterly 25:2 (Summer 1966), 101-116.

B-3821 Beeler, Dorothy, "RACE RIOT IN COLUMBIA, TENNESSEE: FEBRUARY 25-27, 1946," Tennessee Historical Quarterly 39:1 (Spring 1980), 49-61.

B-3822 Bell, Patricia A. and A. Wade Smith, "RACIAL RESIDENTIAL SEGREGA-TION IN THE SUNBELT," Social Indicators Research 16:2 (February 1985), 181-183.

B-3823 Boon, John and William Farmer, "VIOLENCE IN MIAMI: ONE MORE WARN-ING," New South 23:4 (Fall 1968), 28-37.

B-3824 Boulton, Scot W., "DESEGREGATION AND THE OKLAHOMA CITY SCHOOL SYSTEM," Chronicles of Oklahoma 58:2 (Summer 1980), 192-221.

B-3825 Braden, Anne, "BIRMINGHAM, 1956-1979: THE HISTORY THAT WE MADE," Southern Exposure 7:2 (Summer 1979), 48-54.

B-3826 Bullich, Henry Allen, "URBANISM AND RACE RELATIONS," in R. Vance, ed., The Urban South, (1954), 207-229.

B-3827 Burran, James A., "VIOLENCE IN AN 'ARSENAL OF DEMOCRACY': THE BEAUMONT RACE RIOT, 1943," East Texas Historical Journal 14:1 (Spring 1976), 39-52.

B-3828 Butts, J. W. and Dorothy James, "THE UNDERLYING CAUSES OF THE ELAINE RIOT OF 1919," Arkansas Historical Quarterly 20:1 (Spring 1961), 95-104.

B-3829 Carter, Luther J., "DESEGREGATION IN NORFOLK," South Atlantic Quarterly 58:4 (Autumn 1959), 507-520.

B-3830 Carter, Wilmoth A., "NEGRO MAIN STREET AS A SYMBOL OF DISCRIMINA-TION," Phylon 21:3 (1960), 234-242.

B-3831 Cataldo, Everett F., Michael Giles, and Douglas S. Gatlin, "METRO-POLITAN SCHOOL DESEGREGATION: PRACTICAL REMEDY OR IMPRACTICAL IDEAL?" Annals of the American Academy of Political and Social Science 422 (1975), 94-104.

B-3832 Chafe, William, "THE GREENSBORO SIT-INS," Southern Exposure 6:3 (Fall 1978), 78-87.

B-3833 Charity, Ruth Harvey, Christina Davis and Arthur Kinoy, "DANVILLE MOVEMENT: THE PEOPLE'S LAW TAKES HOLD," Southern Exposure 10:4 (July-August 1982), 35-45.

B-3834 Chatfield, Jack, "PORT GIBSON, MISSISSIPPI! A PROFILE OF THE FUTURE?" New South 24:3 (Summer 1969).

B-3835 Christian, Garna L., "THE EL PASO RACIAL CRISES OF 1900," Red River Valley Historical Review 6:2 (Spring 1981), 28-41.

B-3836 Cluster, Dick, "THE BORNING STRUGGLE: THE CIVIL RIGHTS MOVEMENT," Radical America 12:6 (November-December 1978), 9-26.

B-3837 "COALITION RULE IN DANVILLE: A LATE 'NINETEENTH CENTURY RACIST PAMPHLET," Appalachian Journal 1:2 (Spring 1973), 111-114.

B-3838 Cobb, James C., "POLARIZATION IN A SOUTHERN CITY: THE AUGUSTA RIOT AND THE EMERGING CHARACTER OF THE 1970s," Southern Studies 20:2 (Summer 1981), 185-200.

B-3839 Coles, Robert, "NEW ORLEANS, 1960, 'AS BAD AS THEY MAKE IT, THE STRONGER I'LL GET,'" Southern Exposure 7:2 (Summer 1979), 57-60.

B-3840 Cothran, Tilman C., "THE NEGRO PROTEST AGAINST SEGREGATION IN THE SOUTH," Annals of the American Academy of Political and Social Science 357 (January 1965), 65-72.

B-3841 Cothran, Tilman C. and William Phillips Jr., "NEGRO LEADERSHIP IN A CRISIS SITUATION," Phylon 22:2 (1961), 107-118.

B-3842 Coulter, E. Merton, "MESON ACADEMY, LEXINGTON, GEORGIA," Georgia Historical Quarterly 43:2 (June 1958), 125-162.

B-3843 Crowe, Charles, "RACIAL MASSACRE IN ATLANTA, SEPTEMBER 22, 1906," Journal of Negro History 54:2 (April 1969), 150-173.

B-3844 Crowe, Charles, "RACIAL VIOLENCE AND SOCIAL REFORM--ORIGINS OF THE ATLANTA RIOT OF 1906," Journal of Negro History 53:3 (July 1968), 234-256.

B-3845 Daly, Victor R., "A DECADE OF PROGRESS IN RACE RELATIONS IN THE NATION'S CAPITAL," Journal of Intergroup Relations 2:3 (Summer 1961), 252-258.

B-3846 Derrick, W. Edwin and J. Herschel Barnhill, "WITH 'ALL' DELIBERATE SPEED: DESEGREGATION OF THE PUBLIC SCHOOLS IN OKLAHOMA CITY AND TULSA, 1954 TO 1972," Red River Valley Historical Review 6:2 (Spring 1981), 78-90.

B-3847 Dimon, Joseph IV, "CHARLES L. WELTNER AND CIVIL RIGHTS," Atlanta Historical Journal 24:3 (Fall 1980), 57-66.

B-3848 Dinnerstein, Leonard, "SOUTHERN JEWRY AND THE DESEGREGATION CRI-SIS, 1954-1970," American Jewish Historical Quarterly 62:3 (March 1973), 231-241.

B-3849 Dudas, John J. and David B. Longbrake, "PROBLEMS AND FUTURE DI-RECTIONS OF RESIDENTIAL INTEGRATION: THE LOCAL APPLICATION OF FEDERALLY FUNDED PROGRAMS IN DADE COUNTY, FLORIDA," Southeastern Geographer 11:2 (November 1971), 157-168.

B-3850 Dudley, J. Wayne, "HATE ORGANIZATIONS OF THE 1940s: THE COLUMBI-ANS, INC.," Phylon 42:3 (September 1981), 262-274.

B-3851 Dunbar, Leslie, "REFLECTIONS ON THE LATENT REFORM OF THE SOUTH," Phylon 22:3 (1961), 249-257.

B-3852 Duran, Elizabeth Chidester and James A. Duran Jr., "INTEGRATION IN REVERSE AT WEST VIRGINIA STATE COLLEGE," West Virginia History 45 (1983-84), 61-78.

B-3853 Durham, Kenneth R. Jr., "THE LONGVIEW RACE RIOT OF 1919," East Texas Historical Journal 18:2 (1980), 13-24.

B-3854 Dyer, Thomas G., "THE KLAN ON CAMPUS: C. LEWIS FOWLER AND LANIER UNIVERSITY," South Atlantic Quarterly 77:4 (Autumn 1978), 453-469.

B-3855 Eaves, Jehu and Chris Lutz, "MIAMI REBELLION," Southern Exposure 9:1 (Spring 1981), 104-109.

B-3856 Eckford, Elizabeth, "LITTLE ROCK, 1957: 'THE FIRST DAY,'" Southern Exposure 7:2 (Summer 1979), 38-39.

B-3857 Egerton, Joan, "LITTLE ROCK, 1976: 'GOING BACK WOULD BE UNTHINK-ABLE,'" Southern Exposure 7:2 (Summer 1979), 45.

B-3858 Elgie, Robert A., "INDUSTRIALIZATION AND RACIAL INEQUALITY WITHIN THE AMERICAN SOUTH," Social Science Quarterly 61:3-4 (December 1980), 458-472.

B-3859 Elhorst, Hansjorg, "TWO YEARS AFTER INTEGRATION: RACE RELATIONS AT A DEEP SOUTH UNIVERSITY," Phylon 28:1 (Spring 1967), 41-51.

B-3860 Fischer, Roger A., "A PIONEER PROTEST: THE NEW ORLEANS STREET-CAR CONTROVERSY OF 1867," Journal of Negro History 53:3 (July 1968), 219-233.

B-3861 Fleming, Harald C., "THE CHANGING SOUTH AND THE SIT-INS," Journal of Intergroup Relations 2:1 (Winter 1960-61), 56-60.

B-3862 Fly, Jerry W. and George R. Reinhart, "RACIAL SEPARATION DURING THE 1970s: THE CASE OF BIRMINGHAM," Social Forces 58:4 (June 1980), 1255-1262.

B-3863 Flynt, Wayne, "THE ETHICS OF DEMOCRATIC PERSUASION AND THE BIR-MINGHAM CRISIS," Southern Speech Journal 35:1 (Fall 1969), 40-53.

B-3864 Ford, W. Scott, "INTERRACIAL PUBLIC HOUSING IN A BORDER CITY: ANOTHER LOOK AT THE CONTACT HYPOTHESIS," American Journal of Sociology 78:6 (May 1973), 1426-1447.

B-3865 Formwalt, Lee W., "THE CAMILLIA MASSACRE OF 1868: RACIAL VIOLENCE AS POLITICAL PROPAGANDA," Georgia Historical Quarterly 71:3 (Fall 1987), 399-416.

B-3866 Friedman, Murray, "ONE EPISODE IN SOUTHERN JEWRY'S RESPONSE TO DESEGREGATION: AN HISTORICAL MEMOIR," American Jewish Archives 33:2 (November 1981), 170-183.

B-3867 Gaba, Morton J., "SEGREGATION AND A SOUTHERN JEWISH COMMUNITY," Jewish Frontier 21 (October 1954) 12-15.

B-3868 Gardner, Tom and Cynthia Stokes Brown, "THE MONTGOMERY BUS BOY-COTT, Southern Exposure 9:1 (Spring 1981), 12-20.

B-3869 Gavins, Raymond, "URBANIZATION AND SEGREGATION: BLACK LEADERSHIP PATTERNS IN RICHMOND, VIRGINIA, 1900-1920," South Atlantic Quarterly 79:3 (Summer 1980) 257-273.

B-3870 Giljc, Paul A., "'LE MENU PEOPLE' IN AMERICA: IDENTIFYING THE MOB IN THE BALTIMORE RIOTS OF 1812," Maryland Historical Magazine 81:1 (Spring 1986), 50-66.

B-3871 Graham, Hugh Davis, "DESEGREGATION IN NASHVILLE: THE DYNAMICS OF COMPLIANCE," Tennessee Historical Quarterly 25:2 (Summer 1966), 135-154.

B-3872 Granger, Frank, "REACTION TO CHANGE: THE KU KLUX KLAN IN SHREVE-PORT, 1920-1919," North Louisiana Historical Association Journal 9:4 (1978), 219-227.

B-3873 Graves, Carl R., "THE RIGHT TO BE SERVED: OKLAHOMA CITY'S LUNCH COUNTER SIT-INS, 1958-1964," Chronicles of Oklahoma 59:2 (Summer 1981), 152-166.

B-3874 Greenfield, Robert W., "FACTORS ASSOCIATED WITH ATTITUDES TOWARD DESEGREGATION IN A FLORIDA RESIDENTIAL SUBURB," Social Forces 40:1 (October 1961), 31-42.

B-3875 Grigg, Charles M. and Lewis M. Killian, "THE BI-RACIAL COMMITTEE AS A RESPONSE TO RACIAL TENSIONS IN SOUTHERN CITIES," Phylon 23:4 (Winter 1962), 379-382.

B-3876 Grigg, Charles M. and Lewis M. Killian, "RANK ORDERS OF DISCRIMI-NATION OF NEGROES AND WHITES IN A SOUTHERN CITY," Social Forces 39:3 (March 1961), 235-239.

B-3877 Halliburton, R. Jr., "THE TULSA RACE WAR OF 1921," Journal of Black Studies 2:3 (March 1972), 333-358.

B-3878 Harris, Carl V., "REFORMS IN GOVERNMENT CONTROL OF NEGROES IN BIR-MINGHAM, ALABAMA, 1890-1920," Journal of Southern History 38:4 (November 1972), 567-600.

B-3879 Headley, Bernard D., "THE 'ATLANTA TRAGEDY' AND THE RULE OF OFFI-CIAL IDEOLOGY," Journal of Ethnic Studies 14:2 (Summer 1986), 1-28.

B-3880 Hein, Virginia H., "THE IMAGE OF A 'CITY TOO BUSY TO HATE': ATLANTA IN THE 1960's," Phylon 33:3 (Fall 1972), 205-221.

B-3881 Hennessey, Melinda Meek, "RACE AND VIOLENCE IN RECONSTRUCTION NEW ORLEANS: THE 1868 RIOT," Louisiana History 20:1 (Winter 1979), 77-92.

B-3882 Hennessey, Melinda Meek, "RACIAL VIOLENCE DURING RECONSTRUCTION: THE 1876 RIOTS IN CHARLESTON AND CAENHOY," South Carolina Histori-cal Magazine 86:2 (April 1985), 100-112.

B-3883 Hertzberg, Steven, "SOUTHERN JEWS AND THEIR ENCOUNTER WITH BLACKS: ATLANTA, 1850-1915," Atlanta Historical Journal 23:3 (Fall 1979), 7-24.

B-3884 Hill, Mozell C., "RACE ATTITUDES IN OKLAHOMA'S ALL-NEGRO COMMUN-ITY," Phylon 7:3 (1946), 260-268.

B-3885 Hine, William C., "THE 1867 CHARLESTON STREETCAR SIT-INS, A CASE OF SUCCESSFUL BLACK PROTEST," South Carolina Historical Magazine 77:2 (April 1976), 110-114.

B-3886 Holmes, Jack D. L., "THE EFFECTS OF THE MEMPHIS RACE RIOT OF 1856," West Tennessee Historical Society Papers No. 12 (1958), 58-79.

B-3887 Holmes, Jack D. L., "THE UNDERLYING CAUSES OF THE MEMPHIS RACE RIOT OF 1866," Tennessee Historical Quarterly 17:3 (September 1958), 195-221.

B-3888 Howard, Walter, "'A BLOT ON TAMPA'S HISTORY': THE 1934 LYNCHING OF ROBERT JOHNSON,' Tampa Bay History 6:2 (Fall-Winter 1984), 5-18.

B-3889 Hux, Roger K., "THE KU KLUX KLAN IN MACON, 1919-1925," Georgia Historical Quarterly 62:2 (Summer 1978), 155-168.

B-3890 Hwang, Sean-Shong and Steve H. Murdoch, "SEGREGATION IN NONMETRO-POLITAN AND METROPOLITAN TEXAS IN 1980," Rural Sociology 48:4 (Winter 1983), 607-623.

B-3891 Hwang, Sean-Shong, Steven H. Murdock, Banoo Parpia, Rita R. Hamm, "THE EFFECTS OF RACE AND SOCIOECONOMIC STATUS ON RESIDENTIAL SEGREGATION IN TEXAS, 1970-80," Social Forces 63:3 (March 1985), 732-747.

B-3892 Inscoe, John C., "THE CLANSMAN ON STAGE AND SCREEN: NORTH CARO-LINA REACTS," North Carolina Historical Review 64:2 (April 1987), 139-161.

B-3893 Ippolito, Dennis S. and Martin L. Levin, "PUBLIC-REGARDINGNESS, RACE, AND SOCIAL CLASS: THE CASE OF A RAPID TRANSIT REFERENDUM," Social Science Quarterly 51:3 (December 1970), 628-633.

B-3894 Jackson, Luther P., "MANUMISSION IN CERTAIN VIRGINIA CITIES," Journal of Negro History 15:3 (July 1930), 278-314.

B-3895 Jaffe, Andrew, "GRENADA, MISSISSIPPI: PERSPECTIVE ON THE BACK-LASH," New South 21:4 (Fall 1966), 15-27.

B-3896 Johnson, Kenneth R., "SLAVERY AND RACISM IN FLORENCE, ALABAMA, 1841-1862," Civil War History 27:2 (June 1981), 155-171.

B-3897 Johnson, Marie White, "THE COLFAX RIOT OF APRIL, 1873," Louisiana Historical Quarterly 13:3 (July 1930), 391-427.

B-3898 Johnson, Walter, "HISTORIANS JOIN THE MARCH ON MONTGOMERY," South Atlantic Quarterly 79:2 (Spring 1980), 158-174.

B-3899 Jones, Beverly, "BEFORE MONTGOMERY AND GREENSBORO: THE DESEGREGA-TION MOVEMENT IN THE DISTRICT OF COLUMBIA, 1950-53," Phylon 43:2 (June 1982), 144-154.

B-3900 Kennett, Lee, "THE CAMP WADSWORTH AFFAIR," South Atlantic Quarterly 74:2 (SPRING 1975), 197-211.

B-3901 Kharif, Wali R., "BLACK REACTION TO SEGREGATION AND DISCRIMINATION IN POST-RECONSTRUCTION FLORIDA," Florida Historical Quarterly 64:2 (October 1985), 161-173.

B-3902 Killan, Lewis and Charles Grigg, "RACE RELATIONS IN AN URBANIZED SOUTH," Journal of Social Issues 22:1 (January 1966), 20-29.

B-3903 Killian, Lewis M. and Charles U. Smith, "NEGRO PROTEST LEADERS IN A SOUTHERN COMMUNITY," Social Forces 38:3 (March 1960), 253-258.

B-3904 Kotlikoff, Laurence J. and Anton J. Rupert," THE MANUMISSION OF SLAVES IN NEW ORLEANS, 1827-1846," Southern Studies 19:2 (Summer 1980), 172-181.

B-3905 Krause, P. Allen, "RABBIS AND NEGRO RIGHTS IN THE SOUTH, 1954–1967," American Jewish Archives 21:1 (April 1969), 20–47.

B-3906 Kuebler, Edward J., "THE DESEGREGATION OF THE UNIVERSITY OF MARYLAND," Maryland Historical Magazine 71:1 (Spring 1976), 37–49.

B-3907 Kurtz, Michael J., "EMANCIPATION IN THE FEDERAL CITY," Civil War History 24:3 (September 1978), 250–267.

B-3908 Lack, Paul D., "SLAVERY AND VIGILANTISM IN AUSTIN, TEXAS, 1840–1860," Southwestern Historical Quarterly 85:1 (July 1981), 1–20.

B-3909 Lack, Paul D., "URBAN SLAVERY IN THE SOUTHWEST," Red River Valley Historical Review 6:2 (Spring 1981), 8–27.

B-3910 Lamon, Lester C., "TENNESSEE RACE RELATIONS AND THE KNOXVILLE RIOT OF 1919," East Tennessee Historical Society's Publications No. 41 (1969), 67–85.

B-3911 Lawson, Steven F., David R. Colburn, and Darryl Paulson, "GROVE-LAND: FLORIDA'S LITTLE SCOTTSBORO," Florida Historical Quarterly 65:1 (July 1986), 1–26.

B-3912 Leifermann, Henry P., "NOT YET STILL MEANS NEVER: ORANGEBURG, SOUTH CAROLINA," New South 24:4 (Fall 1969), 68–73.

B-3913 Lewis, John, "THE NASHVILLE SIT-INS--NONVIOLENCE EMERGES," Southern Exposure 9:1 (Spring 1981), 30–32.

B-3914 Long, Margaret, "NEIGHBORHOOD TRANSITION: THE MOODS AND MYTHS," New South 21:2 (Spring 1966), 36–45.

B-3915 Lord, J. Dennis, "SCHOOL BUSING AND WHITE ABANDONMENT OF PUBLIC SCHOOLS," Southeastern Geographer 15:2 (November 1975), 81–92.

B-3916 Lord, J. Dennis and John C. Catau, "SCHOOL DESEGREGATION POLICY AND INTRA-SCHOOL DISTRICT MIGRATION," Social Science Quarterly 57:4 (1977), 784–796.

B-3917 Lord, J. Dennis and John C. Catau, "THE SCHOOL DESEGREGATION-RESEGREGATION SCENARIO: CHARLOTTE-MECKLENBURG'S EXPERIENCE," Urban Affairs Quarterly 16:3 (March 1981), 369–376.

B-3918 Lovett, Bobby L., "MEMPHIS RIOTS: WHITE REACTION TO BLACKS IN MEMPHIS, MAY 1865–JULY 1866," Tennessee Historical Quarterly 38:1 (Spring 1979), 9–33.

B-3919 McCain, Ray, "SPEAKING ON SCHOOL DESEGREGATION BY ATLANTA MINIS-TERS," Southern Speech Journal 29:3 (Spring 1964), 256–262.

B-3920 Masterson, Mike, "LITTLE ROCK, 1979: 'THERE HAVE BEEN CHANGES,'" Southern Exposure 7:2 (Summer 1979), 46–47.

B-3921 Masuoka, Jitsuichi, "THE CITY AND RACIAL ADJUSTMENT," Social Forces 27:1 (October 1948), 37–41.

B-3922 Matthews, Jack, "WHAT ARE YOU DOING THERE? WHAT ARE YOU DOING HERE? A VIEW OF THE JESSE HILL FORD CASE," Georgia Review 26:2 (Summer 1972), 121–144.

B-3923 Mayfield, Chris, "LITTLE ROCK: 1957–1960: 'THE MIDDLE GROUND TURNS TO QUICKSAND,'" Southern Exposure 7:2 (Summer 1979), 40–44.

B-3924 Meier, August, "BOYCOTTS OF SEGREGATED STREET CARS, 1894–1909--A RESEARCH NOTE," Phylon 18:3 (1957), 296–297.

B-3925 Meier, August, "THE SUCCESSFUL SIT-INS IN A BORDER CITY: A STUDY IN SOCIAL CAUSATION,' Journal of Intergroup Relations 2:3 (Summer 1961), 230-237.

B-3926 Meier, August and Elliot Rudwick, "THE BOYCOTT MOVEMENT AGAINST JIM CROW STREETCARS IN THE SOUTH, 1900-1906," Journal of American History 55:4 (March 1969), 756-775.

B-3927 Meier, August and Elliot Rudwick, "NEGRO BOYCOTTS OF JIM CROW STREETCARS IN TENNESSEE," American Quarterly 21:4 (Winter 1969), 755-763.

B-3928 Meier, August and Elliot Rudwick, "NEGRO BOYCOTTS OF SEGREGATED STREETCARS IN VIRGINIA, 1904-1907," Virginia Magazine of History and Biography 81:4 (October 1973), 479-487.

B-3929 Miracle, Andrew W. Jr., "FACTORS AFFECTING INTERRACIAL COOPERA- TION: A CASE STUDY OF A HIGH SCHOOL FOOTBALL TEAM," Human Organization 40:2 (Summer 1981), 150-154.

B-3930 Moore, John Hammond, "JIM CROW IN GEORGIA," South Atlantic Quarterly 66:4 (Autumn 1967), 554-565.

B-3931 Morris, Aldon, "BLACK SOUTHERN SIT-IN MOVEMENT: AN ANALYSIS OF INTERNAL ORGANIZATION," American Sociological Review 46:6 (De- cember 1981), 744-767.

B-3932 Muir, Donal E., "THE FIRST YEARS OF DESEGREGATION: PATTERNS OF ACCEPTANCE OF BLACK STUDENTS ON A DEEP-SOUTH CAMPUS, 1963-69," Social Forces 49:3 (March 1971), 372-378.

B-3933 Muller, Mary Lee, 'NEW ORLEANS PUBLIC SCHOOL DESEGREGATION," Louisiana History 17:1 (Winter 1976), 69-88.

B-3934 Murrah, Bill, ed., "THE KNOXVILLE RACE RIOT: 'TO MAKE PEOPLE PROUD,'" Southern Exposure 1:3-4 (Winter 1974), 105-111.

B-3935 Murray, Hugh T. Jr., "THE STRUGGLE FOR CIVIL RIGHTS IN NEW ORLEANS IN 1960: REFLECTIONS AND RECOLLECTIONS," Journal of Ethnic Studies 6:1 (Spring 1978), 25-41.

B-3936 Nash, June, "THE COST OF VIOLENCE," Journal of Black Studies 4:2 (December 1973), 153.

B-3937 [NEW ORLEANS] Southern Exposure 7:2 (Summer 1979), 55-56.

B-3938 "NEW ORLEANS, 1960: 'THE VILEST SORT OF ABUSE,'" Southern Exposure 7:2 (Summer 1979), 63.

B-3939 Norris, Marjorie M., "AN EARLY INSTANCE OF NONVIOLENCE: THE LOUISVILLE DEMONSTRATIONS OF 1870-1871," Journal of Southern History 32:4 (November 1966), 487-504.

B-3940 Ohline, Howard A., "GEORGETOWN, SOUTH CAROLINA: RACIAL ANXIETIES AND MILITANT BEHAVIOR, 1802," South Carolina Historical Magazine 73:3 (July 1972), 130-140.

B-3941 Olson, James S. and Sharon Phair, "THE ANATOMY OF A RACE RIOT: BEAUMONT, TEXAS, 1943," Texana 11:1 (Spring 1973), 64-72.

B-3942 Oppenheimer, Martin, "THE SOUTHERN STUDENT SIT-INS: INTRA-GROUPS RELATIONS AND COMMUNITY CONFLICT," Phylon 27:1 (Spring 1966), 20- 26.

B-3943 Parker, Russel D., "THE BLACK COMMUNITY IN A COMPANY TOWN: ALCOA, TENNESSEE, 1919-1939," Tennessee Historical Quarterly 37:2 (Summer 1978), 203-221.

B-3944 Patrick, Clarence H., "DESEGREGATION IN A SOUTHERN CITY: A
DESCRIPTIVE REPORT," Phylon 25:3 (Fall 1964), 263-269.

B-3945 Paulson, Darryl, "STAY OUT, THE WATER'S FINE: DESEGREGATING
MUNICIPAL SWIMMING FACILITIES IN ST. PETERSBURG, FLORIDA," Tampa
Bay History 4:2 (Fall-Winter 1982), 6-19.

B-3946 Pessen, Edward, "THE SOCIAL CONFIGURATION OF THE ANTEBELLUM CITY:
AN HISTORICAL AND THEORETICAL INQUIRY," Journal of Urban History 2
(1976), 267-305.

B-3947 Pfaff, Eugene, "GREENSBORO SIT-INS," Southern Exposure 9:1 (Spring
1981), 23-28.

B-3948 Quinn, Olive Westbrooke, "THE TRANSMISSION OF RACIAL ATTITUDES
AMONG WHITE SOUTHERNERS," Social Forces 33:1 (October 1954), 41-
47.

B-3949 Rabinowitz, Howard N., "THE CONFLICT BETWEEN BLACKS AND THE POLICE
IN THE URBAN SOUTH, 1865-1900," Historian 39:1 (November 196), 62-
76.

B-3950 Rabinowitz, Howard N., "FROM EXCLUSION TO SEGREGATION: SOUTHERN
RACE RELATIONS, 1865-1890," Journal of American History 63:2
(September 1976), 325-350.

B-3951 Rachleff, Marshall, "ECONOMIC SELF INTEREST VERSUS RACIAL CONTROL:
MOBILE'S PROTEST AGAINST THE JAILING OF BLACK SEAMEN," Civil War
History 25:1 (March 1979), 84-88.

B-3952 Racine, Philip N., "THE KU KLUX KLAN, ANTI-CATHOLICISM, AND
ATLANTA'S BOARD OF EDUCATION, 1916-1927," Georgia Historical
Quarterly 57:1 (Spring 1973), 63-75.

B-3953 Richardson, Joe M., ed., "THE MEMPHIS RACE RIOT AND ITS AFTER-
MATH," Tennessee Historical Quarterly 24:1 (Spring 1965), 63-69.

B-3954 Richardson, Joe M., "'THE NEST OF VILE FANATICS':   WILLIAM N.
SHEATS AND THE ORANGE PARK SCHOOL," Florida Historical Quarterly
64:4 (April 1986), 393-406.

B-3955 Rogers, O. A. Jr., "THE ELAINE RACE RIOTS OF 1919," Arkansas
Historical Quarterly 19:2 (Summer 1960), 142-150.

B-3956 Rudwick, Elliott and August Meier, "NEGRO BOYCOTTS OF SEGREGATED
STREETCARS IN FLORIDA, 1901-1905," Atlantic Quarterly 69:4 (Autumn
1970), 525-533.

B-3957 Ryan, James Gilbert, "THE MEMPHIS RIOTS OF 1866:   TERROR IN A
BLACK COMMUNITY DURING RECONSTRUCTION," Journal of Negro History
62:3 (July 1977), 243-257.

B-3958 Salter, Paul S. and Robert C. Mings, "A GEOGRAPHIC ASPECT OF THE
1968 MIAMI RACIAL DISTURBANCE: A PRELIMINARY INVESTIGATION,"
Professional Geographer 21:2 (March 1969), 79-86.

B-3959 Schafer, Judith Kelleher, "THE IMMEDIATE IMPACT OF NAT TURNER'S
INSURRECTION ON NEW ORLEANS," Louisiana History 21:4 (Fall 1980),
361-376.

B-3960 Schuler, Edgar A., "THE HOUSTON RACE RIOT, 1917," Journal of Negro
History 29:3 (July 1944), 301-338.

B-3961 Scott, William B., "JUDGE J. WATIE'S WARING: ADVOCATE OF
'ANOTHER' SOUTH," South Atlantic Quarterly 77:3 (Summer 1978),
320-334.

B-3962 Sinsheimer, Joe, interview with Sam Block, "NEVER TURN BACK: THE MOVEMENT IN GREENWOOD, MISSISSIPPI," Southern Exposure 15:2 (Summer 1987), 37-50.

B-3963 Spier, William, "A SOCIAL HISTORY OF MANGANESE MINING IN THE BATESVILLE DISTRICT OF INDEPENDENCE COUNTY," Arkansas Historical Quarterly 36:2 (Summer 1977), 130-157.

B-3964 Wagy, Thomas R., "GOVERNOR LeROY COLLINS OF FLORIDA AND THE LITTLE ROCK CRISIS OF 1957," Arkansas Historical Quarterly 38:2 (Summer 1979), 99-115.

B-3965 Wallace, David, "DESEGREGATION IN HOXIE, ARKANSAS: 'RIGHT IN THE SIGHT OF GOD,'" Southern Studies 20:3 (Fall 1981), 311-325.

B-3966 Waller, Altina L., "COMMUNITY, CLASS AND RACE IN THE MEMPHIS RIOT OF 1866," Journal of Social History 18:2 (Winter 1984), 233-246.

B-3967 Weales, Gerald, "PRO-NEGRO FILMS IN ATLANTA, GEORGIA," Phylon 13:4 (1952), 298-305.

B-3968 West, Carroll Van, "PERPETUATING THE MYTH OF AMERICA: SCOTTSBORO AND ITS INTERPRETEES," South Atlantic Quarterly 80:1 (Winter 1981), 36-48.

B-3969 Wieder, Alan, "ONE WHO STAYED: MARGARET CONNER AND THE NEW ORLEANS SCHOOL CRISIS," Louisiana History 26:2 (Spring 1985), 194-201.

B-3970 Williams, Robert, "1957: THE SWIMMING POOL SHOWDOWN," Southern Exposure 8:2 (Summer 1980), 70-72.

B-3971 Wingfield, Marie Gregson, "THE MEMPHIS INTERRACIAL COMMISSION," West Tennessee Historical Society Papers No. 2 (1967), 93-107.

Recreation and Sports

B-3972 Adams, William H., "NEW ORLEANS AS THE NATIONAL CENTER OF BOXING," Louisiana Historical Quarterly 39:1 (January 1956), 92-112.

B-3973 Bain, Kenneth R., Rob Phillips, and Paul D. Travis, "BENSON PARK: SHAWNEE CITIZENS AT LEISURE IN THE TWENTIETH CENTURY," Chronicles of Oklahoma 57:2 (Summer 1979), 164-169.

B-3974 Beck, Earl R., "GERMAN TOURISTS IN FLORIDA: A TWO CENTURY RE-CORD," Florida Historical Quarterly 61:2 (October 1982), 162-180.

B-3975 Bobbitt, Charles, "THE MEMPHIS GOLD CUP," West Tennessee Historical Society Papers No. 30 (1976), 67-82.

B-3976 Brower, Sidney N. and Penelope Williamson, "OUTDOOR RECREATION AS A FUNCTION OF THE URBAN HOUSING ENVIRONMENT," Environment and Behavior 6:3 (September 1974), 295-345.

B-3977 Buchanan, Mrs. E. C., ed., "A RING TOURNAMENT AT TALLALOOSA, 1877," Journal of Mississippi History 16:4 (October 1954), 277-279.

B-3978 Cordell, Harold K., "SUBSTITUTION BETWEEN PRIVATELY AND PUBLICLY SUPPLIED URBAN RECREATIONAL OPEN SPACE," Journal of Leisure Research 8:3 (1976), 160-174.

B-3979 Daniel, W. Harrison, "'THE RAGE' IN THE HILL CITY: THE BEGINNINGS OF BASEBALL IN LYNCHBURG," Virginia Cavalcade 28:4 (Spring 1979), 186-191.

B-3980 Denning, Jeannette Reith, "GOOD TIMES: VACATIONING AT RED BOILING SPRINGS," Tennessee Historical Quarterly 42:3 (Fall 1983), 223-242.

B-3981 Derbes, Max J., "LOCATION ANALYSES OF THE NEW ORLEANS SUPERDOME," Real Estate Issues 10:2 (Fall/Winter 1985), 26-37.

B-3982 Findling, J. E., "THE LOUISVILLE GRAYS' SCANDAL OF 1877," Journal of Sport History 3:2 (Summer 1976), 176-187.

B-3983 Johnson, Guion Griffis, "RECREATIONAL AND CULTURAL ACTIVITIES IN THE ANTE-BELLUM TOWN OF NORTH CAROLINA," North Carolina Historical Review 6:1 (January 1929), 17-37.

B-3984 Jones, Ruth Irene, "HOT SPRINGS: ANTE-BELLUM WATERING PLACE," Arkansas Historical Quarterly 14:1 (Spring 1955), 3-31.

B-3985 Kelley, Arthell, "SULLIVAN-KILRAIN FIGHT, RICHBURG, MISSISSIPPI, JULY 8, 1889," Southern Quarterly 8:2 (January 1970), 135-144.

B-3986 King, Augusta Wylie, "EVALUATION OF THE WHEEL OR THE PERILS OF EARLY BICYCLING IN ATLANTA," Atlanta Historical Bulletin 8:31 (1946), 1-8.

B-3987 Lancaster, John H., "BALTIMORE, A PIONEER IN ORGANIZED BASEBALL," Maryland Historical Magazine 35:1 (March 1940), 32-54.

B-3988 Lawrence, Henry W., "SOUTHERN SPAS: SOURCE OF THE AMERICAN RESORT TRADITION, Landscape 27:2 (1983), 1-12.

B-3989 Lawson, Steven F., "YBOR CITY AND BASEBALL: AN INTERVIEW WITH AL LOPEZ," Tampa Bay History 7:2 (Fall-Winter 1985), 59-76.

B-3990 Lloyd, Robert E. and Roberty Adler, "A COGNITIVE MODEL FOR RECREA-TIONAL SPATIAL BEHAVIOR IN AN URBAN AREA," Southeastern Geographer 20:2 (November 1980), 145-159.

B-3991 Mitchell, Lisle S., "AN EVALUATION OF CENTRAL PLACE THEORY IN A RECREATION CONTEXT: THE CASE OF COLUMBIA, SOUTH CAROLINA," Southeastern Geographer 8 (1968), 46-53.

B-3992 Mitchell, Lisle S. and Paul E. Lovingood Jr., "PUBLIC URBAN RECREATION: AN INVESTIGATION OF SPATIAL RELATIONSHIPS," Journal of Leisure Research 8:1 (1976), 6-20.

B-3993 McGriel, Paul, "WILLIAM FULLER: CHARLESTON'S GENTLEMAN BOXING-MASTER, 1825," South Carolina Historical and Genealogical Magazine 54:1 (1954), 6-14.

B-3994 McKinney, G. B., "NEGRO PROFESSIONAL BASEBALL IN THE UPPER SOUTH IN THE GILDED AGE," Journal of Sport History 3:3 (Winter 1976), 273-280.

B-3995 McMahon, Doreen, "PLEASURE SPOTS IN OLD ATLANTA," Atlanta Histori-cal Bulletin 7:29 (October 1944), 220-234.

B-3996 Olden, Samuel B. Jr., "HOTELS, INNS AND TAVERNS IN MISSISSIPPI, 1830-1860," Journal of Mississippi History 5:4 (October 1943), 171-184.

B-3997 Preston, T. W., "THE NETHERLAND INN AT OLD KINGSPORT," East Ten-nessee Historical Society's Publications No. 4 (January 1932), 32-34.

B-3998 Roberts, Randy, "GALVESTON'S JACK JOHNSON: FLOURISHING IN THE DARK," Southwestern Historical Quarterly 87:1 (July 1983), 37-56.

B-3999 Rosentraub, Mark S. and Samuil R. Nunn, "SUBURBAN CITY, INVESTMENT IN PROFESSIONAL SPORTS: ESTIMATING FOR FISCAL RETURNS OF THE DALLAS COWBOYS AND TEXAS RANGERS TO INVESTOR COMMUNITIES," American Behavioral Scientist 21:3 (1978), 393-414.

B-4000 Russell, Mattie, ed., "THE BILL OF FARE OF THE HOTEL DE VICKSBURG --1863," Journal of Mississippi History 17:4 (October 1955), 282-285.

B-4001 Sarpy, Eleanor Legier, "OFF THE BEATEN PATH IN LOUISIANA," Louisiana Historical Quarterly 54:1 (Winter 1971), 41-57.

B-4002 Scribner, Roberty L., "TWO OUT AND ---?" Virginia Cavalcade 3:4 (Spring 1954), 18-22.

B-4003 Sessoms, H. Douglas and James L. Krug, "MUNICIPAL RECREATION SERVICES IN NORTH CAROLINA," Leisure Sciences 1:1 (1978), 21-34.

B-4004 Simpson, William S. Jr., "1980: THE YEAR RICHMOND WENT 'BASEBALL WILD,'" Virginia Cavalcade 26:4 (Spring 1977), 184-191.

B-4005 Smith, Suanna, "WASHINGTON, MISSISSIPPI: ANTEBELLUM ELYSIUM," Journal of Mississippi History 40:2 (May 1978), 143-166.

B-4006 Somers, Dale A., "A CITY ON WHEELS: THE BICYCLE ERA IN NEW ORLEANS," Louisiana History 8:3 (Summer 1967), 219-238.

B-4007 Somers, Dale A., "WAR AND PLAY: THE CIVIL WAR IN NEW ORLEANS," Mississippi Quarterly 26:1 (Winter 1972-73), 3-28.

B-4008 Sulzby, James E. Jr., "BLOUNT SPRINGS, ALABAMA'S FOREMOST WATERING PLACE OF YESTERYEAR," Alabama Review 2:3 (July 1949), 163-175.

B-4009 Sumner, Jim L., "THE NORTH CAROLINA STATE PROFESSIONAL BASEBALL LEAGUE OF 1902," North Carolina Historical Review 64:3 (July 1987), 247-273.

B-4010 "TRACY AT THE BAT," Black Enterprise 17:2 (September 1986), 52-56.

B-4011 Troubetzkoy, Ulrich, "BOWLS AND SKITTLES," Virginia Cavalcade 9:4 (Spring 1960), 11-16.

B-4012 Van Arsdall, Mai Flournoy Van Deren, "THE SPRINGS AT HARRODSBURG," Register of the Kentucky Historical Society 61:4 (October 1963), 300-328.

B-4013 Ward, Harry M., "RICHMOND SPORTS AT FLOOD TIDE: MAYO ISLAND, 1921-1941," Virginia Cavalcade 34:4 (Spring 1985), 182-191.

Radio, Television, Film, and Communications

B-4014 Ashdown, Raul G., "WTVJ'S MIAMI CRIME WAR: A TELEVISION CRUSADE," Florida Historical Quarterly 58:4 (April 1980), 427-437.

B-4015 Carleton, Eleanor Beatrice, "THE ESTABLISHMENT OF THE ELECTRIC TELEGRAPH IN LOUISIANA AND MISSISSIPPI," Louisiana Historical Quarterly 31:2 (April 1948), 425-490.

B-4016 Devereux, S., "BOOSTERS IN THE NEWSROOM: THE JACKSONVILLE CASE," Columbia Journalism Review 14 (January-February 1976), 38-47.

B-4017 Hamilton, Neal O., "EARLY LOUISVILLE AND THE BLUEGRASS STATIONS," Filson Club History Quarterly 52:2 (April 1978), 147-165.

B-4018 Hunter, Tom, "AUGUSTA AS IT WAS: A NOSTALGIC LOOK AT LOCAL TELE-VISION," Augusta Magazine 12:2 (Summer 1985), 8-12.

B-4019 MacMurdo, Bruce, "IN A FEW HANDS: WHO OWNS THE MEDIA," Southern
       Exposure 2:4 (1975), 51-61.

B-4020 Moore, Harry Estill, "MASS COMMUNICATION IN THE SOUTH," Social
       Forces 29:4 (May 1951), 365-376.

B-4021 Nelson, Richard Alan, "MOVIE MECCA OF THE SOUTH: JACKSONVILLE,
       FLORIDA AS AN EARLY RIVAL TO HOLLYWOOD," Journal of Popular Film
       and Television 8 (Fall 1980), 38-51.

B-4022 Norwood, Beth, "FRENCH BROADCASTING IN LOUISIANA," Southern Speech
       Journal 30:1 (Fall 1964), 46-54.

B-4023 Pusateri, C. Joseph, "RADIO BROADCASTERS AND THE CHALLENGE OF
       TELEVISION: A NEW ORLEANS CASE," Business History Review 54:3
       (Autumn 1980), 303-330.

B-4024 Rada, Stephen E., "MANIPULATING THE MEDIA: A CASE STUDY OF A
       CHICANO STRIKE IN TEXAS," Journalism Quarterly 54:1 (Spring 1977),
       109-113.

B-4025 Rosendahl, Patricia, "NEW ORLEANS' OWN SILENT FILMS," Southern
       Quarterly 23:1 (Fall 1984), 40-46.

B-4026 Schuth, H. Wayne, "THE IMAGE OF NEW ORLEANS ON FILM," Southern
       Quarterly 19:3 and 4 (Spring-Summer 1981), 240-245.

B-4027 Soileau, Jeanne, "MEDIA INFLUENCES ON THE PLAY OF NEW ORLEANS
       CHILDREN," Perspectives on Ethnicity in New Orleans (1981), 32-37.

B-4028 Topper, Martin D. and W. Leigh Wilson, "CABLE TELEVISION: APPLIED
       ANTHROPOLOGY IN A NEW TOWN," Human Organization 35:2 (Summer
       1976), 135-146.

B-4029 Williams, Gilbert A., "PUBLIC TELEVISION'S BLACK PIONEER:
       WHMM TV/32," Phylon 46:4 (December 1985), 363-373.

Religion

B-4030 Abercrombie, Lelia, "EARLY CHURCHES OF PENSACOLA," Florida
       Historical Quarterly 37:3, 4 (January-April 1959), 446-462.

B-4031 Ahrendt, Theodore G., "A HISTORY OF LUTHERANISM IN ATLANTA,"
       Atlanta Historical Journal 14:4 (December 1967), 27-35.

B-4032 Ammerman, Nancy T., "THE CIVIL RIGHTS MOVEMENT AND THE CLERGY IN A
       SOUTHERN COMMUNITY," Sociological Analysis 41:4 (Winter 1980),
       339-350.

B-4033 Baer, Hans A., "BLACK SPIRITUAL ISRAELITES IN A SMALL SOUTHERN
       CITY: ELEMENTS OF PROTEST AND ACCOMMODATION IN BELIEF AND
       ORATORY," Southern Quarterly 23:3 (Spring 1985), 103-124.

B-4034 Baker, Frank, "JOHN WESLEY'S LAST VISIT TO CHARLESTON," South
       Carolina Historical Magazine 78:4 (1977), 265-271.

B-4035 Baker, James T., "THE BATTLE OF ELIZABETH CITY: CHRIST AND ANTI-
       CHRIST IN NORTH CAROLINA," North Carolina Historical Review 54:4
       (Autumn 1977), 393-409.

B-4036 Bauman, Mark K., "HITTING THE SAWDUST TRAIL: BILLY SUNDAY'S
       ATLANTA CAMPAIGN OF 1917," Southern Studies 29:4 (Winter 1980),
       385-399.

B-4037 Becker, Louis D., "UNITARIANISM IN POST-WAR ATLANTA, 1882-1908,"
       Georgia Historical Quarterly 56:3 (Fall 1972), 349-364.

B-4038 Berman, Myron, "RABBI EDWARD NATHAN COLISCH AND THE DEBATE OVER ZIONISM IN RICHMOND, VIRGINIA," American Jewish Historical Quarterly 62:3 (March 1973), 295-305.

B-4039 Berry, Benjamin D., "THE PLYMOUTH CONGREGATIONAL CHURCH OF LOUIS-VILLE, KENTUCKY," Phylon 42:3 (September 1981), 224-232.

B-4040 Beton, Sol, "SHEPHARDIM--ATLANTA," Atlanta Historical Journal 23:3 (Fall 1979), 119-127.

B-4041 Bettersworth, John K., "PROTESTANT BEGINNINGS IN NEW ORLEANS," Louisiana Historical Quarterly 21:3 (July 1938), 823-845.

B-4042 Blied, Benjamin J., "BISHOP VEROT OF SAVANNAH," Georgia Review 5:2 (Summer 1951), 162-168.

B-4043 Blumberg, Janice Rothschild, "THE BOMB THAT HEALED: A PERSONAL MEMOIR OF THE BOMBING OF THE TEMPLE IN ATLANTA, 1958," American Jewish History 73:1 (September 1983), 20-38.

B-4044 Breibart, Solomon, "THE SYNAGOGUES OF KAHAL KADOSH BETH ELOHIM, CHARLESTON," South Carolina Historical Magazine 80:3 (July 1979), 215-235.

B-4045 Breibart, Solomon, "TWO JEWISH CONGREGATIONS IN CHARLESTON, SOUTH CAROLINA BEFORE 1791: A NEW CONCLUSION," American Jewish History 69:3 (March 1980), 360-363.

B-4046 Buice, David, "WHEN THE SAINTS CAME MARCHING IN: THE MORMAN EXPERIENCE IN ANTEBELLUM NEW ORLEANS, 1840-1855," Louisiana History 23:2 (Summer 1982), 221-238.

B-4047 Campbell, Ernest Q. and Thomas F. Pettigrew, "RACIAL AND MORAL CRISIS: THE ROLE OF LITTLE ROCK MINISTERS," American Journal of Sociology 64:5 (March 1959), 509-516.

B-4048 Clarke, Erskine, "AN EXPERIMENT IN PATERNALISM: PRESBYTERIANS AND SLAVES IN CHARLESTON, SOUTH CAROLINA," Journal of Presbyterian History 53:3 (1975), 223-238.

B-4049 Clelland, Donald A., Thomas C. Hood, C. M. Lepsey and Ronald Wim-berley, "IN THE COMPANY OF THE CONVERTED: CHARACTERISTICS OF A BILLY GRAHAM CRUSADE AUDIENCE," Social Analysis 35:1 (1974), 45-56.

B-4050 Coke, Fletch, "CHRIST CHURCH, EPISCOPAL, NASHVILLE," Tennessee Historical Quarterly 38:2 (Summer 1979), 141-157.

B-4051 Coker, William S., "RELIGIOUS CONSENSUSES OF PENSACOLA, 1796-1801," Florida Historical Quarterly 61:1 (July 1982), 54-63.

B-4052 Coleman, Elizabeth Dabney, "BLACK BOANERGES," Virginia Cavalcade 4:3 (Winter 1954), 18-22.

B-4053 Conley, Carolyn, "MAKE FULL PROOF OF THY MINISTRY: LAMARR MOONEY-HAM, THE TRI-CITY BAPTIST TEMPLE, AND THE MORAL MAJORITY," South Atlantic Quarterly 81:2 (Spring 1982), 131-146.

B-4054 Cowett, Mark, "RABBI MORRIS NEWFIELD AND THE SOCIAL GOSPEL: THEOLOGY AND SOCIETAL REFORM IN THE SOUTH," American Jewish Archives 34:1 (April 1982), 52-74.

B-4055 Crews, Clyde F., "HALLOWED GROUND: THE CATHEDRAL OF THE ASSUMP-TION IN LOUISVILLE HISTORY," Filson Club History Quarterly 51:3 (July 1977), 249-261.

B-4056 Cromwell, John W., "FIRST NEGRO CHURCHES IN THE DISTRICT OF COLUM-BIA," Journal of Negro History 7:1 (January 1922), 64-106.

B-4057 Daton, William, "PASCO PIONEERS: CATHOLIC SETTLEMENTS IN SAN
       ANTONIO, ST. LEO AND VICINITY," Tampa Bay History 1:2 (Fall-Winter
       1979), 32-39.

B-4058 Davis, Margaret H., "HARLOTS AND HYMNALS: A HISTORIC CONFRONTA-
       TION OF VICE AND VIRTUE IN WACO, TEXAS," Mid-South Folklore 4:3
       (Winter 1976), 87-94.

B-4059 Elifson, Kirk W. and Joseph Irwin, "BLACK MINISTERS' ATTITUDES
       TOWARD POPULATION SIZE AND BIRTH CONTROL," Sociological Analysis
       38:3 (Fall 1977), 252-257.

B-4060 Faye, Stanley, "THE SCHISM OF 1805 IN NEW ORLEANS," Louisiana
       Historical Quarterly 22:1 (January 1939), 142-165.

B-4061 Fink, Paul M., "METHODISM IN JONESBORO, TENNESSEE," East Tennessee
       Historical Society's Publications No. 22 (1950), 45-59.

B-4062 Fletcher, Mary P., "A REMINISCENCE OF LITTLE ROCK CHURCHES,"
       Arkansas Historical Quarterly 13:3 (Autumn 1954), 257-263.

B-4063 Flynt, Wayne, "RELIGION IN THE URBAN SOUTH: THE DIVIDED RELIGIOUS
       MIND OF BIRMINGHAM, 1900-1930," Alabama Review 30:2 (April 1977),
       108-134.

B-4064 Franch, Michael S., "THE CONGREGATIONAL COMMUNITY IN THE CHANGING
       CITY, 1840-70," Maryland Historical Magazine 71:3 (Fall 1976),
       367-380.

B-4065 Gardner, John H. Jr., "PRESBYTERIANS OF OLD BALTIMORE," Maryland
       Historical Magazine 35:3 (September 1940), 244-255.

B-4066 Gaventa, John, "CASE STUDY: PROPERTY FOR PROPHET," Southern
       Exposure 4:3 (Fall 1976), 101-103.

B-4067 Gerrard, Ginny, "A HISTORY OF THE PROTESTANT EPISCOPAL CHURCH IN
       SHREVEPORT, LOUISIANA, 1839-1916," North Louisiana Historical
       Association Journal 9:4 (1978), 193-203.

B-4068 Gibson, George H., "THE UNITARIAN-UNIVERSALIST CHURCH OF RICH-
       MOND," Virginia Magazine of History and Biography 74:3 (July
       1966), 321-335.

B-4069 Hall, Robert L., "TALLAHASSEE'S BLACK CHURCHES, 1865-1885,"
       Florida Historical Quarterly 58:2 (October 1979), 185-196.

B-4070 Holder, Ray, "METHODIST BEGINNINGS IN NEW ORLEANS 1813-1814,"
       Louisiana History 18:2 (Spring 1977), 171-187.

B-4071 Johnson, David A., "BEGINNINGS OF UNIVERSALISM IN LOUISVILLE,"
       Filson Club History Quarterly 43:2 (April 1969), 173-183.

B-4072 Johnson, Gwen Mills, "CHURCHES AND EVANGELISM IN JACKSON, MISSIS-
       SIPPI, 1920-1919," Journal of Mississippi History 34:4 (November
       1972), 307-330.

B-4073 Johnson, Whittington B., "ANDREW C. MARSHALL: A BLACK RELIGIOUS
       LEADER OF ANTEBELLUM SAVANNAH," Georgia Historical Quarterly 69:2
       (Summer 1985), 173-192.

B-4074 Jolissaint, Van E., "EUROPEAN PRIESTS IN ATLANTA--1914-1939,"
       Atlanta Historical Journal 17:3-4 (Fall-Winter 1972) 53-58.

B-4075 Kaganoff, Nathan M., "AN ORTHODOX RABBINATE IN THE SOUTH: TOBIAS
       GEFFEN, 1870-1970," American Jewish History 73:1 (September 1983),
       56-70.

B-4076 Kalin, Berkley, "RABBI WILLIAM H. FINESHRIBER: THE MEMPHIS YEARS," <u>West</u> <u>Tennessee</u> <u>Historical</u> <u>Society</u> <u>Papers</u> No. 25 (1971), 47-62.

B-4077 Kaslow, Andrew J., "SAINTS AND SPIRITS: THE BELIEF SYSTEM OF AFRO-AMERICAN SPIRITUAL CHURCHES IN NEW ORLEANS," <u>Perspectives</u> <u>on</u> <u>Ethnicity</u> <u>in</u> <u>New</u> <u>Orleans</u> (1981), 61-70.

B-4078 Loveland, Anne C., "THE 'SOUTHERN WORK' OF THE REVEREND JOSEPH C. HARTZELL, PASTOR OF AMES CHURCH IN NEW ORLEANS, 1870-1873," <u>Louisiana</u> <u>History</u> 16:4 (Fall 1975), 391-407.

B-4079 McEwen, H. C. Sr., "FIRST CONGREGATIONAL CHURCH, ATLANTA: 'FOR THE GOOD OF MAN AND THE GLORY OF GOD,'" <u>Atlanta</u> <u>Historical</u> <u>Journal</u> 21:1 (Spring 1977), 129-142.

B-4080 McMillan, Edward L., "RELIGION IN KOSCIUSKO," <u>Journal</u> <u>of</u> <u>Missis-</u><u>sippi</u> <u>History</u> 13:3 (July 1951), 146-164.

B-4081 Martensen, Katherine, "REGION, RELIGION, AND SOCIAL ACTION: THE CATHOLIC COMMITTEE OF THE SOUTH, 1939-1956," <u>Catholic</u> <u>Historical</u> <u>Review</u> 68:2 (April 1982), 249-267.

B-4082 Newman, Harvey K., "PIETY AND SEGREGATION: WHITE PROTESTANT ATTITUDES TOWARD BLACKS IN ATLANTA, 1865-1905," <u>Georgia</u> <u>Historical</u> <u>Quarterly</u> 63:2 (Summer 1979), 238-251.

B-4083 Newman, Harvey K., "THE ROLE OF WOMEN IN ATLANTA'S CHURCHES, 1865-1906," <u>Atlanta</u> <u>Historical</u> <u>Journal</u> 23:4 (Winter 1979-80), 17-30.

B-4084 Newman, Harvey K., "SOME REFLECTIONS ON RELIGION IN NINETEENTH-CENTURY ATLANTA: A RESEARCH NOTE," <u>Atlanta</u> <u>Historical</u> <u>Journal</u> 27:3 (Fall 1983), 47-56.

B-4085 Quinn, Jane, "NUNS IN YBOR CITY: THE SISTERS OF ST. JOSEPH AND THE IMMIGRANT COMMUNITY," <u>Tampa</u> <u>Bay</u> <u>History</u> 5:1 (Spring-Summer 1983), 24-41.

B-4086 Reese, Trevor R., "THE FOUNDING OF ST. PAUL'S CHURCH, AUGUSTA," <u>Georgia</u> <u>Historical</u> <u>Quarterly</u> 42:3 (September 1958), 277-281.

B-4087 Reilly, Timothy F., "HETRODOX NEW ORLEANS AND THE PROTESTANT SOUTH, 1800-1861," <u>Louisiana</u> <u>Studies</u> 12:3 (Fall 1973), 533-552.

B-4088 Reilly, Timothy F., "PARSON CLAPP OF NEW ORLEANS: ANTEBELLUM SOCIAL CRITIC, RELIGIOUS RADICAL, AND MEMBER OF THE ESTABLISH-MENT," <u>Louisiana</u> <u>History</u> 16:2 (Spring 1975), 167-191.

B-4089 Reilly, Timothy F., "SLAVERY AND THE SOUTHWESTERN EVANGELIST IN NEW ORLEANS (1800-1861)," <u>Journal</u> <u>of</u> <u>Mississippi</u> <u>History</u> 41:4 (November 1979), 301-318.

B-4090 Reinders, Robert C., "THE CHURCHES AND THE NEGRO IN NEW ORLEANS, 1850-1860," <u>Phylon</u> 22:3 (1961) 241-248.

B-4091 Reinders, Robert C., "THE LOUISIANA AMERICAN PARTY AND THE CATHO-LIC CHURCH," <u>Mid-America</u> 40:4 (October 1958), 218-228.

B-4092 Rosenswaike, Ira, "THE FOUNDING OF BALTIMORE'S FIRST JEWISH CON-GREGATION: FACT VS. FICTION," <u>American</u> <u>Jewish</u> <u>Archives</u> 28:2 (November 1976), 119-125.

B-4093 Rothschild, Mary Aickin, "THE VOLUNTEERS AND THE FREEDOM SCHOOLS: EDUCATION FOR SOCIAL CHANGE IN MISSISSIPPI," <u>History</u> <u>of</u> <u>Education</u> <u>Quarterly</u> 22:4 (Winter 1982), 401-420.

B-4094 Scott, Ralph G., "THE QUAKER SETTLEMENT OF WRIGHTSBOROUGH, GEOR-GIA," <u>Georgia</u> <u>Historical</u> <u>Quarterly</u> 56:2 (Summer 1972), 210-223.

B-4095 Sengel, William R., "REBELLION IN THE MEETING HOUSE," Virginia Cavalcade 14:1 (Summer 1964), 34–39.

B-4096 Shankman, Arnold, "ATLANTA JEWRY--1900–1930," American Jewish Archives 25:2 (November 1973), 131–155.

B-4097 Sheftall, John McKay, "THE SHEFTALLS OF SAVANNAH: COLONIAL LEADERS AND FOUNDING FATHERS OF GEORGIA JUDAISM," in Proctor, S., ed., Jews of the South, 65–78.

B-4098 Shpall, Leo, "THE FIRST SYNAGOGUE IN LOUISIANA," Louisiana Historical Quarterly 21:2 (April 1938), 518–531.

B-4099 Soden, Dale E., "NORTHERN GEORGIA: FERTILE GROUND FOR THE URBAN MINISTRY OF MARK MATHEWS," Georgia Historical Quarterly 69:1 (Spring 1985), 39–54.

B-4100 Spain, Rufus B., "R. B. C. HOWELL: NASHVILLE BAPTIST LEADER IN THE CIVIL WAR PERIOD," Tennessee Historical Quarterly 14:4 (December 1955), 323–340.

B-4101 Stein, Kenneth W., "A HISTORY OF AHAVATHA ACHIM CONGREGATION, 1887–1927," Atlanta Historical Journal 23:3 (Fall 1979), 107–118.

B-4102 Tabak, Israel, "THE LLOYD STREET SYNAGOGUE OF BALTIMORE: A NATIONAL SHRINE," American Jewish Historical Quarterly 61:4 (June 1972), 342–352.

B-4103 Taylor, A. Reed, "ATLANTA'S CENTRAL PRESBYTERIAN CHURCH," Atlanta Historical Journal 14:3 (September 1969), 103–116.

B-4104 Taylor, Georgia Fairbanks, "THE EARLY HISTORY OF THE EPISCOPAL CHURCH IN NEW ORLEANS, 1805–1840," Louisiana Historical Quarterly 22:2 (April 1939), 428–478.

B-4105 Thompson, Doris, "HISTORY OF AN OZARK UTOPIA," Arkansas Historical Quarterly 14:4 (Winter 1955), 359–373.

B-4106 Tyler, Lyon G., "GOD AND MR. PETIGRU: EPISCOPAL ATTITUDES TOWARD FAITH AND DOCTRINE IN ANTEBELLUM SOUTH CAROLINA," Historical Magazine 52:3 (September 1983), 229–245.

B-4107 Vouga, Anne E., "PRESBYTERIAN MISSIONS AND LOUISVILLE BLACKS: THE EARLY YEARS, 1898–1910," Filson Club History Quarterly 58:3 (July 1984), 310–335.

B-4108 Walker, Randolph Meade, "THE ROLE OF THE BLACK CLERGY IN MEMPHIS," West Tennessee Historical Society Papers No. 32 (1978), 29–47.

B-4109 Webber, Mabel L., ed., "THE RECORDS OF THE QUAKERS IN CHARLES TOWN (1)," South Carolina Historical and Genealogical Magazine 28:1 (January 1927), 22–43.

B-4110 Webber, Mabel L., ed., "THE RECORDS OF THE QUAKERS IN CHARLES TOWN (2)," South Carolina Historical and Genealogical Magazine 28:2 (April 1927), 94–107.

B-4111 Webber, Mabel L., ed., "THE RECORDS OF THE QUAKERS IN CHARLES TOWN (3)," South Carolina Historical and Genealogical Magazine 28:3 (July 1927), 176–197.

B-4112 Whiteman, Maxwell, "NOAH DAVIS AND THE NARRATIVE OF RESTRAINT," Afro-American History Series, Collection 8, Part 1, i–86.

B-4113 Williams, Charles Jr. and Hilda Booker Williams, "CONTEMPORARY VOLUNTARY ASSOCIATIONS IN THE URBAN BLACK CHURCH: THE DEVELOPMENT AND GROWTH OF MUTUAL AID SOCIETIES," Journal of Voluntary Action Review 13:4 (October–December 1984), 19–30.

B-4114 Wooten, Fred T. Jr., "RELIGIOUS ACTIVITIES IN CIVIL WAR MEMPHIS, PART 1," _Tennessee Historical Quarterly_ 3:2 (June 1944), 131-149.

B-4115 Wooten, Fred T. Jr., "RELIGIOUS ACTIVITIES IN CIVIL WAR MEMPHIS, PART 2," _Tennessee Historical Quarterly_ 3:3 (September 1944), 248-272.

Social Problems

B-4116 Aaronson, David E., C. Thomas Dienes, and Michael C. Musheno, "CHANGING THE PUBLIC DRUNKENNESS LAWS: THE IMPACT OF DECRIMINALIZATION," _Law and Society Review_ 12:3 (Spring 1978), 405-436.

B-4117 Adams, Jack E., "THE WELFARE EFFICIENCY OF MOVING FAMILIES INTO PUBLIC HOUSING IN LITTLE ROCK, ARKANSAS," _Land Economics_ 58:2 (May 1982), 217-224.

B-4118 Barbat, Damon, "THE ILLEGITIMATE BIRTH OF THE MAFIA IN NEW ORLEANS," _Southern Studies_ 24:3 (Fall 1985), 343-351.

B-4119 Bates, William M., "NARCOTICS, NEGROES AND THE SOUTH," _Social Forces_ 45:1 (September 1966), 61-67.

B-4120 Bigelow, Martha Mitchell, "BIRMINGHAM'S CARNIVAL OF CRIME, 1871-1910," _Alabama Review_ 3:2 (April 1950), 123-133.

B-4121 Bonner, James C., "THE GEORGIA PENITENTIARY AT MILLEDGEVILLE, 1817-1874," _Georgia Historical Quarterly_ 55:3 (Fall 1971), 303-328.

B-4122 Botein, Barbara, "THE HENNESSY CASE: AN EPISODE IN ANTI-ITALIAN NATIVISM," _Louisiana History_ 20:3 (Summer 1979), 261-280.

B-4123 Centerwall, Brandon S., "RACE, SOCIOECONOMIC STATUS, AND DOMESTIC HOMOCIDE, ATLANTA 1971-72," _American Journal of Public Health_ 74:8 (August 1984), 813-815.

B-4124 Chappell, Gorden T., "'GENTLEMAN JIM': MONTGOMERY'S NOTORIOUS ROBBER," _Alabama Review_ 24:1 (January 1971), 3-16.

B-4125 Christian, Garna L., "NEWTON BAKER'S WAR ON EL PASO VICE," _Red River Valley Historical Review_ 5:2 (Spring 1980), 55-67.

B-4126 Clarke, Stevens H. and Gary G. Koch, "THE INFLUENCE OF INCOME AND OTHER FACTORS ON WHETHER CRIMINAL DEFENDANTS GO TO PRISON,' _Law and Society Review_ 11:1 (Fall 1976), 57-92.

B-4127 Coleman, Alan, "THE CHARLESTON BOOTLEGGING CONTROVERSY, 1915-1918," _South Carolina Historical Magazine_ 75:2 (1974), 77-94.

B-4128 Coulter, E. Merton, "THE ATHENS DISPENSARY," _Georgia Historical Quarterly_ 50:1 (March 1966), 14-36.

B-4129 Courtwright, David T., "THE HIDDEN EPIDEMIC: OPIATE ADDICTION AND COCAINE USE IN THE SOUTH, 1860-1920," _Journal of Southern History_ 49:1 (February 1983), 57.

B-4130 Coxe, John E., "THE NEW ORLEANS MAFIA INCIDENT," _Louisiana Historical Quarterly_ 20:4 (October 1937), 1067-1110.

B-4131 Fraser, Walter J. Jr., "THE CITY ELITE, 'DISORDER' AND THE POOR CHILDREN OF PRE-REVOLUTIONARY CHARLESTON," _South Carolina Historical Magazine_ 84:3 (July 1983), 167-179.

B-4132 Fraser, Walter J. Jr., "CONTROLLING THE POOR IN COLONIAL CHARLES TOWN," _Proceedings of the South Carolina Historical Association_ 50 (1980), 13-30.

B-4133 Furstenberg, Frank F. Jr. and Charles F. Wellford, "CALLING THE
       POLICE: THE EVALUATION OF POLICE SERVICE," Law and Society Review
       7:3 (Spring 1973), 393-406.

B-4134 Galtung, Johan, "A MODEL FOR STUDYING IMAGES OF PARTICIPANTS IN A
       CONFLICT: SOUTHVILLE," Journal of Social Issues 15:4 (1959), 38-
       43.

B-4135 George, Paul S., "THE EVOLUTION OF MIAMI AND DADE COUNTY'S JUDICI-
       ARY, 1896-1930," Tequesta No. 36 (1976), 28-42.

B-4136 George, Paul S., "POLICING MIAMI'S BLACK COMMUNITY, 1896-1930,"
       Florida Historical Quarterly 57:4 (April 1979), 434-450.

B-4137 Georges-Abeyie, Daniel, "THE SOCIAL ECOLOGY OF BOMB THREATS:
       DALLAS, TEXAS," Journal of Black Studies 13:3 (March 1983), 305-
       320.

B-4138 Gibson, Arrell Morgan, "THE ST. AUGUSTINE [INDIAN] PRISONERS," Red
       River Valley Historical Review (Spring 1978), 259-270.

B-4139 Gildrie, Richard P., "LYNCH LAW AND THE GREAT CLARKSVILLE FIRE OF
       1878: SOCIAL ORDER IN A NEW SOUTH TOWN," Tennessee Historical
       Quarterly 42:1 (Spring 1983), 58-75.

B-4140 Griffin, Charles C., "PRIVATEERING FROM BALTIMORE DURING THE SPAN-
       ISH AMERICAN WAR OF INDEPENDENCE," Maryland Historical Magazine
       35:1 (March 1940), 1-25.

B-4141 Hair, William Ivy, "'INQUISITION FOR BLOOD': AN OUTBREAK OF RIT-
       UAL MURDER IN LOUISIANA, GEORGIA AND TEXAS, 1911-1912," Louisiana
       Studies 11:4 (Winter 1972), 274-281.

B-4142 Hall, John A., "NEFARIOUS WRETCHES, INSIDIOUS VILLAINS, AND EVIL
       MINDED PERSONS: URBAN CRIME, REPORTED IN CHARLESTON'S CITY
       GAZETTE IN 1788," South Carolina Historical Magazine 88:1 (January
       1987), 151-168.

B-4143 Hall, John A., "'RIGOUR OF CONFINEMENT WHICH VIOLATES HUMANITY,'
       JAIL CONDITIONS IN SOUTH CAROLINA DURING THE 1790s," Southern
       Studies 24:3 (Fall 1985), 284-294.

B-4144 Harries, Keith D. and Stephen J. Stadler, "AGGRAVATED ASSAULT AND
       THE URBAN SYSTEM: DALLAS, 1980-81," Journal of Environmental
       Systems 15:3 (1985-86), 243-254.

B-4145 Haunton, Richard H., "LAW AND ORDER IN SAVANNAH, 1850-1860,"
       Georgia Historical Quarterly 56:1 (Spring 1972), 1-24.

B-4146 Haynes, Robert V., "THE HOUSTON MUTINY AND RIOT OF 1917,"
       Southwestern Historical Quarterly 76:4 (April 1973), 418-439.

B-4147 Hertz, Hilda and Sue Warren Little, "UNMARRIED NEGRO MOTHERS IN A
       SOUTHERN URBAN COMMUNITY," Social Forces 23:1 (October 1944), 73-
       79.

B-4148 Himes, Joseph S. and Margaret L. Hamlett, "THE ASSESSMENT OF
       ADJUSTMENT OF AGED NEGRO WOMEN IN A SOUTHERN CITY," Phylon 23:2
       (Summer 1962), 139-148.

B-4149 Howington, Arthur F., "VIOLENCE IN ALABAMA: A STUDY OF LATE ANTE-
       BELLUM MONTGOMERY," Alabama Review 27:3 (July 1974), 213-231.

B-4150 Humphrey, David C., "PROSTITUTION AND PUBLIC POLICY IN AUSTIN,
       TEXAS, 1870-1915," Southwestern Historical Quarterly 86:4 (April
       1983), 473-516.

B-4151 Hutcheon, Wallace S. Jr., "THE LOUISVILLE RIOTS OF AUGUST, 1855,"
Register of the Kentucky Historical Society 69:2 (April 1971),
150-172.

B-4152 Ingalls, Robert P., "ANTIRACIAL VIOLENCE IN BIRMINGHAM DURING THE
1930s," Journal of Southern History 47:4 (November 1981), 521-544.

B-4153 Ingalls, Robert P., "LYNCHING AND ESTABLISHMENT VIOLENCE IN TAMPA,
1858-1935," Journal of Southern History 53:4 (November 1987), 613-
644.

B-4154 Ingalls, Robert P., "THE TAMPA FLOGGING CASE: URBAN VIGILANTISM,"
Florida Historical Quarterly 56:1 (July 1977), 13-27.

B-4155 Ivins, Molly, YO-YOS AND SHITKICKERS," Civil Liberties Review 1:4
(November-December 1974), 117-121.

B-4156 Jackson, Joy, "CRIME AND THE CONSCIENCE OF A CITY," Louisiana
History 9:3 (Fall 1968), 229-244.

B-4157 Jackson, Joy J., "PROHIBITION IN NEW ORLEANS: THE UNLIKELIEST OF
CRUSADE," Louisiana History 19:3 (Summer 1978), 261-284.

B-4158 Jacobson, Alvin L., "CRIME TRENDS IN SOUTHERN AND NONSOUTHERN
CITIES: A TWENTY-YEAR PERSPECTIVE," Social Forces 54:1 (September
1975), 226-242.

B-4159 Jones, Newton B., "THE CHARLESTON ORPHAN HOUSE, 1860-1876," South
Carolina Historical Magazine 62:4 (October 1961), 203-214.

B-4160 Jordan, Layton Wayne, "THE METHOD OF MODERN CHARITY: THE
ASSOCIATED CHARITIES SOCIETY OF CHARLESTION, 1888-1920," South
Carolina Historical Magazine 88:1(January 1987), 24-27.

B-4161 Jordan, Layton Wayne, "POLICE POWER AND PUBLIC SAFETY IN ANTE-
BELLUM CHARLESTON: THE EMERGENCE OF A NEW POLICE, 1800-1860,"
South Atlantic Urban Studies 3 (1979), 122-140.

B-4162 Jordan, Philip, "THE CAPITAL OF CRIME," Civil War Times Illustrated 13:10 (February 1975), 4-9, 44-47.

B-4163 Kallison, Frances Rosenthal, "WAS IT A DUEL OR A MURDER?: A STUDY
IN TEXAS ASSIMILATION," American Jewish Historical Quarterly 62:3
(March 1973), 314-320.

B-4164 Karlin, J. Alexander, "THE ITALO-AMERICAN INCIDENT OF 1981 AND THE
ROAD TO REUNION," Journal of Southern History 8:2 (May 1942), 242-
246.

B-4165 Kaser, David, "NASHVILLE'S WOMEN OF PLEASURE IN 1860," Tennessee
Historical Quarterly 23:4 (December 1964), 379-382.

B-4166 Katzman, Martin T., "CONTRIBUTION OF CRIME TO URBAN DECLINE,"
Urban Studies 17:3 (October 1980), 277-286.

B-4167 Kendall, John S., "ACCORDING TO THE CODE," Louisiana Historical
Quarterly 23:1 (January 1940), 141-16168

B-4168 Kendall, John S., "BLOOD ON THE BANQUETT," Louisiana Historical
Quarterly 22:3 (July 1939), 819-856.

B-4169 Kendall, John S., "THE HUMORS OF THE DUELLO," Louisiana Historical
Quarterly 23:2 (April 1940), 445-470.

B-4170 Kendall, John S., "THE HUNTSMEN OF BLACK IVORY," Louisiana Historical Quarterly 24:1 (January 1941), 9-34.

B-4171 Kendall, John S., "NOTES ON THE CRIMINAL HISTORY OF NEW ORLEANS,'
Louisiana Historical Quarterly 34:3 (1951), 147-174.

B-4172 Kendall, John S., "PISTOLS FOR TWO, COFFEE FOR ONE," Louisiana
       Historical Quarterly 24:3 (July 1941), 756-782.

B-4173 Kendall, John S., "THE STRANGE CASE OF MYRA CLARK GAINES,'
       Louisiana Historical Quarterly 20:1 (January 1937), 5-42.

B-4174 Kendall, John S., "WHO KILLA DE CHIEF," Louisiana Historical
       Quarterly 22:2 (April 1939), 492-530.

B-4175 Kennan, Clara B., "WHEN HENRY STARR ROBBED THE BENTONVILLE BANK--
       1893," Arkansas Historical Quarterly 7:1 (Spring 1948), 68-80.

B-4176 Kiebaner, Benjamin Joseph, "PUBLIC POOR RELIEF IN CHARLESTON,
       1800-1860," South Carolina Historical Magazine 55:4 (1955), 210-
       220.

B-4177 Kuchler, Eula Turner, "CHARITABLE AND PHILANTHROPIC ACTIVITIES IN
       ATLANTA DURING RECONSTRUCTION (I)," Atlanta Historical Bulletin
       10:4 (December 1965), 12-53.

B-4178 Kuchler, Eula Turner, "CHARITABLE AND PHILANTHROPIC ACTIVITIES IN
       ATLANTA DURING RECONSTRUCTION (II)," Atlanta Historical Bulletin
       11:1 (March 1966), 20-54.

B-4179 Kurtz, Michael L., "ORGANIZED CRIME IN LOUISIANA HISTORY: MYTH
       AND REALITY," Louisiana History 24:4 (Fall 1983), 355-376.

B-4180 Lack, Paul D., "LAW AND DISORDER IN CONFEDERATE ATLANTA," Georgia
       Historical Quarterly 66:2 (Summer 1982), 171-195.

B-4181 LaSater, Marion Newcomb, "NASHVILLE MAKES A VENTURE," Social
       Forces 11:2 (December 1932), 219-223.

B-4182 Lynch, Ronald G. and Vivian Lord, "PUBLIC SAFETY PROGRAMS: CON-
       SOLIDATING POLICE AND FIRE SERVICES," Popular Government 45:1
       (Summer 1979), 1-8.

B-4183 McCowen, George S. Jr., "THE CHARLES TOWN BOARD OF POLICE, 1780-
       1782: A STUDY IN CIVIL ADMINISTRATION UNDER MILITARY OCCUPATION,"
       Proceedings of the South Carolina Historical Association 34
       (1964), 25-42.

B-4184 Mannard, Joseph G., "THE 1839 BALTIMORE NUNNERY RIOT: AN EPISODE
       IN JACKSONIAN NATIVISM AND SOCIAL VIOLENCE," Maryland Historian
       11:1 (Spring 1980), 13-28.

B-4185 Marchiafava, Louis J., "THE POLICE REFORM MOVEMENT IN HOUSTON,
       1945-1948," East Texas Historical Journal 13:1 (Spring 1975), 43-
       55.

B-4186 Martin, Charles H., "OKLAHOMA'S 'SCOTTSBORO' AFFAIR: THE JESS
       HOLLINS RAPE CASE, 1931-1936," South Atlantic Quarterly 79:2
       (Spring 1980), 175-188.

B-4187 Miller, William D., "MYTH AND THE NEW SOUTH CITY MURDER RATES,"
       Mississippi Quarterly 26:2 (Spring 1973), 143-154.

B-4188 Mitchell, Memory F., "THE GOOD WORKS OF ST. JOHN'S GUILD, 1877-
       1893," North Carolina Historical Review 63:3 (July 1986), 309-339.

B-4189 Molenaer, Harriet, "MADAM LaLAURIE: A CONTEMPORARY FRENCH AC-
       COUNT,' Louisiana Studies 7:4 (Winter 1968), 378-390.

B-4190 Moody, Robert, "THE LORD SELECTED ME," Southern Exposure 7:4
       (Winter 1979), 4-10.

B-4191 Moore, John Hammond, "THE NORFOLK RIOT: 16 APRIL 1866," Virginia
       Magazine of History and Biography 90:2 (April 1982), 155-164.

B-4192 Moseley, Clement Carlton, "THE CASE OF LEO M. FRANK, 1913-1915," Georgia Historical Quarterly 51:1 (March 1967), 42-62.

B-4193 Mulvey, Edward P. and Ann Hicks, "THE PARADOXICAL EFFECT OF A JU-VENILE CODE CHANGE IN VIRGINIA," American Journal of Community Psychology 10:6 (December 1982), 705-722.

B-4194 Musselman, Thomas H., "A CRUSADE FOR LOCAL OPTION: SHREVEPORT, 1951-1952," North Louisiana Historical Association Journal 6:2 (1975), 59-73.

B-4195 Nelli, Humbert S., "THE HENNESSY MURDER AND THE MAFIA IN NEW ORLEANS," Italian Quarterly 19:75-76 (1975), 77-95.

B-4196 Overmyer, Grace, "THE BALTIMORE MOBS AND JOHN HOWARD PAYNE," Maryland Historical Magazine 58:1 (Spring 1963), 54-61.

B-4197 Owens, Harry P., "THE EUFAULA RIOT OF 1874," Alabama Review 16:3 (July 1963), 224-237.

B-4198 Palmer, Early, "THE UNITED WAY AND THR BLACK COMMUNITY IN ATLANTA, GEORGIA," Black Scholar 9:4 (1977), 50-61.

B-4199 Palmer, Gladys L., "THE COMMUNITY CHEST IN VIRGINIA CITIES," Social Forces 6:2 (December 1927), 229-236.

B-4200 Peacock, Jane Bonner, "NELLIE PETERS BLACK: TURN OF THE CENTURY 'MOVER AND SHAKER,'" Atlanta Historical Journal 23:4 (Winter 1979-80), 7-16.

B-4201 Porterfield, Austin L., "CRIME IN SOUTHERN CITIES," in R. Vance, ed., The Urban South (1954), 180-202.

B-4202 Porterfield, Austin L. and Robert H. Talbert, "A DECADE OF DIFFER-ENTIALS AND TRENDS IN SERIOUS CRIMES IN 86 AMERICAN CITIES BY SOUTHERN AND NON-SOUTHERN PAIRS," Social Forces 31:1 (October 1952), 60-68.

B-4203 Rader, Perry Scott, "THE ROMANCE OF AMERICAN COURTS: GAINES VS. NEW ORLEANS," Louisiana Historical Quarterly 27:1 (January 1944), 5-322.

B-4204 Reed, H. Clay, "THE EARLY NEW CASTLE COURT," Delaware History 4:3 (June 1951), 227-245.

B-4205 Reed, John P., "LAW VIEWS AND LAW WAYS OF BLACK AND WHITES IN SUNSHINE CITY," Phylon 35:4 (Winter 1974), 359-367.

B-4206 Reed, Merl E., "FEPC AND THE FEDERAL AGENCIES IN THE SOUTH," Journal of Negro History 65:1 (Winter 1980), 43-56.

B-4207 Reynolds, Terry S., "CISTERNS AND FIRES: SHREVEPORT, LOUISIANA, AS A CASE STUDY OF THE EMERGENCE OF PUBLIC WATER SUPPLY SYSTEMS IN THE SOUTH," Louisiana History 22:4 (Fall 1981), 337-368.

B-4208 Roberts, Derrell C., "ROBERT TOOMBS AND ATLANTA'S NEW SOUTH URBAN PROBLEMS," Atlanta Historical Journal 17:1-2, (Spring-Summer 1972), 58-63.

B-4209 Roblyer, Leslie F., "THE FIGHT FOR LOCAL PROHIBITION IN KNOXVILLE, TENNESSEE, 1970,' East Tennessee Historical Society's Publications No. 26 (1954), 27-37.

B-4210 Rose, Harold M., "THE CHANGING SPATIAL DIMENSION OF BLACK HOMICIDE IN SELECTED AMERICAN CITIES," Journal of Environmental Systems 11:1 (1981-82), 57-80.

B-4211 Ross, Edyth L., "BLACK HERITAGE IN SOCIAL WELFARE: A CASE STUDY OF ATLANTA," Phylon 37:4 (December 1976), 297-307.

B-4212 Ross, Jack C. and Raymond Wheeler, "STRUCTURAL SOURCES OF THREAT TO NEGRO MEMBERSHIP IN MILITANT VOLUNTARY ASSOCIATIONS IN A SOUTHERN CITY," Social Forces 45:4 (June 1967), 583-586.

B-4213 Rousey, Dennis C., "'HIBERNIAN LEATHERHEADS': IRISH COPS IN NEW ORLEANS, 1830-1880," Journal of Urban History 10:1 (November 1983), 61-84.

B-4214 Sanchez-Saavedra, E. M., "AN UNDISCIPLINED SET OF VAGABONDS," Virginia Cavalcade 18:4 (Spring 1969), 41-47.

B-4215 Saunders, Robert M., "CRIME AND PUNISHMENT IN EARLY NATIONAL AMERICA: RICHMOND, VIRGINIA, 1784-1820," Virginia Magazine of History and Biography 86:1 (January 1978), 33-44.

B-4216 Schmier, Louis E., "'NO JEW CAN MURDER': MEMORIES OF TOM WATSON AND THE LICHTENSTEIN MURDER CASE OF 1901," Georgia Historical Quarterly 70:3 (Fall 1986), 433-455.

B-4217 Schultz, Stanley K., "TEMPERANCE REFORM IN THE ANTEBELLUM SOUTH: SOCIAL CONTROL AND URBAN ORDER," South Atlantic Quarterly 83:3 (Summer 1984), 323-339.

B-4218 Shepard, E. Lee, "COURTS IN CONFLICT: TOWN-COUNTY RELATIONS IN POST-REVOLUTIONARY VIRGINIA," Virginia Magazine of History and Biography 85:2 (April 1977), 184-199.

B-4219 Shofner, Jerrell H., "JUDGE HERBERT RIDER AND THE LYNCHING AT LABELLE," Florida Historical Quarterly 59:3 (January 1981), 292-306.

B-4220 Stevens, Michael E., "THE VIGILANT FIRE COMPANY OF CHARLESTON," South Carolina Historical Magazine 87:2 (April 1986), 130-136.

B-4221 Stewart, W. Cassell, "THE PINKERTON-MARONEY INVESTIGATION," Alabama Review 35:3 (July 1982), 163-171.

B-4222 Taskforce on the Homeless, "CAN YOU SEE OUR FACES: IMAGES OF ATLANTA'S HOMELESS," Southern Exposure 15:2 (Summer 1987), 51-55.

B-4223 Tennis, Hall and Dewey S. Knight Jr., "MINORITIES AND JUSTICE IN GREATER MIAMI: A VIEW FROM THE METRO-COURTHOUSE," Urban Resources 2:3 (Spring 1985), 19-25.

B-4224 Thomas, Emory M., "THE RICHMOND BREAD RIOT OF 1863," Virginia Cavalcade 18:1 (Summer 1968), 41-47.

B-4225 Thomas, Emory M., "TO FEED THE CITIZENS: WELFARE IN WARTIME RICHMOND, 1861-1865," Virginia Cavalcade 22:1 (Summer 1972), 22-29.

B-4226 Tournier, Robert E., "URBAN PRESSURES, SOCIAL ISOLATION, AND THE EXERCISE OF DISCRETION BY POLICE OFFICERS," South Atlantic Urban Studies 2 (1978), 203-211.

B-4227 Ulmer, Barbara, "BENEVOLENCE IN COLONIAL CHARLESTON," Proceedings of the South Carolina Historical Association 50 (1980), 1-12.

B-4228 Van Deburg, William L., "HENRY CLAY, THE RIGHT OF PETITION, AND SLAVERY IN THE NATION'S CAPITAL," Register of the Kentucky Historical Society 68:2 (April 1970), 132-146.

B-4229 Vines, Kenneth N., "COURTS AND POLITICAL CHANGE IN THE SOUTH," Journal of Social Issues 22:1 (January 1966), 59-72

B-4230 Wafle, Millard, "LOCATION OF SHOPLIFTERS IN BOCA RATON, FLORIDA," Florida Geographer 15:1 (April 1981), 15-16.

B-4231 Warren, Harris Gaylord, ed., "DOCUMENTS RELATING TO THE ESTABLISH-
MENT OF PRIVATEERS AT GALVESTON, 1816-1817," Louisiana Historical
Quarterly 21:4 (October 1938), 1086-1109.

B-4232 Watts, Eugene J., "THE POLICE IN ATLANTA, 1890-1905," Journal of
Southern History 39:2 (May 1973), 165-182.

B-4233 Weidman, Dennis and J. Bryan Page, "DRUG USE ON THE STREET AND ON
THE BEACH: CUBANS AND ANGLOS IN MIAMI, FLORIDA," Urban Anthropology 11:2 (Summer 1982), 213-236.

B-4234 Wilkerson, Sarah, "NOT SO EASY BUSINESS," Southern Exposure 11:4
(July-August 1983), 19-23.

B-4235 Williams, Marilyn Thornton, "PHILANTHROPY IN THE PROGRESSIVE ERA:
THE PUBLIC BATHS OF BALTIMORE," Maryland Historical Magazine 72:1
(Spring 1977), 118-131.

B-4236 Williams, Martha and Jay Hall, "KNOWLEDGE OF THE LAW IN TEXAS:
SOCIOECONOMIC AND ETHNIC DIFFERENCES," Law & Society Review 7:1
(Fall 1972), 99-118.

B-4237 Wilson, Jon L., "DAYS OF FEAR: A LYNCHING IN ST. PETERSBURG,"
Tampa Bay History 5:2 (Fall-Winter 1983), 4-26.

B-4238 Wiltz, C. J., "FEAR OF CRIME, CRIMINAL VICTIMIZATION AND ELDERLY
BLACKS," Phylon 43:4 (December 1982), 283-294.

B-4239 Wise, Leah, "THE ELAINE MASSACRE," Southern Exposure 1:3, 4
(Winter 1974), 9-32.

B-4240 Wish, Harvey, "THE SLAVE INSURRECTION PANIC OF 1856," Journal of
Southern History 5:2 (May 1939), 206-222.

B-4241 Wolcott, Daniel, "RYVES HOLT, OF LEWES, DELAWARE, 1696-1763,"
Delaware History 8:1 (March 1958), 3-50.

B-4242 Wundram, Ina Jane and R. Barry Ruback, "URBAN RATS: SYMBOL, SYMP-
TOM AND SYMBIOSIS," Human Organization 45:3 (Fall 1986), 212-219.

Theatre

B-4243 Armistead, Margaret Beauchamp,. "THE SAVANNAH THEATER--OLDEST IN
AMERICA," Georgia Review 7:1 (Spring 1953), 50-56.

B-4244 Awsumb, Carl David, "THEATRES OF THE SOUTH: THEATRE MEMPHIS,"
Southern Theatre 19:1 (Winter 1975), 31-33.

B-4245 Bagley, Russell E., "THEATRICAL ENTERTAINMENT IN PENSACOLA, FLORI-
DA: 1882-1892," Southern Speech Journal 17:1 (September 1950),
62-84.

B-4246 Barranger, Milly S., "NEW ORLEANS AS THEATRICAL IMAGE IN PLAYS BY
TENNESSEE WILLIAMS," Southern Quarterly 23:2 (Winter 1985), 38-54.

B-4247 Bloomfield, Maxwell, "WARTIME DRAMA: THE THEATER IN WASHINGTON
(1861-1865)," Maryland Historicla Magazine 64:4 (Winter 1969),
396-411.

B-4248 Bogner, Harold F., "SIR WALTER SCOTT IN NEW ORLEANS, 1818-1832,"
Louisiana Historical Quarterly 21:2 (April 1938), 420-517.

B-4249 Brown, Jared A., "THE THEATER IN THE SOUTH DURING THE AMERICAN
REVOLUTION," Southern Quarterly 18:2 (Winter 1960), 44-59.

B-4250 Christopher, Milbourne, "MAGIC IN EARLY BALTIMORE," Maryland
Historical Magazine 38:4 (December 1943), 323-330.

B-4251 Conner, William H., "THE LIFE AND DEATH OF WILMINGTON'S FIRST THEATRE,' Delaware History 5:1 (March 1952), 3-41.

B-4252 Curtis, Julia, "AUGUSTA'S FIRST THEATRE SEASON: 1790-91," Southern Speech Communication Journal 43:3 (Spring 1978), 283-295.

B-4253 Curtis, Mary Julia, "CHARLES-TOWN'S CHURCH STREET THEATER," South Carolina Historical Magazine 70:3 (July 1969), 149-154.

B-4254 Dart, Henry P., "CABARETS OF NEW ORLEANS IN THE FRENCH COLONIAL PERIOD," Louisiana Historical Quarterly 19:3 (July 1936), 578-583.

B-4255 Davis, Jackson, "DRAMATIC STOCK IN DALLAS, 1920-1925," Southern Speech Journal 29:1 (Fall 1963), 34-46.

B-4256 Deahl, William E. Jr., "BUFFALO BILL'S WILD WEST SHOW IN NEW ORLEANS," Louisiana History 16:3 (Summer 1975), 289-298.

B-4257 deMetz, Kaye, "DANCE DUELS ON NEW ORLEANS STAGES DURING THE NINE-TEENTH CENTURY," Southern Speech Communications Journal 41:3 (Spring 1976), 278-289.

B-4258 deMetz, Kaye, "JUVENILE DANCERS ON NEW ORLEANS STAGE DURING THE EARLY NINETEENTH CENTURY," Southern Theatre 18:4 (Fall 1975), 13-17.

B-4259 deMetz, Kaye, "THEATRICAL DANCING IN NINETEENTH-CENTURY NEW ORLEANS," Louisiana History 21:1 (Winter 1980), 23-42.

B-4260 Dodd, William G., "THEATRICAL ENTERTAINMENT IN EARLY FLORIDA," Florida Historical Quarterly 25:2 (October 1946), 121-174.

B-4261 Dormon, James H., "THESPIS IN DIXIE: PROFESSIONAL THEATER IN CON-FEDERATE RICHMOND," Virginia Cavalcade 28:1 (Summer 1978), 4-13.

B-4262 Fife, Iline, "THE CONFEDERATE THEATER IN GEORGIA," Georgia Review 9:3 (Fall 1955), 305-315.

B-4263 Flannery, James, "SOUTHERN THEATER AND THE PARADOX OF PROGRESS," Southern Exposure 14:3-4 (March-April 1986), 12-17.

B-4264 French, William, "YOU DO ME BETTER 'N I DO: CABBAGETOWN'S ORAL HISTORY PLAY," Southern Exposure 14:3-4 (1986), 66-71.

B-4265 Fuller, Frank Jr., "THEATRES OF THE SOUTH: RICHMOND'S MARSHALL THEATRE," Southern Theatre 17:4 (Summer-Fall 1974), 29-31.

B-4266 Gallant, Carol, "THEATRES OF THE SOUTH: THE OLD OPERA HOUSE OF CHARLES TOWN, WEST VIRGINIA," Southern Theatre 18:3 (Summer 1975), 29-31.

B-4267 Gallegly, Joseph S., "PLAYS AND PLAYERS AT PILLOT'S OPERA HOUSE," Southwestern Historical Quarterly 66:1 (July 1962), 43-58.

B-4268 Gallegly, Joseph S., "THE RENAISSANCE OF THE GALVESTON THEATRE: HENRY GREENWALL'S FIRST SEASON, 1867-1868," Southwestern Histori-cal Quarterly 62:1 (July 1958), 442-456.

B-4269 Gardner, Bettye and Bettye Thomas, "THE CULTURAL IMPACT OF THE HOWARD THEATRE ON THE BLACK COMMUNITY," Journal of Negro History 55:4 (October 1970), 253-265.

B-4270 Gates, William Bryan, "THE THEATRE IN NATCHEZ," Journal of Missis-sippi History 3:2 (April 1941), 71-129.

B-4271 Geary, Helen Brophy, "AFTER THE LAST PICTURE SHOW," Chronicles of Oklahoma 61:1 (Spring 1983), 4-17.

B-4272 Graham, Philip, "SHOWBOATS IN THE SOUTH," Georgia Review 12:2 (Summer 1958), 174-184.

B-4273 Haarbauer, D. Ward, "THE BIRMINGHAM THEATRES OF FRANK O'BRIEN," Southern Theatre 20:3 (Summer 1977), 11-16.

B-4274 Hailey, Robert, "THEATRES OF THE SOUTH: THE ACADEMY OF MUSIC THEATRE," Southern Theatre 17:1 (Fall 1973), 9-11.

B-4275 Harwell, Richard Barksdale, "BRIEF CANDLE: THE CONFEDERATE THEATRE," Proceedings of the American Antiquarian Society 81, part 1 (April 1971), 41-160.

B-4276 Henderson, Jerry, "NASHVILLE IN THE DECLINE OF SOUTHERN LEGITIMATE THEATRE DURING THE BEGINNING OF THE TWENTIETH CENTURY," Southern Speech Journal 29:1 (Fall 1963), 22-33.

B-4277 Henderson, Jerry, "NASHVILLE'S RYMAN AUDITORIUM," Tennessee Historical Quarterly 27:4 (Winter 1968), 305-328.

B-4278 Hickey, Mike, "THEATRES OF THE SOUTH: THE VIRGINIA MUSEUM THEATRE," Southern Theatre 18:4 (Fall 1975), 8-12.

B-4279 Hill, Raymond S., "MEMPHIS THEATRE--FIRST DECADE," West Tennessee Historical Society Papers No. 9 (1955), 48-58.

B-4280 Hill, West T. Jr., "OPENING OF MACAULEY'S THEATRE, LOUISVILLE, KENTUCKY, OCTOBER 4, 1873," Filson Club History Quarterly 32:2 (April 1958), 151-167.

B-4281 Holding, Charles E., "JOHN WILKES BOOTH STARS IN NASHVILLE," Tennessee Historical Quarterly 23:1 (March 1964), 73-79.

B-4282 Hollister, Katharine Stevens, "THE THEATRE IN JACKSON, 1890-1910," Journal of Mississippi History 17:2 (March 1955), 127-134.

B-4283 Hoole, W. Stanley, "CHARLESTON THEATRICALS DURING THE TRAGIC DECADE, 1860-1869," Journal of Southern History 11:4 (Novebmer 1945), 538-546.

B-4284 Hostetler, Paul S., "STUDIES IN SOUTHERN THEATRE HISTORY: THE INFLUENCE OF NEW ORLEANS ON EARLY NINETEENTH CENTURY THEATRE," Southern Speech Journal 29:1 (Fall 1963), 12-19.

B-4285 Kendall, John Smith, "JOSEPH JEFFERSON IN NEW ORLEANS," Louisiana Historical Quarterly 26:4 (October 1943), 1150-1167.

B-4286 Kendall, John Smith, "SARAH BERNHARDT IN NEW ORLEANS," Louisiana Historical Quarterly 26:3 (July 1943), 770-782.

B-4287 Koch, Mary Levin, "ENTERTAINING THE PUBLIC: MUSIC AND DRAMA IN ANTEBELLUM AUGUSTA, MACON, AND COLUMBUS, GEORGIA," Georgia Historical Quarterly 68:4 (Winter 1984), 516-536.

B-4288 Land, Robert H., "THE FIRST WILLIAMSBURG THEATER," William and Mary Quarterly 3rd Series, 5:3 (July 1948), 359-374.

B-4289 Leary, Lewis and Arlin Turner, "JOHN HOWARD PAYNE IN NEW ORLEANS," Louisiana Historical Quarterly 31:1 (January 1948), 110-122.

B-4290 McCall, John Clark Jr., "THE ROXY THEATRE: RECOLLECTIONS OF VAUDEVILLE IN ATLANTA," Atlanta Historical Journal 18:1, 2 (Spring-Summer 1973), 21-26.

B-4291 Maiden, Lewis, "THE THEATRE IN NASHVILLE, 1876-1900," Southern Speech Journal 29:1 (Fall 1963), 20-25.

B-4292 Maiden, Lewis S., "THREE THEATRICAL STARS IN NASHVILLE," Southern Speech Journal 31:4 (Summer 1966), 338-347.

B-4293 Miller, Joseph M., "BOB INGERSOLL COMES TO LOUISVILLE," Filson Club History Quarterly 39:4 (October 1965), 311-319.

B-4294 Moehlenbock, Arthur, "THE GERMAN DRAMA ON THE NEW ORLEANS STAGE," Louisiana Historical Quarterly 26:2 (April 1943), 362-627.

B-4295 Moffatt, Walter, "FIRST THEATRICAL ACTIVITIES IN ARKANSAS," Arkansas Historical Quarterly 12:4 (Winter 1953), 327-332.

B-4296 Neeson, Jack and Margaret Neeson, "FAVORITE WILMINGTON PLAYS BEFORE THE CIVIL WAR," Delaware History 7:3 (March 1957), 262-280.

B-4297 Neeson, Jack H., "FROM SCHOOLHOUSE TO PLAYHOUSE: WILMINGTON'S NON-PROFESSIONAL THEATRE," Delaware History 8:3 (March 1959), 265-293.

B-4298 Niehaus, E. F., "PADDY ON THE LOCAL STAGE AND IN HUMOR: THE IMAGE OF THE IRISH IN NEW ORLEANS, 1820-1862," Louisiana History 5:2 (Spring 1964), 117-134.

B-4299 Overstreet, Robert, "JOHN T. FORD AND THE SAVANNAH THEATER," Southern Speech Communication Journal 38:1 (Fall 1972), 51-60.

B-4300 Peyrouse, Jack, "TURN-OF-THE CENTURY TOURING THEATRE IN SOUTHERN APPALACHIA," Southern Theatre 22:4 (Fall 1979), 3-10.

B-4301 Pusey, William W. III, "THE BEAUTIFUL JERSEY LILY: ENGLISH AC-TRESS LILLIE LANGTRY TOURS VIRGINIA," Virginia Cavalcade 34:3 (Winter 1985), 108-117.

B-4302 Ritchey, David, "COLUMBIA GARDEN: BALTIMORE'S FIRST PLEASURE GARDEN," Southern Speech Communication Journal 39:3 (Spring 1974), 241-247.

B-4303 Ritter, Charles C., "'THE DRAMA IN OUR MIDST'--THE EARLY HISTORY OF THE THEATRE IN MEMPHIS," West Tennessee Historical Society Papers No. 11 (1957), 5-35.

B-4304 Robinson, Emmett, ed., "DR. IRVING'S REMINISCENCES OF THE CHARLES-TON STAGE, (1)," South Carolina Historical and Genealogical Maga-zine 52:1 (February 1951), 26-33.

B-4305 Robinson, Emmett, ed., "DR. IRVING'S REMINISCENCES OF THE CHARLES-TON STAGE, (2)," South Carolina Historical and Genealogical Maga-zine 52:2 (April 1951), 93-106.

B-4306 Robinson, Emmett, ed., "DR. IRVING'S REMINISCENCES OF THE CHARLES-TON STAGE, (3)," South Carolina Historical and Genealogical Maga-zine 52:3 (July 1951), 166-182.

B-4307 Robinson, Emmett, ed., "DR. IRVING'S REMINISCENCES OF THE CHARLES-TON STAGE, (4)," South Carolina Historical and Genealogical Maga-zine 52:4 (October 1951), 225-232.

B-4308 Robinson, Emmett, ed., "DR. IRVING'S REMINISCENCES OF THE CHARLES-TON STAGE, (5)," South Carolina Historical and Genealogical Maga-zine 53:1 (February 1952), 37-47.

B-4309 Rulfs, Donald J., "THE ANTE-BELLUM PROFESSIONAL THEATER IN FAY-ETTEVILLE,' North Carolina Historical Review 31:2 (April 1954), 125-133.

B-4310 Rulfs, Donald J., "THE ANTE-BELLUM PROFESSIONAL THEATER IN RA-LEIGH," North Carolina Historical Review 29:3 (July 1952), 344-348.

B-4311 Rulfs, Donald J., "THE PROFESSIONAL THEATER IN WILMINGTON, 1858-1870," North Carolina Historical Review 28:3 (April 1951), 119-136.

B-4312 Rulfs, Donald J., "THE PROFESSIONAL THEATER IN WILMINGTON, 1870-1900," North Carolina Historical Review 28:2 (July 1951), 316-331.

B-4313 Rulfs, Donald J., "THE PROFESSIONAL THEATER IN WILMINGTON, 1900-1930," North Carolina Historical Review 28:4 (October 1951), 463-485.

B-4314 Rulfs, Donald J., "THE THEATER IN ASHEVILLE FROM 1879 TO 1931," North Carolina Historical Review 36:4 (October 1959), 429-441.

B-4315 Seeker, Edward D., "THE FRENCH THEATRE IN CHARLESTON IN THE EIGHTEENTH CENTURY," South Carolina Historical and Genealogical Magazine 42:1 (Januaary 1941), 1-7.

B-4316 Shelley, Dian Lee, "TIVOLI THEATRE OF PENSACOLA," Florida Historical Quarterly 50:4 (April 1972), 341-351.

B-4317 Sherwood, William, "FIRST THEATRES OF THE SOUTH," Southern Literary Messenger 1:1 (January 1939), 56-59.

B-4318 Shockley, Martin Staples, "FIRST AMERICAN PERFORMANCES OF ENGLISH PLAYS IN RICHMOND BEFORE 1819," Journal of Southern History 13:1 (February 1947), 91-105.

B-4319 Shockley, Martin Staples, "THE RICHMOND THEATRE, 1780-1790," Virginia Magazine of History and Biography 60:3 (July 1952), 421-436.

B-4320 Smither, Neele, "CHARLOTTE CUSHMAN'S APPRENTICESHIP IN NEW ORLEANS," Louisiana Historical Quarterly 31:4 (October 1948), 973-980.

B-4321 Smither, Nellie, "A HISTORY OF THE ENGLISH THEATRE AT NEW ORLEANS, 1806-1842," Louisiana Historical Quarterly 28:1 (January 1945), 85-276; 28:2 (April 1945), 361-572.

B-4322 Stokes, D. Allen, "THE FIRST THEATRICAL SEASON IN ARKANSAS: LITTLE ROCK, 1838-1839," Arkansas Historical Quarterly 23:2 (Summer 1964), 166-183.

B-4323 Swift, Mary Grace, "THE THEATRE D'ORLEANS ON TOUR," Louisiana History 26:2 (Spring 1985), 155-193.

B-4324 Teague, Charlotte Headrick, "THE SAENGER THEATRE, 'ALABAMA'S GREATEST SHOWPLACE,'' Southern Theatre 21:3 (Summer 1978), 25-28.

B-4325 Tedford, Harold, "CIRCUSES IN THE NORTHWEST ARKANSAS BEFORE THE CIVIL WAR," Arkansas Historical Quarterly 26:3 (Fall 1967), 244-256.

B-4326 "THEATRES OF THE SOUTH: THE SPRINGER OPERA HOUSE," Southern Theatre 17:2 (Winter 1974), 8-10.

B-4327 Troubetzkoy, Ulrich, "FROM SOPHOCLES TO ARTHUR MILLER: THE BARTER THEATRE OF VIRGINIA," Virginia Cavalcade 10:1 (Summer 1960), 5-10.

B-4328 Ward, Kathryn Painter, "THE FIRST PROFESSIONAL THEATER IN MARYLAND IN ITS COLONIAL SETTING," Maryland Historical Magazine 70:1 (Spring 1975), 29-44.

B-4329 Ward, Kathryn Painter, "THE MARYLAND THEATRICAL SEASON OF 1760," Maryland Historical Magazine 72:3 (Fall 1979), 335-345.

B-4330 Weisert, John J., "BEGINNINGS OF GERMAN THEATRICALS IN LOUISVILLE," Filson Club History Quarterly 26:4 (October 1952), 347-359.

B-4331 Weisert, John J., "BEGINNINGS OF THE KENTUCKY THEATRE CIRCUIT," Filson Club History Quarterly 34:3 (July 1960), 264-286.

B-4332 Weisert, John J., "AND END AND SEVERAL BEGINNINGS: THE PASSING OF DRAKE'S CITY THEATRE," Filson Club History Quarterly 50:1 (January 1976), 5-28.

B-4333 Weisert, John J., "THE FIRST DECADE AT SAM DRAKE'S LOUISVILLE THEATRE," Filson Club History Quarterly 39:4 (October 1965), 287-310.

B-4334 Weisert, John J., "GOLDEN DAYS AT DRAKE'S CITY THEATRE, 1830-1833," Filson Club History Quarterly 43:3 (July 1969), 255-270.

B-4335 Weiss, David W., "THE CULBRETH THEATRE, THEATRES OF THE SOUTH: CHARLOTTESVILLE, VA," Southern Theatre 17:3 (Spring 1974), 36-40.

B-4336 Wyatt, E. A. IV, "THREE PETERSBURG THEATRES," William and Mary College Historical Magazine 21:2 (April 1941), 83-110.

Transportation

B-4337 Agent, Kenneth R., "WARRANTS FOR LEFT-TURN LANES," Transportation Quarterly 37:1 (January 1983), 99-114.

B-4338 Allen, Gary R., Eugene D. Arnold Jr., and Lester A. Hoel, "STATUS OF INTERCITY BUS SERVICE IN VIRGINIA AND ANTICIPATED IMPACTS OF REGULATING REFORM," Transportation Quarterly 36:4 (October 1982), 597-615.

B-4339 Angel, William D. Jr., "VANTAGE ON THE BAY: GALVESTON AND THE RAILROADS," East Texas Historical Journal 22:1 (1984), 3-18.

B-4340 Antunes, George E. and John P. Plumlee, "THE DISTRIBUTION OF AN URBAN PUBLIC SERVICE: ETHNICITY, SOCIOECONOMIC STATUS, AND BUREAUCRACY AS DETERMINANTS OF THE QUALITY OF NEIGHBORHOOD STREETS," Urban Affairs Quarterly 12:3 (March 1977), 313-332.

B-4341 "ATLANTA SUCCESSFULLY SOLVING ITS LOCAL TRANSPORTATION PROBLEMS," Electric Railway Journal 67 (8 May 1926), 792-797.

B-4342 Baker, Carole, "TRACKING WASHINGTON'S METRO," American Demographics 5:11 (November 1983), 30-35.

B-4343 Baughman, James P., "THE EVOLUTION OF RAIL-WATER SYSTEM OF TRANSPORTATION IN THE GULF SOUTHWEST, 1836-1890," Journal of Southern History 34:3 (August 1968), 357-381.

B-4344 Bederman, Sanford H., "ATLANTA'S INNERCITY RESIDENTS AND THE JOURNEY TO WORK: A SUMMARY OF THREE TRANSPORTATION SURVEYS," Southeastern Geographer 16:1 (May 1976), 62-73.

B-4345 Bixby, Arthur M. Sr., "NORFOLK AND WESTERN'S ROANOKE SHOPS AND ITS LOCOMOTIVES," Railroad History No. 137 (1977), 20-37.

B-4346 Black, J. Thomas, "TRANSPORTATION IN HIGH DENSITY COMMERCIAL CENTERS," Urban Land 42:3 (March 1983), 22-25.

B-4347 Brown, Alexander Crosby, "COLONIAL WILLIAMSBURG'S CANAL SCHEME," Virginia Magazine of History and Biography 86:1 (January 1978), 26-32.

B-4348 Brownell, Blaine A., "THE AUTOMOBILE IN SOUTHERN CITIES IN THE 1920's," American Quarterly 24:1 (March 1972), 20-44.

B-4349 Brownell, Blaine A., "THE NOTORIOUS JITNEY AND THE URBAN TRANSPORTATION CRISIS IN BIRMINGHAM IN THE 1920's," Alabama Review 25:2 (April 1972), 105-118.

B-4350 Buffington, Milton W., "CARS ACROSS THE COUNTRYSIDE," Virginia Cavalcade 15:2 (Autumn 1965) 14-22.

B-4351 Burt, Jesse C., "EDMUND W. COLE AND THE STRUGGLE BETWEEN NASHVILLE AND LOUISVILLE AND THEIR RAILROADS, 1879-1880," Filson Club History Quarterly 26:2 (April 1952), 112-132.

B-4352 Burt, Jesse C. Jr., "FOUR DECADES OF THE NASHVILLE, CHATTANOOGA AND ST. LOUIS RAILWAY, 1873-1916," Tennessee Historical Quarterly 9:2 (June 1950), 99-130.

B-4353 Campbell, Walter E., "PROFIT, PREJUDICE, AND PROTEST: UTILITY COMPETITION AND THE GENERATION OF JIM CROW STREETCARS IN SAVANNAH, 1905-1907," Georgia Historical Quarterly 70:2 (Summer 1986), 197-231.

B-4354 Chang, Semoon, "FORECASTING PASSENGER ENPLANEMENTS OF A MUNICIPAL AIRPORT: THE CASE OF MOBILE, ALABAMA," Review of Regional Studies 7:3 (Winter 1977), 13-19.

B-4355 Coleman, Elizabeth Dabney, "THE NIGHT RIDE THAT MADE ROANOKE," Virginia Cavalcade 4:1 (Summer 1954), 9-13.

B-4356 Cotterill, R. S., "MEMPHIS RAILROAD CONVENTION, 1849," Tennessee Historical Magazine 4:2 (June 1918), 83-94.

B-4357 Cotterill, R. S., "SOUTHERN RAILROADS, 1850-1860," Journal of American History 10:4 (March 1924), 396-405.

B-4358 Crocker, Helen Bartler, "STEAMBOATS FOR BOWLING GREEN," Filson Club History Quarterly 46:1 (January 1972), 9-23.

B-4359 Cruickshank, A., "HARTSFIELD ATLANTA INTERNATIONAL AIRPORT," Geography 66, part 1:290 (January 1981), 60-63.

B-4360 Dajani, J., M. M. Egan and M. B. McElroy," THE REDISTRIBUTIVE IMPACT OF THE ATLANTA MASS TRANSIT SYSTEM," Southern Economic Journal 42:1 (July 1975), 49-60.

B-4361 Davis, Aurora E., "THE DEVELOPMENT OF THE MAJOR COMMERCIAL AIRLINES IN DADE COUNTY, FLORIDA: 1945-1970," Tequesta No. 32 (1972), 3-16.

B-4362 Davis, Sid, "MARTA--A REASSESSMENT," Atlanta Economic Review 28:1 (January February 1978), 52-55.

B-4363 Dew, Lee A., "OWENSBORO'S DREAM OF GLORY: A RAILROAD TO RUSSELL-VILLE," Filson Club History Quarterly 52:1 (January 1978), 26-47.

B-4364 Dew, Lee A., "OWENSBORO'S 'PAPER' INTERURBANS," Filson Club History Quarterly 57:2 (April 1983), 207-222.

B-4365 Doherty, Herbert J. Jr., "JACKSONVILLE AS A NINETEENTH-CENTURY RAILROAD CENTER," Florida Historical Quarterly 58:4 (April 1980), 373-386.,

B-4366 Doss, Chriss, "CULLMAN COAL AND COKE COMPANY RAILROAD," Alabama Review 37:4 (October 1984), 243-256.

B-4367 Ellis, Herman A., "THE GROWTH OF THE GREYHOUND BUS SERVICE IN THE SOUTHEAST," Register of the Kentucky Historical Society 61:1 (January 1963), 1-21.

B-4368 Fabian, Lawrence J., "PEOPLE MOVERS: THE EMERGENCE OF SEMI-PUBLIC TRANSIT," Traffic Quarterly 35:4 (October 1981), 557-568.

B-4369 Falkner, Murry C., "THE COMING OF THE MOTOR CAR," Southern Review 10:1 (January 1974), 170-180.

B-4370 Farkas, Z. Andrew, "COSTS AND BENEFICIARIES OF ATLANTA MASS TRANSIT," Atlanta Economic Review 27:4 (July-August 1977), 50-54.

B-4371 George, Paul S., "TRAFFIC CONTROL IN EARLY MIAMI," Tequesta No. 37 (1977), 3-18.

B-4372 Goff, John H., "THE STEAMBOAT PERIOD IN GEORGIA," Georgia Historical Quarterly 12:3 (September 1928), 236-254.

B-4373 Grant, H. Roger, "ARKANSAS'S 'PAPER INTERURBANS,'" Arkansas Historical Quarterly 39:1 (Spring 1980), 53-63.

B-4374 Grant, H. Roger, "'INTERURBANS ARE THE WAVE OF THE FUTURE': ELECTRIC RAILWAY PROMOTION IN TEXAS," Southwestern Historical Quarterly 84:1 (July 1980), 29-48.

B-4375 Grant, H. Roger, "MEMPHIS AND THE INTERURBAN AREA," Tennessee Historical Quarterly 46:1 (Spring 1987), 43-48.

B-4376 Griselle, Sherman and Herbert S. Levinson, "CO-OPERATIVE EXPRESS-WAY PLANNING IN THE TULSA METROPOLITAN AREA," Traffic Quarterly 13:1 (January 1959), 112-127.

B-4377 Hanks, Dorothy M., "SHREVEPORT'S FIRST ELECTRIC STREET CAR," Louisiana Studies 7:2 (Summer 1968), 179-182.

B-4378 Harwood, Herbert H. Jr., "MT. CLARE STATION, AMERICA'S OLDEST: OR IS IT?" Railroad History 139 (1978), 39-53.

B-4379 Herzberg, James, "SPEED AND GROWTH: THE DEVELOPMENT OF THE GULF FREEWAY," Houston Review 4 (Fall 1982), 113-136.

B-4380 Hildrith, Charles W.., "RAILROADS OUT OF PENSACOLA, 1833-1883," Florida Historical Quarterly 37:3-4 (January-April 1959), 397-417.

B-4381 Holmes, William F., "THE NEW CASTLE AND FRENCHTOWN TURNPIKE AND RAILROAD COMPANY, 1809-1830: PART I, TURNPIKES ACROSS THE PENIN-SULA," Delaware History 5:1 (April 1962), 71-104.

B-4382 Holmes, William F., "THE NEW CASTLE AND FRENCHTOWN TURNPIKE AND RAILROAD COMPANY, 1809-1830: PART II, CANAL VERSUS RAILROAD," Delaware History 5:2 (October 1962), 152-180.

B-4383 Holmes, William F., "THE NEW CASTLE AND FRENCHTOWN TURNPIKE AND RAILROAD COMPANY, 1809-1830: PART III, FROM HORSES TO LOCOMO-TIVES," Delaware History 5:3 (April 1963), 235-270.

B-4384 Hudson, Patricia L., "THE OLD ANDERSON ROAD: LIFELINE TO CHATTA-NOOGA," Tennessee Historical Quarterly 42:2 (Summer 1983), 165-178.

B-4385 Hunnicutt, J. M. Jr., "NASHVILLE'S LOADING-ZONE POLICY," Traffic Quarterly 13:2 (April 1959), 260-282.

B-4386 Klima, Don L., "BREAKING OUT: STREETCARS AND SUBURBAN DEVELOP-MENT, 1872-1900," Atlanta Historical Society 26:2-3 (Summer-Fall 1982), 67-82.

B-4387 Lakshmanan, T. R., "AN APPROACH TO THE ANALYSIS OF INTRAURBAN LOCATION APPLIED TO THE BALTIMORE REGION," Economic Geography 40:4 (October 1964), 348-370.

B-4388 Laws, Forrest, "THE RAILROAD COMES TO TENNESSEE: THE BUILDING OF THE LAGRANGE AND MEMPHIS," West Tennessee Historical Society Papers No. 30 (1976), 24-42.

B-4389 Livingood, James W., "CHATTANOOGA: A RAIL JUNCTION OF THE OLD SOUTH," Tennessee Historical Quarterly 6:3 (September 1947), 230-250.

B-4390 McCormick, Kyle, "CHARLESTON'S RAILROAD," West Virginia History 21:3 (April 1960), 197-199.

B-4391 McGuire, Peter S., "ATHENS AND THE RAILROADS: THE GEORGIA AND THE NORTHEASTERN, PT. I," Georgia Historical Quarterly 18:1 (March 1934), 1-26.

B-4392 McGuire, Peter S., "ATHENS AND THE RAILROADS: THE NORTHEASTERN EXTENSION; THE MACON AND NORTHERN; AND THE GEORGIA, CAROLINA, AND NORTHERN. PART II," Georgia Historical Quarterly 18:2 (June 1934), 118-144.

B-4393 MacFadyen, J. Levere, "THIS TEXAS SEAWAY SHOULDN'T WORK—BUT DOES," Smithsonian 16:7 (October 1985), 88-99.

B-4394 Maraffa, Thomas A. and Don Kiel, "AIR SERVICE TO CITIES ABANDONED BY PIEDMONT AVIATION SINCE DEREGULATION,' Southeastern Geographer 25:1 (May 1985), 16-29.

B-4395 Marti, Bruce E., "CHANGES IN MARITIME TRAFFIC OF THE PORT OF JACKSONVILLE," Florida Geographer 17:1 (August 1983), 1-10.

B-4396 Martin, Jean, "MULE TO MARTA, VOL. I," Atlanta Historical Journal 19:2 (1975), 1-112.

B-4397 Martin, Jean, "MULE TO MARTA, VOL. II," Atlanta Historical Bulletin 20:4 (Winter 1976), 1-208.

B-4398 Mehrling, John C., "THE MEMPHIS AND OHIO RAILROAD," West Tennessee Historical Society Papers No. 22 (1968), 52-61.

B-4399 Meyers, Frederic, "ORGANIZATION AND COLLECTIVE BARGAINING IN THE LOCAL MASS TRANSPORTATION INDUSTRY IN THE SOUTHEAST," Southern Economic Journal 15:4 (April 1949), 425-440.

B-4400 Miller, Nory, "WASHINGTON METRO: IT WORKS AND LOOKS GOOD," Ekistics 43:156 (March 1977), 171-178.

B-4401 Millet, Donald J., "SOUTHWEST LOUISIANA ENTERS THE RAILROAD AGE: 1880-1900," Louisiana History 24:2 (Spring 1983), 165-183.

B-4402 Mitchelson, Ronald L. and James O. Wheeler, "ANALYSIS OF AGGREGATE FLOWS: THE ATLANTA CASE," in Susan Hanson, ed., The Geography of Urban Transportation, (1986), 119-153.

B-4403 Mitchelson, Ronald L. and James S. Fisher, "COMMUTING COST VISI-BILITY: A CONTEMPORARY CASE STUDY," Southeastern Geographer 21:2 (November 1981), 130-147.

B-4404 Moore, John Hammond, "ATLANTA'S HANSON CAR," Atlanta Historical Bulletin 12:2 (June 1967), 16-29.

B-4405 Muir, Andrew Forest, "RAILROADS COME TO HOUSTON, 1857-1861," Southwestern Historical Quarterly 64:1 (July 1960), 42-63.

B-4406 Neeley, Mary Ann, "'THE LIGHTNING ROUTE,': THE DEVELOPMENT OF THE ELECTRIC STREETCAR AND ITS EFFECT ON MONTGOMERY, 1885-1900," Alabama Review 60:4 (October 1987), 243-258.

B-4407 Odom, Mackie, "THE INTRODUCTION AND EXPANSION OF RAILROAD LINES IN MISSISSIPPI, 1830-1973," Mississippi Geographer 2:1 (Spring 1974), 51-60.

B-4408 Olmstead, Florence, "OLD CITY AND SUBURBAN CAR LINES," Georgia Historical Quarterly 28:3 (September 1944), 138-142.

B-4409 Olsen, Richard J. and G. W. Westley, "REGIONAL DIFFERENCES IN THE
       GROWTH OF OVERNIGHT TRUCK TRANSPORT MARKETS, 1950-1970," Review of
       Regional Studies 4, Sup. (1973), 53-59.

B-4410 Page, John H., "I-66 CASE STUDY: EVOLUTION PROCESS OF TOMORROW'S
       URBAN HIGHWAYS," Transportation Quarterly 37:4 (October 1983),
       493-510.

B-4411 Peeples, Vernon, "CHARLOTTE HARBOR DIVISION OF THE FLORIDA SOUTH-
       ERN RAILROAD," Florida Historical Quarterly 58:3 (January 1980),
       291-302.

B-4412 Pitts, Robert Loy, "THE DEMAND FOR BUS TRANSPORTATION IN HOUSTON--
       AN ANALYSIS OF PRICE AND SERVICE SENSITIVITY," American Economist
       21:1 (Spring 1977), 30-33.

B-4413 Polanis, Stanley F., "SIGNAL COORDINATION AND FUEL EFFICIENCY:
       WINSTON-SALEM'S EXPERIENCE," Transportation Quarterly 38:2 (April
       1984), 283-296.

B-4414 Potter, Paul E., "URBAN RESTRUCTURING: ONE GOAL OF THE NEW
       ATLANTA TRANSIT SYSTEM," Traffic Quarterly 33:1 (January 1979),
       45-60.

B-4415 Provenzo, Eugene F. Jr., "ST. PETERSBURG-TAMPA AIRBOAT LINE,"
       Florida Historical Quarterly 48:1 (July 1979), 72-77.

B-4416 Reed, Merl E., "GOVERNMENT INVESTMENT AND ECONOMIC GROWTH:
       LOUISIANA'S ANTEBELLUM RAILROADS," Journal of Southern History
       28:2 (May 1962), 183-201.

B-4417 Reichenburger, Donovan, "WINGS OVER WAYNOKA," Chronicles of
       Oklahoma 65:2 (Summer 1987), 116-131.

B-4418 Reidy, Jeanne P., "BOCA GRANDE: THE TOWN THE RAILROAD BUILT,"
       Tampa Bay History 4:1 (Spring-Summer 1982), 21-32.

B-4419 Ristroph, Paul L., "NEW ORLEANS' SEVEN-CENT BUS FARE," Traffic
       Quarterly 13:3 (July 1959), 402-407.

B-4420 Rose, F. P., "THE SPRINGFIELD WAGON COMPANY," Arkansas Historical
       Quarterly 10:1 (Spring 1951), 95-103.

B-4421 Rosenburg, Leon J. and Grant M. Davis, "DALLAS AND ITS FIRST RAIL-
       ROAD," Railroad History No. 135 (1976), 34-42.

B-4422 Ross, Catherine L., "MEASURING TRANSPORTATION SYSTEM EFFECTIVE-
       NESS," Journal of Urban Affairs 5:4 (Fall 1983), 299-314.

B-4423 Scribner, Robert L. and W. Edwin Hemphil," RICHMOND'S ELECTRIC
       STREETCAR SYSTEM," Virginia Cavalcade 8:2 (Autumn 1958), 21-31.

B-4424 Seely, Bruce E., "WILMINGTON AND ITS RAILROADS: A LASTING CON-
       NECTION," Delaware History 19:1 (Spring-Summer 1980), 1-19.

B-4425 Siegling, H. Carter, "THE BEST FRIEND OF CHARLESTON," South
       Carolina History Illustrated 1:1 (February 1970), 19-23, 71.

B-4426 Sioussat, St. George L., "MEMPHIS AS A GATEWAY TO THE WEST: A
       STUDY IN THE BEGINNINGS OF RAILWAY TRANSPORTATION IN THE OLD
       SOUTHWEST," [Part I] Tennessee Historical Magazine 3:1 (March
       1917), 1-27.

B-4427 Sioussat, St. George L., "MEMPHIS AS A GATEWAY TO THE WEST: A
       STUDY IN THE BEGINNINGS OF RAILWAY TRANSPORTATION IN THE OLD
       SOUTHWEST," [Part II] Tennessee Historical Magazine 3:2 (June
       1917), 77-114.

B-4428 Southerland, Henry Leon Jr., "THE FEDERAL ROAD, GATEWAY TO
ALABAMA, 1806-1836," Alabama Review 39:2 (April 1986), 96-119.

B-4429 Sprague, Stuart S., "KENTUCKY AND THE CINCINNATI-CHARLESTON
RAILROAD, 1835-1839," Register of the Kentucky Historical Society
73:2 (April 1975), 122-135.

B-4430 Stanley, William R. and Thomas F. Baucom, "SOME SPATIAL COMPONENTS
OF REGIONAL AIR SERVICE DEMAND IN THE SOUTHEAST," Southeastern
Geographer 12:2 (November 1972), 145-154.

B-4431 Stansfield, Charles A., "CHANGES IN THE GEOGRAPHY OF PASSENGER
LINER PORTS: THE RISE OF THE SOUTHEASTERN FLORIDA PORTS,"
Southeastern Geographer 17:1 (May 1977), 25-32.

B-4432 Starling, Robert B., "THE PLANK ROAD MOVEMENT IN NORTH CAROLINA,"
North Carolina Historical Review 16:2 (April 1939), 147-173.

B-4433 Stewart, Peter C., "RAILROADS AND URBAN RIVALRIES IN ANTEBELLUM
EASTERN VIRGINIA," Virginia Magazine of History and Biography 81:1
(January 1973), 3-22.

B-4434 Wetherington, Mark V., "STREETCAR CITY: KNOXVILLE, TENNESSEE,
1876-1947," East Tennessee Historical Society Publications No. 54,
55 (1982-1983), 70-110.

B-4435 Wilkstrom, Debbie, "THE HORSE-DRAWN STREET RAILWAY: THE BEGINNING
OF PUBLIC TRANSPORTATION IN SHREVEPORT," North Louisiana Historical Association Journal 7:3 (1976), 83-90.

B-4436 Willis, Stanley, "'TO LEAD VIRGINIA OUT OF THE MUD': FINANCING
THE OLD DOMINION'S PUBLIC ROADS, 1922-1924," Virginia Magazine of
History and Biography 94:4 (October 1986), 425-452.

B-4437 Wise, David Owen and Marguerite Dupree, "THE CHOICE OF THE AUTOMO-
BILE FOR URBAN PASSENGER TRANSPORTATION: BALTIMORE IN THE 1920s,"
South Atlantic Urban Studies 2 (1978), 153-179.

B-4438 Wolbrink, Donald H. and Frederic M. Robinson, "TOURISTS AND
TRAFFIC IN HAWAII AND IN MIAMI BEACH, FLORIDA," Traffic Quarterly
13:1 (January 1959), 90-111.

B-4439 Zegeer, Charles V. and Robert C. Deen, "IDENTIFICATION OF HAZARD-
OUS LOCATIONS ON CITY STREETS," Traffic Quarterly 31:4 (October
1977) 549-570.

Urban Renewal

B-4440 Barnes, William R., "A NATIONAL CONTROVERSY IN MINIATURE: THE
DISTRICT OF COLUMBIA STRUGGLE OVER PUBLIC HOUSING AND REDEVELOP-
MENT, 1943-46," Prologue 9:2 (1977), 91-104.

B-4441 Byrne, Robert and Douglas Porter, "A UDAG EXAMPLE: THE RADISSON
WILMINGTON HOTEL," Urban Land 39:6 (June 1980), 5-10.

B-4442 Darlow, Arthur, "MIAMI TO UPGRADE ITS DOWNTOWN," American City 74
(August 1959), 123-127.

B-4443 Eisman, D. E., "BEALE STREET REDEVELOPMENT: A COST-BENEFIT
ANALYSIS," Mid-South Business Journal 2:2 (April 1982), 15-20.

B-4444 Goldfield, David R., "PRIVATE NEIGHBORHOOD REDEVELOPMENT AND DIS-
PLACEMENT: THE CASE OF WASHINGTON D. C.," Urban Affairs Quarterly
15:4 (June 1980), 453-468.

B-4445 Harrison, Glen, "GENTRIFICATION IN KNOXVILLE, TENNESSEE: A STUDY
OF THE FOURTH AND GILL NEIGHBORHOOD," Urban Geography 4:1
(January-March 1983), 40-53.

B-4446 Humphries, Barry K., "BEAUMONT, TEXAS: ONE APPROACH TO CBD REDEVELOPMENT," Urban Land 33 (September 1974), 16-27.

B-4447 Ikemma, William N., "REVITALIZING INNER-CITY MINORITY COMMUNITIES: THE BLACK NEIGHBORHOOD-BASED BUSINESS ENVIRONMENT IN HOUSTON," Urbanism Past and Present No. 4 (1977), 11-18.

B-4448 Jacobs, Barry, "INNER CITIES: SAVANNAH LANDMARK," Southern Exposure 8:1 (Spring 1980), 48-54.

B-4449 Jenne, Kurt, "COMMUNITY DEVELOPMENT BLOCK GRANTS: THE FIRST FIVE YEARS," Popular Government 45:4 (Spring 1980), 1-14.

B-4450 Jones, Malcolm, "PEOPLE, PLACE, PERSISTENCE: A VICTORY FOR NEIGHBORHOODS," Southern Exposure 5:1 (Spring 1977), 66-74.

B-4451 Jones, Malcolm, "THE WORKABLE PROGRAM OF A SOUTHERN METROPOLIS, ATLANTA, GEORGIA," Phylon 19:1 (1958), 60-63.

B-4452 Laska, S. B., J. M. Seaman and D. R. McSeneney, "INNER CITY REIN-VESTMENT: NEIGHBORHOOD CHARACTERISTICS AND SPATIAL PATTERNS OVER TIME," Urban Studies [Essex] 19:2 (May 1982), 155-166.

B-4453 Lawrence, David M., "DOWNTOWN REVITALIZATION: AN EXPLORATION OF LEGAL AND FINANCIAL ISSUES," Popular Government 46:1 (Summer 1980), 10-16.

B-4454 Lee, Barrett A., and Paula M. Mergenhagen, "IS REVITALIZATION DETECTABLE? EVIDENCE FROM FIVE NASHVILLE NEIGHBORHOODS," Urban Affairs Quarterly 19:4 (June 1984), 511-538.

B-4455 Little, Charles E., "ATLANTA RENEWAL GIVES POWER TO THE COMMUNI-TIES," Smithsonian 7:4 (1974), 100-107.

B-4456 McConnell, Dennis D., "INVESTING IN NEIGHBORHOOD REVITALIZATION," Atlanta Economic Review 28:2 (March-April 1978), 22-27.

B-4457 Rash, James Dennis, "PRIVATELY FUNDED REDEVELOPMENT IN NORTH CAROLINA," Urban Land 42:10 (October 1983), 2-7.

B-4458 Richards, Carol and Jonathan Rowe, "RESTORING A CITY: WHO PAYS THE PRICE," Working Papers for a New Society 4:4 (1977), 54-61.

B-4459 Short, Dale, "BIRMINGHAM RECLAIMS ITS DOWNTOWN," Place 3:5 (May 1983), 4-6.

B-4460 Sinclair, Stephen, "SPIRIT SQUARE: HOW CHARLOTTE, NORTH CAROLINA, REVITALIZED ITS DOWNTOWN," Cultural Post 6 (September-October 1980), 18-21.

B-4461 Stapleton, Lee Ellen, "JACKSONVILLE, FLA. BUYS A FACELIFT," South Magazine 7:2 (February 1980), 50-54.

B-4462 Tournier, Robert E., "CITIES AS PEOPLE, CITIES AS PLACES: URBAN REVITALIZATION AND URBAN CONFLICT," Journal of Urban Affairs 6:2 (Spring 1984), 141-150.

B-4463 Waite, Otis, "BIRMINGHAM'S MAGNIFICENT FACELIFT," 7:4 (April 1980), 42-49.

B-4464 Weaver, Robert C., "SOUTHERN COMFORT: A POSSIBLE MISAPPLICATION OF FEDERAL FUNDS," Journal of Integroup Relations 1:3 (Summer 1960), 14-20.

B-4465 Wickham, DeWayne, "BALTIMORE: WHERE BLACK POLITICIANS GOT IN ON URBAN RENEWAL," Black Enterprise 9 (August 1978), 37-39, 41-42.

B-4466 Wishneff, Brian and Douglas Eckel, "ROANOKE, VIRGINIA," Urban Land 44:11 (November 1985), 22-27.

Unclassified

B-4467 Bederman, Sanford H. and James R. Miller, "DATA BASE COMPLEXITIES
       AND PROBLEMS IN THE ATLANTA S.M.S.A.--A PLEA FOR STANDARDIZATION,"
       Atlanta Economic Review 23:5 (September-October 1973), 34-41.

B-4468 Bookchin, Murray, "TOWARD A VISION OF THE URBAN FUTURE," in D.
       Perry, Ed., The Rise of the Sunbelt Cities, (1977), 259-276.

B-4469 Brownell, Blain A., "THE URBAN SOUTH COMES OF AGE, 1900-1940," in
       B. Brownell, ed., The City in Southern History, (1977), 123-158.

B-4470 Bryan, Violet H., "LAND OF DREAMS: IMAGE AND REALITY IN NEW
       ORLEANS," Urban Resources 1:4 (Spring 1984), 29-35.

B-4471 Carstensen, Laurence W. Jr., "TIME-DISTANCE MAPPING AND TIME-SPACE
       CONVERGENCE: THE SOUTHERN UNITED STATES," Southeastern Geographer
       21:2 (November 1981), 67-83.

B-4472 Trout, Robert O., "RURAL-URBAN DEPENDENCY RATIOS IN LOUISIANA,"
       Louisiana Studies 5:4 (Winter 1966), 269-277.

B-4473 Vance, Rupert B. and Sara Smith, "METROPOLITAN DOMINANCE AND
       INTEGRATION," in R. Vance, ed., The Urban South, (1954), 114-134.

B-4474 White, Dana F. and Timothy J. Crimmins, "URBAN STRUCTURE, ATLANTA:
       AN INTRODUCTION," Atlanta Historical Journal 26:2-3 (Summer Fall
       1982), 6-12.

Monographs

Architecture and Historic Preservation

C-1 Acker, Marian Francis, GLIMPSES OF OLD MOBILE, Mobile, AL: Gill Printing and Stationery Co., 1955.

C-2 Alexander, Ann C., PERSPECTIVES ON A RESORT COMMUNITY: HISTORIC BUILDINGS INVENTORY, SOUTHERN PINES, NORTH CAROLINA, Southern Pines: Town of Southern Pines, 1983.

C-3 American Institute of Architects, Dallas Chapter, DALLASITES: AN ANTHOLOGY OF ARCHITECTURE AND OPEN SPACES, Dallas: AIA, 1978.

C-4 Anderson, Elizabeth B., ANNAPOLIS, A WALK THROUGH HISTORY, Centerville, MD: Tidewater Publishers, 1984.

C-5 Andrews, Wayne, PRIDE OF THE SOUTH: SOCIAL HISTORY OF SOUTHERN ARCHITECTURE, New York: Atheneum, 1979.

C-6 Arnell, Pater and Ted Bickford, eds., SOUTHWEST CENTER: THE HOUSTON COMPETITION, New York, NY: Rizzoli, 1983.

C-7 Arrigo, Joseph A., THE FRENCH QUARTER AND OTHER NEW ORLEANS SCENES, GRETNA, LA: Pelican Publishing Co., 1984, C 1976.

C-8 ATLANTA HISTORIC RESOURCES WORKBOOK, Atlanta: The Commission, 1981.

C-9 Autry, William O. Jr., AN ARCHAEOLOGICAL, ARCHITECTURAL, AND HISTORIC CULTURAL RESOURCES RECONNAISSANCE OF THE NORTHEAST METROPOLITAN NASHVILLE TRANSPORTATION CORRIDOR, Nashville: Tanasi Anthropological Research Associates, 1982.

C-10 Beeson, Leola Selman, THE ONE HUNDRED YEARS OF THE OLD GOVERNORS' MANSION, MILLEDGEVILLE, GEORGIA, 1838-1938, Macon: The J. W. Burke Company, 1938.

C-11 Beirne, Rosamund Randall and Edith Rossiter, THE HAMMOND-HARWOOD HOUSE AND ITS OWNERS, Annapolis, MD: 1941.

C-12 Birmingham Historical Society, DOWNTOWN BIRMINGHAM: ARCHITECTURAL AND HISTORICAL WALKING TOUR GUIDE, Birmingham: The Society; National Bank of Birmingham, 1977.

C-13 Bishir, Catherine W. and Lawrence S. Earley, eds., EARLY TWENTIETH-CENTURY SUBURBS IN NORTH CAROLINA: ESSAYS ON HISTORY, ARCHITECTURE, AND PLANNING, Raleigh: Division of Archives and History, Department of Cultural Resources, 1985.

C-14 Black, David R., HISTORIC ARCHITECTURAL RESOURCES OF DOWNTOWN ASHEVILLE, NORTH CAROLINA, Raleigh: Archaeology and Historic Preservation Section, Division of Archives and History, 1979-1980.

C-15 Brazeal, Celia Stokes, et al., HISTORIC ARCHITECTURE OF HAMILTON, NORTH CAROLINA, Raleigh: Archaeology and Historic Preservation Section, Division of Archives and History, 1979-1980.

C-16 Broward, Robert C., THE ARCHITECTURE OF HENRY JOHN KLUTHO: THE PRAIRIE SCHOOL IN JACKSONVILLE, Jacksonville: University of North Florida Press, 1983.

C-17 Bruce, Curt, THE GREAT HOUSES OF NEW ORLEANS, New York: Knopf, 1977.

C-18 Bryan, John M., AN ARCHITECTURAL HISTORY OF THE SOUTH CAROLINA COLLEGE, 1801-1855, Columbia: University of South Carolina Press, 1976.

C-19 THE BUILDINGS OF BILOXI: AN ARCHITECTURAL SURVEY, Biloxi, MS: City of Biloxi, 1976.

C-20 Bureau of Governmental Research, New Orleans, PLAN AND PROGRAM FOR THE PRESERVATION OF THE VIEUX CARRE: HISTORIC DISTRICT DEMONSTRATION STUDY, New Orleans, 1968.

C-21 Cain, Helen, AN ILLUSTRATED GUIDE TO THE MISSISSIPPI GOVERNOR'S MANSION, Jackson: University Press of Mississippi, 1984.

C-22 Chambers, S. Allen Jr., LYNCHBURG: AN ARCHITECTURAL HISTORY, Charlottesville: University Press of Virginia, 1981.

C-23 Charleston, S.C. Civic Services Committee, THIS IS CHARLESTON, A SURVEY OF THE ARCHITECTURAL HERITAGE OF A UNIQUE AMERICAN CITY . . . (Text by Samuel Gaillard Stoney), Charleston: Charleston Art Association, 1944.

C-24 Christian, Frances Archer and Susznne William Massie, HOMES AND GARDENS IN OLD VIRGINIA, Richmond: Garrett and Massie, Inc., 1931.

C-25 Christovitch, Mary Louise, Roulhac Toledano, Betsy Swanson, and Pat Holden, eds., NEW ORLEANS ARCHITECTURE VOLUME II: THE AMERICA SECTOR, Gretna, LA: Pelican Publishing Company, 1972.

C-26 Christovitch, Mary Louise, Sally Kittredge Evans, and Roulhac Toledano, NEW ORLEANS ARCHITECTURE: VOLUME V: THE ESPLANADE RIDGE, Gretna, LA: Pelican Publishing Company, 1977.

C-27 Colonial Williamsburg, THE RALEIGH TAVERN, Richmond: 1932.

C-28 Cooper, J. Wesley, ANTE-BELLUM HOUSES OF NATCHEZ, Natchez: Southern Historical Publications, 1970.

C-29 Cruise, Boyd and Merle Horton, SIGNOR FARANTA'S IRON THEATRE, New Orleans: Historic New Orleans Collection, 1982.

C-30 Curl, Donald W., MIZNER'S FLORIDA: AMERICAN RESORT ARCHITECTURE, Cambridge: MIT Press, 1984.

C-31 Curtis, Nathaniel Cortlandt, NEW ORLEANS; ITS OLD HOUSES, SHOPS, AND PUBLIC BUILDINGS, Philadelphia: J. B. Lippincott Company, 1933.

C-32 Davidson, William H., ARCHITECTURAL HERITAGE OF WEST POINT (GA.)--
LANETT (ALA.) IN THE CHATTAHOOCHEE VALLEY, West Point: Chattahoochee Valley Historical Society, 1975.

C-33 Davis, Deering, et al., ALEXANDRIA HOUSES, 1750-1830, New York:
Architectural Book Publishing Company, 1946.

C-34 Davis, Deering, ANNAPOLIS HOUSES, 1700-1775, New York: Architectural Book Publishing Company, 1947.

C-35 Davis, Deering, Stephen P. Dorsey, and Ralph C. Hall, GEORGETOWN
HOUSES OF THE FEDERAL PERIOD: WASHINGTON, D. C., 1780-1830, New
York: Architectural Book Publishing Company, 1944.

C-36 Davis, William Columbus, THE COLUMNS OF ATHENS, GEORGIA'S CLASSIC
CITY, Athens: 1951.

C-37 Delaney, Caldwell, DEEP SOUTH, Mobile, AL: The Haunted Book Shop,
1942.

C-38 Donaghey, George W., BUILDING A STATE CAPITOL, Little Rock: Parke-
Harper Company, 1937.

C-39 Dorsey, Jasper N., THE COBB HOMES OF ATHENS, Washington, GA: 1966.

C-40 Dorsey, John and James D. Dilts, ed., A GUIDE TO BALTIMORE ARCHI-
TECTURE, Centreville, MD: Tidewater Publishers, 1981.

C-41 Dulaney, Paul S., THE ARCHITECTURE OF HISTORIC RICHMOND, Charlottesville: University Press of Virginia, 1968.

C-42 Dunsavage, Lyn and Virginia Talkington, THE MAKING OF A HISTORIC
DISTRICT: SWISS AVENUE, DALLAS, TEXAS, Washington: Preservation
Press, 1975.

C-43 FRANKLIN HOUSE HOTEL HISTORY, ATHENS, GEORGIA, Atlanta: Group Five
Architects and Designers, 197-.

C-44 Friends of the Cabildo, NEW ORLEANS ARCHITECTURE, Gretna, LA:
Pelican Publishing Company, 1971.

C-45 Giza, Joanne and Catharine F. Black, GREAT BALTIMORE HOUSES: AN
ARCHITECTURAL AND SOCIAL HISTORY, Baltimore: Maclay & Associates,
Inc., 1982.

C-46 Glass, Brent D. and Pat Dickinson, BADIN, A TOWN AT THE NARROWS: AN
HISTORICAL AND ARCHITECTURAL SURVEY, Albermarle, NC: Stanley
County Historic Properties Commission, 1982.

C-47 Glassie, Henry, FOLK HOUSING IN MIDDLE VIRGINIA, Knoxville:
University of Tennessee Press, 1975.

C-48 Gleason, David K., THE GREAT HOUSES OF NATCHEZ, Jackson: University
Press of Mississippi, 1986.

C-49 Glennon, John Francis and Rosemary Glennon, WHERE TIME BEARS WITNESS
TO SOUND BUILDING, Mobile, AL: First National Bank, 1935.

C-50 Goode, James M., CAPITAL LOSSES: A CULTURAL HISTORY OF WASHINGTON'S
DESTROYED BUILDINGS, Washington, D. C.: Smithsonian Institution
Press, 1979.

C-51 Goolrick, John T., OLD HOMES AND HISTORY AROUND FREDERICKSBURG,
Richmond, VA: Garrett and Massie, 1929.

C-52 Graham, Eleanor, ed., NASHVILLE: A SHORT HISTORY AND SELECTED
BUILDINGS, Nashville: Historical Commission of Metropolitan
Nashville-Davidson County, TN, 1974.

C-53 Griffin, Frances, OLD SALEM: AN ADVENTURE IN HISTORIC PRESERVATION,
Winston-Salem, NC: Old Salem, Inc., 1970.

C-54 Harrap, Neil and Carole Harrap, THE GARDEN DISTRICT OF NEW ORLEANS,
New Orleans: Harrap, 1969.

C-55 Harrington, Jean Carl, SEARCH FOR THE CITTIE OF RALEGH: ARCHEOLOGI-
CAL EXCAVATIONS AT FORT RALEIGH NATIONAL HISTORIC SITE, NORTH CARO-
LINA, Washington: Government Printing Office, 1962.

C-56 Harris, W. Stuart, A SHORT HISTORY OF MARION, PERRY COUNTY, ALABAMA:
ITS HOMES AND ITS BUILDINGS, Camden, AL: Alabama-Tombigbee Regional
Commission, 1975.

C-57 Hatch, Charles E. Jr., JAMESTOWN, VIRGINIA: THE TOWNSITE AND ITS
STORY, Washington: National Park Service, 1957.

C-58 Hopkins, George D. Jr., URBAN ECOLOGY THROUGH THE ADAPTIVE USE OF
EXISTING BUILDINGS: A SELECTED BIBLIOGRAPHY, Monticello, IL: Vance
Bibliographies, 1978.

C-59 Huber, Leonard V., Peggy McDowell, and Mary Louise Cristovitch, NEW
ORLEANS ARCHITECTURE VOLUME III. THE CEMETERIES, Gretna, LA:
Pelican Publishing Company, 1974.

C-60 Huber, Leonard Victor and Samuel Wilson Jr., THE BASILICA ON JACKSON
SQUARE: THE HISTORY OF THE ST. LOUIS CATHEDRAL AND ITS PREDECES-
SORS, 1727-1965, New Orleans: St. Louis Cathedral, 1969.

C-61 Huger Smith, Alice R. and D. E. Huger Smith, THE DWELLING HOUSES OF
CHARLESTON, SOUTH CAROLINA, Philadelphia: J. B. Lippincott Company,
1917.

C-62 Hurley, June, THE DON CE-SAR STORY, St. Petersburg Beach: Partner-
ship Press, 1975.

C-63 Jones, Carleton, LOST BALTIMORE LANDMARKS: A PORTFOLIO OF VANISHED
BUILDINGS, Baltimore: Mackay Associates, 1982.

C-64 Jumonville, Florence M., THE VIEUX CARRE SURVEY, New Orleans:
Historic New Orleans Collection, 1981.

C-65 Kell, Jean Bruyere, BEAUFORT, NORTH CAROLINA IN COLOR, Beaufort, NC:
J. B. Kell, 1983.

C-66 Kell, Jean Bruyere, THE OLD PORT TOWN: BEAUFORT, NORTH CAROLINA,
Beaufort, NC: J. B. Kell, 1980.

C-67 Kempe, Helen, PELICAN GUIDE TO OLD HOMES OF MISSISSIPPI, [V. I.
NATCHEZ AND THE SOUTH; V. II. COLUMBUS AND THE NORTH], Gretna, LA:
Pelican Publishing Company, 1977.

C-68 Kocher, A. Lawrence and Howard Dearstone, COLONIAL WILLIAMSBURG:
ITS BUILDINGS AND GARDENS, Williamsburg: Colonial Williamsburg,
Inc., 1949.

C-69 Lancaster, Clay, VESTIGES OF THE VENERABLE CITY: A CHRONICLE OF
LEXINGTON, KENTUCKY, Lexington: Lexington-Layette County Historic
Commission, 1978.

C-70 Lancaster, Clay, EUTAW: THE BUILDERS AND ARCHITECTURE OF AN ANTE-
BELLUM SOUTHERN TOWN, Eutaw, AL: Green County Historical Society,
1979.

C-71 Larew, Marilynn M., BEL AIR: THE TOWN THROUGH ITS BUILDINGS,
Edgwood, MD: Town of Bel Air and the Maryland Historical Trust,
1981.

C-72 Lea, Diane E. and Claudia Roberts, AN ARCHITECTURAL AND HISTORICAL
      SURVEY OF TRYON, NORTH CAROLINA, Raleigh, NC: Archaeology and His-
      toric Preservation Section, Division of Archives and History, 1980.

C-73 Lee, Mary Ann, AN INVENTORY OF HISTORIC ARCHITECTURE, MONROE, NC,
      Monroe: City of Monroe, 1978.

C-74 Letsinger, Philip S., INVENTORY OF HISTORIC ARCHITECTURE OF MAXTON,
      NORTH CAROLINA, Maxton: Maxton Historical Society, 1982.

C-75 Lewis, Kenneth E., CAMDEN: A FRONTIER TOWN, Columbia, SC: Insti-
      tute of Archaeology and Anthropology, University of South Carolina,
      Anthropological Studies, No. 2, 1976.

C-76 Little-Stokes, Ruth, AN INVENTORY OF HISTORIC ARCHITECTURE, GREENS-
      BORO, N. C., Greensboro: City of Greensboro, 1976.

C-77 Lounsbury, Carl, THE ARCHITECTURE OF SOUTHPORT [N.C.], Southport:
      Southport Historical Society, 1979.

C-78 Lyon, Elizabeth Anne Mack, ATLANTA ARCHITECTURE: THE VICTORIAN
      HERITAGE, Atlanta: Atlanta Historical Society, 1976.

C-79 MacMillan, Emma Woodward, WILMINGTON'S VANISHED HOUSES AND BUILD-
      INGS, Raleigh: Edwards and Broughton, 1966.

C-80 Manucy, Albert, THE HOUSES OF ST. AUGUSTINE, St. Augustine: St.
      Augustine Historical Society, 1962.

C-81 Maroon, Fred, MAROON ON GEORGETOWN, Charlottesville, VA: Thomasson-
      Grant and Howell, 1985.

C-82 Marsh, Kenneth Frederick, ATHENS, GEORGIA'S COLUMNED CITY, Ashe-
      ville, NC: Biltmore Press, 1964.

C-83 Marsh, Kermit B., ed., THE AMERICAN INSTITUTE OF ARCHITECTS GUIDE TO
      ATLANTA, Atlanta: Atlanta Chapter of the American Institute of
      Architects, 1975.

C-84 Mastin, Bettye Lee, FAMED HOMES SINCE DESTROYED STILL EXISTED IN
      1888 [2 SHEETS], Lexington: 1963.

C-85 Mazyck, Arthur and Gene Waddell, CHARLESTON IN EIGHTEEN EIGHTY-
      THREE, Easley, SC: Southern Historical Press, 1983.

C-86 Mearns, Kate, CENTRAL CITY HISTORIC BUILDINGS INVENTORY, ROCKY
      MOUNT, NORTH CAROLINA, Rocky Mount: Rocky Mount Central City
      Revitalization Corporation, 1979.

C-87 Miller, Ruth M. and Ann T. Andress, WITNESS TO HISTORY: CHARLES-
      TON'S OLD EXCHANGE AND PROVOST DUNGEON, Orangeburg, SC: Sandlapper
      Publishing Company, 1986.

C-88 Milward, Burton, THE HUNT-MORGAN HOUSE, Lexington, KY: The Blue
      Grass Trust for Historic Preservation, 1979.

C-89 Mitchell, Mary, GLIMPSES OF GEORGETOWN, PAST AND PRESENT, Washing-
      ton, DC: Road Street Press, 1983.

C-90 Mobile (AL) City Planning Commission, NINETEENTH CENTURY MOBILE
      ARCHITECTURE: AN INVENTORY OF EXISTING BUILDINGS, Mobile: The
      Commission, 1974.

C-91 Moe, Christine, PRESERVATION AND THE HUMAN SCALE IN NEW ORLEANS AND
      LOUISIANA, Monticello, IL: Vance Bibliographies, 1979.

C-92   Montgomery Museum of Fine Arts and Diane J. Gingole, SPACES AND
       PLACES: VIEWS OF MONTGOMERY'S BUILT ENVIRONMENT, Montgomery: The
       Museum, 1978.

C-93   Moore, Gay Montague, SEAPORT IN VIRGINIA: GEORGE WASHINGTON'S
       ALEXANDRIA, Richmond: Garrett and Massie, Inc., 1949.

C-94   Moran, Francis T., A HISTORICAL SKETCH OF THE ST. LOUIS CATHEDRAL
       OF NEW ORLEANS, METROPOLITAN CHURCH BUILD IN 1794, New Orleans:
       1959.

C-95   Morgan, William, LOUISVILLE: ARCHITECTURE AND THE URBAN ENVIRON-
       MENT, Dublin: W. L. Bauhan, 1979.

C-96   Manford, Robert Beverley Jr., RICHMOND HOMES AND MEMORIES, Rich-
       mond: Garrett and Massie, Inc., 1936.

C-97   Murphy, Ann Melanie, AN INVENTORY OF HISTORIC ARCHITECTURE, HENDER-
       SON, NORTH CAROLINA, Raleigh: Archaeology and Historic Presenta-
       tion Section, Division of Archives and History, 1979/1980.

C-98   Murtaugh, William J., MORAVIAN ARCHITECTURE AND TOWN PLANNING,
       Chapel Hill: University of North Carolina Press, 1967.

C-99   McGee, E. Alan, ATLANTA AT HOME: PHOTOGRAPHS, Atlanta, GA: Perry
       Communications, 1979.

C-100 Nelson, Lucy G., THE HISTORY OF OAKLEIGH, AN ANTE-BELLUM MANSION IN
       MOBILE, Mobile, AL: Gill Printing and Stationary Company, 1956.

C-101 Newcomb, Rexford, ARCHITECTURE IN OLD KENTUCKY, Urbana: University
       of Illinois Press, 1952.

C-102 North Carolina Executive Mansion Fine Arts Committee, THE EXECU-
       TIVE MANSION, RALEIGH, NORTH CAROLINA, Raleigh: North Carolina
       Department of Cultural Resources, 1978.

C-103 Norwood, Martha F., A HISTORY OF THE WHITE HOUSE TRACT, RICHMOND
       COUNTY, GEORGIA, 1756-1975, Atlanta: Historic Preservation Sec-
       tion, Georgia Department of Natural Resources, 1975,

C-104 Owen, Mary Barrow, ed., OLD SALEM, NORTH CAROLINA, Winston-Salem,
       NC: Winston Printing Company, 1941.

C-105 Phillips, Laura A., REIDSVILLE, NORTH CAROLINA: AN INVENTORY OF
       HISTORIC AND ARCHITECTURAL RESOURCES, Raleigh, NC: Archaeology and
       Historic Preservation Section, Division of Archives and History,
       1981.

C-106 Portman, John Calvin, THE ARCHITECT AS DEVELOPER, New York:
       McGraw-Hill, 1976.

C-107 Pratt, Dorothy and Richard, A GUIDE TO EARLY AMERICAN HOMES--SOUTH,
       New York: McGraw Hill Publishing Company, 1956.

C-108 Radoff, Morris Leon, BUILDINGS OF THE STATE OF MARYLAND AT ANNA-
       POLIS, Annapolis: Hall of Records Commission, 1954.

C-109 Rogner, E. A., THE PENTAGON: 'A NATIONAL INSTITUTION': ITS
       HISTORY, ITS FUNCTION, ITS PEOPLE, Alexandria: D'Or Press, 1984.

C-110 Roth, Darlene R. and Steve Grable, THE REO BUILDING, A HISTORY,
       Atlanta: MARTA, 1978.

C-111 Sawyer, Elizabeth M. and Jane Foster Matthews, THE OLD IN NEW
       ATLANTA: A DIRECTORY OF HOUSES, BUILDINGS, AND CHURCHES BUILT
       PRIOR TO 1915, STILL STANDING IN THE MID-1970s IN ATLANTA AND
       ENVIRONS, Atlanta: JEMS Publications, 1976.

C-112 Satterfield, Carolyn Green, HISTORIC SITES OF JEFFERSON COUNTY, Birmingham: Jefferson County Historical Commission, 1976.

C-113 Schumann, Marguerite E., ed., GRAND OLD LADIES: NORTH CAROLINA ARCHITECTURE DURING THE VICTORIAN ERA, Charlotte, NC: East Woods Press, 1984.

C-114 Schumann, Marguerite E., STONES, BRICKS & FACES: A WALKING GUIDE TO DUKE UNIVERSITY, Durham, NC: Duke University Office of Publications, 1976.

C-115 Schumann, Marguerite E. with Virginia Terrell-Lathrop, BRICKS AND PEOPLE: A WALKING GUIDE TO THE UNIVERSITY OF NORTH CAROLINA AT GREENSBORO, Greensboro, NC: Alumni Association of the University of North Carolina at Greensboro, 1973.

C-116 Scott, Mary Wingfield, HOUSES OF OLD RICHMOND, Richmond: The Valentine Museum, 1941.

C-117 Scully, Arthur Jr., JAMES DAKIN, ARCHITECT: HIS CAREER IN NEW YORK AND THE SOUTH, Baton Rouge: Louisiana State University Press, 1973.

C-118 Severns, Kenneth, SOUTHERN ARCHITECTURE: 350 YEARS OF DISTINCTIVE AMERICAN BUILDINGS, New York: Dutton Company, 1981.

C-119 Shivers, Natalie W., THOSE OLD PLACID ROWS: THE AESTHETIC AND DEVELOPMENT OF THE BALTIMORE ROWHOUSE, Baltimore: Maclay & Associates, 1981.

C-120 Shoemaker, Mary Macahon, AN INVENTORY OF HISTORICAL ARCHITECTURE IN THE TOWN OF SMITHFIELD, 1977, Smithfield: Town of Smithfield, 1977-78.

C-121 A SHORT HISTORY OF THE EARLY DAYS OF BLUFFTON, SOUTH CAROLINA, Bluffton: Bluffton Historical Presentation Society, 1983.

C-122 Simons, Albert and Samuel Lapham Jr., THE EARLY ARCHITECTURE OF CHARLESTON, Columbia: University of South Carolina Press, 1927.

C-123 Smith, Eugenia B., CENTERVILLE, VIRGINIA: ITS HISTORY AND ARCHITECTURE, Fairvax, VA: Fairfax Office of Planning, 1973.

C-124 Smith, H. McKelden, ARCHITECTURAL RESOURCES, AN INVENTORY OF HISTORIC ARCHITECTURE: HIGH POINT, JAMESTOWN, GIBSONVILLE, GUILORD COUNTY [N.C.], Raleigh: Historic Preservation Society, 1980.

C-125 Smith, Hubert, A CENTURY OF PRIDE: THE ARKANSAS STATE CAPITOL, Little Rock: Arkansas State Capitol Association, 1982.

C-126 Smoot, Betty Carter, DAYS IN AN OLD TOWN, Alexandria, VA: 1934.

C-127 Stanforth, Deirdre, ROMANTIC NEW ORLEANS, New York: Viking Press, 1977.

C-128 Starbuck, James C., THE BUILDINGS OF ATLANTA, Monticello, IL: Vance Bibliographies, 1978 [A-26].

C-129 Thompson, Bailey, HISTORIC SHREVEPORT: A GUIDE, Shreveport: Shreveport Publishing Corporation, 1980.

C-130 Toledano, Roulhac, FAUBOURG TREME AND THE BAYOU ROAD, Gretna, LA: Pelican Publishing Company, 1980.

C-131 Toledano, Roulhac and Mary Louise Christovitch, NEW ORLEANS ARCHITECTURE, VOL. VI: FAUBOURG TREME AND THE BAYOU ROAD, Gretna, LA: Pelican Publishing Company, Inc., 1980.

C-132 Tomlinson, Doug and David Dillon, DALLAS ARCHITECTURE, 1936 TO
      1986, Austin, TX: Texas Monthly Press, 1985.

C-133 VILLAGE CREEK: AN ARCHITECTURAL AND HISTORICAL RESOURCES SURVEY OF
      ENSLEY, EAST BIRMINGHAM, AND EAST LAKE, THREE VILLAGE CREEK NEIGH-
      BORHOODS, CITY OF BIRMINGHAM, Birmingham, AL: Birmingham Histori-
      cal Society, 1985.

C-134 Waterman, Thomas Tileston, THE DWELLINGS OF COLONIAL AMERICA,
      Chapel Hill: University of North Carolina Press, 1950.

C-135 White, Marjorie Longenecker, AN ARCHITECTURAL AND HISTORICAL TOUR
      OF DOWNTOWN BIRMINGHAM, Birmingham, AL: Birmingham Historical
      Society, 1977.

C-136 Williford, William B., THE GLORY OF COVINGTON, Atlanta: Cherokee
      Publishing Company, 1973.

C-137 Wilson, Samuel, THE CABILDO ON JACKSON SQUARE: THE COLONIAL PER-
      IOD, 1723-1803, Gretna, LA: Pelican Publishing Company, Inc.,
      1973.

C-138 Wilson, Samuel Jr., THE CREOLE FAUBOURGS, Gretna, LA: Pelican
      Publishing Company, 1974.

C-139 Wilson, Samuel, Jr. THE PRESBYTERE ON JACKSON SQUARE, New Orleans,
      LA: Friends of the Cabildo, 1981.

C-140 Wilson, Samuel Jr., THE VIEUX CARRE, NEW ORLEANS: ITS PLAN, ITS
      GROWTH, ITS ARCHITECTURE, New Orleans: Bureau of Governmental
      Research, 1968.

C-141 Wilson, Samuel Jr. and Bernard Lemann, THE LOWER GARDEN DISTRICT,
      Gretna, LA: Pelican Publishing Company, 1971.

C-142 Winthrop, Robert P., ARCHITECTURE IN DOWNTOWN RICHMOND, Richmond:
      Junior Board of Historic Richmond Foundation, 1982.

C-143 Wrenn, Tony P., WILMINGTON, NORTH CAROLINA: AN ARCHITECTURAL AND
      HISTORICAL PORTRAIT, Charlottesville: The University Press of Vir-
      ginia, 1984.

Archaeology

C-144 Bushnell, David Jr., NATIVE VILLAGE SITES EAST OF THE MISSISSIPPI,
      Bureau of American Ethnology Bulletin 69, Washington: Government
      Printing Office, 1919.

C-145 Bowen, William R. and Linda F. Carnes, ARCHAEOLOGICAL IMPACT STUD-
      IES OF THE MARTA EAST AND WEST LINES, FEBRUARY 15, 1976-FEBRUARY
      14, 1977, Atlanta: Department of Anthroplogy, Georgia State
      University, unpublished report, 1977.

C-146 Carnes, Linda F. and Roy S. Dickens Jr., ARCHAEOLOGICAL IMPACT
      STUDIES ON THE MARTA NORTH AND SOUTH LINES, Atlanta: Department
      of Anthropology, Georgia State University, unpublished report,
      1979.

C-147 Cotter, John L., ARCHAEOLOGICAL EXCAVATION AT JAMESTOWN, VIRGINIA,
      Washington, DC: National Park Service, 1958.

C-148 Cotter, John L. and J. Paul Hudson, NEW DISCOVERIES AT JAMESTOWN,
      Washington, DC: Government Printing Office, 1957.

C-149 Council, Bruce and Nicholas Honerkamp, THE UNION RAILYARDS SITES:
      INDUSTRIAL ARCHAEOLOGY IN CHATTANOOGA, TENNESSEE, Jeffrey L. Brown
      Institute of Archaeology, University of Tennessee at Chattanooga
      and Tennessee Valley Association Publications in Anthropology #38,
      1984.

C-150 Deagan, Kathleen, SPANISH ST. AUGUSTINE: THE ARCHAEOLOGY OF A
      COLONIAL CREOLE COMMUNITY, Studies in Historical Archaeology, New
      York: Academic Press, 1983.

C-151 Dickens, R. S., ed., ARCHAEOLOGY OF URBAN AMERICA, New York:
      Academic Press, 1982.

C-152 Honercamp, Nicholas, AN ARCHAEOLOGICAL INVESTIGATION OF THE
      CHARLESTON CONVENTION CENTER SITE, CHARLESTON, SOUTH CAROLINA,
      Chattanooga: Jeffrey L. Brown Institute of Archaeology, University
      of Tennessee at Chattanooga, 1982.

C-153 Honercamp, Nicholas, COLONIAL LIFE ON THE GEORGIA COAST, St. Simons
      Island, GA: Fort Frederica Association, 1977.

C-154 Honercamp, Nicholas, R. Bruce Council, and Charles H. Fairbanks,
      THE REALITY OF THE CITY: URBAN ARCHAEOLOGY AT THE TELFAIR SITE,
      SAVANNAH, GEORGIA, Chattanooga, TN: The Jeffrey L. Brown Institute
      of Archaeology, The University of Tennessee, 1983.

C-155 Reeves, Ally K. and William D. Reeves, ARCHIVAL EVALUATION OF
      FLOODWALL ALIGNMENT, NEW ORLEANS, LOUISIANA, New Orleans: U. S. A.
      Engineer District, N. O., 1982.

C-156 Shephard, Steven J., THE VOLUNTEER IN ALEXANDRIA ARCHAEOLOGY,
      Alexandria, VA: Alexandria Urban Archaeological Program, 1981.

C-157 Yonge, Samuel H., THE SITE OF OLD "JAMES TOWNE," 1607-1698,
      Richmond, VA: Hermitage Press, 1907.

Art

C-158 Cochran, J. O., BATTLE OF ATLANTA. STORY OF THE CYCLORAMA,
      Atlanta: Johnson Dallis Company, 1917.

C-159 Edmunds, Mary Lewis Rucker, THE PHOTOGRAPHY OF JOHN WALKER FRY:
      THE IMMEDIATE WORLD AND DISTANT VISTAS . . . INCLUDING AN INTIMATE
      HISTORY OF GREENSBORO, Winston-Salem, NC: Hunter Publishing
      Company, 1982.

C-160 Gandy, Joan W. and Thomas H. Gandy, NORMAN'S NATCHES, AN EARLY
      PHOTOGRAPHER AND HIS TOWN, Jackson: University Press of Missis-
      sippi, 1978.

C-161 Historic New Orleans Collection, ALFRED R. WAND: SPECIAL ARTIST
      ON ASSIGNMENT, New Orleans: Historic New Orleans, 1979.

C-162 Historic New Orleans Collection, ORLEANS GALLERY: THE FOUNDERS,
      New Orleans: Historic New Orleans Collection, 1982.

C-163 Holmes, Jack D., PENSACOLA'S CIVIL WAR ART: BENJAMIN LABREE AND
      THOMAS NAST, [s.l.: s.n., 1985]

C-164 Hoobler, James A. et al., ART WORK OF NASHVILLE, 1894-1901: [INDEX
      OF HISTORIC SITES], [s.l.: s.n.], 1984.

C-165 Kurtz, Wilbur G., ATLANTA AND THE OLD SOUTH: PAINTINGS AND DRAW-
      INGS BY WILBUR G. KURTZ, ARTIST AND HISTORIAN, Atlanta: American
      Lithograph Company, 1969.

C-166 Kurtz, Wilbur G., THE ATLANTA CYCLORAMA, THE STORY OF THE FAMED
      BATTLE OF ATLANTA, Atlanta: City of Atlanta, 1954.

C-167 Middleton, Margaret S., HENRIETTA JOHNSON OF CHARLES TOWN, SOUTH
      CAROLINA: AMERICA'S FIRST PASTELLIST, Columbia: University of
      South Carolina Press, 1966.

C-168 Middleton, Margaret Simons, JEREMIAH THEUS: COLONIAL ARTIST OF
      CHARLES TOWN, Columbia: University of South Carolina Press, 1953.

C-169 Morris, Joan Perry and Lee H. Warner, THE PHOTOGRAPHS OF ALVAN S.
      HARPER, TALLAHASSEE, 1885-1910, Tallahassee: University Presses of
      Florida, 1983.

C-170 Smith, Margaret D. and Mary L. Tucker, PHOTOGRAPHY IN NEW ORLEANS:
      THE EARLY YEARS, 1840-1865, Baton Rouge: Louisiana State Univer-
      sity Press, 1982.

Artisans and Crafts

C-171 Albright, Frank P., JOHANN LUDWIG EBERHARDT AND HIS SALEM CLOCKS,
      Chapel Hill: University of North Carolina Press for Old Salem,
      1978.

C-172 Bayless, Charles, CHARLESTON IRONWORK, Orangeburg, SC: Sandlapper
      Publishing Company, 1986.

C-173 Bivins, John Jr., THE MORAVIAN POTTERS IN NORTH CAROLINA, Chapel
      Hill: University of North Carolina Press for Old Salem, Inc, 1972.

C-174 Bridenbaugh, Carl, THE COLONIAL CRAFTSMEN, New York: New York
      University Press, 1950.

C-175 Burton, E. Milby, CHARLESTON FURNITURE, 1700-1825, Columbia: Uni-
      versity of South Carolina Press, 1970 [1955].

C-176 Burton, E. Milby, SOUTH CAROLINA SILVERSMITHS, 1690-1860, Charles-
      ton: The Charleston Museum, 1942.

C-177 Deas, Alston, THE EARLY IRONWORK OF CHARLESTON, Columbis, SC:
      Bostich and Thornley, 1941.

C-178 Dew, Charles B., IRONMAKER TO THE CONFEDERACY: JOSEPH R. ANDERSON
      AND THE TREDEGAR IRON WORKS, New Haven: Yale University Press,
      1966.

C-179 Howard, Annie Shillito, ENCHANTMENT IN IRON: MOBILE, Mobile:
      Rapier House Publications, 1950.

C-180 Ingate, Margaret Rose, MOBILE IRONWORK, [s. 1.:   s.n., 1964]

C-181 Katzenbery, Dena S., BALTIMORE ALBUM QUILTS, Baltimore: The
      Baltimore Museum of Art, 1981.

C-182 McMultrie, Douglas Crawford, EARLY PRINTING IN NEW ORLEANS, 1764-
      1810, New Orleans: Searcy & Pfaff, 1929.

C-183 Ormond, Suzanne and Mary E. Irvine, LOUISIANA'S ART NOVEAU: THE
      CRAFTS OF THE NEWCOMB STYLE, Gretna, LA: Pelican Publishing
      Company, 1976.

C-184 Vlack, John Michael, CHARLESTON BLACKSMITH: THE WORK OF PHILIP
      SIMMONS, Athens: University of Georgia Press, 1981.

C-185 Walsh, W. Richard, CHARLESTON'S SONS OF LIBERTY: A STUDY OF THE
      ARTISANS, 1763-1789, Columbia: University of South Carolina Press,
      1959.

Arts and Culture

C-186 Reid, Alfred S., ed., THE ARTS IN GREENVILLE, 1800-1960, Green-ville, SC: Keys Printing Company, 1960.

C-187 Rutledge, Anna Wells, ARTISTS IN THE LIFE OF CHARLESTON. THROUGH COLONY AND STATE FROM RESTORATION AND RECONSTRUCTION, Philadelphia: American Philosophical Society, 1949.

C-188 Severens, Martha and Charles L. Wyrick Jr., CHARLES FRASER OF CHARLESTON: ESSAYS ON THE MAN, HIS ART AND HIS TIMES, Charleston: Carolina Art Association, 1983.

C-189 Stewart, Rick, LONE STAR REGIONALISM: THE DALLAS NINE AND THEIR CIRCLE, 1928-1945, Austin, TX: Texas Monthly Press.

Business and Economics

C-190 Alabama University, Bureau of Business Research, MOBILE, AN ECO-NOMIC APPRAISAL, University, AL: University of Alabama, 1949.

C-191 Allan, William, THE LIFE AND WORK OF JOHN McDONOGH, Baltimore: Press of Friedewald, 1886.

C-192 Amos, Harriet A., COTTON CITY: URBAN DEVELOPMENT IN ANTEBELLUM MOBILE, University, AL: University of Alabama Press, 1985.

C-193 Arkwright, Preston Stanley, THE AUGUSTA CANAL, AN EXPLANATION OF THE PROPOSED LEASE OF THE CANAL AND ITS ELECTRIFICATION, [text of speech] August 2, 1929.

C-194 Associates of Louisville Municipal College, University of Louis-ville, Louisville Urban League, and Central Colored High School, A STUDY OF BUSINESS AND EMPLOYMENT AMONG NEGROES IN LOUISVILLE, Louisville, KY: 1944.

C-195 Athens, GA Chamber of Commerce, ATHENS, GEORGIA, IN THE HEART OF EXPANSION, A VERY PLEASANT PLACE TO LIVE, Athens: 1959.

C-196 ATHENS' COMMERCIAL, AGRICULTURAL, INDUSTRIAL, EDUCATIONAL INTER-ESTS, Athens: Athens Banner, 1906.

C-197 Atherton, Lewis E., THE SOUTHERN COUNTRY STORE, 1800-1860, Baton Rouge: Louisiana State University Press, 1949.

C-198 Augusta Exchange, THE INDUSTRIAL ADVANTAGES OF AUGUSTA, GEORGIA . . ., Augusta: Akehurst, 1893.

C-199 Avery, Isaac Wheeler, and others, CITY OF ATLANTA: A DESCRIPTIVE, HISTORICAL AND INDUSTRIAL REVIEW OF THE GATEWAY CITY OF THE SOUTH, Louisville: The Inter-State Publishing Company, 1892-93.

C-200 Baker, Henry Givens, RICH'S OF ATLANTA: THE STORY OF A STORE SINCE 1867, Atlanta: 1953.

C-201 Ball, T., THE PORT OF HOUSTON: HOW IT CAME TO PASS, Houston: Houston Chronicle and Houston Post, 1936.

C-202 Ballinger, Kenneth, MIAMI MILLIONS: THE DANCE OF THE DOLLARS IN THE GREAT FLORIDA LAND BOOM OF THE NINETEEN-TWENTIES, Miami: The Franklin Press, 1936.

C-203 BALTIMORE, AMERICA'S FIFTH LARGEST NEGRO MARKET, Baltimore, MD: Afro-American Company, 1946.

C-204 Bancroft, Frederic, SLAVE-TRADING IN THE OLD SOUTH, Baltimore: J. H. Furst Company, 1931.

C-205 Biles, Roger, MEMPHIS IN THE GREAT DEPRESSION, Knoxville: University of Tennessee Press, 1986.

C-206 BIRMINGHAM'S LEBANESE: THE EARTH TURNED TO GOLD, Birmingham, AL: Birmingfind, 19--.

C-207 Blassingame, John W., BLACK NEW ORLEANS, 1860-1880, Chicago: University of Chicago Press, 1973.

C-208 Blythe, LeGette, WILLIAM HENRY BELK: MERCHANT OF THE SOUTH, Chapel Hill: University of North Carolina Press, 1950.

C-209 Bobo, James R., THE NEW ORLEANS ECONOMY; PRO BONO PUBLICO?, New Orleans: University of New Orleans, 1975.

C-210 Brown, Byron B., EXPORT-EMPLOYMENT MULTIPLIER ANALYSIS OF A MAJOR INDUSTRIAL COMMUNITY; A STUDY OF BASIC AND TOTAL EMPLOYMENT IN THE HOUSTON METROPOLITAN AREA, Houston: University of Houston, 1964.

C-211 Brown, David E., NORTH CAROLINA: NEW DIRECTIONS FOR AN OLD LAND: AN ILLUSTRATED HISTORY OF TAR HEEL BUSINESS AND INDUSTRY, Northridge, CA: Windsor Publications, Inc., 1985.

C-212 Brown, James R., AN ANALYSIS OF THE BIRMINGHAM ECONOMY, Tuscaloosa: University of Alabama, 1959.

C-213 Bruckey, Stuart, ROBERT OLIVER, MERCHANT OF BALTIMORE, 1783-1819, Baltimore: Johns Hopkins Press, 1956.

C-214 Catledge, Oraien E., CABBAGETOWN, Austin, TX: University of Texas Press, 1985.

C-215 Caudill, Harry M., THEIRS BE THE POWER: THE MOGULS OF EASTERN KENTUCKY, Urbana: University of Illinois Press, 1983.

C-216 Chapman, James Emory and William H. Wells, FACTORS IN INDUSTRIAL LOCATION IN ATLANTA, 1946-1955, Atlanta: Georgia State College of Business Administration, 1958.

C-217 Charleston, SC Civic Services Committee, CHARLESTON GROWS: AN ECONOMIC SOCIAL AND CULTURAL PORTRAIT OF AN OLD COMMUNITY IN THE NEW SOUTH. THE CHARLESTON STORY, BY HERBERT RAVENELL SASS, Charleston: Carolina Art Association, 1949.

C-218 Childs, William T., JOHN McDONOGH: HIS LIFE AND WORK, Baltimore: Meyer & Thalheimer, 1939.

C-219 Citizens and Southern National Bank Georgia, GROWING ATLANTA, 1946 . . . 1953, Atlanta: 1953.

C-220 The City Builder, WHAT'S MADE IN ATLANTA AND WHO MAKES IT, Atlanta: 1919.

C-221 City of Atlanta, A DESCRIPTIVE HISTORICAL AND INDUSTRIAL REVIEW OF THE GATEWAY CITY OF THE SOUTH, Louisville, KY: Inter-state Publishing Company, 1892-93.

C-222 Clark, James A. and Michael T. Halbouty, SPINDLETOP, New York: Random House, 1952.

C-223 Clark, John G., NEW ORLEANS, 1718-1812: AN ECONOMIC HISTORY, Baton Rouge: Louisiana State University Press, 1970.

C-224 Clowse, Converse D., MEASURING CHARLESTON'S OVERSEAS COMMERCE, 1717-1767: STATISTICS FROM THE PORT'S NAVAL LISTS, Washington, DC: University Press of America, 1981.

C-225 Cobb, James C., THE SELLING OF THE SOUTH: THE SOUTHERN CRUSADE FOR INDUSTRIAL DEVELOPMENT, Baton Rouge: Louisiana State University Press, 1982.

C-226 Coker, William S., THE FINANCIAL HISTORY OF PENSACOLA'S SPANISH PRESIDIOS, 1698-1763, Pensacola: Pensacola Historical Society, 1979.

C-227 Cotner, Robert C., et al., TEXAS CITIES AND THE GREAT DEPRESSION, Austin, TX: Texas Memorial Museum, 1973.

C-228 Curry, Leonard P., RAIL ROUTES SOUTH: LOUISVILLE'S FIGHT FOR THE SOUTHERN MARKET, 1865-1872, Lexington: University of Kentucky Press, 1969.

C-229 Dill, Alonzo Thomas, CHESAPEAKE: PIONEER PAPERMAKER: A HISTORY OF THE COMPANY AND ITS COMMUNITY, Charlottesville: University Press of Virginia, 1968.

C-230 Donelson, Cathalynn, MOBILE, SUNBELT CENTER OF OPPORTUNITY, Northridge, CA: Windsor Publications, Inc., 1986.

C-231 Edge, Sarah Simms, JOEL HURT AND THE DEVELOPMENT OF ATLANTA, Atlanta: Atlanta Historical Bulletin, No. 37, 1955.

C-232 Eller, Ronald D., MINERS, MILLHANDS AND MOUNTAINEERS: INDUSTRIALIZATION OF THE APPALACHIAN SOUTH, 1880-1930, Knoxville: University of Tennessee Press, 1982.

C-233 Furino, Antonio, AN INDUSTRIAL PRODUCTION INDEX FOR THE HOUSTON ECONOMIC AREA, Houston: University of Houston, 1966.

C-234 Georgia. State Engineering Experiment Station, Atlanta, ECONOMIC PROFILE OF DALLAS, GEORGIA, Atlanta: Georgia Institute of Technology, 1974.

C-235 Goerch, Carl, DURHAM LIFE, 1906-1963: A CORPORATE BIOGRAPHY, TRACING THE ORIGIN AND GROWTH OF THE DURHAM LIFE INSURANCE COMPANY, Raleigh, NC: Edwards and Broughton, 1963.

C-236 Gottwald, Floyd D., ALBEMARLE, FROM PINES TO PACKAGING; 75 YEARS OF PAPERMAKING PROGRESS, 1887-1962, New York: Newcomen Society in North America, 1962.

C-237 Gray, Lewis Cecil, HISTORY OF AGRICULTURE IN THE SOUTHERN UNITED STATES TO 1860, 2 vols, Washington: The Carnegie Institute of Washington, 1933.

C-238 Green, Fletcher M., THE ROLE OF THE YANKEE IN THE OLD SOUTH, (Mercer University, Lamar Memorial Lectures, No. 11), Athens: University of Georgia Press, 1972.

C-239 Green, George D., FINANCE AND ECONOMIC DEVELOPMENT IN THE OLD SOUTH: LOUISIANA BANKING, 1804-1861, Stanford: Stanford University Press, 1972.

C-240 Green, James L., METROPOLITAN ECONOMIC REPUBLICS: A CASE STUDY IN REGIONAL ECONOMIC GROWTH, Athens: University of Georgia Press, 1965.

C-241 Hales, Charles A., THE BALTIMORE CLEARING HOUSE, Baltimore: The Johns Hopkins Press, 1940.

C-242 Haley, J. Evetts, CHARLES SCHREINER, GENERAL MERCHANDISE: THE STORY OF A COUNTRY STORE, Austin, TX: Texas State Historical Association, 1944.

C-243 Harman, Joyce Elizabeth, TRADE AND PRIVATEERING IN SPANISH FLORIDA,
      1732-1763, St. Augustine, FL: St. Augustine Historical Society,
      1969.

C-244 Harris, Leon, MERCHANT PRINCES: AN INTIMATE HISTORY OF JEWISH
      FAMILIES WHO BUILT GREAT DEPARTMENT STORES, New York: Harper and
      Row, 1979.

C-245 Hartness, Richard L. Sr., WITTSBURG, ARKANSAS: CROWLEY'S RIDGE
      STEAMBOAT RIVERPORT, 1848-1890, Wynne, AK: Cross Country Histori-
      cal Society, Inc., 1979.

C-246 Hartshorn, Truman A., et al., METROPOLIS IN GEORGIA: ATLANTA'S
      RISE AS A MAJOR TRANSACTION CENTER, Cambridge, MA: Ballinger,
      1976.

C-247 Hassinger, Bernice Shield, HENDERSON STEEL, BIRMINGHAM'S FIRST
      STEEL, Birmingham: Hassinger, 1978.

C-248 Hearden, Patrick J., INDEPENDENCE AND EMPIRE: THE NEW SOUTH'S
      COTTON MILL CAMPAIGN, 1865-1901, DeKalb, IL: Northern Illinois
      University Press, 1982.

C-249 Henry, James P., RESOURCES OF THE STATE OF ARKANSAS, WITH DESCRIP-
      TION OF COUNTIES, RAILROADS, MINES, AND THE CITY OF LITTLE ROCK,
      Little Rock: Price and M'clure, printers, 1872.

C-250 Henson, Margaret Sweet, SAMUEL MAY WILLIAMS: EARLY TEXAS ENTRE-
      PRENEUR, College Station: Texas A & M University Press, 1976.

C-251 Herget, J. Barlow and Dee Reid, INSIDERS GUIDE TO THE TRIANGLE OF
      NORTH CAROLINA: RALEIGH, CARY, DURHAM, CHAPEL HILL, Manteo, NC:
      Storie Mcowen, 1986.

C-252 Hertzberg, Stevern, STRANGERS WITHIN THE GATE CITY: THE JEWS OF
      ATLANTA, 1845-1915, Philadelphia: Jewish Publication Society of
      America, 1978.

C-253 Hoffecker, Carol E., WILMINGTON, DELAWARE: PORTRAIT OF AN INDUS-
      TRIAL CITY, 1830-1910, Charlottesville, VA: University Press of
      Virginia, 1974.

C-254 Hollander, Jacob H., THE FINANCIAL HISTORY OF BALTIMORE, Baltimore:
      Johns Hopkins University Press, 1899.

C-255 Holly, Byron, THE ENLARGED AUGUSTA CANAL, AUGUSTA, GA., ITS CAPA-
      CITY FOR THE MANUFACTURE OF COTTON GOODS . . ., New York: Corlies,
      Macy & Company, 1875.

C-256 Hooner, Calvin B. and B. V. Rackford, ECONOMIC RESOURCES AND
      POLICIES OF THE SOUTH, New York: McMillan, 1951.

C-257 House, Ray, CHANGES IN WHOLESALING IN MEMPHIS--SHELBY COUNTY,
      TENNESSEE, 1948 TO 1963, Memphis: Memphis State University, 1968.

C-258 Huff, Sarah, MY 80 YEARS IN ATLANTA, Atlanta: 1937.

C-259 Jenkins, Herbert T., FOOD, FAIRS AND FARMERS' MARKETS IN ATLANTA:
      RECOLLECTIONS . . . ON THE EARLY DAYS, GROWTH AND EXPANSION OF THE
      PRODUCE BUSINESS AND ITS INFLUENCE UPON THE CITY OF ATLANTA,
      Atlanta: Emory University, 1977.

C-260 Juhn, Daniel S., GROWTH AND CHANGING COMPOSITION OF INTERNATIONAL
      TRADE THROUGH THE PORT OF NEW ORLEANS, 1955-1964, New Orleans:
      Louisiana State University in New Orleans, 1967.

C-261 Kilbourne, Richard Holcombe, LOUISIANA COMMERCIAL LAW: THE ANTE-
      BELLUM PERIOD, Baton Rouge: Louisiana State University School of
      Law, 1980.

C-262 Klein, Maury, GREAT RICHMOND TERMINAL: A STUDY OF BUSINESSMEN AND
      BUSINESS STRATEGY, Charlottesville, VA: University Press of Vir-
      ginia, 1970.

C-263 Livingood, James W., THE PHILADELPHIA-BALTIMORE TRADE RIVALRY,
      1780-1860, Harrisburg: Pennsylvania Historical and Museum Commiss-
      ion, 1947.

C-264 Ludwig, Armin K., et al., RADIAL FREEWAYS AND THE GROWTH OF OFFICE
      SPACE IN THE CENTRAL CITIES, Washington, DC: U. S. Department of
      Transportation, Federal Highway Administration, Office of Program
      and Policy Planning.

C-265 Mahau, Joseph B., COLUMBUS: GEORGIA'S FALL LINE "TRADING TOWN,"
      Northridge, CA: Windsor Publications, Inc., 1986.

C-266 Martin, Harold H., THREE STRONG PILLARS: THE STORY OF TRUST COM-
      PANY OF GEORGIA, Atlanta: Trust Company of Georgia, 1974.

C-267 Martin, Richard A., THE CITY MAKERS, Jacksonville, FL: Convention
      Press, 1972.

C-268 Martin, Robert L, THE CITY MOVES WEST: ECONOMIC AND INDUSTRIAL
      GROWTH IN CENTRAL WEST TEXAS, Austin: University of Texas Press,
      1969.

C-269 Martinez, Raymond Joseph, THE STORY OF THE RIVER FRONT AT NEW
      ORLEANS, New Orleans: Industries Publishing Agency, 1955.

C-270 May, Earl Chapin, PRINCIPIO TO WHEELING, 1715-1945: A PAGEANT OF
      IRON AND STEEL, New York: Harper and Brothers, 1945.

C-271 Memphis and Shelby County Planning Commission, METROPOLITAN MEM-
      PHIS: ITS PEOPLE, ITS ECONOMY: THE OUTLOOK FOR THE POPULATION AND
      ECONOMY OF METROPOLITAN MEMPHIS, Memphis: 1965.

C-272 Metropolitan Richmond Chamber of Commerce, WHO'S WHO IN METROPOLI-
      TAN RICHMOND BUSINESS [11th ed.], Richmond, VA: The Chamber, 1984.

C-273 Mitchell, Broadus, WILLIAM GREGG, FACTORY MASTER OF THE OLD
      SOUTH, Chapel Hill: University of North Carolina Press, 1928.

C-274 Mitchell, Robert D., COMMERCIALISM AND FRONTIER: PERSPECTIVES ON
      THE EARLY SHENANDOAH VALLEY, Charlottesville, VA; University Press
      of Virginia, 1977.

C-275 Mobile, AL First National Bank, HIGHLIGHTS OF 75 YEARS IN MOBILE
      FIRST NATIONAL BANK, MOBILE, ALA., 75TH ANNIVERSARY, 1865-1940,
      [Mobile, 1940].

C-276 McFerrin, John Berry, CALDWELL AND COMPANY: A SOUTHERN FINANCIAL
      EMPIRE, Nashville: Vanderbilt University Press, 1969.

C-277 McKnight, Tom Lee, MANUFACTURING IN DALLAS; A STUDY OF EFFECTS,
      Austin: Bureau of Business Research, University of Texas, 1956.

C-278 THE NATIONAL TRADE REVIEW. DEVOTED TO COMMERCIAL, EDUCATIONAL,
      MANUFACTURING AND AGRICULTURAL INTERESTS, Clarksville, TN: May,
      1895, reprint ed.

C-279 New Orleans, World's Industrial and Cotton Centennial Exposition,
      1884-1885, OFFICIAL CATALOGUE . . ., New Orleans: J. S. Rivers,
      1885.

C-280 O'Conner, Roderick F., TUFTED TEXTILES: AN INDUSTRY AT THE CROSS-ROADS, Atlanta: Georgia Institute of Technology, 1967.

C-281 Odom, Marianne, THE BUSINESSES THAT BUILT SAN ANTONIO, San Antonio, TX: Living Legacies, 1985.

C-282 Papenfuse, Edward C., IN PURSUIT OF PROFIT: THE ANNAPOLIS MERCHANTS IN THE ERA OF THE AMERICAN REVOLUTION, 1763-1805, Baltimore: Johns Hopkins University Press, 1975.

C-283 Parkins, A. E., THE SOUTH: ITS ECONOMIC AND GEOGRAPHIC DEVELOPMENT, New York: John Wiley & Sons, Inc., 1938.

C-284 Payne, Peter Lester and Lance Edwin Davis, THE SAVINGS BANK OF BALTIMORE, 1818-1866: A HISTORICAL AND ANALYTICAL STUDY, Johns Hopkins University Studies in Historical and Political Science No. 2, Series 1954, Baltimore: Johns Hopkins Press, 1956.

C-285 Poll, Solomon, THE HASIDIC COMMUNITY OF WILLIAMSBURG: A STUDY IN THE SOCIOLOGY OF RELIGION, New York: Schocken Books, 1969.

C-286 Pringle, Robert, THE LETTERBOOK OF ROBERT PRINGLE, 1737-1745, Columbia: University of South Carolina Press, 1972.

C-287 Ragsdale, Kenneth, QUICKSILVER: TERLINGUA AND THE CHISOS MINING COMPANY, College Station: Texas A & M University Press, 1976.

C-288 Reagan, Alice E., H. I. KIMBALL, ENTREPRENEUR, Atlanta: Cherokee Publishing Company, 1983.

C-289 Reed, Merl E., NEW ORLEANS AND THE RAILROADS: THE STRUGGLE FOR COMMERCIAL EMPIRE, 1830-1860, Baton Rouge: Louisiana State University Press for Louisiana Historical Association, 1966.

C-290 Research Atlanta, AIRPORT CAPACITY AND ECONOMIC GROWTH IN ATLANTA, Atlanta: Research Atlanta, 1979.

C-291 Research Atlanta, ECONOMIC DEVELOPMENT IN ATLANTA, Atlanta: Research Atlanta, 1978.

C-292 Research Atlanta, COMMERCIAL REVITALIZATION IN ATLANTA, Atlanta: Research Atlanta, 1978.

C-293 Robert, Joseph C., ETHYL: A HISTORY OF THE CORPORATION AND THE PEOPLE WHO MADE IT, Charlottesville, VA: The University Press of Virginia, 1983.

C-294 Robert, Joseph Clark, THE TOBACCO KINGDOM: PLANTATION, MARKET AND FACTORY IN VIRGINIA AND NORTH CAROLINA, 1800-1860, Durham: Duke University Press, 1938.

C-295 Robinson, George Oscar, THE CHARACTER OF QUALITY; THE STORY OF GREENWOOD MILLS, A DISTINGUISHED NAME IN TEXTILES, [Greenwood, SC: 1964].

C-296 Rose, Warren, THE ECONOMIC IMPACT OF THE PORT OF HOUSTON, 1958-1963, Houston: University of Houston, 1965.

C-297 Rosenberg, Leon Joseph, SANGERS': PIONEER TEXAS MERCHANTS, Austin: Texas State Historical Association, 1978.

C-298 Rowell, Raymond J. Sr., VULCAN IN BIRMINGHAM, Birmingham: Birmingham Park and Recreation Board, 1972.

C-299 Rukert, Norman G., FEDERAL HILL, A BALTIMORE NATIONAL HISTORIC DISTRICT, Baltimore: Bodine & Associates, 1980.

C-300 Rukert, Norman G., HISTORIC CANTON: BALTIMORE'S INDUSTRIAL HEART-
      LAND . . . AND ITS PEOPLE, Baltimore: Bodine & Associates, 1978.

C-301 Rutter, F. R., THE SOUTH AMERICAN TRADE OF BALTIMORE, Baltimore:
      The Johns Hopkins Press, 1897.

C-302 Satterfield, Carolyn Green, McWANE INC.: THE HISTORY OF A FAMILY
      BUSINESS, Birmingham: 1981.

C-303 Savannah River Improvement Commission, PORT AUGUSTA, A GREAT NEW
      INLAND PORT LOCATED AT THE HEAD OF NAVIGATION ON THE SAVANNAH RIVER
      . . ., Augusta: The Commission, 1937.

C-304 Schaffer, William A., George D. Houser, and Robert A. Weinbeig, THE
      ECONOMIC IMPACT OF THE BRAVES ON ATLANTA: 1966, Atlanta: Georgia
      Institute of Technology, 1967.

C-305 Sellers, Leila, CHARLESTON BUSINESS ON THE EVE OF THE AMERICAN
      REVOLUTION, Chapel Hill: University of North Carolina Press, 1934.

C-306 Shartar, Martin and Norman Shanin, THE WONDERFUL WORLD OF COCA-
      COLA, Atlanta: Perry Communications, 1978.

C-307 Shofner, Jerrell H., DANIEL LADD: MERCHANT PRINCE OF FRONTIER
      FLORIDA, Gainesville: University Presses of Florida, 1978.

C-308 Siegel, Stanley E., HOUSTON: CHRONICLE OF THE SUPERCITY ON BUFFALO
      BAYOU, Woodland Hills, CA: Windsor Publicaitons, 1983.

C-309 Sigafoos, Robert A., COTTON ROW TO BEALE STREET: A BUSINESS
      HISTORY OF MEMPHIS, Memphis: Memphis State University Press, 1979.

C-310 Sinclair, Harold, THE PORT OF NEW ORLEANS, Garden City, NY:
      Doubleday, Doran & Company, Inc., 1942.

C-311 Sisco, Paul Hardman, THE RETAIL FUNCTION OF MEMPHIS, Chicago:
      University of Chicago, Department of Geography Research Paper No.
      37, 1954.

C-312 Soltow, J. H., THE ECONOMIC ROLE OF WILLIAMSBURG, Charlottesville,
      VA: University Press of Virginia, 1965.

C-313 Stepick, Alex, THE BUSINESS COMMUNITY OF LITTLE HAITI, Miami:
      Haitian Task Force, 1984.

C-314 Stevens, William, ANVIL OF ADVERSITY: BIOGRAPHY OF A FURNITURE
      PIONEER, New York: Popular Library, 1968.

C-315 Stokes, Durward T., COMPANY SHOPS: THE TOWN BUILT BY A RAILROAD,
      Winston-Salem: John F. Blair, 1981.

C-316 Tang, Anthony M., ECONOMIC DEVELOPMENT IN THE SOUTHERN PIEDMONT,
      1860-1950: ITS IMPACT ON AGRICULTURE, Chapel Hill: University of
      North Carolina Press, 1958.

C-317 Texas University Bureau of Business Research, BIG SPRING, TEXAS; A
      STUDY IN ECONOMIC POTENTIAL, Austin: 1959.

C-318 Van Deusen, John G., THE ANTE-BELLUM SOUTHERN COMMERCIAL CONVEN-
      TIONS, Durham, ND: Duke University Press, 1926.

C-319 VIEWS OF ATLANTA AND THE COTTON STATES AND INTERNATIONAL EXPOSI-
      TION, Columbus, OH: Ward, 1895.

C-320 WASHINGTON'S 28% PLUS MARKET: A CONSUMER ANALYSIS OF THE NEGRO
      MARKET IN WASHINGTON, Washington, DC: The Afro-American, 1942.

C-321 Watters, Pat, COCA-COLA: AN ILLUSTRATED HISTORY, Garden City, NY:
      Doubleday, 1978.

C-322 Weare, Walter B., BLACK BUSINESS IN THE NEW SOUTH: A SOCIAL HIS-
      TORY OF THE NORTH CAROLINA MUTUAL LIFE INSURANCE COMPANY, Urbana:
      University of Illinois Press, 1973.

C-323 Weber, Dickinson, A COMPARISON OF TWO OIL CITY BUSINESS CENTERS
      (ODESSA-MIDLAND, TEXAS), Chicago: University of Chicago, Depart-
      ment of Geography Research Paper, 1958.

C-324 Weigall, T. H., BOOM IN PARADISE, New York: Alfred H. King, 1932.

C-325 Wender, Herbert, SOUTHERN COMMERCIAL CONVENTIONS, 1837-1859,
      Baltimore: The Johns Hopkins Press, 1930.

C-326 Westfall, L. Glenn, KEY WEST: CIGAR CITY U. S. A., Key West, FL:
      Historic Key West Preservation Board, 1984.

C-327 WHY, THE ATLANTA JOURNAL, Atlanta: Atlanta Journal, 1935.

C-328 Wilds, John, JAMES W. PORCH AND THE PORT OF NEW ORLEANS, New Or-
      leans: International Trade Mart, Thomson-Shore, Printers, 1984.

C-329 WILLIAMS' CLARKESVILLE DIRECTORY, CITY GUIDE AND BUSINESS MIRROR,
      Vol. 1-1859-'60, Clarkesville: C. O. Faxon, 1859, reprint ed.

C-330 Williams, Handy Jr. and Noel A. D. Thompson, AN ECONOMIC STUDY OF
      THE ALABAMA BLACK BELT, Tuskegee: Tuskegee Institute, Alabama,
      1975.

C-331 White, Marjorie Longenecker, THE BIRMINGHAM DISTRICT: AN INDUS-
      TRIAL HISTORY AND GUIDE, Birmingham: Birmingham Historical
      Society, 1981.

C-332 Wier, Sadye H. with John F. Makszalek, A BLACK BUSINESSMAN IN WHITE
      MISSISSIPPI, Jackson: The University Press of Mississippi, 1977.

C-333 Woodman, Harold D., KING COTTON AND HIS RETAINERS: FINANCING AND
      MARKETING THE COTTON CROP OF THE SOUTH, 1800-1925, Lexington: Uni-
      versity of Kentucky Press, 1968.

C-334 Woofter, Thomas Jackson, . . . THE NEGROES OF ATHENS, GEORGIA,
      Athens: Phelps-Stokes Fellowship Studies, N. 1, 1913.

C-335 Young, John R., RISING HOUSTON SALES: RETAIL, WHOLESALE, AND
      SERVICE BUSINESS: 1963 AND 1958 COMPARISON, Houston: University
      of Houston, 1966.

Ecology and Environment

C-336 Cooney, Loraine M., GARDEN HISTORY OF GEORGIA, 1733-1933, Atlanta:
      The Peachtree Garden Club, 1933.

C-337 Cowdrey, Albert E., THIS LAND, THIS SOUTH: AN ENVIRONMENTAL HIS-
      TORY, Lexington: University Press of Kentucky, 1983.

C-338 Dutton, Joan Parry, PLANTS OF COLONIAL WILLIAMSBURG: HOW TO IDENT-
      IFY 200 OF COLONIAL AMERICA'S FLOWERS, HERBS, AND TREES, Williams-
      burg: The Colonial Williamsburg Foundation, 1979.

C-339 Herrick, Stephen Marion and H. E. LeGrand, GEOLOGY AND GROUND-WATER
      RESOURCES OF THE ATLANTA AREA, GEORGIA, Atlanta: U. S. Department
      of the Interior, 1949.

C-340 Memphis Garden Club, MEMPHIS & MID-SOUTH GARDEN GUIDE, Memphis,
      TN: The Memphis Garden Club, 1954.

C-341 Rainbolt, Victor, THE TOWN THAT CLIMATE BUILT, Miami: Parker Art Printing Association, 1924.

C-342 Ricco, Joseph H., et al., DEVELOPMENT OF A HYDROLOGIC CONCEPT FOR THE GREATER MOBILE METROPOLITAN-URBAN ENVIRONMENT, University, AL: Geological Survey of Alabama, Bulletin 106, 1973.

C-343 Ricco, Joseph F. and Conrad A. Gazzier, HISTORY OF THE WATER SUPPLY OF THE MOBILE AREA, ALABAMA, University, AL: Geological Survey of Alabama, Circular 92, 1973.

C-344 Sorrels, William, MEMPHIS' GREATEST DEBATE: A QUESTION OF WATER, Memphis: Memphis State University Press, 1970.

C-345 Stone, Doris M., THE GREAT PUBLIC GARDENS OF THE EASTERN UNITED STATES, New York: Pantheon Books, 1982.

Education

C-346 Atlanta University, ATLANTA UNIVERSITY, 1865-1965, Atlanta: 1965.

C-347 Augusta College, Augusta, Georgia, INSTITUTIONAL SELF-STUDY, Augusta: 1963.

C-348 Bacote, Clarence Albert, THE STORY OF ATLANTA UNIVERSITY; A CENTURY OF SERVICE, 1865-1965, Atlanta: Atlanta University, 1969.

C-349 Baird, W. David, MEDICAL EDUCATION IN ARKANSAS, 1879-1979, Memphis: Memphis State University Press, 1979.

C-350 Battle, Kemp Plummer, HISTORY OF THE UNIVERSITY OF NORTH CAROLINA, Raleigh, NMC: Edwards & Broughton Printing Company, 1907-1912.

C-351 Betterswort, John K., PEOPLE'S COLLEGE: A HISTORY OF MISSISSIPPI STATE, University, AL: University of Alabama Press, 1953.

C-352 Bird, William Ernest, THE HISTORY OF WESTERN CAROLINA COLLEGE: THE PROGRESS OF AN IDEA, Chapel Hill: University of North Carolina Press, 1963.

C-353 Boney, F. N., A PICTORIAL HISTORY OF THE UNIVERSITY OF GEORGIA, Athens: University of Georgia Press, 1984.

C-354 Bowles, Elizabeth Ann, A GOOD BEGINNING, THE FIRST FOUR DECADES OF THE UNIVERSITY OF NORTH CAROLINA AT GREENSBORO, Chapel Hill: University of North Carolina Press, 1969.

C-355 Brittain, Marion L., THE STORY OF GEORGIA TECH, Chapel Hill: University of North Carolina Press, 1948.

C-356 Brooks, Lyman Bucker, UPWARD: A HISTORY OF NORFOLK STATE UNIVER-SITY (1925-1975), Washington, DC: Howard University Press, 1983.

C-357 Campbell, Clarice T. and Oscar Allan Rogers Jr., MISSISSIPPI: THE VIEW FROM TUGALOO, Jackson: University Press of Mississippi, 1979.

C-358 Callcott, George H., A HISTORY OF THE UNIVERSITY OF MARYLAND, Baltimore: Maryland Historical Society, 1966.

C-359 Cashin, Edward J., A HISTORY OF AUGUSTA COLLEGE, Augusta: Augusta College Press, 1976.

C-360 Cashin, Edward J., THE QUEST: A HISTORY OF PUBLIC EDUCATION IN RICHMOND COUNTY, Augusta: Richmond Co. Board of Education, 1985.

C-361 Chamberlain, Ruth, THE SCHOOL OF NURSING OF THE MEDICAL COLLEGE OF SOUTH CAROLINA--ITS STORY, Columbia,: R. L. Bryan Company, 1970.

C-362 Conkin, Paul K., GONE WITH THE IVY: A BIOGRAPHY OF VANDERBILT
UNIVERSITY, Knoxville: University of Tennessee Press, 1985.

C-363 Cooper, Waller Raymond, SOUTHWESTERN AT MEMPHIS, 1848-1948,
Richmond: 1949.

C-364 Covington, James W. and C. Herbert Laub, THE STORY OF THE UNIVER-
SITY OF TAMPA, Tampa: University of Tampa Press, 1955.

C-365 Cross, George L., BLACKS IN WHITE COLLEGES: OKLAHOMA'S LANDMARK
CASES, Norman: University of Oklahoma Press, 1975.

C-366 Cross, George L., THE UNIVERSITY OF OKLAHOMA AND WORLD WAR II: A
PERSONAL ACCOUNT, 1941-1946, Norman: University of Oklahoma Press,
1980.

C-367 Dansby, B. Baldwin, A BRIEF HISTORY OF JACKSON COLLEGE; A TYPICAL
STORY OF THE SURVIVAL OF EDUCATION AMONG NEGROES IN THE SOUTH,
Jackson: Jackson College, [1953].

C-368 Duffy, John, THE TULANE UNIVERSITY MEDICAL CENTER: ONE HUNDRED AND
FIFTY YEARS OF MEDICAL EDUCATION, Baton Rouge: Louisiana State
University Press, 1984.

C-369 Dyer, John P., TULANE: THE BIOGRAPHY OF A UNIVERSITY, 1834-1965,
New York: Harper & Row, 1966.

C-370 Dyer, Thomas G., THE UNIVERSITY OF GEORGIA: A BICENTENNIAL HIS-
TORY, 1785-1985, Athens: University of Georgia Press, 1985.

C-371 Ecke, Melvin W., FROM IVY STREET TO KENNEDY CENTER: CENTENNIAL
HISTORY OF THE ATLANTA PUBLIC SCHOOL SYSTEM, Atlanta: Atlanta
Boartd of Education, 1972.

C-372 Ellison, Rhoda Coleman, HISTORY OF HUNTINGTON COLLEGE, 1854-1954,
University, AL: University of Alabama Press, 1954.

C-373 Esslinger, Deane R., FRIENDS FOR TWO HUNDRED YEARS: A HISTORY OF
BALTIMORE'S OLDEST SCHOOL, Baltimore: Frends School Publishers,
1983.

C-374 Gobbel, Luther Lafayette, GREENSBORO COLLEGE, 1935-1952: MY SEVEN-
TEEN YEARS AS ITS PRESIDENT: WITH A RESUME OF THE YEARS BEFORE
1935, Greensboro: Greensboro College Alumni Association, 1977.

C-375 Govan, Gilbert E. and James W. Livingood, THE UNIVERSITY OF CHATTA-
NOOGA: SIXTY YEARS, Chattanooga: University of Chattanooga, 1947.

C-376 Griffin, Frances, "LESS TIME FOR MEDDLING": A HISTORY OF SALEM
ACADEMY AND COLLEGE, 1772-1866, Winston-Salem: John F. Blair,
1979.

C-377 Guilday, Peter K., THE LIFE AND TIMES OF JOHN ENGLAND, FIRST BISHOP
OF CHARLESTON (1786-1842), New York: The American Press, 1927.

C-378 Hamilton, Green Polonius, BOOKER T. WASHINGTON HIGH SCHOOL: RETRO-
SPECTIVE, PROSPECTIVE FROM 1889 TO 1927, Memphis: [SIN] 1927.

C-379 Henderson, Arachibald, THE CAMPUS OF THE FIRST STATE UNIVERSITY,
Chapel Hill: University of North Carolina Press, 1949.

C-380 Hollis, Daniel Walker, UNIVERSITY OF SOUTH CAROLINA: COLLEGE TO
UNIVERSITY (Vol. II), Columbia: University of South Carolina
Press, 1956.

C-381 Hunter, Henry Reid, THE DEVELOPMENT OF PUBLIC SECONDARY SCHOOLS IN
ATLANTA, GEORGIA, 1845-1937, Nashville: George Peabody College for
Teachers, 1939.

C-382 Lamar, Joseph Rucker, TRUSTEES OF RICHMOND ACADEMY OF AUGUSTA, GEORGIA; THEIR WORK DURING THE EIGHTEENTH CENTURY, IN THE MANAGEMENT OF A SCHOOL, A TOWN AND A CHURCH, Augusta: the author, 1910.

C-383 Leflar, Robert A., THE FIRST HUNDRED YEARS, CENTENNIAL HISTORY OF THE UNIVERSITY OF ARKANSAS, Fayetteville, AK: The University of Arkansas Foundation, Inc., 1972.

C-384 Lynch, Kenneth M., MEDICAL SCHOOLING IN SOUTH CAROLINA 1823-1969, Columbia: R. L. Bryan Company, 1970.

C-385 Marshall, Edward Chauncy, HISTORY OF THE UNITED STATES NAVAL ACADEMY . . . ., New York: D. Van Nostrand, 1862.

C-386 Mims, Edwin, HISTORY OF VANDERBILT UNIVERSITY, Nashville: Vanderbilt University Press, 1946.

C-387 Montgomery, James R., Stanley Folmsbee, and Lee S. Greene, TO FOSTER KNOWLEDGE: A HISTORY OF THE UNIVERSITY OF TENNESSEE, 1794-1970, Knoxville: The University of Tennessee Press, 1984.

C-388 McCallie, Eleanor Grace, DON'T SAY 'YOU,' SAY 'WE': THE FOUNDING OF GIRLS' PREPARATORY SCHOOL, 1906-1918, Chattanooga: The Bruiser Press, 1982.

C-389 McMath, Robert C. Jr., ENGINEERING THE NEW SOUTH: GEORGIA TECH, 1885-1985, Athens: University of Georghia Press, 1985.

C-390 Neyland, Ludell W. and Joan W. Riley, THE HISTORY OF FLORIDA AGRICULTURAL AND MECHANICAL UNIVERSITY, Gainesville: University of Florida Press, 1963.

C-391 Nicks, Roy S., ed., COMMUNITY COLLEGES OF TENNESSEE: THE FOUNDING AND EARLY YEARS, Memphis: Memphis State University Press, 1979.

C-392 Peter, Robert, TRANSYLVANIA UNIVERSITY, ITS ORIGIN, RISE, DECLINE, AND FALL, Louisville: J. P. Morton & Company, Printers, 1896 [Filson Club Publications #11].

C-393 Plummer, Kenneth M., A HISTORY OF WEST VIRGINIA WESLEYAN COLLEGE, 1890-1965, Buckhannon: West Virginia Wesleyan College Press, 1965.

C-394 Powell, William S., THE FIRST STATE UNIVERSITY: A PICTORIAL HISTORY OF THE UNIVERSITY OF NORTH CAROLINA, Chapel Hill: University of North Carolina Press, 1972.

C-395 Proctor, Samuel and Wright Langley, GATOR HISTORY: THE UNIVERSITY OF FLORIDA--A PICTORAL HISTORY, [s.l.]: South Star Publishers, 1986.

C-396 Rankins, Walter Herbert, HISTORIC AUGUSTA AND AUGUSTA COLLEGE, Augusta, KY: 1947.

C-397 Record, Wilson and Jane Cassels Record, eds., LITTLE ROCK, U. S. A., San Francisco: Chandler Publishing Company, 1960.

C-398 Reid, Alfred Sandlin, FURMAN UNIVERSITY: TOWARD A NEW IDENTITY, 1925-1975, Durham, NC: Duke University Press, 1976.

C-399 Richardson, Joe M., A HISTORY OF FISK UNIVERSITY, 1865-1946, University, AL: The University of Alabama Press, 1980.

C-400 Richmond County, GA Public Schools, REPORT ON THE PUBLIC SCHOOLS OF RICHMOND COUNTY AND CITY OF AUGUSTA, 1ST--18--, Augusta: J. L. Gow, Printer.

C-401 Roper, James E., SOUTHWESTERN AT MEMPHIS, 1948-1975, Memphis: Southwestern, 1975.

C-402 Rumbly, Rose, A CENTURY OF CLASS: ONE HUNDRED YEAR HISTORY OF PUBLIC EDUCATION IN DALLAS, Austin, TX: Eakin Press, 1984.

C-403 Schumann, Marguerite E., THE FIRST STATE UNIVERSITY: A WALKING GUIDE, Chapel Hill: University of North Carolina Press, 1972.

C-404 Sellers, James Benson, HISTORY OF THE UNIVERSITY OF ALABAMA, University, AL: University of Alabama Press, 1953.

C-405 Stevenson, George J., INCREASE IN EXCELLENCE: A HISTORY OF EMORY AND HENRY COLLEGE, New York: Appleton-Century-Crofts, 1963.

C-406 Stewart, Frank Ross, Mrs., DOCTOR CLARENCE WILLIAM DAUGETTE, THE BIOGRAPHY OF AN EDUCATOR, Centre, AL: Stewart University Press, 1982.

C-407 Stoops, Martha, THE HERITAGE: THE EDUCATION OF WOMEN AT ST. MARY'S COLLEGE, RALEIGH, NORTH CAROLINA, Raleigh: St. Mary's College, 1983.

C-408 Talbert, Charles g., THE UNIVERSITY OF KENTUCKY: THE MATURING YEARS, Lexington, KY: University Press of Kentucky, 1965.

C-409 Tebeau, Charlton W., THE UNIVERSITY OF MIAMI: A GOLDEN ANNIVERSARY HISTORY, 1926-1976, Coral Gables, FL: University of Miami Press, 1976.

C-410 Terry, Adolphine Fletcher, CHARLOTTE STEPHENS: LITTLE ROCK'S FIRST BLACK TEACHER, Little Rock: Academic Press of Arkansas, 1973.

C-411 Turrentine, Samuel Bryant, A ROMANCE OF EDUCATION; A NARRATIVE IN-CLUDING RECOLLECTIONS AND OTHER FACTS CONNECTED WITH GREENSBORO COLLEGE, Greensboro, NC: Piedmont Press, 1946.

C-412 Wilson, Louis R., UNIVERSITY OF NORTH CAROLINA, 1900-1930: THE MAKING OF A MODERN UNIVERSITY, Chapel Hill: University of North Carolina Press, 1957.

C-413 Wolfe, Suzanne R., THE UNIVERSITY OF ALABAMA: A PICTORIAL HISTORY, University, AL: University of Alabama Press, 1983.

Ghost Towns

C-414 Brinkley, Louis Barnes, THE DESERTED SYCAMORE VILLAGE OF CHEATHAM COUNTY, Pleasant View, TN: The author, 1980.

C-415 Harris, W. Stuart, DEAD TOWNS OF ALABAMA, University, AL: The University of Alabama Press, 1977.

C-416 Jones, Charles Colcock Jr., THE DEAD TOWNS OF GEORGIA, Savannah: Morning News Steam Printing House, 1878.

C-417 Morris, John W., GHOST TOWNS OF OKLAHOMA, Norman: University of Oklahoma Press, 1977.

C-418 McIlvaine, Paul, THE DEAD TOWN OF SUNBURY, GEORGIA, Hendersonville, GA: The author [1971].

C-419 Roddy, Vernon, THE LOST TOWN OF BLEDSOESBOROUGH, TENNESSEE: ITS BEGINNING, ITS END: TWO ESSAYS IN THE RECORD OF TENNESSEE'S UPPER CUMBERLAND OF OLD, [Tennessee]: Upper Country People Probe, 1984.

C-420 Warnke, James R., THE GHOST TOWNS AND SIDE ROADS OF FLORIDA, Boynton Beach, FL: Roving Photographers & Associates, Inc., 1979.

Growth, Development and Land Use

C-421 ACTION AT THE CORE: A BLUEPRINT FOR ATLANTA, Atlanta: Hammer and
Company, 1959.

C-422 ATLANTA 2000, Atlanta: GA: Atlanta Chamber of Commerce, 1973.

C-423 Ballard, Steven C. and Thomas E James, Eds., THE FUTURE OF THE
SUNBELT: MANAGING GROWTH AND CHANGE, New York: Praeger, 1983.

C-424 Brownell, Blaine A., THE URBAN ETHOS IN THE SOUTH 1920-1930, Baton
Rouge: Louisiana State University Press, 1975.

C-425 Behrman, Martin, CIVIC DEVELOPMENT: PROGRESS OF CITY OF NEW
ORLEANS IN PAST TEN YEARS, New Orleans: [s.m.], 1913.

C-426 Bertelson, David, THE LAZY SOUTH, New York: Oxford University
Press, 1967.

C-427 Blumstein, James F. and Benjamin Walter, eds., GROWING METROPOLIS:
ASPECTS OF DEVELOPMENT IN NASHVILLE, Nashville: Vanderbilt University Press, 1975.

C-428 Brantley, William Henderson, THE STORY OF BAYOU CHATUGUE, OR, CAST
IRON PIPE AND PAPER MILLS IN EARLY ALABAMA, Birmingham: [s.n.,
1938].

C-429 Chapin, F. Stuart Jr. and others, IN THE SHADOW OF A DEFENSE PLANT:
A STUDY OF URBANIZATION IN RURAL SOUTH CAROLINA . . ., Chapel
Hill: University of North Carolina Press, 1954.

C-430 Clark, Thomas D., A PIONEER SOUTHERN RAILROAD FROM NEW ORLEANS TO
CAIRO, Chapel Hill: University of North Carolina Press, 1936.

C-431 Davidson, Claud M., A SPATIAL ANALYSES OF SUBMETROPOLIS SMALL TOWN
GROWTH, Austin: Bureau of Business Research, University of Texas,
1972.

C-432 Gaston, Paul M., THE NEW SOUTH CREED: A STUDY IN SOUTHERN MYTH-
MAKING, New York: Alfred A. Knopf, Inc., 1970.

C-433 GOALS FOR DALLAS, Dallas, TX: Goals for Dallas, 1966.

C-434 Goldfield, David R., URBAN GROWTH IN THE AGE OF SECTIONALISM: VIR-
GINIA 1847-1861, Baton Rouge: Louisiana State University Press,
1977.

C-435 Gorsuch, Edwin N. and Dudley S. Hinds, THE FUTURE OF ATLANTA'S
CENTRAL CITY, Atlanta: Georgia State University, 1977.

C-436 Hamer, Andrew Marshall, ed., URBAN ATLANTA: REDEFINING THE ROLE OF
THE CITY, Research Monograph No. 84, Atlanta: College of Business
Administration, Georgia State University, 1980.

C-437 Hansen, Niles M., INTERMEDIATE-SIZE CITIES AS GROWTH CENTERS:
APPLICATIONS FOR KENTUCKY, THE PIEDMONT CRESCENT, THE OZARKS, AND
TEXAS, New York: Praeger Publishers, 1971.

C-438 Hill, Carole S. and Robert E. Garren, ATLANTA INTERNATIONAL:
PROBLEMS AND PROSPECTS, Atlanta: Georgia State University, 1976.

C-439 Ivey, John Eli, et al., BUILDING ATLANTA'S FUTURE, Chapel Hill:
University of North Carolina Press, 1948.

C-440 Jones, Joe H., DALLAS-FORT WORTH: REGIONAL GROWTH INFLUENCING
TRANSPORTATION PLANNING, Austin: University of Texas, 1965.

C-441 Kiang, Ying-Cheng, A TALE OF TWO CITIES, Jacksonville, FL:
Jacksonville University, 1969.

C-442 Larsen, Lawrence H., THE RISE OF THE URBAN SOUTH, Lexington:
University of Kentucky Press, 1985.

C-443 Laws, Kevin John, CHANGING LAND USE: PEACHTREE STREET, ATLANTA: A
CASE STUDY IN SEQUENT OCCUPANCE, Athens: University of Georgia,
1978.

C-444 Naylor, Thomas H. and James Clotfelter, STRATEGIES FOR CHANGE IN
THE SOUTH, Chapel Hill: University of North Carolina, 1975.

C-445 O'Brien, Michael, THE IDEA OF THE AMERICAN SOUTH, 1920-1941, Baltimore: Johns Hopkins University Press, 1979.

C-446 Papenfuse, Edward C. and Joseph M. Coale III, THE HAMMOND-HARWOOD
HOUSE ATLAS OF HISTORICAL MAPS OF MARYLAND, 1608-1908, Baltimore:
Johns Hopkins University Press, 1982.

C-447 Payne-Maxie Consultants, Blayney-Dyett, Urban and Regional Planners, THE LAND USE AND URBAN DEVELOPMENT IMPACTS OF BELTWAYS: CASE
STUDIES, Washington, DC: U. S. Government Printing Office, June
1980.

C-448 Perry, David and Alfred Watkins, eds., THE RISE OF THE SUNBELT
CITIES, Beverly Hills: Sage, 1978.

C-449 Platt, Harold L., CITY BUILDING IN THE NEW SOUTH: THE GROWTH OF
PUBLIC SERVICES IN HOUSTON, TEXAS, 1830-1910, Philadelphia: Temple
University Press, 1983.

C-450 Pogue, Nell C., SOUTH CAROLINA ELECTRIC AND GAS COMPANY, 1846-1964,
Columbia: 1964.

C-451 Poland, Charles Preston, FROM FRONTIER TO SUBURBIA, Marceline, MO:
Walsworth Publishing Company, 1976,

C-452 Pred, Allan R., URBAN GROWTH AND THE CIRCULATION OF INFORMATION,
THE UNITED STATES SYSTEM OF CITIES, Cambridge, MA: Harvard
University Press, 1973.

C-453 Reed, John Shelton and Daniel Joseph Singal, eds., REGIONALISM AND
THE SOUTH: SELECTED PAPERS OF RUPERT VANCE, Chapel Hill: University of North Carolina Press, 1982.

C-454 Research Atlanta, WHICH WAY ATLANTA? A TREND ANALYSIS OF METRO-
POLITAN ATLANTA'S POPULATION, SCHOOLS, EMPLOYMENT AND INCOME,
HEALTH, TAXES AND HOUSING, Atlanta: 1973.

C-455 Sawyers, Larry and William K. Tabb, eds., SUNBELT/SNOWBELT: URBAN
DEVELOPMENT AND REGIONAL RESTRUCTURING, New York: Oxford University Press, 1983.

C-456 Sears, Joan Niles, THE FIRST ONE HUNDRED YEARS OF TOWN PLANNING IN
GEORGIA, Atlanta: Cherokee Publishing Company, 1979.

C-457 Shingleton, Royce, RICHARD PETERS: CHAMPION OF THE NEW SOUTH,
Macon: Mercer University Press, 1985.

C-458 Smallwood, James M., URBAN BUILDER: THE LIFE AND TIMES OF STANLEY
DRAPER, Norman: University of Oklahoma Press, 1977.

C-459 Sofen, Edward, THE MIAMI METROPOLITAN EXPERIMENT: METROPOLITAN
ACTION STUDIES 2, Bloomington: Indiana University Press, 1963.

C-460 Weinstein, Bernard L. and Robert E. Firestone, REGIONAL GROWTH AND
DECLINE IN THE UNITED STATES: THE RISE OF THE SUNBELT AND THE
DECLINE OF THE NORTHEAST, New York: Praeger, 1978.

C-461 Wheat, Leonard F., URBAN GROWTH IN THE NONMETROPOLITAN SOUTH, Lexington, MA: Lexington Books, D. C. Heath and Company, 1976.

C-462 Wheeler, Kenneth W., TO WEAR A CITY'S CROWN: THE BEGINNINGS OF URBAN GROWTH IN TEXAS, 1836-1865, Cambridge: Harvard University Press, 1968.

C-463 White, Dana F. and Victor A. Kromer, eds., OLMSTED SOUTH: OLD SOUTH CRITIC/NEW SOUTH PLANNER, Westport, CT: Greenwood, 1979.

C-464 Wolff, Reinhold P., MIAMI METRO: THE ROAD TO URBAN UNITY, Coral Gables: University of Miami Press, 1960.

Hazards and Disasters

C-465 Anderson, Dan Robert and Maurice Weinrobe, EFFECTS OF A NATURAL DISASTER ON LOCAL MORTGAGE MARKETS: THE PEARL RIVER FLOOD IN JACKSON, MISSISSIPPI, APRIL 1979, Boulder: University of Colorado, 1980.

C-466 Davis, F. Edgar, SOUVENIR VIEWS OF AUGUSTA'S BIG FIRE, MARCH 22, 1916, Savannah: M. S. & D. A. Byck Company, Printers, 1916.

C-467 Harrison, Benjamin, ACRES OF ASHES; THE STORY OF THE GREAT FIRE THAT SWEPT OVER THE CITY OF JACKSONVILLE, FLORIDA, ON THE AFTERNOON OF FRIDAY, MAY 3, 1901, Jacksonville: J. A. Holloman, [1901].

C-468 Hederman, T. M. Jr., ed., THE GREAT FLOOD, Jackson, MS: Clarion Ledger/Jackson Daily News, 1979.

C-469 National Fire Protection Association, AUGUSTA, GEORGIA CONFLAGRATION, MARCH 22-23, 1916 . . . ., Boston, 1916.

C-470 WALA-TV News, FREDERIC [VIDEORECORDING]: THE WINDS OF DESTRUCTION, 1979.

Health

C-471 Charleston, SC City Council, REPORT OF THE COMMITTEE OF THE CITY COUNCIL OF CHARLESTON UPON THE EPIDEMIC YELLOW FEVER OF 1858, Charleston: Walker, Evans and Company, 1859.

C-472 Dain, Norman, DISORDERED MINDS: THE FIRST CENTURY OF EASTERN STATE HOSPITAL IN WILLIAMSBURG, VIRGINIA, 1766-1866, Williamsburg: Colonial Williamsburg Foundation, 1971.

C-473 Davidson, Chalmers G., FRIEND OF THE PEOPLE: THE LIFE OF DR. PETER FAYSSOUX, OF CHARLESTON, SOUTH CAROLINA, Columbia, SC: The Medical Association of South Carolina, 1950.

C-474 Duffy, John, SWORD OF PESTILENCE: THE NEW ORLEANS YELLOW FEVER EPIDEMIC OF 1853, Baton Rouge: Louisiana State University Press, 1966.

C-475 AN ENVIRONMENTAL HEALTH REPORT OF AUGUSTA, GEORGIA, AUGUST 3-8, 1964, Augusta: Richmond County, 1964.

C-476 Haworth, Brend A., OUT OF THE BLACK BAG: A MEDICAL HISTORY OF HIGH POINT, NORTH CAROLINA, High Point, NC: Guilford County Medical Auxiliary, [1975].

C-477 Henley, Ruth N., SANATORIUM TO MEDICAL CENTER: THE HISTORY OF PIEDMONT HOSPITAL: PIEDMONT HOSPITAL, 1905-1985, Atlanta: Amersand Studios, 1984.

C-478 Leake, Chauncey D., ed., YELLOW FEVER IN GALVESTON, REPUBLIC OF
      TEXAS, 1839. AN ACCOUNT OF THE GREAT EPIDEMIC, BY ASHBEL SMITH,
      M.D., A.M., EX-SURGEON GENERAL OF THE TEXIAN ARMY, TOGETHER WITH A
      BIOGRAPHICAL SKETCH BY CHAUNCEY D. LEAKE, AND STORIES OF THE MEN
      WHO CONQURED YELLOW FEVER, Austin: University of Texas Press,
      1951.

C-479 Livingood, James W., CHATTANOOGA AND HAMILTON COUNTY MEDICAL
      SOCIETY: THE PROFESSION AND ITS COMMUNITY, Chattanooga:
      Chattanooga and Hamilton County Medical Society, 1983.

C-480 Meredith, Owen and Lee Seitz, A HISTORY OF THE AMERICAN RED CROSS
      IN NASHVILLE, TENNESSEE, Nashville: privately printed, 1980.

C-481 Merritt, Webster, A CENTURY OF MEDICINE IN JACKSONVILLE AND DUVAL
      COUNTY, Gainesville: University of Florida Press, 1949.

C-482 NINETY YEARS OF SERVICE 1873-1963: THE STORY OF ST. LUKE'S HOSPI-
      TAL, JACKSONVILLE, FLORIDA, Jacksonville: 1963.

C-483 Steiner, Lewis Henry, REPORT OF LEWIS H. STEINER, M.D. . . ., New
      York: A. D. F. Randolph, 1862.

C-484 Waring, Joseph Ioor, A HISTORY OF MEDICINE IN SOUTH CAROLINA, 1670-
      1825, Charleston: The South Carolina Medical Association, 1964.

History and Geography

C-485 Acheson, Sam, edited by Lee Milazzo, DALLAS YESTERDAY, Dallas:
      Southern Methodist University Press, 1977.

C-486 Acker, Marian Francis, ETCHINGS OF OLD MOBILE, Mobile, AL: Press
      of Gill Printing and Stationery Company, 1938.

C-487 Adams, George Rollie and Ralph Jerry Christian, NASHVILLE, A PIC-
      TORIAL HISTORY, Norfolk, VA: Donning Company/Publishers, 1981.

C-488 Adams, Walter M., NORTH LITTLE ROCK: THE UNIQUE CITY: A HISTORY,
      Little Rock: August House, 1986.

C-489 Adicks, Richard and Donna M. Neely, OVIEDO: BIOGRAPHY OF A TOWN,
      Orlando: Executive Press, 1979.

C-490 Aiken, Leona Taylor, DONELSON, TENNESSEE: ITS HISTORY AND LAND-
      MARKS, Nashville: Donelson History Book Committee, 1969.

C-491 Alabama Land Improvement Co., ANNISTON, ALABAMA IN NORTH ALABAMA:
      THE MODEL CITY OF THE SOUTH, Baltimore: Record Printing House,
      1885.

C-492 An Alabamian, SHEFFIELD, ALABAMA: ITS PRESENT AND FUTURE WITH A
      STORY OF HINDA'S CANE OR THE LOST TRIBES, Nashville: Southern
      Methodist Publishing House, 1885.

C-493 Alexander, James (Mary Rawlings, ed.), EARLY CHARLOTTESVILLE, Char-
      lottesville: The Michie Company, 1942.

C-494 Allen, Ethan, HISTORICAL NOTICES OF ST. ANN'S PARISH IN ANN ARUNDEL
      COUNTY, MARYLAND, EXTENDING FROM 1649 TO 1857, Baltimore: J. B.
      Des Forges, 1857.

C-495 Allen, Ivan Earnest, THE ATLANTA SPIRIT, ALTITUDE AND ATTITUDE,
      Atlanta: Allen-Marshall Company, 1948.

C-496 Allen, Ivan, ATLANTA FROM THE ASHES, Atlanta: Ruralist Press,
      1928.

C-497 Allen, Martha Norbuen, ASHEVILLE AND LAND OF THE SKY, Charlotte:
      Heritage House, 1960.

C-498 Allston, Elizabeth W., CHRONICLES OF CHICORA WOOD, New York:
      Charles Scribner's Sons, 1922.

C-499 Alperin, Lynn M., CUSTODIANS OF THE COAST: HISTORY OF THE UNITED
      STATES ARMY ENGINEERS AT GALVESTON, Galveston District: U. S. Army
      Corps of Engineers, 1977.

C-500 Anderson, Alan D., THE ORIGIN AND RESOLUTION OF AN URBAN CRISIS:
      BALTIMORE, 1890-1930, Baltimore: Johns Hopkins University Press,
      1977.

C-501 Andrews, Christopher Columbus, HISTORY OF THE CAMPAIGN OF MOBILE
      . . ., New York: D. Van Nostrand, 1867.

C-502 Arnade, Charles W., THE SEIGE OF ST. AUGUSTINE IN 1702, Gaines-
      ville: University of Florida Press, 1959.

C-503 Arnett, Ethel Stephens, GREENSBORO, NORTH CAROLINA: THE COUNTY
      SEAT OF GUILFORD, Chapel Hill: University of North Carolina Press,
      1955.

C-504 Arthur, Stanley Clisby, OLD NEW ORLEANS, New Orleans: Harmanson,
      1936.

C-505 Ashton, Jacqueline, BOCA RATON, FROM PIONEER DAYS TO THE FABULOUS
      TWENTIES, Boca Raton, FL: Dedication Press, 1979.

C-506 Ashton, Jacqueline, BOCA RATON PIONEERS AND ADDISON MIZNER, Boca
      Raton, FL: [s.n.] 1981.

C-507 Askins, Norman Davenport, RHODES MEMORIAL HALL, Atlanta: Georgia
      Department of Archives and History, 1980.

C-508 Athens, GA, ATHENS, GEORGIA, HOME OF THE UNIVERSITY OF GEORGIA,
      1801-1951, Athens: 1951.

C-509 Athens, GA, HAND-BOOK OF ATHENS AND SOUVENIR OF THE CARNIVAL,
      OCTOBER 1 TO 6, 1900, Athens: [s.n.], 1900.

C-510 Athens, GA Chamber of Commerce, ATHENS, CLASSIC CITY. THE
      METROPOLIS OF NORTH-EAST GEORGIA, Athens: The Chamber, 1913.

C-511 Athens, GA Chamber of Commerce, ATHENS, GEORGIA, Athens: 192?

C-512 Atkins, Leah Rawls, THE VALLEY AND THE HILLS: AN ILLUSTRATED HIS-
      TORY OF BIRMINGHAM AND JEFFERSON COUNTY, Woodland Hills, CA:
      Windsor Publicaitons, Inc., 1981.

C-513 Atkins, Leah Rawls with Flora Jones Beaners, THE JONES FAMILY OF
      HUNTSVILLE ROAD, Birmingham: L. R. Atkins, 1981.

C-514 Atlanta, Chamber of Commerce, SOUVENIR ALBUM, ATLANTA, GEORGIA,
      Atlanta: Foote and Davies, 1911.

C-515 Atlanta. Convention and Tourist Bureau, ATLANTA; THE PINNACLE
      CITY, Atlanta: 1930.

C-516 Atlanta. Convention and Tourist Bureau, ATLANTA'S OFFICIAL SONG
      BOOK . . ., Atlanta: 1935.

C-517 ATLANTA: A CITY OF THE MODERN SOUTH, American Guide Series,
      Federal Writers Project, New York: Smith and Durrell, 1942.

C-518 ATLANTA: A NATIONAL CITY, Atlanta: Atlanta Chamber of Commerce,
      1970.

C-519 ATLANTA CENTENNIAL YEAR BOOK, 1837-1937, Atlanta: Franklin Printing Company, 1937.

C-520 ATLANTA: 89 NATURAL COLOR VIEWS, Atlanta: Aerial Photography
Services, 1978.

C-521 THE ATLANTA EXPOSITION AND SOUTH ILLUSTRATED, Chicago: Alder Art
Publishing Company, 1895.

C-522 ATLANTA FACTS BOOK, Atlanta: Atlanta Chamber of Commerce, 1983.

C-523 ATLANTA IN YOUR POCKET, Woodbury, NY: Barron's, 1981.

C-524 ATLANTA, METROPOLIS OF THE SOUTHEAST, Atlanta: Atlanta Guide
Publishing Company, 1928.

C-525 ATLANTA OF TODAY: SOUVENIR, 1903, [s.l.: s.n.], 1903.

C-526 ATLANTA RESURGENS, Atlanta: First National Bank of Atlanta, 1971.

C-527 Augusta, GA, AUGUSTA BICENTENNIAL, MAY 12TH TO 18TH, Augusta:
Phoenix Printing Company, 1935.

C-528 Augusta Herald, A HANDBOOK OF THE AUGUSTA AREA, Augusta: Walton
Print Company, 1947.

C-529 Aycock, Roger D., ALL ROADS TO ROME, Roswell, GA: W. H. Wolfe
Associates, 1981.

C-530 Babcock, Bernie (Smade), YESTERDAY AND TODAY IN ARKANSAS, Little
Rock: Jordan and Foster Printing Company, 1917.

C-531 Bacon, Eve, OAKLAND: THE EARLY YEARS, Chuluota, FL: The Meklee
House, 1975-76.

C-532 Bacon, Eve, ORLANDO: A CENTENNIAL HISTORY, Chuluota, FL: Mecklee
House, 1975-77 [2 vols].

C-533 Bailey, Ronald H., et al., THE BATTLES FOR ATLANTA: SHERMAN MOVES
EAST, Alexandria, VA: Time-Life Books, 1985.

C-534 Bake, William A. and James J. Kilpatrick, THE AMERICAN SOUTH:
TOWNS AND CITIES, Birmingham: Oxmoor House, Inc., 1982.

C-535 Baldwin, William P., THE VISIBLE VILLAGE: McCLELLANVILLE, 1860-
1945, Summerville: Privately printed, 1984.

C-536 Bales, John B., ed., DIXIE DATELINE: A JOURNALISTIC PORTRAIT OF
THE CONTEMPORARY SOUTH, New Series, No. 1, Houston: Rice University Series, 1983.

C-537 Bane, Michael and Ellen Moor, TAMPA: YESTERDAY, TODAY, AND
TOMORROW, Tampa, FL: Mishler & King Publishers, 1981.

C-538 Barclay, R. E., DUCKTOWN, BACK IN RAHT'S TIME, Chapel Hill: The
University of North Carolina, 1946.

C-539 Barnstone, Howard, THE GALVESTON THAT WAS, New York: Macmillan
Company, 1966.

C-540 Barringer, Bugs, Dot Barringer and Lila Chesson, ROCKY MOUNT: A
PICTORIAL HISTORY, Norfolk, VA: Donning Company, 1977.

C-541 Barrow, Elfrida DeRenne and Laura Palmer Bell, ANCHORED YESTERDAYS:
THE LOG BOOK OF SAVANNAH'S VOYAGE ACROSS A GEORGIA CENTURY, IN TEN
WATCHES, Savannah: Review Publishing and Printing Company, 1923.

C-542 Bartholomew, Ed Ellsworth, THE HOUSTON STORY: A CHRONICLE OF THE CITY OF HOUSTON AND THE TEXAS FRONTIER FROM THE BATTLE OF SAN JACINTO TO THE WAR BETWEEN THE STATES, 1836-1865, Houston: Frontier Press of Houston, 1951.

C-543 Bartley, Numan V., THE CREATION OF MODERN GEORGIA, Athens: University of Georgia Press, 1983.

C-544 Battey, George M. Jr., HISTORY OF ROME AND FLOYD COUNTY, GEORGIA, Atlanta: Webb, 1922.

C-545 Battle, Kemp Plummer, THE EARLY HISTORY OF RALEIGH, THE CAPITAL CITY OF NORTH CAROLINA, Raleigh, NC: Edwards & Broughton, 1893.

C-546 Beach, Marie, ed., GUIDE TO RICHMOND, Midlothian, VA: Prides Crossing, Ltd., 1976.

C-547 Beckett, Hazel W., GROWING UP IN DALLAS, Austin: Wind River Press, 1985.

C-548 Beeson, Leola Selman, HISTORY STORIES OF MILLEDGEVILLE AND BALDWIN COUNTY, Macon: The J. W. Burke Company, 1943.

C-549 Beirne, Francis F., BALTIMORE: A PICTURE HISTORY, 1958-1968, Baltimore: Bodine, 1968.

C-550 Beirne, Francis F. and Carleton Jones, BALTIMORE: A PICTURE HISTORY, Baltimore: Bodine and Associates, Inc. and Maclay and Associates, Inc., 1982.

C-551 Bell, James W., LITTLE ROCK HANDBOOK, Author, 1980.

C-552 Bell, Robert E., A BIBLIOGRAPHY OF MOBILE, ALABAMA, University of Alabama Studies, No. 11, University, AL: University of Alabama Press, 1956.

C-553 Berins, Jane and Madilyn Samuels, NEW ORLEANS Q & A: TRIVIAL QUESTIONS, TERRIFIC ANSWERS, New Orleans: Royale Publishers, 1985.

C-554 Beryl, Frank, A PICTORAL HISTORY OF PIKESVILLE, MARYLAND, Towson, MD: Baltimore County Public Library, 1982.

C-555 Besson, J. A. B., HISTORY OF EUFAULA, ALABAMA, THE BLUFF CITY OF THE CHATTAHOOCHEE, Franklin Steam Printing House, 1875.

C-556 Bethell, John A., BETHELL'S HISTORY OF POINT PINELLAS, St. Petersburg: Great Outdoors Publishing Company, 1962.

C-557 Betts, Edward Chanbees, EARLY HISTORY OF HUNTSVILLE, ALABAMA, 1804 TO 1870, Montgomery: The Brown Printing Company, 1916.

C-558 Bill, Alfred Hoyt, THE BELEAGUERED CITY: RICHMOND, 1861-1865, New York: Alfred A. Knopf, 1946.

C-559 Birmingham Centennial Corporation, PORTRAIT OF BIRMINGHAM, ALABAMA, Birmingham, 1971.

C-560 BIRMINGHAM HERITAGE HIKE GUIDE, Birmingham: Birmingham Historical Society, 1979.

C-561 Blackman, E. V., MIAMI AND DADE COUNTY, FLORIDA: ITS SETTLEMENT, PROGRESS AND ACHIEVEMENT, Washington, DC: V. Raenbolt, 1921.

C-562 Blankenstein, Mark E. and Chester Phillips, ROTARY IN BATON ROUGE, OVER SIXTY YEARS OF SERVICE, 1918-1980, Baton Rouge: Moran Ind., 1980.

C-563 Bloodworth, Bertha E. and Alton C. Morris, PLACES IN THE SUN: THE HISTORY AND ROMANCE OF FLORIDA PLACE NAMES, Gainesville: The University Presses of Florida, 1978.

C-564 Blossom, Virgil T., IT HAS HAPPENED HERE, New York: Harper, 1959.

C-565 Blue, Matthew P., HISTORY OF MONTGOMERY, Montgomery: Society of Pioneers, 1959. [repr. 1878 ed.]

C-566 Blum, Ethel, MIAMI ALIVE, New York: Alive Publications, 1981.

C-567 Blythe, LeGette, et al., CHARLOTTE AND MECKLENBURG COUNTY, NORTH CAROLINA TODAY, Charlotte, NC: Crabtree Press, 1967.

C-568 Blythe, LeGette and Charles R. Brockman, HORNET'S NEST: THE STORY OF CHARLOTTE AND MECKLENBURG CONTY, Charlotte: McNally of Charlotte, 1961.

C-569 Boagni, Ethel Hass, MADISONVILLE LOUISIANA, Hammond, LA: Carr Printing, Inc., 1980.

C-570 Boley, Henry, LEXINGTON IN OLD VIRGINIA, Richmond: Garrett and Massie, 1936.

C-571 Bondurant, Agnes M., POE'S RICHMOND, Richmond: Garrett and Massie, Inc., 1942.

C-572 Bonner, James C., MILLEDGEVILLE, GEORGIA'S ANTEBELLUM CAPITAL, Athens: University of Georgia Press, 1978.

C-573 Booth, Pat, PALM BEACH, New York: Ballentine Books, 1986.

C-574 Boyd, William Kenneth, THE STORY OF DURHAM: CITY OF THE NEW SOUTH, Durham: Duke University Press, 1925.

C-575 Boylston, Elise Reid, ATLANTA: ITS LORE, LEGENDS, AND LAUGHTER, Doraville, GA: Foote and Davies, 1968.

C-576 Brantley, William H., THREE CAPITALS: A BOOK ABOUT THE FIRST THREE CAPITALS OF ALABAMA, ST. STEPHENS, HUNTSVILLE, AND CABAWA, Boston: Merrymount Press, 1947.

C-577 Bridenbaugh, Carl, JAMESTOWN, 1544-1699, New York: Oxford University Press, 1980.

C-578 BRIDGEPORT, ALABAMA: 1890-1900, Chattanooga: The Brodt Printing Company, 1900.

C-579 Bridges, George C., MEMPHIS IN PICTURES: WELCOMING YOU TO MEMPHIS AND THE NEW SOUTH [3 p.], Memphis: S. C. Loof, 1940.

C-580 Bridwell, Ronald E., ". . . THAT WE SHOULD HAVE A PORT . . .": A HISTORY OF THE PORT OF GEORGETOWN, SOUTH CAROLINA, 1732-1865, Georgetown: The Georgetown Times, 1982.

C-581 Brindley, Mabel, A HISTORY OF COLLINSVILLE, ALABAMA, Collinsville: Study Club of Collinsville, 1970.

C-582 Brown, Alexander Crosby, ed., NEWPORT NEWS' 325 YEARS, Newport News, VA: The Newport News Golden Anniversary Corporation, 1946.

C-583 Brown, Charles, A BRIEF BIOGRAPHY OF PHILLIP A. HOLLAND: LOCAL BLACK HISTORIAN, Birmingham: Forniss Printing Company, 1977.

C-584 Brown, Douglas Summers, A CITY WITHOUT COBWEBS: A HISTORY OF ROCK HILL, SOUTH CAROLINA, Columbia: University of South Carolina Press, 1953.

C-585 Brown, James E., GOT A CRAYON? COLORING CHARLESTON, Charleston: Walker, Evans & Cogswell Company, 1975.

C-586 Brown, Kent R., FAYETTEVILLE [ARK.]: A PICTORIAL HISTORY, Norfolk: Donning Company, 1982.

C-587 Browne, Gary Lawson, BALTIMORE IN THE NATION, 1789-1861, Chapel Hill: University of North Carolina Press, 1980.

C-588 Browne, Jefferson B., KEY WEST: THE OLD AND THE NEW, St. Augustine, 1912; facsimile ed., Gainesville, 1973.

C-589 Brownell, Blaine A. and David R. Goldfield, eds., THE CITY IN SOUTHERN HISTORY, Port Washington, NY: National University Publications, 1977.

C-590 Brownlee, Fambrough L., WINSTON-SALEM: A PICTORIAL HISTORY, Norfolk: Donning Company, 1977.

C-591 Bruce, Carolyn Hale, ROANOKE: A PICTORIAL HISTORY, Norfolk: Donning Company, 1976.

C-592 Bruton, Quintilla Geer and David E. Bailey, Jr., PLANT CITY: ITS ORIGINS AND HISTORY, St. Petersburg, FL: Valkyrie Press, 1977.

C-593 Buchanan, James E., ed., HOUSTON: A CHRONOLOGICAL AND DOCUMENTARY HISTORY, 1519-1970, Dobbs Ferry, NY: Oceana Publications, 1975.

C-594 Buchanan, James E., ed., MIAMI: A CHROMOLOGICAL AND DOCUMENTARY HISTORY, 1513-1977, Dobbs Ferry, NY: Oceana Publications, 1978.

C-595 Buker, George E., SUN, SAND AND WATER: A HISTORY OF THE JACKSONVILLE DISTRICT, U. S. ARMY CORPS OF ENGINEERS, 1821-1975, Atlanta: Government Printing Office, 1981.

C-596 Burdett, Harold N., YESTERYEAR IN ANNAPOLIS, Cambridge, MD: Tidewater Publishers, 1974.

C-597 Burkhardt, Ann M., TOWN WITHIN A CITY: A HISTORY OF FIVE POINTS SOUTH NEIGHBORHOOD, Birmingham: Birmingham Historical Society, 1982.

C-598 Burt, Jesse C., NASHVILLE: ITS LIFE AND TIMES, Nashville: Tennessee Book Company, 1959.

C-599 Burton, E. Milby, SEIGE OF CHARLESTON, 1861-1865, Columbia: University of South Carolina Press, 1970.

C-600 Bushnell, David I., THE FIVE MONACAN TOWNS IN VIRGINIA, 1607, Washington, DC: Government Printing Office, 1890.

C-601 Butler, William J., FORT SMITH PAST AND PRESENT; A HISTORICAL SUMMARY, Little Rock: International Graphics, 1972.

C-602 Byrd, Sam, SMALL TOWN SOUTH, Boston: Houghton Mifflen Company, 1942.

C-603 Cable, Mary, LOST NEW ORLEANS, Boston: Houghton Mifflin Company, 1980.

C-604 Caldwell, Bettie D., ed., FOUNDERS AND BUILDERS OF GREENSBORO, 1808-1908, Greensboro, NC: J. J. Stone, 1925.

C-605 Call, Cora Pinkley, EUREKA SPRINGS, STAIR-STEP-DOWN: A BACKGROUND HISTORY OF THE FAMOUS NORTHWEST ARKANSAS TOWN THAT CLIMBS THE HILLS, Eureka Springs, AK: Echo Press, 1952.

C-606 Callahan, Helen, AUGUSTA: A PICTORIAL HISTORY, Norfolk, VA: The Donning Company/Publishers, 1980.

C-607 Calvert, Jesse, HISTORY OF JONESVILLE, [n.p. 1971].

C-608 Cameron, William E., PETERSBURG, THE COCADE CITY, 1894.

C-609 Campbell, Davis W., LEST WE FORGET, privately printed, 1952.

C-610 Campbell, William Simeon, ONE HUNDRED YEARS OF FAYETTEVILLE, 1828–1928, Jefferson City, MO: c. 1928.

C-611 Capers, Gerald M., THE BIOGRAPHY OF A RIVER TOWN: MEMPHIS, ITS HEROIC AGE, Chapel Hill: University of North Carolinna Press, 1939.

C-612 Capers, Gerald M., OCCUPIED CITY: NEW ORLEANS UNDER THE FEDERALS, 1862–1865, Lexington: University of Kentucky Press, 1965.

C-613 Carmer, Carl, FRENCH TOWN, New Orleans: Pelican Publishing House, 1968.

C-614 Carmichael, Virginia, THIS IS FREDERICKSBURG, Richmond, VA: The Deitz Press, Inc., 1957.

C-615 Carpenter, Bonnie, OLD MOUNTAIN CITY, San Antonio: Naylor Company, 1970.

C-616 Carter, Hodding, WHERE MAIN STREET MEETS THE RIVER, New York: Rinehart & Company, Inc., 1952–1953.

C-617 Carter, Hodding, ed., THE PAST AS PRELUDE: NEW ORLEANS 1718–1968, New Orleans: Pelican Publishing House, 1968.

C-618 Carter, Samuel III, BLAZE OF GLORY: THE FIGHT FOR NEW ORLEANS, 1814–1815, New York: St. Martin's Press, 1971.

C-619 Carter, Samuel III, THE SEIGE OF ATLANTA, 1864, New York: St. Martin's Press, 1973.

C-620 Cashin, Edward J., AUGUSTA AND THE AMERICAN REVOLUTION, Darien, GA: Richmond County Historical Society, 1975.

C-621 Cashin, Edward J., ed., COLONIAL AUGUSTA: KEY OF THE INDIAN COUNTRY, Macon, GA: Mercer University Press, 1986.

C-622 Casseday, Ben, THE HISTORY OF LOUISVILLE FROM ITS EARLIEST SETTLEMENT TILL THE YEAR 1852, Louisville: Hull and Brothers, 1852.

C-623 Castellanos, Henry C., NEW ORLEANS AS IT WAS, Baton Rouge: Louisiana STate University Press, 1979.

C-624 Caveda, F. F., LIBBY LIFE: EXPERIENCES OF A PRISONER OF WAR IN RICHMOND, VIRGINIA, 1863–64, Washington: University Press of America, 1985 (reprint, 1865).

C-625 THE CENTENNIAL ALBUM, Books I and II, Alexandria, LA: McCormic and Company, Inc., 1983.

C-626 Chamber of Commerce of the New Orleans Area, NEW ORLEANS: FACTS ABOUT THE CITY, New Orleans: The Chamber, 1931.

C-627 Chamberlain, Hope Summerell, OLD DAYS IN CHAPEL HILL. BEING THE LIFE AND LETTERS OF CORNELIA PHILLIPS SPENCER, Chapel Hill: The University of North Carolina Press, 1926.

C-628 Chandler, Julian A. C. et al., eds., THE SOUTH IN THE BUILDING OF
THE NATION, Richmond, VA: The Southern Historical Publication
Society, 1909.

C-629 Chapman, Berlin Basil, THE FOUNDING OF STILLWATER: A CASE STUDY IN
OKLAHOMA HISTORY, Stillwater: Oklahoma Agricultural and Mechanical
College, 1948.

C-630 Charleston, SC Civic Services Committee, CHARLESTON GROWS; AN ECO-
NOMIC, SOCIAL AND CULTURAL PORTRAIT OF AN OLD COMMUNITY IN THE NEW
SOUTH, Charleston: Carolina Art Association, 1949.

C-631 CHARLESTON: SOUTH CAROLINA, Charleston: Carolina Art Association,
1963.

C-632 Chesney, Allen, ed., CHATTANOOGA ALBUM: THIRTY-TWO HISTORIC POST-
CARDS, Knoxville: The University of Tennessee Press, 1983.

C-633 Chesson, Michael B., RICHMOND AFTER THE WAR, 1865-1890, Richmond:
Virginia State Library, 1981.

C-634 Christian, W. Asbury, RICHMOND: HER PAST AND PRESENT, Richmond,
VA: L. H. Jenkins, 1912.

C-635 The City of Raleigh, HISTORICAL SKETCHES FROM ITS FOUNDAITON,
Raleigh: Edwards and Broughton, 1887.

C-636 THE CIVIL WAR AT CHARLESTON, Charleston: Post-Courier, 1966.

C-637 Claiborne, Jack, JACK CLAIBORNE'S CHARLOTTE, Charlotte: Charlotte
Pub., 1974.

C-638 Clark, Thomas D., ed., SOUTH CAROLINA: THE GRAND TOUR, 1780-1865,
Columbia: University of South Carolina Press, 1973.

C-639 Clarke, Edward Young, ILLUSTRATED HISTORY OF ATLANTA, Atlanta:
J. P. Harrison, 1877.

C-640 Claxon, Erie, MEMPHIS MEMORIES, Memphis: Claxton, 1977.

C-641 Clay, Grady, ALLEYS: A HIDDEN RESOURCE, Louisville: Grady Clay
and Company, 1978.

C-642 Clay, James W., ed (with D. M. Orr), METROLINA ATLAS, Chapel Hill:
University of North Carolina Press, 1972.

C-643 Clayton, James D., ANTEBELLUM NATCHEZ, Baton Rouge: Louisiana
State University Press, 1968.

C-644 Clem, Gladys Bauserman, IT HAPPENED AROUND STAUNTON IN VIRGINIA,
Staunton: McClure Printing Company, 1964.

C-645 Clift, G. Glenn, HISTORY OF MAYSVILLE AND MASON COUNTY [KENTUCKY],
Lexington: Transylvania Printing Company, 1936.

C-646 Clinton, Matthew William, TUSCALOOSA, ALABAMA: ITS EARLY DAYS,
1816-1865, Tuscaloosa: The Zonta Club, 1958.

C-647 Cobbs, Aleathea and Annie S. Howard, AROUND THE YEAR IN MOBILE
[1702-1914], Mobile: Cobbs, Howard & Watkins, 1923.

C-648 Cochran, Louis, HALLELUJAH, MISSISSIPPI, New York: Duell, Sloan
and Pearce, 1955.

C-649 Coker, William S. and Hazel P. Coker, THE SEIGE OF MOBILE, 1780,
Pensacola, FL: Perdido Bay Press, 1982.

C-650 Coleman, J. Winston Jr., THE SQUIRE'S SKETCHES OF LEXINGTON,
Lexington, KY: Henry Clay Press, 1972.

C-651 Coleman, James C. and Irene S. Coleman, GUARDIANS ON THE GULF: PENSACOLA FORTIFICATIONS, 1698-1980, Pensacola: Pensacola Historical Society, 1982.

C-652 Coleman, James J. Jr., ANTOINE DE ST. MAXENT: THE SPANISH-FRENCHMAN OF NEW ORLEANS, New Orleans: Pelican Publishing House, 1968.

C-653 Coleman, Kenneth, ed., ATHENS, 1861-1865: AS SEEN THROUGH LETTERS IN THE UNIVERSITY OF GEORGIA LIBRARIES, Athens, GA: University of Georgia Press, 1969.

C-654 Coleman, Kenneth, CONFEDERATE ATHENS, Athens: University of Georgia Press, 1967.

C-655 Coleman, William Head, HISTORICAL SKETCH BOOK AND GUIDE TO NEW ORLEANS AND ENVIRONS, New York: W. H. Coleman, 1885.

C-656 Colourpicture Publishing Company, NEW ORLEANS, [s.l.]: Colourpicture Publishing Company, 1981.

C-657 The Commercial Appeal, Memphis, CENTENNIAL EDITION, JAN. 1, 1940, Memphis: 1940.

C-658 Connelly, John Lawrence, NORTH NASHVILLE AND GERMANTOWN: YESTERDAY AND TODAY, Nashville: North High Association, nd (c. 1983-84).

C-659 Conrad, Glenn R. comp, NEW IBERIA: ESSAYS ON THE TOWN AND ITS PEOPLE, Lafayette, LA: Center for Louisiana Studies, 1979.

C-660 Cook, Bruce, THE HISTORY OF McRAE, ARKANSAS, Searcy, AK: Harding University Press, 1981.

C-661 Cook, D. Louise, GUIDE TO THE MANUSCRIPT COLLECTIONS OF THE ATLANTA HISTORICAL SOCIETY, Atlanta: The Society, 1976.

C-662 Cooper, Walter Gerald, OFFICIAL HISTORY OF FULTON COUNTY, Atlanta: Walter W. Brown Publishing Company, 1934.

C-663 Copeland, Catherine, BRAVEST SURRENDER: A PETERSBURG PATCHWORK, Richmond, VA: The Press of Whitlet & Shepperson, 1961.

C-664 Coppinger, Margaret Brown, Herschel Gower, Samuel B. Howell, and Georgianna D. Overby, eds., BEERSHEBA SPRINGS: 150 YEARS, 1833-1983, A HISTORY AND A CELEBRATION, Beersheba Springs, TN: Beersheba Springs Historical Society, 1983.

C-665 Coppock, Paul R., MEMPHIS MEMOIRS, Memphis: Memphis State University Press, 1980.

C-666 Coppock, Paul R., MEMPHIS SKETCHES, Memphis: Friends of Memphis and Shelby County Libraries, 1976.

C-667 Corley, Florence Flemming, CONFEDERATE CITY, AUGUSTA, GEORGIA, 1860-1865, Columbia, SC: University of South Carolina Press, 1960.

C-668 Coulter, E. Merton, OLD PETERSBURG AND THE BROAD RIVER VALLEY OF GEORGIA: THEIR RISE AND DECLINE, Athens: University of Georgia Press, 1965.

C-669 Coulter, E. Merton, THE SOUTH DURING RECONSTRUCTION, Batron Rouge: Louisiana State University Press, 1947.

C-670 Cowan, Walter G., John C. Chase, Charles L. Dufour, O. K. LeBlanc, and John Wilds, NEW ORLEANS, YESTERDAY AND TODAY: A GUIDE TO THE CITY, Baton Rouge: Louisiana State University Press, 1983.

C-671 Cowett, Mark, BIRMINGHAM'S RABBI: MORRIS NEWFIELD AND ALABAMA, 1895-1940, University, AL: University of Alabama Press, 1986.

C-672 Cox, Christopher, A KEY WEST COMPANION, New York: St. Martin's Press, 1983.

C-673 Cox, Jacob Dolson, ATLANTA, New York: C. Scribner's Sons, 1903.

C-674 Crabb, Alfred Leland, JOURNEY TO NASHVILLE: A STORY OF THE FOUND- ING, New York: Bobbs-Merrill company, Inc., 1957.

C-675 Crabb, Alfred Leland, NASHVILLE, THE PERSONALITY OF A CITY, Indianapolis: The Bobbs-Merrill Company, Inc., 1960.

C-676 Cram, Mildred, OLD SEAPORT TOWNS OF THE SOUTH, New York: Dodd, Mead, 1917.

C-677 Craven, Wesley Frank, THE SOUTHERN COLONIES IN THE 17TH CENTURY, 1607-1689, Baton Rouge: Louisiana State University Press.

C-678 Crawford, Charles W. ed., MEMPHIS MEMORIES: THIRTY-TWO HISTORIC POSTCARDS, Knoxville: The University of Tennessee Press, 1983.

C-679 Crawford, Charles W., YESTERDAY'S MEMPHIS, Miami: Seemann Publishing Company, 1976.

C-680 Creekmore, Betsey B., KNOXVILLE, Knoxville: University of Tennes- see Press, 1958.

C-681 Crockett, Norman L., THE BLACK TOWNS, Lawrence, KS: Regents Press of Kansas, 1979.

C-682 Crown, John A., THIS IS ATLANTA, Atlanta: Atlanta Board of Real- tors, 1973.

C-683 Cruikshank, George M., A HISTORY OF BIRMINGHAM AND ITS ENVIRONS, Chicago: Lewis Publishing Company, 1920.

C-684 Currie, James T., ENCLAVE: VICKSBURG AND HER PLANTATIONS, 1863- 1870, Jackson: University Press of Mississippi, 1980.

C-685 Current, Richard N., NORTHERNIZING THE SOUTH, Athens: University of Georgia Press, 1983.

C-686 Cumming, Mary Gardner (Smith), TWO CENTURIES OF AUGUSTA: A SKETCH, Augusta: Ridgely-Tidwell-Ashe, 1926.

C-687 Cunningham, Cornelia, ATLANTA, CITY OF TODAY; A SKETCHBOOK, Atlanta: Darby, 1933.

C-688 Cunningham, Robert E., STILLWATER, WHERE OKLAHOMA BEGAN, Still- water: Arts and Humanities Council of Stillwater, Oklahoma, 1969.

C-689 Cunningham, Robert E., STILLWATER THROUGH THE YEARS, Stillwater: Arts and Humanities Council of Stillwater, Oklahoma, 1974.

C-690 Dabney, Virginius, RICHMOND: THE STORY OF A CITY, Garden City: Doubleday and Company, 1976.

C-691 Dall, Caroline Wells, BARBARA FRITCHIE. A STUDY, Boston: Roberts Brothers, 1892.

C-692 Dalton, Lawrence, HISTORY OF TOWNS AND COMMUNITIES IN RANDOLF COUNTY, ARKANSAS, Pocahontas: Pocahontas Federal Savings and Loan Association, [1963].

C-693 Darter, Oscar H., COLONIAL FREDERICKSBURG AND NEIGHBORHOOD IN PERSPECTIVE, New York: Twayne, 1957.

C-694 Dashiell, Segar Cofer, SMITHFIELD: A PICTORIAL HISTORY, Norfolk: Donning Company/Publishers.

C-695 Datnow, Claire-Louise, DOWNTOWN--AN OUTDOOR CLASSROOM, Birmingham: Birmingham Historical Society, 1981.

C-696 Davidson, William F., DUNEDIN THRU THE YEARS, 1850-1978, Charlotte, NC: Delmar Printing Company, 1978.

C-697 Davis, Arthur Kyle, THREE CENTURIES OF AN OLD VIRGINIA TOWN: THE STORY OF PETERSBURG, ITS HISTORY AND MEMORIALS, Richmond, VA: W. C. Hill, Printers, 1923.

C-698 Davis, Arthur Kyle, ed., VIRGINIA COMMUNITIES IN WAR TIME, Virginia: War History Commission Publications, 1926-27.

C-699 Davis, Burke, GETTING TO KNOW JAMESTOWN, New York: Coward, McCann and Geoghegan, 1971.

C-700 Davis, Burke, A WILLIAMSBURG GALAXY, New York: Holt, Rinehart and Winston, 1968.

C-701 Davis, J. E., JAMESTOWN AND HER NEIGHBORS ON VIRGINIA'S HISTORIC PENINSULA, Richmond, VA: Garrett & Massie, Inc., 1928.

C-702 Davis, James D., HISTORY OF MEMPHIS, Memphis: Hite, Crumpton and Kelly, 1873.

C-703 Davis, James D., THE HISTORY OF THE CITY OF MEMPHIS, ALSO THE "OLD TIMES PAPERS," Memphis: West Tennessee Historical Society reprint, 1972.

C-704 Davis, John L., HOUSTON: A HISTORICAL PORTRAIT, Austin: Encino Press, 1983.

C-705 Davis, Louise Littleton, NASHVILLE TALES, Gretna, LA: Pelican Publishing Company, 1981.

C-706 Davis, Thomas Frederick, HISTORY OF EARLY JACKSONVILLE, FLORIDA; BEING AN AUTHENTIC RECORD OF EVENTS FORM THE EARLIEST TIMES TO AND INCLUDING THE CIVIL WAR, Jacksonville: H. & W. B. Drew, 1911.

C-707 Davis, Thomas Frederick, HISTORY OF JACKSONVILLE, FLORIDA AND VICINITY, 1513 TO 1924, Jacksonville: Florida Historical Society, 1925.

C-708 Deadrick, Lucile, ed., HEART OF THE VALLEY: A HISTORY OF KNOXVILLE, TENNESSEE, Knoxville, TN: East Tennessee Historical Society, 1976.

C-709 Dean, Susie Kelly, ON ST. ANDREWS BAY, 1911-1917: A SEQUEL, Tampa: Sylvia Dean Harbert, 1969.

C-710 Dean, Susie Kelly, THE TAMPA OF MY CHILDHOOD, 1897-1907, Tampa: Sylvia Dean Harbert, 1966.

C-711 Debo, Angie, TULSA: FROM CREEK TOWN TO OIL CAPITAL, Norman: University of Oklahoma Press, 1943.

C-712 DeBolt, Margaret Wayt, SAVANNAH: A HISTORICAL PORTRAIT, Virginia Beach, VA: Donning Company, 1976.

C-713 deCoste, Frederik, TRUE TALES OF OLD ST. AUGUSTINE, St. Petersburg: Great Outdoors Publishing Company, 1966.

C-714 Degler, Carl N., PLACE OVER TIME: THE CONTINUITY OF SOUTHERN DISTINCTIVENESS, Baton Rouge: Louisiana State University Press, 1977.

C-715 DeGrummond, Jane Lucas, <u>RENATO BELUCHE, SMUGGLER, PRIVATEER, AND
PATRIOT, 1780-1860</u>, Baton Rouge: Louisiana State University Press,
1983.

C-716 Delaney, Caldwell, <u>CONFEDERATE MOBILE: A PICTORIAL HISTORY</u>,
Mobile: Haunted Book Shop, 1971.

C-717 Delaney, Caldwell, ed., <u>CRAIGHEAD'S MOBILE</u>, Mobile: Haunted Book
Shop, 1968.

C-718 Delaney, Caldwell, <u>A MOBILE SEXTET: PAPERS READ BEFORE THE ALABAMA
HISTORICAL ASSOCIATION, 1952-1971</u>, Mobile: The Haunted Book Shop,
1981.

C-719 Delaney, Caldwell, <u>MOBILE'S HAUNTED BOOK SHOP: A SENTIMENTAL
REMINISCENCE</u>, Mobile: The Haunted Bookshop, 1986.

C-720 Delaney, Caldwell, <u>THE PHOENIX VOLUNTEER FIRE COMPANY OF MOBILE,
1838-1880</u>, Mobile, AL: Museum Mobile, 1967.

C-721 Delaney, Caldwell, <u>REMEMBER MOBILE</u>, Mobile, AL: 1948.

C-722 Delaney, Caldwell, <u>THE STORY OF MOBILE</u>, Mobile: Gill Printing
Company, 1953.

C-723 Dellquest, Augustus Wilfried, <u>HISTORIC AUGUSTA, A BRIEF DESCRIPTION
OF THE MONUMENTS AND PLACES OF HISTORICAL INTEREST</u> . . ., Augusta:
A. W. Deelquest Book Company, 1917.

C-724 DeSpain, Richard and Ralph Megna, <u>MORE THAN A MEMORY: LITTLE
ROCK'S HISTORIC QUAPAW QUARTER</u>, Little Rock: Rose Publishing
Company, 1981.

C-725 DeVore, Harry L., <u>CITY OF THE MARDI GRAS</u>, New York: The Beech-
hurst Press, 1946.

C-726 Diettrich, Sigismond DeR., <u>MIAMI</u>, Garden City: Doubleday, 1960,
rev. ed. 1964.

C-727 Dinkins, J. Lester, <u>DUNNELLON--BOOMTOWN OF THE 1890'S; THE STORY OF
RAINBOW SPRINGS AND DUNNELLON</u>, St. Petersburg: Great Outdoors Publishing Company, 1969.

C-728 Dixon, Richard Remy, <u>OLD ALGIERS: A STORY OF ALGIERS, YESTERDAY
AND TODAY</u>, Algiers, LA: Algiers Annexation to New Orleans Centennial Committee, 1980.

C-729 Dodd, Donald B. and Wynell S. Dodd, <u>HISTORICAL STATISTICS OF THE
SOUTH, 1790-1970</u>, University, AL: University of Alabama Press,
1973.

C-730 Dombhart, John Martin, <u>HISTORY OF WALKER COUNTY [ALABAMA], ITS
TOWNS AND ITS PEOPLE</u>, Thornton, AK: Cayce Publishing Company,
1937.

C-731 Dorsey, John, <u>MOUNT VERNON PLACE: AN ANECDOTAL ESSAY WITH 66
ILLUSTRATIONS</u>, Baltimore: Maclay & Associates, 1983.

C-732 Douglas, W. Lovett, <u>HISTORY OF DUNEDIN</u>, St. Petersburg: Great
Outdoors Publishing Company, 1965.

C-733 Dowdey, Clifford, <u>EXPERIMENT IN REBELLION</u>, Garden City: Doubleday,
1946.

C-734 Downs, Fane and Roy Flukinger, <u>ABILENE: AN AMERICAN CENTENNIEL</u>,
Austin: University of Texas Press, 1982.

C-735 Doyle, Don H., NASHVILLE IN THE NEW SOUTH, 1880-1930, Knoxville: University of Tennessee Press, 1985.

C-736 Dozier, Linda, THE ATLANTA COLOR BOOK, Atlanta: Happy Times Corp., 1975.

C-737 DuBose, John Witherspoon, JEFFERSON COUNTY AND BIRMINGHAM, ALABAMA: HISTORICAL AND BIOGRAPHICAL, 1887, Easley, SC: Southern Historical Press, 1976.

C-738 Dufore, Charles L., THE NIGHT THE WAR WAS LOST, Garden City, NJ: Doubleday and Company, Inc., 1960.

C-739 Duke, Maurice and Daniel P. Jordan, A RICHMOND READER, 1733-1983, Chapel Hill: University of North Carolina Press, 1983.

C-740 Dunn, Hampton, TAMPA: A PICTORIAL HISTORY, Norfolk, VA: Donning Company, 1985.

C-741 Dunn, Hampton, YESTERDAY'S CLEARWATER, Miami: E. A. Seemann Publishing, Inc., 1973.

C-742 Dunn, Hampton, YESTERDAY'S LAKELAND, Lakeland, FL: City of Lakeland, 1976.

C-743 Dunn, Hampton, YESTERDAY'S ST. PETERSBURG, Miami: E. A. Seemann Publishing, Inc., 1973.

C-744 Dunn, Hampton, YESTERDAY'S TALLAHASSEE, Miami: E. A. Seeman Publishing Company, 1974.

C-745 Dunn, Hampton, YESTERDAY'S TAMPA, Miami: E. A. Seeman Publishing, Inc., 1972.

C-746 Durden, Robert Franklin, THE DUKES OF DURHAM, 1865-1929, Durham: Duke University Press, 1975.

C-747 Durrett, Reuben T., THE CENTENARY OF LOUISVILLE, Louisville: John P. Morton and Company, 1893. Filson Club Publications No. 8.

C-748 Earle, Carville V., THE EVOLUTION OF A TIDEWATER SETTLEMENT SYSTEM: ALL HALLOWS PARISH, MARYLAND, 1650-1783, Research Paper No. 170, Chicago: Department of Geography, University of Chicago, 1975.

C-749 Eaton, Clement, THE GROWTH OF SOUTHERN CIVILIZATION, 1790-1860, New York: Harper & Row, 1961.

C-750 Eaves, Charles Dudley and C. A. Hutchinson, POST CITY, TEXAS, Austin: Texas State Historical Association, 1952.

C-751 Ebaugh, Laura Smith, BRIDGING THE GAP; A GUIDE TO EARLY GREENVILLE, SOUTH CAROLINA, Greenville, SC: Greenville County Events, SC Tricentennial, 1970.

C-752 Eckenrode, H. J., ed., RICHMOND: CAPITAL OF VIRGINIA, Richmond: Whittet & Shepperson, 1938.

C-753 Edwards, Jim, THE VANISHED SPLENDOR II: A POSTCARD ALBUM OF OKLAHOMA CITY, Oklahoma City: Abalache Book Shop, 1983.I

C-754 Edwards, Jim, THE VANISHED SPLENDOR III: POSTCARD MEMORIALS OF OKLAHOMA CITY, Oklahoma City: Abalache Bookshop, 1985.

C-755 Edwards, Jim and Hal Ottaway, THE VANISHED SPLENDOR, Oklahoma City: Abalache Book Shop Publishing Company, 1982.

C-756 Elias, George S., HERITAGE AND HORIZONS, [s.l.]: John B. Roberts Company, 1961.

C-757 Eller, Ernest McNeill, "THE HOUSES OF PEACE," BEING A HISTORICAL, LEGENDARY, AND CONTEMPORARY ACCOUNT OF THE MORAVIANS AND THEIR SETTLEMENT OF SALEM IN NORTH CAROLINA, New York: Fleming H. Revell, 1937.

C-758 Ellison, Rhoda Coleman, HISTORY AND BIBLIOGRAPHY OF ALABAMA NEWS-PAPERS IN THE NINETEENTH CENTURY, University, AL: University of Alabama Press, 1954.

C-759 Ellsworth, Lucius and Linda Ellsworth, PENSACOLA, THE DEEP WATER CITY, Tulsa: Continental Heritage Press, 1982.

C-760 ELYTON-WEST END: BIRMINGHAM'S FIRST NEIGHBORHOOD, Birmingham: Birmingfind, [19--].

C-761 Egerton, John, NASHVILLE: THE FACES OF TWO CENTURIES, 1780-1980, Nashville: PlusMedia, 1979.

C-762 Egloff, Fred R., EL PASO LAWMAN G. W. CAMPBELL, College Station, TX: Creative Publishing Company, 1982.

C-763 Embrey, Alvin T., HISTORY OF FREDERICKSBURG, VIRGINIA, Richmond: Old Dominion Press, 1937.

C-764 Engelbrecht, Jacob, THE DIARY OF JACOB ENGELBRECHT, 1818-1878, Frederick, MD: Historical Society of Frederick County, 1976.

C-765 Evans, Oliver Wendell, NEW ORLEANS, New York: Macmillan, 1959.

C-766 Fairbanks, George R., THE HISTORY AND ANTIQUITIES OF THE CITY OF ST. AUGUSTINE, FLORIDA, Gainesville: The University Presses of Florida, 1975.

C-767 Fairey, Jack, THE QUIZZICAL QUEST OF ATLANTA, Atlanta: T. A. Wilson, 1945.

C-768 Fancher, Betsy, SAVANNAH: A RENAISSANCE OF THE HEART, Garden City, NY: Doubleday Company, Inc., 1976.

C-769 Federal Writers' Project, HOUSTON: A HISTORY AND GUIDE, St. Clair Shores, MI: Scholarly Press, 1977, c1942.

C-770 Federal Writers' Project, NEW ORLEANS, Boston: Houghton Mifflin, 1938.

C-771 Federal Writers' Project, SEEING ST. AUGUSTINE, St. Augustine: The Record Company, 1937.

C-772 Federal Writers' Project, Georgia, AUGUSTA, Augusta: Tidwell Print, Supply Company, 1938.

C-773 Federal Writers' Program, Georgia, SAVANNAH, Savannah: Review Printing Company, 1937.

C-774 Felder, Paula S., FORGOTTEN COMPANIONS: THE FIRST SETTLERS OF SPOTSYLVANIA COUNTY AND FREDERICKSBURG TOWN . . ., Fredericksburg, VA: Historic Publications of Fredericksburg, 1982.

C-775 Fields, Mamie Gavin with Karen Fields, LEMON SWAMP AND OTHER PLACES: A CAROLINA MEMOIR, New York: The Free Press, 1983.

C-776 Fink, Paul M., JONESBORO, THE FIRST CENTURY OF TENNESSEE'S FIRST TOWN, Johnson City: Tennessee State Planning Commission, 1972.

C-777 First White House Association, THE FIRST WHITE HOUSE OF THE CON-FEDERACY, MONTGOMERY, ALABAMA, Montgomery, 1958 [1930].

C-778 Fitzgerald, Ruth Coder, A DIFFERENT STORY: A BLACK HISTORY OF
FREDERICKSBURG, STAFFORD, AND SPOTSYLVANIA, VIRGINIA, Greensboro,
NC: Unicorn, 1979.

C-779 Fleming, Berry (compiler), AUTOBIOGRAPHY OF A CITY IN ARMS:
AUGUSTA, GEORGIA, 1861-1865, Augusta: Richmond County Historical
Society, 1976.

C-780 Fleming, Berry, (compiler), AUTOBIOGRAPHY OF A COLONY: THE FIRST
HALF-CENTURY OF AUGUSTA, GEORGIA, Athens: University of Georgia
Press, 1957.

C-781 Fleming, Vivian Minor, BATTLES OF FREDERICKSBURG AND CHANCELLORS-
VILLE, VIRGINIA, Richmond: W. C. Hill Printing company, 1921.

C-782 Flemming, Vivian Minor, HISTORICAL PERIODS OF FREDERICKSBURG, 1608-
1861, Fredericksburg, VA: Fredericksburg Library Association, 1921.

C-783 Forman, Henry C., JAMESTOWN AND ST. MARY'S: BURIED CITIES OF
ROMANCE, Baltimore: Johns Hopkins Press, 1938.

C-784 Forman, L. Ronald, AUDUBON PARK: AN URBAN EDEN, Baton Rouge:
Friends of the Zoo, 1985.

C-785 Fornell, Earl Wesley, THE GALVESTON ERA: THE TEXAS CRESCENT ON THE
EVE OF SUCCESSION, Austin: University of Texas Press, 1961.

C-786 Foster, William Lovelace and Kenneth Trist Urquhart, eds.,
VICKSBURG: SOUTHERN CITY UNDER SIEGE, New Orleans: The Historic
New Orleans Collection, 1982.

C-787 Fountain, Clara G., DANVILLE: A PICTORIAL HISTORY, Virginia Beach,
VA: Donning Company, Publishers.

C-788 Foushee, Ola Maie, AVALON: A NORTH CAROLINA TOWN OF JOY AND
TRAGEDY, Chapel Hill: BOOKS, 1977.

C-789 Fraser, Charles, A CHARLESTON SKETCH BOOK, 1796-1806, Charleston:
Carolina Art Association [1941].

C-790 Fries, Adelade L., THE ROAD TO SALEM, Chapel Hill: The University
of North Carolina Press, 1944.

C-791 Fries, Adelade L. and others, FORSYTH: A COUNTY ON THE MARCH,
Chapel Hill: University of North Carolina Press, 1949.

C-792 Fripp, Gayle Hicks, GREENSBORO, A CHOSEN CENTER: AN ILLUSTRATED
HISTORY, Woodland Hills, CA: Windsor Publications, 1982.

C-793 Fuermann, George, THE FACE OF HOUSTON, Houston: Press of Premier,
1963.

C-794 Fuermann, George, HOUSTON: THE FEAST YEARS, AN ILLUSTRATED ESSAY,
Houston: Press of Premier, 1962.

C-795 Fuermann, George, HOUSTON: THE ONCE AND FUTURE CITY, Garden City,
NY: Doubleday and Company, 1971.

C-796 Foscue, Edwin J., GATLINBURG, GATEWAY TO THE GREAT SMOKIES, Dallas:
University Press in Dallas, 1946.

C-797 Gamel, Faye, ATLANTA IMAGES: A GUIDE TO THE PHOTOGRAPH COLLECTIONS
OF THE ATLANTA HISTORICAL SOCIETY, Atlanta: Atlanta Historical
Society, 1978.

C-798 Garrett, Franklin Miller, ATLANTA AND ENVIRONS, New York: Lewis
Historical Publishing Company, 1954.

C-799 Garrett, Franklin M., VIGNETTE HISTORY OF ATLANTA, Atlanta: Commerce Club, 1971.

C-800 Garrett, Franklin Miller, YESTERDAY'S ATLANTA, Miami: E. A. Seeman
Publisher, 1971.

C-801 Garvey, Joan B. and Mary Lou Winter, BEAUTIFUL CRESCENT: A HISTORY
OF NEW ORLEANS, New Orleans: Garmer Press, Inc., 1984.

C-802 Gates, Grace Hooten, GLIMPSES: EARLY ANNISTON, 1872-1884, Anniston, AL: 1970.

C-803 Gates, Grace Hooten, THE MODEL CITY OF THE NEW SOUTH: ANNISTON,
ALABAMA, Huntsville: Strode Publishers, 1978.

C-804 Genthe, Arnold, IMPRESSIONS OF OLD NEW ORLEANS; A BOOK OF PICTURES,
New York: G. H. Doran, 1926.

C-805 Georgia. University Institute for the Study of Georgia Problems,
SURVEY OF ATHENS AND CLARKE COUNTY, GEORGIA [4 vol.], Athens: The
University, 1944-45.

C-806 Gibbon, David and Ted Smart, eds., ATLANTA, A PICTURE BOOK TO
REMEMBER HER BY, New York: Crescent, 1979.

C-807 Giduz, Roland, WHO'S GONNA COVER 'EM UP? CHAPEL HILL UNCOVERED
SINCE--1950-1985: FEATURING A NEWSMAN'S NOTEPAD, Chapel Hill, NC:
Citizen Publishing, 1985.

C-808 Gillespie, LaRoux K., IRETON, OKLAHOMA: FORGOTTEN PIONEER TOWN,
Kansas City, MO: Family History and Genealogy, 1986.

C-809 Gleasner, Diana, CHARLOTTE: TOUCH OF GOLD, Charlotten, NC: East
Woods Press, 1983.

C-810 Gleason, David K., OVER NEW ORLEANS: AERIAL PHOTOGRAPHS, Baton
Rouge: Louisiana State University Press, 1983.

C-811 Godown, Marian Bailey and Alberta Colcord Rawchuck, YESTERDAY'S
FORT MYERS, Miami: E. A. Seemann Publishing, Inc., 1975.

C-812 Goerch, Carl, OCRACOKE, Raleigh, NC: Edwards and Broughton Company, 1956.

C-813 Golden, Virginia N., A HISTORY OF TALLASSEE FOR TALLASSEEANS, Tallassee: Tallassee Mills of Mount Vertnon-Woodberry Mills, 1949.

C-814 Goldfield, David R., COTTON FIELDS AND SKYSCRAPERS: SOUTHERN CITY
AND REGION, 1607-1980, Baton Rouge: Louisiana State University
Press, 1982.

C-815 Goodwin, Rutherford, A BRIEF AND TRUE REPORT FOR THE TRAVELER CON-
CERNING WILLIAMSBURG IN VIRGINIA, Richmond: Dietz Printing Company, 1935.

C-816 Goolrick, John T., FREDERICKSBURG AND THE CAVALIER COUNTRY, Richmond, VA: Garrett and Massie, 1935.

C-817 Goolrick, John T., HISTORIC FREDERICKSBURG, Richmond, VA: Whittet
and Shepperson, 1922.

C-818 Goolrick, William K., REBELS RESURGENT: FREDERICKSBURG TO CHANCEL-
LORSVILLE, Alexandria, VA: Time-Life Books, 1985.

C-819 Goodwin, Rutherford, WILLIAMSBURG IN VIRGINIA, Richmond: August
Dietz & Son, 1935.

C-820 Gott, John K., A HISTORY OF MARSHAL (FORMERLY SALEM) FAUQUIER
COUNTY, VIRGINIA, Middleburg, VA: Denlinger's, 1959.

C-821 Govan, Gilbert E. and James W. Livingood, THE CHATTANOOGA COUNTRY, 1540-1951: FROM TOMAHAWKS TO TVA, New York: E. P. Dutton & Company, Inc., 1952.

C-822 Graff, Mary G., MANDARIN ON THE ST. JOHNS, University of Florida Press, 1953.

C-823 Graghan, S. J., SAINT FERDENAND DE FLORISSANT: THE STORY OF AN ANCIENT PARISH, Chicago: Loyola University Press, 1923.

C-824 Graham, Leroy, BALTIMORE: THE NINETEENTH CENTURY BLACK CAPITAL, Washington, DC: University Press of America, 1982.

C-825 Graham, Thomas, THE AWAKENING OF ST. AUGUSTINE. THE ANDERSON FAMILY AND THE OLDEST CITY, 1821-1924., St. Augustine: St. Augustine Historical Society, 1978.

C-826 Graves, Lawrence L., ed., A HISTORY OF LUBBOCK, Lubbock, TX: West Texas Museum Association, 1962.

C-827 Green, A. C., DALLAS U.S.A., Austin, TX: Texas Monthly Press, 1984.

C-828 Green, Constance McLaughlin, WASHINGTON. VOLUME II. CAPITAL CITY, 1879-1950, Princeton, NJ: Princeton University Press, 1963.

C-829 Green, Constance McLaughlin, WASHINGTON: A HISTORY OF THE CAPITAL, 1800-1950 [2 vols], Princeton, NJ: Princeton University Press, 1962-63.

C-830 Green, Fletcher M. and J. Isaac Copeland, THE OLD SOUTH [a bibliography], Arlington Heights, IL: AHM Publishing Corporation, 1980.

C-831 Green, Margaret Sprout, LAKE MARY BEGINNINGS: AND THE ROARING TWENTIES IN LAKE MARY AND STANFORD, FLORIDA, Chuluota, FL: Mickler House, 1986.

C-832 Greene, A. C., DALLAS: THE DECIDING YEARS--A HISTORICAL PORTRAIT, Austin, TX: Encino Press, 1974.

C-833 Greer, Virginia, MOBILE: TALK ABOUT A TOWN!, Mobile, AL: Attic Salt Press, 1985.

C-834 Griffin, Thomas Kurtz, NEW ORLEANS: A GUIDE TO AMERICA'S MOST INTERESTING CITY, Garden City, NY: Doubleday, 1964.

C-835 Griffin, Thomas Kurtz, THE PELICAN GUIDE TO NEW ORLEANS: TOURING AMERICA'S MOST INTERESTING CITY, Gretna: Pelican Publishing Company, 1983.

C-836 Griffith, Helen, DAUNTLESS IN MISSISSIPPI: THE LIFE OF SARAH A. DICKEY, 1838-1904, Northampton, MA: Metcalf Publishing Company, 1965.

C-837 Griffin, William A., ANTE-BELLUM ELIZABETH CITY: THE HISTORY OF A CANAL TOWN, Elizabeth City: Roanoke Press, Inc., 1970.

C-838 Grismer, Karl H., THE STORY OF FORT MYERS, St. Petersburg: St. Petersburg Printing Company, 1949.

C-839 Grismer, Karl H., THE STORY OF SARASOTA, Sarasota: M. E. Russell, 1946.

C-840 Grismer, Karl H., TAMPA, A HISTORY OF THE CITY OF TAMPA AND THE TAMPA BAY REGION OF FLORIDA, St. Petersburg: St. Petersburg Publishing Company, 1950.

C-841 Groene, Bertram H., ANTE-BELLUM TALLAHASSEE, Tallahassee: Heritage Foundation, 1971.

C-842 A GUIDE TO MANUSCRIPT SOURCES IN THE SPECIAL COLLECTIONS DEPARTMENT FOR ATLANTA, GEORGIA, Atlanta: Emory University, 1978.

C-843 Gute, Fredericka Doel and Katherine Brash Jeter, HISTORICAL PROFILE --SHREVEPORT 1850, Shreveport, LA: Shreveport Committee of the National Society of the Colonial Dames in America in the State of Louisiana, 1982.

C-844 Haagen, Victor B., THE PICTORIAL HISTORY OF HUNTSVILLE, 1805-1865, Meriden, CN: Meriden Gravure Company, 1963.

C-845 Hagan, Jane Gray, THE STORY OF DANVILLE, New York: Stratford House, 1950.

C-846 Hairston, Lora Beatrice Wade, A BRIEF HISTORY OF DANVILLE, VIRGINIA, 1728-1954, Richmond, VA: The Dietz Press, Inc., 1955.

C-847 Hajos, Albin, HAJOS' ATHENS, GA. PHOTO-GRAVUERS, Brooklyn, NY: Albertyne Company, 1900.

C-848 Hall, Louise Fortune, A HISTORY OF DAMASCUS, VIRGINIA 1793-1950, Abingdon, VA: The John Anderson Press, 1950.

C-849 Hallam, George, RIVERSIDE REMEMBERED, Jacksonville, FL: Drummond Press, 1976.

C-850 Hamilton, Peter J., THE CHEVALIER D'IBERVILLE, SOME CONSIDERATIONS OF THE LIFE OF A GREAT PIONEER, Mobile: Historic Mobile Preservation Society, 1948.

C-851 Hamilton, Peter J., THE FOUNDING OF MOBILE, 1702-1718, STUDIES IN THE HISTORY OF THE FIRST CAPITAL OF THE PROVINCE OF LOUISIANA, WITH MAP SHOWING ITS RELATION TO THE PRESENT CITY, Mobile: Commercial Printing Company, 1911.

C-852 Hamilton, Peter J., A LITTLE BOY IN CONFEDERATE MOBILE, Mobile: Colonial Mobile Book Shop, 1947.

C-853 Hamilton, Peter J., MOBILE OF THE FIVE FLAGS . . ., Mobile: The Gill Printing Company, 1913.

C-854 Hamilton, Peter J., Charles G. Summersell, ed., COLONIAL MOBILE, University, AL: The University of Alabama Press, 1976 [1897].

C-855 Hammond, Nathaniel Job, WHY ATLANTA SHOULD BE THE SEAT OF GOVERNMENT, Atlanta, 1877?

C-856 HAND BOOK OF THE CITY OF ATLANTA, Atlanta: Southern Industrial Publishing Company, 1898.

C-857 Handy, Mary Olivia, HISTORY OF FORT SAM HOUSTON, San Antonio: Naylor Company, 1951.

C-858 Hannau, Hans W., NEW ORLEANS, Garden City, NY: Doubleday Company, Inc., 1968.

C-859 Harden, William, HISTORY OF SAVANNAH AND SOUTH GEORGIA, Chicago: Lewis Publishing Company, 1913.

C-860 Harden, William, RECOLLECTIONS OF A LONG AND SATISFYING LIFE, Savannah: Review Printing Company, 1934.

C-861 Hardy, John, SELMA: HER INSTITUTIONS AND HER MEN, Selma: Times Book and Job Office, 1879.

C-862 Harkins, John E., METROPOLIS ON THE AMERICAN NILE, AN ILLUSTRATED HISTORY OF MEMPHIS AND SHELBY COUNTY, Woodland Hills, CA: West Tennessee Historical Society and Windsor Publications, Inc., 1982.

C-863 Harney, Karen, ST. AUGUSTINE AND ST. JOHNS COUNTY, A PICTORIAL HISTORY, Virginia Beach, VA: Donning Company, 1979.

C-864 Harrell, Virginia Calohan, VICKSBURG AND THE RIVER, Jackson: University Press of Mississippi, 1982.

C-865 Harris, W. Stuart, ALABAMA PLACE NAMES, Huntsville, AL: The Strode Publlishers, 1982.

C-866 Harrison, Marion Clifford, HOME TO THE COCADE CITY; THE PARTIAL BIOGRAPHY OF A SOUTHERN TOWN, Richmond, VA: The House of Dietz, Publishers, 1942.

C-867 Harshaw, Lou, ASHEVILLE: PLACES OF DISCOVERY, Lakemont, GA: Copple House Books, 1980.

C-868 Harshaw, Lou, THE GOLD OF DAHLONEGA: THE FIRST MAJOR GOLD RUSH IN NORTH AMERICA, Asheville, NC: Hexagon Company, 1976.

C-869 Haselden, Willis J., MOORESVILLE, NORTH CAROLINA: THE EARLY YEARS, Mooresville: Chamber of Commerce, 1967.

C-870 Hassell, Joan, ed., MEMPHIS, 1800-1900 [3 vols], New York: Nancy Powers & Company, Publishers, Inc., 1982.

C-871 Hawkins, Van, HAMPTON/NEWPORT NEWS: A PICTORIAL HISTORY, Virginia Beach, VA: The Donning Company/Publishers, Inc., 1975.

C-872 Hayes, Charles R., THE DISPERSED CITY: THE CASE OF PIEDMONT, NORTH CAROLINA, Chicago: University of Chicago, Department of Geography Research Paper No. 173, 1976.

C-873 Hearin, Emily Staples, CANOPY OF OAKS, Mobile: Streetscapes, Inc., 1986.

C-874 Hearin, Emily Staples, DOWNTOWN GOES UPTOWN, Mobile: First Southern Federal Savings and Loan Association, 1983.

C-875 Heltzler, Michael J., ed. by Richard N. Cote, HISTORIC GOOSE CREEK, SOUTH CAROLINA, 1670-1980, Easley, SC: Southern Historical Press, 1983.

C-876 Hemperley, Marion R., CITIES, TOWNS AND COMMUNITIES OF GEORGIA BE-TWEEN 1847-1962: 8500 PLACES AND THE COUNTY IN WHICH LOCATED, Easley, SC: Southern Historical Press, 1980.

C-877 Henderson, P. F., A SHORT HISTORY OF AIKEN AND AIKEN COUNTY, Columbia, SC: R. L. Bryan Company, 1951.

C-878 Henley, John C. Jr., THIS IS BIRMINGHAM: THE STORY OF THE FOUNDING AND GROWTH OF AN AMERICAN CITY, Birmingham: Southern University Press, 1960.

C-879 Henrici, Holice H., SHREVEPORT SAGA, Shreveport, LA: Henrici, 1977.

C-880 Henrici, Holice H., SHREVEPORT, THE BEGINNINGS, Lafayette, LA: University of Southwest Louisiana Center for Louisiana Studies, 1986.

C-881 Hermann, Bernard, NEW ORLEANS, Baton Rouge: Louisiana State University Press, 1980.

C-882 Hermann, Janet Sharp, THE PURSUIT OF A DREAM, New York: Oxford University Press, 1981.

C-883 Higgenbotham, Jay, MOBILE, CITY BY THE BAY, Mobile: Azelea City Printers, [1968].

C-884 Higginbotham, Jay, OLD MOBILE: FORT LOUIS DE LA LOUISIANE, 1702-1711, Mobile: Museum of the City of Mobile, 1977.

C-885 Hildreth, Charles H. and Merlin G. Cox, HISTORY OF GAINESVILLE, FLORIDA, 1854-1979, Gainesville: Alachua County Historical Society, 1981.

C-886 Hinojosa, Gilberto Miguel, A BORDERLANDS TOWN IN TRANSITION: LAREDO, 1755-1870, College Station, TX: Texas A & M University Press, 1983.

C-887 HISTORIC CAMDEN, SOUTH CAROLINA, West Chester, PA: National Heritage Corporation, 1976.

C-888 HISTORY OF FREDERICA, Waycross, GA: Waycross Journal, 1913.

C-889 Hoehling, A. A. and Mary Hoehling, THE DAY RICHMOND DIED, San Diego: A. S. Barnes and Company, 1981.

C-890 Hoehling, Adolph A., LAST TRAIN FROM ATLANTA, New York: T. Yoseloff, 1958.

C-891 Hoehling, A. A., et al., eds., VICKSBURG: 47 DAYS OF SEIGE, Englewood cliffs, NJ: Prentice-Hall, 1969.

C-892 Hogan, William Ransom and Edwin Adams Davis, eds., WILLIAM JOHNSON'S NATCHEZ: THE ANTE-BELLUM DIARY OF A FREE NEGRO, Baton Rouge: Louisiana State University Press, 1951.

C-893 Hollifield, Mollie, AUBURN: LOVELIEST VILLAGE OF THE PLAIN, Auburn, AL: Bulletin Publishing Company, 1955.

C-894 Hollis, Daniel Webster, A BRIEF HISTORY OF COLUMBIA, Columbia, SC: 1968 [8p].

C-895 Hollis, Daniel Webster, SUMTER, SOUTH CAROLINA, Sumter, SC: s.n. 1976?

C-896 Hoobler, James A., CITIES UNDER THE GUN: IMAGES OF OCCUPIED NASHVILLE AND CHATTANOOGA, Nashville, TN: Rutledge Hill Press, 1986.

C-897 Hoobler, James A., ed., NASHVILLE MEMORIES: THIRTY-TWO HISTORIC POSTCARDS, Knoxville: The University of Tennessee Press, 1983.

C-898 Hoole, William Stanley, A CHECK-LIST AND FINDING-LIST OF CHARLESTON PERIODICALS, 1732-1864, Durham: Duke University Press, 1936.

C-899 Hoover, Edwin C., CITY GUIDE, GREATER NEW ORLEANS AREA, New Orleans: Echo Publications, 1982.

C-900 Horn, Stanley F., DECISIVE BATTLE OF NASHVILLE, Baton Rouge: Louisiana State University Press, 1956.

C-901 Hornady, John R., ATLANTA, YESTERDAY, TODAY AND TOMORROW, [n.p.] American Cities Book Company, 1922.

C-902 Hornaday, John Randolf, THE BOOK OF BIRMINGHAM, New York: Dodd, Mead and Company, 1921.

C-903 House, Robert B., THE LIGHT THAT SHINES: CHAPEL HILL 1912-1916, Chapel Hill: University of North Carolina Press, 1964.

C-904 Howard, James, BIG D IS FOR DALLAS: CHAPTERS IN THE TWENTIETH-CENTURY HISTORY OF DALLAS, Austin: University Co-operative Society, 1957.

C-905 Hoyt, James A., THE PHOENIX RIOT, NOVEMBER 8, 1898, Greenwood, SC: s.n. 1938?

C-906 Huber, Leonard V., NEW ORLEANS: A PICTORIAL HISTORY, New York: Crown Publishers, 1971.

C-907 Huff, Erma, UP HIGH AND DOWN MAIN IN PUGHTOWN, W. VA., N.W. Cumberland, WV: Hancock Courier Printing Company, 1981.

C-908 Hull, Augustus Longstreet, ANNALS OF ATHENS, GEORGIA, 1801-1901, Danielsville, GA: Heritage Papers, 1978.

C-909 Hull, Augustus Longstreet, SKETCHES OF ATHENS, GEORGIA FROM 1830 TO 1865, Athens: Woman's Work Printers, 1893.

C-910 Hume, Ivor Noel, MARTIN'S HUNDRED [Va], New York: Alfred A. Knopf, 1982.

C-911 Hutchins, Fred L., WHAT HAPPENED IN MEMPHIS, Kingsport: The Author, 1965.

C-912 Huttenhauer, Helen G., YOUNG SOUTHERN PINES, Southern Pines, NC: Morgan/Hubbars, 1980.

C-913 Hutton, Ralph B., updated by H. V. Longley, THE HISTORY OF ELKTON, Elkton, VA: Elkton Independence Bicentennial Commission, 1976.

C-914 Hynds, Ernest C., ANTEBELLUM ATHENS AND CLARKE COUNTY, GEORGIA, Athens: University of Georgia Press, 1974.

C-915 Ingate, Margaret Rose, HISTORY IN TOWNS: MOBILE, ALABAMA, Reprint from Antiques Magazine, 1964.

C-916 Isenhour, Judith C., KNOXVILLE: A PICTORIAL HISTORY, Norfolk, VA: Donning Company, 1978.

C-917 J-D Enterprises, ATLANTA: ATLAS AND FOLDING MAP, Atlanta, 1970.

C-918 Jackson, Eugene Beauharnais, THE ROMANCE OF HISTORIC ALEXANDRIA, A GUIDE TO THE OLD CITY, Atlanta: A. B. Caldwell Publishing Company, 1921.

C-919 Jackson, Luther T., PHOEBUS: A PICTORIAL HISTORY, Hampton, VA: by the author, 1976.

C-920 Jackson, Melinda H., PRIVATEERS IN CHARLESTON, 1793-1796, Smithsonian Studies in History and Technology, No. 1 (Washington): Smithsonian Institution Press, 1969.

C-921 Jackson, Page S., AN INFORMAL HISTORY OF ST. PETERSBURG, St. Petersburg: Great Outdoors Publishing Company, 1962.

C-922 Jackson, Walter Mahan, THE STORY OF SELMA, Decatur, AL: privately printed, 1954.

C-923 Jacksonville, Fla. Chamber of Commerce, JACKSONVILLE AND FLORIDA FACTS, Jacksonville: H. & W. B. Drew Company, 1906.

C-924 JACKSONVILLE: THE STORY OF A DYNAMIC COMMUNITY, 1872-1972, Jacksonville, TX: Jacksonville Centennial Corporation, 1972.

C-925 James, D. Clayton, ANTEBELLUM NATCHEZ, Baton Rouge: Louisiana State University Press, 1968.

C-926 Jamison, Chipp, ATLANTA: A CELEBRATION, Atlanta: Perry Communications, 1978.

C-927 Janvier, Carmalite, WHIMSICAL MADAM NEW ORLEANS, New Orleans: Robt. H. True Company, 1928.

C-928 Jenkins, James S., VIEWING GREENVILLE AND PITT COUNTY NEAR THE TURN OF THE CENTURY, Greenville, NC: The author, 1965.

C-929 Jenkins, William H. and John Knox, THE STORY OF DECATUR, ALABAMA, Decatur: Decatur Printing, 1970.

C-930 Jett, Dora Chinn, MINOR SKETCHES OF MAJOR FOLK AND WHERE THEY SLEEP; THE OLD MASONIC BURYING GROUND, FREDERICKSBURG, VIRGINIA, Richmond: Old Dominion Press, 1928.

C-931 Johnson, Charles W. and Charles O. Jackson, CITY BEHIND A FENCE OAK RIDGE, TENNESSEE, 1942-1946, Knoxville: University of Tennessee Press, 1981.

C-932 Johnson, Helen DuBois, A VIGNETTE OF MOBILE, 1775-1976, Mobile: [s.n.], 1976.

C-933 Johnston, J. S., ed., MEMORIAL HISTORY OF LOUISVILLE FROM ITS FIRST SETTLEMENT TO THE YEAR 1896, Chicago: American Biographical Publishing Company, 1896. (2 vol.?)

C-934 Jones, Charles Colcock, MEMORIAL HISTORY OF AUGUSTA, GEORGIA; FROM ITS SETTLEMENT IN 1735 TO THE CLOSE OF THE EIGHTEENTH CENTURY, Syracuse: D. Mason & Company, 1890.

C-935 Jones, Charles Colcock, SOME EARLY MEMORIES CONNECTED WITH AUGUSTA, Augusta: 1883.

C-936 Jones, D. Clayton, ANTEBELLUM NATCHEZ, Baton Rouge: Louisiana State University Press, 1968.

C-937 Jordan, Weymouth T., ANTE-BELLUM ALABAMA: TOWN AND COUNTRY, Tallahassee: The Florida State University, Florida State University Studies, No. 27, 1957.

C-938 Junior League of Augusta, Ga., AUGUSTA, YESTERDAY AND TODAY, Augusta, 1950.

C-939 Kane, Harnett T., THE GOLDEN COAST, Garden City, NY: Doubleday & Company, 1959.

C-940 Kane, Harnett T., QUEEN NEW ORLEANS: CITY BY THE RIVER, New York: William Morrow & Company, 1949.

C-941 Keith, Robert C., BALTIMORE HARBOR: A PICTURE HISTORY, Baltimore: Ocean World Publishing Company Inc., 1982.

C-942 Kell, Jean Bruyere, HISTORIC BEAUFORT, NORTH CAROLINA: A PICTORIAL PROFILE, Greenville: National Printing Company, 1977.

C-943 Kell, Jean Bruyere, WHEN THE PIRATES CAME TO BEAUFORT, Beaufort NC: J. B. Kell, 1982.

C-944 Kelley, Sarah Foster, GENERAL JAMES ROBERTSON: THE FOUNDER OF NASHVILLE, Nashville: privately printed, 1980.

C-945 Kelly, Jacques, BYGONE BALTIMORE: A HISTORICAL PORTRAIT, Norfolk, VA: Donning Company, 1982.

C-946 Kemler, Edgar, IRREVERENT MR. MENCKEN, Boston: Atlantic-Little, Brown and Company, 1950.

C-947 Kemp, John R., NEW ORLEANS, Woodland Hills, CA: Windsor Publications, 1981.

C-948 Kendall, John Smith, THE HISTORY OF NEW ORLEANS, Chicago: The Lewis Publishing Company, 1922.

C-949 Kendrick, Baynard, H., ORLANDO, A CENTURY PLUS, Orlando: Sentinel
       Star Company, 1976.

C-950 Kerr, Bettie L. and John Wright Jr., LEXINGTON: A CENTURY IN
       PHOTOGRAPHS, Lexington, KY: Lexington-Fayette County Historical
       Commission, 1984.

C-951 Kimbrough, Emily, SO NEAR AND YET SO FAR, New York: Harper and
       Brothers, 1955.

C-952 Kimmel, Stanley Preston, MR. DAVIS'S RICHMOND, New York: Coward-
       McCann, Inc., 1958.

C-953 King, G. Wayne, RISE UP SO EARLY: A HISTORY OF FLORENCE COUNTY,
       SOUTH CAROLINA, Spartanburg: Reprint Company Publishers, 1981.

C-954 King, Grace E., NEW ORLEANS, THE PLACE AND THE PEOPLE, New York:
       Macmillan, 1911.

C-955 King, Spencer B. Jr., DARIEN: THE DEATH AND REBIRTH OF A SOUTHERN
       TOWN, Macon: Mercer University Press, 1981.

C-956 Kirkland, Thomas J. and Robert M. Kennedy, HISTORIC CAMDEN VOL I,
       Columbia, SC: The State Printing Company, 1905.

C-957 Kishpaugh, Robert A., AMERICA'S MOST HISTORIC CITY.   FREDERICKS-
       BURG, A GUIDE TO ITS POINTS OF INTEREST, Fredericksburg, VA: R. A.
       Kishpaugh, 1922.

C-958 Kishpaugh, Robert A., pub., HISTORIC FREDERICKSBURG, Fredericks-
       burg: Stationery and Printing, 1920.

C-959 Kitchens, Ben E., GUNBOATS AND CAVALRY: A HISTORY OF EASTPORT,
       MISSISSIPPI, Florence, AL: Thornwood Book Publishers, 1986.

C-960 Klonsky, Arthur J. and Jane Sobel, NEW ORLEANS, Toronto: Skyline
       Press: Oxford University Press, 1985.

C-961 Knight, Lucian Lamar, HISTORY OF FULTON COUNTY, GEORGIA, NARRATIVE
       AND BIOGRAPHICAL, Atlanta: A. H. Cawston, 1930.

C-962 Knight, Oliver, FORT WORTH: OUTPOST ON THE TRINITY, Norman: Uni-
       versity of Oklahoma Press, 1953.

C-963 Kohn, Peter, THE CRADLE: ANATOMY OF A TOWN--FACT AND FICTION, New
       York: Vantage Press, 1969.

C-964 Kolb, Carolyn, NEW ORLEANS: AN INVITATION TO DISCOVER ONE OF
       AMERICA'S MOST FASCINATING CITIES, Garden City, NY: Doubleday and
       Company, 1972.

C-965 Kostyu, Joel A. and Frank A. Kostyu, DURHAM: A PICTORIAL HISTORY,
       Norfolk: Donning Company, 1978.

C-966 Kowert, Elise, OLD HOMES AND BUILDINGS OF FREDERICKSBURG,
       Fredericksburg, TX: Fredericksburg Publishing Company, 1977.

C-967 Kurtz, Wilbur G., HISTORIC ATLANTA; A BRIEF STORY OF ATLANTA AND
       ITS LANDMARKS, Atlanta: Conger Printing Company, 1929.

C-968 Kwilecki, Paul, UNDERSTANDINGS: PHOTOGRAPHS OF DECATUR COUNTY,
       GEORGIA, Chapel Hill: University of North Carolina Press, 1981.

C-969 Kyle, F. Clayson, IMAGES: A PICTORIAL HISTORY OF COLUMBUS,
       GEORGIA, Norfolk: The Donning Company Publishers, 1986.

C-970 Lamar, Curt, ed., A HISTORY OF ROSEDALE, MISSISSIPPI, 1876-1976,
       Spartenburg, SC: Reprint Company, 1976.

C-971 LaMonte, Edward S., GEORGE B. WARD, BIRMINGHAM'S URBAN STATESMAN: AN ESSAY IN HONOR OF MERVYN H. STERNE, Birmingham, AL: Birmingham Public Library, 1974.

C-972 Lane, Mills, ed., THE RAMBLER IN GEORGIA, Savannah: The Beehive Press, 1973.

C-973 Lane, Mills, SAVANNAH REVISITED: A PICTORIAL HISTORY Savannah: The Beehive Press, 1969.

C-974 Langley, Joan and Wright Langley, KEY WEST: IMAGES OF THE PAST, Key West: Christopher C. Bell and Edwin O. Swift, 1982.

C-975 Langley, Joan and Wright Langley, OLD KEY WEST IN 3-D, Key West: Langley Press, 1986.

C-976 Langley, Joan and Wright Langley, YESTERDAY'S ASHEVILLE, Miami: E. A. Seemann Publishing, Inc., 1975.

C-977 Lankevich, George J., comp. and ed., ATLANTA: A CHRONOLOGICAL AND DOCUMENTARY HISTORY, Dobbs Ferry, NY: Oceana Publications, Inc., 1978.

C-978 Larsmell, Lynda, RUGBY: A BRAVE FAILURE, A BRAVE SUCCESS, Rugby: Rugby Restoration Press, 1975.

C-979 Latrobe, Benjamin Henry Boneval, ed. by Samuel Wilson Jr., IMPRESSIONS RESPECTING NEW ORLEANS: DIARY & SKETCHES, 1818-1820, New York: Columbia University Press, 1951.

C-980 Lauterer, Jock, ONLY IN CHAPEL HILL, A PHOTOGRAPHIC ESSAY, Chapel Hill: School of Journalism Foundation of North Carolina, 1967.

C-981 Lawrence, Alexander A., STORM OVER SAVANNAH: THE STORY OF COUNT D'ESTAING AND THE SEIGE OF THE TOWN IN 1779, Athens: University of Georgia Press, 1951.

C-982 Lawrence, Robert, DALLAS TODAY, Dallas: Taylor Publishing Company, 1985.

C-983 Leavenworth, Geoffrey, HISTORIC GALVESTON, Houston: Herring Press, 1985.

C-984 Leavitt, Mel, A SHORT HISTORY OF NEW ORLEANS, San Francisco: Lexico's, 1982.

C-985 Leiding, Harriette K., CHARLESTON: HISTORIC AND ROMANTIC, Philadelphia: J. B. Lippincott, 1931.

C-986 Leiserson, Avery, ed., THE AMERICAN SOUTH IN THE 1960s, New York: Praeger, 1964.

C-987 Leland, Isabella A., CHARLESTON: CROSSROADS OF HISTORY, Woodland Hills, CA: Charleston Trident Chamber of Commerce/Windsor Publications, 1980.

C-988 Lesy, Michael, REAL LIFE: LOUISVILLE IN THE TWENTIES, New York: Pantheon Books, 1976.

C-989 Letcher, John Seymour, ONLY YESTERDAY IN LEXINGTON, VIRGINIA, Verona, VA: McClure Press, 1976.

C-990 Levkoff, Alice F., Robert Levkoff, and N. S. Whitelau, CHARLESTON COME HELL OR HIGH WATER, Columbia, SC: R. L. Bryan Company, 1976.

C-991 Lewis, David L., DISTRICT OF COLUMBIA: A BICENTENNIAL HISTORY, New York: W. W. Norton and Company, 1976.

C-992   Lewis, Elizabeth W., HOUSTON: STAR OF THE REPUBLIC: 1836 TO 1846, Toe Run Press, 1985.

C-993   Lewis, Pierce F., NEW ORLEANS--THE MAKING OF AN URBAN LANDSCAPE, Cambridge, MA: Ballinger Publishing Company, 1976.

C-994   Lewis, Willie Newbury, WILLIE, A GIRL FROM A TOWN CALLED DALLAS, College Station: Texas A & M University Press, 1984.

C-995   Linehan, Mary Collar, EARLY LANTANA, HER NEIGHBORS AND MORE, St. Petersburg, FL: Byron Kennedy and Company, 1979.

C-996   Linsley, Judith Walker and Ellen Walker Rienstra, BEAUMONT: A CHRONICLE OF PROMISE, AN ILLUSTRATED HISTORY, Windsor Hills, CA: Windsor Publications, 1982.

C-997   Little, John P., HISTORY OF RICHMOND, Richmond: The Diltz Press, 1933.

C-998   Livingood, James W., A HISTORY OF HAMILTON COUNTY, TENNESSEE, Memphis: Memphis State University Press, 1981.

C-999   Lockerman, Doris, DISCOVER ATLANTA, New York: Simon & Schuster, 1969.

C-1000 Longbrake, David B. and Woodrow W. Nichols, Jr., SUNSHINE AND SHADOWS IN METROPOLITAN MIAMI, Cambridge, MA: Ballinger Publishing Company, 1976.

C-1001 Longstreet, R. J., THE STORY OF MOUNT DORA, FLORIDA, Mount Dora: Mount Dora Historical Society, 1960.

C-1002 Louisville Abstract & Loan Association, ATLAS OF THE CITY OF LOUISVILLE, KY., 1876, Louisville: Reprint Standard Printing Company, 1974, 1876.

C-1003 Loving, Robert S., DOUBLE DESTINY; THE STORY OF BRISTOL, TENNESSEE-VIRGINIA, Bristol: King Printing Company, 1955.

C-1004 Lucas, Marion Brunson, SHERMAN AND THE BURNING OF COLUMBIA, College Station, TX: Texas A & M University Press, 1976.

C-1005 Luraghi, Richard, THE RISE AND FALL OF THE PLANTATION SOUTH, New York: New Viewpoints, 1978.

C-1006 Lutz, Francis E., A RICHMOND ALBUM, Richmond: Garrett & Massie, 1937.

C-1007 Lutz, Frances E., RICHMOND IN WORLD WAR II, Richmond: Dietz Press, 1951.

C-1008 Lynn, Stuart M., NEW ORLEANS, New York: Bonanza Books, 1949.

C-1009 MacArthur, William J., ed., OLD KNOXVILLE: THIRTY-TWO HISTORIC POSTCARDS, Knoxville: The University of Tennessee Press, 1982.

C-1010 MacDowell, Claire Leavitt, CHRONOLOGICAL HISTORY OF WINTER PARK, FLORIDA, Winter Park: Orange Press, 1950.

C-1011 MADISONVILLE, W.P.A. Federal Writers' Project, Department of Archives and History, Jackson, MI.

C-1012 Mahan, Joseph B., A HISTORY OF CASSVILLE, GEORGIA, Cassville, GA: Cassville High School Publication, 1976 (repr. 1950 ed.).

C-1013 Maloney, Walter, SKETCH OF THE HISTORY OF KEY WEST, FLORIDA, Newark, 1876; facsimile ed., Gainesville, 1968.

C-1014 Manning, Warren Henry, WARREN H. MANNING'S CITY PLAN OF BIRMING-
HAM, Birmingham, AL: 1919.

C-1015 Mansfield, James Roger, A HISTORY OF EARLY SPOTSYLVANIA, Orange,
VA: Green Publishers, 1977.

C-1016 Marquez, Hudson, MONKEY ISLAND . . . A FANTASTIC GUIDE TO NEW
ORLEANS, [s.l.]. Faust Publishing Company, 1986.

C-1017 Marsh, Blanche, CHARLOTTE, CAROLINA'S QUEEN CITY, Columbia, SC:
R. L. Bryan Company, 1967.

C-1018 Marsh, Blanche, HITCH UP THE BUGGY, Greenville, SC: A Press,
1977.

C-1019 Marshall, A. J., THE AUTOBIOGRAPHY OF MRS. A. J. MARSHALL, AGE 84
YEARS, Pine Bluff, AR: Adams-Wilson Printing Company, 1897.

C-1020 Marszalek, John F., ed., THE DIARY OF MISS EMMA HOLMES, 1861-1866,
Baton Rouge; Louisiana State University Press, 1979.

C-1021 Marth, Del, YESTERDAY'S SARASOTA, Miami: Seemann Publishing,
Inc., 1977.

C-1022 Martin, Harold H., ATLANTA AND ENVIRONS . . . 1940-1976, V. III,
Atlanta: Atlanta Historical Society; Athens: University of
Georgia Press, 1987.

C-1023 Martin, Thomas H., ATLANTA AND ITS BUILDERS, A COMPREHENSIVE
HISTORY OF THE GATE CITY OF THE SOUTH, Atlanta: Century Memorial
Publishing Company, 1902.

C-1024 Martinez, Raymond J. and Jack D. L. Holmes, NEW ORLEANS: FACTS
AND LEGENDS, New Orleans: Hope Publications, 1969.

C-1025 Mastin, Bettye Lee, LEXINGTON 1779: PIONEER KENTUCKY, AS DES-
CRIBED BY EARLY SETTLERS, Lexington: Lexington-Fayette County
Historic Commission, 1979.

C-1026 Mastin, Bettye Lee, LIBERTY HALL [2 sheets], Lexington, KY: n.p.
1962.

C-1027 Mastin, Bettye Lee, QUICK GLIMPSES OF PLEASANT HILL, INTERESTING
FACTS; A WALKING TOUR WITH MAP TO ACCOMPANY VISITORS TO SHAKER-
TOWN, Lexington, KY: Richard S. DeCamp, 1969.

C-1028 Mathews, Charles Elijah and Anderson Browns, HIGHLIGHTS OF 100
YEARS IN MOBILE, Mobile, AL: First National Bank, 1965.

C-1029 Mell, Edward Baker, REMINISCENCES OF ATHENS, Athens: 1957.

C-1030 Melosi, Martin V., DALLAS-FORT WORTH: POLITICS, ECONOMY, AND
DEMOGRAPHY SINCE WORLD WAR II, Public Administration Series
Bibliography, Monticello, IL: Vance Bibliographies, June 1982.

C-1031 MEMPHIS MENUS: A COLLECTION OF MENUS FROM MEMPHIS' FINER
RESTAURANTS, Memphis: Sunbelt, Inc., 1982.

C-1032 Merrens, Harry Roy, COLONIAL NORTH CAROLINA IN THE EIGHTEENTH
CENTURY: A STUDY IN HISTORICAL GEOGRAPHY, Chapel Hill: University of North Carolina Press, 1964.

C-1033 Meyers, Rose, A HISTORY OF BATON ROUGE, 1699-1912, Baton Rouge:
Louisiana State University Press, 1976.

C-1034 Miami, Florida Chamber of Commerce, OUTWITTING WINTER, Miami:
Graydon E. Bevis, Inc., 1934.

C-1035 Miers, Earl S., THE WEB OF VICTORY: GRANT AT VICKSBURG, New York:
        Knopf, 1955.

C-1036 Miers, Earl Schenck, WHEN THE WORLD ENDED, THE DIARY OF EMMA
        LeCONTE, New York: Oxbord University Press, 1957.

C-1037 Milburn, Douglas, HOUSTON, A SELF PORTRAIT, Houston: Herring
        Press, 1986.

C-1038 Milburn, Douglas, ed., HOUSTON-IN-THE-ROUND: PANORAMIC PHOTO-
        GRAPHS OF THE CITY, 1903-1983, Houston: Houston Public Library,
        1983.

C-1039 Miller, Mark, MOUNT WASHINGTON, BALTIMORE SUBURB: A HISTORY
        REVEALED THROUGH PICTURES AND NARRATIVE, Baltimore: GBS Publish-
        ers, 1981.

C-1040 Miller, Paul W., ed., ATLANTA: CAPITAL OF THE SOUTH, New York:
        Oliver Durell, Inc., 1949.

C-1041 Miller, Ray, RAY MILLER'S GALVESTON, Houston: Cordovan Press,
        1983.

C-1042 Miller, Ray, RAY MILLER'S HOUSTON, Houston: Cordovan Press, 1982.

C-1043 Miller, William D., MEMPHIS DURING THE PROGRESSIVE ERA, 1900-1917,
        Memphis: The Memphis State University Press, 1957.

C-1044 Mitchell, George, PONCE DE LEON: AN INTIMATE PORTRAIT OF AT-
        LANTA'S MOST FAMOUS AVENUE, Atlanta: Argonne Books, 1983.

C-1045 Mitchell, Mary, DIVIDED TOWN, Barre, MA: Barre Publishers, 1968.

C-1046 Mitchell, Mary (Atkinson), ANNAPOLIS VISIT: A PHOTOGRAPHIC ESSAY
        ON MARYLAND'S ANCIENT CITY, Barre, MA: Barre Publishers, 1969.

C-1047 MOCCASIN BEND, CHATTANOOGA, TENNESSEE, Washington: Urban Land
        Institute, 1982.

C-1048 Mode, Robert L., NASHVILLE, ITS CHARACTER IN A CHANGING AMERICA.
        PROCEEDINGS OF A SYMPOSIUM PRESENTED AT VANDERBILT UNIVERSITY,
        OCTOBER 18, 1980, Nashville: Office of University Publications,
        Vanderbilt University, 1981.

C-1049 Molloy, Robert, CHARLESTON: A GRACIOUS HERITAGE, New York: D.
        Appleton-Century, 1947.

C-1050 Monaco, Arto, COLORING BOOK OF ATLANTA, Chamblee, GA: Atlanta
        News Agency, 1969.

C-1051 Moore, Edith Wyatt, NATCHEZ-UNDER-THE-HILL, Natchez, MS: Southern
        Historical Publications, Inc., 1958.

C-1052 Moore, Francis, A VOYAGE TO GEORGIA . . . CONTAINING AN ACCOUNT OF
        THE SETTLING OF THE TOWN OF FREDERICA . . . ALSO A DESCRIPTION OF
        THE TOWN . . . OF SAVANNAH, London: J. Robinson, 1944.

C-1053 Moore, Virginia, SCOTTSVILLE ON THE JAMES: AN INFORMAL HISTORY,
        Charlottesville, VA: The Jarman Press, 1969.

C-1054 Mordecai, Samuel, RICHMOND IN BY-GONE DAYS, Richmond, VA: George
        M. West, 1856. Reprint ed., Arno Press, Inc., 1975.

C-1055 Mormino, Gary R. and Anthony P. Pizzo, TAMPA: THE TREASURE CITY,
        Tulsa, OK: Continental Heritage Press, 1983.

C-1056 Morris, Allen, FLORIDA PLACE NAMES, Coral Gables: University of
        Miami Press, 1974.

C-1057 Mugnier, George Francois, NEW ORLEANS AND BAYOU COUNTRY; PHOTO-GRAPHS (1880-1910), Barre, MA: Barre Publishers, 1972.

C-1058 Muir, Helen, MIAMI, U.S.A., New York: Holt, 1953.

C-1059 Muncy, Lee, SEARCY, ARKANSAS: A FRONTIER TOWN GROWS UP WITH AMERICA, Searcy: Harding Press, 1976.

C-1060 Murray, Malcolm, ATLAS OF ATLANTA, THE 1970's, Tuscaloosa: University of Alabama Press, 1974.

C-1061 Muscat, Beth T. and Mary A. Nerley, THE WAY IT WAS: EIGHTEEN FIFTY TO NINETEEN THIRTY: PHOTOGRAPHS OF MONTGOMERY AND HER CENTRAL ALABAMA NEIGHBORS, Montgomery: Landmarks Foundation, 1985.

C-1062 McAshan, Marie P., A HOUSTON LEGACY: ON THE CORNER OF MAIN AND TEXAS, Houston: Hutchins House, 1985.

C-1063 McCabe, Gillie Cary, THE STORY OF AN OLD TOWN--HAMPTON, VIRGINIA, Richmond: Old Dominion Press, 1929.

C-1064 McCall, H. G., A SKETCH, HISTORICAL AND STATISTICAL, OF THE CITY OF MONTGOMERY . . ., Montgomery, AL: W. D. Brown and Company, 1885.

C-1065 McCampbell, Coleman, SAGA OF A FRONTIER SEAPORT, Dallas: South-West Press, 1934.

C-1066 McCarty, John L., MAVERICK TOWN: THE STORY OF OLD TASCOSA, Nor-man: University of Oklahoma Press, 1946.

C-1067 McCarty, Kenneth G. Jr., ed., HATTIESBURG: A PICTORIAL HISTORY, Jackson: University Press of Mississippi, 1982.

C-1068 McComb, D. G., HOUSTON: A HISTORY, Austin, TX: University of Texas Press, 1981.

C-1069 McComb, David, HOUSTON: THE BAYOU CITY, Austin: University of Texas Press, 1969.

C-1070 McCowen, George Smith Jr., THE BRITISH OCCUPATION OF CHARLESTON, 1780-82, Columbia: University of South Carolina Press, 1972.

C-1071 McCuddy, Robin, THIS IS MEMPHIS, Memphis: Memphis Board of Real-tors, 1974.

C-1072 McDill, Raus, VIRGINIA PLACE NAMES: DERIVATIONS, HISTORICAL USES, Verona, VA: McClure Press, 1969.

C-1073 McDonald, Michael J. and William Bruce Wheeler, KNOXVILLE, TENNES-SEE: CONTINUITY AND CHANGE IN AN APPALACHIAN CITY, Knoxville: University of Tennessee Press, 1983.

C-1074 McDonald, William L., DALLAS REDISCOVERED: A PHOTOGRAPHIC CHRONI-CLE OF URBAN EXPANSION, 1870-1925, Dallas: Dallas Historical Society, 1978.

C-1075 McDonough, James Lee and Thomas L. Connely, FIVE TRAGIC HOURS: THE BATTLE OF FRANKLIN, Knoxville: University of Tennessee Press, 1983.

C-1076 McEachern, Leora Hiatt, HISTORY OF ST. JAMES PARISH, 1729-1979, Wilmington, NC: s.n., 1985?

C-1077 McEachin, Archibald Bruce, THE HISTORY OF TUSCALOOSA: 1816-1880, University, AL: Confederate Publishing Company, 1977.

C-1078 McElreath, Walter, WALTER McELREATH: AN AUTOBIOGRAPHY, Macon:
       Mercer University Press, 1984.

C-1079 McGovern, James R. ed., ANDREW JACKSON AND PENSACOLA, Pensacola:
       Pensacola Bicentennial Commission, 1974.

C-1080 McGovern, James R., ed., COLONIAL PENSACOLA, Pensacola: Pensacola
       Bicentennial Commisison, 1974.

C-1081 McGovern, James R., THE EMERGENCE OF A CITY IN THE MODERN SOUTH:
       PENSACOLA 1900-1945, Pensacola, FL: The Author, distributed by
       the University of West Florida Bookstore.

C-1082 McIver, Stuart B., FORT LAUDERDALE AND BROWARD COUNTY: AN ILLUS-
       TRATED HISTORY, Woodland Hills, CA: Windsor Publications, Inc.,
       1983.

C-1083 McIver, Stuart I., YESTERDAY'S PALM BEACH, Miami: E. H. Seemann,
       1976.

C-1084 McKinney, John C. and Edgar T. Thompson, ed., THE SOUTH IN CON-
       TINUITY AND CHANGE, Durham, NC: Duke University Press, 1965.

C-1085 McLaurin, Ann M., ed., GLIMPSES OF SHREVEPORT, Natchitoches, LA:
       Northwestern State University Press, 1985.

C-1086 McLaurin, A. Melton and Michael V. Thompson, THE IMAGE OF PROG-
       RESS: ALABAMA PHOTOGRAPHS, 1872-1917, University, AL: University
       of Alabama Press, 1980.

C-1087 McLendon, James, PIONEER IN THE FLORIDA KEYS: THE LIFE AND TIMES
       OF DEL LAYTON, Miami: E. A. Seemann Publishers, 1976.

C-1088 McMillan, Malcolm Cook, YESTERDAY'S BIRMINGHAM, Miami: E. A.
       Seemann Publishers, 1975.

C-1089 McMurtrie, Douglas Crawford, LOUISIANA IMPRINTS, 1768-1810,
       Hattiesburg, MI: The Book Farm, 1942.

C-1090 McMurtrie, Henry, SKETCHES OF LOUISVILLE, Louisville: S. Penn,
       1819.

C-1091 McNeely, Stanley Blake, BITS OF CHARM IN OLD MOBILE, Mobile, AL:
       Gill Printing and Stationery Company, 1946.

C-1092 McRaven, William Henry, NASHVILLE: "ATHENS OF THE SOUTH," Chapel
       Hill: Scheer & Jervis, 1949.

C-1093 Nardini, Louis Raphael, NO MAN'S LAND: A HISTORY OF EL CAMINO
       REAL, New Orleans: Pelican Publishing Company, 1961.

C-1094 NASHVILLE: CONSERVING A HERITAGE, Nashville: Historical Commis-
       sion of Metropolitan Nashville-Davidson County, 1977.

C-1095 Nast, Lenora Heilig, Lawrence N. Krause, and R. C. Monk, eds.,
       BALTIMORE: A LIVING RENAISSANCE, Baltimore: Historic Baltimore
       Society, Inc., 1982.

C-1096 Neville, Bert and Nellie Neville, A GLANCE AT EARLY SELMA; SCENES
       OF SELMA, ALABAMA, 1820-1920, Selma, AL: 1968.

C-1097 New Orleans Progressive Union, NEW ORLEANS; WHAT TO SEE AND HOW TO
       SEE IT; A STANDARD GUIDE TO THE CITY OF NEW ORLEANS, New Orleans:
       Press of Louisiana Printing Company, 1909.

C-1098 Newport News History Commission, NEWPORT NEWS DURING THE SECOND
       WORLD WAR, Newport News: Newport News, History Commission, 1948.

C-1099 Newson, D. Earl, DRUMRIGHT, THE GLORY DAYS OF A BOOM TOWN, Perskins, OK: Evans Publications, 1985.

C-1100 Nickel, Janice F., ed., KNOW KNOXVILLE, Strode, 1982.

C-1101 Nixon, H. C., POSSUM TROT: RURAL COMMUNITY, SOUTH, Norman: University of Oklahoma Press, 1941.

C-1102 Norman, Benjamin Moore, ed. by Matthew J. Schott, NORMAN'S NEW ORLEANS AND ENVIRONS, Baton Rouge: Louisiana State University Press, 1976, c. 1845.

C-1103 Norris, Clarence and Sybil D. Washington, THE LAST OF THE SCOTTSBORO BOYS: AN AUTOBIOGRAPHY, New York: G. P. Putnam's Sons, 1979.

C-1104 Norris, J. E., ed., HISTORY OF THE LOWER SHENANDOAH VALLEY . . . CITIES, TOWNS, AND VILLAGES . . ., Chicago: A Warner, 1890.

C-1105 Obear, Katharine Theus, THROUGH THE YEARS IN OLD WINSBORO, Columbia, SC: The R. L. Bryan Company, 1940.

C-1106 Odum, Howard W., SOUTHERN REGIONS OF THE UNITED STATES, Chapel Hill: University of North Carolina Press, 1936.

C-1107 O'Keefe, Patrick, GREENSBORO: A PICTORIAL HISTORY, Norfolk, VA: Donning Company, 1977.

C-1108 OLD REMINISCENCES OF AUGUSTA: AND NEW INDUSTRIES SINCE THE CIVIL WAR, Augusta: s.n., 19?

C-1109 Olson, Sherry H., BALTIMORE: THE BUILDING OF AN AMERICAN CITY, Baltimore: Johns Hopkins University Press, 1980.

C-1110 Oppenheimer, Evelyn and Bill Porterfield, eds., THE BOOK OF DALLAS, Garden City, NJ: Doubleday, 1976.

C-1111 Ornelas-Struve, Carole M. and Frederick L. Coulter, MEMPHIS, 1800–1900 (3 vol.), New York: N. Powers, 1982.

C-1112 Osborne, J. A., WILLIAMSBURG IN COLONIAL TIMES, Richmond: The Dietz Press, 1935.

C-1113 Ottaway, Hal N. and Jim L. Edwards, THE VANISHED SPLENDOR: POSTCARD VIEWS OF EARLY OKLAHOMA CITY, Oklahoma City: Abalache Bookshop, 1982.

C-1114 Palfrey, Francis Winthrop, . . . THE ANTIETAM AND FREDERICKSBURG, New York: C. Scribner's Cons, 1902 [c. 1881].

C-1115 Panagopoulos, E. P., NEW SMYRNA: AN EIGHTEENTH CENTURY GREEK ODYSSEY, Gainesville: University of Florida Press, 1966.

C-1116 Parks, Arva Moore, THE MAGIC CITY--MIAMI, Tulsa: Continental Heritage Press, Inc., 1981.

C-1117 Parramore, Thomas C., THE ANCIENT MARITIME VILLAGE OF MURFREESBOROUGH: 1787-1825, Murfreesborough, Johnson Publishing Company, 1969.

C-1118 Patrick, Rembert W., THE FALL OF RICHMOND, Baton Rouge: Louisiana State University Press, 1960.

C-1119 Peck, Elisabeth S., BEREA'S FIRST CENTURY, 1855-1955, Lexington: University of Kentucky Press, 1955.

C-1120 Pember, Phoebe Yates [author], Bell Irwin Wiley [ed.], A SOUTHERN WOMAN'S STORY: LIFE IN CONFEDERATE RICHMOND, Jackson, TN: McCowart-Mercer Press, Inc., 1959.

C-1121 Pent, R. F., THE HISTORY OF TARPON SPRINGS, St. Petersburg: Great
       Outdoors Publishing Company, 1964.

C-1122 Perdue, Theda, NATIONS REMEMBERED: AN ORAL HISTORY OF THE FIVE
       CIVILIZED TRIBES, 1865-1907, Westport, CN: Greenwood Press, 1980.

C-1123 Peters, James E., ARLINGTON NATIONAL CEMETERY: SHRINE TO AMERI-
       CA'S HEROS, Kensington, MD: Woodbine House, 1986.

C-1124 Peters, Thelma, BISCAYNE COUNTY, 1870-1926, Miami: Banyon Books,
       1981.

C-1125 Peters, Thelma, LEMON CITY: PIONEERING ON BISCAYNE BAY, Miami:
       Banyan Books, 1976.

C-1126 Philips, Shine, BIG SPRING, THE CASUAL BIOGRAPHY OF A PRAIRIE
       TOWN, New York: Prentice-Hall, 1946.

C-1127 Pinkley-Call, Cora, EUREKA SPRINGS, STAIR-STEP-TOWN, Eureka
       Springs, AR: 1952.

C-1128 PIONEER CITIZENS' HISTORY OF ATLANTA, 1833-1902, Atlanta: Byrd
       Printing company, 1902.

C-1129 Pioneers Club, EARLY DAYS IN BIRMINGHAM, Birmingham: Birmingham
       Publishing Company, 1937.

C-1130 Pizzo, Anthony P., TAMPA TOWN 1824-1886: CRACKER VILLAGE WITH A
       YANKEE ACCENT, Miami: Hurricane House Publishers, 1968.

C-1131 Plunkett, Kitty, MEMPHIS: A PICTORIAL HISTORY, Norfolk, VA:
       Donning Company/Publishers, 1976.

C-1132 Pointdexter, Charles, RICHMOND: AN ILLUSTRATED HANDBOOK OF THE
       CITY AND BATTLE FIELDS, Richmond, VA: The Mermitage Press, Inc.,
       1907.

C-1133 Polk, Stella Gipson, MASON AND MASON COUNTY: A HISTORY, Austin:
       Pemberton Press, 1966.

C-1134 Porter, Glenn and William H. Mulligan Jr., BALTIMORE HISTORY:
       WORKING PAPERS FROM THE REGIONAL ECONOMIC HISTORY RESEARCH CENTER,
       v. 4, No. 1-2, Wilmington, DE: Eleutherian Mills-Hayley Founda-
       tion, 1981.

C-1135 Porterfield, Lula, CHRISTIANSBURG, MONTGOMERY COUNTY, VIRGINIA,
       Racford, VA: Edmonds Printing Company, 1981.

C-1136 Powell, Lyman P., ed., HISTORIC TOWNS OF THE SOUTHERN STATES, New
       York: G. P. Putnam's Sons, 1900.

C-1137 Powell, William S., NORTH CAROLINA GAZETTEER, Chapel Hill:
       University of North Carolina Press, 1968.

C-1138 Pratt, Theodore, THAT WAS PALM BEACH, St. Petersburg: Great
       Outdoors Publishing Company, 1968.

C-1139 Protopappas, John J. and Lin Brown, WASHINGTON ON FOOT: 24 WALK-
       ING TOURS OF WASHINGTON, D. C., OLD TOWN ALEXANDRIA, HISTORIC
       ANNAPOLIS, Washington, DC: Smithsonian Press, 1984.

C-1140 Quinn, S. J., THE HISTORY OF THE CITY OF FREDERICKSBURG, VIRGINIA,
       Richmond, VA: The Hertmitage Press, 1908.

C-1141 Rabac, Glenn A., THE CITY OF COCOA BEACH: THE FIRST SIXTY YEARS,
       The City, n.d.

C-1142 Radoff, Morris Leon, THE STATE HOUSE AT ANNAPOLIS, Annapolis, Hall of Records Publication No. 17, 1972.

C-1143 RALEIGH: A GUIDE TO NORTH CAROLINA'S CAPITAL, Raleigh: The Raleigh Fine Arts Society, Inc., 1975.

C-1144 Ranck, George W., BOONESBOROUGH: ITS FOUNDING, PIONEER STRUGGLES, INDIANA EXPERIENCES, TRANSYLVANIA DAYS, AND REVOLUTIONARY ANNALS, Louisville: John P. Morton and Company, 1901.

C-1145 Rankin, Hugh F., THE GOLDEN AGE OF PIRACY, New York: Holt, Rinehart and Winston, Inc., 1969.

C-1146 Rawlings, Mary, A SHORT HISTORY OF CHARLOTTESVILLE, Charlottesville: The Michie Company, 1949.

C-1147 Rawls, Carolina, THE JACKSONVILLE STORY, A PICTORIAL RECORD OF A FLORIDA CITY, Jacksonville: Jacksonville's Fifty Years of Progress Association, 1950.

C-1148 Rayburn, Otto Ernest, THE EUREKA SPRINGS STORY, Eureka Springs, AR: The Times-Echo Press, 1954.

C-1149 Read, Daisy I., NEW LONDON [VA]: TODAY AND YESTERDAY, Lynchburg, VA: J. P. Bell Company, 1950.

C-1150 THE READY HAND BOOK TO ATHENS, GEORGIA AND VICINITY, Athens: D. W. McGregor, 1903.

C-1151 Reap, James, ATHENS, A PICTORIAL HISTORY, Virginia Beach, VA: Donning Company, 1982.

C-1152 Reaves, Bill, A BRIEF HISTORY OF WILMINGTON, N. C., s.n. 1977.

C-1153 Reaves, Bill, HISTORY OF BURGAW, NC, PENDEE COUNTY, Burgaw: Burgaw Centennial Book Committee, 1979.

C-1154 Reaves, Bill, SOUTHPORT (SMITHVILLE): A CHRONOLOGY, Southport, NC: Southport Historical Society, 1978.

C-1155 Redway, George William, FREDERICKSBURG; A STUDY IN WAR, New York: Macmillan, 1906.

C-1156 Reed, Wallace Putnam, ed., HISTORY OF ATLANTA, GEORGIA, WITH ILLUSTRATIONS AND BIOGRAPHICAL SKETCHES OF SOME OF ITS PROMINENT MEN AND PIONEEERS, Syracuse, NY: D. Mason & Company, 1889.

C-1157 Reese, Trevor Richard, FREDERICA, COLONIAL FORT AND TOWN; ITS PLACE IN HISTORY, St. Simons Island, GA: Fort Frederica Association, 1969.

C-1158 Reeves, Sally K. Evans, et al., GRAND ISLE ON THE GULF, Metairie, LA: Jefferson Parish Historical commission, 1979.

C-1159 Reeves, Sally K. Evans, et al., HISTORIC CITY PARK: NEW ORLEANS, New Orleans: Friends City Park, 1982.

C-1160 Register, James, SHADOWS OF OLD NEW ORLEANS, Baton Rouge: Claitors Book Store, 1967.

C-1161 Reinders, Robert C., END OF AN ERA: NEW ORLEANS, 1850-1860, New Orleans: Pelican Publishing Company, 1964.

C-1162 Reps, John W., TIDEWATER TOWNS: CITY PLANNING IN COLONIAL VIRGINIA AND MARYLAND, Williamsburg: Colonial Williamsburg Foundation, 1972.

C-1163 Rhea, Linda, HUGH SWINTON LEGARE, A CHARLESTON INTELLECTUAL, Chapel Hill: University of North Carolina Press, 1934.

C-1164 Rhett, James Moore III and John Carson Hay Steele, CHARLESTON THEN AND NOW, Columbia, SC: The R. L. Bryan Company, 1974.

C-1165 Rhett, Robert Goodwin, CHARLESTON, AN EPIC OF CAROLINA, Richmond: Garrett and Massie, Inc., 1940.

C-1166 Rice, Otis K., CHARLESTON AND THE KANAWHA VALLEY: AN ILLUSTRATED HISTORY, Woodland Hills, CA: Windsor Publications, Inc., 1981.

C-1167 Rich, Linda G., Joan Clark Netherwood, Elinor B. Cahn, NEIGHBOR-HOOD: A STATE OF MIND, Baltimore: Johns Hopkins University Press, 1981.

C-1168 Richards, Ira Don, STORY OF A RIVERTOWN, LITTLE ROCK IN THE NINETEENTH CENTURY, Arkadelphia, AR: privately printed, 1969.

C-1169 Richards, J. Nobel, FLORIDA'S HIBISCUS CITY: VERO BEACH, Melbourne: Brevard Graphics, Inc., 1968.

C-1170 Rico, Paul, THIS IS MY NEW ORLEANS, New Orleans: W. A. Simms and Company, 1968.

C-1171 Rightor, Henry, STANDARD HISTORY OF NEW ORLEANS, LOUISIANA, Chicago: The Lewis Publishing Company, 1900.

C-1172 Riley, Edward M. and Charles E. Hatch Jr., eds., JAMESTOWN IN THE WORDS OF CONTEMPORARIES, Washington, DC: U. S. National Park Service, 1944.

C-1173 Rinhart, Floyd and Marion Rinhart, VICTORIAN FLORIDA, Atlanta: Peachtree Press, 1986.

C-1174 Rister, Carl Coke, FORT GRIFFIN ON THE TEXAS FRONTIER, Norman: University of Oklahoma Press, 1956.

C-1175 Roberts, Bruce and Frances Griffin, OLD SALEM IN PICTURES, Charlotte: McNally and Loftin, 1966.

C-1176 Roberts, Chalmers M., WASHINGTON PAST AND PRESENT: A PICTORIAL HISTORY OF THE NATION'S CAPITAL, Washington: Public Affairs Office, 1950.

C-1177 Robertson, Linda Shirley, et al., SOUTH CAROLINA'S INTERNATIONAL GREENVILLE: A GUIDE, Greenville, SC: Writers Unlimited, 1982.

C-1178 Roeber, A. G., ed., A NEW ENGLAND WOMAN'S PERSPECTIVE ON NORFOLK, VIRGINIA, 1801-1802: EXCERPTS FROM THE DIARY OF RUTH HENSHAW BASCOM, Worchester, MI: American Antiquarian Society, 1979 [Proceedings of the American Antequarian Society, v. 88, pt. 2, October 1979].

C-1179 Rogers, George C. Jr., CHARLESTON IN THE AGE OF THE PINCKNEYS, Norman, OK: University of Oklahoma Press, 1969.

C-1180 Rondthaler, Edward, THE MEMORABILIA OF FIFTY YEARS, 1877 TO 1927, Raleigh: Edwards and Broughton, 1928.

C-1181 Roper, James E., THE FOUNDING OF MEMPHIS, 1818-1820, Memphis: Memphis Sesquicentennial, Inc., 1970.

C-1182 Rosales, Francisco A. and Barry J. Kaplan, eds., HOUSTON: A TWENTIETH CENTURY URBAN FRONTIER, Port Washington, NY: Associated Faculty Press, Inc., 1983.

C-1183 Rose, Willie Lee, REHEARSAL FOR RECONSTRUCTION: THE PORT ROYAL EXPERIMENT, London: Oxford University Press, 1964.

C-1184 Rosen, Robert, A SHORT HISTORY OF CHARLESTON, San Francisco: Lexikos, 1982.

C-1185 Ross, Fitzgerald (author), Richard Barksdale Harwell (editor), CITIES AND CAMPS OF THE CONFEDERATE STATES, Urbana: The University of Illinois Press, 1958 (1865).

C-1186 Rouse, Parke Jr., COWS ON THE CAMPUS: WILLIAMSBURG IN BYGONE DAYS, Richmond: The Dietz Press, 1973.

C-1187 Rouse, Parke Jr., RICHMOND IN COLOR, New York: Hastings House, Publishers, 1978.

C-1188 Rowe, Hugh J., HISTORY OF ATHENS AND CLARKE COUNTY, 1923, Athens: McGregor Company, Printers, 1923.

C-1189 Rowland, Arthur Ray, A GUIDE TO THE STUDY OF AUGUSTA AND RICHMOND COUNTY, GEORGIA, Augusta: Richmond County Historical Society, 1967.

C-1190 Rowland, Arthur Ray and Helen Callahan, YESTERDAY'S AUGUSTA, Miami: E. A. Seemann Publishing Company, 1976.

C-1191 Rukert, Norman G., THE FELLS POINT STORY, Baltimore: Bodine & Associates, 1976.

C-1192 Rukert, Norman G., FORT McHENRY: HOME OF THE BRAVE, Baltimore: Bodine, 1983.

C-1193 Rukert, Norman G., THE PORT: PRIDE OF BALTIMORE, Baltimore: Bodine & Associates, Inc., 1982.

C-1194 Russell, Lucy Phillips, A RARE PATTERN, Chapel Hill: The University of North Carolina Press, 1957.

C-1195 Russell, Phillips, THE WOMAN WHO RANG THE BELL: THE STORY OF CORNELIA PHILLIPS SPENCER, Chapel Hill: University of North Carolina Press, 1949.

C-1196 Rust, Jeanne Johnson, A HISTORY OF THE TOWN OF FAIRFAX, Washington, DC: Moore and Moore, Inc., 1960.

C-1197 Sanford, James K., ed., RICHMOND: HER TRIUMPHS, TRAGEDIES, AND GROWTH, Richmond, VA: Metropolitan Richmond Chamber of Commerce, 1975.

C-1198 Santerre, George Henry, DALLAS' FIRST HUNDRED YEARS, 1856-1956, Dallas: Book Craft, 1956.

C-1199 Saunders, H. G., GUIDE TO ATLANTA WITH LATEST REVISED MAP OF THE CITY, Atlanta: The Author, 1889.

C-1200 Saunders, W. L., THE COLONIAL RECORDS OF NORTH CAROLINA, Raleigh: P. M. Hale, Printer to the State, 1886-1890.

C-1201 Scheel, Eugene M., THE STORY OF PURCELLVILLE, LOUDOUN COUNTY, VIRGINIA, Berryville, VA: Virginia Book Company, 1977.

C-1202 Scheel, Rolfe F., HISTORY OF FORT MYERS BEACH, FLORIDA, Fort Myers Beach, FL: Island Press, 1980.

C-1203 Schertz, Helen Pitkin, A WALK THROUGH FRENCH TOWN IN NEW ORLEANS, New Orleans: New Orleans Journal, 1924?

C-1204 Schlegel, Marvin W., CONSCRIPTED CITY: NORFOLK IN WORLD WAR II, Norfolk: Norfolk War History Commission, 1951.

C-1205 Schmidt, Ruby, ed., FORT WORTH AND TARRANT COUNTY: A HISTORICAL GUIDE, Fort Worth, TX: Texas Christian University Press, 1984.

C-1206 Schnore, Leo F., THE NEW URBAN HISTORY: QUANTITATIVE EXPLORATIONS BY AMERICAN HISTORIANS, Princeton: Princeton University Press, 1975.

C-1207 Schumann, Marguerite E., STROLLING AT STATE: A WALKING GUIDE TO NORTH CAROLINA STATE UNIVERSITY, Raleigh, NC: North Carolina State Alumni Association, [1973].

C-1208 Scott, Mary Wingfield, OLD RICHMOND NEIGHBORHOODS, Richmond: Whittet & Shepperson, 1950.

C-1209 Scruggs, Philip Lightfoot, THE HISTORY OF LYNCHBURG, 1786-1946, Lynchburg, VA: J. P. Bell Company, Inc., 1972.

C-1210 Seawell, Meade, EDGEHEEL ENTRY: TALE OF A TARHEEL TOWN, Raleigh: Edwards & Broughton, 1970.

C-1211 Seib, Philip M., DALLAS: CHASING THE URBAN DREAM, Dallas: Pressworks, 1986.

C-1212 Seidman, P. K. (as told to James Cortese), THE MAN WHO LIKES MEMPHIS, A MEMOIR OF FORTY YEARS PASSED BY, Memphis: The Cornation Press, 1975.

C-1213 Sesnovich, Arthur, ed., ATLANTA'S PLACES AND FACES, Atlanta: Phoenix Periodicals, 1984.

C-1214 Sewall, Rufus K., SKETCHES OF ST. AUGUSTINE, Gainesville: The University Presses of Florida, 1976.

C-1215 Shavin, Norman, THE ATLANTA CENTURY . . . MARCH 4, 1860-MAY 20, 1860, Atlanta: Atlanta Journal-Constitution, 1960.

C-1216 Shavin, Norman, ATLANTA THEN, ATLANTA NOW, Atlanta: Capricorn Corp., 1975.

C-1217 Shavin, Norman, OLD ATLANTA, Atlanta: Century House, 1969.

C-1218 Shavin, Norman, UNDERGROUND ATLANTA, Atlanta: Capricorn Corp., 1973.

C-1219 Shavin, Norman, WHATEVER BECAME OF ATLANTA, Atlanta: Capricorn Corp., 1984.

C-1220 Shavin, Norman, THE WORLD OF ATLANTA, Atlanta: Capricorn Corp., Inc., 1983.

C-1221 Shavin, Norman and Bruce Galphin, ATLANTA: TRIUMPH OF A PEOPLE, AN ILLUSTRATED HISTORY, Atlanta: Capricorn Corp., 1982.

C-1222 Sherrill, Chris and Roger Aiello, KEY WEST THE LAST RESORT, Key West, FL: The Key West Book and Card Company, 1978.

C-1223 Shibley, Ronald E., HISTORIC FREDERICKSBURG: A PICTORIAL HISTORY, Norfolk, Donning, 1976.

C-1224 Shibley, Ronald E. and N. Jane Iseley, FREDERICKSBURG, Fredericksburg: Historic Fredericksburg Foundation, Inc., 1977.

C-1225 Shingleton, Royce, RICHARD PETERS: CHAMPION OF THE NEW SOUTH, Macon: Mercer University Press, 1985.

C-1226 Shofner, Jerrell H., HISTORY OF APOPKA AND NORTHWEST ORANGE COUNTY, FLORIDA, Apopka, FL: Apopka Historical Society, 1982.

C-1227 Shofner, Jerrell H., ORLANDO: THE CITY BEAUTIFUL, Tulsa, OK: Continental Heritage Press, 1984.

C-1228 Shore, Allen J., CITIES IN THE COMMONWEALTH: TWO CENTURIES OF URBAN LIFE IN KENTUCKY, Lexington: University Press of Kentucky, 1982.

C-1229 Sibley, Celestine, PEACHTREE STREET, U.S.A.; AN AFFECTIONATE PORTRAIT OF ATLANTA, Garden City, NY: Doubleday, 1963.

C-1230 Sibley, Marilyn McAdams, THE PORT OF HOUSTON: A HISTORY, Austin: University of Texas Press, 1968.

C-1231 Siddons, Anne Rivers, GO STRAIGHT ON PEACHTREE, Garden City, NY: Dolphin Books, 1978.

C-1232 Sieg, Edward Chan, EDEN ON THE MARSH: AN ILLUSTRATED HISTORY OF SAVANNAH, Northridge, CA: Windsor Publications, Inc., 1985.

C-1233 Siegel, Martin, NEW ORLEANS: A CHRONOLOGICAL AND DOCUMENTARY HISTORY, 1539-1970, Dobbs Ferry, NY: Oceana Publications, 1975.

C-1234 Siegel, Stanley E., HOUSTON: A CHRONICLE OF THE SUPER CITY ON BUFFALO BAYO, Woodland Hills, CA: Windsor Publications, 1983.

C-1235 Simmons, William T. and L. Brooks Lindsay, CHARLOTTE AND MECKLEN-BURG COUNTY: A PICTORIAL HISTORY, Norfolk: Donning Company, 1977.

C-1236 Simms, William Gilmore, CHARLESTON AND HER SATIRISTS: A SCRIBBLE-MENT, Charleston: James A. Burges, 1848..

C-1237 Simms, William Gilmore, SACK AND DESTRUCTION OF THE CITY OF COLUMBIA, S.C., Columbia, SC: Power Press of Daily Phoenix, 1865.

C-1238 Simons, Albert and Samuel Lapham, Jr., eds., CHARLESTON, SOUTH CAROLINA, New York: Press of the American Institute of Archi-tects, Inc., 1927.

C-1239 Simpkins, F.B., THE SOUTH, OLD AND NEW, New York: Alfred A. Knopf, 1949.

C-1240 Sinclair, W. R., TARHSELIA, NORTH CAROLINA, Charlotte, NC: CLCB Press, 1985.

C-1241 Slappey, Pansy Aiken, A MAN AND HIS CITY, BROWN HAYES AND ATLANTA; THE STORY OF A MAN'S PASSION FOR THE PROTECTION OF THE HEART OF HIS CITY, Atlanta: Southern Publications Society, 1961.

C-1242 Smith, Charles William, OLD CHARLESTON, Richmond: The Dial Press, 1933.

C-1243 Smith, D. E. Huger, A CHARLESTONIAN'S RECOLLECTIONS, 1846-1913, Charleston: Carolina Art Association, 1950.

C-1244 Smith, Jean Herron, SNICKERSVILLE: THE BIOGRAPHY OF A VILLAGE, Miamisburg, OH: Miamisburg News, 1970.

C-1245 Smiley, Nixon, YESTERDAY'S MIAMI, Miami: A. Seemann, 1977.

C-1246 Smith, Sidney Adair, ed., MOBILE: 1861-1865; NOTES AND A BIBLI-OGRAPHY, Chicago: Wyvern Press of S.F.E., Inc., [1964].

C-1247 Smith, Simon, TOADVINE IN ITS HEYDAY, privately printed, 1960.

C-1248 Sobel, Jane and Arthur J. Klonsky, ATLANTA, Toronto, Canada: Skyline Press, 1985.

C-1249 Sobel, Jane, Arthur J. Klonsky and Christine Gehman, A SOUTHERN CELEBRATION: CHARLESTON AND SAVANNAH PROCLAIMED, Toronto: Sky-line Press, 1985.

C-1250 Society of Pioneers, A HISTORY OF MONTGOMERY IN PICTURES, Montgom-
       ery: The Society of Pioneers, 1963.

C-1251 Sommers, Richard J., RICHMOND REDEEMED: THE SEIGE AT PETERSBURG,
       Garden City: Doubleday and Company, Inc., 1981.

C-1252 Spence, Ruth, BIBLIOGRAPHY OF BIRMINGHAM, ALABAMA, 1872-1972,
       Birminghamn: Oxmoor Press, 1973.

C-1253 Spence, Vernon Gladden, JUDGE LEGETT OF ABILENE: A TEXAS FRONTIER
       PROFILE, College Station: Texas A & M University Press, 1977.

C-1254 Spence, Vernon Gladden, PIONEER WOMEN OF ABILENE, Burnet, TX:
       Eakin Press, 1981.

C-1255 Spratling, William Philip, SHERWOOD ANDERSON AND OTHER FAMOUS
       CREOLES, Austin: University of Texas Press, 1967.

C-1256 Squires, William Henry Tappey, PETERSBURG, VA.: A COLLECTION OF
       VIRGINIANA ANENT PETERSBURG AND VICINITY. . . ., Norfolk, VA:
       1941.

C-1257 Stackpole, Edward James, DRAMA ON THE RAPPAHANNOCK: THE FRED-
       ERICKSBURG CAMPAIGN, Harrisburg, PA: Military Service Publishing
       Company, [1957].

C-1258 Stagg, Brian, DEER LODGE, TENNESSEE: ITS LITTLE-KNOWN HISTORY,
       n.p.: the Author, 1964.

C-1259 Stagg, Brian L., THE DISTANT EDEN, TENNESSEE'S RUGBY COLONY,
       Knoxville: Paylor Publications, 1973.

C-1260 Staples, Charles R., HISTORY OF PIONEER LEXINGTON, Lexington:
       Lexington-Fayette Historic Commission, 1973 (reprint).

C-1261 Starkey, Marion L., THE FIRST PLANTATION: HISTORY OF HAMPTON AND
       ELIZABETH CITY COUNTY, VIRGINIA, 1607-1887, Hampton: Houston
       Printing and Publishing House, 1936.

C-1262 Steelman, Joseph F., ed., OF TAR HEEL TOWNS, SHIPBUILDERS, RECON-
       STRUCTIONISTS AND ALLIANCEMEN: PAPERS IN NORTH CAROLINA HISTORY,
       Greenville: East Carolina University Publications, Department of
       History, Vol. 5, 1981.

C-1263 Stegeman, John F., THESE MEN SHE GAVE: CIVIL WAR DIARY OF ATHENS,
       GEORGIA, Athens: University of Georgia Press, 1964.

C-1264 Stein, R. Conrad, THE STORY OF ARLINGTON NATIONAL CEMETARY,
       Chicago: Childrens Press, 1979.

C-1265 Stewart, Roy P., BORN GROWN: AN OKLAHOMA CITY HISTORY, Oklahoma
       City: Fidelity Bank, 1974.

C-1266 Stieghorst, Junann J., BAY CITY AND MATAGORDA COUNTY: A HISTORY,
       Austin: Pemberton Press, 1965.

C-1267 Stokes, Durward T., AUCTION AND ACTION: HISTORICAL HIGHLIGHTS OF
       GRAHAM, NORTH CAROLINA, Graham, NC: City of Graham, NC, 1985.

C-1268 Stokes, Thomas L., THE SAVANNAH, New York: Rinehart and Company,
       Inc., 1951.

C-1269 Stolpen, Steve, CHAPEL HILL: A PICTORIAL HISTORY, Norfolk:
       Donning Company, 1978.

C-1270 Stolpen, Steve, RALEIGH: A PICTORIAL HISTORY, Norfolk: Donning
       Company, 1977.

C-1271 Stoughton, Gertrude K., TARPON SPRINGS: THE EARLY YEARS, Tarpon
        Springs, FL: Tarpon Springs Area Historical Society, 1976.

C-1272 Strahan, Clarles Morton, CLARKE COUNTY, GA. AND THE CITY OF
        ATHENS, Athens: C. P. Byrd, printer, 1893.

C-1273 Strom, Ann Miller, THE PRAIRIE CITY: A HISTORY OF KYLE, TEXAS,
        1880-1980, Burnet, TX: Nortex Press: Eakin Publications, 1981.

C-1274 Suarez, Annette McDonald, A SOURCE BOOK ON THE EARLY HISTORY OF
        CUTHBERT AND RANDOLPH COUNTY GEORGIA, Atlanta: Cherokee Publish-
        ing Company, 1982.

C-1275 Sulzby, James Frederick, ARTHUR W. SMITH, A BIRMINGHAM PIONEER,
        1855-1944, Birmingham, AL: 1961.

C-1276 Sulzby, James Frederick, BIRMINGHAM, AS IT WAS, IN JACKSON COUNTY,
        ALABAMA, Birmingham: Birmingham Printing Company, 1944.

C-1277 Sulzby, James Frederick, BIRMINGHAM SKETCHES; FROM 1871 THROUGH
        1921, Birmingham: Birmingham Printing Company, 1945.

C-1278 Summersell, Charles Grayson, MOBILE: HISTORY OF A SEAPORT TOWN,
        University, AL: University of Alabama Press, 1949.

C-1279 Sumter, Thomas S., STATESBURG AND ITS PEOPLE Sumpter: Sumpter
        Printing Company, 1949.

C-1280 Sylvester, C. Doughty, PRESENTING A PICTORICAL HISTORY OF AUGUSTA,
        GEORGIA, Augusta: Wel-com-in Publications, 1962.

C-1281 Tanner, John Thomas, A HISTORY OF ATHENS: AND INCIDENTALLY OF
        LIMESTONE COUNTY, ALABAMA, University, AL: Confederate Publishing
        Company, 1978.

C-1282 Tate, William, STROLLS AROUND ATHENS, Athens, GA: Observer Press,
        1975.

C-1283 Taylor, Donald Ransom, OUT OF THE PAST--THE FUTURE: A HISTORY OF
        HAMPTON, VIRGINIA, Hampton: Prestige Press, Inc., 1960.

C-1284 Taylor, Elberta, BIRMINGHAM IS MY HOME, Birmingham: Birmingham
        Printing Company, 1940.

C-1285 Taylor, James, NEW ORLEANS ON THE HALF SHELL: A NATIVE'S GUIDE TO
        THE CRESCENT CITY, New Orleans: New Bohemian Press, 1981.

C-1286 Taylor, Owen M., THE HISTORY OF ANNAPOLIS, THE CAPITAL OF MARY-
        LAND. . ., Baltimore: Turnbull Brothers, 1872.

C-1287 Teal, Harney S., RIDES ABOUT CAMDEN, 1853 & 1873, Columbia, SC:
        McDonald Letter Shop, 196189

C-1288 Tellier, Mark, ST. AUGUSTINE'S PICTURES OF THE PAST: A SECOND
        DISCOVERY, St. Augustine: The Author, 1979.

C-1289 Ten Eick, Virginia Elliot, HISTORY OF HOLLYWOOD, Hollywood, FL:
        The City of Hollywood, 1966.

C-1290 Terrell, Lloyd Preston, BLACKS IN AUGUSTA: A CHRONOLOGY, 1741-
        1977, Augusta: Preston Publications, 1977.

C-1291 Thomas, Emory M., THE CONFEDERATE STATE OF RICHMOND: A BIOGRAPHY
        OF THE CAPITAL, Austin: University of Texas Press, 1971.

C-1292 Thomas, Jane, OLD DAYS IN NASHVILLE, TENNESSEE, REMINISCENSES,
        Nashville: Publishing House, 1897; reprint, Nashville: Charles
        Elder, Bookseller and Publisher, 1969.

C-1293 Thomas, Samuel, LOUISVILLE SINCE THE TWENTIES, Louisville: The
       Courier-Journal and the Louisville Times, 1978.

C-1294 Thomas, Samuel W., ed., VIEWS OF LOUISVILLE SINCE 1766, Louis-
       ville: The Courier-Journal and the Louisville Times, 1971.

C-1295 Thomas, Samuel W. and William Morgan, OLD LOUISVILLE: THE VIC-
       TORIAN ERA, Louisville: Data Courier, Inc., 1975.

C-1296 Thomas, William H. B., GORDONSVILLE, VIRGINIA: HISTORIC CROSS-
       ROADS TOWN, Verona, VA: McClure Press, 1971.

C-1297 Thomas, William H. B., ORANGE, VIRGINIA: STORY OF A COURTHOUSE
       TOWN, Verona, VA: McClure Press, 1972.

C-1298 Thomason, Michael and Milton McLaurin, MOBILE: AMERICAN RIVER
       CITY, Mobile: Easter Publishing Company, 1975.

C-1299 Thomson, Bailey and Patricia L. Meador, SHREVEPORT: A PHOTO-
       GRAPHIC REMEMBRANCE, 1873-1849, Baton Rouge: Louisiana State
       University Press, 1986.

C-1300 Thornthwaite, Charles Warren, LOUISVILLE, KENTUCKY: A STUDY IN
       URBAN GEOGRAPHY, Berkeley: University of California Press, 1929.

C-1301 Tidwell, Oliver Cromwell Jr., BELLE MEADE PARK, Nashville:
       privately printed, 1983.

C-1302 Tintagil Club, OFFICIAL GUIDE TO THE CITY OF MONTGOMERY, ALABAMA,
       1948, Montgomery, 1948.

C-1303 Tolles, Zonira Hunter, BONNIE MELROSE, THE EARLY HISTORY OF MEL-
       ROSE, FLORIDA, Gainesville: Storter Printing Company, Inc., 1982.

C-1304 Travelog Publishing Company, GREATER MIAMI, SOUTH FLORIDA, AND THE
       KEYS, Coral Gables: John S. Griffith, 196?.

C-1305 Trim, Laura, SHORT TRIPS IN AND AROUND DALLAS, Dallas, TX: LDT
       Press, 1984.

C-1306 Trowbridge, J. T., SOUTH: A TOUR OF ITS BATTLE FIELDS & RUINED
       CITIES, Ayer Company, American Negro, His History and Literature
       Series, No. 2, 1969, repr. of 1866 ed.

C-1307 True, Ransom, JAMESTOWN: A GUIDE TO OLD TOWN, Richmond, VA: The
       Association for the Preservation of Virginia Antiquities.

C-1308 Uhlendorf, B. A., trans., THE SEIGE OF CHARLESTON: WITH AN AC-
       COUNT OF THE PROVINCE OF SOUTH CAROLINA: DIARIES AND LETTERS OF
       HESSIAN OFFICERS, Ann Arbor: University of Michigan Press, 1938.

C-1309 Unibook, Inc., eds., HOUSTON: CITY OF DESTINY, New York:
       Macmillan, 1980.

C-1310 Urguhart, Kenneth Trist, ed., VICKSBURG: SOUTHERN CITY UNDER
       SEIGE, New Orleans: The Historic New Orleans Collection, 1980.

C-1311 Valentine, Orpha, LAFAYETTE; ITS PAST, PEOPLE, AND PROGRESS, Baton
       Rouge, LA: Moran Publishing Corp., 1980.

C-1312 Vance Rupert B. and Nicholas J. Demerath, THE URBAN SOUTH, Chapel
       Hill: University of North Carolina Press, 1954.

C-1313 Vance, Rupert Bayless, John Shelton Reed and Daniel Joseph Singal,
       eds., REGIONALISM AND THE SOUTH: SELECTED PAPERS OF RUPERT VANCE,
       Chapel Hill: University of North Carolina Press, 1982.

C-1314 Van Court, Catherine, IN OLD NATCHEZ, New York: Doubleday, Doran and Company, Inc., 1937.

C-1315 Vandal, Gilles, THE NEW ORLEANS RIOT OF 1866: ANATOMY OF A TRAGEDY, Lafayette, Center for Louisiana Studies at the University of Southwestern Louisiana, 1983.

C-1316 Van der Veer, Virginia, ALABAMA: A BICENTENNIAL HISTORY, New York: W. W. Norton Company, 1977.

C-1317 Vaughn-Roberson, Courtney and Glen Vaughn-Roberson, CITY IN THE OSAGE HILLS: A HISTORY OF TULSA, OKLAHOMA, Boulder, CO: Pruett Publishing Company, 1984.

C-1318 Verner, Elizabeth O'Neill, MELLOWED BY TIME, A CHARLESTON NOTE-BOOK, Columbia, SC: Bostich and Thornley, Inc., 1941.

C-1319 Vickers, James, RALEIGH, CITY OF OAKS: AN ILLUSTRATED HISTORY, Woodland Hills, CA: Windsor Publications, 1982.

C-1320 Vickers, James, et al., CHAPEL HILL: AN ILLUSTRATED HISTORY, Chapel Hill, NC: Barclay Publishers, 1985.

C-1321 Voges, Nettie Allen, OLD ALEXANDRIA: WHERE AMERICA'S PAST IS PRESENT, McLean, VA: EPM Publicaitons, 1975.

C-1322 Walker, Carrol, NORFOLK: A TRICENTENNIAL PICTORIAL HISTORY, Virginia Beach, VA: Donning Company/Publishers.

C-1323 Waller, William, ed., NASHVILLE IN THE 1890s, Nashville: Vanderbilt University Press, 1970.

C-1324 Waller, William, NASHVILLE, 1900-1910, Nashville: Vanderbilt University Press, 1972.

C-1325 Walton, Frank L., SHUBUTA. A BRIEF STORY ABOUT SHUBUTA ON THE BANKS OF THE CHICKASAWHOY, Shubuta, MS: Shubuta Memorial Association, 1947.

C-1326 Ward, David, CITIES AND IMMIGRANTS: A GEOGRAPHY OF CHANGE IN NINETEENTH CENTURY AMERICA, New York: Oxford University Press, 1971.

C-1327 Ward, Harry M., RICHMOND: AN ILLUSTRATED HISTORY, Northridge, CA: Windsor Publications, Inc., 1985.

C-1328 Ward, Harry M. and Harold E. Greer Jr., RICHMOND DURING THE REVOLUTION, 1775-83, Charlottesville: University Press of Virginia, 1977.

C-1329 Ward, James Robertson and Dena Elizabeth Snodgrass, OLD HICKORY'S TOWN, AN ILLUSTRATED HISTORY OF JACKSONVILLE, Jacksonville: Florida Publishing Company, 1982.

C-1330 Warren, Marion, et al.,"THE TRAIN'S DONE BEEN AND GONE": AN ANNAPOLIS PORTRAIT, 1859-1910: A PHOTOGRAPHIC COLLECTION, Annapolis, MD: M. E. Warren, 1981.

C-1331 Waterbury, Jean Parker, THE OLDEST CITY: ST. AUGUSTINE, SAGA OF SURVIVAL, St. Augustine, FL: St. Augustine Historical Society, 1983.

C-1332 Waugh, Elizabeth Culbertson, NORTH CAROLINA'S CAPITAL, RALEIGH, Chapel Hill: University of North Carolina Press, 1969.

C-1333 Wayne, Flynt, MONTGOMERY, AN ILLUSTRATED HISTORY, Woodland Hills, CA: Windsor Publications, 1980.

C-1334 Wertenbaker, Thomas J., NORFOLK: HISTORIC SOUTHERN PORT, Durham:
       Duke University Press, 1962 [c. 1951].

C-1335 Wertenbaker, Thomas Jefferson, THE OLD SOUTH. THE FOUNDING OF
       AMERICAN CIVILIZATION, New York: Charles Scribner's Sons, 1942.

C-1336 Weatherly, Andrew Earl, THE FIRST HUNDRED YEARS OF HISTORIC
       GILFORD, 1771-1871, Greensboro: Greensboro Printing Company,
       1972.

C-1337 Weaver, C. E., SKETCHES OF ATLANTA, GEORGIA; GATE CITY OF THE
       SOUTH, Atlanta: Central Publishing Company, 193-.

C-1338 Weaver, John D., THE BROWNSVILLE RAID, New York: W. W. Norton and
       Company, 1970.

C-1339 Webb, Sheyann and Rachel West Nelson as told to Frank Sikora,
       SELMA, LORD, SELMA: GIRLHOOD MEMORIES OF THE CIVIL-RIGHTS DAYS,
       University, AL: The University of Alabama Press, 1980.

C-1340 Weeks, Linton, CLARKSDALE & COAHOMA COUNTY: A HISTORY, Clarks-
       dale, MS: Carnegie Public Library, 1982.

C-1341 Weeks, Linton, CLEVELAND: A CENTENIAL HISTORY, 1886-1986 (sic),
       Cleveland, MS: City of Cleveland, 1985 (sic.).

C-1342 Weidling, Philip J. and August Burghard, CHECKERED SUNSHINE: THE
       STORY OF FORT LAUDERDALE, 17934-1955, Gainesville: University of
       Florida Press, 1966.

C-1343 Wharton, Clarence R., GAIL BORDEN, PIONEER, San Antonio: Naylor
       Company, 1941.

C-1344 Wheeler, Richard, SWORD OVER RICHMOND. AN EYEWITNESS HISTORY OF
       McCLELLAN'S PENINSULA CAMPAIGN, New York: Harper & Row, 1986.

C-1345 Whitmore, Nancy F. and Timothy L, Cannon, FREDERICK: A PICTORAL
       HISTORY, Norfolk: Donning Company, 1981.

C-1346 Wickham, Joan, SAINT AUGUSTINE FLORIDA 1565-1965, Worcester, MA:
       Achille J. St. Onge, 1967.

C-1347 Wilkinson, Eliza (Caroline Gilman, ed.), LETTERS OF ELIZA WILLIAMS
       DURING THE INVASION AND POSSESSION OF CHARLESTON, SOUTH CAROLINA,
       BY THE BRITISH IN THE REVOLUTIONARY WAR, New York: S. Colman,
       1839.

C-1348 Williams, Caroline, LOUISVILLE SCENE, Garden City, NY: Doubleday
       and Company, 1970.

C-1349 Williams, Charlean, THE OLD TOWN SPEAKS; WASHINGTON, HEMPSTEAD
       COUNTY, ARKANSAS, GATEWAY TO TEXAS, 1935; CONFEDERATE CAPITAL,
       1863, Houston: Anson Jones Press, 1951.

C-1350 Williams, Emma Inman, HISTORIC MADISON: THE STORY OF JACKSON AND
       MADISON COUNTY FROM THE PREHISTORIC MOUNDBUILDERS TO 1917, Jack-
       son, TN: Madison County Historical Society, 1946.

C-1351 Williams, Mack H., IN OLD FORT WORTH, Fort Worth: News-Tribune,
       1977.

C-1352 Williford, William Bailey, PEACHTREE STREET, ATLANTA, Athens:
       University of Georgia Press, 1962.

C-1353 Wilson, Everett B., EARLY SOUTHERN TOWNS, South Brunswick: A. S.
       Barnes & Company, 1967.

C-1354 Wilson, George O., TODAY AND TOMORROW BECOME YESTERDAY: THE CITY
        OF DALTON AND THE COUNTY OF WHITFIELD IN THE STATE OF GEORGIA
        . . ., Dalton, GA: [Dalton-Whitfield County Bicentennial Com-
        mission?], 1976.

C-1355 Wilson, John, CHATTANOOGA'S STORY, Chattanooga: Chattanooga News-
        Free Press, 1980.

C-1356 Wilson, John, THE PATTEN CHRONICLE: THE STORY OF A GREAT CHATTA-
        NOOGA FAMILY, Chattanooga: R. McDonald, 1986?.

C-1357 Windhorn, Stan and Wright Langley, YESTERDAY'S KEY WEST, Miami:
        E. A. Seemann Publishing Company, 1973.

C-1358 Winningham, Geoff, GOING TEXAN, THE DAYS OF THE HOUSTON LIVESTOCK
        SHOW AND RODEO, Houston: Marvis P. Kelsey, Jr., 1972.

C-1359 Winningham, Geoff and Al Reinert, A PLACE OF DREAMS: HOUSTON, AN
        AMERICAN CITY, Houston, TX: Rice University Press, 1986.

C-1360 Winters, Ralph L., HISTORICAL SKETCHES OF ADAMS, ROBERTSON COUNTY,
        TENNESSEE, AND PORT ROYAL, MONTGOMERY COUNTY, TENNESSEE, FROM 1779
        TO 1868, Clarkesville, TN: The Author, 1968.

C-1361 Wolcott, Reed, ROSE HILL, New York: G. P. Putnam's Sons, 1976.

C-1362 Wolle, Petyer, Francis Griffin, ed., THE THREE FORKS OF MUDDY
        CREEK, Winston-Salem: Old Salem, Inc., 1984.

C-1363 Womack, Walter, McMINNVILLE AT A MILESTONE, 1810-1860, McMinn-
        ville: Standard Publishing Company, Inc., 1960.

C-1364 Wood, Louisa F., BEHIND THOSE GARDEN WALLS IN HISTORIC SAVANNAH,
        Savannah: Historic Savannah Foundation, 1982.

C-1365 Woodward, C. Vann, ORIGINS OF THE NEW SOUTH, 1877-1913, Baton
        Rouge: Louisiana State University Press, 1951.

C-1366 Woodward, William, FRENCH QUARTER ETCHINGS OF OLD NEW ORLEANS, New
        Orleans: The Magnolia Press, The American Academy of History,
        1938.

C-1367 Woodworth, Karl, FIND YOUR OWN WAY IN DOWNTOWN ATLANTA: A WALKING
        TOUR AND STREET LEVEL GUIDE TO THE "MAGIC CITY OF THE SOUTH,"
        Atlanta: Woodworth, 1976.

C-1368 Wooldridge, John, HISTORY OF NASHVILLE, TENNESSEE, WITH FULL OUT-
        LINE OF THE NATURAL ADVANTAGES, ACCOUNTS OF THE MOUND BUILDERS,
        INDIAN TRIBES, EARLY SETTLEMENT, ORGANIZATION OF THE METRO DIS-
        TRICT, AND GENERAL AND PARTICULAR HISTORY OF THE CITY DOWN TO THE
        PRESENT TIME, Nashville: Methodist Publishing House, 1890;
        reprint Nashville: Charles Elder, Bookseller, 1970.

C-1369 Wooley, Carolyn Murray, THE FOUNDING OF LEXINGTON, 1775 TO 1776,
        Lexington: Lexington-Fayette County Historic Commission, 1975.

C-1370 Wootten, Bayard and Samuel Gaillard Stoney, CHARLESTON. AZELEAS
        AND OLD BRICKS, Boston: Houghton Mifflin Company, 1939.

C-1371 Work Projects Administration, HOUSTON: A HISTORY AND A GUIDE,
        Houston, TX: Anson Jones, 1942.

C-1372 Wright, John D. Jr., LEXINGTON: HEART OF THE BLUEGRASS, Lexing-
        ton: Lexington-Fayette County Historic Commission, 1983.

C-1373 Writers' Program, ATLANTA, A CITY OF THE MODERN SOUTH, New York:
        Smith and Durrell, 1942.

C-1374 Writers' Program, Georgia, THE MACON GUIDE AND OCMULGEE NATIONAL MONUMENT, Macon, GA: J. W. Burke Company, 1939.

C-1375 Writers' Program, North Carolina, RALEIGH, CAPITAL OF NORTH CARO-LINA, New York: AMS Press, 1975, c. 1942.

C-1376 Writers' Program of the Works Progress Administration in the State of Texas, HOUSTON: A HISTORY AND GUIDE, Houston: American Guide Series, 1942.

C-1377 Writers' Program, Virginia, ROANOKE; STORY OF COUNTY AND CITY, Roanoke: Stone Printing and Manufacturing Company, 1942.

C-1378 Yater, George H., TWO HUNDRED YEARS AT THE FALLS OF THE OHIO: A HISTORY OF LOUISVILLE AND JEFFERSON COUNTY, Louisville: Heritage Corporation, 1979.

C-1379 Young, Harold, et al., VICKSBURG BATTLEFIELD MONUMENTS: A PHOTO-GRAPHIC RECORD, Jackson: University Press of Mississippi, 1984.

C-1380 Young, Samuel Oliver, TRUE STORIES OF OLD HOUSTON AND HOUSTONIANS: HISTORICAL AND PERSONAL SKETCHES, Galveston: O. Springer, 1913.

C-1381 Zeiss, Betsy, THE OTHER SIDE OF THE RIVER: HISTORICAL CAPE CORAL, privately printed, 1983.

C-1382 Zibart, Carl F., YESTERDAY'S NASHVILLE, Miami: E. A. Seemann Publishing, Inc., 1976.

Housing and Neighborhoods

C-1383 Bullard, Robert D., HOUSING ALLOWANCE IN THE SEVENTIES: AN ASSESSMENT OF HOUSTON'S HOUSING ASSISTANCE PAYMENT PROGRAM, Houston: Texas Southern University, 1977.

C-1384 Bullard, Robert D. and Donald L. Tryman, HOUSING MOBILITY IN THE HOUSTON METROPOLITAN AREA: A SURVEY OF HUD ASSISTED FAMILY DEVELOPMENT, Houston: Demographic Environs Research, 1980.

C-1385 Frye, Robert J., HOUSING AND URBAN RENEWAL IN ALABAMA, University, AL: Bureau of Public Administration, University of Alabama, 1965.

C-1386 Glazer, Nathan and Davis McEntire, eds., STUDIES IN HOUSING AND MINORITY GROUPS, Berkeley: University of California Press, 1960.

C-1387 Reissman, Leonard, et al., HOUSING DISCRIMINATION IN NEW ORLEANS, New Orleans: Tulane Urban Studies Center, Tulane University, 1970.

C-1388 Wolff, Reinhold P. and David Gellogly, NEGRO HOUSING IN THE MIAMI AREA: EFFECTS OF THE POSTWAR HOUSING BOOM, Coral Gables: University of Miami, 1951.

C-1389 Vogt, Lloyd, NEW ORLEANS HOUSES: A HOUSE-WATCHERS GUIDE, Gretna, LA: Pelican Publishing Company, Inc., 1985.

Journalism

C-1390 Acheson, Sam, 35,000 DAYS IN TEXAS: A HISTORY OF THE DALLAS NEWS AND ITS FORBEARS, New York: Macmillan Company, 1938.

C-1391 Allsop, Fred W., HISTORY OF THE ARKANSAS PRESS FOR A HUNDRED YEARS AND MORE, Little Rock: Parke-Harper Publishers, 1922.

C-1392 Baker, Thomas Harrison, THE MEMPHIS COMMERCIAL APPEAL: THE HIS-
TORY OF A SOUTHERN NEWSPAPER, Baton Rouge: Louisiana State
University Press, 1971.

C-1393 Bell, Earl L. and Kenneth C. Crabbe, THE AUGUSTA CHRONICLE:
INDOMITABLE VOICE OF DIXIE, 1785-1960, Athens: University of
Georgia Press, 1960.

C-1394 Carney, Robert, WHAT HAPPENED AT THE ATLANTA TIMES, Atlanta:
Business Press, 1969.

C-1395 Chambers, Lenoir and Joseph E. Shank, SALT WATER & PRINTERS INK:
NORFOLK AND ITS NEWSPAPERS, 1865-1965, Chapel Hill: University of
North Carolina Press, 1967.

C-1396 Claiborne, Jack, THE CHARLOTTE OBSERVER: ITS TIME AND PLACE,
Chapel Hill: University of North Carolina Press, 1986.

C-1397 Cohen, Hennig, THE SOUTH CAROLINA GAZETTE, 1732-1775, Columbia:
University of South Carolina Press, 1953.

C-1398 Dabney, Thomas Ewing, ONE HUNDRED GREAT YEARS: THE STORY OF THE
TIMES-PICAYUNE FROM ITS FOUNDING TO 1940, Baton Rouge: Louisiana
State University Press, 1944.

C-1399 Daniel, John M., THE RICHMOND EXAMINER DURING THE WAR, New York:
by the author, 1868.

C-1400 Darden, Robert F., DRAWING POWER: KNOTT, FICKLEN, AND McCLANAHAN,
EDITORIAL CARTOONISTS OF THE DALLAS MORNING NEWS, Waco: Markham
Press Fund, 1983.

C-1401 Dealey, Ted, THREE MEN OF TEXAS, AND A TEXAS INSTITUTION, "THE
DALLAS MORNING NEWS," New York: Newcomen Society in North
America, 1957.

C-1402 Elliot, Robert Neal Jr., THE RALEIGH REGISTER, 1799-1863, James
Sprunt Studies in History and Political Science, Volume 36, Chapel
Hill: University of North Carolina Press, 1955.

C-1403 Evans, Herclon J., THE NEWSPAPER PRESS IN KENTUCKY, Lexington:
University Press of Kentucky, 1976.

C-1404 Graham, Hugh Davis, CRISIS IN PRINT: DESEGREGATION AND THE PRESS
IN TENNESSEE, Nashville: Vanderbilt University Press, 1967.

C-1405 Griffin, Richard W., NEWSPAPER STORY OF A TOWN: A HISTORY OF
DANVILLE, KENTUCKY, Danville: Advocate-Messenger and the Kentucky
Advocate, 1965.

C-1406 Hall, Grover C., HONORING R. F. HUDSON AND COMMEMORATING HIS
FIFTIETH YEAR WITH THE MONTGOMERY ADVERTISER, 1903-1952, Montgomery, AL: Brown Printing Company, 1953.

C-1407 Harkey, Ira B. Jr., THE SMELL OF BURNING CROSSES: AN AUTOBIO-
GRAPHY OF A MISSISSIPPI NEWSPAPERMAN, Jacksonville, IL: Harris
Wolfe and Company, 1967.

C-1408 Hederman, Robert M. Jr., THE HEDERMAN STORY; A SAGA OF THE PRINTED
WORD IN MISSISSIPPI, New York: Newcomen Society in North America, 1966.

C-1409 Hollis, Daniel Webster III, AN ALABAMA NEWSPAPER TRADITION:
GROVER C. HALL AND THE HALL FAMILY, University, AL: The University of Alabama Press, 1983.

C-1410 Hoole, W. Stanley, ALIAS SIMON SUGGS: THE LIFE AND TIMES OF
       JOHNSON JONES HOOPER, University, AL: University of Alabama
       Press, 1952.

C-1411 Houzeau, Jean-Charles (David C. Rankin, ed; Gerald F. Denoult,
       transl.), MY PASSAGE AT THE NEW ORLEANS TRIBUNE: A MEMOIR OF THE
       CIVIL WAR ERA, Baton Rouge: Louisiana State University Press,
       1984.

C-1412 Jacobs, Howard, LET'S GO TO PRESS: THE STORY OF THE TIMES-
       PICAYUNE AND NEW ORLEANS STATES ITEM, New Orleans: Times-
       Picayune, 197-.

C-1413 Kneebone, John T., SOUTHERN LIBERAL JOURNALISTS AND THE ISSUE OF
       RACE, 1920-1944., Chapel Hill: University of North Carolina
       Press, 1985.

C-1414 Logan, Rayford W., ed., THE ATTITUDE OF THE SOUTHERN WHITE PRESS
       TOWARD NEGRO SUFFRAGE, 1932-1940, Washington: The Founding
       Publishers, 1940.

C-1415 Quenzel, Carrol Hunter, EDGAR SNOWDEN, SR., VIRGINIA JOURNALIST
       AND CIVIC LEADER, Charlottesville: Bibliographical Society of the
       University of Virginia, 1954.

C-1416 Reynolds, Donald E., EDITORS MAKE WAR: SOUTHERN NEWSPAPERS IN THE
       SECESSION CRISIS, Nashville: Vanderbilt University Press, 1970.

C-1417 Rogers, Ernest, PEACHTREE PARADE, Atlanta: Tupper and Love, 1956.

C-1418 Ross, Margaret, ARKANSAS GAZETTE: THE EARLY YEARS, 1819-1866,
       Little Rock: Arkansas Gazette Foundation, 1969.

C-1419 Rubin, Louis D. Jr., et al., THE HISTORY OF SOUTHERN LITERATURE,
       Baton Rouge: Louisiana State University Press, 1985.

C-1420 Sass, Herbert Ravenel, OUTSPOKEN, Columbia: University of South
       Carolina Press, 1953.

C-1421 Sharpe, Ernest, G. B. DEALEY OF THE DALLAS NEWS, New York: Holt,
       1955.

C-1422 Sibley, Marilyn McAdams, LONE STARS AND STATE GAZETTES: TEXAS
       NEWSPAPERS BEFORE THE CIVIL WAR, College Station, TX: Texas A & M
       University Press, 1983.

C-1423 Smiley, Nixon, KNIGHTS OF THE FOURTH ESTATE: THE STORY OF THE
       MIAMI HERALD, Miami: E. A. Seemann Publishing, Inc., 1975.

C-1424 Suggs, Henry Lewis, ed., THE BLACK PRESS IN THE SOUTH, 1865-1979,
       Westport: Greenwood Press, 1983.

C-1425 U. S. Works Projects Administration, Georgia, AUGUSTA NEWSPAPER
       DIGEST. COMPILED FROM FILES OF THE AUGUSTA CHRONICLE, 1861-72,
       Augusta: WPA, 193-.

C-1426 Veale, Frank, THE ATLANTA TIMES INSIDE STORY, Greenville, GA:
       Gresham Printing Company, 1965.

C-1427 Wheeler, Joseph Towne, THE MARYLAND PRESS, 1777-1790, Baltimore:
       The Maryland Historical Society, 1938.

C-1428 Wilds, John, AFTERNOON STORY, A CENTURY OF THE NEW ORLEANS STATES-
       ITEM, Baton Rouge: Louisiana State University Press, 1976.

Labor and Employment

C-1429 Beifuss, Joan Turner, AT THE RIVER I STAND: MEMPHIS, THE 1968 STRIKE AND MARTIN LUTHER KING, Memphis: B & W Books, 1985.

C-1430 Bergland, Abraham, George Talmage Starnes and Frank Traver deVyver, LABOR IN THE INDUSTRIAL SOUTH, University, VA: Institute for Research in the Social Sciences, 1930.

C-1431 Byerly, Victoria, HARD TIMES COTTON MILL GIRLS: PERSONAL HIS-TORIES OF WOMANHOOD AND POVERTY IN THE SOUTH, Boston, MA: South End Press, 1985.

C-1432 Christian, Marcus, NEGRO IRONWORKERS IN LOUISIANA, 1718-1900, Gretna, LA: Pelican Publishing Company, 1972.

C-1433 Conway, Mimi, RISE GONNA RISE, A PORTRAIT OF SOUTHERN TEXTILE WORKERS, New York: Anchor Press/Doubleday, 1979?

C-1434 Fink, Gary M. and Merl E. Reed, eds., ESSAYS IN SOUTHERN LABOR HISTORY: SELECTED PAPERS, SOUTHERN LABOR HISTORY CONFERENCE, 1976, Westport, CN: Greenwood Press, 1977.

C-1435 Golden, Claudia Dale, URBAN SLAVERY IN THE AMERICAN SOUTH 1820-1860: A QUANTITATIVE HISTORY, Chicago: University of Chicago Press, 1976.

C-1436 Herring, Harriet Laura, WELFARE WORK IN MILL VILLAGES: THE STORY OF EXTRA-MILL ACTIVITIES IN NORTH CAROLINA, Chapel Hill: 1929.

C-1437 Marshall, F. Ray, LABOR IN THE SOUTH, Cambridge, MA: Harvard University Press, 1966.

C-1438 Menefee, Selden and Orin C. Cassmore, THE PECAN SHELLERS OF SAN ANTONIO, Washington, DC: Works Progress Administration, U.S. Government Printing Office, 1940.

C-1439 McLaurin, Melton Alonza, PATERNALISM AND PROTEST: SOUTHERN COTTON MILL WORKERS AND ORGANIZED LABOR, 1875-1905, Westport: Greenwood Publishing Company, 1971.

C-1440 Phillips, Ulrich B., LIFE AND LABOR IN THE OLD SOUTH, Boston: Little, Brown, 1931.

C-1441 Rachleff, Peter J., BLACK LABOR IN THE SOUTH: RICHMOND, VIRGINIA, 1865-1890, Philadelphia: Temple University Press, 1984.

C-1442 Sellars, James Benson, SLAVERY IN ALABAMA, University, AL: University of Alabama Press, 1950.

C-1443 Stanback, Thomas M. and Thierry J. Noyelle, CITIES IN TRANSITION: CHANGING JOB STRUCTURES IN ATLANTA, DENVER, BUFFALO, PHOENIX, COLUMBUS (OHIO), NASHVILLE, AND CHARLOTTE, Totowa, NJ: Allonheld, Osmun, 1981.

C-1444 Starobin, Robert S., INDUSTRIAL SLAVERY IN THE OLD SOUTH, New York: Oxford University Press, 1970.

C-1445 United States Work Projects Administration, THE PECAN SHELLERS OF SAN ANTONIO: THE PROBLEM OF UNDERPAID AND UNEMPLOYED MEXICAN LABOR, Washington, DC: U.S. Government Printing Office, 1940.

C-1446 Wade, Richard C., SLAVERY IN THE CITIES: THE SOUTH 1820-1860, New York: Oxford University Press, 1964.

C-1447 Yellin, David Gilmer and Carol Lynn Yellin, THE MEMPHIS MULTI-MEDIA ARCHIVAL PROJECT: THE 1968 SANITATION WORKERS' STRIKE: FINAL REPORT TO THE NATIONAL ENDOWMENT FOR THE HUMANITIES, Memphis: J. W. Brister Library, 1974.

Life, Culture and Social Organization

C-1448 Abbott, Shirley, WOMENFOLK: GROWING UP DOWN SOUTH, New Haven:
Tichnor & Fields, 1983.

C-1449 Acton, Hul-Cee Marcus, THE PIERIAN CLUB OF BIRMINGHAM, WITH BIO-
GRAPHIES OF MEMBERS AND MEMORIES OF EAST LAKE, Birmingham: Banner
Press, 1962.

C-1450 Albaugh, June Middleton and Rose Lyon Traylor, COLLIRINE, THE
QUEEN HILL, Montgomery: Herff Jones--Paragon Press, 1977.

C-1451 Allen, Martha M., GEORGETOWN'S YESTERYEARS: THE PEOPLE REMEMBER,
Georgetown, TX: Georgetown Heritage, 1985.

C-1452 Amos, Harriet Elizabeth, COTTON CITY: URBAN DEVELOPMENT IN
ANTEBELLUM MOBILE, University, AL: University of Alabama Press,
1985.

C-1453 Anchor, Shirley, MEXICAN AMERICANS IN A DALLAS BARRIO, Tucson:
University of Arizona Press, 1978.

C-1454 Andrews, Johnnie and William David Higgins, CREOLE MOBILE: A
COMPENDIUM OF THE COLONIAL FAMILIES OF THE CENTRAL GULF COAST,
1702-1813, Prichard, AL: Bienville Historical Society, 1974.

C-1455 Armstrong, Louis, SATCHMO: MY LIFE IN NEW ORLEANS, New York:
Prentice-Hall, Inc., 1954.

C-1456 Asbury, Herbert, THE FRENCH QUARTER: AN INFORMAL HISTORY OF THE
NEW ORLEANS UNDERWORLD, New York: Alfred A. Knopf Company, 1936.

C-1457 Athens, Georgia Public Schools, A COMMUNITY STUDY OF ATHENS IN
RELATION TO PERSISTANT PROBLEMS OF LIVING, Athens: s.n., 19--?

C-1458 Atlanta Fire Department, PROMPT TO ACTION: ATLANTA FIRE DEPART-
MENT 1860-1960; 100 YEARS OF ORGANIZED FIRE PROTECTION, Atlanta:
1961.

C-1459 Atlanta Public Forum, AN INTRODUCTION TO SOCIAL SERVICE AGENCIES
IN ATLANTA, Atlanta: 1938.

C-1460 Ayers, H. Brandt and Thomas H. Naylor, eds., YOU CAN'T EAT
MAGNOLIAS, New York: McGraw-Hill, 1972.

C-1461 Bailess, R. R., et al., eds., VINTAGE VICKSBURG, Vicksburg:
Vicksburg Junior Auxilliary, 1985.

C-1462 Bauxbaum, Edwin C., THE GREEK AMERICAN GROUP OF TARPON SPRINGS,
FLORIDA: A STUDY OF ETHIC IDENTIFICATION AND ACCULTURATION,
[s.l.]. Ayer Company, Publishers, 1981.

C-1463 Beirne, Francis F., THE AMIABLE BALTIMORIANS, New York: Dutton,
1951.

C-1464 Beneke, Lynda, ed., A GRAND HERITAGE: A CULINARY LEGACY OF
COLUMBUS, MISSISSIPPI, Columbus: Heritage Academy, 1983.

C-1465 Berkeley, Edmund and Dorothy Smith Berkeley, DR. ALEXANDER GARDEN
OF CHARLES TOWN, Chapel Hill: University of North Carolina Press,
1969.

C-1466 Berman, Myron, RICHMOND'S JEWRY, 1769-1976: SHABBAT IN SHOCKOE,
Charlottesville, VA: University Press of Virginia, 1979.

C-1467 Bethel, Elizabeth Rauh, PROMISED LAND: A CENTURY OF LIFE IN A
NEGRO COMMUNITY, Philadelphia: Temple University Press, 1981.

C-1468 Blackwelder, Julia Kirk, WOMEN OF THE DEPRESSION: CASTE AND CULTURE IN SAN ANTONIO, 1929-1939, College Station: Texas A & M University Press, 1984.

C-1469 Bonge, Lyle, THE SLEEP OF REASON. LYLE BONGE'S ULTIMATE ASH-HAULING MARDI GRAS PHOTOGRAPHS, New York: Jargon Society, 1974.

C-1470 Bonner, James C., ed., THE JOURNAL OF A MILLEDGEVILLE GIRL, 1861-1867, Athens: University of Georgia Press, 1964.

C-1471 Borchert, James, ALLEY LIFE IN WASHINGTON: FAMILY, COMMUNITY, RELIIGON, AND FOLKLIFE IN THE CITY, 1850-1870, Urbana: University of Illinois Press, 1980.

C-1472 Bowes. Frederick P. THE CULTURE OF EARLY CHARLESTON, Chapel Hill: University of North Carolina Press, 1942.

C-1473 Bragg, Emma W., SCRAPBOOK: SOME FAMILY REMINISCENCES OF A NATIVE NASHVILLE SEPTUAGENARIAN, Nashville, TN: E. W. Bragg, 1985.

C-1474 Bridenbaugh, Carl, CITIES IN THE WILDERNESS: THE FIRST CENTURY OF URBAN LIFE IN AMERICA, 1625-1742, New York: The Ronald Press Company, 1938.

C-1475 Bridenbaugh, Carl, MYTHS AND REALITIES--SOCIETIES OF THE COLONIAL SOUTH, Baton Rouge: Louisiana State University Press, 1952.

C-1476 Brown, Mrs. Douglas Summers, A HISTORY OF LYNCHBURG'S PIONEER QUAKERS AND THEIR MEETING HOUSE, 1754-1936, Lynchburg, VA: J. P. Bell Company, Inc., 1936.

C-1477 Brown, Letitia Wood, FREE NEGROES IN THE DISTRICT OF COLUMBIA, 1790-1846, New York: Oxford University Press, 1972.

C-1478 Buck, Polly S., THE BLESSED TOWN: OXFORD, GEORGIA, AT THE TURN OF THE CENTURY, Chapel Hill, NC: Algonquin Books, 1986.

C-1479 Burton, Orville Vernon and Robert C. McMath, Jr., eds., CLASS, CONFLICT, AND CONSENSUS: ANTEBELLUM SOUTHERN COMMUNITY STUDIES, Westport, CT: Greenwood Press, 1980.

C-1480 Burton, Orville Vernon and Robert C. McMath Jr., eds., TOWARD A NEW SOUTH? STUDIES IN POST-CIVIL WAR SOUTHERN COMMUNITIES, Westport, CT: Greenwood Press, 1982.

C-1481 Butt, William, CHURCHILL DOWNS MUSEUM BOOK, Louisville: Harmony House Publishing Company, 1986.

C-1482 Campbell, Randolf B., A SOUTHERN COMMUNITY IN CRISIS: HARRISON COUNTY, TEXAS, 1850-1880, Austin: Texas State Historical Association, 1983.

C-1483 Carleton, David L., MILL AND TOWN IN SOUTH CAROLINA, 1880-1920, Baton Rouge: Louisiana State University Press, 1982.

C-1484 Cash, Joseph, THE MIND OF THE SOUTH, New York: Knopf, 1941.

C-1485 Catledge, Oraien E., CABBAGETOWN, Austin: University of Texas Press, 1985.

C-1486 Chapin, F. Stuart Jr., et al., IN THE SHADOW OF A DEFENSE PLANT: A STUDY OF URBANIZATION IN RURAL SOUTH CAROLINA, Chapel Hill: 1954.

C-1487 Cobb, James C., INDUSTRIALIZATION AND SOUTHERN SOCIETY, 1877-1984, Lexington: University Press of Kentucky, 1984.

C-1488 Cochran, Jean D., AUGUSTA-RICHMOND COUNTY PUBLIC LIBRARY SINCE
        1949: A HISTORY OF FIFTEEN YEARS (1949-64), Augusta: s.n., 1964.

C-1489 Coleman, William Head, LA CUSINE CREOLE, New York: W. H. Coleman,
        1885.

C-1490 Cooke, John, Ed., PERSPECTIVES ON ETHNICITY IN NEW ORLEANS, New
        Orleans: The Committee on Ethnicity in New Orleans, 1980.

C-1491 Cooper, Patyricia Irvin and Glen McAnick, MAP AND HISTORICAL
        SKETCH OF THE OLD ATHENS CEMETERY, JACKSON STREET, ATHENS,
        GEORGIA, Athens: Old Athens Cemetery Foundation, Inc., 1983.

C-1492 Cortes, Carlos, ed., THE CUBAN EXPERIENCE IN THE UNITED STATES,
        New York: Arno Press, 1980.

C-1493 Couch, W. T., ed., CULTURE IN THE SOUTH, Chapel Hill: University
        of North Carolina Press, 1934.

C-1494 Coulter, E. Merton, THE OTHER HALF OF OLD NEW ORLEANS, University,
        LA: Louisiana State University Press, 1939.

C-1495 Craighead, Erwin, FROM MOBILE'S PAST: SKETCHES OF MEMORABLE
        PEOPLE AND EVENTS, Mobile, AL: The Powers Printing Company, 1925.

C-1496 Craighead, Erwin, MOBILE: FACT AND TRADITION, NOTEWORTHY PEOPLE
        AND EVENTS, Mobile, AL: The Powers Printing Company, 1930.

C-1497 Crane, Katherine Elizabeth, BLAIR HOUSE, PAST AND PRESENT: AN
        ACCOUNT OF ITS LIFE AND TIMES IN THE CITY OF WASHINGTON, Washing-
        ton, DC: Department of State, 1945.

C-1498 Creighton, Wilbur F., A PAGE FROM NASHVILLE'S HISTORY: THE
        FOSTER-CREIGHTON STORY, Nashville: The Author, 1974.

C-1499 Crete, Liliane, DAILY LIFE IN LOUISIANA, 1815-1830, Baton Rouge:
        Louisiana State University Press, 1981.

C-1500 Cumming, Katharine Jane Hubbell [W. Kirk Wood, ed.], A NORTHERN
        DAUGHTER AND A SOUTHERN WIFE: THE CIVIL WAR REMINISCENCES AND
        LETTERS OF KATHERINE H. CUMMING, 1860-1865, Augusta: Richmond
        County Historical Society, 1976.

C-1501 Curry, Leonard P., THE FREE BLACK IN URBAN AMERICA, 1800-1850,
        Chicago: University of Chicago Press, 1981.

C-1502 Dallas, Southern Methodist University, CROSSROADS COMMUNITY STUDY
        FOR DALLAS, TEXAS, Dallas: 1970.

C-1503 Davenport, F. Garvin, CULTURAL LIFE IN NASHVILLE ON THE EVE OF THE
        CIVIL WAR, Chapel Hill: University of North Carolina Press, 1941.

C-1504 Davis, Allison, Burleigh B. Gardner and Mary R. Gardner, DEEP
        SOUTH: A SOCIAL ANTHROPOLOGICAL STUDY OF CASTE AND CLASS,
        Chicago: The University of Chicago Press, 1941.

C-1505 Davis, Arthur Kyle, NORFOLK CITY IN WAR TIMES: A COMMUNITY
        HISTORY, [Richmond? 1925].

C-1506 Davis, Edwin A. and William R. Hogan, THE BARBER OF NATCHEZ, Port
        Washington, NY: Kennikat Press, 1972.

C-1507 Dawe, Louise Belote, TO IRVINGTON WITH LOVE: ITS MEMORIES AND
        SOME OF ITS BEST RECIPES, Richmond, VA: Whitlet & Shepperson,
        n.d.

C-1508 Dawson, Sarah Morgan, ed., A CONFEDERATE GIRL'S DIARY, Blooming-
        ton: Indiana University Press, 1960.

C-1509 Dealey, Ted, DIAPER DAYS OF DALLAS, Nashville: Abingdon Press, 1966.

C-1510 Debo, Angie, PRAIRIE CITY: THE STORY OF AN AMERICAN COMMUNITY, New York: A. A. Knopf, 1944.

C-1511 DeBolt, Margaret Wayt, SAVANNAH SPECTRES AND OTHER STRANGE TALES, Norfolk, VA: Donning Company, 1984.

C-1512 DeBolt, Margaret Wayt with Emma R. Law, SAVANNAH SAMPLER COOKBOOK, Norfolk, VA: Donning, 1978.

C-1513 Delaney, Caldwell, MADAME OCTAVIA WALTON LE VERT: THE SOUTH'S MOST FAMOUS BELLE, Mobile: Historic Mobile Preservation Society, 1961.

C-1514 Delaney, Caldwell and Cornelia McDuffie Turner, INFANT MYSTICS: THE FIRST HUNDRED YEARS, Mobile, AL: 1968.

C-1515 Delery, Linda, ed., NINETEEN EIGHTY-FOUR WORLD'S FAIR: THE OFFICIAL GUIDEBOOK, New Orleans: Picayune Press, 1984.

C-1516 Dinnerstein, Leonard and Mary Dale Palsson, ed., JEWS IN THE SOUTH, Baton Rouge: Louisiana State University Press, 1973.

C-1517 Dollard, John, CASTE AND CLASS IN A SOUTHERN TOWN, New Haven: Yale University Press, 1937.

C-1518 Dormon, James H., THE PEOPLE CALLED CAJUNS: AN INTRODUCTION TO ETHNOHISTORY, Lafayette: Center for Louisiana Studies, 1983.

C-1519 Dorson, Richard M., NEGRO TALES FROM PINE BLUFF, ARKANSAS AND CALVIN, MICHIGAN, Bloomington: Indiana University Press, 1958.

C-1520 Durrett, Dan and Dana F. White, AN-OTHER ATLANTA: THE BLACK HERITAGE: A BICENTENNIAL TOUR, Atlanta: The History Group, 1975.

C-1521 DuVal, Benjamin T., OLD FORT SMITH, CULTURAL CENTER ON THE SOUTHWESTERN FRONTIER, Little Rock: Pioneer Press, 1965.

C-1522 Earle, John R., Dean D. Knudsen, and Donald W. Shriner Jr., SPINDLES AND SPIRES: A RE-STUDY OF RELIGION AND SOCIAL CHANGE IN GASTONIA, Atlanta: John Knox Press, 1976.

C-1523 Elovitz, Mark H., A CENTURY OF JEWISH LIFE IN DIXIE: THE BIRMINGHAM EXPERIENCE, University, AL: University of Alabama Press, 1974.

C-1524 Evans, Eli N., THE PROVINCIALS: A PERSONAL HISTORY OF JEWS IN THE SOUTH, New York: Atheneum, 1973.

C-1525 Evans, Paul Fairfax, CITY LIFE: A PERSPECTIVE FROM BALTIMORE 1968-1978, Columbia, MD: C. H. Fairfax Company, 1981.

C-1526 Faulkner, William, NEW ORLEANS SKETCHES, New York: Random House, 1958.

C-1527 Figh, Margaret Gillis and Kathryn Tucker Windham, 13 ALABAMA GHOSTS AND JEFFRY, Huntsville: Strode Publishing, 1969.

C-1528 Flack, J. Kirkpatric, DESIDERATUM IN WASHINGTON: THE INTELLECTUAL COMMUNITY IN THE CAPITAL CITY 1870-1900, Cambridge: Schenkman, 1975.

C-1529 Fleming, Berry, 199 YEARS OF AUGUSTA'S LIBRARY: A CHRONOLOGY, Athens: University of Georgia Press, 1949.

C-1530 Flynt, J. Wayne, DIXIE'S FORGOTTEN PEOPLE: THE SOUTH'S POOR WHITES, Bloomington: The University of Indiana Press, 1979.

C-1531 Flynt, J. Wayne and Dorothy S. Flynt, SOUTHERN POOR WHITES: A SELECTED ANNOTATED BIBLIOGRAPHY OF PUBLISHED SOURCES, New York: Garlan Publishing, Inc., 1981.

C-1532 Frank, Fedora Small, BEGINNINGS ON MARKET STREET: NASHVILLE AND HER JEWRY 1861-1901, Nashville: The Author, 1976.

C-1533 Frank, Fedora Small, FIVE FAMILIES AND EIGHT YOUNG MEN: NASHVILLE AND HER JEWRY 1850-1861, Nashville: Tennessee Book Company, 1962.

C-1534 Fuerman, George, HOUSTON: LAND OF THE BIG RICH, Garden City, NJ: Doubleday, 1951.

C-1535 Fuller, Walter, ST. PETERSBURG AND ITS PEOPLE, St. Petersburg: Great Outdoors Publishing Company, 1972.

C-1536 Gamble, Thomas, SAVANNAH DUELS AND DUELLISTS, 1733-1877. (Annals of Savannah, vol. I), Savannah: Review Publishing and Printing Company, 1923.

C-1537 Gandolfo, Henri A., METAIRIE CEMETERY: AN HISTORICAL MEMOIR, New Orleans: Stewart Enterprises, Inc., 1982.

C-1538 Garcia, Mario T., DESERT IMMIGRANTS: THE MEXICANS OF EL PASO, 1880-1920, New Haven: Yale University Press, 1981.

C-1539 Ginsberg, Louis, HISTORY OF THE JEWS IN PETERSBURG, 1789-1950, Petersburg, VA: 1954.

C-1540 Gongaware, George J., THE HISTORY OF THE GERMAN FRIENDLY SOCIETY OF CHARLESTON, SOUTH CAROLINA, 1766-1916, Richmond: Garrett and Massie, Publishers, 1935.

C-1541 Graham, Eleanor and Mary Glenn Hearne, NASHVILLE FAMILIES AND HOMES: PARAGRAPHS FROM NASHVILLE HISTORY LECTURE SERIES, 1979-81, Nashville: Public Library of Nashville and Davidson County, 1983.

C-1542 Green, Ben, FINEST KIND: A CELEBRATION OF A FLORIDA FISHING VILLAGE, Macon: Mercer University Press, 1985.

C-1543 Greenberg, Mrs. David J., THROUGH THE YEARS: A STUDY OF THE RICHMOND JEWISH COMMUNITY, Richmond: Richmond Jewish Community Council, 1955.

C-1544 Grove, Dorothy Haverty, CULTURAL ATLANTA AT A GLANCE, Atlanta: Foote & Davies, 1950?

C-1545 Gwin, Yolande, YOLANDE'S ATLANTA: FROM THE HISTORICAL TO THE HYSTERICAL, Atlanta: Peachtree Publishers, 1983.

C-1546 Hall, A. Oakey, ed. by Henry A. Kmen, THE MANHATTANER IN NEW ORLEANS: OR, PHASES OF "CRESCENT CITY" LIFE, Baton Rouge: Louisiana State University Press, 1976.

C-1547 Hamilton, Green Polonius, THE BRIGHT SIDE OF MEMPHIS: A COMPENDIUM OF INFORMATION CONCERING THE COLORED PEOPLE . . . , Memphis, TN: 1908.

C-1548 Hardy, Arthur, NEW ORLEANS MARDI GRAS GUIDE, New Orleans: A. Hardy and Associates, 1985.

C-1549 Hareven, Tamara K., ed., ANONYMOUS AMERICANS: EXPLORATIONS IN NINETEENTH-CENTURY SOCIAL HISTORY, Englewood Cliffs, NJ: Prentice Hall, 1971.

C-1550 Harris, J. William, PLAIN FOLK AND GENTRY IN A SLAVE SOCIETY:
WHITE LIBERTY AND BLACK SLAVERY IN AUGUSTA'S HINTERLANDS,
Middletown, CT: Wesleyan University Press, 1985.

C-1551 Harrison, Constance (Cary), BELHAVEN TALES; CROW'S NEST; UNA AND
KING DAVID, New York: The Century Company, 1892.

C-1552 Hearin, Emity Staples and Kathryn T. DeCelle, QUEENS OF MOBILE
MARDI GRAS, 1893-1986, Mobile: Museum Mobile, 1986.

C-1553 Herring, Harriet L., PASSING OF THE MILL VILLAGE: REVOLUTION IN A
SOUTHERN INSTITUTION, Chapel Hill: University of North Carolina
Press, 1949.

C-1554 Herring, Harriet L., SOUTHERN INDUSTRY AND REGIONAL DEVELOPMENT,
Chapel Hill: University of North Carolina Press, 1940.

C-1555 Hill, Reuben, J. Jall Moss and Claudine G. Writas, EDDYVILLE'S
FAMILIES: A STUDY OF PERSONAL AND FAMILY ADJUSTMENTS SUBSEQUENT
TO THE RAPID URBANIZATION OF A SOUTHERN TOWN, Chapel Hill:
Institute for Research in Social Science, 1953.

C-1556 Holmes, Jack D., NEW ORLEANS DRINKS AND HOW TO MIX THEM, New
Orleans: Hope Publications, 1973.

C-1557 Honorkamp, Nick, COLONIAL LIFE ON THE GEORGIA COAST, St. Simon's
Island: Fort Frederica Association, Inc., 1977.

C-1558 Huber, Leonard V., CLASPED HANDS, SYMBOLISM IN NEW ORLEANS CEME-
TERIES, Lafayette, LA: The Center for Louisiana Studies, University of Southwestern Louisiana, 1982.

C-1559 Hudspeth, Ron, LIVING, LOVING, LAUGHING, DYING, AND CRYING ON
PEACHTREE, Atlanta: Peachtree Publishers, 1980.

C-1560 Hutchins, Myldred Flanigan, RED CLAY: TRUE STORIES ABOUT PEOPLE
WHO LIVED IN AND AROUND THE SMALL TOWN OF AUBURN, GEORGIA, Lakemont, GA: Copple House Books, 1981.

C-1561 Ingle, Edward, THE NEGRO IN THE DISTRICT OF COLUMBIA, Baltimore:
The Johns Hopkins Press, 1893.

C-1562 Jackson, George, SIXTY YEARS IN TEXAS, Dallas, TX: Wilkinson
Printing Company, 1908.

C-1563 Jacobs, Howard, CHARLIE THE MOLE AND OTHER DROLL SOULS, Gretna,
LA: Pelican, 1973.

C-1564 Jennings, M. Kent, COMMUNITY INFLUENTIALS AND THE ELITES OF
ATLANTA, London: Free Press of Glencoe, 1964.

C-1565 Johnson, Michael P. and James L. Roark, eds., NO CHARIOT LET DOWN:
CHARLESTON'S FREE PEOPLE OF COLOR ON THE EVE OF THE CIVIL WAR,
Chapel Hill: University of North Carolina Press, 1984.

C-1566 Johnson, Thomas Cary Jr., SCIENTIFIC INTERESTS IN THE OLD SOUTH,
New York: D. Appleton-Century Company, 1936.

C-1567 Jones, Katherine M., LADIES OF RICHMOND: CONFEDERATE CAPITAL, New
York: Bobbs-Merrill Company, Inc., 1962.

C-1568 Junior League of the Palm Beaches, Inc., PALM BEACH ENTERTAINS,
New York: Coward, McCann & Geo. Megan, 1976.

C-1569 Kaganoff, Nathan M. and Milvin I. Urofsky, eds., "TURN TO THE
SOUTH:" ESSAYS ON SOUTHERN JEWRY, Charlottesville: University
Press of Virginia, 1979.

C-1570 Kalisch, Philip Arthur, THE ENOCH PRATT FREE LIBRARY: A SOCIAL
       HISTORY, Metuchen, NJ: Scarecrow Press, 1969.

C-1571 Kimball, Solon T. and Marion Pearsall, THE TALLADEGA STORY,
       University, AL: University of Alabama Press, 1954.

C-1572 Kinney, Robert, THE BACHELOR IN NEW ORLEANS, New Orleans: Bormon
       House, 1942.

C-1573 Knotts, Tom, SEE YANKEETOWN: HISTORY AND REMINISCENCES, Yankee-
       town: Withlacoochee Press, 1970.

C-1574 Korn, Bertram W., THE EARLY JEWS OF NEW ORLEANS, Waltham, MA:
       American Jewish Historical Society, 1969.

C-1575 Krueger, Max Amadeus Paulus, ed. by Marily McAdams Sibley, SECOND
       FATHERLAND: THE LIFE AND FORTUNES OF A GERMAN IMMIGRANT, College
       Station: Texas A & M University Press, 1976.

C-1576 LaCour, Arthur Burton, NEW ORLEANS MASQUERADE: CHRONICLES OF
       CARNIVAL, New Orleans: Pelican Publishing Company, 1957.

C-1577 Larson, Mel, SKID ROW STOPGAP, THE MEMPHIS STORY, Wheaton, IL:
       Van Kampen Press, 1950.

C-1578 LEARNING FROM GALVESTON, Learning From the USA: What Makes Cities
       Livable Series, New York: Institute for Environmental Action,
       1983.

C-1579 Leavitt, Mel, GREAT CHARACTERS OF NEW ORLEANS, San Francisco:
       Lexikos, 1984.

C-1580 Lebsock, Suzanne, THE FREE WOMEN OF PETERSBURG: STATUS AND
       CULTURE IN A SOUTHERN TOWN, New York: W. W. Norton & Company,
       1984.

C-1581 Lee, Don Chang, ACCULTURATION OF KOREAN RESIDENTS IN GEORGIA, San
       Francisco: R. and E. Research Associates, 1975.

C-1582 Leech, Margaret, REVEILLE IN WASHINGTON, 1860-1865, New York:
       Harper and Row, 1941.

C-1583 Lewis, H. H. Walker, THE RULE DAY CLUB: BALTIMORE, MARYLAND,
       Baltimore: Maryland Historical Society, 1980.

C-1584 Liddeel, Viola Goode, A PLACE OF SPRINGS, University, AL:
       University of Alabama Press, 1979.

C-1585 Lillard, Stewart, MEIGS COUNTY, TENNESSEE: A DOCUMENTED ACCOUNT
       OF ITS EUROPEAN SETTLEMENT AND GROWTH, Sewanee: University of the
       South Press, 1975.

C-1586 Loewen, James W., THE MISSISSIPPI CHINESE: BETWEEN BLACK AND
       WHITE, Cambridge, MA: Harvard University Press, 1971.

C-1587 Lynch, Hollis R., THE BLACK URBAN CONDITION: A DOCUMENTARY
       HISTORY, 1866-1971, New York: Thomas Y. Crowell, Co., 1973.

C-1588 Magdal, Edward and Jon L. Wakelyn, THE SOUTHERN COMMON PEOPLE:
       STUDIES IN NINETEENTH-CENTURY SOCIAL HISTORY, Westport, CT:
       Greenwood Press, 1980.

C-1589 Mahopatra, M. K., THE URBAN OMBUDSMAN AND COMMUNITY EXPECTATIONS
       STRUCTURE IN LEXINGTON, KENTUCKY, Atlanta: Southern Education
       Foundation, 1982.

C-1590 Main, Gloria L., TOBACCO COLONY: LIFE IN EARLY MARYLAND, 1650-
       1720, Princeton, NJ: Princeton University Press.

C-1591 Marcus, Jacob Rader, AMERICAN JEWRY: THE JEWS OF PENNSYLVANIA AND THE SOUTH 1655-1790, Philadelphia: Jewish Publication Society of America, 1955.

C-1592 Marinbach, Bernard, GALVESTON: ELLIS ISLAND OF THE WEST, Albany: State University of New York Press, 1983.

C-1593 Martin, Margaret Rhett, CHARLESTON GHOSTS, Columbia: University of South Carolina Press, 1963.

C-1594 Martinez, Raymond J., THE IMMORTAL MARGARET HAUGHERY, New Orleans: Industries Publishing, 1956.

C-1595 Matthews, Antoinette Johnson, OAKDALE ROAD, ATLANTA, GA., DEKALB COUNTY; ITS HISTORY AND ITS PEOPLE, Atlanta: Atlanta Historical Society, 1972.

C-1596 Mauer, George J., WHO'S WHO IN METRO ORLANDO, Orlando: G. J. Mauer, 1986.

C-1597 Mehden, Fred R. von der, ed., THE ETHNIC GROUPS OF HOUSTON, Houston, TX: Rice University Studies, 1984.

C-1598 Merrens, H. Roy, THE COLONIAL SOUTH CAROLINA SCENE: CONTEMPORARY VIEWS, 1697-1774, Columbia: University of South Carolina Press, 1977.

C-1599 Miller, Elinor and Eugene D. Genovese, PLANTATION, TOWN, AND COUNTRY: ESSAYS ON THE LOCAL HISTORY OF AMERICAN SLAVE SOCIETY, Urbana: University of Illinois Press, 1974.

C-1600 Mitchell, Mary A., CHRONICLES OF GEORGETOWN LIFE, Cabin John, MD: Seven Locks Press, 1986.

C-1601 Mobley, Joe A., JAMES CITY: A BLACK COMMUNITY IN NORTH CAROLINA, 1863-1900, Raleigh: North Carolina Department of Cultural Resources, Division of Archives and History, 1981.

C-1602 Mormino, Gary R. and George E. Pozzetta, THE IMMIGRANT WORLD OF YBOR CITY: ITALIANS AND THEIR LATIN NEIGHBORS IN TAMPA, 1885-1985, Urbana: University of Illinois Press, 1987.

C-1603 Morris, Sylvanus, STROLLS ABOUT ATHENS DURING THE EARLY SEVENTIES, Athens: 1912?

C-1604 Muniz, Jose Rivers, LOS CUBANOS EN TAMPA, Havana: Revista Bimestre Cubana, 1958.

C-1605 McIlwaine, Shields, MEMPHIS DOWN IN DIXIE, New York: E. P. Dutton and Company, Inc., 1948.

C-1606 McPheeters, Annie L., NEGRO PROGRESS IN ATLANTA, GEORGIA, 1961-70, A Selective Bibliography on Race and Human Relations, Atlanta, 1972.

C-1607 Niehaus, Earl F., THE IRISH IN NEW ORLEANS, 1800-1860, Baton Rouge: Louisiana State University Press, 1965.

C-1608 Ney, John, PALM BEACH: THE PLACE, THE PEOPLE, ITS PLEASURES AND PALACES, Boston: Little, Brown and Company, 1966.

C-1609 Nix, Harold L., AUGUSTA-RICHMOND COUNTY TASK FORCE STUDY, Athens: University of Georgia Press, [1970?].

C-1610 NOTABLE MEN OF ATLANTA AND GEORGIA, Atlanta: [s.n.], 1913.

C-1611 O'Brien, Michael and David Moltke-Hansen, eds., INTELLECTUAL LIFE IN ANTEBELLUM CHARLESTON, Knoxville: University of Tennessee Press, 1985.

C-1612 Ogburn, W. F., SOCIAL CHARACTERISTICS OF CITIES, Chicago: The
       International City Managers' Association, 1937.

C-1613 Olien, Roger M. and Diana Davids Olien, OIL BOOMS: SOCIAL CHANGE
       IN FIVE TEXAS TOWNS, Lincoln: University of Nebraska Press, 1982.

C-1614 Osborne, Mitchel L., MARDI GRAS!: A CELEBRATION, New Orleans:
       Picayune Press, 1981.

C-1615 Owsley, F. L., PLAIN FOLK OF THE OLD SOUTH, Baton Rouge: Louisi-
       ana State University Press, 1949.

C-1616 Parlier, Gertrude Dana and others, PURSUITS OF WAR: THE PEOPLE OF
       CHARLOTTESVILLE AND ALBERMARLE COUNTY, VIRGINIA, IN THE SECOND
       WORLD WAR, Charlottesville: Albermarle County Historical Society,
       1948.

C-1617 Pattillo, Lois, LITTLE ROCK ROOTS: BIOGRAPHIES IN ARKANSAS BLACK
       HISTORY: THE LIVES OF BLACKS WHO HAVE MADE HISTORY IN ARKANSAS
       SINCE 1900, Little Rock: Lois Pattillo Books, 1981.

C-1618 Pease, William H. and Jane H. Pease, THE WEB OF PROGRESS: PRIVATE
       VALUES AND PUBLIC STYLES IN BOSTON AND CHARLESTON, 1828-1843, New
       York: Oxford University Press, 1985.

C-1619 Perdue, Robert E., THE NEGRO IN SAVANNAH, 1865-1900, Hicksville,
       NY: Exposition Press, 1973.

C-1620 Phillibec, William W. and Clyde B. McCory with Harry C. Dilling-
       ham, THE INVISIBLE MINORITY: URBAN APPALACHIANS, Lexington:
       University Press of Kentucky, 1981.

C-1621 Pope, Liston, MILLHANDS AND PREACHERS: A STUDY OF GASTONIA, New
       Haven, CT: Yale University Press, 1942.

C-1622 Prince, William Meade, THE SOUTHERN PART OF HEAVEN, New York:
       Rinehart & Company, Inc., 1950.

C-1623 Proctor, Samuel and Louis Schmier, JEWS OF THE SOUTH, Macon:
       Mercer University Press, 1984.

C-1624 Quan, Robert Seto, LOTUS AMONG THE MAGNOLIAS; THE MISSISSIPPI
       CHINESE, Jackson: University Press of Mississippi, 1982.

C-1625 Ravenal, Mrs. St. Julien, CHARLESTON: THE PLACE AND THE PEOPLE,
       New York: Macmillan, 1906.

C-1626 Rayford, Julian Lee, CHASIN' THE DEVIL ROUND A STUMP, Mobile, AL:
       American Print Company, 1962.

C-1627 RECIPES AND REMINISCENSES OF NEW ORLEANS, VOL. II, [s.l.]:
       Ursuline, 1981.

C-1628 Reese, Morton Lamar, comp., CEMETERY RECORDS, MAINLY FROM RICHMOND
       COUNTY, Augusta: 1948.

C-1629 Reissman, Leonard, PROFILE OF A COMMUNITY: SOCIOLOGICAL STUDY OF
       THE NEW ORLEANS JEWISH COMMUNITY, New Orleans: Jewish Federation
       of New Orleans, 1958.

C-1630 Reissman, Leonard, et al., SOCIOLOGICAL ASPECTS OF COMMUNITY RE-
       NEWAL IN BATON ROUGE, LOUISIANA, Baton Rouge: Community Renewal
       Program, City-Parish Planning Commission, 1970.

C-1631 Remington, Patricia W., POLICING, THE OCCUPATION AND THE INTRODUC-
       TION OF FEMALE OFFICERS: AN ANTHROPOLOGIST'S STUDY, Washington,
       DC: The University Press of America, 1981.

C-1632 Reznikoff, Charles and Uriah Z. Engleman, THE JEWS OF CHARLESTON: A HISTORY OF AN AMERICAN JEWISH COMMUNITY, Philadelphia: Jewish Publication Society of America, 1950.

C-1633 Richmond, Marie LaLiberte, IMMIGRANT ADAPTION AND FAMILY STRUCTURE AMONG CUBANS IN MIAMI, FLORIDA, New York: Arno Press, 1980 [1974].

C-1634 Ripley, Eliza Moore, SOCIAL LIFE IN OLD NEW ORLEANS: BEING RE-COLLECTIONS OF MY GIRLHOOD, New York: Appleton and Company, 1912.

C-1635 Roark, Eldon, MEMPHIS BRAGABOUTS: AMAZING CHARACTERS I HAVE MET, New York: McGraw-Hill Book Company, Inc., 1945.

C-1636 Rogers, John William, THE LUSTY TEXANS OF DALLAS, New York: Dutton, 1951.

C-1637 Rose, Al, STORYVILLE, NEW ORLEANS: BEING AN AUTHENTIC, ILLUSTRAT-ED ACCOUNT OF THE NOTORIOUS RED-LIGHT DISTRICT, University, AL: University of Alabama Press, 1974.

C-1638 Roy, F. Hampton and Charles Witsell, HOW WE LIVED: LITTLE ROCK AS AN AMERICAN CITY, Little Rock: August House, Inc., December 1983.

C-1639 Rubin, Saul Jacob, THIRD TO NONE: THE SAGA OF SAVANNAH JEWRY, 1733-1983, Savannah: Congregation Mickve Israel, 1983.

C-1640 Rutledge, S. (Anna Wells Rutledge, postscript), THE CAROLINA HOUSEWIFE, OR HOUSE AND HOME: BY A LADY OF CHARLESTON, Charles-ton: S. S. S. Publishers [1963], reprint 1947 ed.

C-1641 Saxon, Lyle, FABULOUS NEW ORLEANS, New York: Century Company, 1928.

C-1642 Saxon, Lyle, Edward Dreyer and Robert Tallant, GUMBO YA-YA, A COLLECTION OF LOUISIANA FOLK TALES, Boston: Houghton Mifflin and Company, 1945.

C-1643 Schmier, Louis E., ed., REFLECTIONS OF SOUTHERN JEWRY, THE LETTERS OF CHARLES WESSOLOWSKY, 1878-1879, Macon: Mercer University Press, 1982.

C-1644 Shiners, Louise Shingleton, A TABLE BY THE DAYLIGHT: THE COCHRAN YEARS, Augusta: [s.n.], 1975.

C-1645 Shofner, Jerrell H. and Linda V. Ellsworth, eds., ETHNIC MINORI-TIES IN GULF COAST SOCIETY, Pensacola: Gulf Coast History and Humanities Conference, 1979.

C-1646 Shugg, R. W., ORIGINS OF CLASS STRUGGLE IN LOUISIANA, Baton Rouge: Louisiana State University Press, 1939.

C-1647 Sims, Patsy, NEW ORLEANS: THE PASSING PARADE, New Orleans: Picayune Press, 1980.

C-1648 Smith, Guy L. III, A HOUSE FOR JOSHUA: THE BUILDING OF THE KNOX-VILLE ZOO, Knoxville, TN: University of Tennessee Press, 1985.

C-1649 Smith, Michael P., SPIRIT WORLD: PATTERNS IN THE EXPRESSIVE FOLK CULTURE OF AFRO-AMERICAN NEW ORLEANS: PHOTOGRAPHS AND JOURNAL, New Orleans: New Orleans Urban, 1984.

C-1650 Smith, T. Lynn and C. A. McMahan, eds., THE SOCIOLOGY OF URBAN LIFE, New York: The Dryden Press, 1951.

C-1651 SOCIAL BLIGHT AND NEIGHBORHOOD RENEWAL IN ATLANTA, Atlanta: Community Council of the Atlanta Area, Inc., Research Center, 1967.

C-1652 Speizman, Morris, THE JEWS OF CHARLOTTE: A CHRONICLE WITH COMMEN-
       TARY AND CONJECTURE, Charlotte: McNally and Loftin, 1978.

C-1653 Stall, Gaspar J. "Buddy," PROUD, PECULIAR NEW ORLEANS: THE INSIDE
       STORY, Baton Rouge, LA: Claitor's Publishing Division, 1984.

C-1654 Stanard, Mary Newton, RICHMOND, ITS PEOPLE AND ITS STORY, Phila-
       delphia: J. B. Lippincott Company, 1923.

C-1655 Standard, Diffee William, COLUMBUS, GEORGIA, IN THE CONFEDERACY:
       THE SOCIAL AND INDUSTRIAL LIFE OF THE CHATTAHOOCHEE RIVER PORT,
       New York: William-Frederick Press, 1954.

C-1656 Stanforth, Deirdre, CREOLE! THE LEGENDARY CUISINE OF NEW ORLEANS
       . . . PLUS FASCINATNG LORE FOR THE COOK, Gretna, LA: Pelican
       Publishing Company, 1986, c 1969.

C-1657 Stanforth, Deirdre, THE NEW ORLEANS RESTAURANT COOKBOOK, New York:
       Doubleday and Company, Inc., 1968.

C-1658 Starr, S. Frederick, NEW ORLEANS UNMASQUED: BEING A WAGWIT'S AF-
       FECTIONATE SKETCHES OF A SINGULAR AMERICAN CITY, New Orleans:
       Edition Dedeaux, 1985.

C-1659 Stepick, Alex, HAITIANS IN MIAMI: AN ASSESSMENT OF THEIR BACK-
       GROUND AND POTENTIAL, Dialogue #12, Occasional Papers Series,
       Latin American and Caribbean Center, Florida International
       University, 1982.

C-1660 Stuck, Goodloe, ANNIE McCUNE: SHREVEPORT MADAM, Baton Rouge, LA:
       Moran Publishing Corp., 1981.

C-1661 Tallant, Robert, MARDI GRAS, Garden City, NY: Doubleday, 1948.

C-1662 Tallant, Robert, VOODOO IN NEW ORLEANS, New York: Macmillan
       Company, 1941.

C-1663 Tassin, Myron, BACCHUS, Gretna, LA: Pelican Publishing Company,
       1975.

C-1664 Tassin, Myron, MARDI GRAS AND BACCHUS: SOMETHING OLD, SOMETHING
       NEW, Gretna, LA: Pelican Publishing Company, 1984.

C-1665 Tate, James H., KEEPER OF THE FLAME: THE STORY OF ATLANTA GAS
       LIGHT COMPANY, 1856-1985, Atlanta: The Company, 1985.

C-1666 Taylor, Alrutheus Ambush, THE NEGRO IN TENNESSEE, 1865-1880,
       Washington: The Associated Publishers, Inc., 1941.

C-1667 Taylor, Carter, THE AUGUSTA SURVEY; A COMMUNITY IMPROVEMENT STUDY
       OF AUGUSTA AND RICHMOND COUNTY . . ., Augusta: Augusta Kiwanis
       Club, 1924.

C-1668 Thomas, Gail, ed., IMAGINING DALLAS, Dallas, TX: Pegasus Founda-
       tion, 1982.

C-1669 Taylor, Rosser H., ANTE-BELLUM SOUTH CAROLINA: A SOCIAL AND CUL-
       TURAL HISTORY, Chapel Hill: University of North Carolina Press,
       1942.

C-1670 Thurmond, Michael L., A STORY UNTOLD: BLACK MEN AND WOMEN IN
       ATHENS HISTORY, Athens: Clarke County School District, 1978.

C-1671 Tinker, Edward Larocque, CREOLE CITY: ITS PAST AND ITS PEOPLE,
       New York: Longmans, Green and Company, 1953.

C-1672 Tobias, Henry J., THE JEWS IN OKLAHOMA, Norman: University of
       Oklahoma Press, 1980.

C-1673 Tobias, Thomas J., THE HEBREW ORPHAN SOCIETY OF CHARLESTON, S. C., Charleston: Hebrew Orphan Society, 1957.

C-1674 Tolles, Zonira Hunter, SHADOWS IN THE SAND: A HISTORY OF THE LAND AND THE PEOPLE IN THE VICINITY OF MELROSE, FLORIDA, Keystone Heights, FL: Tolles, 1976.

C-1675 Tonkin, Leroy F. Jr., ALABAMA COMMUNITIES IN PERSPECTIVE, Montgomery: Alabama Development Office, 1973.

C-1676 Turitz, Leo and Evelyn Turitz, JEWS IN EARLY MISSISSIPPI, Jackson: University Press of Mississippi, 1983.

C-1677 von der Mehden, Fred R., THE ETHNIC GROUPS OF HOUSTON, Houston: Rice University Studies [No. 3], 1984.

C-1678 Wade, Richard C., THE URBAN FRONTIER: PIONEER LIFE IN EARLY PITTSBURGH, CINCINNATI, LEXINGTON, LOUISVILLE, AND ST. LOUIS, Chicago: University of Chicago Press, 1967.

C-1679 Waring, George E. Jr., THE SEWERAGE OF MEMPHIS, U.S.A. (London, 1881).

C-1680 Warner, Lee H. and Mary B. Eastland, TALLAHASSEE: DOWNTOWN TRANSITIONS, Tallahassee: Brokaw-McDougall House, 1976.

C-1681 Watkins, C. Malcolm, THE CULTURAL HISTORY OF MARLBOROUGH, VIRGINIA, Washington, DC: Smithsonian Institution Bulletin 253, 1968.

C-1682 Weeks, Linton, MEMPHIS: A FOLK HISTORY, Little Rock: Parkhurst, 1982.

C-1683 Weiner, Jonathan M., SOCIAL ORIGINS OF THE NEW SOUTH: ALABAMA, 1860-1885, Baton Rouge: Louisiana State University, 1978.

C-1684 Wertenbaker, Thomas J., THE GOLDEN AGE OF COLONIAL CULTURE, New York: New York University Press, 1941.

C-1685 Western and Atlantic Railroad, MARDI GRAS IN NEW ORLEANS, ITS ANCIENT AND MODERN OBSERVANCE, Atlanta: Barrow, the Printer, 1873?

C-1686 Whitaker, R. H., WHITAKER'S REMINISCENCES, INCIDENTS AND ANECDOTES . . ., Raleigh, NC: Edwards & Broughton, 1905.

C-1687 Wickiser, Ralph Lewanda, et al., MARDI GRAS, New York: H. Holt, 1948.

C-1688 Wikramanayake, Marina, A WORLD IN SHADOW: THE FREE BLACK IN ANTEBELLUM SOUTH CAROLINA, Columbia: University of South Carolina Press, 1973.

C-1689 Willford, William Bailey, AMERICUS THROUGH THE YEARS: THE FIRST ONE HUNDRED AND TWENTY-FIVE YEARS OF A GEORGIA TOWN AND ITS PEOPLE, 1831-1956, Atlanta: 1960.

C-1690 Williams, Joyce E., BLACK COMMUNITY CONTROL: A STUDY OF TRANSITION IN A TEXAS GHETTO, New York: Praeger, 1973.

C-1691 Wilson, John Stainback, ATLANTA AS IT IS; BEING A BRIEF SKETCH OF ITS EARLY SETTLERS, GROWTH, SOCIETY . . . ETC., New York: Little, Rennie & Company, Printers, 1871.

C-1692 Wood, Maude Talmage, ONCE UPON A TIME, Athens, GA: Classic Press, 1977.

C-1693 Wooley, Rita Paschal, SKETCHES OF LIFE IN LITTLE ROCK: 1836 TO
       1850, BASED ON THE F. W. TRAPNALLS, [s.l.: s.n., 1981].

C-1694 Wright, George C., LIFE BEHIND A VEIL: BLACKS IN LOUISVILLE,
       KENTUCKY, 1865-1930, Baton Rouge: Louisiana State University
       Press, 1985.

C-1695 Wright, Louis Booker, BAREFOOT IN ARCADIA, Columbia: University
       of South Carolina Press, 1974.

C-1696 Vesperi, Maria D., CITY OF GREEN BENCHES: GROWING OLD IN A NEW
       DOWNTOWN, Ithica: Cornell University Press, 1985.

C-1697 Yater, George H., FLAPPERS, PROHIBITION AND ALL THAT JAZZ: LOUIS-
       VILLE REMEMBERS THE TWENTIES: AN ESSAY, Louisville: Museum of
       History and Science, 1984.

C-1698 Young, James Sterling, THE WASHINGTON COMMUNITY, 1800-1828, New
       York: Columbia University Press, 1966.

C-1699 Young, Perry, THE MYSTICK KREWE: CHRONICLES OF COMUS AND HIS KIN,
       New Orleans: Louisiana Heritage Press, 1969.

Literature

C-1700 Arthur, Ella (Bentley), SONGS OF A CREOLE CITY, AND OTHER POEMS,
       New Orleans: Harmanson, 1950.

C-1701 Boudreau, Amy, MIGHTY MISSISSIPPI AND NEW ORLEANS, Baton Rouge:
       Claitor's Publishing Company, 1967.

C-1702 Boudreau, Amy, POEMS OF THE VIEUX CARRE, NEW ORLEANS' FRENCH
       QUARTER, Baton Rouge: Claitor's Publishing Denision, 1979.

C-1703 Brown, Steven F., ed., CONTEMPORARY LITERATURE IN BIRMINGHAM: AN
       ANTHOLOGY, Birmingham: Thunder City Press, 1983.

C-1704 Cutrer, Thomas W., PARNASSUS ON THE MISSISSIPPI: THE SOUTHERN
       REVIEW AND THE BATON ROUGE LITERARY COMMUNITY, 1935-1942, Baton
       Rouge: Louisiana State University Press, 1984.

C-1705 Flanders, Bertram Holland, EARLY GEORGIA MAGAZINES: LITERARY
       PERIODICALS TO 1865, Athens, GA: University of Georgia Press,
       1944.

C-1706 Gabel, Leona C., FROM SLAVERY TO THE SORBONNE AND BEYOND: THE
       LIFE AND WRITINGS OF ANNA J. COOPER, Northhampton, MA: Department
       of History of Smith College, Smith College Studies in History,
       Vol. 49, 1982.

C-1707 McMurtrie, Douglas C., EARLY PRINTING IN NEW ORLEANS, 1764-1810,
       WITH A BIBLIOGRAPHY OF THE ISSUES OF THE LOUISIANA PRESS, New
       Orleans: Searcy & Pfaff, 1929.

C-1708 Rubin, Louis D., NO PLACE ON EARTH: ELLEN GLASGOW, JAMES BRANCH
       CABELL, AND RICHMOND-IN-VIRGINIA, Austin: University of Texas
       Press, 1959.

C-1709 Saint-Amand, Mary Scott, A BALCONY IN CHARLESTON, Richmond:
       Garrett and Massie, Inc., 1941.

C-1710 Simms, William G., ed., THE CHARLESTON BOOK: A MISCELLANY IN
       PROSE AND VERSE, Charleston, SC: S. Hart, 1845.

C-1711 Wingfield, Marshall, LITERARY MEMPHIS, A SURVEY OF ITS WRITERS AND
       WRITINGS, memphis: west Tennessee Historical Society, 1942.

Music

C-1712 Bane, Michael, WHITE BOY SINGIN' THE BLUES: THE BLACK ROOTS OF WHITE ROCK, New York: Penguin Books, 1982.

C-1713 Baron, John H., ed., PIANO MUSIC FRON NEW ORLEANS, 1851-1898, New York: Da Capo Press, 1980.

C-1714 Broven, John, RHYTHM AND BLUES IN NEW ORLEANS, Gretna, LA: Pelican Publishing Company, 1978.

C-1715 Broven, John, SOUTH TO LOUISIANA: THE MUSIC OF THE CAJUN BAYOUS, Bretna, LA: Pelican Publishing Company, 1983.

C-1716 Chilton, John, A JAZZ NURSERY: THE STORY OF THE JENKINS' ORPHAN- AGE BANDS, London: Bloomsbury Book Shop, 1980.

C-1717 Crawford, Ralston, MUSIC IN THE STREET: PHOTOGRAPHS OF NEW ORLEANS BY RALSTON CRAWFORD, New Orleans: Historic New Orleans Collection, 1983.

C-1718 Gillock, William, NEW ORLEANS JAZZ STYLES, Cincinnati: Willis Music Company, 1966.

C-1719 Gombosi, Marilyn, A DAY OF SOLEMN THANKSGIVING: MORAVIAN MUSIC FOR THE FOURTH OF JULY, 1783, IN SALEM, NORTH CAROLINA, Chapel Hill: University of North Carolina Press, 1977.

C-1720 Handy, William C., FATHER OF THE BLUES; AN AUTOBIOGRAPHY New York: The Macmillan Company, 1941.

C-1721 Hemphill, Paul, THE NASHVILLE SOUND: BRIGHT LIGHTS AND COUNTRY MUSIC, New York: Simon and Schuster, 1970.

C-1722 Kmen, Henry A., MUSIC IN NEW ORLEANS: THE FORMATIVE YEARS, 1791- 1841, Baton Rouge: Louisiana State University Press, 1966.

C-1723 Lee, George W., BEALE STREET WHERE THE BLUES BEGAN, New York: R. O. Ballou, 1934.

C-1724 Lomax, John III, NASHVILLE: MUSIC CITY, U.S.A., New York: Abrams, 1985.

C-1725 Martinez, Ramond J., PORTRAITS OF NEW ORLEANS JAZZ: ITS PEOPLES AND PLACES, New Orleans: Hope Publications, 1971.

C-1726 McCorkle, Donald Macomber, THE COLLEGIUM MUSICUM SALEM: ITS MUSIC, MUSICIANS AND IMPORTANCE, Winston-Salem: Moravian Music Foundation, 1956.

C-1727 McKee, Margaret and Fred Chisenhall, BEALE BLACK AND BLUE: LIFE AND MUSIC ON BLACK AMERICA'S MAIN STREET, Baton Rouge: Louisiana State University Press, 1981.

C-1728 Roussel, Hubert, THE HOUSTON SYMPHONY ORCHESTRA: 1913-1971, Austin: University of Texas Press, 1972.

C-1729 Savage, William W. Jr., SINGING COWBOYS AND ALL THAT JAZZ: A SHORT HISTORY OF POPULAR MUSIC IN OKLAHOMA, Norman: University of Oklahoma Press, 1983.

C-1730 Stoutamire, Albert, MUSIC OF THE OLD SOUTH: COLONY TO CONFEDER- ACY, Rutherford: Fairleigh Dickinson University Press, 1972.

C-1731 Tassin, Myron and Jerry Henderson, FIFTY YEARS AT THE GRAND OLE OPRY, Gretna, LA: Pelican Publishing Company, 1975.

Politics and Government

C-1732 Abbott, Carl, THE NEW URBAN AMERICA: GROWTH AND POLITICS IN SUN-
       BELT CITIES, Chapel Hill: University of North Carolina Press,
       1981.

C-1733 Allen, Ivan and Paul Hemphill, MAYOR: NOTES ON THE SIXTIES, New
       York: Simon and Schuster, 1971.

C-1734 Alley, Cal, CAL ALLEY, Memphis: Memphis State University Press,
       1973.

C-1735 Alvey, Edward Jr., THE STREETS OF FREDERICKSBURG, Fredericksburg,
       VA: The Mary Washington College Foundation, Inc., 1978.

C-1736 Alyea, Paul E. and Blanche R. Alyea, FAIRHOPE, 1894-1954: THE
       STORY OF A SINGLE TAX COLONY, University, AL: University of
       Alabama Press, 1956.

C-1737 Atlanta City Hall Men's Club, OUR CITY, ATLANTA, Atlanta, 1963.

C-1738 Aulis, Jack, 75 YEARS OF SERVICE: A HISTORY OF THE NORTH CAROLINA
       LEAGUE OF MUNICIPALITIES, Raleigh: North Carolina League of
       Municipalities, 1982.

C-1739 Bain, Chester W., ANNEXATION IN VIRGINIA, Charlottesville: Uni-
       versity Press of Virginia, 1966.

C-1740 Bain, Chester W., "A BODY INCORPORATE": THE EVOLUTION OF CITY-
       COUNTY SEPARATION IN VIRGINIA, Charlottesville: University Press
       of Virginia, 1967.

C-1741 Barker, Jacob, INCIDENTS IN THE LIFE OF JACOB BARKER OF NEW
       ORLEANS, LOUISIANA, Washington: [s.n.], 1855.

C-1742 Baxter, William, PEA RIDGE AND PRAIRIE GROVE, Van Buren: Press
       Argus reprint (1958) of 1864 ed. (Cincinnati).

C-1743 Behrman, Martin, MARTIN BEHRMAN OF NEW ORLEANS: MEMOIRS OF A CITY
       BOSS, Baton Rouge: Louisiana State University Press, 1977.

C-1744 Behrman, Martin, NEW ORLEANS: A HISTORY OF THREE GREAT PUBLIC
       UTILITIES: SEWERAGE, WATER AND DRAINAGE AND THEIR INFLUENCE UPON
       THE HEALTH AND PROGRESS OF A BIG CITY, New Orleans: Brandoo
       Printers, [1914?].

C-1745 Bernard, Richard M. and Bradley R. Rice, SUNBELT CITIES: POLITICS
       AND GROWTH SINCE WORLD WAR II, Austin: University of Texas Press,
       1983.

C-1746 Beth, Loren P., THE POLITICS OF MIS-REPRESENTATION; RURAL-URBAN
       CONFLICT IN THE FLORIDA LEGISLATURE, Baton Rouge: Louisiana State
       University Press, 1962.

C-1747 Billings, Dwight B. Jr., PLANTERS AND THE MAKING OF A "NEW SOUTH":
       CLASS, POLITICS AND DEVELOPMENT IN NORTH CAROLINA 1865-1900,
       Chapel Hill: University of North Carolina Press, 1979.

C-1748 Bolner, James, ed., LOUISIANA POLITICS: FESTIVAL IN A LABYRINTH,
       Baton Rouge: Louisiana State University Press, 1982.

C-1749 Bornhaldt, Laura, BALTIMORE AND EARLY PAN-AMERICANISM: A STUDY IN
       THE BACKGROUND OF THE MONROE DOCTRINE, Northhampton, MA: Smith
       College Studies in History, v. 34, 1949.

C-1750 Brown, Charlie, CHARLIE BROWN REMEMBERS ATLANTA: MEMOIRS OF A
       PUBLIC MAN, Columbia, SC: R. L. Bryan, Company, 1982.

C-1751 Burgess, Margaret Elaine, NEGRO LEADERSHIP IN A SOUTHERN CITY, Chapel Hill: University of North Carolina Press, 1962.

C-1752 Carleton, Don E., RED SCARE: RIGHT-WING HYSTERIA, FIFTIES FANATI-CISM AND THEIR LEGACY IN TEXAS, Austin: Texas Monthly Press, 1985.

C-1753 Cassell, Frank A., MERCHANT CONGRESSMAN IN THE YOUNG REPUBLIC: SAMUEL SMITH OF MARYLAND, 1852-1839, Madison: University of Wisconsin Press, 1971.

C-1754 Church, Annette and Roberta Church, THE ROBERT R. CHURCHES OF MEMPHIS: A FATHER AND SON WHO ACHIEVED IN SPITE OF RACE, Ann Arbor, MI: The authors, n.d.

C-1755 Clark, Thomas D., HELM BRUCE, PUBLIC DEFENDER: BREAKING LOUIS-VILLE'S GOTHIC POLITICAL RING, 1905, Louisville: The Filson Club, 1974.

C-1756 Cook, Howard, SWIFTER THAN EAGLES--BILL WHITE AND THE BATTLE OF ATHENS, Athens, TN: Friendly City Publishing Company, 1981.

C-1757 Crenson, Matthew A., NEIGHBORHOOD POLITICS, Cambridge, MA: Harvard University Press, 1983.

C-1758 Crooks, James B., POLITICS AND PROGRESS: THE RISE OF URBAN PRO-GRESSIVISM IN BALTIMORE, 1895 TO 1911, Baton Rouge: Louisiana State University Press, 1968.

C-1759 Daniels, Bruce B., ed., TOWN AND COUNTRY: ESSAYS ON THE STRUCTURE OF LOCAL GOVERNMENT IN THE AMERICAN COLONIES, Middletown, CT: Wesleyan University Press, 1978.

C-1760 Davidson, Chandler, BIRACIAL POLITICS; CONFLICT AND COALITION IN THE METROPOLITAN SOUTH, Baton Rouge: Louisiana State University Press, 1972.

C-1761 Davis, William Hardy, AIMING FOR THE JUGULAR IN NEW ORLEANS, Port Washington, NY: Ashley Books, 1976.

C-1762 Dibble, Ernest F., ANTE-BELLUM PENSACOLA AND THE MILITARY PRESENCE, PENSACOLA: PENSACOLA/ESCAMBIA DEVELOPMENT COMMISSION, 1974.

C-1763 DILL, ALONZO THOMAS, GOVERNOR TRYON AND HIS PALACE, Chapel Hill: University of North Carolina Press, 1955.

C-1764 Ferry-Hanly Advertising Company, THE STORY OF MAYOR BEHRMAN'S NATIONAL CAMPAIGN TO ADVERTISE NEW ORLEANS: AND ITS ADVANTAGES TO THE ENTIRE UNITED STATES, New Orleans: The Company, 1918.

C-1765 Frye, Robert J. and John A. Dyer, THE CITY MANAGER SYSTEM IN ALABAMA, University: University of Alabama Press, 1961.

C-1766 Gavins, Raymond, THE PERILS AND PROSPECTS OF SOUTHERN BLACK LEADERSHIP: GORDON BLAINE HANCOCK, 1884-1970, Durham, NC: Duke University Press, 1977.

C-1767 Goodall, Leonard E., URBAN POLITICS IN THE SOUTHWEST, Tempe: Institute of Public Administration, Arizona State University, 1967.

C-1768 Harris, Carl Vernon, POLITICAL POWER IN BIRMINGHAM, 1871-1921, (Twentieth-Century American Series), Knoxville: University of Tennessee Press, 1977.

C-1769 Harvard, William and Loren P. Beth, THE POLITICS OF MIS-
REPRESENTATION: RURAL-URBAN CONFLICT IN THE FLORIDA LEGISLATURE,
Baton Rouge: Louisiana State University Press, 1961.

C-1770 Harvard, William and Floyd L. Corty, RURAL-URBAN CONSOLIDATION:
THE MERGER OF GOVERNMENTS IN THE BATON ROUGE AREA, Baton Rouge:
Louisiana State University Press, 1964.

C-1771 Hass, Edward F., DeLESSEPS S. MORRISON AND THE IMAGE OF REFORM:
NEW ORLEANS POLITICS, 1946-1961, Baton Rouge: Louisiana State
University Press, 1974.

C-1772 Haugh, James Bertram, POWER AND INFLUENCE IN A SOUTHERN CITY:
COMPARED WITH THE CLASSIC COMMUNITY POWER STUDIES OF THE LYNDS,
HUNTER, VIDICH AND BENSMAN, AND DAHL, Washington, DC: University
Press of America, 1980.

C-1773 Hawkins, Brett W., NASHVILLE METRO: THE POLITICS OF CITY-COUNTY
CONSOLIDATION, Nashville: Vanderbilt University Press, 1966.

C-1774 Henderson, William D., GILDED AGE CITY: POLITICS, LIFE AND LABOR
IN PETERSBURG, VIRGINIA, 1874-1889, Lhm, MDS: University Press of
America, 1980.

C-1775 Hoffecker, Carol E., SEWAGE WORKS IN WILMINGTON, DELAWARE, 1810-
1910, Chicago: Public Works Historical Society, 1982.

C-1776 Howard, Lawrence Vaughn and Robert S. Friedman, GOVERNMENT IN
METROPOLITAN NEW ORLEANS, New Orleans: Tulane University, 1959.

C-1777 Howe, William Wirt, MUNICIPAL HISTORY OF NEW ORLEANS, Baltimore:
Johns Hopkins University, 1889.

C-1778 Hunnicutt, James W., THE CONSPIRACY UNVEILED: THE SOUTH SACRI-
FICED; OR THE HORRORS OF SECESSION, Philadelphia: J. B. Lippincott and Company, 1963.

C-1779 Hunter, Floyd, COMMUNITY POWER SUCCESSION: ATLANTA'S POLICY-
MAKERS REVISTED, Chapel Hill: University of North Carolina Press,
1980.

C-1780 Inger, Morton, POLITICS AND REALITY IN AN AMERICAN CITY: THE NEW
ORLEANS SCHOOL CRISIS OF 1960, New York: Center for Urban Education, 1969.

C-1781 Jackson, Joy J., NEW ORLEANS IN THE GILDED AGE: POLITICS AND
URBAN PROGRESS, 1880-1896, Baton Rouge: Louisiana State University Press, 1969.

C-1782 Jennings, Thelma, THE NASHVILLE CONVENTION: SOUTHERN MOVEMENT FOR
UNITY, 1848-1851, Memphis: Memphis State University Press, 1980.

C-1783 Johnson, David R., John A. Booth, and Richard J. Harris, eds., THE
POLITICS OF SAN ANTONIO: COMMUNITY, PROGRESS, AND POWER, Lincoln:
University of Nebraska Press, 1983.

C-1784 Kammer, Gladys, Charles D. Farris, John M. DeGrone, and Alfred B.
Clubok, CITY MANAGERS IN POLITICS, AN ANALYSIS OF MANAGER TENURE
AND TERMINATION, Gainesville: University of Florida Press, 1962.

C-1785 Kammer, Gladys M., Charles D. Farris, John M. DeGrone, and Alfred
B. Clubok, THE URBAN POLITICAL COMMUNITY: PROFILES IN TOWN
POLITICS, Boston: Houghton Mifflin Company, 1963.

C-1786 Kemp, John R., ed., MARTIN BEHRMAN OF NEW ORLEANS: MEMOIRS OF A
CITY BOSS, Baton Rouge: Louisiana State University Press, 1977.

C-1787 Krefetz, Sharon Perlman, WELFARE POLICY MAKING AND CITY POLITICS, New York: Praeger Publishers, 1976.

C-1788 Langley, Michael, PROTECTION OF MINORITY POLITICAL PARTICIPATION ABANDONED IN SUPREME COURT'S RULING ON MOBILE ELECTIONS, Mobile: Voter Education Project, 1980.

C-1789 Lanier, Robert A., MEMPHIS IN THE TWENTIES: THE SECOND TERM OF MAYOR ROWLETT PAINE, 1924-1928, Memphis: Zenda Press, 1979.

C-1790 Lennon, Donald R. and Ida Brooks Kellam, THE WILMINGTON TOWN BOOK, 1743-1778, Raleigh: Division of Archives and History, North Carolina Department of Cultural Resources, 1973.

C-1791 Lotz, Aileen R., METROPOLITAN DADE COUNTY: TWO-TIER GOVERNMENT IN ACTION, Boston: Allyn and Bacon, 1984.

C-1792 Lyons, William E., THE POLITICS OF CITY-COUNTY MERGER: THE LEXINGTON-FAYETTE COUNTY EXPERIENCE, Lexington: University Press of Kentucky, 1977.

C-1793 MacManus, Susan A., FEDERAL AID TO HOUSTON, Washington, DC: Brookings Institution, 1983.

C-1794 Marando, Vincent Louis, METROPOLITAN DECISION-MAKING: RAPID TRANSIT IN ATLANTA, Athens: University of Georgia, 1973.

C-1795 Martin, Harold H., WILLIAM BERRY HARTSFIELD: MAYOR OF ATLANTA, Athens: University of Georgia Press, 1978.

C-1796 Martin, Richard, CONSOLIDATION: JACKSONVILLE, DUVAL COUNTY; THE DYNAMICS OF URBAN POLITICAL REFORM, Jacksonville: Crawford Publishing Company, 1968.

C-1797 Martinez, Raymond J., ROUSSEAU--THE LAST DAYS OF SPANISH NEW ORLEANS . . ., New Orleans: Hope Publications, 1975.

C-1798 Miller, William D., MR. CRUMP OF MEMPHIS, Baton Rouge: Louisiana State University Press, 1964, Greenwood Press, reprint, 1981.

C-1799 Moeser, John V. and Rutledge M. Dennis, THE POLITICS OF ANNEXATION: OLIGARCHIC POWER IN A SOUTHERN CITY, Cambridge, MA: Schenkman Publishing Company, 1982.

C-1800 Parker, Joseph B., THE MORRISON ERA: REFORM POLITICS IN NEW ORLEANS, Gretna, LA: Pelican Publishing Company, 1974.

C-1801 Peirce, Neal R., THE DEEP SOUTH STATES OF AMERICA: PEOPLE, POLITICS, AND POWER IN THE SEVEN DEEP SOUTH STATES, New York: W. W. Norton & Company, Inc., 1974.

C-1802 Perrenod, Virginia M., SPECIAL DISTRICTS, SPECIAL PURPOSES: FRINGE GOVERNMENTS AND URBAN PROBLEMS IN THE HOUSTON AREA, College Station: Texas A & M University Press, 1984.

C-1803 Petersburg, VA, Chamber of Commerce of Petersburg, Inc., THE CITY OF PETERSBURG, VA. THE BOOK OF ITS CHAMBER OF COMMERCE, Petersburg: George W. Engelhardt, 1894.

C-1804 Pride, Richard A. and David Woodward, THE BURDEN OF BUSING: THE POLITICS OF DESEGREGATION IN NASHVILLE, TENNESSEE, Knoxville: University of Tennessee Press, 1985.

C-1805 Raisty, Lloyd B., MUNICIPAL GOVERNMENT AND ADMINISTRATION IN GEORGIA, Athens: University of Georgia Press, 1941.

C-1806 Reissman, Leonard, et al., THE NEW ORLEANS VOTER: A HANDBOOK OF POLITICAL DESCRIPTION, New Orleans: Tulane University, 1955.

C-1807 Reynolds, George M., MACHINE POLITICS IN NEW ORLEANS, 1897-1926, New York: Columbia University Press, 1936.

C-1808 Sansing, David G. and Carroll Waller, A HISTORY OF THE MISSISSIPPI GOVERNOR'S MANSION, Jackson: University Press of Mississippi, 1977.

C-1809 Silver, Christopher, TWENTIETH-CENTURY RICHMOND: PLANNING, POLI-TICS, AND RACE, Knoxville: University of Tennessee Press, 1984.

C-1810 Soule, Leon Cyprian, THE KNOW NOTHING PARTY IN NEW ORLEANS: A REAPPRAISAL, Baton Rouge: Louisiana Historical Association, 1961.

C-1811 Speed, Thomas, THE POLITICAL CLUB: DANVILLE, KENTUCKY 1786-1790, Louisville: John P. Morton and Company, 1894, Filson Club Publication No. 9.

C-1812 Spritzer, Lorraine N., THE BELLE OF ASHBY STREET: HELEN DOUGLAS MANKEN AND GEORGIA POLITICS, Athens: University of Georgia Press, 1982.

C-1813 Steinberg, Alfred, THE BOSSES, New York: Macmillan Company, 1972.

C-1814 Strong, Donald S., URBAN REPUBLICANISM IN THE SOUTH, University, AL: University of Alabama, Bureau of Public Administration, 1960.

C-1815 Thomas, Thaddeus P., CITY GOVERNMENT OF BALTIMORE, Baltimore: The Johns Hopkins Press, 1896.

C-1816 Thometz, Carol, THE DECISION MAKERS: THE POWER STRUCTURE OF DALLAS, Dallas: Southern Methodist Press, 1963.

C-1817 Tucker, David M., LIEUTENANT LEE OF BEALE STREET, Nashville: Vanderbilt University Press, 1971.

C-1818 Tucker, David M., MEMPHIS SINCE CRUMP: BOSSISM, BLACKS AND CIVIC REFORMERS, 1849-1968, Knoxville: University of Tennessee Press, 1980.

C-1819 Vines, Kenneth N., REPUBLICANISM IN NEW ORLEANS, New Orleans: Tulane University, 1955.

C-1820 Vines, Kenneth N., TWO PARTIES FOR SHREVEPORT, New York: Holt, 1959.

C-1821 Watts, Eugene J., THE SOCIAL BASES OF CITY POLITICS: ATLANTA 1865-1903, (Contributions to American History, No. 73), Westport, CT, Greenwood Press, 1978.

C-1822 Wright, William E., MEMPHIS POLITICS: A STUDY IN RACIAL BLOC VOT-ING, New York: McGraw-Hill, 1962.

Population

C-1823 Bryant, Ellen S., CHANGES IN COMMUTING IN MISSISSIPPI FROM 1960 TO 1970, Mississippi State: Mississippi State University, Department of Sociology and Rural Life Bulletin 897, October 1981.

C-1824 Diaz-Briquets and Lisandro Perez, THE CUBAN IMMIGRATION, 1959-1966 AND ITS IMPACT ON MIAMI-DADE COUNTY, FLORIDA, Coral Gables: University of Miami, 1967.

C-1825 Fussell, Richard, A DEMOGRAPHIC ATLAS OF BIRMINGHAM, 1960-1970, University, AL: The University of Alabama Press, 1975.

C-1826 Goodman, Allen C. and Ralph B. Taylor, THE BALTIMORE NEIGHBORHOOD FACT BOOK, 1970 AND 1980, Baltimore: Center for Metropolitan Planning and Research, The Johns Hopkins University, 1983.

C-1827 Hamilton, C. Horace, RURAL-URBAN MIGRATION IN NORTH CAROLINA 1920 TO 1930, Raleigh, North Carolina Agricultural Experiment Station Bulletin 195, 1934.

C-1828 Jenna, William W. Jr., METROPOLITAN MIAMI: A DEMOGRAPHIC OVER-VIEW, Coral Gables: University of Miami Press, 1974.

C-1829 Murdock, Steve H., R. L. Skrabanek, Sean-Shong Hwang, and Rita R. Hamm, CITY AND SMALL TOWN POPULATION GROWTH IN TEXAS IN THE 1970's, College Station: Texas A & M University, Department of Rural Sociology, Technical Report No. 18-5, 1981.

C-1830 McMahan, Chalmers A., THE PEOPLE OF ATLANTA: A DEMOGRAPHIC STUDY OF GEORGIA'S CAPITAL CITY, Athens: University of Georgia Press, 1950.

C-1831 Poston, Dudley C. Jr. and Robert H. Willer, THE POPULATION OF THE SOUTH: STRUCTURE AND CHANGE IN SOCIAL DEMOGRAPHIC CONTEXT, Austin: University of Texas Press, 1981.

C-1832 Rosenquist, Carl Martin and Walter Gordon Browder, . . . FAMILY MOBILITY IN DALLAS, TEXAS, 1923-1938, Austin: University of Texas, 1942.

C-1833 Ross, Elmer L., FACTORS IN RESIDENCE PATTERNS AMONG LATIN AMERI-CANS IN NEW ORLEANS, LOUISIANA: A STUDY IN ANTHROPOLOGICAL METHODOLOGY, New York: Arno Press, 1980 [1973].

C-1834 Smith, David M., INEQUALITY IN AN AMERICAN CITY: ATLANTA 1960-1970, London: Occasional Paper No. 17, Department of Geography, Queen Mary College, University of London, 1981.

C-1835 Smith, David M., INEQUALITY IN ATLANTA, GEORGIA 1960-1980, London: Occasional Paper No. 25, Department of Geography and Earth Science, Queen Mary College, University of London, January 1985.

C-1836 United States. Bureau of the Census, URBAN ATLAS: TRACT DATA FOR STANDARD METROPOLITAN STATISTICAL AREAS: ATLANTA, GEORGIA, Washington, DC: The Bureau, 1975.

C-1837 United States. Work Projects Administration, Georgia, POPULA-TION; A STUDY OF FAMILY MOVEMENTS AFFECTING AUGUSTA, GEORGIA, 1899-1939, Augusta: Federal Works Agency, WPA, 1942.

C-1838 United States. Work Projects Administration, Georgia, . . . A STATISTICAL STUDY OF CERTAIN ASPECTS OF THE SOCIAL AND ECONOMIC PATTERN OF THE CITY OF ATLANTA, GEORGIA. . ., Atlanta, 1939.

C-1839 University of Texas, THE USE OF CITY DIRECTORIES IN THE STUDY OF URBAN POPULATION: A METHODOLOGICAL NOTE, Austin: The University of Texas, 1942.

Race Relations

C-1840 Anderson, Margaret, THE CHILDREN OF THE SOUTH, New York: Farrar, Straus and Geroux, 1966.

C-1841 Baldwin, James, THE EVIDENCE OF THINGS NOT SEEN, New York: Holt, Rinehart and Winston, 1985.

C-1842 Barnes, Catherine A., JOURNEY FROM JIM CROW: THE DESEGREGATION OF SOUTHERN TRANSIT, New York: Columbia University Press, 1983.

C-1843 Barrett, Russell H., INTEGRATION AT OLE MISS, Chicago: Quadrangle Books, 1965.

C-1844 Bates, Daisy (Gatson), THE LONG SHADOW OF LITTLE ROCK, A MEMOIR, New York: David McKay Company, 1963.

C-1845 Carter, Dan T., SCOTTSBORO: A TRAGEDY OF THE AMERICAN SOUTH, Baton Rouge: Louisiana State University Press, 1969.

C-1846 Carter, Hodding, A TALE OF TWO CITIES, [Stanford, CA: Stanford University, 1965?]

C-1847 Cartwright, Joseph H., THE TRIUMPH OF JIM CROW: TENNESSEE RACE RELATIONS IN THE 1880s, Knoxville: University of Tennessee Press, 1976.

C-1848 Chafe, William H., CIVILITIES AND CIVIL RIGHTS: GREENSBORO, NORTH CAROLINA, AND THE BLACK STRUGGLE FOR FREEDOM, New York: Oxford University Press, 1980.

C-1849 Charleston, S.C., . . . NEGRO PLOT. AN ACCOUNT OF THE LATE INTENDED INSURRECTION AMONG A PORTION OF THE BLACKS OF THE CITY OF CHARLESTON, Boston: J.W. Ingraham, 1822.

C-1850 Colburn, David R., RADICAL CHANGE AND COMMUNITY CRISIS: ST. AUGUSTINE, FLORIDA, 1887-1980, New York: Columbia University Press, 1985.

C-1851 Crawford, Fred Roberts, Harney Gates and James Congers, CIVIL AGGRESSION AND URBAN DISORDERS, ATLANTA, GEORGIA, 1967, Atlanta: Emory University, 1967?

C-1852 Cross, George Lynn, PROFESSORS, PRESIDENTS, AND POLITICIANS: CIVIL RIGHTS AND THE UNIVERSITY OF OKLAHOMA, 1890-1968, Norman: University of Oklahoma Press, 1981.

C-1853 Crowe, Charles, SOUTHERN REPRESSION AND BLACK RESISTANCE: 1900, 1917 AND 1932.

C-1854 Cunningham, W. J., AGONY AT GALLOWAY: ONE CHURCH'S STRUGGLE WITH SOCIAL CHANGE, Jackson: University Press of Mississippi, 1980.

C-1855 Ellsworth, Scott, DEATH IN A PROMISED LAND: THE TULSA RACE RIOT OF 1921, Baton Rouge: Louisiana State University Press, 1982.

C-1856 Fager, Charles E., SELMA, 1965, New York: Scribner, 1974.

C-1857 Garrow, David J., PROTEST AT SELMA, MARTIN LUTHER KING, JR., AND THE VOTING RIGHTS ACT OF 1965, New Haven, CT: Yale University Press, 1978.

C-1858 Gay, William T., MONTGOMERY, ALABAMA: A CITY IN CRISIS, New York: Exposition Press, 1957.

C-1859 Gordon, J. A., NIGHTRIDERS, Birmingham: BRALGO Publications, 1966.

C-1860 Green, Constance McLaughlin, THE SECRET CITY: A HISTORY OF RACE RELATIONS IN THE NATION'S CAPITAL, Princeton: Princeton University Press, 1967.

C-1861 Greene, Karen, PORTER-GAND SCHOOL: THE NEXT STEP, Easley, SC: Southern Historical Press, 1982.

C-1862 Guzman, Jessie P., CRUSADE FOR CIVIC DEMOCRACY: THE STORY OF THE TUSKEGEE CIVIC ASSOCIATION, 1941-1970, New York: Vantage Press, 1984.

C-1863 Hair, William Ivy, CARNIVAL OF FURY: ROBERT CHARLES AND THE NEW
       ORLEANS RACE RIOT OF 1900, Baton Rouge: Louisiana State Univer-
       sity Press, 1976.

C-1864 Huckaby, Elizabeth, CRISIS AT CENTRAL HIGH: LITTLE ROCK, 1957-58,
       Baton Rouge: Louisiana State University Press, 1980.

C-1865 Hutcheson, John D., RACIAL ATTITUDES IN ATLANTA, Atlanta: Emory
       University, 1973.

C-1866 Jackson, Kenneth T., THE KU KLUX KLAN IN THE CITY, 1915-1930, New
       York: Oxford University Press, 1967.

C-1867 Jacoway, Elizabeth and David R. Colburn, eds., SOUTHERN BUSINESS-
       MEN AND DESEGREGATION, Baton Rouge: Louisiana State University
       Press, 1982.

C-1868 King, Martin Luther Jr., STRIDE TOWARD FREEDOM: THE MONTGOMERY
       STORY, New York: Harper, 1958.

C-1869 Lane, Ann J., THE BROWNSVILLE AFFAIR: NATIONAL CRISIS AND BLACK
       REACTION, Port Washington, NY: Kennikat Press, 1971.

C-1870 Meltzer, Ida S., MONTGOMERY BUS STORY, Brooklyn, NY: Book-Lab,
       1980.

C-1871 Mikell, Robert Mosley, SELMA, Northport, AL: A.S. Press, 1965.

C-1872 Miller, Marilyn, THE BRIDGE AT SELMA, Morristown, NJ: Silver
       Burdett, 1985. [Juvenile Literature].

C-1873 Morgan, Charles, TIME TO SPEAK, New York: Holt, Rinehart and
       Winston, 1979.

C-1874 Morgan, Charles, Morland, J. Kenneth, LUNCH-COUNTER DESEGREGATION
       IN CORPUS CHRISTI, GALVESTON, AND SAN ANTONIO, TEXAS, Atlanta:
       Southern Regional Council, 1960.

C-1875 Morris, Willie, YAZOO: INTEGRATION IN A DEEP-SOUTHERN TOWN, New
       York: Harper and Row, 1971.

C-1876 McPheeters, Annie L., NEGRO PROGRESS IN ATLANTA, GEORGIA, 1950-
       1960; A SELECTIVE BIBLIOGRAPHY ON HUMAN RELATIONS FROM FOUR
       ATLANTA NEWSPAPERS, Atlanta: West Hunter Branch, Atlanta Public
       Library, 1964.

C-1877 McPheeters, Annie L., NEGRO PROGRESS IN ATLANTA, GEROGIA, 1961-
       1970; A SELECTIVE BIBLIOGRAPHY ON RACE AND HUMAN RELATIONS FROM
       FOUR ATLANTA NEWKSPAPERS, Atlanta, 1972.

C-1878 Persons, Albert C., THE TRUE SELMA STORY: SEX AND CIVIL RIGHTS,
       Birmingham: Esco Publishers, 1965.

C-1879 Porter, Bruce and Marvin Dunn, THE MIAMI RIOT OF 1980: CROSSING
       THE BOUNDS, Lexington, MA: Heath, 1984.

C-1880 Prather, H. Leon Sr., WE HAVE FAHINA CITY: WILMINGTON RACIAL
       MASSACRE AND COUP OF 1898, London: Farleigh Dickinson University
       Press, 1984.

C-1881 Proudfoot, Merril, DIARY OF A SIT-IN, Chapel Hill: University of
       North Carolina Press, 1962.

C-1882 Rabinowitz, Howard N., RACE RELATIONS IN THE URBAN SOUTH, 1865-
       1900, (Urban Life in America Series), New York: Oxford University
       Press, 1978.

C-1883 Salter, John R., JACKSON, MISSISSIPPI: AN AMERICAN CHRONICLE OF
STRUGGLE AND SCHISM, Hicksville, NY: Exposition Press, 1979.

C-1884 Southern Regional Council, AUGUSTA, GEORGIA AND JACKSON STATE UNI-
VERSITY, SOUTHERN EPISODES IN A NATIONAL TRAGEDY, Atlanta,1970.

C-1885 Stanfield, J. Edwin, IN MEMPHIS: MIRROR TO AMERICA?, Atlanta:
Southern Regional Council, 1968.

C-1886 Stevenson, Janet, THE MONTGOMERY BUS BOYCOTT, DECEMBER, 1955:
AMERICAN BLACKS DEMAND AN END TO SEGREGATION, New York: Watts [a
focus book], 1971.

C-1887 United States. Congress, House Select Committee on the Memphis
Riots, MEMPHIS RIOTS AND MASSACRES, Washington: The Committee,
1866.

C-1888 Williams, Lee E. and Lee E. Williams II, ANATOMY OF FOUR RACE
RIOTS: RACIAL CONFLICT IN KNOXVILLE, ELAINE [ARKANSAS], TULSA AND
CHICAGO, 1919-1921, Hattiesburg: University and College Press of
Mississippi, 1972.

C-1889 Wolff, Miles, LUNCH AT THE FIVE AND TEN: THE GREENSBORO SIT-INS.
A CONTEMPORARY HISTORY, New York: Stein and Day, 1970.

Recreation and Sports

C-1890 Athens-Clarke County Planning Commission, RECREATION--OPEN SPACE,
ATHENS AND CLARKE COUNTY, GEORGIA, Atlanta: Georgia Department of
Community Development, 1974.

C-1891 Berry, Evalena, SUGAR LOAF SPRINGS: HEBER'S ELEGANT WATERING
PLACE, Conway, AR: Renee Road Press, 1985.

C-1892 Bisher, Furman, THE ATLANTA FALCONS: VIOLENCE AND VICTORY,
Englewood Cliffs, NJ: Prentice-Hall, 1973.

C-1893 Bisher, Furman, MIRACLE IN ATLANTA; THE ATLANTA BRAVES STORY,
Cleveland: World Publishing Company, 1966.

C-1894 Buckley, Jean and Liz Getz, ATLANTA GUIDE TO STREET RUNNING,
Atlanta: The Camera & Eye, 1978.

C-1895 Chipman, Donald, THE DALLAS COWBOYS AND THE NFL, Norman:
University of Oklahoma Press, 1970.

C-1896 Cross, George L., PRESIDENT'S CAN'T PUNT: THE OU FOOTBALL
TRADITION, Norman: University of Oklahoma Press, 1977.

C-1897 Duls, Louisa DeSaussure, THE STORY OF LITTLE SWITZERLAND,
Richmond, VA: Whitlet and Shepperson.

C-1898 Eller, Buddy, Gene Middleton and Donald E. O'Brien, THE AMAZING
BRAVES: AMERICA'S TEAM, Atlanta: Philmay Enterprises, 1982.

C-1899 Fields, Robert Ashley, TAKE ME OUT TO THE CROWD: TED TURNER AND
THE ATLANTA BRAVES, Huntsville, AL: Strode Publishers, 1977.

C-1900 Fox, William P. and Franklin Ashley, HOW 'BOUT THEM GAMECOCKS,
Columbia: University of South Carolina Press, 1985.

C-1901 Frisbie, Louise K., FLORIDA'S FABLED INNS, Burton, FL: Imperial
Publishing Company, 1980.

C-1902 Huber, Jim, THE BABES OF WINTER: AN INSIDE HISTORY OF ATLANTA
FLAMES HOCKEY, Huntsville, AL: Strode Publishers, 1975.

C-1903 Keith, Harold, OKLAHOMA KICKOFF: AN INFORMAL HISTORY OF THE FIRST TWENTY-FIVE YEARS AT THE UNIVERSITY OF OKLAHOMA AND OF THE AMUSING HARDSHIPS THAT ATTENDED ITS PIONEERING, Norman: University of Oklahoma Press, 1978.

C-1904 Paige, David, THE DALLAS COWBOYS: AN ILLUSTRATED HISTORY, New York: Harper & Row, 1981.

C-1905 Quattlebaum, Julian K., THE GREAT SAVANNAH RACES, Athens: University of Georgia Press, Brown Thrasher Books, 1983.

C-1906 Rice, Russell, THE WILDCAT LEGACY: A PICTORIAL HISTORY OF KENTUCKY BASKETBALL, Virginia Beach, VA: JCP Corp. of Virginia, 1982.

C-1907 Rice, Russell, THE WILDCATS: A STORY OF KENTUCKY FOOTBALL, Huntsville, AL: Strode Publishers, 1975.

C-1908 Roberts, Clifford, THE STORY OF THE AUGUSTA NATIONAL GOLF CLUB, Garden City, NY: Doubleday, 1976.

C-1909 Rubin, Louis D. Jr., THE BOLL WEEVIL AND THE TRIPLE PLAY, Charleston, SC: Tradd Street Press, 1979.

C-1910 Schenck, Noella L., WINTER PARK'S OLD ALABAMA HOTEL, Winter Park, FL: Anna Publishing, 1982.

C-1911 Somers, Dale A., THE RISE OF SPORTS IN NEW ORLEANS, 1850-1900, Baton Rouge: Louisiana State University Press, 1972.

C-1912 Sorrels, William Wright and Charles F. Holmes, MEMPHIS STATE FOOTBALL: THE FIGHTING TIGERS, Huntsville, AL: Strode Publishers, 1981.

C-1913 Stegeman, John, THE GHOSTS OF HERTY FIELD: EARLY DAYS ON A SOUTHERN GRIDIRON, Athens: University of Georgia Press, 1966.

C-1914 Stowers, Carlton, DALLAS COWBOYS: THE FIRST TWENTY-FIVE YEARS, Dallas, TX: Taylor Publishers, 1984.

C-1915 Sulzby, James F. Jr., HISTORIC ALABAMA HOTELS AND RESORTS, University, AL: University of Alabama Press, 1960.

C-1916 Sulzby, James Frederick, BLOUNT SPRINGS: ALABAMA'S FOREMOST WATERING PLACE OF YESTERYEAR, Birmingham: s.n. 1949.

C-1917 Taylor, Dawson, THE MASTERS: AN ILLUSTRATED HISTORY, San Diego: A. S. Barnes, 1981.

Religion

C-1918 Anderson, Nola, THE LAKESIDE STORY: ONE HUNDRED YEARS OF HISTORY, Little Rock: August House, 1986.

C-1919 Augusta, GA First Presbyterian Church, MEMORIAL OF THE CENTENNIAL ANNIVERSARY OF THE FIRST PRESBYTERIAN CHURCH, AUGUSTA, GEORGIA, Philadelphia: Press of Allen, Lane and Scott, 1904.

C-1920 Bezou, Henry C., LOURDES ON NAPOLEON AVENUE: AN ACCOUNT OF THE PARISH OF OUR LADY OF LOURDES, NEW ORLEANS COMMEMORATING ITS SEVENTY-FIFTY ANNIVERSARY, New Orleans: Congregation of Notre Dame de Lourdes Church, 1980.

C-1921 Bezou, Henry C., METAIRIE: A TONGUE OF LAND TO PASTURE: AN ACCOUNT OF THE DEVELOPMENT OF THE FAITH COMMUNITY . . ., Gretna, LA: Pelican Publishers, 1973.

C-1922 Bezou, Henry C., TENT TO TEMPLE: THE STORY OF ST. PHILIP NERI
       PARISH, METAIRIE, LOUISIANA, Metairie, LA: Congregation of St.
       Philip Neri Roman Catholic Church, 1985.

C-1923 Blanton, Wyndham B., THE MAKING OF A DOWNTOWN CHURCH, Richmond:
       The John Knox Press, 1945.

C-1924 Blumberg, Janice Rothschild, ONE VOICE: RABBI JACOB M. ROTHSCHILD
       AND THE TROUBLED SOUTH, Macon: Mercer University Press, 1985.

C-1925 Clapp, Theodore, AUTOBIOGRAPHICAL SKETCHES AND RECOLLECTIONS:
       DURING A 35 YEARS RESIDENCE IN NEW ORLEANS, Boston: Phillips,
       Sampson, 1957.

C-1926 Clewell, John H., A HISTORY OF WACHOVIA IN NORTH CAROLINA, New
       York: Doubleday, Page and Company, 1902.

C-1927 Colley, Van Buren, HISTORY OF THE DIOCESAN SHRINE OF THE IMMACU-
       LATE CONCEPTION, Atlanta: Diocesan Shrine of the Imaculate Con-
       ception, 1955.

C-1928 Crabb, Aldred LeLand (introduction), SEVEN EARLY CHURCHES OF NASH-
       VILLE, Nashville: Charles Elder, Bookseller, 1972.

C-1929 Davies-Rodgers, Ellen, THE GREAT BOOK: CALVARY PROTESTANT EPISCO-
       PAL CHURCH, MEMPHIS, SHELBY COUNTY, TENNESSEE, Memphis: Planta-
       tion Press, 1973.

C-1930 Davis, John H., ST. MARY'S CATHEDRAL, MEMPHIS, Jackson: McCowat-
       Mercer Press, 1958.

C-1931 Duffy, John, ed., PARSON CLAPP OF THE STRANGERS' CHURCH OF NEW
       ORLEANS, Baton Rouge: Louisiana State University Press, 1957.

C-1932 Grant, Dorothy Fremont, JOHN ENGLAND: AMERICAN CHRISTOPHER,
       Milwaukee: The Bruce Publishing Company, 1949.

C-1933 Helmhold, F. Wilbur, SELMA: THE GOSPEL AT WORK, Birmingham:
       Banner Press, 1983.

C-1934 Helmhold, F. Wilbur, ed., SEVENTY-FIVE YEARS, CENTRAL PARK BAPTIST
       CHURCH, BIRMINGHAM, ALABAMA, 1910-1985, Birmingham: Banner Press,
       1985.

C-1935 Hitz, Alex M., A HISTORY OF THE CATHEDRAL OF ST. PHILIP, DIOCESE
       OF ATLANTA, ATLANTA, GEORGIA, OF THE PROTESTANT EPISCOPAL CHURCH,
       Atlanta: Cathedral Chapter, 1947?

C-1936 Holifield, E. Brooks, THE GENTLEMEN THEOLOGIANS: AMERICAN
       THEOLOGY IN SOUTHERN CULTURE, 1795-1860, Durham: Duke University
       Press, 1978.

C-1937 Jordan, Isabella S., A CENTURY OF SERVICE: FIRST BAPTIST CHURCH,
       AUGUSTA, GEORGIA, Augusta: 1921?

C-1938 King, Martin Luther, DADDY KING: AN AUTOBIOGRAPHY, New York:
       Marron, 1980.

C-1939 Lamar, Joseph Rucker, FIRST DAYS OF ST. PAUL'S CHURCH, AUGUSTA,
       GEORGIA [unpublished paper], Augusta: 1910?

C-1940 Lewis, Thomas P., CONDENSED HISTORICAL SKETCH OF TABERNACLE BAP-
       TIST CHURCH, AUGUSTA, GEORGIA; FROM ITS ORGANIZATION IN 1885 TO
       FEBRUARY, 1904 . . . ., Augusta: Georgia Baptist Book Printers,
       1904.

C-1941 Loveland, Anne C., SOUTHERN EVANGELICALS AND THE SOCIAL ORDER,
       1800-1860, Baton Rouge: Louisiana State University Press, 1980.

C-1942 May, James William, THE GLENN MEMORIAL STORY: A HERITAGE IN TRUST: A HISTORY OF THE UNITED METHODIST CHURCH ON THE EMORY UNIVERSITY CAMPUS, Nashville: Parthenon Press, 1985.

C-1943 Miller, Randal M. and Jon L. Wakelyn, eds., CATHOLICS IN THE OLD SOUTH: ESSAYS ON CHURCH AND CULTURE, Macon: Mercer University Press, 1983.

C-1944 McKim, Randolph Harrison, WASHINGTON'S CHURCH. AN HISTORICAL SKETCH OF OLD CHRIST CHURCH, ALEXANDRIA, VIRGINIA . . ., Alexandria: Press of Bell's Sons, 1886.

C-1945 Newman, Harvey Knupp, THE VISION OF ORDER: WHITE PROTESTANT CHRISTIANITY IN ATLANTA, 1865-1906, Atlanta: s.n., 1977.

C-1946 Rogers, Ebenezer Platt, A BRIEF HISTORY OF THE FIRST PRESBYTERIAN CHURCH, IN AUGUSTA, GEO., . . ., Charleston: Steam Power Press of Walker and James, 1851.

C-1947 Rothschild, Janice O., AS BUT A DAY: THE FIRST HUNDRED YEARS, 1867-1967, Atlanta: Hebrew Benevolent Congregation, the Temple, 1967.

C-1948 Sellers, James Benson, THE FIRST METHODIST CHURCH OF TUSCALOOSA, ALABAMA, 1818-1968, Tuscaloosa, AL: Westherford Printing Company, 1968.

C-1949 Simms, James M., FIRST COLORED BAPTIST CHURCH IN NORTH AMERICA, Philadelphia: J. B. Lippincott Company, 1888.

C-1950 Smith, George Gilman, A HUNDRED YEARS OF METHODISM IN AUGUSTA, GA, Augusta, GA: Richards & Shaver, printers, 1898.

C-1951 Stein, Kenneth W., A HISTORY OF THE AHAVATH ACHIM CONGREGATION, 1887-1977, Atlanta: Standard Press, 1978.

C-1952 Stokes, Durward T., A HISTORY OF GRAHAM PRESBYTERIAN CHURCH, Graham, NC: by the author, 1984.

C-1953 Symms, Marion S., comp., A BRIEF HISTORY OF THE FIRST BAPTIST CHURCH, Augusta: Walton Printing Company, 1945.

C-1954 Tebeau, Charlton W., SYNAGOGUE IN THE CENTRAL CITY: TEMPLE ISRAEL OF GREATER MIAMI, 1920-1922, Miami: University of Miami Press, 1972.

C-1955 TRINITY METHODIST EPISCOPAL CHURCH, SOUTH ATLANTA, GEORGIA . . . 1854-1935, Atlanta: 1935.

C-1956 Tucker, David M., BLACK PASTORS AND LEADERS: THE MEMPHIS CLERGY, 1819-1972, Memphis: Memphis State University Press, 1975.

C-1957 Weatherspool, William W., IT WAS DONE, Atlanta: Morris Brown College Press, 1945.

C-1958 Williams, Chauncy C., THE STORY OF ST. PAUL'S CHURCH, AUGUSTA, GEORGIA, A.D. 1750-1906, Augusta?: 1906?

Social Problems

C-1959 Cantwell, Edward, A HISTORY OF THE CHARLESTON POLICE FORCE FROM THE INCORPORATION OF THE CITY, 1783-1908, Charleston: J. J. Furlong, 1908.

C-1960 Coulter, E. Merton, THE OTHER HALF OF NEW ORLEANS. SKETCHES OF
       CHARACTERS AND INCIDENTS FROM THE RECORDER'S COURT OF NEW ORLEANS
       IN THE EIGHTEEN FORTIES AS REPORTED IN THE PICAYUNE, University,
       LA: Louisiana State University Press, 1939.

C-1961 Dettlinger, Chet with Jeff Prugh, THE LIST, Atlanta: Phelmay
       Enterprises, Inc., 1983.

C-1962 Dinnerstein, Leonard, THE LEO FRANK CASE, New York: Columbia
       University Press, 1968.

C-1963 Durrett, J. J. and W. G. Stromquist, A STUDY OF VIOLENT DEATHS
       REGISTERED IN ATLANTA, BIRMINGHAM, MEMPHIS AND NEW ORLEANS FOR THE
       YEARS 1921 AND 1922, Memphis: Davis Print Company, 1923?

C-1964 Frankel, Sandor, BEYOND A REASONABLE DOUBT, New York: Stein and
       Day, 1971.

C-1965 Gambino, Richard, VENDETTA: A TRUE STORY OF THE WORST LYNCHING IN
       AMERICA, THE MASS MURDER OF ITALIAN-AMERICANS IN NEW ORLEANS IN
       1891, THE VICIOUS MOTIVATIONS BEHIND IT, AND THE TRAGIC REPERCUS-
       SIONS THAT LINGER TO THIS DAY, Garden City, NY: Doubleday and
       Company, Inc., 1977.

C-1966 Golden, Harry, A LITTLE GIRL IS DEAD, New York: World Publishers,
       1965.

C-1967 Hayne, Robert V., A NIGHT OF VIOLENCE: THE HOUSTON RIOT OF 1917,
       Baton Rouge: Louisiana State University Press, 1976.

C-1968 HISTORY OF THE ATLANTA POLICE DEPARTMENT, Atlanta: Policemen's
       Relief Association, 1898.

C-1969 Hoffer, Frank William, Delbert Martin Mann, and Floyd Nelson
       House, THE JAILS OF VIRGINIA: A STUDY OF THE LOCAL PENAL SYSTEM,
       New York: D. Appleton-Century Company Inc., 1933.

C-1970 Hoole, W. Stanley, THE BIRMINGHAM HORRORS, Huntsville, AL: The
       Strode Publishers, Inc., 1980.

C-1971 Jenkins, Herbert T., FORTY YEARS ON THE FORCE: 1932-1972; HERBERT
       JENKINS REMINISCES ON HIS CAREER WITH THE ATLANTA POLICE DEPART-
       MENT, Atlanta: Emory University, 1973.

C-1972 Jenkins, Herbert T., KEEPING THE PEACE; A POLICE CHIEF LOOKS AT
       HIS JOB, New York: Harper & Row, 1970.

C-1973 Jenkins, James S., MURDER IN ATLANTA! SENSATIONAL CRIMES THAT
       ROCKED THE NATION, Atlanta: Cherokee Publishing Company, 1981.

C-1974 Kantor, Seth, WHO WAS JACK RUBY?, New York: Everest House, 1978.

C-1975 Marchiafava, Louis J., THE HOUSTON POLICE, 1878 TO 1948, Houston:
       William Marsh Rice University, 1977.

C-1976 Martin, Charles H., THE ANGELO HERNDON CASE AND SOUTHERN JUSTICE,
       Baton Rouge: Louisiana State University Press, 1976.

C-1977 Mathias, William Jefferson and Stuart Anderson, HORSE TO HELICOP-
       TER; FIRST CENTURY OF THE ATLANTA POLICE DEPARTMENT, Atlanta:
       Georgia State University, 1973.

C-1978 Thomas, Josiah, SIX SECONDS IN DALLAS, New York: Bernard Geis,
       1967.

C-1979 Udderzook, William Eachus, THE GOSS-UDDERZOOK TRAGEDY: BEING A
       HISTORY OF A STRANGE CASE OF DECEPTION AND MURDER, Baltimore:
       Baltimore Gazette Printers, 1873.

C-1980 Weisberg, Harold, OSWALD IN NEW ORLEANS, New York: Parallax Publishing Company, Inc., 1967.

C-1981 Wilbanks, William, MURDER IN MIAMI: AN ANALYSIS OF HOMOCIDE PATTERNS IN DADE COUNTY (MIAMI) FLORIDA, 1917-1983, Lanham, MD: University Press of America, 1984.

C-1982 Williams, Jack Kenny, VOGUES IN VILLANY: CRIME AND RETRIBUTION IN ANTE-BELLUM SOUTH CAROLINA, Columbia: University of South Carolina Press, 1959.

C-1983 Woodroof, Horace, STONE WALL COLLEGE, Nashville: Aurora Publishers Inc., 1970.

Theatre

C-1984 Adams, Henry W., THE MONTGOMERY THEATRE 1822-1835, University, AL: University of Alabama Press, 1955.

C-1985 Ashby, Clifford and Suzanne DePauw May, TROUPING THROUGH TEXAS: HARLEY SADLER AND HIS TENT SHOW, Bowling Green, OH: Bowling Green University Popular Press, 1982.

C-1986 Dormon, James H., THEATER IN THE ANTE BELLUM SOUTH, 1815-1861, Chapel Hill: University of North Carolina Press, 1967.

C-1987 Hoole, W. Stanley, THE ANTE-BELLUM CHARLESTON THEATRE, Tuscaloosa: University of Alabama Press, 1946.

C-1988 Jones, Margo, THEATRE-IN-THE-ROUND, New York: Rinehart, 1951.

C-1989 LeGardeur, Rene J. Jr., THE FIRST NEW ORLEANS THEATRE, 1792-1803, New Orleans: Leeward Books, 1963.

C-1990 Patrick, J. Max, SAVANNAH'S PIONEER THEATER FROM ITS ORIGIN TO 1810, Athens: University of Georgia Press, 1953.

C-1991 Ritchey, David, comp. and ed., A GUIDE TO THE BALTIMORE STAGE IN THE EIGHTEENTH CENTURY: A HISTORY AND DAY BOOK CALENDAR, Westport, CT: Greenwood Press, 1982.

C-1992 Shockley, Martin Staples, THE RICHMOND STAGE, 1784-1812, Charlottesville: University Press of Virginia, 1977.

C-1993 Smither, Neele K., A HISTORY OF THE ENGLISH THEATRE AT NEW ORLEANS, 1806-1842, New York: B. Blom [1967, c 1944].

C-1994 Watson, Charles S., ANTEBELLUM CHARLESTON DRAMATISTS, University, AL: University of Alabama Press, 1976.

C-1995 Willis, Eola, THE CHARLESTON STAGE IN THE EIGHTEENTH CENTURY, Columbia: The State Company, 1924.

Transportation

C-1996 August, Perez & Associates, THE LAST LINE: A STREETCAR NAMED ST. CHARLES, Gretna, LA: Pelican Publushers, 1980, c. 1973.

C-1997 Bambach, Richard O. and William E. Borah, AN ANALYSIS OF THE REPORTS ON THE RIVERFRONT EXPRESSWAY, New Orleans: 1966.

C-1998 Baumbach, Richard O. Jr. and William E. Borah, THE SECOND BATTLE OF NEW ORLEANS: A HISTORY OF THE VIEUX CARRE RIVERFRONT EXPRESSWAY CONTROVERSY, University, AL: University of Alabama Press, 1981.

C-1999 Borah, William E., MISSISSIPPI RIVER BRIDGE AUTHORITY'S APPLICA-
       TION TO THE UNITED STATES COAST GUARD FOR A PERMIT TO CONSTRUCT A
       BRIDGE ACROSS THE MISSISSIPPI RIVER . . ., 1970.

C-2000 Carson, O. E. THE TROLLEY TITANS: A MOBILE HISTORY OF ATLANTA,
       Glendale, CA: Interurban Press, 1981.

C-2001 Charlton, Elbridge Harper, STREET RAILWAYS OF NEW ORLEANS, Los
       Angeles: I.L. Swett, 1955.

C-2002 Clark, Ira G., THEN CAME THE RAILROADS: THE CENTURY FROM STEAM TO
       DIESEL IN THE SOUTHWEST, Norman: University of Oklahoma Press,
       1958.

C-2003 Costa, Louis, STREETCAR GUIDE TO UPTOWN NEW ORLEANS, New Orleans:
       TransiTour, Inc., 1981, c. 1980.

C-2004 Costa, Louis, Andre Neff and Peter Raarup, THE STREETCAR GUIDE TO
       UPTOWN NEW ORLEANS, New Orleans: TransiTour, Inc., 1980.

C-2005 Hennick, Louis C. and Elbridge Harper Charlton, LOUISIANA, ITS
       STREET AND INTERURBAN RAILWAYS, Shreveport: 1962.

C-2006 Hennick, Louis C. and Elbridge Harper Charlton, STREETCARS OF NEW
       ORLEANS, Gretna, LA: Pelican Publishing Company, 1965.

C-2007 Jenkins, Herbert T., ATLANTA AND THE AUTOMOBILE, Atlanta: Emory
       University, 1977.

C-2008 Langley, A. M., TROLLYS IN THE VALLEY; A HISTORY OF THE STREET AND
       INTERURBAN RAILWAYS OF AUGUSTA, GEORGIA, NORTH AUGUSTA, SOUTH
       CAROLINA, THE HORSE CREEK VALLEY, AIKEN, SOUTH CAROLINA, n.p.,
       1972.

C-2009 Lewis, W. David and Wesley Phillips Newton, DELTA: THE HISTORY OF
       AN AIRLINE, Athens: University of Georgia Press, 1979.

C-2010 Memphis Transit Authority, MASS TRANSPORTATION STUDIES IN MEMPHIS;
       TRANSIT SYSTEM'S HISTORY, 1956-1965; SUBURBAN RIDERSHIP DEMONSTRA-
       TION PROJECT, Memphis: Memphis Transit Authority, 1965.

C-2011 Preston, Howard L., AUTOMOBILE AGE ATLANTA: THE MAKING OF A
       SOUTHERN METROPOLIS, 1900-1935, Athens: The University of Georgia
       Press, 1979.

C-2012 Stoner, John F., THE RAILROADS OF THE SOUTH, 1865-1900, Chapel
       Hill: University of North Carolina Press, 1955.

C-2013 Summers, Mark W., RAILROADS, RECONSTRUCTION, AND THE GOSPEL OF
       PROSPERITY, Princeton, NJ: Princeton University Press, 1984.

Geographic Index

ABILENE, TX [B] 1821; [C] 734, 1255

ABINGTON, VA [B] 4327

ADAMS, TN [C] 1360

AIKEN, SC [C] 838, 2009

ALABAMA [A] 95, 209, 320; [B] 228, 565, 703, 704, 705, 806, 844, 964, 965, 973, 974, 975, 1166, 1281, 1381, 1397, 1432, 1435, 1471, 1473, 1477, 1608, 1695, 2053, 2308, 2478, 2485, 2492, 2531, 2537, 3020, 3023, 3094, 3113, 3373, 3718, 4428; [C] 330, 415, 428, 730, 758, 865, 938, 1061, 1086, 1316, 1442, 1527, 1675, 1683, 1765, 1915, 1916

ALBANY, GA [A] 222; [B] 270, 2285, 3836

ALBEMARLE, VA [B] 2169; [C] 236

ALCOA, TN [B] 947, 2172, 2173, 3943

ALEXANDER CITY, AL [C] 1409

ALEXANDRIA, LA [B] 1159, 1426, 2702, 2945; [C] 625, 918

ALEXANDRIA, VA [A] 361, 491, 644, 759; [B] 9, 40, 83, 707, 917, 935, 2088, 2346, 3465; [C] 33, 93, 126, 151, 156, 1139, 1321, 1415, 1551, 1944

ALGIERS, LA [C] 728

ALLARDT, TN [B] 1728

ALTUS, OK [B] 2494

AMARILLO, TX [B] 2487

AMERICUS, GA [B] 2105, 2771, 3009; [C] 1689

ANDERSONVILLE, GA [B] 1962

ANDREWS, SC [B] 2577

ATLANTA (CONTINUED)

3247, 3250, 3251, 3253, 3273, 3276, 3282, 3283, 3297, 3298, 3353,
3362, 3364, 3366, 3377, 3392, 3403, 3413, 3420, 3421, 3441, 3483,
3504, 3505, 3508, 3511, 3512, 3539, 3551, 3552, 3553, 3558, 3565,
3585, 3602, 3604, 3613, 3614, 3624, 3645, 3647, 3648, 3653, 3655,
3659, 3662, 3664, 3674, 3678, 3698, 3749, 3753, 3754, 3755, 3756,
3780, 3781, 3784, 3799, 3800, 3801, 3813, 3817, 3843, 3844, 3847,
3854, 3879, 3880, 3883, 3893, 3914, 3967, 3986, 3995, 4031, 4035,
4036, 4037, 4043, 4074, 4075, 4079, 4082, 4083, 4084, 4096, 4101,
4103, 4123, 4177, 4178, 4180, 4192, 4198, 4200, 4208, 4210, 4211,
4216, 4222, 4232, 4242, 4264, 4290, 4341, 4344, 4348, 4359, 4360,
4362, 4370, 4396, 4397, 4402, 4403, 4404, 4414, 4422, 4451, 4455,
4456, 4467, 4474; [C] 5, 8, 78, 83, 99, 103, 106, 111, 128, 158,
165, 166, 199, 200, 214, 216, 219, 220, 221, 231, 244, 247, 252,
258, 259, 264, 266, 288, 290, 291, 292, 304, 306, 319, 321, 327,
339, 346, 355, 371, 381, 389, 405, 421, 422, 435, 436, 438, 439,
443, 447, 454, 457, 477, 495, 496, 507, 514, 515, 516, 517, 518,
519, 520, 521, 522, 523, 524, 525, 526, 533, 575, 619, 639, 661,
662, 673, 682, 687, 736, 767, 797, 799, 800, 806, 842, 855, 856,
890, 901, 917, 927, 962, 968, 978, 1000, 1023, 1024, 1041, 1045,
1051, 1061, 1079, 1129, 1156, 1199, 1213, 1215, 1216, 1217, 1218,
1219, 1220, 1221, 1225, 1229, 1231, 1241, 1248, 1337, 1352, 1367,
1373, 1394, 1417, 1426, 1443, 1458, 1460, 1486, 1521, 1545, 1546,
1560, 1565, 1582, 1596, 1607, 1611, 1632, 1651, 1665, 1691, 1733,
1737, 1750, 1779, 1794, 1795, 1813, 1821, 1830, 1834, 1835, 1836,
1838, 1841, 1851, 1865, 1866, 1876, 1877, 1892, 1893, 1894, 1924,
1927, 1935, 1938, 1945, 1947, 1951, 1961, 1962, 1963, 1966, 1968,
1971, 1972, 1973, 1976, 1977, 2000, 2007, 2011

AUBURN, AL [B] 1232, 1864; [C] 893

AUBURN, GA [C] 1560

AUGUSTA, GA [A] 26, 39, 319, 538, 668, 711; [B] 108, 115, 486, 717, 718,
791, 862, 1089, 1092, 1137, 1209, 1493, 1495, 1498, 1682, 1703,
1707, 1753, 1850, 2143, 2186, 2193, 2224, 2225, 2228, 2356, 2364,
2388, 2446, 2447, 2448, 2625, 2688, 2754, 2810, 2972, 3022, 3103,
3215, 3272, 3387, 3429, 3446, 3477, 3532, 3575, 3582, 3587, 3668,
3676, 3682, 3838, 4018, 4086, 4252, 4287; [C] 193, 198, 255, 303,
347, 359, 360, 382, 396, 400, 466, 469, 475, 527, 528, 606, 620,
621, 667, 686, 713, 723, 779, 780, 934, 935, 938, 1108, 1189, 1190,
1280, 1290, 1393, 1425, 1488, 1500, 1529, 1550, 1609, 1628, 1644,
1667, 1837, 1884, 1908, 1917, 1919, 1937, 1939, 1940, 1946, 1950,
1954, 1958, 2008

AUGUSTA, KY [B] 197

AURARIA, GA [B] 1276

AUSTIN, TX [A] 797, 851, 858; [B] 488, 501, 788, 960, 1869, 2258, 3908,
4150, 4236

AVALON, NC [C] 788

BADIN, NC [C] 46

BAINBRIDGE, GA [B] 1830; [C] 968

BALTIMORE, MD [A] 43, 44, 54, 56, 76, 87, 88, 97, 116, 123, 139, 153,
163, 260, 279, 301, 313, 341, 374, 376, 465, 626, 630, 643, 662,
727, 756, 758, 791, 792, 799, 814, 821, 826, 827, 829, 855; [B] 27,
65, 66, 88, 112, 224, 239, 326, 336, 343, 377, 380, 415, 417, 427,
432, 438, 490, 520, 523, 536, 548, 558, 563, 572, 594, 595, 597,
598, 658, 665, 666, 672, 710, 719, 720, 726, 738, 760, 775, 785,
792, 793, 800, 803, 832, 841, 875, 876, 896, 902, 927, 954, 955,

BALTIMORE (CONTINUED)
    970, 979, 1001, 1016, 1019, 1084, 1108, 1152, 1165, 1190, 1216,
    1241, 1253, 1254, 1332, 1408, 1419, 1444, 1465, 1503, 1516, 1520,
    1564, 1578, 1587, 1619, 1711, 1712, 1713, 1743, 1761, 1790, 1836,
    1906, 1960, 2007, 2029, 2056, 2067, 2072, 2116, 2117, 2118, 2119,
    2155, 2180, 2227, 2344, 2370, 2371, 2372, 2378, 2389, 2394, 2420,
    2501, 2519, 2550, 2575, 2576, 2596, 2698, 2750, 2772, 2773, 2779,
    2789, 2791, 2827, 2838, 2847, 2849, 2886, 2910, 2911, 2912, 2956,
    2965, 3005, 3018, 3037, 3052, 3083, 3104, 3127, 3153, 3161, 3204,
    3211, 3218, 3230, 3231, 3232, 3237, 3277, 3324, 3332, 3343, 3349,
    3378, 3425, 3444, 3454, 3518, 3519, 3601, 3608, 3623, 3631, 3637,
    3649, 3671, 3693, 3694, 3743, 3745, 3746, 3747, 3763, 3870, 3878,
    3925, 3976, 3987, 4065, 4092, 4102, 4112, 4140, 4184, 4196, 4235,
    4250, 4302, 4387, 4437, 4465; [C] 40, 63, 119, 181, 203, 212, 213,
    241, 254, 263, 284, 299, 300, 301, 358, 373, 446, 447, 494, 500,
    550, 587, 731, 824, 945, 946, 1039, 1095, 1109, 1134, 1167, 1191,
    1192, 1193, 1463, 1525, 1570, 1583, 1749, 1753, 1757, 1758, 1787,
    1815, 1826, 1979, 1991

BARKSDALE, LA [B] 3406

BARLOW, KY [B] 1597

BARTONSVILLE, NC [B] 899

BATESVILLE, AR [B] 226, 1057, 1184, 1660, 2360

BATON ROUGE, LA [A] 170, 199, 744; [B] 234, 1643, 1653, 1843, 2562,
    2695, 3275, 3354, 3859; [C] 562, 784, 1033, 1508, 1630, 1704, 1770

BAUXITE, AR [B] 1654

BAY CITY, TX [C] 1266

BAY SPRINGS, MS [B] 1282

BAYOU CHATUGUE, LA [C] 428

BAYTOWN, TX [A] 75

BEAUFORT, NC [B] 900, 1413, 2182, 2924; [C] 65, 66, 942, 943

BEAUFORT, SC [B] 2260, 2551

BEAUMONT, TX [B] 837, 3358, 3502, 3827, 3941, 4446; [C] 222, 996

BECKLEY, WV [B] 541

BEERSHEBA SPRINGS, TN [B] 3660, 3661; [C] 664

BEL AIR, VA [C] 71

BELLA VISTA, AR [B] 2255

BELLE GLADE, FL [B] 3773

BELLE MEADE PARK, TN [C] 1301

BELTON, TX [B] 3027

BENTONVILLE, AR [B] 4175

BETHABARA, NC [B] 47

BEREA, KY [B] 1163, 1935; [C] 1119

BERTRANDVILLE, LA [B] 2963

BIG SPRING, TX [C] 317, 1126

BILOXI, MS [B] 257, 434, 1437, 2287; [C] 19

BIRMINGHAM, AL [A] 241, 294, 371, 451, 466, 572, 681, 753, 801 [B] 203,
    205, 208, 254, 421, 435, 440, 448, 529, 567, 706, 1005, 1042, 1048,
    1094, 1097, 1099, 1106, 1162, 1491, 1526, 1696, 2068, 2150, 2422,
    2680, 2726, 2758, 3024, 3214, 3234, 3238, 3330, 3473, 3702, 3807,
    3825, 3862, 3863, 4054, 4063, 4120, 4152, 4273, 4348, 4349, 4459,
    4463; [C] 12, 112, 133, 135, 247, 298, 331, 512, 513, 559, 560,
    671, 683, 696, 737, 760, 878, 902, 971, 1014, 1088, 1129, 1252,
    1275, 1276, 1277, 1284, 1449, 1523, 1703, 1768, 1825, 1934, 1963,
    1970

BISCAYNE BAY, FL [A] 671

BLACKBURN, OK [B] 1933

BLAKELEY, AL [B] 2171

BLANFORD, VA [B] 192

BLEDSOESBOROUGH, TN [C] 419

BLOUNT SPRINGS, AL [B] 4008; [C] 1916

BLUFFTON, SC [C] 121

BLYTHEVILLE, AR [B] 655

BOCA GRANDE, FL [B] 4418

BOCA RATON, FL [B] 1472, 4230; [C] 505, 506

BOLEY, OK [B] 1941, 3564, 3884

BOONESBOROUGH, KY [C] 1144

BOWLING GREEN, KY [B] 1936, 4358

BREMOND, TX [B] 1000

BRENHAM, TX [B] 1523

BREWTON, AL [A] 358; [B] 2246

BRICEVILLE, TN [B] 1579

BRIDGEPORT, AL [C] 578

BRINKELY, AR [B] 1984, 1985, 1986

BRISTOL, TN [B] 3156, 3414; [C] 1003

BRISTOL, VA [B] 3156, 3414; [C] 1003

BROOKSVILLE, FL [B] 2366

BROWNSVILLE, TN [B] 1167

BROWNSVILLE, TX [A] 308; [B] 412, 659, 813; [C] 1338, 1869

BROWNTOWN, SC [B] 671

BRUNSWICK, GA [B] 977

BRUNSWICK, NC [A] 690; [B] 2064

CHAMPAGNOLLE, AR [B] 1752

CHANCELLORSVILLE, VA [C] 781, 818

CHAPEL HILL, NC [A] 244; [B] 260, 2850, 3509, 3818; [C] 251, 350, 379,
   394, 403, 412, 627, 807, 903, 980, 1194, 1195, 1269, 1320, 1622

CHARLESTON, SC [A] 28, 29, 32, 68, 69, 100, 124, 174, 258, 277, 297,
   367, 391, 534, 566, 589, 599, 602, 639, 645, 649, 670, 675, 718,
   752; [B] 45, 49, 57, 58, 59, 63, 116, 139, 150, 207, 238, 245, 267,
   349, 381, 409, 454, 460, 468, 470, 473, 479, 481, 503, 519, 547,
   611, 640, 675, 713, 725, 801, 808, 814, 815, 869, 870, 871, 901,
   989, 990, 991, 998, 999, 1023, 1026, 1107, 1115, 1141, 1217, 1229,
   1230, 1383, 1418, 1425, 1518, 1519, 1521, 1528, 1532, 1555, 1566,
   1567, 1617, 1661, 1691, 1786, 1813, 1835, 1873, 2015, 2048, 2075,
   2115, 2134, 2135, 2136, 2230, 2231, 2232, 2233, 2261, 2262, 2266,
   2267, 2284, 2296, 2306, 2307, 2310, 2312, 2340, 2407, 2437, 2438,
   2507, 2534, 2567, 2579, 2608, 2709, 2711, 2755, 2786, 2816, 2818,
   2826, 2832, 2833, 2859, 2862, 2890, 2891, 2907, 2953, 2971, 2979,
   2981, 2982, 3029, 3030, 3034, 3080, 3085, 3101, 3140, 3144, 3146,
   3151, 3212, 3245, 3259, 3313, 3344, 3346, 3352, 3355, 3367, 3379,
   3389, 3418, 3474, 3531, 3587, 3589, 3594, 3615, 3626, 3684, 3700,
   3714, 3716, 3726, 3882, 3885, 3960, 3993, 4034, 4044, 4045, 4048,
   4106, 4109, 4110, 4111, 4130, 4132, 4142, 4143, 4159, 4160, 4161,
   4176, 4183, 4220, 4227, 4253, 4283, 4304, 4305, 4306, 4307, 4308,
   4315, 4390, 4425, 4429, 4462; [C] 23, 61, 85, 87, 122, 152, 167,
   168, 172, 175, 176, 177, 184, 185, 187, 188, 204, 217, 224, 286,
   305, 361, 377, 384, 471, 473, 484, 498, 585, 599, 631, 636, 775,
   789, 898, 920, 985, 987, 990, 1020, 1049, 1070, 1163, 1164, 1165,
   1166, 1179, 1184, 1236, 1238, 1242, 1243, 1249, 1308, 1318, 1347,
   1370, 1465, 1472, 1540, 1565, 1593, 1611, 1618, 1625, 1632, 1640,
   1673, 1684, 1709, 1710, 1716, 1849, 1861, 1909, 1932, 1959, 1987,
   1994, 1995

CHARLESTON, WV [B] 1793, 2867, 3315, 3852, 4266

CHARLOTTE, NC [A] 84, 99, 382, 478, 496, 667, 694, 764, 870; [B] 662,
   828, 1082, 1489, 2793, 3056, 3089, 3233, 3916, 3917, 4126, 4127,
   4460; [C] 567, 568, 637, 809, 1017, 1235, 1396, 1443, 1652, 1897

CHARLOTTESVILLE, VA [A] 335, 368, 809; [B] 158, 1147, 1175, 1177, 1575,
   1625, 1630, 1631, 1632, 1633, 1926, 1948, 2016, 2217, 2247, 2451,
   4335; [C] 493, 1146, 1616

CHATTANOOGA, TN [A] 298, 342; [B] 195, 667, 823, 1902, 1918, 1919, 1958,
   2076, 2077, 2140, 2439, 2477, 2505, 3318, 4352, 4384, 4389; [C]
   149, 375, 388, 479, 632, 821, 896, 998, 1047, 1355, 1356

CHEROKEE, GA [B] 1060, 2367

CHERRYVILLE, NC [B] 2796

CHESTNUT HILL, TN [B] 3689

CHILDSBURG, AL [B] 2263

CHRISTIANSBURG, VA [C] 1135

CHUCALISSA, TN [B] 2147

CHURCH HILL, VA [B] 235

CLAIBORNE, AL [B] 1724

CLARKSDALE, MS [C] 1340

CLARKSVILLE, TN [A] 329; [B] 1015, 1649, 2350, 4139; [C] 278

COUNCIL GROVE, OK [B] 1652

COVINGTON, KY [B] 743, 1533, 1946, 2623; [C] 136

CRISFIELD, MD [B] 1033

CROSSETT, AR [B] 1657

CROWLEY, LA [B] 1934

CULLMAN, AL [B] 4366

CUSHMAN, AR [B] 3963

CUTHBERT, GA [C] 1274

DAHLONEGA, GA [B] 600, 2042, 2941; [C] 868

DALLAS, GA [C] 234

DALLAS, TX [A] 94, 384, 386, 565, 616, 699, 781; [B] 74, 95, 126, 283,
    398, 500, 507, 540, 631, 660, 683, 734, 773, 847, 861, 952, 1080,
    1234, 2349, 2390, 2402, 2616, 3221, 3316, 3385, 3413, 3638, 4137,
    4144, 4155, 4255, 4421; [C] 3, 42, 132, 189, 264, 277, 402, 431,
    433, 440, 485, 547, 827, 832, 904, 982, 994, 1030, 1074, 1110,
    1198, 1211, 1305, 1390, 1400, 1401, 1453, 1502, 1509, 1636, 1669,
    1816, 1832, 1866, 1895, 1904, 1914, 1974, 1978, 1988

DALTON, GA [B] 842, 1024, 2663; [C] 280, 1354

DAMASCUS, VA [C] 848

DANVILLE, KY [A] 453; [B] 404, 969, 1173, 2212, 3833, 3837; [C]
    1405, 1811

DANVILLE, VA [A] 165; [C] 787, 845, 846

DARDANELLE, AR [B] 1921

DARIEN, GA [B] 2071, 3640, 3690; [C] 955

DECATUR, AL [C] 929

DECATUR, GA [B] 1727, 2130

DEER LODGE, TN [C] 1258

DELAWARE [A] 24, 702; [B] 25, 457, 509, 688, 1011, 1031, 1264, 1384,
    3383

DEMOPOLIS, AL [B] 2276

DENMARK, TN [B] 1825

DENTON, TX [A] 629

DISNEY WORLD, FL [B] 1078, 2889

DISSTON CITY, FL [B] 2547

DONALDSVILLE, LA [B] 3607

DONCASTER, MD [B] 1297

DONELSON, TN [C] 490

EUDORA, AR [B] 1603

EUFAULA, AL [B] 306, 333, 3341, 4197; [C] 555

EUREKA SPRINGS, AR [B] 1795, 2187; [C] 605, 1127, 1148

EUTAW, AL [B] 3340; [C] 70

FAIRFAX, VA [B] 1369, 2245; [C] 1196

FAIRFIELD, AL [B] 2170

FAIRHOPE, AL [C] 1736

FAYETTEVILLE, AR [B] 1062; [C] 383, 586, 610, 1019, 1742

FAYETTEVILLE, NC [B] 2591, 4309

FAYETTEVILLE, WV [B] 2038

FELLS POINT, MD [C] 1191

FERNANDINA, FL [A] 145, 353; [B] 2552

FINCASTLE, VA [B] 1512, 2152

FITZGERALD, GA [B] 1905, 2731, 3265

FLORENCE, AL [B] 571, 731, 1176, 3896

FLORENCE, SC [B] 2039, 2200; [C] 953

FLORIDA [A] 118, 191, 205, 229, 524, 634, 714, 790; [B] 593, 669, 849,
    883, 919, 925, 945, 1014, 1116, 1211, 1334, 1337, 1453, 1853, 1866,
    1944, 2166, 2250, 2251, 2376, 2560, 2574, 2620, 2686, 2706, 2765,
    3059, 3256, 3257, 3264, 3319, 3543, 3627, 3808, 3809, 3901, 3956,
    3964, 3974, 4260; [C] 420, 563, 823, 1056, 1173, 1746, 1769, 1784,
    1785, 1901

FLOWERDEN, VA [B] 18

FORT BLISS, TX [A] 67

FORT GRIFFIN, TX [C] 1174

FT. LAUDERDALE, FL [A] 627; [B] 138, 1805, 3038, 3773; [C] 1082, 1342

FORT McHENRY, MD [C] 1192

FORT MORGAN, AL [B] 2824

FORT MYERS, FL [C] 811, 838, 1202

FORT SAM HOUSTON, TX [C] 857

FORT SMITH, AR [B] 91, 2504; [C] 601, 1521

FORT VALLEY, GA [B] 1050

FORT WORTH, TX [A] 148, 386; [B] 111, 247, 500, 504, 773, 847, 2145; [C]
    962, 1205, 1351

FRANKFORT, KY [B] 2008, 2294, 3322; [C] 1026

FRANKLIN, TN [A] 329; [B] 166, 320; [C] 1075

FRANKLINVILLE, KY [B] 1277

FREDERICA, DE [B] 2091, 2129

FREDERICK, MD [B] 218, 927; [C] 483, 691

FREDERICKSBURG, VA [A] 166, 879; [B] 961, 1303, 1389, 1738, 1833, 2133,
    2134, 2209, 2242, 2243, 3116; [C] 51, 164, 614, 693, 764, 774, 778,
    781, 782, 816, 817, 818, 930, 957, 958, 966, 1114, 1140, 1155,
    1223, 1224, 1257, 1735

FREDERICKSBURG, TX [A] 12

FREDERICA, GA [A] 8; [B] 44, 161; [C] 153, 888, 1052, 1157

FRENCHBURG, KY [B] 2795

FRENCHTOWN, DE [B] 4381, 4382, 4383

FULLERTON, LA [B] 609, 1091

GADSDEN, AL [A] 443; [B] 2670, 2677

GAINESVILLE, FL [A] 53, 208, 261, 327, 332; [B] 53, 698, 1507, 2814; [C]
    390, 885

GAINESVILLE, GA [A] 605

GALLOWAY, MS [C] 1854

GALVESTON, TX [A] 48, 120, 338, 707; [B] 36, 347, 552, 838, 1484, 1515,
    1524, 1582, 1787, 1860, 2572, 2668, 2690, 3443, 3516, 3533, 3561,
    3762, 3998, 4231, 4268, 4339, 4379; [C] 250, 478, 499, 539, 785,
    983, 1041, 1343, 1578, 1592, 1874

GALVESTOWN, LA [B] 2240

GARLAND, TX [B] 3503

GASTONIA, NC [B] 920, 2603, 2645, 2691, 2722, 3216; [C] 1522, 1621

GATLINBURG, TN [A] 59, 81; [B] 700; [C] 796

GEORGIA [A] 256, 268, 331; [B] 694, 695, 767, 865, 879, 931, 1110, 1336,
    1364, 1440, 1449, 1694, 2291, 2518, 2671, 2708, 2738, 2741, 3336,
    3350, 3428, 3557, 3703, 3765, 3930, 4099, 4262, 4372; [C] 336, 416,
    456, 543, 876, 972, 1557, 1581, 1705, 1805, 1812, 1813

GEORGETOWN, DC [B] 308, 402, 1349, 2879; [C] 35, 81, 89, 1046, 1600

GEORGETOWN, SC [B] 1954, 2265, 3940; [C] 580

GEORGETOWN, TX [C] 1451

GERMANNA, KY [B] 2144

GERMANTOWN, LA [B] 1648, 2030

GERMANTOWN, TN [B] 1745; [C] 658

GIBBON, OK [B] 1286

GIBSONVILLE, NC [C] 124

GILBERT, AR [B] 4015

GILFORD, WV [C] 1336

GLADEVILLE, VA [B] 1959

GLEN ALLAN, MS [A] 300

GLENNVILLE, AL [B] 2769

GLOUCESTERTOWN, VA [B] 2290

GLUCHSTADT, MS [B] 3619

GOLDSBORO, NC [A] 142

GOODLETTSVILLE, TN   [A] 329

GOOSE CREEK, SC [C] 875

GORDONSVILLE, VA [B] 2299; [C] 1296

GRAFORD, TX [A] 523

GRAHAM, NC [A] 251; [B] 2605; [C] 1267, 1952

GRAHAMTON, KY [B] 916

GRAND ISLE, LA [C] 1158

GRANITVILLE, SC [B] 854, 2326; [C] 273

GREENBELT, MD [B] 1995

GREENSBORO, NC [A] 245, 557, 771; [B] 431, 748, 888, 948, 1064, 1446,
     2026, 2400, 2453, 2687, 2906, 3162, 3386, 3476, 3617, 3832, 3899,
     3947; [C] 76, 115, 159, 354, 374, 411, 503, 604, 792, 1107, 1848,
     1889

GREENVILLE, AL [B] 668

GREENVILLE, MS [B] 2568, 3108; [C] 616, 1586, 1624, 1846

GREENVILLE, NC [A] 476, 577; [B] 1118, 2697, 2701, 2710; [C] 928

GREENVILLE, SC [B] 2159; [C] 186, 398, 751, 1018, 1177

GREENWOOD, MS [B] 3962

GREENWOOD, SC [C] 295

GRENADA, MS [B] 3895

GRIFFIN, GA [B] 1664

GROVELAND, FL [B] 3911

GULF PORT CITY, TX [B] 618

GULFPORT, MS [B] 1537

GUTHRIE, OK [B] 263, 265, 1674, 1978

HAINES CITY, FL [B] 1656

HALIFAX, NC [B] 399

HOUSTON (CONTINUED)

    1371, 1376, 1380, 1384, 1534, 1597, 1678, 1728, 1760, 1793, 1802, 1853, 1967, 1975

HOWWEN-IN-THE-HILLS, FL [B] 779

HOUMA, LA [B] 3063

HOXIE, AR [B] 1186, 3965

HUMBOLT, TN [B] 3922

HUNTINGTON, WV [B] 641

HUNTSVILLE, AL [B] 1003, 1715, 1993; [C] 557, 576, 844

HURST, TX [B] 3060

IAMONIA, FL [B] 895

INDIAN SPRINGS, GA [B] 1943

INEZ, TX [B] 2533

IRETON, OK [C] 808

IRVINGTON, TX [B] 3999

IRVINGTON, VA [C] 1507

JACINTO, MS [B] 1729

JACKSBORO, TN [B] 2883

JACKSON, LA [B] 1240

JACKSON, MS [A] 40, 212, 580, 778; [B] 84, 241, 1164, 1681, 2465, 3814, 4072, 4282; [C] 465, 468, 1408, 1808, 1883, 1884

JACKSON, TN [B] 857

JACKSONBORO, SC [B] 164, 1865, 2270

JACKSONPORT, AR [B] 2338

JACKSONVILLE, AL [A] 295; [C] 406

JACKSONVILLE, FL [A] 217, 285, 288, 468, 606; [B] 87, 561, 889, 1113, 1153, 1565, 1600, 1607, 1769, 1770, 1819, 2025, 2112, 2113, 2114, 2192, 2462, 2516, 2705, 3226, 3262, 3314, 3455, 3831, 3876, 4016, 4021, 4365, 4395, 4461; [C] 16, 267, 441, 467, 481, 482, 595, 706, 707, 849, 923, 924, 1147, 1329, 1791, 1796

JAMES CITY, NC [C] 1601

JAMESTOWN, VA [A] 3, 4; [B] 26, 125, 202, 225, 471, 482, 483, 484, 1556, 1589, 1953, 1999, 2059, 2160, 2241, 2264, 2385, 2996, 3041; [C] 57, 124, 148, 149, 157, 577, 699, 701, 783, 1172, 1307

JAMESTOWN, TN [C] 149

JEFFERSON, LA [B] 1937

JENSEN BEACH, FL [B] 1072

LAREDO, TX [A] 730; [C] 886

LAUREL, MS [A] 106; [B] 768

LAWRENCEVILLE, VA [A] 224

LAWTON, OK [B] 1867

LAYTON, DE [C] 1087

LEBANON. TN [B] 2061

LEMON CITY, FL [B] 2757; [C] 1215

LEMON SWAMP, FL [C] 775

LENOIR, NC [C] 314

LENOIR CITY, TN [A] 42

LEVI, TN [B] 1392

LEWES, DE [B] 4241

LEXINGTON, GA [B] 3842

LEXINGTON, KY [A] 252, 315, 484; [B] 118, 153, 271, 390, 538, 634, 1081,
    1095, 1533, 1741, 2009, 2124, 2365, 2396, 2777, 3014, 3183, 3387,
    3490, 3559, 3797, 3864, 4331, 4337; [C] 69, 84, 408, 650, 950,
    1025, 1027, 1369, 1372, 1589, 1678, 1792

LEXINGTON, MD [B] 1863

LEXINGTON, SC [B] 41

LEXINGTON, VA [B] 34, 833, 1215, 2314; [C] 570, 989, 1260

LINTON, KY [B] 1646

LITHONIA SPRINGS, GA [B] 3852

LITTLE ROCK, AR [A] 169, 254, 784, 852; [B] 251, 330, 362, 394, 831,
    1178, 1194, 1258, 1407, 1720, 1851, 2210, 2466, 2503, 2538, 2539,
    2719, 3393, 3495, 3534, 3681, 3820, 3841, 3856, 3857, 3920, 3923,
    3966, 4047, 4062, 4117, 4295, 4322; [C] 38, 125, 249, 349, 397,
    410, 488, 530, 551, 564, 724, 1168, 1418, 1617, 1638, 1693 1844,
    1864

LONDON, KY [B] 2715

LONGVIEW, TX [B] 3853

LORANGER, LA [B] 1269

LOUISIANA [A] 45, 101, 229, 540, 735, 794; [B] 429, 638, 934, 1272,
    1400, 1963, 2399, 2522, 2689, 2704, 2894, 3062, 3312, 3368, 3616,
    3657, 3687, 3692, 3699, 3723, 3791, 4001, 4015, 4022, 4179, 4416,
    4472; [C] 239, 951, 1499, 1646, 1707, 1715, 1748, 1813

LOUISVILLE, KY [A] 16, 19, 22, 34, 93, 102, 160, 210, 215, 242, 304,
    377, 456, 460, 464, 475, 514, 547, 583, 593, 636, 647, 657, 672,
    677, 705, 761, 766, 812, 837, 841, 854, 865, 869, 874; [B] 159,
    191, 480, 513, 830, 1096, 1128, 1157, 1172, 1386, 1497, 1509, 1510,
    1517, 1533, 1678, 1690, 1702, 1766, 1817, 1828, 2047, 2081, 2082,
    2083, 2091, 2125, 2126, 2127, 2128, 2348, 2387, 2425, 2457, 2475,
    2523, 2612, 2615, 2635, 2721, 2787, 2790, 2829, 2830, 2834, 2839,
    2854, 2933, 2934, 3000, 3087, 3137, 3138, 3179, 3180, 3269, 3285,
    3299, 3325, 3536, 3537, 3540, 3580, 3651, 3679, 3702, 3744, 3772,

LOUISVILLE (CONTINUED)

> 3939, 3982, 4017, 4039, 4055, 4071, 4107, 4151, 4280, 4293, 4330, 4332, 4333, 4334, 4351, 4401; [C] 95, 194, 228, 264, 447, 622, 641, 766, 933, 988, 1002, 1090, 1293, 1294, 1295, 1300, 1348, 1378, 1481, 1678, 1694, 1697, 1757

LOWNDESBORO, AL [B] 315

LUBBOCK, TX [B] 2781; [C] 826

LUFKIN, TX [B] 583

LYNCH, KY [B] 2027

LYNCHBURG, TN [B] 566

LYNCHBURG, VA [A] 845, 879; [B] 81, 1130, 1722, 3098, 3461, 3894, 3979, 4274; [C] 22, 1209, 1476

LYNNVILLE, TN [B] 2291, 2292

LYON, MS [B] 129

LYSTRA, KY [B] 1277

MACON, GA [A] 6, 39, 334, 553; [B] 67, 229, 255, 335, 986, 1044, 1061, 1079, 1155, 2041, 2059, 2095, 2146, 2580, 3103, 3539, 3889, 4287; [C] 1374

MADISON, AR [B] 2853

MADISON, GA [B] 1773, 2470

MADISON, TN [C] 1350

MADISONVILLE, LA [C] 569

MADISONVILLE, MS [C] 1011

MANAKIN TOWN, VA [B] 3579

MANCHE, MS [B] 580

MANCHESTER, TN [B] 1299

MANDARIN, FL [C] 822

MARCHE, AR [B] 3750

MARIETTA, GA [B] 2319

MARION, MS [B] 3501; [C] 56

MARLBOROUGH, VA [C] 1681

MARSHALL, TX [A] 844

MARSHALLVILLE, GA [B] 2254

MARTIN, TN [B] 2106, 2298

MARTINS HUNDRED, VA [C] 910

MARTINSBURG, WV [B] 2607

MARTINVILLE, LA [B] 3026

MARYLAND [B] 732, 742, 745, 1022, 1181, 1322, 1859, 2548, 2633, 3381, 3472, 3612, 4064, 4329; [C] 270, 446, 748, 1427, 1590, 1753, 1759

MARYVILLE, TN [B] 947, 1208

MASARYKTOWN, FL [B] 3777

MASON, TX [C] 1133

MAYSVILLE, KY [C] 645

MAXTON, NC [C] 74

MECKLENBURG, NC [B] 1785, 2248, 3917, 3918

MELROSE, FL [C] 1303, 1674

MEMPHIS, TN [A] 110, 122, 167, 255, 275, 344, 389, 442, 449, 458, 474, 483, 513, 610, 652, 653, 658, 687, 689, 691, 714, 717, 722, 824, 825, 830; [B] 2, 85, 86, 127, 230, 346, 414, 453, 506, 511, 530, 588, 772, 824, 898, 929, 963, 983, 1046, 1047, 1073, 1074, 1102, 1114, 1140, 1205, 1233, 1310, 1313, 1316, 1398, 1530, 1535, 1541, 1542, 1558, 1559, 1560, 1586, 1590, 1627, 1666, 1669, 1718, 1719, 1721, 1744, 1749, 1750, 1751, 1778, 1826, 1841, 1998, 2004, 2065, 2092, 2121, 2188, 2199, 2220, 2221, 2325, 2433, 2435, 2441, 2445, 2559, 2564, 2570, 2588, 2589, 2598, 2606, 2644, 2665, 2759, 2836, 2855, 2881, 2893, 2944, 2997, 3131, 3170, 3171, 3181, 3223, 3243, 3244, 3271, 3395, 3396, 3413, 3423, 3436, 3440, 3452, 3496, 3510, 3513, 3514, 3535, 3628, 3717, 3766, 3767, 3771, 3789, 3794, 3886, 3887, 3918, 3953, 3957, 3966, 3971, 3975, 4076, 4108, 4244, 4279, 4303, 4348, 4356, 4375, 4388, 4398, 4426, 4427, 4443; [C] 205, 257, 271, 309, 311, 340, 344, 363, 378, 401, 579, 611, 640, 657, 665, 666, 678, 679, 702, 703, 862, 870, 911, 1031, 1043, 1071, 1111, 1131, 1181, 1212, 1392, 1429, 1447, 1547, 1577, 1605, 1635, 1679, 1682, 1711, 1712, 1720, 1723, 1727, 1734, 1789, 1798, 1813, 1817, 1818, 1822, 1866, 1885, 1887, 1912, 1929, 1930, 1958, 1963, 2010

MERIDIAN, MS [A] 291; [B] 953

METAIRIE, LA [C] 1921, 1922

MIAMI, FL [A] 107, 132, 257, 259, 269, 490, 495, 525, 719, 724, 746, 747, 816; [B] 110, 122, 196, 363, 369, 603, 669, 715, 716, 845, 867, 908, 1049, 1323, 1362, 1374, 1380, 1390, 1394, 1450, 1452, 1468, 1506, 1583, 1621, 1671, 1707, 1784, 1810, 1819, 1829, 2090, 2099, 2108, 2109, 2174, 2249, 2352, 2423, 2424, 2541, 2652, 2724, 2799, 2823, 2842, 2843, 3166, 3210, 3281, 3296, 3329, 3400, 3459, 3515, 3544, 3570, 3584, 3596, 3621, 3633, 3704, 3705, 3722, 3729, 3742, 3773, 3798, 3823, 3849, 3855, 3958, 4014, 4135, 4223, 4361, 4371, 4442; [C] 5, 202, 313, 324, 341, 409, 459, 464, 561, 566, 594, 726, 1000, 1034, 1058, 1087, 1116, 1124, 1125, 1245, 1304, 1388, 1423, 1633, 1659, 1828, 1879, 1954, 1981

MIAMI BEACH, FL [A] 13, 127; [B] 69, 75, 131, 1705, 1706, 4438

MIDDLEBURG, OK [B] 1480

MIDDLESBORO, KY [B] 976

MIDDLESBORO, TN [B] 355

MIDLAND, SC [B] 585

MIDLAND, TX [C] 323

MILLEDGEVILLE, GA [B] 77, 219, 1677; [C] 10, 548, 572, 1470

NACOGDOCHES, TX [A] 796

NASHOBA, TN [C] 762

NASHVILLE, TN [A] 72, 152, 247, 290, 542, 607, 609, 654, 656, 687, 763,
    770, 833, 864, 865; [B] 76, 92, 133, 135, 141, 163, 233, 256, 291,
    318, 319, 321, 351, 436, 462, 554, 636, 721, 897, 912, 913, 978,
NASHVILLE (CONTINUED)

        1009, 1013, 1109, 1112, 1127, 1133, 1150, 1158, 1179, 1198, 1199,
        1225, 1248, 1249, 1252, 1305, 1436, 1474, 1501, 1548, 1586, 1610,
        1651, 1655, 1745, 1762, 1771, 1982, 1983, 1991, 2006, 2084, 2102,
        2103, 2104, 2111, 2272, 2273, 2377, 2412, 2417, 2421, 2486, 2490,
        2555, 2556, 2776, 2805, 2812, 2816, 2892, 2951, 3012, 3025, 3044,
        3047, 3048, 3064, 3140, 3145, 3174, 3195, 3198, 3206, 3208, 3222,
        3317, 3320, 3322, 3331, 3335, 3388, 3415, 3436, 3449, 3469, 3509,
        3542, 3630, 3785, 3871, 3913, 4050, 4059, 4066, 4100, 4165, 4181,
        4276, 4277, 4281, 4291, 4292, 4348, 4351, 4352, 4385, 4454; [C] 9,
        52, 164, 362, 386, 427, 480, 487, 598, 658, 674, 675, 705, 735,
        761, 897, 900, 944, 1048, 1092, 1094, 1292, 1301, 1323, 1324, 1368,
        1382, 1443, 1473, 1498, 1503, 1506, 1532, 1541, 1721, 1724, 1731,
        1773, 1782, 1804, 1928, 1983

NASSAU, FL [A] 455

NATCHEZ, MS [A] 14, 333, 342, 807; [B] 102, 156, 782, 1504, 1692, 1987,
    2122, 2148, 2354, 3065, 3361, 4270; [C] 28, 48, 67, 160, 643, 892,
    925, 936, 1051, 1314, 1504

NATCHEZ-UNDER-THE-HILL, MS [B] 2122

NATCHITOCHES, LA [B] 361, 1687, 1688, 1818, 2357; [C] 1093

NEDERLAND, TX [B] 3568

NEW BERN, NC [A] 21, 346, [B] 136, 474, 1644, 1796, 1797, 1798, 1799,
    1800, 1801, 1802, 1803; [C] 1763

NEW CASTLE, DE [A] 24, 303; [B] 253, 345, 426, 3401, 3611, 4204, 4381,
    4382, 4383

NEW HANOVER, GA [A] 692; [B] 1274

NEW IBERIA, LA [B] 121; [C] 659

NEW LONDON, VA [B] 2252, 2269; [C] 1149

NEW MARKET, VA [B] 472

NEW ORLEANS, LA [A] 10, 35, 37, 45, 50, 51, 61, 101, 113, 119, 138,
    158,159, 176, 179, 182, 185, 203, 220, 273, 287, 324, 339, 373,
    390, 454, 467, 519, 528, 531, 532, 536, 540, 549, 555, 586, 604,
    622, 638, 641, 646, 651, 655, 665, 674, 678, 697, 701, 729, 736,
    737, 782, 817, 818, 828, 832, 835, 839, 846, 847, 848, 850, 853,
    868, 875; [B] 97, 98, 99, 100, 114, 130, 140, 155, 165, 240, 247,
    248, 249, 250, 258, 259, 284, 287, 325, 337, 364, 367, 406, 407,
    410, 423, 451, 477, 492, 508, 512, 528, 532, 543, 546, 549, 573,
    574, 575, 576, 579, 624, 625, 626, 653, 677, 680, 684, 723, 733,
    740, 753, 782, 783, 807, 855, 858, 866, 906, 923, 924, 932, 940,
    941, 956, 966, 971, 972, 982, 994, 1010, 1018, 1020, 1052, 1066,
    1125, 1131, 1159, 1161, 1183, 1188, 1203, 1204, 1223, 1228, 1246,
    1316, 1333, 1368, 1410, 1459, 1460, 1505, 1514, 1536, 1543, 1544,
    1545, 1546, 1553, 1554, 1557, 1558, 1561, 1562, 1563, 1569, 1570,
    1571, 1581, 1602, 1605, 1606, 1614, 1615, 1624, 1634, 1637, 1638,
    1639, 1640, 1641, 1698, 1700, 1701, 1726, 1735, 1742, 1746, 1779,
    1780, 1781, 1782, 1783, 1807, 1812, 1827, 1838, 1858, 1909, 1937,
    1967, 1969, 2002, 2003, 2019, 2021, 2023, 2031, 2032, 2043, 2049,
    2054, 2058, 2161, 2162, 2196, 2201, 2202, 2204, 2214, 2234, 2238,

NORTH CAROLINA (CONTINUED)

   3458, 3489, 3523, 3646, 3779, 3892, 3983, 4003, 4009, 4432, 4449,
   4453, 4457; [C] 13, 113, 294, 602, 642, 1032, 1200, 1262, 1436,
   1555, 1738, 1747, 1827

NORTH SPRINGFIELD, VA [B] 812

NORVILLE, OK [B] 3751

OAK RIDGE, TN [A] 299; [B] 1672, 2339, 2428, 2861, 2884, 3359; [C] 931

OAKLAND, FL [C] 531

OCALA, FL [B] 2529

OCEAN SPRINGS, MS [A] 356

OCMULGEE FIELDS, GA [B] 1949

OCRACOKE, NC [C] 812

ODESSA, TX [C] 323

OHIOPIOOMINGO, KY [B] 1277

OKLAHOMA [A] 600, 859; [B] 639, 817, 1366, 1370, 1393, 1480, 1549, 1907,
   2510, 2569, 2593, 2871, 3824, 4186, 4271; [C] 365, 417, 1122, 1510,
   1672

OKLAHOMA CITY, OK [A] 172, 470, 713, 775; [B] 562, 693, 1331, 1847,
   2415, 2821, 3491, 3846, 3873; [C] 753, 754, 755, 1113, 1265, 1729

ONANCOCK, VA [B] 3819

OPELIKA, AL [B] 668

ORANGE, VA [C] 1297

ORANGE PARK, FL [B] 3954

ORANGEBURG, SC [A] 760; [B] 3912

ORLANDO, FL [A] 479; [B] 778, 1095, 1403, 1404, 1420, 1429, 2327, 2889;
   [C] 532, 949, 1227, 1596

OSCEOLA, AR [B] 2359

OTTERBEIM, KY [B] 1668

OVIEDO, FL [C] 489

OWENSBORO, KY [B] 657, 4363, 4364

OXFORD, GA [C] 1478

OXFORD, MS [A] 392; [B] 1806, 3128, 4369; [C] 1843

PADUCAH, KY [B] 3037

PALM BEACH, FL [A] 13, 58, 507; [B] 119, 232, 334, 422, 505, 1699, 2313,
   2315; [C] 573, 1083, 1138, 1568, 1608

PAMPLIN, VA [B] 51

PANAMA CITY, FL [A] 568

PRINCEVILLE, NC [B] 2948

PUGHTOWN, WV [C] 907

PURCELLVILLE, VA [C] 1201

PURDY, TN [B] 1635

PURRYSBURGH, SC [A] 579; [B] 2268

RADFORD, VA [B] 848

RADNOR, SC [B] 2270

RALEIGH, NC [A] 231, 245, 250, 478, 497, 620, 660; [B] 23, 261, 366,
     1412, 1437, 1601, 2069, 2434, 2840, 2908, 2919, 3721, 3830, 3978,
     4188, 4310, [C] 14, 27, 55, 102, 251, 407, 447, 545, 635, 1143,
     1207, 1270, 1319, 1332, 1375, 1402, 1686

RAYVILLE, LA [B] 602

RED BOILING SPRINGS, TN [B] 3980

REDEEMER, AL [B] 2629

REIDSVILLE, NC [C] 105

RESTON, VA [B] 1568, 2898

RICHBURG, MS [B] 3985

RICHMOND, KY [B] 1142

RICHMOND, VA [A] 115, 136, 363, 385, 461, 673, 704, 804; [B] 37, 71,
     145, 188, 365, 373, 400, 437, 447, 461, 524, 531, 564, 633, 728,
     1008, 1075, 1129, 1154, 1238, 1378, 1443, 1455, 1511, 1527, 1739,
     1740, 1772, 1804, 1837, 1956, 2010, 2035, 2036, 2037, 2074,
     2197, 2275, 2280, 2300, 2355, 2430, 2444, 2543, 2563, 2619, 2634,
     2713, 2785, 3017, 3086, 3111, 3112, 3122, 3123, 3134, 3141, 3147,
     3150, 3228, 3240, 3241, 3339, 3399, 3419, 3424, 3460, 3507, 3573,
     3590, 3620, 3636, 3691, 3702, 3866, 3869, 3894, 4002, 4004, 4013,
     4038, 4068, 4214, 4215, 4224, 4225, 4261, 4265, 4278, 4318, 4319,
     4423; [C] 24, 41, 96, 116, 142, 204, 262, 272, 293, 546, 558, 571,
     624, 633, 634, 690, 733, 739, 752, 952, 997, 1007, 1054, 1118
     1120, 1132, 1187, 1197, 1208, 1251, 1291, 1327, 1328, 1399, 1441,
     1466, 1543, 1567, 1654, 1708, 1766, 1809, 1923, 1992

RIO GRANDE CITY, TX [B] 2578

RIVERSIDE, FL [C] 849

ROANOKE, VA [A] 173; [B] 424, 988, 3081, 3191, 4355, 4466; [C] 591, 1377

ROCK HILL, SC [C] 584

ROCKINGHAM, NC [B] 3287

ROCKWOOD, TN [B] 872

RODNEY, MS [B] 1283

ROME, GA [B] 3268; [C] 529, 544

ROOSEVELT CITY, AL [B] 2151

ROSE HILL, NC [C] 1361

ROSEDALE, MS [C] 970

SCOTTSBORO, TN [B] 372, 1012, 3968

SCOTTSVILLE, VA [A] 862; [B] 811, [C] 1053

SEARCY, AR [A] 77, 783; [C] 1059

SEASIDE, FL [B] 577

SELMA, AL [B] 984, 1200, 2532, 3380; [C] 861, 922, 1096, 1339, 1856,
   1857, 1871, 1872, 1878, 1933

SEMINOLE, FL [B] 2742

SEVIERVILLE, TN [B] 478

SEWANEE, TN [B] 1123

SHAKERTOWN, KY [C] 1027

SHARON, MS [B] 1231

SHAWNEE, OK [B] 3470, 3973

SHEFFIELD, AL [B] 881; [C] 492

SHREVEPORT, LA [A] 360, 744; [B] 391, 556, 805, 1306, 1714, 1777, 1945,
   2226, 2277, 2278, 3872, 4067, 4194, 4207, 4377, 4435; [C] 129, 879,
   880, 1085, 1299, 1660, 1820

SHUBUTA, MS [C] 1325

SMITHFIELD, NC [C] 120, 694, 1154

SNICKERSVILLE, VA [C] 1244

SOMERVILLE, TX [A] 577

SOUTH [A] 32, 65, 70, 71, 80, 86, 104, 121, 143, 150, 151, 181, 200,
   207, 213, 214, 227, 262, 276, 286, 359, 383, 387, 444, 446, 447,
   459, 488, 504, 518, 529, 539, 545, 546, 556, 563, 571, 575, 581,
   591, 595, 597, 598, 611, 614, 659, 669, 679, 685, 686, 709, 725,
   734, 738, 740, 742, 745, 765, 773, 776, 808, 810, 815, 819, 840,
   856, 863, 878, 880, 881, 882; [B] 93, 94, 132, 458, 487, 489, 521,
   522, 526, 544, 545, 550, 551, 556, 582, 596, 599, 606, 608, 615,
   616, 630, 632, 637, 642, 649, 673, 690, 692, 701, 714, 741, 746,
   750, 751, 761, 765, 766, 796, 821, 827, 852, 859, 877, 884, 885,
   886, 891, 903, 904, 910, 914, 915, 921, 942, 957, 976, 985, 1002,
   1030, 1034, 1039, 1040, 1045, 1051, 1053, 1055, 1083, 1098, 1114,
   1124, 1144, 1148, 1219, 1226, 1246, 1262, 1314, 1315, 1317, 1318,
   1319, 1321, 1325, 1326, 1327, 1335, 1338, 1339, 1340, 1342, 1343,
   1347, 1348, 1350, 1351, 1353, 1357, 1358, 1360, 1363, 1367, 1376,
   1385, 1391, 1399, 1401, 1411, 1414, 1416, 1421, 1427, 1428, 1438,
   1439, 1441, 1445, 1448, 1451, 1457, 1458, 1463, 1466, 1467, 1469,
   1475, 1481, 1483, 1485, 1487, 1490, 1572, 1584, 1676, 1697, 1704,
   1730, 1765, 1775, 1791, 1815, 1822, 1823, 1848, 1849, 1913, 1914,
   1915, 1932, 1951, 1952, 1972, 1977, 1981, 1992, 2001, 2013, 2028,
   2045, 2073, 2096, 2158, 2163, 2164, 2165, 2175, 2183, 2194, 2207,
   2382, 2405, 2411, 2426, 2431, 2452, 2461, 2464, 2472, 2483, 2491,
   2571, 2581, 2583, 2605, 2613, 2614, 2617, 2618, 2622, 2627, 2628,
   2630, 2636, 2664, 2675, 2679, 2681, 2684, 2685, 2696, 2716, 2717,
   2733, 2740, 2801, 2809, 2811, 2815, 2819, 2822, 2877, 2878, 2887,
   2896, 2901, 2903, 2905, 2926, 2939, 2987, 2988, 3011, 3021, 3068,
   3069, 3076, 3119, 3129, 3136, 3139, 3142, 3155, 3173, 3176, 3242,
   3248, 3249, 3252, 3258, 3274, 3302, 3305, 3321, 3345, 3376, 3409,
   3412, 3413, 3527, 3538, 3560, 3562, 3567, 3576, 3581, 3603, 3642,
   3656, 3663, 3675, 3686, 3701, 3712, 3713, 3727, 3734, 3739, 3740,
   3741, 3759, 3760, 3761, 3793, 3796, 3803, 3816, 3822, 3826, 3840,
   3851, 3858, 3861, 3875, 3902, 3905, 3924, 3926, 3931, 3942, 3946,

TALBOTTON, GA [B] 1285

TALLADEGA, AL [B] 2316, 2317; [C] 1571

TALLAHASSEE, FL [A] 103, 128, 312, 321, 511, 592, 751, 769; [B] 586, 892, 893, 894, 1134, 1508, 1708, 1930, 2219, 2391, 2870, 2975, 3319, 3903, 4069; [C] 169, 744, 813, 841, 1680

TALLALOOSA, MS [B] 3977

TALLAPOOSA, GA [B] 1006

TALLASSEE, AL [B] 1980

TAMPA, FL [A] 157, 234, 263, 508, 623, 698, 703; [B] 21, 38, 39, 54, 142, 272, 354, 389, 446, 463, 464, 465, 592, 605, 623, 661, 1035, 1595, 1716, 1759, 1760, 1968, 2024, 2079, 2080, 2138, 2139, 2142, 2366, 2397, 2467, 2640, 2641, 2659, 2660, 2661, 2662, 2676, 2683, 2760, 2761, 2762, 2864, 2865, 2954, 2984, 3007, 3433, 3434, 3435, 3455, 3641, 3708, 3709, 3724, 3725, 3728, 3788, 3888, 3989, 4085, 4153, 4154, 4212, 4411, 4415; [C] 364, 537, 709, 710, 740, 745, 840, 1055, 1130, 1602, 1604

TARBORO, NC [B] 2471

TARHSELIA, NC [C] 1240

TARPON SPRINGS, FL [A] 517, 726; [B] 1628, 3634, 3720, 3778; [C] 1121, 1271, 1462

TASCOSA, OK [C] 1066

TECUMSEH, AL [B] 937

TEN MILE, MS [B] 1809

TENNESSEE [A] 49, 125, 237, 493, 503; [B] 128, 237, 627, 628, 654, 724, 727, 771, 949, 950, 1004, 1025, 1149, 1180, 1396, 1764, 1854, 1862, 2291, 2292, 2301, 2342, 2526, 2753, 2806, 3384, 3644, 3811, 3815, 3901, 3927, 4053; [C] 391, 1404, 1585, 1813, 1847

TENOXTITLAN, TX [B] 2097

TERLINGUA, TX [C] 287

TEXARKANA, AR [B] 749

TEXAS [A] 55, 109, 190, 239, 264, 272, 515, 522, 632, 683, 788, 795; [B] 204, 356, 590, 622, 645, 739, 776, 1366, 1454, 2101, 2427, 2592, 2631, 2678, 2942, 2947, 3004, 3278, 3357, 3404, 3480, 3484, 3488, 3595, 3737, 3758, 3812, 3890, 3891, 4024, 4374, 4393; [C] 227, 242, 268, 297, 437, 462, 1422, 1482, 1562, 1575, 1613, 1690, 1752, 1829, 1985

TEXAS CITY, TX [B] 1525

THOMASVILLE, GA [A] 131; [B] 358, 3010

THURBER, TX [B] 2669

THURMOND, VA [B] 2303

TIFTON, GA [A] 477; [B] 2922

TOADVINE, AL [C] 1247

TONTITOWN, AR [B] 3654, 3683, 3748

TRACY CITY, TN [B] 2573

TRANSYLVANIA, KY [A] 502

TRIADELPHIA, MD [B] 1295

TRIANA, AL [B] 1090

TROY, AL [B] 794, 2337, 3200

TRYON, NC [C] 72

TULANE, LA [B] 130, 1183

TULIP, AR [B] 1243, 2271

TULLAHOMA, TN [B] 737

TULSA, OK [A] 218, 354, 471; [B] 1021, 1028, 1029, 1087, 2408, 2873,
    2958, 3846, 3877, 4376; [C] 711, 1317, 1855, 1888

TUPELO, MS [A] 233; [B] 607, 936, 1496

TUSCALOOSA, AL [A] 798; [B] 5, 1731, 1732, 1979, 2509, 4032; [C] 646,
    1077, 1948

TUSKEGEE, AL [A] 209, 216; [B] 851, 882, 1136, 1187, 1189, 3390; [C]
    1862

TYLER, TX [B] 3316

TYREE SPRINGS, TN [B] 1288

TYSON'S CORNER, VA [B] 1857

UNIVERSITY, AL [C] 404, 413

VALDESE, NC [B] 3194

VALDOSTA, GA [B] 946, 2311, 3752

VANOSS, OK [B] 1480

VERO BEACH, FL [B] 809; [C] 1169

VICKSBURG, MS [A] 73, 305, 366, 648; [B] 928, 3554, 4000; [C] 684, 786,
    864, 891, 1035, 1310, 1379, 1461

VICTORIO, OK [B] 3751

VINTON, MS [B] 629

VIRGINIA [A] 31, 225, 248; [B] 25, 82, 103, 143, 144, 168, 169, 170,
    171, 172, 173, 174, 175, 176, 177, 178, 179, 180, 181, 182, 183,
    184, 185, 214, 215, 221, 279, 297, 300, 324, 328, 375, 396, 397,
    456, 539, 752, 829, 834, 839, 890, 918, 1007, 1022, 1036, 1119,
    1237, 1273, 1298, 1402, 1422, 1461, 1478, 1556, 1915, 2449, 2464,
    2848, 3328, 3445, 3563, 3652, 3928, 4011, 4095, 4193, 4199, 4218,
    4301, 4338, 4350, 4433, 4436; [C] 24, 47, 294, 434, 698, 820, 1072,
    1162, 1739, 1740, 1759, 1969

WACHOVIA, NC [B] 1939

WACO, TX [A] 628, 789; [B] 2335, 2792, 3028, 4058

WAGONER, OK [B] 1642, 2353

WARM SPRINGS, GA [B] 353, 2363

WARREN, AR [B] 958

WARRENTON, NC [B] 1145

WASHINGTON, AR [B] 1931; [C] 1349

WASHINGTON, DC [A] 17, 112, 197, 280, 284, 328, 375, 393, 512, 520, 551,
     625, 633, 637, 738, 787, 792, 805, 811, 820, 822, 831; [B] 89, 90,
     107, 109, 117, 132, 157, 167, 190, 193, 194, 198, 199, 209, 212,
     244, 252, 262, 275, 308, 310, 329, 330, 370, 374, 402, 403, 416,
     428, 433, 442, 491, 493, 498, 499, 502, 510, 516, 518, 523, 525,
     729, 812, 911, 1104, 1168, 1169, 1203, 1206, 1214, 1244, 1250,
     1265, 1442, 1629, 1774, 1912, 1922, 1924, 2044, 2198, 2373, 2374,
     2393, 2406, 2414, 2418, 2520, 2653, 2672, 2825, 2962, 3035, 3040,
     3202, 3310, 3323, 3342, 3462, 3520, 3528, 3583, 3711, 3738, 3743,
     3764, 3845, 3899, 3907, 4056, 4116, 4162, 4228, 4247, 4269, 4342,
     4400, 4440, 4444, 4458; [C] 35, 50, 109, 320, 828, 829, 991, 1139,
     1176, 1471, 1477, 1497, 1528, 1561, 1582, 1699, 1706, 1860, 1964

WASHINGTON, GA [B] 1658, 2282

WASHINGTON, MS [B] 1683, 4005

WATERFORD, VA [B] 1088, 2229

WAYCROSS, GA [B] 2040, 2916, 3370

WAYNESBORO, GA [B] 3555

WAYNOKA, OK [B] 4417

WENTWORTH, NC [B] 1763

WEST PALM BEACH, FL [B] 2347, 2392

WEST POINT, GA [C] 32

WEST POINT, VA [C] 270

WEST VIRGINIA [A] 175, 448; [B] 879, 1406, 2502, 2530, 2651, 2798; [C]
     270

WHEELING, WV [B] 1793, 2005, 2154, 2442, 2530, 3219

WHITE BLUFF, TN [B] 3769

WHITEHAVEN, TN [B] 1392

WILLIAMSBURG, VA [B] 162, 186, 227, 282, 292, 298, 317, 332, 340, 418,
     449, 467, 485, 939, 1577, 1599, 2022, 2223, 2318, 3091, 3506, 4288,
     4347; [C] 68, 285, 312, 338, 472, 700, 815, 819, 1112, 1145, 1186,
     1684

WILMINGTON, DE [A] 192, 253, 370, 378, 587, 642, 654, 692, 780; [B] 466,
     581, 612, 689, 799, 853, 1011, 1032, 1242, 1423, 1804, 2100, 2460,
     2479, 2591, 2743, 2866, 3033, 3159, 3175, 3348, 3632, 4251, 4296,
     4297, 4424, 4441; [C] 1775

WILMINGTON, NC [B] 801, 1437, 3458, 3936, 4311, 4312, 4313; [C] 79, 143,
     253, 1076, 1152, 1790, 1880

WINCHESTER, KY [A] 330

Subject Index

ACCULTURATION [A] 517, 518

ADVERTISING [A] 94, 147

AGEE, JAMES [B] 3079

AGNES SCOTT [B] 1151

AGRICULTURE [A] 123, 227, 684; [B] 616, 714, 750, 822, 982, 1026, 1051, 2492, 3283, 3351; [C] 237, 259

AIR CONDITIONING [B] 2740

AIR FORCE, U.S. [B] 3406

AIR QUALITY [A] 207

AIRLINES (AIR SERVICE) [B] 819, 2446, 2866, 4354, 4359, 4361, 4394, 4415, 4417, 4430; [C] 2009

AIRPORTS [A] 468; [C] 290

ALABAMA MEDICAL COLLEGE [B] 1106

ALBANIANS [B] 3043

ALBANY STATE COLLEGE [A] 222

ALDEN, AUGUSTUS E. [B] 3388

ALEXANDER, WILLIAM [B] 745

ALEXANDER CITY OUTLOOK [C] 1409

ALEXANDRIA GAZETTE [C] 1415

ALLEY, CAL [C] 1734

ALLEYS [A] 284, 811; [C] 641

AMELUNG GLASS FACTORY [B] 27

AMERICAN RED CROSS [C] 480

ATLANTA GEORGIAN [A] 429

ATLANTA INTELLIGENCER [B] 2512

ATLANTA INQUIRER [A] 437

ATLANTA JOURNAL [A] 429; [C] 327

ATLANTA MAGAZINE [A] 188

ATLANTA TIMES [A] 419; [C] 1394, 1426

ATLANTA UNIVERSITY [A] 509; [B] 1111, 1120, 1170, 1251; [C] 346, 348

ATLANTA WEEKLY [B] 2527

ATLANTA WORLD [A] 437

AUDUBON PARK [C] 784

AUGUSTA CANAL [C] 255

AUGUSTA CHRONICLE [C] 1393, 1425

AUGUSTA COLLEGE [C] 347, 359, 360, 396

AUSTIN, STEPHEN F. [B] 2258

AUTOMOBILES [B] 909, 4350, 4369, 4437; [C] 2007, 2011

BAILEY HOUSE [A] 261

BALTIMORE AFRO AMERICAN [B] 2550

BALTIMORE CLEARING HOUSE [C] 241

BALTIMORE SPICE COMPANY [B] 970

BANKING [A] 62, 79, 101, 105, 113, 155, 193; [B] 616, 635, 684, 831, 832, 930, 949, 950, 960, 1004, 1054, 1056, 1057; [C] 239, 241, 275, 276

BANKOKENTUCKY [A] 93

BANNER OF THE SOUTH [B] 2447

BAPTIST [B] 1167, 3025, 4053, 4100

BARILI, ALFREDO [B] 3197

BASCOMB, RUTH HENSHAW [C] 1178

BASEBALL [B] 3979, 3982, 3989, 3994, 4002, 4004

BATHS (PUBLIC) [B] 2750, 4235

BATTERTON, IRA A. [A] 430

BAUER, A. G. [B] 104

BAYOU ROAD [C] 130

BEALE STREET [A] 658, 689; [B] 85, 1998, 2065, 3223, 4443; [C] 309, 1723, 1727, 1817

BEHRMAN, MARTIN [B] 3526; [C] 1743, 1764, 1786

BELK, WILLIAM HENRY [C] 208

BELL FACTORY [B] 1003

BELTWAYS [C] 447

BELUCHE, RENATO [C] 715

BEREA COLLEGE [B] 1163

BICYCLING [B] 3986, 4006

BINGHAM, ROBERT WORTH [B] 3299

BLACKS, (GENERAL) [A] 71, 72, 115, 128, 158, 197, 336, 364, 412, 476,
    478, 514, 538, 551, 553, 564, 579, 582, 594; [B] 683, 905, 1071,
    1328, 1665, 1903, 1917, 1957, 2238, 2323, 2357, 3572, 3658, 3781,
    3782, 3786; [C] 207, 680, 778, 824, 892, 1103, 1386, 1387, 1388,
    1467, 1477, 1501, 1519, 1520, 1547, 1561, 1584, 1587, 1601, 1606,
    1619, 1666, 1670, 1690, 1994;

(ARCHITECTS) [A] 17

(ARTISANS) [A] 28, 30, 31, 32; [B] 468, 478, 590; [C] 1432

(ARTISTS) [A] 38; [B] 452

(BIOGRAPHY) [C] 583, 1506, 1617, 1754

(BUSINESS) [B] 542, 557, 567, 569, 590, 624, 653, 741, 756, 817,
    874, 973, 1001, 1017, 1048, 3533, 4447

(CREOLE) [A] 287

(CRIME) [A] 813; [B] 2802, 2803, 3817

(ECONOMICS) [A] 313, 541, 606; [B] 820, 825, 826, 830, 831, 835,
    851, 882, 911, 923, 3816; [C] 203, 320, 322, 332, 334

(EDUCATION) [A] 209, 210, 211, 215, 216, 222, 509; [B] 1115,
    1120, 1127, 1143, 1146, 1148, 1149, 1152, 1153, 1156, 1162,
    1168, 1169, 1170, 1173, 1174, 1175, 1178, 1179, 1180, 1187,
    1195, 1202, 1203, 1205, 1206, 1211, 1213, 1214, 1216, 1219,
    1225, 1227, 1235, 1237, 1239, 1244, 1245, 1248, 1249, 1250,
    1251, 1252, 1253, 1255, 1262, 1264, 1265, 1266, 1267, 2390,
    2403, 2410, 3824, 3831, 3841, 3842, 3846, 3852, 4093; [C]
    346, 348, 365, 367, 378, 399, 406

(FREE) [A] 423, 516, 531, 534, 604; [C] 1565, 1688

(HEALTH) [A] 282; [B] 1580, 1584, 1588, 1603, 1628

(HOUSING) [A] 381; [B] 2375, 2394, 2399, 2402, 2407, 2411, 2413,
    2418, 2419, 2422, 2423, 2425, 2426, 2982, 3628, 3670, 3711,
    3741, 3813, 3822, 3849, 3864

(JOURNALISM) [A] 405, 427; [B] 2489, 2492, 2503, 2507, 2518,
    2532, 2550, 2554, 2569; [C] 1425

(LABOR AND EMPLOYMENT) [A] 442, 448, 450, 451, 453; [B] 766,
    2588, 2589, 2595, 2605, 2624, 2629, 2631, 2647, 2648, 2651,
    2652, 2671, 2680, 2696, 2701, 2705, 2706, 2711, 2725, 2726;
    [C] 194

(LEADERSHIP AND POLITICS) [A] 632, 658, 660, 663, 664, 665, 673,
    676, 678, 689, 692, 698, 701, 708, 709, 714, 748, 749, 763,

BLACKS CONTINUED

CHARLES, ROBERT [C] 1863

CHARLESTON COURIER [B] 3567

CHARLESTON MARINE SCHOOL [B] 1107

CHARLESTON MERCURY [A] 391, 425, 670

CHARLESTON NEWS AND COURIER [C] 1420

CHARLOTTE OBSERVER [A] 424; [C] 1396

CHARMICHAEL, STOKLEY [B] 2006, 2975

CHATTANOOGA NEWS [A] 421

CHATTANOOGA REBEL [B] 2505

CHEMICALS (INDUSTRY) [A] 192

CHESAPEAKE, COMPANY [C] 229

CHICAGO SCHOOL [A] 34

CHICANOS [B] 4024

CHILDREN [B] 2614, 2664, 3805, 3817, 4027, 4130, 4131

CHINESE [A] 521, 567, 615; [B] 2606, 3555, 3575, 3586, 3587, 3676,
    3680, 3682, 3737; [C] 1586, 1624

CHIPPENDALE [A] 29

CHISOS MINING COMPANY [C] 287

CHOLERA [B] 1533, 1534, 1550

CHOPIN, KATE [B] 3084

CHURCH, ROBERT R. [C] 1754

CHURCH, ROBERT R. JR. [B] 3243

CIGAR, INDUSTRY [B] 2574, 2638, 2640, 2641, 2659, 2660, 2683, 3433,
    3434, 3435; [C] 326

CITY DIRECTORIES [C] 1839

CITY PLANS [A] 229

CIVIL WAR [A] 119, 292, 305, 360, 363, 366, 370, 422, 440, 528, 716;
    [B] 786, 813, 893, 926, 984, 1631, 1632, 1633, 1649, 2519, 2563,
    3260, 3318, 3423, 3592, 3731, 4007, 4114, 4115, 4128, 4255

CLAPP, PARSON [C] 1931

CLARK, LARDNER [B] 912, 913

CLOCKS [C] 171

CLOTHING, INDUSTRY [A] 64; [B] 2956

COAL [A] 175, 448; [B] 962, 974, 976, 1406, 2629, 2633, 2656, 4366

COBBS, HAMMER [B] 2453

COCA-COLA [B] 578; [C] 306, 321

D [A] 402

DAILY SOUTH CAROLINIAN [A] 440

DALLAS COWBOYS [B] 3999; [C] 1895, 1904, 1914

DALLAS MORNING NEWS [C] 1400, 1401

DALLAS NEWS [C] 1390, 1421

DALLAS NINE [C] 189

DANCE [A] 197, 651, 839; [B] 4257, 4258, 4259

DANIELS, JOHN [B] 775

DARE, VIRGINIA [B] 3081

DAUGHETTE, CLARENCE WILLIAM [C] 406

DAVIS, NOAH [B] 4112

DAWSON, FRANCIS WARRINGTON [B] 2450

DEALEY, G. B. [C] 1421

DEBUTANTS [A] 565

DELINQUENCY [A] 809, 814, 821, 830, 831

DELTA AIRLINES [B] 819; [C] 2011

DEMOCRATS [A] 672

DENTISTRY [B] 1594

DEPARTMENT STORES [A] 87, 169

DEPRESSION, ECONOMIC [A] 44, 75, 90, 93, 127, 155, 569; [B] 753, 887,
     919, 1669, 2026; [C] 205, 227

DESEGREGATION [A] 71, 750, 759, 761, 762, 767, 768, 769, 770, 771, 775,
     784

DEXTER, ANDREW [B] 2218

D'IBERVILLE, CHEVALIER [C] 851

DICKEY, JAMES [B] 3130

DICKEY, SARAH A. [C] 329

DIX, JOHN A. [B] 786

DON CE-SAR [C] 62

DORTCH, ELLEN [B] 3351

DOTHAM EAGLE [B] 1401

DOWN'S SYNDROME [A] 280

DRAPER, STANLEY [C] 458

DRUGS [B] 3053, 3066, 4119, 4129, 4233

DUELS [C] 1536

FEDERAL HILL [C] 299

FERTILITY [A] 720, 731, 734, 797

FESTIVALS [B] 2797, 2841, 3042

FILIPINOS [B] 3616

FILM [B] 4021, 4025, 4026

FINCH, WILLIAM [B] 3236

FINANCE [A] 101, 153

FISHING [A] 141, 145

FIRE DEPARTMENTS [B] 2644, 2861, 2892, 2893, 3064, 3269, 3270, 3280, 3337, 4220

FIRES [B] 996, 4139, 4207; [C] 466, 469

FISK UNIVERSITY [B] 1179, 1225, 1249; [C] 399

FITZPATRICK, JOHN [B] 3301

FLAG OF THE UNION [A] 432

FLOOD WALLS [C] 155

FLOODS [C] 465

FLORIDA AGRICULTURAL AND MECHANICAL UNIVERSITY [C] 390

FLORIDA STATE UNIVERSITY [B] 1134, 1135

FLOUR [A] 97, 163; [B] 564, 954, 955

FOLKLORE [A] 523; [B] 2471, 2522, 2566, 2724, 27670, 2761, 2762, 2787, 2788, 2790, 2795, 2858, 2924, 2984, 2985

FOOD [B] 1618, 2841, 3316, 4000; [C] 1464, 1489, 1507, 1512, 1556, 1568, 1627, 1656

FOOTBALL [B] 3999

FOREIGN TRADE [A] 60, 68; [C] 224, 260, 301

FORSYTH, JOHN [B] 2474

FORT WORTH STOCKYARDS COMPANY [A] 148

FORTS [C] 55

FOSTER, REV. W. L. [C] 1309

FRANK, LEO [A] 429; [B] 3604, 4192; [C] 1962, 1966

FRANKLIN HOUSE [C] 43

FRASER, CHARLES [C] 188

FREE PRESS [A] 414

FRENCH [A] 35; [B] 477, 3132, 3579, 3580, 3699, 4022

FRENCH QUARTER [B] 2031; [C] 7, 1366, 1456

FRIENDS SCHOOL [C] 373

FRITCHIE, BARBARA [C] 691

FROELICHER, HANS JR. [B] 3472

FRY, JOHN WALKER [C] 159

FUNERALS [A] 559, 597; [B] 931, 2767, 3042, 3052, 3070

FURMAN UNIVERSITY [C] 398

FURNITURE [A] 29, 85; [B] 674; [C] 175, 314

GALLOWAY COLLEGE [B] 1193

GALVESTON MOVEMENT [A] 338

GALVESTON WHARF COMPANY [A] 48

GAMECOCKS [C] 190

GARDEN, DR. ALEXANDER [C] 1465

GARDENS [C] 68, 336, 340, 345

GAYARRE, CHARLES [B] 3114

GEFFIN, TOBIAS [B] 3096, 4075

GENERAL MAGAZINE AND IMPARTIAL REVIEW [B] 3153

GENTRIFICATION [A] 377; [B] 4445

GEOLOGY [C] 339

GEORGIA TECHNOLOGICAL INSTITUTE [C] 355, 389

GERMANS [A] 239, 542, 628; [B] 472, 2143, 2199, 2310, 2704, 2821, 3179,
     3180, 3218, 3219, 3440, 3591, 3592, 3593, 3619, 3651, 3673, 3710,
     4294, 4330; [C] 1540, 1575

GHOST TOWNS [B] 2510, 3977; [C] 414-420

GHOSTS [B] 2883, 2900, 3013; [C] 1511, 1527, 1593

GILLESPIE, DIZZY [B] 3203

GILMAN, CAROLINE [B] 2437; [C] 1709

GIRL'S PREPARATORY SCHOOL [C] 388

GLASGOW, ELLEN [C] 1708

GODCHAUX, LEON [B] 1020

GORDON, JEAN [B] 2899

GORDON, KATE [B] 2899

GRADY, HENRY W. [B] 646, 709, 2451, 3441, 3483

GRAIN [B] 961

GREENVILLE MOUNTAINEER [B] 2568

GRAND OPERA HOUSE [A] 846

GREAT RICHMOND TERMINAL [C] 262

GREAT SPECKLED BIRD [A] 401; [B] 2476

GREEKS [A] 517, 726; [B] 1628, 2530, 3613, 3614, 3634, 3637, 3720, 3772, 3778, 3785; [C] 1115, 1121, 1271, 1462

GREENSBORO COLLEGE [C] 374, 411

GREENSBORO WATCHMAN [B] 2453

GREENWOOD MILLS [C] 295

GREGG, WILLIAM [B] 854; [C] 273

GREY, FRANCIS [B] 1743

GREYHOUND BUS LINES [B] 4367

GULF LUMBER COMPANY [B] 1091

HALL, GROVER C. [C] 1409

HAMMOND-HARWOOD HOUSE [C] 446

HAMPTON INSTITUTE [B] 1174

HANCOCK, GORDON BLAIN [C] 1766

HANDICAPPED [A] 813

HANDY, WILLIAM C. [C] 1720

HARPER, ALVAN S. [C] 169

HARRIS, EZEKIEL [B] 2289

HARRIS, JULIAN [B] 2524

HARTSFIELD, WILLIAM BERRY [C] 1795

HATIANS [A] 525, 747; [B] 1362, 1725, 3570, 3627, 3704, 3705, 3773; [C] 313, 1659

HAUGHERY, MARGARET [C] 1594

HAY HOUSE [B] 229, 255

HAYNIE, HUGH [B] 2475

HAZARDS [A] 271

HEALTH [A] 272, 273, 275, 281, 286

HEARST, W. [A] 429

HEIMAN, ALDOPHIS [B] 318, 338, 339

HENDERSON, RICHARD [B] 2486

HENDERSON STEEL [C] 247

HENNING, WILLIAM JOHN [B] 2143

HERNDON, ALONZO F. [B] 756

IMMIGRANTS [A] 512, 517, 521, 525, 526, 532, 537, 540, 542, 543, 550, 567, 573, 603, 626, 719, 726, 746, 747; [B] 1595, 2582, 2601, 2661, 2708, 2954, 3561, 3701, 3789, 3795, 3796, 3809, 3812

IMMIGRATION [A] 359, 513, 560, 610, 622, 623; [C] 1824

INDIANS, AMERICAN [A] 612; [B] 669, 815, 1282, 1949, 1992, 2147, 2335, 2824, 3556, 3609, 3694, 3718, 3751, 3798, 4138; [C] 144, 1122

INDUSTRIAL DEVELOPMENT [A] 52, 71, 77, 91, 92, 150, 160, 164, 226, 233, 237, 238, 241, 725; [C] 196, 198, 199, 210, 211, 216, 220, 221, 225, 253, 268, 331, 1108, 1554

INDUSTRIAL LOCATION [A] 54, 66, 70, 858; [C] 216

IRISH [A] 586, 603; [B] 2709, 3582, 3648, 3664, 3714, 3717, 3771, 4298; [C] 1607

IRON [A] 116; [B] 793, 873, 937, 976, 984, 1042, 2657, 2680; [C] 270

IRON THEATRE [C] 29

IRONWORK [C] 172, 177, 178, 180, 184, 1432

ITALIANS [A] 540, 626; [B] 2513, 2601, 2954, 2984, 2985, 3006, 3334, 3479, 3577, 3654, 3683, 3692, 3695, 2696, 3708, 3709, 3728, 3748, 3757, 3787, 3788, 4122, 4164, 4174, 4195; [C] 1602, 1965

I. W. W. [B] 2689

JACKSON, ANDREW [B] 3422, 3494

JACKSON DAILY NEWS [A] 433; [C] 1408

JACKSON, JAMES M. [B] 1621

JACKSON, MAYNARD [B] 3362

JACKSON COLLEGE [C] 367

JACKSON STATE UNIVERSITY [C] 1884

JACKSON SQUARE [C] 60, 94, 137, 139

JACKSONVILLE STATE TEACHERS COLLEGE [C] 406

JAILS [B] 1764

JAPANESE [A] 94

JENKINS, HERBERT C. [C] 1971

JEWISH [A] 45, 429, 520, 532, 535, 573, 624, 801, 806, 824, 829; [B] 570, 734, 760, 762, 1000, 1028, 1045, 1064, 1141, 1147, 1292, 1961, 2389, 2731, 2749, 2815, 2831, 2836, 2837, 2894, 2916, 2920, 2921, 3008, 3009, 3010, 3015, 3085, 3096,3551, 3552, 3585, 3589, 3590, 3595, 3604, 3605, 3612, 3615, 3620, 3623, 3630, 3631, 3632, 3636, 3637, 3638, 3653, 3671, 3700, 3716, 3726, 3730, 3731, 3735, 3743, 3744, 3745, 3746, 3747, 3749, 3752, 3756, 3762, 3763, 3764, 3774, 3775, 3776, 3780, 3794, 3804, 3848, 3866, 3867, 3883, 3905, 4038, 4040, 4043, 4044, 4045, 4054, 4075, 4076, 4092, 4096, 4097, 4098, 4101, 4102, 4192; [C] 244, 252, 285, 1466, 1516, 1523, 1524, 1532, 1533, 1539, 1543, 1569, 1574, 1591, 1623, 1629, 1632, 1639, 1640, 1652, 1672, 1673, 1676, 1924, 1947, 1951, 1954, 1962

JITNEYS [B] 4349

JOHN BIRCH SOCIETY [B] 1188

JOHN FOX HOUSE [B] 41

JOHNSON, A. N. [B] 2429

JOHNSON, GERALD W. [B] 3105

JOHNSON, J. FRED [B] 1053

JOHNSON, JAMES WELDON [B] 1111

JOHNSON, LYNDON [B] 3338

JOHNSON, WILLIAM [C] 892

JOURNALISM [A] 188; [B] 3229, 3252, 3283, 3319, 4142

KEMP, HENRY [B] 2821

KENDALL, GEORGE WILKINS [B] 2497

KENDIG, BERNARD [B] 994

KENNEDY, JOHN F. [C] 1978

KENT, RICHARD [B] 3429

KENT STATE UNIVERSITY [A] 778

KENTUCKY GAZETTE [B] 2468

KEY, ROBERT [B] 78

KIMBALL, HANIBAL I. [A] 154; [B] 3441; [C] 288

KING, MARTIN LUTHER [C] 1429, 1857, 1938

KINSHIP [A] 549, 572

KLUTHO, HENRY JOHN [C] 16

KNIGHTS OF LABOR [B] 2633, 2647

KNOW NOTHINGS [B] 3285; [C] 1810

KOREANS [A] 137; [B] 864, 865; [C] 1581

KRONIKALS OF THE TIMES [B] 2836

KU KLUX KLAN [A] 439; [B] 2441, 2524, 2800, 3023, 3024, 3854, 3872, 3889, 3892, 3952; [C] 1866

KUDZU [B] 2465

KURTZ, WILBUR G. [C] 165

LA PRENSA [A] 397

LA RAZA [A] 601

LA RESISTENCIA [B] 2661

LABOR [A] 28, 29, 30, 31, 32, 53, 143, 189, 442-467; [B] 2395, 2440, 2571, 3307, 3433, 3434, 3549

LABREE, BENJAMIN [C] 163

LACY, ROGER [B] 1682

LADD, DANIEL [C] 307

LAMAR, GAZAWAY [B] 630

LAND, VACANT [A] 481

LAND SUBSIDENCE [A] 373

LAND USE [A] 204, 468-486, 792, 793; [C] 1047

LANGSTON UNIVERSITY [B] 1245

LANGTRY, LILLIE [B] 4301

LANGUAGE [A] 587, 589

LANIER UNIVERSITY [B] 3854

LANNOM, G. S., JR. [B] 737

LATINS [B] 1035, 3541, 3544, 3621; [C] 1833

LATROBE, BENJAMIN HENRY [B] 437, 3288

LAZINESS [A] 276

LAW [C] 261, 763

LAW ENFORCEMENT [A] 812, 823

LEAD [A] 277

LEBANESE [B] 843; [C] 206

LECONTE, EMMA [C] 1036

LEE, LIEUTENANT [C] 1817

LEGARE, HUGH SWINTON [C] 1163

LEGETT, JUDGE [C] 1253

LEISURE [B] 1018, 2966, 3059

LEVERT, MADAM OCTAVIA WALTON [C] 1513

LEWIS, JERRY LEE [B] 3213

LIBERTY HALL ACADEMY [B] 34

LIBRARIES [A] 487-508; [B] 1765, 1937, 2754, 2756, 2757, 2782, 2791, 2928, 2951, 3018, 3071, 3075, 3113, 3326, 3397; [C] 1488, 1529, 1570, 1644

LILY-TULIP COMPANY [B] 862

LIMNOLOGY [A] 199

LIND, JENNY [B] 3182

LITERATURE [A] 638-643; [B] 2603, 2611, 3036, 3510

LITTLE HAITI [A] 525; [C] 313

LIVESTOCK [A] 148

LLANO, LOUIS [B] 3410

LOCOMOTIVES [B] 917

LONG, EARL [B] 3375

LONG, HUEY P. [B] 3244, 3463

LOST TRIBES [C] 492

LOUISIANA STATE UNIVERSITY [B] 1159, 3859

LOUISVILLE MEDICAL INSTITUTE [B] 1172

LOUISVILLE MUNICIPAL COLLEGE [A] 210, 761

LOYALISTS [A] 682

LOYLESS, THOMAS W. [B] 2448

LUCEY, ROBERT E. [A] 55

LUMBEES [B] 3693, 3694

LUMBER [A] 86, 106; [B] 583, 675, 676, 677, 678, 679, 768, 958, 1091

LUTHERANS [B] 4031

LUZENBERG, CHARLES ALOYSIUS [B] 1569

LYLE, JOHN BLAIR [B] 833

LYNCHBURG COLLEGE [B] 1130

LYNCHING [A] 777; [B] 2433, 2493, 2564, 3028, 3478, 3888, 4139, 4153, 4219, 4237

MADDOX, F. E. [B] 749

MADSTONES [B] 1597

MAFIA [B] 4118, 4122, 4130, 4168, 4174, 4195

MAGAZINES [A] 188, 387, 420, 640; [B] 3086, 3089, 3099, 3101, 3112, 3136, 3146, 3148

MAGNOLIA [B] 3086

MANEGAULT, GABRIEL [B] 640

MANKEN, HELLEN DOUGLAS [C] 1812

MAPS [C] 446

MARDI GRAS [B] 2938, 2946, 2998, 3217; [C] 725, 1469, 1548, 1552, 1576, 1614, 1626, 1661, 1662, 1663, 1664, 1685, 1687, 1699

MARKETING [A] 170

MARKETS [A] 50

MARSHALL, MRS. A. J. [C] 1019

MARSHALL, ANDEW C. [B] 4073

MARYLAND GAZETTE [B] 2548

MARTA [C] 145, 146

MARTIN, BOYD [A] 841

MASSAGE PARLORS [B] 3035

MAURY, MASON [A] 34

MAYBANK, BERNET [B] 3259

MEAD, LUCIA AMES [B] 3276

MENCKEN, H. L. [B] 3104; [C] 946

MEDICAL COLLEGE OF GEORGIA [B] 1137

MEDICAL COLLEGE OF SOUTH CAROLINA [C] 361

MEDICINE [A] 415; [B] 1106, 1119, 1137, 1166, 1172, 1238, 1753; [C]
    349, 361, 368, 384, 1465

MELROSE, BONNIE [C] 1303

MEMPHIS APPEAL [A] 389

MEMPHIS COMMERCIAL APPEAL [A] 388, 395; [B] 2441; [C] 1392

MEMPHIS DAILY APPEAL [B] 2435, 2445

MEMPHIS UNION APPEAL [B] 2435

MENNONITES [B] 3652

MENUS [C] 1031

MERCHANTS [A] 100, 102, 146, 174

MERCIER, ALFRED [B] 3132

MEREWETHER'S WEEKLY [B] 2570

MESTIZAJE [A] 524

MESTIZO [A] 7

METHODISTS [B] 1150, 4061, 5071

MEXICANS [A] 457, 537, 550, 584, 601, 635, 797; [B] 2674, 2781, 2942,
    3356, 3610, 3736; [C] 1438, 1445, 1453, 1538

MIAMI HERALD [C] 1423

MIDWAY INC. [A] 64

MIGRATION [A] 718, 736, 740, 742, 743; [B] 1192, 3546, 3558, 3562,
    3563, 3567, 3574, 3578, 3617, 3629, 3642, 3643, 3644, 3650, 3656,
    3662, 3663, 3674, 3679, 3689, 3802, 3805; [C] 1827

MILK [A] 151

MILITARY [B] 3352, 3359

MORTUARY ART [B] 3052, 3054

MOUNT VERNON PLACE [C] 731

MUSEUMS [B] 147, 193, 206, 247, 273, 296, 419, 438, 504, 520, 527, 1813, 2967, 2978

MUSIC [A] 644-656; [B] 3510, 4017, 4274, 4277, 4287; [C] 1456, 1712-1731

McCARTHYISM [B] 3261

McCUNE, ANNIE [C] 1660

McDONOGH, JOHN [B] 2032, 3127; [C] 191, 218

McELREATH, WALTER [C] 1078

McGILL, RALPH [B] 2515

McLAUGHLIN, "MISS LENNIS" [A] 672

McWANE INCORPORATED [C] 302

NAACP [A] 766; [B] 2588, 3411

NASHVILLE LYCEUM [B] 1112, 1917

NATION, CARRIE [B] 2843

NATIONAL FOREST POLICY [A] 200

NATIONAL TRADE REVIEW [C] 278

NATIONAL URBAN LEAGUE [B] 3425

NEAL, JOHN R. [B] 1195

NEIGHBORHOODS [A] 372, 377, 533, 674, 872, 873; [C] 597, 760, 1208

NIEMAN-MARCUS [B] 631, 734

NEW DEAL [A] 90; [B] 3382

NEW ORLEANS ACADEMY OF MUSIC THEATRE [A] 646, 655, 835

NEW ORLEANS CABILDO [A] 324

NEW ORLEANS DAILY PICAYUNE [A] 390

NEW ORLEANS DEMOCRAT [B] 2482

NEW ORLEANS DOUBLE DEALER [B] 2443

NEW ORLEANS L'UNION [A] 417

NEW ORLEANS PICAYUNE [B] 2497, 2500; [C] 1398, 1412

NEW ORLEANS STATES ITEM [C] 1412, 1428

NEW ORLEANS TIMES [B] 2482

NEW ORLEANS TRIBUNE [A] 417; [B] 2458; [C] 1411

NEW SOUTH [A] 294, 385, 668

NEWFIELD, RABBI MORRIS [A] 801

NEWS MEDIA [A] 412, 620, 786, 787

NICHOLSON, ELIZA JANE POITERENT [A] 390

NILES, HEZEKIAH [B] 2479

NORFOLK JOURNAL AND GUIDE [A] 427, 434; [B] 2554

NORFOLK STATE UNIVERSITY [C] 356

NORTH CAROLINA MUTUAL LIFE INSURANCE COMPANY [C] 322

NORTH CAROLINA STATE UNIVERSITY [C] 1207

NORTHERNERS [B] 2784

OCHS, ADOLPH S. [B] 2477

OCOMULGEE OLD FIELDS [A] 6

O'CONNER, FLANNERY [B] 3118

OFFICES [A] 114, 195

OIL [A] 98; [B] 604, 619, 769, 804; [C] 222, 323, 711, 1613

OLIVER, ROBERT [C] 213

OLMSTEAD, FREDERICK LAW [B] 159

OPERA [A] 651, 846

ORION [B] 3148

ORLEANS GALLERY [C] 162

ORPHANS [C] 1594, 1673, 1716

OSBORNE, SELLER [B] 2460

OXFORD EAGLE [A] 392

PACA HOUSE [B] 48

PACKER, CHARLES MACK [A] 777

PAINE, ROWLETT [C] 1789

PALMER, CHARLES F. [A] 680

PAPER, [A] 156; [C] 229, 236, 428

PARKS [B] 1096, 1103, 1444, 3397

PARKS, WILLIAM [B] 3091

PEABODY HOTEL [A] 302

PEACHTREE STREET [C] 443, 1352

PENSACOLA NEWS JOURNAL [A] 400

RELIGION [A] 408, 678, 752, 797–806; [B] 60, 83, 108, 270, 319, 320,
     346, 427, 1150, 1263, 1747, 2102, 2135, 2464, 2767, 2829, 2830,
     3025, 3377, 3502, 3573, 3700, 3814, 3919, 4030–4115; [C] 285,
     1466, 1516, 1522, 1523, 1524, 1532, 1533, 1539, 1543, 1569, 1574,
     1591, 1623, 1629, 1632, 1639, 1643, 1652, 1854, 1918–1958

RENT [A] 374

REO BUILDING [C] 110

REPUBLICANS [A] 669, 685; [C] 1814, 1819

RESORTS [A] 325; [B] 1296, 1710, 1736; [C] 2, 1891, 1901, 1915, 1916

RETAIL TRADE [A] 42, 74, 84, 99, 112, 167

REVIEWER, THE [B] 3141

REX HOSPITAL [B] 1601

RICH'S DEPARTMENT STORE [B] 784; [C] 200

RICHMOND, MARY [A] 826

RICHMOND ACADEMY [C] 382

RICHMOND COLLEGE [B] 1129

RICHMOND COMPILER [B] 2430

RICHMOND EXAMINER [A] 413; [C] 1399

RICHMOND LANCASTERIAN SCHOOL [B] 1154

RICHMOND PLANET [A] 385; [B] 2444

RIOTS [A] 107, 692, 755, 778, 782; [B] 1712, 1827, 2623, 2819, 2785,
     3022, 3051, 3067, 3340, 3341, 3343, 3442, 3468, 3488, 3501, 3819,
     3821, 3823, 3827, 3828, 3838, 3843, 3844, 3865, 3870, 3881, 3882,
     3887, 3910, 3918, 3934, 3941, 3953, 3955, 3957, 3960, 3966, 4146,
     4150, 4184, 4191, 4196, 4197, 4224; [C] 905, 1855, 1863, 1887,
     1888, 1967

RIPLEY, ELIZA MOORE [C] 1634

RITCHIE, THOMAS [B] 1154

RIVERS, PEARL [B] 3185

RIVERSIDE COTTON MILLS [B] 969

ROADS [A] 859, 861; [B] 1464, 2925, 4379, 4381, 4383, 4410, 4428, 4432,
     4436

ROBB, JAMES [B] 684

ROBERTS, ALBERT [B] 2555, 2556

ROBERTSON, GEN. JAMES [C] 941

ROCK 'N' ROLL [A] 653

ROCKEFELLER SANITARY COMMISSION [A] 276

ROGER WILLIAMS UNIVERSITY [B] 1252

ROGERS, NICHOLAS [B] 66

ROOT, SIDNEY [B] 840

ROSE, FRED [A] 656

ROSE MAGAZINES [B] 2437

ROTARY CLUBS [C] 562

ROTHSCHILD, JACOB M. [C] 1924

RUBBER [B] 2677

RUBY, JACK [C] 1974

RUFFIN, EDMOND [B] 2517

RUMALLAH-AMERICANUS [A] 217

RUSSELL, LUCY PHILLIPS [C] 1194

RUSSELL'S MAGAZINE [B] 3089

RUSSIANS [B] 760, 1028, 1181

RUTHERFORD, THOMAS [B] 2275

SADLER, HARLEY [C] 1985

ST. CHARLES THEATRE [A] 850, 853

ST. LAWRENCE SEAWAY [A] 76

ST. LOUIS CATHEDRAL [C] 60, 94

ST. MARY'S COLLEGE [C] 404

ST. MAXENT, ANTOINE DE [C] 652

ST. PAUL'S COLLEGE [A] 224

ST. PETERSBURG TIMES [B] 2469

SALEM ACADEMY AND COLLEGE [C] 376

SANBORN FIRE INSURANCE COMPANY [A] 473

SALEM COLLEGE [B] 1257

SANITATION [B] 2804

SASS, HERBERT RAVENELL [C] 217

SAVANNAH MORNING NEWS [B] 2528

SAVINGS BANK OF BALTIMORE [C] 284

SAVOY THEATRE [A] 16

SCHIFF, JACOB H. [B] 3561, 3762

SCHIZOPHRENIA [A] 283

SCHOBER, GOTTLIEB [B] 992

SCHREINER, CHARLES [C] 242

STRIP CLUBS [B] 2763

SUBURBS [A] 24, 198, 234, 245, 455; [C] 13, 1039

SUGAR [B] 934, 966

SUGGS, SIMON [C] 1409

SUFFRAGE [A] 577

SUICIDE [B] 3574

SUNDAY TIMES [B] 2559

SUNDAY, BILLY [B] 4036

SWISS [B] 3600, 3660, 3661

SYLVESTER, JAMES JOSEPH [B] 1147

SYPHAX, WILLIAM [B] 1214

SYRIAN-LEBANESE [B] 2730

TALLADEGA COLLEGE [A] 209

TANNEHILLE, WILKINS [B] 636

TEAS, THOMAS S. [B] 782

TELEGRAPH [B] 4015

TELEVISION [A] 786; [B] 4014, 4016, 4018, 4018, 4029

TEMPERANCE [B] 2842, 2843

TEXTILES [A] 168, 265, 445, 459; [B] 702, 703, 842, 854, 907, 916,
     1003, 2577, 2603, 2612, 2614, 2618, 2623, 2625, 2639, 2655, 2663,
     2666, 2673, 2684, 2687, 2716, 2722, 2728, 2878, 2963, 3216; [C]
     280, 295, 1431, 1433

THACKERAY [B] 3013

THEATRE [A] 646, 651, 655, 833-854; [B] 4243-4336; [C] 29, 1984-1995

THEUS, JEREMIAH [C] 168

TIMES-PICAYUNE [C] 1398, 1412

TIMROD, HENRY [A] 440

TOBACCO [A] 133; [B] 51, 2643; [C] 294

TOOMBS, ROBERT [B] 4208

TORNADOS [A] 271; [B] 2788

TOURISM [A] 58, 59, 144; [B] 716, 807, 845, 3974

TRADE CENTERS [A] 51, 89, 162, 184

TRANSPORTATION [A] 180, 190, 245, 468, 477, 486, 677, 813, 857-867; [B]
     540, 2062, 2377, 2925, 3282, 3291, 3790, 3860, 3893, 4337-4439;
     [C] 9, 145, 146, 149, 228, 245, 264, 289, 290, 440, 447, 1794,
     1842, 1868, 1870, 1886, 1996-2013

TREDEGAR IRON WORKS [C] 178

TREME, FAUBOURG [C] 130

TRENT, ALPHONSO [B] 3205

TRUCKING [B] 4409

TRUST COMPANY OF GEORGIA [C] 266

TRYON, GOV. [C] 1763

TURNER, NAT [B] 3959

TULANE THEATRE [A] 847

TULANE UNIVERSITY [C] 368, 369

TURNER, TED [C] 1899

TUSKEGEE INSTITUTE [A] 209, 216; [B] 1540

TVA [A] 228, 421, 504; [B] 936, 1046; [C] 821

TWAIN, MARK [B] 3081

TYLER COURIER-TIMES [A] 406

TYLER MORNING TELEGRAPH [A] 406

TYPHUS [B] 1564

TYSON, ELISHA [A] 757

TYSON AND JONES BUGGY COMPANY [B] 922

U.A.W. [B] 2637

UNCLE REMUS'S MAGAZINE [B] 3126

UNION RAILYARD [C] 149

UNIONS [B] 721, 2574, 2581, 2589, 2599, 2600, 2601, 2602, 2605, 2607,
    2609, 2633, 2637, 2647, 2661, 2662, 2663, 2665, 2666, 2668, 2669,
    2677, 2680, 2685, 2689, 2690, 2705, 2710, 2713, 2718, 2727

UNIVERSITY OF ALABAMA [B] 3932; [C] 404, 413

UNIVERSITY OF ARKANSAS [B] 1062, 1202, 1235, 1236; [C] 383

UNIVERSITY OF CHATTANOOGA [C] 375

UNIVERSITY OF DELAWARE [B] 1264

UNIVERSITY OF FLORIDA [C] 395

UNIVERSITY OF GEORGIA [B] 1126, 1160, 1256; [C] 353, 370, 1913

UNIVERSITY OF KENTUCKY [C] 408, 1906, 1907

UNIVERSITY OF LOUISIANA [B] 1246

UNIVERSITY OF LOUISVILLE [A] 761; [B] 2934

UNIVERSITY OF MARYLAND [B] 3906; [C] 358

WASHINGTON, JESSIE [B] 3028

WATER [A] 108, 198, 201, 202, 205, 206, 208; [B] 3288, 3294, 3298,
    3414, 4207; [C] 339, 342, 343, 344, 428

WATERMAN, CHARLES M. [B] 3254

WELLS, IDA B. [B] 2564

WESLEYAN COLLEGE [B] 1155

WESSOLOWSKY, CHARLES [C] 1643

WEST VIRGINIA STATE COLLEGE [B] 3852

WEST VIRGINIA WESLEYAN COLLEGE [C] 393

WESTERN CAROLINA COLLEGE [C] 352

WHALING [B] 853

WHEELER, JOHN FOSTER [B] 2504

WHEELING DAILY INTELLEGENCER [A] 422

WHEELING GAZETTE [B] 2530

WHEELING INTELLEGENCER [B] 2442

WHITESTONE, HENRY [A] 22

WHOLESALE TRADE [A] 78, 110, 117, 136, 138, 152, 180

WILDCATS [C] 1906

WILDE, OSCAR [B] 3094

WILDE, RICHARD HENRY [B] 1246

WILLIAM AND MARY [B] 340

WILLIAM'S CLARKESVILLE DIRECTORY, CITY GUIDE AND BUSINESS MIRROR [C]
    329

WILLIAMS, ELIZA [C] 1347

WILLIAMS, SAMUEL MAY [C] 250

WILLIAMS, TENNESSEE [B] 3082, 4246

WINCHESTER, MARCUS [B] 2221

WITCHCRAFT [B] 2850, 2864, 2970

WINERIES [B] 693, 1973, 2011

WOLFE, THOMAS [B] 3120, 3150, 3509

WOMEN [A] 126, 189, 221, 341, 453, 536, 577, 605, 613, 631, 660, 826;
    [B] 187, 382, 535, 835, 1004, 1114, 1124, 1145, 1151, 1155, 1167,
    1210, 1215, 1224, 1256, 1473, 1549, 2491, 2561, 2584, 2585, 2586,
    2590, 2616, 2626, 2632, 2638, 2643, 2658, 2674, 2687, 2725, 2736,
    2747, 2755, 2782, 2810, 2834, 2835, 2850, 2854, 2870, 2886, 2917,
    2918, 2983, 2987, 3027, 3033, 3081, 3084, 3085, 3093, 3098, 3100,
    3104, 3115, 3118, 3133, 3134, 3142, 3143, 3158, 3182, 3185, 3202,
    3216, 3276, 3279, 3332, 3351, 3483, 3484, 3565, 3610, 3709, 3762,
    4010, 4083, 4085, 4147, 4148, 4200, 4320; [C] 372, 388, 407, 410,

List of Journals Surveyed

AMERICAN JOURNAL OF PUBLIC HEALTH

AMERICAN JOURNAL OF SOCIOLOGY

AMERICAN MUSIC

AMERICAN POLITICAL SCIENCE REVIEW

AMERICAN PRESERVATION

AMERICAN SCHOLAR

AMERICAN SOCIOLOGICAL REVIEW

AMERICAN SPEECH

AMERICAN QUARTERLY

AMERICAS

ANNALS OF THE AMERICAN ACADEMY OF POLITICAL AND SOCIAL SCIENCE

ANNALS OF THE ASSOCIATION OF AMERICAN GEOGRAPHERS

ANNALS OF REGIONAL SCIENCE

ANTHROPOLOGICAL QUARTERLY

ANTIPODE

ANTIQUES

APPALACHIAN JOURNAL

ARCHAEOLOGY

ARCHEOLOGICAL SOCIETY OF VIRGINIA--QUARTERLY BULLETIN

ARCHITECTURAL RECORD

ARKANSAS HISTORICAL QUARTERLY

ART IN AMERICA

ATLANTA ECONOMIC REVIEW

ATLANTA HISTORICAL JOURNAL

ATLANTIC MONTHLY

AZTLAN

BLACK BOOKS BULLETIN

BLACK ENTERPRISE

BLACK REVIEW

BUSINESS ATLANTA

BUSINESS HISTORY REVIEW

CAPITOL STUDIES

CATHOLIC HISTORICAL REVIEW

CENTRAL STATES ARCHAEOLOGICAL JOURNAL

CHRONICLES OF OKLAHOMA

CITIES

CITY

CIVIL LIBERTIES REVIEW

CIVIL WAR HISTORY

CIVIL WAR TIMES ILLUSTRATED

COLUMBIA JOURNALISM REVIEW

CONFERENCE ON HISTORICL SITE ARCHAEOLOGY PAPERS

CRISIS

CURRENT MUSICOLOGY

DELAWARE HISTORY

DEMOGRAPHY

EARLY AMERICAN LIFE

EAST TENNESSEE HISTORICAL SOCIETY PUBLICATIONS

EAST TEXAS HISTORICAL JOURNAL

ECONOMIC GEOGRAPHY

EDUCATION AND URBAN SOCIETY

EIGHTEENTH CENTURY LIFE

EKISTICS

ENVIRONMENT AND BEHAVIOR

ESCRIBANO

ETHNIC GROUPS

ETHNIC AND RACIAL STUDIES

ETHNOHISTORY

EXPLORATIONS IN ECONOMIC HISTORY

FEMINIST STUDIES

FILSON CLUB HISTORY QUARTERLY

FLORIDA ANTHROPOLOGIST

FLORIDA GEOGRAPHER

FLORIDA HISTORICAL QUARTERLY

FLORIDA SCIENTIST

FREEDOMWAYS

GARDEN DESIGN

GEOGRAPHICAL REVIEW

GEOGRAPHY

GEOGRAPHY AND THE URBAN ENVIRONMENT

GEORGIA HISTORICAL QUARTERLY

GEORGIA JOURNAL

GEORGIA LIFE

GEORGIA REVIEW

GEOSCIENCE AND MAN

GREAT PLAINS JOURNAL

GROWTH AND CHANGE

HABITAT INTERNATIONAL

HISTORIC PRESERVATION

HISTORICAL ARCHAEOLOGY

HISTORICAL GEOGRAPHY NEWSLETTER

HISTORICAL MAGAZINE OF THE PROTESTANT EPISCOPAL CHURCH

HISTORIAN

HISTORY OF EDUCATION QUARTERLY

HISTORY WORKSHOP

HORIZON

HUMAN ORGANIZATION

INTERNATIONAL JOURNAL OF URBAN AND REGIONAL RESEARCH

INTERNATIONAL MIGRATION

INTERNATIONAL MIGRATION REVIEW

JEWISH JOURNAL OF SOCIOLOGY

JEWISH SOCIAL STUDIES

JOURNAL OF ALABAMA ARCHAEOLOGY

JOURNAL OF THE AMERICAN ACADEMY OF RELIGION

JOURNAL OF AMERICAN CULTURE

JOURNAL OF AMERICAN ETHNIC HISTORY

JOURNAL OF AMERICAN HISTORY

JOURNAL OF AMERICAN STUDIES

JOURNAL OF BLACK STUDIES

JOURNAL OF THE COMMUNITY DEVELOPMENT SOCIETY

JOURNAL OF COUNTRY MUSIC

JOURNAL OF CULTURAL GEOGRAPHY

JOURNAL OF THE EARLY REPUBLIC

JOURNAL OF ECONOMIC HISTORY

JOURNAL OF ENVIRONMENTAL SYSTEMS

JOURNAL OF ETHNIC STUDIES

JOURNAL OF FAMILY HISTORY

JOURNAL OF GARDEN HISTORY

JOURNAL OF HISTORICAL GEOGRAPHY

JOURNAL OF THE HISTORY OF MEDICINE AND ALLIED SCIENCES

JOURNAL OF INTERDISCIPLINARY HISTORY

JOURNAL OF INTERGROUP RELATIONS

JOURNAL OF LEISURE RESEARCH

JOURNAL OF LIBRARY HISTORY

JOURNAL OF MISSISSIPPI HISTORY

JOURNAL OF MODERN HISTORY

JOURNAL OF NEGRO HISTORY

JOURNAL OF POLITICAL SCIENCE

JOURNAL OF POLITICS

JOURNAL OF POPULAR CULTURE

JOURNAL OF PSYCHOHISTORY

JOURNAL OF SOCIAL HISTORY

JOURNAL OF SOCIAL ISSUES

JOURNAL OF SOUTHERN HISTORY

JOURNAL OF SPORT HISTORY

JOURNAL OF URBAN AFFAIRS

JOURNAL OF URBAN ECONOMICS

JOURNAL OF URBAN HISTORY

JOURNAL OF VOLUNTARY ACTION RESEARCH

JOURNALISM HISTORY

JOURNALISM QUARTERLY

KENTUCKY FOLKLORE RECORD

LABOR HISTORY

LAND ECONOMICS

LANDSCAPE

LANDSCAPE ARCHITECTURE

LANDSCAPE PLANNING

LAW AND SOCIETY REVIEW

LEISURE SCIENCES

LINCOLN REVIEW

LOUISIANA HISTORICAL QUARTERLY

LOUISIANA HISTORY

MANUSCRIPTS

MARYLAND HISTORIAN

MARYLAND HISTORICAL MAGAZINE

MID-AMERICA

MID-SOUTH FOLKLORE

MIDWEST QUARTERLY

MILITARY AFFAIRS

MISSISSIPPI QUARTERLY

NEW ORLEANS REVIEW

NEW SOUTH

NORTH AMERICAN ARCHAEOLOGIST

NORTH CAROLINA FOLKLORE JOURNAL

NORTH CAROLINA HISTORICAL REVIEW

NORTH GEORGIA JOURNAL

NOTEBOOK--SOUTH CAROLINA ARCHAEOLOGY AND ANTHROPOLOGY

PERSPECTIVES IN AMERICAN HISTORY

PHYLON QUARTERLY

POLICE JOURNAL

POLITICAL SCIENCE QUARTERLY

POPULAR GOVERNMENT

PROFESSIONAL GEOGRAPHER

PROGRESSIVE ARCHITECTURE

PUBLIUS

QUALITATIVE SOCIOLOGY

QUARTERLY JOURNAL OF THE LIBRARY OF CONGRESS

RADICAL AMERICA

RADICAL HISTORY REVIEW

REAL ESTATE ISSUES

REASON

RED RIVER VALLEY HISTORICAL REVIEW

REGIONAL SCIENCE PERSPECTIVES

REGIONAL SCIENCE AND URBAN ECONOMICS

REGISTER OF THE KENTUCKY HISTORICAL SOCIETY

REVIEW OF BLACK POLITICAL ECONOMY

REVIEW OF REGIONAL STUDIES

REVIEW OF SOCIAL ECONOMY

RICHMOND COUNTY HISTORY

RURAL SOCIOLOGY

SEWANEE REVIEW

SIGNS

SMITH COLLEGE STUDIES IN HISTORY

SMITHSONIAN

SOCIAL FORCES

SOCIAL INDICATORS AND RESEARCH

SOCIAL PROBLEMS

SOCIAL SCIENCE HISTORY

SOCIAL SCIENCE AND MEDICINE

SOCIAL SCIENCE QUARTERLY

SOCIOLOGICAL SPECTRUM

SOCIOLOGICAL QUARTERLY

SOCIOLOGY AND SOCIAL RESEARCH

SOUTH ATLANTIC QUARTERLY

SOUTH ATLANTIC URBAN STUDIES

SOUTH BUSINESS

SOUTH CAROLINA ANTIQUITIES

SOUTH CAROLINA HISTORICAL MAGAZINE

SOUTH CAROLINA HISTORY ILLUSTRATED

SOUTHEASTERN ARCHAEOLOGY

SOUTHEASTERN GEOGRAPHER

SOUTHEASTERN GEOLOGY

SOUTHERN ACCENTS

SOUTHERN ECONOMIC JOURNAL

SOUTHERN EXPOSURE

SOUTHERN FOLKLORE QUARTERLY

SOUTHERN FUNERAL DIRECTOR

SOUTHERN HISTORICAL RESEARCH MAGAZINE

SOUTHERN HOSPITALS

SOUTHERN HUMANITIES REVIEW

SOUTHERN LITERARY JOURNAL

SOUTHERN LITERARY MESSENGER

SOUTHERN MEDICAL JOURNAL

SOUTHERN OBSERVER

SOUTHERN QUARTERLY

SOUTHERN QUARTERLY REVIEW

SOUTHERN REVIEW

SOUTHERN SPEECH COMMUNICATION JOURNAL

SOUTHERN STUDIES

SOUTHERN THEATRE

SOUTHWEST REVIEW

SOUTHWESTERN HISTORICAL QUARTERLY

SOUTHWESTERN LOUISIANA JOURNAL

STUDIES IN POPULAR CULTURE

TAMPA BAY HISTORY

TENNESSEE ARCHAEOLOGIST

TENNESSEE FOLKLORE SOCIETY BULLETIN

TENNESSEE HISTORICAL QUARTERLY

TENNESSEE VALLEY PERSPECTIVE

TEQUESTA

TEXANA

TRANSPORTATION QUARTERLY

URBAN AFFAIRS QUARTERLY

URBAN ANTHROPOLOGY

URBAN ECOLOGY

URBAN EDUCATION

URBAN GEOGRAPHY

URBAN GEORGIA

URBAN LAND

URBAN LEAGUE REVIEW

URBAN LIFE AND CULTURE

URBAN RESOURCES

URBAN REVIEW

URBAN AND SOCIAL CHANGE REVIEW

URBAN STUDIES

VIRGINIA CAVALCADE

VIRGINIA GEOGRAPHER

VIRGINIA MAGAZINE OF HISTORY AND BIOGRAPHY

VIRGINIA QUARTERLY REVIEW

VIRGINIA SOCIAL SCIENCE JOURNAL

WEST TENNESSEE HISTORICAL SOCIETY PAPERS

WEST VIRGINIA HISTORY

WILLIAM AND MARY QUARTERLY

About the Compiler

CATHERINE L. BROWN, a resident of Oceanside, California, has been a planner for the Georgia Department of Defense, a program coordinator for the U.S.-Georgia China Council, and a library assistant.